Assessment in Special and Inclusive Education

ASSESSMENT IN SPECIAL AND INCLUSIVE EDUCATION

FOURTEENTH EDITION

JAMES E. YSSELDYKE

ERIN A. CHAPARRO

AMANDA M. VANDERHEYDEN

pro·ed
An International Publisher

800-897-3202 Fax 800-397-7633
www.proedinc.com

1301 W. 25th St., Suite 300
Austin, TX 78705-4248
800-897-3202 Fax 800-397-7633
www.proedinc.com

LIBRARY OF CONGRESS CATALOGING-IN-PUBLICATION DATA

Names: Ysseldyke, James E., author. | Chaparro, Erin A., author. |
  VanDerHeyden, Amanda M., author.
Title: Assessment in special and inclusive education / James E. Ysseldyke,
  Erin A. Chaparro, Amanda M. VanDerHeyden.
Description: Fourteenth edition. | Austin, TX : PRO-ED, An International
  Publisher, [2023] | Includes bibliographical references and index.
Identifiers: LCCN 2022019156 (print) | LCCN 2022019157 (ebook) | ISBN
  978-1-4164-1202-1 (paperback) | ISBN 978-1-4164-1203-8 (ebook)
Subjects: LCSH: Educational tests and measurements--United States. |
  Special education--United States. | Remedial teaching--United States.
Classification: LCC LB3051 .S245 2022 (print) | LCC LB3051 (ebook) | DDC
  371.26--dc23/eng/20220512
LC record available at https://lccn.loc.gov/2022019156
LC ebook record available at https://lccn.loc.gov/2022019157

Art Director: Jason Crosier
Designer: Bookbright Media
This book is designed in Iowan Old Style and Franklin Gothic.

Printed in the United States of America

1 2 3 4 5 6 7 8 9 10   31 30 29 28 27 26 25 24 23 22

CONTENTS

PART I: OVERVIEW AND IMPORTANT CONSIDERATIONS

PART II: PROVIDING SUPPORT AND MONITORING STUDENT PROGRESS

PART III: USING FORMAL MEASURES

PART IV: USING ASSESSMENT INFORMATION TO MAKE EDUCATIONAL DECISIONS

List of Figures

The following figures appear within Online Resource 4.1:

List of Tables

The following table appears within Online Resource 4.1:

Table A   Scores Earned on Two Tests Administered by Ms. Smith to Her Arithmetic Class

List of Boxes

Resources (Online)

PREFACE

The title for this fourteenth edition, *Assessment in Special and Inclusive Education,* remains unchanged and reflects the fact that in this textbook we continue to be concerned about assessing the performance and progress of students with disabilities, regardless of whether their education occurs in general or special education settings. We are also concerned with assessment to identify and address the needs of students requiring additional academic and social-emotional support that occurs in classrooms. Educational assessment has undergone substantial change since the first publication of *Assessment in Special and Inclusive Education* in 1978. Improvement and expansion in assessment tools and strategies are certainly evident. New models and technologies for assessment in school settings have emerged in an attempt to more comprehensively and yet also efficiently address the needs of students today. Federal laws, regulations, and guidelines related to school assessment practices have been revised in attempts to promote improvements in student outcomes, and they are in the midst of revision as we complete this most recent edition.

Throughout these changes, we have remained committed to assessment approaches that promote data-based decision making, and we believe that many concepts and ideas presented in the original edition are still essential for our readers to understand and apply. Philosophical differences continue to divide the assessment community. Disputes continue over the value of standardized and nonstandardized test administration, objective and subjective scoring, generalizable and nongeneralizable measurement, interpersonal and intrapersonal comparisons, and so forth. In the midst of these differences, we believe students and society are best served by the objective, reliable, and valid assessment of student abilities and skills and by meaningful links between assessment results and intervention.

Our position is based on several conclusions. First, the Individuals With Disabilities Education Act (IDEA) requires objective assessment, largely because it usually leads to better decision making. Second, we are encouraged by the substantial improvement in assessment devices and practices over the past 40-plus years. Third, although some alternatives are merely unproven, other innovative approaches to assessment—especially those that celebrate subjectivity—have severe shortcomings that have been understood since the early 1900s. Fortunately, much of the initial enthusiasm for those approaches has waned. Fourth, we believe it is unwise to abandon effective procedures without substantial evidence that the proposed alternatives really are better. Too often, we learned that an educational innovation was ineffective after it had already failed far too many students.

Our focus is on assessment that matters; assessment that will bring important changes that enhance the lives of the students served. By equipping our readers with knowledge and understanding of key assessment concepts and principles that can be readily applied in school settings, we believe they will be prepared to engage in work that will indeed improve the academic and social-emotional outcomes of the students they serve.

The Audience for This Book

Assessment in Special and Inclusive Education, fourteenth edition, is intended for a first course in assessment taken by those whose careers require understanding and informed use of assessment data. The primary audience is made up of those who are or will be teachers in special education at the elementary or secondary level. The secondary audience is the large support system for special educators: school psychologists, child development specialists, counselors, educational administrators, nurses, reading specialists, school social workers, speech and language specialists, and specialists in therapeutic recreation. Additionally, in today's reform climate, many classroom teachers enroll in the assessment course as part of their own professional development. In writing for those who are taking their first course in assessment, we have assumed no prior knowledge of measurement and statistical concepts.

Purpose

Students with disabilities have the right to an appropriate evaluation and to an appropriate education in the least restrictive educational environment. Those who assess have a tremendous responsibility; assessment results are used to make decisions that directly and significantly affect students' lives. Those who assess are responsible for knowing the tests and procedures they use and for understanding the limitations of those tests and procedures. Decisions about a student's eligibility for special education and related services must be based on accurate and reliable information; decisions about how and where to educate students with disabilities must be based on accurate and reliable data. Best practices in assessment can help support the learning and development of not just those with disabilities, but all students needing a variety of different levels of support, and so we intend for many of the concepts presented to facilitate best practices for all students, and not just those with disabilities.

New to This Edition

The fourteenth edition continues to offer straightforward and clear coverage of basic assessment concepts, evenhanded evaluations of standardized tests in each domain, and illustrations of applications to the decision-making process. All chapters have been updated, several have been revised substantially, and a few have been eliminated to allow for a clear focus on assessment that matters for promoting academic and social-emotional outcomes. Five chapters are entirely new to this edition.

Overall Changes

Throughout the revision process, our primary goal was to focus on essential assessment concepts, principles, and practices necessary for serving students in school settings. The development and availability of assessment tools, particularly for the purpose of systematic monitoring of student progress, have increased dramatically in recent years, and websites now provide information to facilitate our readers' own reviews of these tools. Therefore, instead of providing numerous detailed reviews of available instruments, we decided to focus our efforts on effectively communicating the key characteristics readers should look for when evaluating the multitude of options available. We have further focused this edition on basic information necessary for generalists (as opposed to specialists) who are seeking to use assessment to improve academic and social-emotional functioning of school-age students. As such, we have reduced coverage of topics that are not closely aligned with this purpose. Furthermore, instead of including a separate chapter on technology, we have incorporated discussion of new technologies within the chapters with which they most closely align. Finally, we know that many school systems are moving toward use of models involving a multi-tiered system of supports (MTSS), and we therefore considered it necessary to provide more background for readers on these models for assessment and intervention. In doing so, we revised the associated chapters to focus on basic assessment concepts and principles that are important to understand when applying these models, defined important keywords that are increasingly being used in the application of these models, and provided examples of how these models are applied in schools. Overall, our goal is to provide readers with a comprehensive textbook that provides easy access to the assessment concepts and ideas necessary to facilitate the academic and social–emotional competence of all students in schools today.

New Features

In addition to important content revisions, we have incorporated several new pedagogical features across chapters.

- At the beginning of each chapter, we now display specific learning objectives.
- Keywords are bolded, with definitions included in the narrative.
- One to three "Progress Monitoring Checks" are included in each chapter. These enable the reader periodically to check their understanding of the content in the textbook.
- Advanced content, which is for students in upper-level or graduate courses, is uniquely formatted to convey that it is advanced material, and is included in an online resources section.
- Stakeholder Perspectives are included throughout the textbook. These are personal perspectives written by teachers, administrators, parents, or even students reflecting their views on specific topics being covered in the text.
- Tables of test overviews are included in relevant chapters. These include lists of tests in the domains for the specific chapter, information regarding the authors, publisher, and date of publication, lists of skills assessed by each of the tests, information on the nature of the norm group for each test, and information on reliability and validity of each test. These tables provide readers with a quick overview of the test instruments available in each domain.

Major Chapter Revisions

Although all chapters that were maintained for the fourteenth edition have been updated, major updates were made in the following chapters:

Chapter 1: Assessment and Decision Making in Schools

Revised to provide a brief introduction to basic assessment concepts and themes that are elaborated on in later chapters. Major additions were made in conceptualizing the diversity of students who attend today's schools. A clearer model of the kinds of assessment decisions made in schools was included.

Chapter 2: A Principled Approach to Assessment and Decision Making

This is a new chapter in which we describe fundamental principles and values that ought to drive the assessment and decision-making process. These are the values we hold and used as we wrote the book.

Chapter 3: Laws, Ethical Codes, and Professional Standards That Impact Assessment

This chapter was rewritten to reflect changes in new laws, ethical codes, and professional standards since the 2017 edition.

Chapter 6: Cultural and Linguistic Considerations in Assessment and Decision Making

This chapter was entirely rewritten to reflect contemporary thinking about cultural diversity, culturally responsive practices, and the impact on assessment and new considerations regarding assessment of students who are linguistically diverse.

Chapter 7: Assessment in Multi-Tiered Systems of Support

This is a completely rewritten chapter on assessment approaches within MTSS and RTI models.

Chapter 8: Monitoring Student Progress Toward Instructional Goals

This is a significantly rewritten chapter to reflect major changes in progress monitoring since publication of the thirteenth edition.

Chapter 10: Screening

This is a new chapter focusing on universal screening and the use of screening measures to make decisions about students. The chapter provides a link to Tools Charts that include reviews of screening measures on the website of the National Center on Intensive Intervention.

Chapter 15: Using Oral and Written Language Measures and Measures of Receptive Vocabulary

In the thirteenth edition we included a chapter on measures of oral language. Measures of receptive vocabulary were reviewed and discussed in the chapter on cognitive assessment. This new chapter provides a comprehensive review of the very many language measures used in schools today.

Chapter 16: Using Measures of Perception and Perceptual-Motor Skills

This new chapter provides a comprehensive overview of assessment of measures of visual and auditory perception and of perceptual-motor skills. We point out the significant problems inherent in using these measures in efforts to plan instructional interventions for students.

Chapter 19: Accessibility Supports and Accommodations

The provision of accessibility supports and accommodations is rapidly changing in the assessment of students with disabilities and English learners. This required the significant updating of the content of this chapter and inclusion of information regarding new rules, regulations, and state education agency guidelines. We provide the very latest up-to-date information along with links to websites where the latest information can be found.

Chapter 24: How to Read and Understand Psychoeducational Reports and State Assessment Reports

This chapter is new to this edition and to the book. Users have requested a chapter on how to read psychoeducational reports. We have refrained from including such a chapter in the past because of the wide variability in practice and because it is difficult to train readers for just what might be included in such reports. We now include a basic chapter on this topic. We also included a section on reading state assessment reports because teachers today are expected to be able to read and understand the reports on the annual assessments administered in their states.

We deleted two chapters that were focused on classroom assessments, one on teacher-made tests of achievement and one on managing classroom assessments. Users of the text told us that they found these chapters were not helpful, with the exception of some of the information on using technology. We incorporated the technology information into other chapters.

Revised Tests

Several tests that are very commonly used to assess students with disabilities have been released with new editions. Reviews of the following recently updated tests are included in corresponding chapters of the book:

- *Woodcock-Johnson Tests of Achievement and Cognitive Abilities–Fourth Edition* (WJ-ACH-4; WJ-COG-4)
- *Wechsler Intelligence Scales for Children–Fifth Edition* (WISC-V)
- *Oral and Written Language Scales–Second Edition* (OWLS-2)
- *Behavior Assessment System for Children–Third Edition* (BASC-3)
- *Gray Oral Reading Test–Fifth Edition* (GORT-5)
- *Diagnostic Achievement Battery–Fourth Edition* (DAB-4)

Major changes have taken place in the test publication industry since we published the first edition of *Assessment in Special and Inclusive Education* in 1978. At that time, tests were published by as many as a dozen publishers and even university centers or institutes. Over the years, a series of consolidations, takeovers in the industry, and buyouts has occurred so that today there are two major publishers of tests used in schools: Pearson, Inc. and PRO-ED, Inc. Along with these a number of publishers (Academic Therapy Publications, Riverside Publishing, MHS, and Stoelting) continue to publish from one to a handful of tests. We list publishers of tests in the test review tables we include in chapters 12, 13, 14, 15, 16, 17, and 18.

Organization

Part I, "Overview and Important Considerations," places testing in the broader context of assessment. We describe the fundamental foundations for assessment practices in schools.

- In Chapter 1, "Assessment and Decision Making in Schools," we describe the need to effectively support diverse students in schools today and introduce basic concepts and principles that will be covered in greater depth later in the book. We stress the fact that students' differing levels of skills require different levels of supports. We describe the kinds of assessment information collected on students and the kinds of decisions made using that information.

- In Chapter 2, "A Principled Approach to Assessment and Decision Making," we describe fundamental principles that underlie effective assessment in special and inclusive education. We also describe our (the authors') values, beliefs, and perspectives that informed our thinking throughout the development of this textbook and that we believe ought to guide assessment and decision making practices in today's schools.

- In Chapter 3, "Laws, Ethical Codes, and Professional Standards That Impact Assessment," we discuss the ways assessment practices are regulated and mandated by legislation and litigation, as well as various ethical principles that may be used to guide assessment practices.

- In Chapter 4, "Test Scores and Norms," we describe the commonly used ways to quantify test performance and provide interpretative data. We distinguish criterion-referenced, standards-referenced, and norm-referenced interpretation of assessment data and describe important considerations in the construction and interpretation of norms.

- In Chapter 5, "Technical Requirements: Reliability and Validity," we explain the basic measurement concepts of reliability and validity.

- In Chapter 6, "Cultural and Linguistic Considerations in Assessment and Decision Making," we discuss the cultural and linguistic diversity of students who attend today's schools and how that affects assessment practices, talk about how to incorporate culturally responsive practices into the assessment process, and describe best practices when working with culturally and linguistically diverse families and caregivers.

Part II, "Providing Support and Monitoring Student Progress," provides fundamental information about practices for gathering assessment information during the instructional process and using that information to make decisions about if and when to make changes in interventions.

- In Chapter 7, "Assessment in Multi-Tiered Systems of Supports," we identify and describe RTI and MTSS concepts that underlie school assessment practices, describe fundamental assumptions in RTI, describe dimensions of assessment for MTSS models, and provide evidence for RTI and MTSS.

- In Chapter 8, "Monitoring Student Progress Toward Instructional Goals," we describe effective progress monitoring tools, curriculum-based measures, alternative methods for setting instructional goals and making changes in instructional interventions, and discuss alternative instructional frameworks that can be used along with progress monitoring to inform instructional changes.

In Part III, "Using Formal Measures," the use of tests to make decisions about students in specific areas like reading, mathematics, and cognition are discussed with a focus on necessary practices and the merits and shortcomings of specific tests.

- In Chapter 9, "How to Evaluate a Test," we describe specific steps one should go through in evaluating the technical adequacy and usefulness of a test.
- In Chapter 10, "Screening," the dual purpose of screening, program evaluation and individual risk assessment, is described. Features of effective academic screening are described and the technical features of accuracy, sensitivity, and specificity are explained.
- Chapter 11, "Assessing Behavior Through Observation," explains the major concepts in conducting systematic observations of student behavior.

The next six chapters in Part III provide an overview of various domains that are assessed in schools using formal measures and reviews the most frequently used measures: Chapter 12, "Assessment of Academic Achievement With Multiple-Skills Measures"; Chapter 13, "Using Diagnostic Reading Measures"; Chapter 14, "Using Diagnostic Mathematics Measures"; Chapter 15, "Using Oral and Written Language Measures and Measures of Receptive Vocabulary"; Chapter 16, "Using Measures of Perception and Perceptual-Motor Skills"; Chapter 17, "Using Measures of Intelligence and Cognitive Processes"; Chapter 18, "Using Measures of Social and Emotional Behavior"; and Chapter 19, "Accessibility Supports and Accommodations."

In Part IV, "Using Assessment Information to Make Educational Decisions," we discuss the most important decisions educators make on behalf of students with disabilities.

- In Chapter 20, "Using Assessment Information to Make Intervention Decisions," we discuss the decisions that are made prior to a student's referral for special education and those that are made in special education settings.
- In Chapter 21, "Using Assessment Information to Make Diagnostic/Eligibility Decisions," we discuss the role of multidisciplinary teams and the process for determining a student's eligibility for special education and related services. In a new section, we describe approaches using information on a student's Response to Intervention in making eligibility decisions.

- In Chapter 22, "Using Assessment Information to Make Accountability Decisions," we explain the legal requirements for states and districts to meet the standards of No Child Left Behind and IDEA and discuss important considerations in making decisions about how a student participates in the accountability program.
- In Chapter 23, "Principles and Practices for Collaborative Teams," we provide an overview of communicating with school teams about assessment and decision making. We also include information about the characteristics of effective school teams, strategies for effectively communicating assessment information to parents and students, and the rules concerning data sharing.
- Chapter 24, "How to Read and Understand Psychoeducational Reports and State Assessment Reports," is included to help users understand the content of psychoeducational reports. The second half of this chapter is devoted to helping readers understand and interpret the content of state assessment reports.

Online Resources for Instructors

Instructor's Manual With Test Bank

An online instructor's manual accompanies this book. It contains information to assist the instructor in designing the course, including sample syllabi, discussion questions, teaching and learning activities, field experiences, learning objectives, and additional online resources. For assessment support, the updated test bank includes true–false, multiple-choice, matching, short-answer, and essay questions for each chapter.

PowerPoint Lecture Slides

These vibrant Microsoft PowerPoint lecture slides for each chapter assist instructors with their lectures by providing concept coverage using images, figures, and tables directly from the textbook.

ACKNOWLEDGMENTS

Dr. John Salvia, Professor Emeritus of Special Education at Pennsylvania State University, deserves special recognition and acknowledgement for his role as a major founding author of this book. Together with Jim Ysseldyke, John authored the first edition in 1978 and was a co-author on 12 subsequent editions of the book. His vision, ideas, commitment to technical quality, and integrity in assessment were present in every edition and are clearly evident in this edition. John is a wonderful professional colleague and his voice is clear in this book. We thank him for his insights, clarity of writing, and friendship over the years. Dr. Sara (Bolt) Witmer, Associate Professor of School Psychology at Michigan State University, assisted with preparation of the tenth edition of this book and joined the author team for the eleventh edition in 2009. She served as a co-author of the eleventh through thirteenth editions. Her valued contributions also live on in several of the chapters of this text. We thank Sara for her many contributions over the years.

Several valued professional colleagues assisted us by editing specific chapters of this textbook. Dr. Martha Thurlow, Emeritus Director of the National Center on Educational Outcomes at the University of Minnesota, and one of the nation's experts on large-scale assessment practices for students with disabilities, provided extensive editorial assistance for chapters 19, 22, and 24. Dr. Mitchell Yell, Professor of Special Education at the University of South Carolina, and author of the textbook *The Law and Special Education*, provided editorial assistance with Chapter 3. Dr. Bob Lichtenstein, Professor Emeritus of Psychology at William James College and author of *High Impact Assessment Reports*, provided assistance with Chapter 24. Dr. Kathleen Cohen-Strickland, Research Associate Professor at the University of Oregon, provided editorial assistance for Chapter 18, "Using Measures of Social and Emotional Behavior."

We would also like to acknowledge the originator of the following figures: Figure 7.3 "Oregon MTSS Teaming Framework" and Figure 20.1 "TIPS Framework." Both are reprinted with permission from Educational and Community Supports at the University of Oregon (copyright 2021). We thank Rob Richardson, Professor of School Psychology at the University of Tennessee, for providing the psychological report example that appears in Resource 24.1. We would like to thank our colleagues at the Heartland Area Education Agency, Amy Pickering, Dorothy Landon, and Rebecca Carver for providing us with an example report that showcases their functional assessment practices in Resource 24.2.

We thank the following people who provided their insight via the Stakeholder Perspectives.

Meghan Anderson Kindergarten Teacher, Rialto Unified School District	Chapter 1
John Salvia, PhD Professor Emeritus of Special Education, College of Education, Pennsylvania State University	Chapter 5
Donna Y. Ford, PhD Distinguished Professor, College of Education and Human Ecology, Ohio State University	Chapter 6
James L. Moore III, PhD Vice Provost for Diversity and Inclusion, Chief Diversity Officer, Ohio State University	
Mr. Casey Sovo, MA Arts in Teaching Education Program Administrator, Bureau of Indian Education	Chapter 6
Naomi Brahim, EdD Director of MTSS Behavior, Jefferson County Schools, Louisville, Kentucky	Chapter 7
Kim Hosford, PhD School Psychologist, Southern Oregon Education Service District and Ashland School District	Chapter 8
Lisa L. Persinger, PhD Faculty, Northern Arizona University	Chapter 12
Jared Campbell, MEd Statewide Lead for Mathematics Initiative, Pennsylvania Training and Technical Assistance Network (PaTTAN)	Chapter 14
Amy VanOrman, MA, CCC-SLP Speech-Language Pathologist, Greenville Public Schools, Greenville, Michigan	Chapter 15

Douglas Fuchs, PhD
 Research Professor, Vanderbilt University and
   Institute Researcher, American Institutes for
   Research
	Chapter 16

Dan Reschly, PhD Professor Emeritus, Vanderbilt University, Department of Special Education	Chapter 17
Ileana Umaña, MA, NCSP, BCBA School Psychology Doctoral Candidate, Texas A&M University	Chapter 18
Sheryl Lazarus, PhD Director, National Center on Educational Outcomes, University of Minnesota	Chapter 19
Savannah Treviño-Casias, MA Graduate Student, Arizona State	Chapter 19
Reina Chehayeb, MA Doctoral Student in School Psychology, Northeastern University	Chapter 20

Chanda Telleen, EdS, NCSP, Doctoral
   Candidate
 Educational Consultant, Pennsylvania Training
   and Technical Assistance Network
	Chapter 23

Tina Lawson, EdD Educational Consultant, Pennsylvania Training and Technical Assistance Network	
Kristen Hood, LMSW School Social Worker, Waverly Community Schools, Waverly, Michigan	Chapter 23

We'd also like to extend our thanks to the editorial staff at PRO-ED, particularly Beth Donnelly, Beth Allen, Kathy Synatschk, and Don Hammill, for their support of our vision to continue the legacy of this seminal textbook. Beth Donnelly did an outstanding job editing and keeping us organized and on time, which was no small feat. We also send our gratitude to Kristen Schrauben, Associate Professor at Grand Valley State University, who once again brought her professional expertise, thoroughness, and instructor's eye to the Instructor's Manual.

We thank our families for their enduring support through the preparation of this text. Finally, we'd like to thank you, the reader. Whether you're a student or a professor, we thank you for your commitment to improving the lives of students.

Jim Ysseldyke
University of Minnesota
Minneapolis, MN

Erin Chaparro
University of Oregon
Eugene, OR

Amanda VanDerHeyden
Education Research and Consulting
Daphne, AL

PART I

Overview and Important Considerations

CHAPTER 1

Assessment and Decision Making in Schools

LEARNING OBJECTIVES

1. Understand the diversity of students who attend today's schools and how this diversity affects assessment and decision-making practices.
2. Know that students have individual differences in skills and behaviors and how these differences can require different levels of support to succeed in school.
3. Describe four ways in which assessment information is collected.
4. Explain four kinds of educational decisions made using assessment information.
5. Understand that significant improvements in assessment have happened and continue to happen.

In this information age, gathering and using information based on data for the purpose of making decisions is of paramount importance, from big decisions concerning one's career to little decisions such as what to have for dinner. **Assessment** is the process of gathering information for the purpose of making decisions. This textbook is about gathering information (assessment data) for the purpose of making decisions for and about children and youth in special and inclusive educational settings. Those who assess have a tremendous responsibility; assessment results are used to make decisions that directly and significantly affect students' lives. Those who assess are responsible for knowing the assessments and procedures they use and for understanding the limitations of those assessments and procedures; they are responsible for being data-informed decision makers. Decisions about a student's eligibility for special education and related services, as well as decisions about how and where to educate students with disabilities, must be based on accurate and reliable data. Best practices in assessment can help support the learning and development of not just those with disabilities, but all students needing a variety of different levels of support. The concepts presented in this text are intended to facilitate best practices for all students, especially for the hundreds of thousands of students who struggle in school.

Precise, accurate assessment is one driving focus in this book, for if the data collection process is flawed, the decision-making process will be flawed. Flawed decision making risks harming students. You will learn about using various forms of data collection: record collection, interviewing, observation, and testing. The emphasis is on precision: knowing how to gather information in the most reliable and valid ways and knowing how to pick and choose the most technically adequate tests that are available.

Good decision making with attention to useful, equitable, and low-cost assessment processes is a second driving force of this text. A critical tenet of data-based decision making in schools is that the assessment team must know in advance what type of decision is needed and drive the data-collection process to yield technically adequate data for that particular decision. Data-Based Decision Making (DBDM) requires facility with data sources, data-collection procedures, decisions, and potential consequences of decisions inside school contexts. In school settings many different kinds of decisions are made, and each kind of decision requires different data, different data-collection procedures, and often different decision-making processes. For example, the process of deciding who should receive special education services is different than the process of deciding how to teach a student. Different kinds of data are needed, and the process of using the data differs. As a profession there is a better knowledge base about the process of deciding who should receive special education services (making eligibility decisions) than there is about deciding how to teach individual struggling students (making instructional decisions).

The kinds of data that school personnel collect on students and the kinds of decisions they make using the data are described in this chapter. First, though, consider the diversity of students who attend today's schools and the kinds of educational supports they need in order to be successful.

Diverse Students and Educational Supports

Students who attend U.S. schools today are a more diverse group than in the past, and they are diverse in many ways. In this section, the racial/ethnic, geographic, socio-economic, and linguistic diversity that characterizes students in today's classrooms is described. Finally, diversity in skill development and diversity in opportunity to learn, the two aspects that have the greatest impact on instructional planning, are highlighted. Those who assess students must always take various forms of diversity into account. We highlight them because they have a direct effect on the decisions made for and about students. Failure to take diversity into account may lead to serious errors that may harm students, including errors in test selection, administration, scoring, interpretation, and decision making.

TABLE 1.1

Racial and Ethnic Composition and Percentage of Students Receiving Free and Reduced-Price Lunch (FRPL) in Some Large Representative U.S School Districts

School District	Enrollment	Afr Am	White	Lat/ Hisp	Nat Am	Asian	Elig FRPL
The School District of Philadelphia	202,944	52%	14%	21%	1%	7%	65%
Los Angeles Unified School District	596,937	10%	9%	73%	-	4%	82%
Chicago Public Schools	340,658	35%	11%	46%	-	4%	79%
Houston Independent School District	209,309	9%	9%	62%	-	4%	79%
Cherry Creek School District, CO	55,839	10%	65%	14%	-	8%	5%
Minneapolis Public Schools	36,357	36%	38%	17%	3%	6%	40%
Baldwin County Public Schools, AL	31,000	9%	83%	5%	1%	1%	12%

Note. This table was constructed by the authors by researching websites for individual school districts or government websites and gathering the most recent data available. The data are intended to be representative rather than exact. Percentages are rounded off and thus do not always sum to 100. Websites used include the following:

- The School District of Philadelphia: philasd.org/fast-facts.
- Los Angeles Unified School District: achieve.lausd.net/site
- Chicago Public Schools: illinoisreportcard.com
- Houston Independent School District: houstonisd.org
- Cherry Creek School District, CO: nces.ed.gov
- Minneapolis Public Schools: mpls.k12.mn.us
- Baldwin County Public Schools, AL: nces.ed.gov

Racial and Ethnic Diversity

When most people think about diversity they think about it as a matter of race or ethnicity. It is clear that today's schools are very diverse. The data in Table 1.1 provide a picture of the racial/ethnic diversity of different school districts in the nation (e.g., the race/ethnicity of 52% of the students attending the Philadelphia Schools is African American, while 21% of the students are Latino/Hispanic; 10% of the students attending the Los Angeles Unified School District are African American, while 73% are Latino/Hispanic).

Geographic Diversity

Depending where one teaches, the composition of classrooms looks very different. The racial/ethnic makeup of students attending the School District of Philadelphia is very different than that of students attending the Los Angeles Unified School District. Moreover, the racial/ethnic makeup of schools within districts can differ considerably, and within states, the composition of school districts differs as a function of whether the schools are located in urban, suburban, or rural areas.

Socioeconomic Diversity

Large numbers of students who attend today's schools come from high-risk environments, especially poverty environments. Risk intersects in a number of ways in schools. Factors like race and poverty do not necessarily convey risk directly, but there is a strong co-occurrence of poverty and other factors that are known to negatively impact learning. For example, children living in poverty have a higher likelihood of attending schools that are relatively less well-resourced than wealthier schools. These schools may experience a higher staff turnover rate. Research is beginning to unpack the ways in which children's unique background characteristics can signify elevated risk and intersect with other instructional events to produce inequitable outcomes.

Another way to think about equity gaps is to instead consider them as opportunity gaps. With different investments, learning can often readily be improved. For example, imagine a child who lives in a high-poverty setting and attends a poorly resourced school. That child happens to be a child who needs to experience highly effective reading instruction to learn to read, and that child does not receive highly effective reading instruction. Compensatory processes (e.g., tutoring, supplemental intervention programs) may simultaneously be less available. Thus, poverty can be thought of as a factor that, when intersected with other instructional events and unique student needs, can produce poor learning and even illiteracy. At the same time, such negative effects can be overcome when systems recognize educational need and react with effective compensatory strategies. There are major differences between school districts and even between schools within school districts in the numbers of students who are eligible for free and reduced-priced lunches (a marker for poverty or low socioeconomic status). In Table 1.1 we show the numbers of students in representative U.S. school districts who receive free or reduced-price lunches.

Linguistic Diversity

In 2018, 10% of the nation's schoolchildren were English learners, ranging from 0.8% in West Virginia to 19.4% in California (nces.ed.gov/program/coe/indicator/cgf), according to data from the National Center for Education Statistics. The number of EL students has risen significantly since 2019. Importantly, in the Chicago Public Schools, for example, students spoke 110 *different* languages, while the majority of teachers speak only English. Linguistic diversity is often partnered with cultural diversity and in research studies these students are grouped together as culturally and linguistically diverse students. Speaking multiple languages is cognitively beneficial, a strength that linguistically diverse students bring to their classrooms. However, most academically oriented tests have not been designed with this population in mind. If one of the requirements of the law is that students must be assessed in their native language or mode of communication, how do we assure that students are assessed appropriately in their native language and in English? Diversity of student characteristics such as race, ethnicity, and language beckon educators to responsibly reflect on school-based assessment practices. Throughout this textbook, we provide you with what we call Stakeholder Perspectives. These are firsthand, frontline views from professionals in the schools, some experts, and parents who provide you as readers with their perspectives on the important issues you are reading about. The first such perspective appears on the next page and is provided by Meghan Anderson, a veteran kindergarten teacher from Rialto Unified School District in California. Ms. Anderson describes the diversity of students enrolled in her classroom.

Diversity in Skill Development

In addition to student characteristics derived from their family life there are other aspects of diversity that are more influenced by school-based experiences. Students demonstrate a significant range of academic skills; for example, in some large urban environments, 75% of sixth graders are reading more than 2 years below grade level, and there is as much as a 10-year range in skill level in math in a sixth-grade classroom. It is critical that teachers and related services personnel assess the skill development of individual students within classrooms to differentiate instruction for students.

It is always necessary to match the level of instruction that occurs for individual students to their level of skill development if one is to expect them to succeed and make progress through the curriculum. If instruction is understood as an interaction between the learner, the teacher, and the broader instructional environment, then instruction is the variable that we can best adjust to improve the fit between the student, the teacher's behavior, and the environment to improve student learning. Learning can best be described as a very predictable outcome of instruction. When learning is not occurring, assessment teams must ask, "What is wrong with the instruction?" Too often, assessment teams only ask, "What is wrong with the learner?"

Meghan Anderson, Kindergarten Teacher, Rialto Unified School District

I have been an elementary teacher in the Rialto Unified School district for 17 years. Of those 17 years, I worked with kindergarten students for 14 years (12 years as a teacher and 2 years as the kindergarten math coach). Rialto has a diverse population, with 97% minority enrollment and 88% free and reduced-price lunch eligibility; 20% of students are English language learners.

For many students, kindergarten is their first experience in a formal school setting. These students arrive at school with diverse backgrounds and experiences. Some of the different types of diversity include skill, linguistic, and cultural diversity. Some arrive on the first day of school already with many foundational skills such as alphabet knowledge, concepts about print, ability to write their name, and the experience of being read to on a regular basis. They understand the difference between a letter and a number. Others will need help finding their name on their cubby, have never held a pencil or scissors before, will pick up a book upside down and backward, and see letters, numbers, and words as random symbols that yet to have meaning to them. They have a diverse range of skills and abilities. While many students come into kindergarten with a rich vocabulary in the English language, others may have a rich vocabulary in Spanish or another language with little or no exposure to the English language. Cultural diversity is seen through a variety of races, religions, and ethnicities of students and their families.

In my classroom, I look for ways to support individual differences that will also facilitate instruction and assessment. For example, some students are unable to sit for extended periods of time. I provide movement breaks which allows students to stand rather than sit at their table. Sometimes I provide some kind of flexible seating. These are easy ways I can be flexible to enhance the learning environment for all of my students. When assessing students, I understand that inability to demonstrate proficiency may not be that a student doesn't understand the concept. In some cases, an incorrect answer might be due to how the question is asked, level of language proficiency, lack of exposure, or how comfortable the student is in the testing environment. I strive to keep an open mind so that I can understand the true reasons behind slower rates of learning or incorrect answers.

As a kindergarten teacher, it is important for me to value and celebrate the different experiences, backgrounds, and cultures that students bring to the classroom. Through this I can build authentic and meaningful relationships with students and their families. I can select materials, literature, activities, and teaching strategies that build connections between what they already understand and their learning needs. I can help students to recognize, honor, and celebrate diversity amongst their classmates. I attended a training once highlighting that students need mirrors and windows in their life and classrooms. When students see themselves in others that would be considered a mirror. As a Caucasian women I may not be a mirror for many of my students, but I can provide windows through diverse literature and experiences.

Diversity in Opportunity to Learn

The students who attend today's schools come from different cultural, economic, linguistic, and experiential backgrounds. Whenever we assess students it is critical that we take their background experiences and opportunities into account. It is always necessary for us to ask the extent to which a student has had the opportunity to learn the material we are assessing. In fact, several disability conditions cannot be formally assigned unless and until a special education planning team can show that a student has had an opportunity to learn content being assessed and has failed to learn that content. Opportunity to learn can be impacted by a wide range of variables including disability, mobility, and quality of instruction.

Throughout this textbook we will be stressing the two most important diversity factors to be considered in assessment: diversity in skill development and diversity in opportunity to learn. These two encompass the other aspects of diversity and have the greatest implications for planning instruction and interventions that will lead to improved student competence.

Schools are intended to provide *all* students with the skills and competencies they need to enhance their lives and the lives of their fellow citizens. School personnel are expected to provide all students with a predetermined set of competencies, usually those specified in individual state education standards. This function would be extremely difficult even if all students entered school with the same abilities, life experiences, and competencies and even if all students learned in the same way and at the same rate. However, they do not. For example, it is the first day of school at Tuskegee Elementary, and several students show up for kindergarten:

- Yanis is dropped off at the front door. He speaks no English and the school staff had no idea he was coming.
- Griffin comes knowing how to read, print, add, and subtract.
- Muhammad is afraid to come to school and cries when his mother tries to leave.
- Kamryn and her mother arrive with a folder that includes all of her preschool records, her immunization and medical records, and reports from the two psychologists she has been seeing since age 2.
- Emma doesn't show up. The school has her name on a list and her completed registration records, and notes from a social worker indicate that she is eligible for free and reduced-price lunch.

Not only do students not begin school with the same skills and abilities, but they make progress through the curriculum at different rates and have different instructional needs. For example, midway through first grade, Sally has picked up all she has been taught with no additional help. She just "gets it." Charles needs instruction specifically targeted to help him master letter–sound correspondence; he sees a tutor twice a week. Joe needs so much help that he receives intensive special education services.

More than 7.1 million children and youth with disabilities (approximately 14% of the school-age population) received special education and related services during the

2018–2019 school year (National Center for Education Statistics, 2019). Most of these children and youth are attending schools in their own neighborhoods in classes with their peers—this was not always the case in the past—and fewer students with disabilities receive special education services in separate buildings or separate classes.

The focus of this book is on students in both special and inclusive education. **Special education** is a set of unique educational services and supports provided to students with disabilities who meet particular disability criteria; these may include services provided in separate settings or services provided in settings including both students with and without disabilities. **Inclusive education** refers to educational approaches that facilitate learning of all students, including those with and without disabilities, within the same environment.

Methods of Collecting Assessment Information

When most people hear the term *assessment*, they think of testing. Assessment is broader than testing. **Testing** consists of administering a particular set of questions to an individual or group of individuals to obtain a score. That score is the end product of testing. A test is only one of several assessment techniques or procedures for gathering information. During the process of assessment, data from record reviews, interviews, observations and tests all come into play. To be most efficient, it can be helpful to first seek relevant information through a review of records, followed by interviews with those with special expertise and those who know the individuals well, and then through observations. The use of testing can be reserved for the collection of more targeted information that can inform instructional changes, and for those decisions that require the use of very current and highly precise information about student skills and behavior. You may find it helpful to think of the mnemonic "RIOT" (record review, interview, observations, and tests), first used by Kenneth Howell (Hosp et al., 2014; Howell & Morehead, 1987) as a handy way to remember the four ways of collecting assessment information.

1.1
ONLINE
RESOURCE

Record Review

Record review is an assessment method involving review of student cumulative records or medical records. In student records, school personnel retain demographic information, previous test scores, attendance data, and teacher verified comments about student behavior and performance. Assessors nearly always examine the prior records of the individual students with whom they work. These might include health records, prior school records, or records of prior evaluations. Record reviews are useful in documenting when problems first appeared, their severity, and the interventions attempted. Similarly, record reviews are helpful when a student has not previously demonstrated difficulties. Assessors may also review the nature of instructional demands in classrooms and compare these to products of individual students' work in order to get at any discrepancies between the skills students have and the nature of tasks they are being asked to complete.

Interviews

Recollections, or recalled observations and interpretations of behavior and events, are frequently used as an additional source of information. People who are familiar with the student can be very useful in providing information through interviews and rating scales. An **interview** is an assessment method involving a conversation between two or more people where questions are asked by the interviewer to elicit facts or statements from the interviewee. Interviews can range in structure from casual conversations to highly structured processes in which the interviewer has a predetermined set of questions that are asked in a specified sequence. For example, the interviewer might ask the teacher questions such as, "If you notice _____ is off task, how do you refocus his/her attention?" or, "Which instructional modifications have been effective with _____ ?" Unstructured interviews are discussions with loosely defined questions and open-ended responses. The interviewer asks questions such as "Tell me about how _____ 's behavior in class compares to that of his/her classmates." Semi-structured interviews include a standardized set of questions and open-ended responses. Structured interviews standardize both the questions and possible responses. Examples of structured interviews are the *Behavioral Assessment Scale for Children-2* (Reynolds & Kamphaus, 2015) and the *Gilliam Autism Rating Scale 3* (Gilliam, 2014). Generally, the more structured the interview, the more accurate are the comparisons of the results of several different interviews. Rating scales can be considered the most formal type of structured interview. Rating scales allow questions to be asked in a standardized way and to be accompanied by the same stimulus materials, and they provide a standardized and limited set of response options. Surveys can serve as formal interviews. Students can be asked to complete surveys about their own performance or to provide feedback on an instructional placement.

Observations

Observations can provide highly accurate, detailed, verifiable information not only about the person being assessed but also about the surrounding contexts. **Observations** can be categorized as either nonsystematic or systematic. In *nonsystematic, or informal, observation*, the observer simply watches an individual in his or her environment and notes the behaviors, characteristics, and personal interactions that seem significant. In *systematic observation*, the observer sets out to observe one or more precisely defined behaviors. The observer specifies observable events that define the behavior and then counts the frequency or measures the frequency, duration, amplitude, or latency of the behaviors.

Tests

A **test** is a predetermined set of questions or tasks for which predetermined types of behavioral responses are sought. Tests are particularly useful because they permit tasks and questions to be presented in exactly the same way to each person evaluated. Because a tester elicits and scores behavior in a predetermined and consistent manner, the performances of several different test takers can be compared no matter who does the testing. Hence, tests tend to make many contextual factors in assessment consistent for all those tested. The price of this consistency is that the predetermined questions, tasks, and responses may not be equally relevant to all students. Tests yield two types of information—quantitative and qualitative. *Quantitative data are observations that have been tabulated or otherwise given numerical values.* They are the actual scores achieved on the test. An example of quantitative data is Lee's score of 80 on her math test. *Qualitative data are pieces of information collected based on nonsystematic and unquantified observations.* These may consist of other observations made while a student is tested; they tell us how Lee achieved her score. For example, Lee may have solved all of the addition and subtraction problems with the exception of those that required regrouping. When tests are used, we usually want to know both the scores and how the student earned those scores.

1.1

PROGRESS MONITORING CHECK

Making Assessment Decisions

Educators and related services personnel who work in schools will gather and use assessment information to make decisions for or about students. Table 1.2 lists the kinds of decisions school personnel make using assessment information. The four kinds of decisions listed are those long accepted and currently used in the field (Eunice Kennedy Shriver National Institute of Child Health and Human Development, NIH, DHHS, 2000; National Center on Intensive Intervention, 2013).

TABLE 1.2

Educational Decisions Made Using Assessment Information

Kinds of Decisions	Decisions Made Using Assessment Information
Screening	Are there unrecognized problems?
Diagnostic	Is the student eligible for special education services? Does the student meet the criteria for a condition? Does the student need special education services?
Instructional Planning and Monitoring	What to teach. How to teach. Progress monitoring.
Outcomes	Is the student meeting individual goals? Are state standards being met at the individual, classroom, district, and state level?

Screening Decisions

Screening decisions involve the collection of assessment information to decide whether students have unrecognized problems. Educators now know that it is very important to identify physical, academic, or behavior problems early in students' school careers. Early identification enables us to develop treatments or interventions that may alleviate or eliminate difficulties. School personnel engage in universal screening (they test everyone) for some kinds of potential problems. All young children are screened for vision or hearing problems with the understanding that identification of sensory problems allows us to prescribe corrective measures (glasses, contacts, hearing aids, or amplification equipment) that will prevent sensory problems from serving as a barrier to learning. All students are required to have a physical examination, and most students are assessed for "school readiness" prior to entrance into school. Academic screening tests typically are given to all students in regular classes to identify students who are discrepant from an expected level of performance. Such screening is called universal screening. When all students are screened, school personnel usually use screening measures to ascertain the extent to which general education instruction is meeting the needs of all students and to identify specific students who may need supplemental supports to be successful.

Diagnostic and Eligibility Decisions

Diagnostic decisions must be made when students experience academic or behavior difficulties. Diagnostic tests pinpoint which specific skill or behavior deficits may be stopping students from meeting goals or standards. Then instructional programs to remediate or compensate for those skill deficits must be designed. One kind of diagnostic decision is to identify a student as meeting the criteria for a specific disability condition. We refer to these decisions as eligibility decisions.

Eligibility decisions involve the collection and use of assessment information to decide whether a student meets the state criteria for a disability condition and also needs special education services to be successful in school. Note the two-part nature of eligibility decisions. Before a student may be declared eligible for special education services, he or she must be shown to be exceptional (have a disability) *and* to have special learning needs. This is an important point especially relevant to assessment in schools. It is not enough to be disabled *or* to have special learning needs.

Students can have a disability and not require special education services. For example, they can be hearing impaired, and the impairment may not be interfering with their academic performance. Similarly, students can have special learning needs but not meet the state criteria for being declared disabled. For example, there is no federal mandate for provision of special education services to students with behavior disorders, and in many states students with behavior disorders are not eligible for special education services (students need to be identified as emotionally disturbed to receive special education services). Students who receive special education (1) have diagnosed disabilities and (2) need special education services to achieve educational outcomes.

In addition to the classification system employed by the federal government, every state has an education code that specifies disability types or categories. States may have different names for the same disability. For example, in California, some students are called "deaf" or "hard of hearing"; in other states, such as Colorado, the same kinds of students are called "hearing impaired." States may expand special education services to provide for students who have disabilities that are not listed in the Individuals With Disabilities Education Act (IDEA), but states may not exclude service provision to students who have disabilities listed in IDEA. Finally, while a state may provide students labeled as gifted with special programs and protections, these students are not included in the IDEA and are not entitled to federal funding for special education. We expand on these concepts in Chapter 21, "Using Assessment Information to Make Diagnostic/Eligibility Decisions." In later chapters, we describe diagnostic assessment in reading, mathematics, written language, cognition, and social-emotional functioning.

Instructional Planning and Modification Decisions

Instructional planning and **modification decisions** involve the collection of assessment information for planning individualized instruction or making changes in the instruction students are receiving. Data on instructional planning and modification provides information about what can be done to enhance a students' competence and build their capacity. Inclusive education teachers are able to take a standard curriculum and plan instruction based on it. Although curricula vary from district to district—largely as a function of the values of community and school—they are appropriate for most students at a given age or grade level. However, what should teachers do for those students whose academic and behavioral skills differ significantly from their peers or from district standards? These students need special help to benefit from classroom curriculum and instruction, and school personnel must gather data to plan special programs for these students.

Three kinds of decisions are made in instructional planning: (1) instructional planning—deciding what to teach, (2) instructional strategies—deciding how to teach, and (3) progress monitoring—measuring how much progress is being made.

Deciding What to Teach

Instructional planning, or deciding what to teach, involves content decisions made on the basis of a systematic analysis of the skills that students do and do not have relative to expected skill proficiencies in a content area at a grade level. Expected milestone proficiencies can be specified on an instructional calendar by taking the state standards for a grade level and mapping them out logically over the number of instructional weeks that are available for teaching those understandings. Assessment of student mastery of these skills at key intervals helps teachers decide whether students have specific competencies. Test information may be used to determine placement in reading groups or assignment to specific compensatory or remedial programs. Some teachers use computer adaptive tests to identify specific skill-development standing. Teachers also use information gathered from observations and interviews in deciding what to teach.

Deciding How to Teach

There is no way to decide ahead of time how to teach specific individual students because teaching is recursive process that involves the teacher responding to the student as learning occurs. There are instructional methods, approaches, or strategies that are generally more effective than others. In fact, one of the provisions of the Every Student Succeeds Act, the major federal law governing delivery of elementary and secondary education, states that schools are to use "evidence-based" instructional practices. There are a number of interventions with empirical evidence to support their use with students with special needs. Many websites are devoted to evidence-based teaching, including the National Center on Intensive Intervention (intensiveintervention.org), the National Center on Response to Intervention (rti4success.org), Intervention Central (interventioncentral.org), and the What Works Clearinghouse from the U.S. Department of Education (ies.ed.gov/ncee/wwc/). These are, however, compilations of practices that are generally more effective than others. Thus, test results alone do not tell us how to teach. Instructional tactics must be selected from those with efficacy data and aligned to the instructional goals of the classroom and the students' skill proficiencies. The best way to decide how to teach is to teach and to gather data on the extent to which our instructional approaches produce effective outcomes. When they do, we continue them, and when they don't, we change them until we find approaches that move students toward their goals. This is why good instructional decision making always includes progress monitoring.

Progress Monitoring

School personnel **monitor student progress** to make two kinds of instructional decisions: (1) Is the student making adequate progress toward individual goals?, and (2) Is the student making adequate progress toward state standards?

Teachers and related services personnel regularly assess the specific skills that students do or do not have in specified academic content areas such as decoding words, comprehending what they read, performing math calculations, solving math problems, or writing. Monitoring progress allows them to know whether the student's rate of acquisition will allow the completion of all instructional goals within the time allotted (e.g., by the end of the school year or by the completion of secondary education). The data are collected for the purpose of making decisions about what to teach and the level at which to teach. For example, students who have mastered single-digit addition need no further instruction (although they may still need practice) in single-digit addition. Students who do not demonstrate those skills need further instruction. The specific goals and objectives for students who receive special education services are listed in their Individualized Education Programs (IEPs).

Teachers monitor progress toward the competencies they want students to attain so that they can modify instruction or interventions that are not having desired outcomes. Progress may be monitored continuously or periodically to ensure students have acquired the information and skills being taught, can maintain the newly acquired skills and information over time, and can appropriately generalize the newly acquired skills and information. The IEPs of students who receive special education services must contain statements about the methods that will be used to assess their progress toward attaining individualized goals. In any case, the information is used to make decisions about whether the instruction or intervention is working and whether there is a need to alter instruction.

A second kind of progress monitoring decision is one in which school personnel monitor student progress toward specific state standards. State education agency personnel set goals/standards/expectations for performance of schools, classes, and individual students. All states have identified academic content and performance standards that specify what students are expected to learn in reading, mathematics, social studies, science, and so forth. Moreover, states are required by law to have in place a system of assessments aligned with their goals/standards/expectations. The assessments that are used to identify the standing of groups are also used to ascertain if individuals have met or exceeded state standards/goals.

Outcomes Decisions

School personnel use assessment data to make two kinds of outcomes decisions. The first outcomes decision considers whether or not students have met their individual instructional goals, and whether students, classrooms, districts and states have met state standards. Data gathered from standardized tests, computer-adaptive tests, or curriculum-based measures are used to ascertain whether or not students have met their individual goals or objectives. A school team might review the number of students with IEPs and review what percentages of those students met their yearly goals.

The second kind of outcomes assessment is seen in state or federal accountability assessments where the focus is on the extent to which students, classrooms, districts, or states have met state standards. The assessments used typically are state tests. Under the provisions of the Every Student Succeeds Act (ESSA, 2015), schools, school districts, and state education agencies are held accountable for individual student performance and progress. School districts must report annually to their state's department of education the performance of all students, including students with disabilities, on tests the state requires students to take. By law, states, districts, and individual schools must demonstrate that the students they teach are making adequate yearly progress (AYP). When it is judged by the state that a school is not making AYP, or when specified subgroups of students (disadvantaged students, students with disabilities, or specific racial/ethnic groups) are not making AYP, sanctions are applied. The school is said to be a school in need of improvement. The nature of sanctions changes over time. Proactive school teams will review their data gathered from state assessments to self-evaluate what percentage of students are meeting grade-level standards. These outcome deci-sions can be used to guide important decisions pertaining to professional development or curriculum purchases.

The Assessment Process

The assessment and decision-making process differs for individual students, but there are commonalities in the sequence of activities that take place. Figure 1.1 shows the flow of activities from initial concern by a classroom teacher to the implementation of supplemental and targeted or intensive interventions in the general education class-room. Student progress is monitored and, depending on how students perform, they either receive more or less intensive services. Also illustrated is the fact that assessment information is collected for the purpose of deciding whether students are eligible for special education services and for the purpose of making accountability decisions. This simple chart is intended to illustrate the process in general. Recognize that for individual students, the process may include some extra steps, and certainly that it takes varying amounts of time for different individuals to proceed through the steps. Recognize also that many students with disabilities receive special education services before they enter school. This is especially true for students who are blind, deaf, have medical conditions that interfere with learning, or have multiple disabilities.

Let's walk through the steps in the assessment and decision-making process. A stu-dent, let's call her Sara, is enrolled in an elementary general education classroom. Uni-versal screening (screening tests given to all students in her grade) reveals a difference between her reading level (the observed level on the screening test) and the level of the materials in which she is placed. A decision is made to move to targeted interventions (Tier 2 of a Response to Intervention [RTI] approach) in an effort to attempt to over-come Sara's deficit in reading skills. The problem is verified, alternative hypotheses are generated about how best to address the problem, interventions are tried, and progress monitoring assessment data are collected. If sufficient progress is not observed after ap-plication of multiple interventions, a decision is made to move to more intensive (Tier 3) interventions. Once sufficient attempts at intervening in a variety of ways are made, Sara may be referred to a multidisciplinary team for further assessment to determine her eligibility for special education services. Decisions about eligibility must be made by a multidisciplinary team of professionals, which includes general and special educators, administrators, school psychologists, and others depending on the nature of the case. The multidisciplinary team in partnership with caregivers or parents develops an IEP, specifying short- and long-term objectives for Sara and the specific instructional ap-proaches that will be used to achieve those objectives. It is expected that the long-term goals will be based on the state education standards. The goals are thus often called standards-based goals.

Implicit in these mutually supportive requirements for general education accountabil-ity, special education eligibility (including child find), and standards-aligned goals for

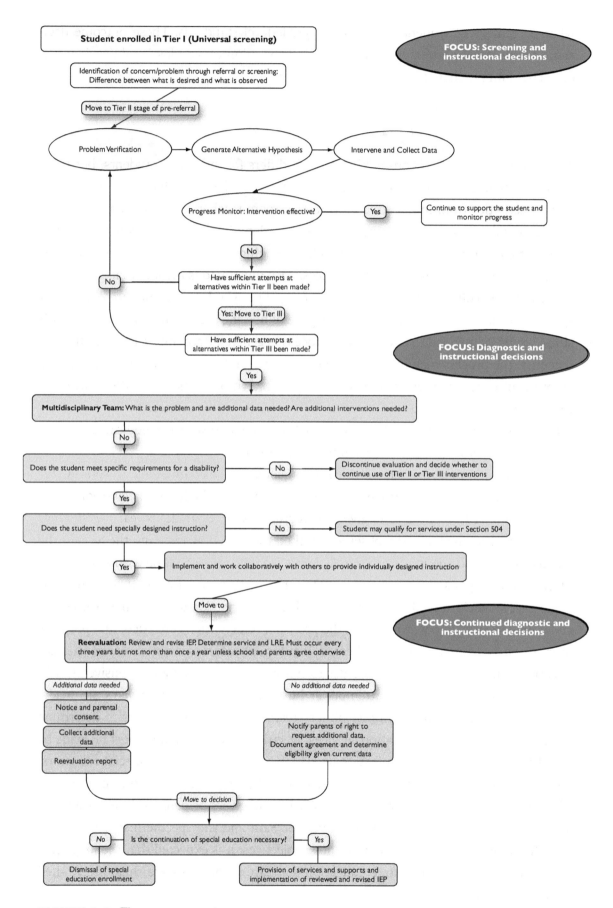

FIGURE 1.1. The assessment process.

students in special education is every child's right to a free and appropriate public education. The aspiration is to provide all children with an optimal opportunity for learning during school and this aspiration is the basis for (a) universal screening to detect educational need, (b) intervention as a remediation and prevention activity in general instruction, rigorous expectations for all learners, and (c) ultimately an IEP that provides the necessary supports for students with disabilities to have grade-level success. Admittedly, we have a long way to go in attaining these aspirations, but as school personnel engaged in assessment, it is important to remember the purpose of the procedures we follow when determining eligibility and serving eligble students.

When students receive special education services, teachers are expected to monitor progress toward IEP goals. School personnel are also required to periodically review the extent to which the student continues to be eligible for special education services, and if not, they must discontinue such services. Special education teachers and school psychologists are often in a leadership position to develop and carry out special education plans and to ensure that parents and caregivers understand the assessment data gathered and the plan developed.

Why Learn About Assessment in Special and Inclusive Education?

Educational professionals must assess and must understand the results of assessments that they and others administer. Assessment is a critical practice that serves the purpose of matching instruction to the level of students' skills, monitoring student progress, modifying instruction, and working hard to enhance student competence. It is a critical component of teaching, and so it is necessary for teachers to have good skills in assessment and a good understanding of assessment information.

Although assessment can be an intimidating topic for practicing professionals as well as individuals training to become professionals, learning its different important facets helps people become less apprehensive. Educational assessments always have consequences that are important for students and their families. We can expect that good assessments lead to good decisions—decisions that facilitate a student's progress toward the desired goal (especially long term) of becoming a happy, well-adjusted, independent, productive member of society. Poor assessments can slow, stop, and sometimes reverse progress. The assessment process can also be intimidating because there is so much to know; a student of assessment can easily get lost in the details of measurement theory, legal requirements, teaching implications, and national politics.

1.2
PROGRESS
MONITORING
CHECK

Ensuring Fairness in Assessment

We indicated that in each chapter we would include a section on ensuring fairness in assessment. In this first chapter we have already touched on a number of important considerations that help ensure fairness. Those who assess students must always be concerned about the extent to which the assessment instruments they use and the assessment process itself is fair for the many different kinds of students who attend today's schools. They must ask questions such as: "Is the test appropriate for the purpose—that is, for the decision I want to make?" "Is the student I am testing included in the norm group of the test I am using?" "Will the test I am using provide the information needed to choose interventions that will improve the academic and behavioral competence of the student I am assessing?" By keeping these questions and others like them always in mind, assessment procedures and processes should be fairer and in the best interests of students.

PROGRESS 1.1
MONITORING CHECK

1. How might racial/ethnic and diversity in skill development affect assessment practices in a school?
2. Think about two of your friends who have had quite different opportunities to learn. How might their different backgrounds affect their performance on a college admissions exam?
3. Horatio transfers into Ms. Young's fourth-grade class in November of the academic year. Ms. Young asks you how she can identify what skills Horatio has. What do you advise her?
4. Identify four ways to gather information on students and describe one of those methods in detail.
5. What is meant by individual differences? Why is it important to take individual differences into account as we try to identify ways to support students in order to help them be successful in school?

PROGRESS 1.2
MONITORING CHECK

1. Identify four kinds of educational decisions made using assessment information.
2. We discussed two necessary things that must be demonstrated to declare a student eligible for special education services. What are those two?
3. When school personnel make instructional planning and monitoring decisions, what three kinds of decisions do they make?
4. What is the best way to decide how to teach a student?

CHAPTER 2

A Principled Approach to Assessment and Decision Making

LEARNING OBJECTIVES

1. Identify and understand the fundamental principles that underlie effective and appropriate assessment in special and inclusive education.
2. Understand the authors' values, beliefs, and perspectives regarding assessment and decision making in order to inform your own thinking about assessment.

Models, methods, and materials used for assessment are constantly evolving. In the past four decades that this book has been written and updated, school personnel have engaged in many different assessment practices, both good and bad. We highlight here some fundamental considerations that we believe are important to understand as you learn more about assessment. A comprehensive understanding of these concepts will help you as you seek to apply assessment knowledge in your school-based practices. These are basic principles that we believe ought to underlie your thinking about assessment and assessment practices. They certainly form the cornerstone of our beliefs and attitudes about how and why we assess students. We hope you will read these and use them as your own lens as you read the remainder of this text.

Fairness Is Paramount

Fairness is a guiding principle in assessment and throughout this textbook because it is at the heart of our principled approach to assessment. We want you always to be thinking about fairness as you learn about assessing students in special and inclusive education. What is not fair cannot be accurate and useful for systems and, as a result, can bring measurable harm to the students we aim to help. School personnel should work always to maximize fairness in assessment. This means choosing tests that are technically adequate and that are relevant to improved instructional outcomes. This means always administering tests according to standard procedures and always taking into account the nature of students' social and cultural backgrounds. A principled and fair approach to assessment means taking into account learning histories and opportunities to learn and always being sensitive to individual differences and disabilities.

Assessment practices should do no harm. If they do not result in improved educational outcomes for students, then they can be considered harmful. In many of the chapters of this text we include a specific section examining how to ensure fairness in assessment. For example, in Chapter 13, "Using Diagnostic Reading Measures," we discuss how to make diagnostic reading assessment work in the best interests of students. The end goal being to ensure that they get appropriate reading instruction that is at their level and that moves them forward as rapidly as possible to attain their individual goals and meet state standards. In Chapter 21, "Using Assessment Information to Make Diagnostic/Eligibility Decisions," we describe methods that minimize bias and are in the best interests of the students we serve when deciding who should receive special education services. The theme of fair assessments used in the best interest of students is one of our foundational principles that you will find throughout this book.

Individual Students Need Different Levels of Support to Succeed

Teachers and related services personnel are responsible for providing education matched to the needs of students with few skills and those with highly developed skills in the same class. No matter what level of skills they bring with them and no matter how motivated students are to learn, it is our job to enhance their competence and to build the capacity of schools together with families, community organizations, churches and other agencies that influence students' development to meet their needs. In a larger social context, the assessor or a case coordinator must take into account these multiple influences when assessing students and developing supports to meet individual student needs. For example, the tutoring Rosa is receiving at the community center could actually be confusing rather than clarifying. Or we may find that a really effective way to help Muhammad is to work with the local Somali neighborhood organization that provides students with homework help. An understanding that we are all citizens and members of a variety of communities can enhance our effectiveness when we take into account these multiple perspectives and systems. To discuss all these influences is beyond the scope of this text, yet we will be taking many such factors into consideration as we talk about appropriate assessment and decision making in school settings.

Effective use of assessment tools is one means by which educators can fulfill the promise of providing instruction that matches students' needs with the goal of enabling each individual student to be successful in attaining the educational state and federal standards of learning. School personnel use assessment results to decide who gets what kinds of support and the level of instructional intensity needed by a student, how instruction will be delivered, and the extent to which instruction is working. Instruction falls along a continuum from differentiated to personalized to individualized instruction. As you move from differentiated to personalized to individualized instruction, it is increasingly customized to the learner based upon student assessment data, which also becomes more detailed.

Differentiated instruction is a process that involves matching the content and instructional approach to individual students' learning needs in order to accelerate the learning of all students. Within one first grade class, some students may not have mastered single-digit addition and subtraction, whereas other students may have mastered this skill and be ready to learn the strategies of carrying and borrowing associated with double-digit addition and subtraction. Some students may need the teacher to provide 10 examples of regrouping within a double-digit additional problem and other students may need just two examples. Only with appropriate and ongoing assessment can one ensure that the content and instructional approaches selected truly match students' needs, and that they are effective. Generally, differentiated instruction is informed by ongoing formative assessment in the classroom. This assessment can be informal as it will occur recursively during instruction so that the teacher can determine what skills students have mastered and which skills require additional instruction. Because this assessment is needed to drive instruction each day, it is not time-consuming or intensive assessment, but rather brief and very targeted. Knowledge and application of best practices in assessment can help a teacher identify where each student's current skill level and deliver instruction at that level, thereby providing differentiated instruction that optimizes student learning.

Personalized instruction is typically delivered to individual students by a teacher or instructional aid or via computer-based instructional tools. Regardless of the delivery method, individual student data is taken into consideration when developing the academic goals, content, and instructional delivery so that the combined effort is personalized. Computer-based intervention systems offer advantages that were not available in the previous decades of personalized instruction implementation. These systems can be easy to use because the assessment and instruction is automated (i.e., delivered via the computer), but the results of the assessments and their linkage to intervention changes in subsequent sessions is largely hidden from the teacher. Theoretically, because the intervention is adjusted from session to session based upon collected data, personalized instruction represents a more intensive intervention effort. Research studies examining the effects on student learning for differentiated and personalized instruction have been mixed.

Individualized intervention that is actively managed by the teacher with assessments selected by the teacher with consideration to local learning expectations and the current instructional plan can produce positive effects on student learning. Equipping teachers to understand how assessment choices lead to individualized intervention is an important goal of this book. We encourage you to think of differentiation as a logical method to organize core or universal classroom instruction, recognizing that learners bring different needs to your instruction each day. Individualized instruction is more commonly found in special education settings. For example, you can plan to deliver an extension of a lesson or a reteach of a lesson and sort groups of students based on informal assessment during the first lesson. This differentiated instruction can be partnered with individualized instruction for those students who need additional opportunities to learn and master the content. Ultimately, assessing child performance and delivering intensive intervention in small groups and one-on-one with students is the most high-yield action in terms of student learning gains and is only possible with accurate and fair assessment. Every chapter in this book is built from the principle that assessment used effectively is a tool to be used by educators to match student need to appropriate instruction and intervention and minimizes bias and maximizes cultural and community resources toward that goal. We will focus on this process in each of the diagnostic assessment chapters.

Different Decisions May Require Collection of Different Data Types

Decisions made within school settings vary considerably in terms of the consequences or stakes attached. In some cases, decisions may have relatively minor implications for student learning. For instance, a high school teacher may want information to decide whether to focus more instructional time during a particular class period on the causes of the Civil War or whether it would be better to move on to teaching about the various battles in the war. In this case, the teacher might quickly develop a brief measure to find out whether the majority of the class knows several identified causes of the war. In other cases, a decision may have major implications for students. For example, determining whether a student has a disability and qualifies for special education services can have lifelong implications for the student's future. Such a diagnostic decision should be informed by data that are collected systematically over time using measures that have strong evidence of reliability (i.e., they measure consistently) and validity (i.e., they measure what they propose to measure). Although data with strong technical characteristics (i.e., reliability and validity) are desirable, they are not always necessary, and they do not guarantee that sound decisions are made as a result. In some cases, reliance on a high standard for reliability and validity may prolong decision-making that needs to be made more quickly to be effective. It is therefore important to consider the stakes of the decision being made to know how technically adequate the assessment tools should be. Chapters 4 ("Test Scores and Norms") and 5 ("Technical Requirements: Reliability and Validity") provide information on technical characteristics that should be considered when deciding which assessment tools to use. Chapters 10 ("Screening"), 12 ("Assessment of Academic Achievement With Multiple-Skills Measures"), 13 ("Using Diagnostic Reading Measures"), 14 ("Using Diagnostic Mathematics Measures"), 15 ("Using Oral and Written Language Measures and Measures of Receptive Vocabulary"), and 18 ("Using Measures of Social and Emotional Behavior") describe assessment processes that are used when making decisions, some with high- and some with low-stake impacts.

Individual Students Need Different Assessment Methods

Test developers typically try to make their tests accessible to a wide range of individuals. However, characteristics of how the test is administered, how those being tested are expected to provide their responses, and characteristics of the norm group to whom students are compared may influence the extent to which a given test is appropriate for a particular student. For example, some tests that are intended to measure math skills are written in a way that students ultimately need to have vision and competent reading skills to understand the test items. Such a test may not accurately measure the math skills of a student who is blind or has a reading disability. Students who do not have proficiency with the English language or who are from particularly unique cultures may not have the prerequisite language and cultural knowledge to demonstrate their cognitive abilities on cognitive tests that have been developed and normed in mainstream U.S. culture. For example, a child who has just relocated from a small, rural farming community in Puerto Rico may not be familiar with a chimney in a house. In such a case, not knowing the meaning of the word *chimney* results only from a lack of familiarity due to life experience. Although test developers are careful to remove items that could carry such bias, teachers should always be aware of the potential for bias in items that can come into play based on a student's life history. In such cases, one must be careful to either identify and use tests that are more appropriate for students with the given characteristics, consider accessibility options to allow the test to be more appropriate for the given student, or use alternative methods of assessment. Chapters 6 ("Cultural and Linguistic Considerations in Assessment and Decision Making") and 7 ("Assessment in Multi-Tiered Systems of Support") discuss important considerations for the assessment of two unique groups of students: those who are non-native English speakers (i.e., English learners, emerging bilingual, limited English proficient students) and those who have disabilities. Chapter 22 ("Using Assessment Information to Make Accountability

Decisions") highlights important considerations for effectively including students with disabilities in accountability assessment programs.

Only Present Behavior Is Observed

When students take tests, we only observe what they do. We never observe the full range of what they can do. If a student correctly solves half of the single-digit addition problems on a math test, we know that she correctly solved half of the single-digit addition problems. We do not know that she *can* only correctly solve half of the problems, can add single-digit addition problems involving 3s, or will do so in the future. Any statement about future performance or capability is an *inference*. Many factors determine a student's performance on a given day on a given test and it is important to remember that we only observe what the student *does*, not what he or she *can do*. One of our pet peeves and a shared annoyance of any competent assessor is observing a colleague using the results of student performance on a specific test to infer what a student can or cannot do. In life it is best not to assume or make unfounded predictions. The same is true in the world of education and assessment. Teachers can make it a habit to describe student performance on tests that eliminate phrases such as "was able" or "can complete" and instead use phrases such as "performed 15 problems correctly and made three errors" or "completed" or simply "scored." Fairness in the assessment process can be maintained by only describing the behaviors and skills demonstrated.

Avoid High-Inference Decision Making

In the assessment process we typically make inferences about a student's level and rate of progress using a sample of information. However, a high level of inference making can be problematic. Inference making is particularly evident and potentially problematic when (a) there are only a few items or tasks that sample a particular behavior or skill of interest, and (b) the skills needed to complete the items or tasks do not adequately reflect the skills targeted for measurement. For example, use of a brief three-item multiple choice test to measure a student's math problem-solving skills involves a high level of inference because (a) it includes just a few items, and (b) the task ultimately requires mere selection from the listed responses for each item rather than actual completion of a math problem. A student could (merely by chance!) earn a high score on such a test and not ultimately have strong math problem-solving skills. In such a situation, the inference that the resulting test score offers an accurate indication of the student's math problem-solving skills would be incorrect. A test requiring less inference would be one that requires the student to actually solve the problem on his or her own, without providing a list of potentially correct responses.

Furthermore, some constructs currently being measured in school settings are only tangentially related to academic and social-emotional skills. When tests of these constructs are used, high-level inferences are needed to connect the information in a way that can meaningfully inform instruction. For example, although there is information to suggest that short-term memory (a construct commonly measured on tests of intelligence) is related to academic performance, knowing that a student performed low on a test of short-term memory does not provide targeted guidance on what or how to teach. Although it may suggest a student needs more repetitions to master a particular skill, one could arrive at that conclusion with greater confidence if they more directly measured the number of repetitions the student required to learn something.

One of the authors of this book participated in a review of a student's eligibility evaluation. The evaluation team elected to conduct and consider the results of a cognitive battery of assessments and to analyze the resulting subtest scores to determine if a weakness could be detected relative to stronger subtest and cluster scores. All of the student's scores were in the average range of performance with only one exception. She had one subtest score, which was estimated on the basis of her ability to recall a list of 30 common items (ball, horse, fish) following completion of two different testing tasks intended to introduce a delay (about 8 minutes in her case) between the time at which the items were shown and the time at which she was asked to recall the names of as many items as she could within a 45-second window. This score—delayed item recall—was lower than her other scores but still within the typical range. The student also had ample academic screening and progress monitoring data with and without intervention delivered by a reading coach. Because this student had been absent from school approximately 50% of every school year for every year she had been in school, intervention response data were especially important to rule out lack of instruction as causal to her poor reading performance. The student attained twice the rate of growth necessary to determine a successful Response to Intervention during the four weeks of reading intervention that she received with a reading coach. Nonetheless, this student was incorrectly determined eligible for specific learning disability by the evaluation team. The reason cited for her eligibility was repeatedly that she had a discrepancy or significant weakness in the area of memory. This conclusion was based on a single subtest embedded within a number of other assessment activities on a single day with an adult she did not know and using an artificial task as memory tests often do. Despite overwhelming evidence that she performed in the average range on academic achievement tests (need was not demonstrated), that she had missed a substantial amount of instruction and did appear in the risk range on reading screening, and that when given targeted reading intervention by the school's reading coach, in 4 weeks' time, she performed outside of the risk range, this team concluded that she was eligible for special education. Her subsequent service in special education did not resolve her absenteeism problems, and though her academic performance remained in the average range, her annual review continued to reference her "substantial memory problem." Surely, the overwhelming evidence of her capacity to learn to read (at her first review, she read in the average range) was a superior test of her memory capacity than a single subtest that was artificial and administered by an adult she did not really know. This example highlights that the decision to include specific assessments and to weigh some assessment findings more heavily than others must be thoughtful in order to provide free and appropriate public education to students and to avoid the potential for harm that can result from a more restrictive educational placement or even the expectations of her family and teachers because of a now-codified, but probably incorrect, conclusion about her memory capacity and her ability to learn.

It is our belief that one should avoid use of assessment tools that require a high level of inference making, especially when making high-stakes decisions such as special education eligibility. This is because results obtained through use of such tools may (a) misrepresent the students' actual skills, and (b) lead to conclusions that are not helpful for informing instruction. Instead, we prefer direct measurement of actual academic and behavioral skills that can be altered through instruction. Characteristics and examples of direct assessment are described in Chapter 11. Part III, "Using Formal Measures," includes information on assessment tools that vary considerably in the level of inference required for instructional decision making.

2.1

PROGRESS MONITORING CHECK

Accurately Collect, Score, Interpret, and Communicate Assessment Information

Assessment tools often have very specific rules about how they are to be administered and scored. These rules are developed to ensure that the tool allows for accurate and meaningful measurement of the target skill. Deviation from these rules can result in scores that do not accurately reflect a student's level of competence in the targeted area and ultimately lead to poor decision making. Therefore, great care must be taken to ensure that the data are collected carefully and with due attention to any administration and scoring rules.

However, merely attending to accuracy in the collection of data is not enough. The data are only helpful if they are used in an appropriate manner for decision making. All too often we hear of situations in which schools have collected a large amount of data but the data are not used to facilitate improvements in instruction. This may be because no one has or takes the time to interpret and use them, they don't have the capacity to understand and interpret the data, or they use them in ways that they were not intended to be used. Before data are even collected, it is important to clarify how the data will be used and ensure that the use of the given data for the given purpose is justified. In many cases, data are used to inform the decisions made by teams of individuals. In these cases, it is important to ensure that the assessment information is communicated well to all team members. Chapter 3, "Laws, Ethical Codes, and Professional Standards That Impact Assessment," discusses laws and ethics surrounding the collection and use of data in school settings, and Chapter 23, "Principles and Practices for Collaborative Teams," offers ideas for ensuring that data are communicated well to team members.

Keep Assessment Instructionally Relevant

The fundamental purpose of assessment is gathering information that leads to improvement in students' competencies in relevant domains of behavior and achievement. Assessment that is related to and supports the development of effective interventions is worthwhile and clearly in the best interests of individuals, families, schools, communities, and society. Many assessment practices in schools today are irrelevant and unnecessary. You will read about examples of some of these in chapters on assessment of perception and perceptual-motor functioning and on assessment of cognitive processes. Some of these assessments do not lead to interventions that improve student competence in relevant domains of behavior and achievement. Many assessments are technically inadequate, so the information they provide is not useful for anything. Other practices provide information of heuristic interest only. Throughout this text you will hear us preaching the message of instructionally relevant assessment practices. There is no more critical purpose of assessment than to improve school outcomes for students by providing useful information for teachers. When teams conduct assessments that fall short of this goal, it is not only inefficient or a poor use of limited resources but is also potentially harmful because it can lead to inaccurate decisions and worse outcomes for students.

2.2
*PROGRESS
MONITORING
CHECK*

Principled Assessment Practices Are Dynamic

Educational personnel regularly change their assessment practices. New federal or state laws, regulations, or guidelines specify and, in some cases, mandate, new assessment practices. New tests become available and old ones go away. States change their special education eligibility criteria and technological advances enable us to gather data in new and more efficient ways. The population of students attending schools also changes, bringing new knowledge to the educational personnel who are working to enhance the academic and behavioral competence of all students. Therefore, although this chapter is focused on highlighting key concepts that are universal, it is important to note that one of those concepts is ultimately that assessment practices change. By becoming familiar with the fundamental concepts presented here and throughout this book, we anticipate that you will have the beginning skills to evaluate future assessment practices and adopt those practices that both meet legal and ethical guidelines and ultimately help to promote student learning.

PROGRESS

2.1

MONITORING CHECK

1. What questions would you ask yourself in examining the extent to which assessment practices are fair for a student?

2. What factors should be taken into account in making a decision about whether a specific test is appropriate to administer to a student?

3. Why is it important to make low-inference decisions?

PROGRESS

2.2

MONITORING CHECK

1. Why is it important to administer a test precisely as a test manual says it should be administered?

2. How do you know if an assessment is instructionally relevant?

3. What is the bottom line in fairness?

CHAPTER 3

Laws, Ethical Codes, and Professional Standards That Impact Assessment

LEARNING OBJECTIVES

1. List the major laws that affect assessment, along with the specific provisions (e.g., Individualized Education Program, least restrictive environment, and due process provisions) of the laws.
2. Describe broad ethical principles and standards for assessment that have been developed by professional associations and learn about a process for how to proceed ethically in ambiguous situations.
3. Explain how test standards promote the development of tests with greater technical adequacy.

Much of the practice of assessing students is the direct result of federal laws, court rulings, and professional standards and ethics. Federal laws, such as Section 504 of the Rehabilitation Act of 1973 and the Individuals With Disabilities Education Act of 1990 (IDEA), mandate when and how students must be assessed. Specifically, the IDEA requires data collection and decisions by teams of teachers, school psychologists and related services personnel before students are determined to be eligible for special education services. Federal laws also mandate an Individualized Education Program (IEP) for every eligible student with a disability, instructional objectives for each of these students derived from a comprehensive individualized assessment, and the provision of an annual report by the states to the U.S. Department of Education on the academic performance of all students, including students with disabilities (SWD). Professional associations go beyond federal laws and court rulings (e.g., the Council for Exceptional Children, the National Association of School Psychologists, the American Psychological Association, and the National Education Association) by specifying standards for good professional practice and ethical principles to guide the behavior of those who assess students.

Laws

Laws, rules, and regulations change frequently. They are fueled by information provided to policymakers that convinces them the respective changes will be helpful. Changes often come about when there is a lack of clarity in the existing laws, rules, and regulations, as evidenced by court cases that are needed to clarify how the law should be interpreted in various ambiguous situations. As you read this chapter, we suggest that you enter "IDEA changes," or "ESSA changes" into a search engine and read the latest changes to the law.

It is very important to understand the history of federal legislation on the education and assessment of individuals with disabilities and the changes that have taken place over time in the laws that govern assessment practices. Prior to 1975, there was no federal requirement that students with disabilities attend school or that schools should make an effort to teach them. Requirements for school attendance were decided on a state-by-state basis, and they differed and were applied differently among states. Since the mid-1970s, the delivery of services to students in special and inclusive education has been governed by federal laws. An important federal law, **Section 504 of the Rehabilitation Act of 1973**, gave individuals with disabilities equal access to programs and services funded by federal monies. In 1975, Congress passed the **Education for All Handicapped Children Act (EHA) (Public Law 94-142)**, which was the first law to prescribe specific instructional and assessment requirements for serving and identifying students with disabilities in need of specially designed instruction. The law was reauthorized, amended, and updated in 1986, 1990, 1997, and 2004. In 1990, the law was given a new name, the **Individuals With Disabilities Education Act**. As with other reauthorizations, it included updated provisions for identifying and serving students with disabilities. To reflect contemporary practices, Congress replaced references to "handicapped children" with "children with disabilities." The 2004 amendments to IDEA were titled the **Individuals With Disabilities Education Improvement Act** to highlight the fact that the major intent of the law is to improve educational services for students with disabilities.

The **2001 Elementary and Secondary Education Act** (formerly **No Child Left Behind [NCLB]** and now titled **Every Student Succeeds Act [ESSA]**) was another federal law that was especially important to contemporary assessment practices because it required that states report to the U.S. Department of Education every year data on the performance and progress of all students. States receive the information from districts, so this law required that school districts report to state departments of education on the performance and progress of all students, including students with disabilities and English learners. Table 3.1 lists the federal laws that are especially important to assessment practices. The major new provisions of each law are highlighted.

TABLE 3.1

Major Federal Laws and Their Key Provisions Relevant to Assessment

Act	Provisions
Section 504 of the Rehabilitation Act of 1973 (Public Law 93-112)	It is illegal to deny participation in activities or benefits of programs, or to in any way discriminate against a person with a disability solely because of the disability. Individuals with disabilities must have equal access to programs and services. Auxiliary aids must be provided to individuals with impaired speaking, manual, or sensory skills.
Family Educational Rights and Privacy Act (FERPA) (Public Law 93-380)	Educational agencies that accept federal funding must grant parents the opportunity to inspect and challenge student records, as well as require parent consent for release of identifiable data. Once the child turns 18, these rights are transferred to the child.
Education for All Handicapped Children Act of 1975 (EHA) (Public Law 94-142)	Students with disabilities have the right to a free, appropriate public education. Schools must have on file an Individualized Education Program for each student determined to be eligible for services under the act. Parents have the right to inspect school records on their children. When changes are made in a student's educational placement or program, parents must be informed. Parents have the right to challenge what is in records or to challenge changes in placement. Students with disabilities have the right to be educated in the least restrictive educational environment. Students with disabilities must be assessed in ways that are considered fair and nondiscriminatory. They have specific protections.
1986 Amendments to the Education for All Handicapped Children Act (EAHCA) (Public Law 99-457)	All rights of the Education for All Handicapped Children Act are extended to preschoolers with disabilities. Each school district must conduct a multidisciplinary assessment and develop an individualized family service plan for each preschool child with a disability.

Individuals With Disabilities Education Act of 1990 (IDEA) (Public Law 101-476)	The Education for All Handicapped Children Act is further revised and the name is changed. Two new disability categories (traumatic brain injury and autism) are added to the definition of students with disabilities. A comprehensive definition of transition services is added.
1990 Americans With Disabilities Act (ADA)	Guarantees equal opportunity to individuals with disabilities in employment, public services, transportation, state and local government services, and telecommunications.
1997 Amendments to the Individuals With Disabilities Education Act (IDEA) (Public Law 105-17)	The amendments add a number of significant provisions to IDEA and restructure the law. A number of changes in the Individualized Education Program and participation of students with disabilities in state and district assessments are mandated. Significant provisions on mediation of disputes and discipline of students with disabilities are added.
2001 Elementary and Secondary Education Act (No Child Left Behind Act [NCLB]; Public Law 107-110)	Targeted resources are provided to help ensure that disadvantaged students have access to a quality public education (funds Title I). The act aims to maximize student learning, provide for teacher development, and enhance school system capacity. The act requires states and districts to report on annual yearly progress for all students, including students with disabilities. The act provides increased flexibility to districts in exchange for increased accountability. The act gives parents whose children attend a school on a state "failing schools list" for 2 years the right to transfer their children to another school. Students in "failing schools" for 3 years are eligible for supplemental education services.
2004 Reauthorization of IDEA (Individuals With Disabilities Education Improvement Act)	New approaches are introduced to prevent overidentification by race or ethnicity. States must have measurable annual objectives for students with disabilities. States may not require districts to use severe discrepancy between ability and achievement in identifying students with learning disabilities.
2008 Americans With Disabilities Act Amendments (ADAA)	The act further defines and clarifies criteria necessary for determining whether a student has a disability under ADA and Section 504.
2015 Every Student Succeeds Act (ESSA) (reauthorization of Elementary and Secondary Education Act)	All children must be provided a significant opportunity to receive a fair, equitable, and high-quality education. Educational achievement gaps will be closed.

Every Student Succeeds Act

The Every Student Succeeds Act (PL 114-95), signed into law on December 10, 2015, is the nation's main education law for all public schools. This law reauthorized the Elementary and Secondary Education Act and replaced NCLB, which had been in place since 2001. The purpose of the law was "to provide all children significant opportunity to receive a fair, equitable, and high-quality education, and to close educational achievement gaps" (20 U.S.C.§ 6301). In ESSA, Congress required states to specify goals and standards for all students. State department of education personnel in each state must submit plans to the U.S. Department of Education indicating their state standards and how they will measure the numbers of students who have met those standards. The status of state plans can be reviewed at ESSA.org.

State education personnel must adopt "challenging" academic standards and are required to test students in Grades 3 through 8 in reading and math and once in high school. All students, including those in special education, must be assessed on grade-level tests. Only 1% of students overall (10% of those in special education) can be given an alternative assessment.

ESSA requires each state to choose a minimum of five ways to measure student performance. The first four are academic indicators that are mandatory: academic achievement, academic progress, English language proficiency, and high school graduation rate. States must set goals for students. The goals are supposed to help struggling students, especially those in special education, keep up, catch up, and close the achievement gap with other students.

Each year state department of education personnel must report to the U.S. Department of Education the numbers of students who meet state standards by individual schools within their state. They must disaggregate their data by subgroup, reporting separately by gender, race/ethnicity, and disability category subgroup. Each state's department of education personnel must specify a minimum number for each subgroup. This is so that the identification of individual students is protected. For example, if there are only three students with cognitive disabilities in the Crosby-Ironton School District in Minnesota, reporting on the performance of those students would run the risk of divulging the scores of one of the three individual students or compromising those students' right to privacy with regard to their test data.

There are sanctions for failure to meet state standards. At least once every 3 years a statewide category of schools needing Comprehensive Support and Improvement (CSI) must be identified. Then states must identify:

1. Not less than the lowest performing 5% of all schools receiving Title I funding,
2. All public high schools failing to graduate one third or more of their students, and
3. Certain other public schools that have subgroups of students performing as poorly as the lowest 5% of Title I students.

ESSA pertains to all students, including those on IEPs and 504 Plans. It encourages schools to expand personalized learning and requires states to involve parents in the accountability process.

Section 504 of the Rehabilitation Act of 1973

Section 504 of the Rehabilitation Act of 1973 is civil rights legislation that prohibits discrimination against persons with disabilities and is sometimes referred to as a law ensuring access. According to the act:

> No otherwise qualified handicapped individual shall, solely by reason of his handicap, be excluded from the participation in, be denied the benefits of, or be subjected to discrimination in any program or activity receiving federal financial assistance (Rehabilitation Act of 1973, Section 504, 29 U.S.C. § 794(a)).

Section 504 (1) prohibits schools from excluding students with disabilities from any activities solely because of their disability, (2) requires schools to take reasonable steps to prevent harassment based on disability, and (3) requires schools to make those accommodations necessary to enable students with disabilities to participate in all its activities and services (Jacob et al., 2022). If the Office of Civil Rights (OCR) of the U.S. Department of Education finds that a state education agency (SEA) or local education agency (LEA) is not in compliance with Section 504, and that a state or district chooses not to act to correct the noncompliance, the OCR may withhold federal funds from that State or local education agency.

Most of the provisions of Section 504 were incorporated into and expanded in the Education for All Handicapped Children Act of 1975 (Public Law 94-142) and are a part of IDEA. Section 504 is broader than IDEA and its predecessors because its provisions are not restricted to a specific age group or to education. Section 504 has been used to secure services for students with conditions not formally listed in the disabilities education legislation. The most frequent of these conditions are attention-deficit disorder (ADD) and attention-deficit/hyperactivity disorder (ADHD). Unlike IDEA, Section 504 does not provide any funds to schools. Yet, any school that receives federal funds for any purpose at all must comply with the provisions of Section 504 or they may lose their funds. And, to make matters more complex, Section 504 and the Americans With Disabilities Act Amendments of 2008 require that schools must provide students with the necessary accommodations to participate in individual and standards-based assessments. It is illegal to refuse to let students use accommodations (e.g., extra time, testing sessions broken into short intervals, or sign language) necessary to be successful in school and/or to participate in individual or standards-based assessment. Those who assess students are required to evaluate the extent to which they are eligible for accommodations in classrooms and/or those necessary to take tests. The accommodations must always be determined by a group of people (usually the child study or IEP team) and they must be based on individual student need rather than on disability type or category.

Individuals With Disabilities Education Act

When Congress passed the Education for All Handicapped Children Act in 1975, it included four major requirements relative to assessment: an IEP for each student with a disability, protection in evaluation procedures, education in the least restrictive appropriate environment (LRE), and due process rights. The provisions of federal law continued with the 2004 reauthorized Individuals With Disabilities Education Improvement Act.

Individualized Education Program Provisions

Public Law 94-142 (the Education for All Handicapped Children Act of 1975) specified that all students with disabilities have the right to a free and appropriate public education (FAPE) and that schools must have an IEP for each student with a disability who is determined to need specially designed instruction. An **Individualized Education Program (IEP)** is a legal document that describes the services that are to be provided to a student with a disability who qualifies for special education services. In the IEP, school personnel must specify the annual goals and short-term objectives[1] of the instructional program. IEPs must be based on a comprehensive assessment conducted by a multidisciplinary team. We stress that assessment data are collected for the purpose of helping team members specify the components of the IEP. The team must specify not only goals and objectives but also plans for implementing the instructional program. They must specify how and when progress toward accomplishment of objectives will be evaluated. Note that specific assessment activities that form the basis of the program are listed within the IEP, as are specific instructional goals or objectives. IEPs are to be formulated by a multidisciplinary child study team that meets with the parents. Parents have the right to agree or disagree with the contents of the program as specified in the IEP.

In the amendments in the 1997 reauthorization of IDEA, Congress mandated a number of changes to the IEP. The core IEP team was expanded to include both a special education teacher and a general education teacher. The 1997 law also specified that students with disabilities are to be included in state- and district-wide assessments and that states must report annually on the performance and progress of all students, including students with disabilities. The IEP team must decide whether the student will take the assessments with or without accommodations or take an alternate assessment.

Protection in Evaluation Procedures Provisions

Congress included a number of specific requirements in Public Law 94-142 (EHA). These requirements were designed to protect students and help ensure that assessment procedures and activities would be fair, equitable, and nondiscriminatory. Specifically, Congress mandated eight provisions:

---

1. Many states do not require short-term objectives except for students who take the alternate assessment for alternate achievement standards (see Chapter 20).

1. Tests are to be selected and administered so as to be racially and culturally non-discriminatory.
2. To the extent feasible, students are to be assessed in their native language or primary mode of communication (e.g., American Sign Language).
3. Tests must have been validated for the specific purpose for which they are used.
4. Tests must be administered by trained personnel following the instructions for administration provided by the test producer.
5. Tests used with students must include those designed to provide information about specific educational needs, not just a general intelligence quotient.
6. Decisions about students are to be based on more than their performance on a single test.
7. Evaluations are to be made by a multidisciplinary team that includes at least one teacher or other specialist with knowledge in the area of suspected disability.
8. Children must be assessed in all areas related to a specific disability, including—where appropriate—health, vision, hearing, social and emotional status, general intelligence, academic performance, communicative skills, and motor skills.

In passing the 1997 amendments and the 2004 amendments, Congress reauthorized these provisions.

Least Restrictive Environment Provisions

In writing the 1975 Education for All Handicapped Children Act, Congress wanted to ensure that, to the greatest extent appropriate, students with disabilities would be placed in settings that would maximize their opportunities to interact with students without disabilities. **Least Restrictive Environment (LRE)** is now defined in Section 612(a)(5) (A) of IDEA 2004, which requires:

> To the maximum extent appropriate, children with disabilities . . . are educated with children who are not disabled, and special classes, separate schooling, or other removal of children with disabilities from the regular educational environment occurs only when the nature or severity of the disability of a child is such that education in regular classes with the use of supplementary aids and services cannot be achieved satisfactorily.

The LRE provisions arose out of court cases in which state and federal courts had ruled that when two equally appropriate placements were available for a student with a disability, the most normal (that is, least restrictive) placement was preferred. The LRE provisions were reauthorized in all revisions of the law.

Due Process Provisions

In Public Law 94-142, the Education for All Handicapped Children Act, Congress specified the procedures that schools and school personnel would have to follow to ensure due process in decision making. Specifically, when a decision affecting identification, evaluation, or placement of a student with disabilities is to be made, the student's parents or guardians must be given both the opportunity to be heard and the right to have an impartial due process hearing to resolve conflicting opinions.

Schools must provide opportunities for parents to inspect the records that are kept on their children and to challenge material that they believe should not be included in those records. Parents have the right to have their child evaluated by an independent professional and to have the results of that evaluation considered when psychoeducational decisions are made. In addition, parents must receive written notification before any education agency can begin an evaluation that might result in changes in the placement of a student.

In the 1997 amendments to IDEA, Congress specified that states must offer mediation as a voluntary option to parents and educators as an initial part of dispute resolution. If mediation is not successful, either party may request a due process hearing. The due process provisions were reauthorized in the 2004 IDEA.

No Child Left Behind Act of 2001

The No Child Left Behind Act of 2001 was signed into law on January 8, 2002, and was the reform of the federal Elementary and Secondary Education Act. It has been replaced in its entirety by the Every Student Succeeds Act of 2015.

2004 Reauthorization of IDEA

The Individuals With Disabilities Education Act was reauthorized in 2004. Several of the new requirements of the law have special implications for assessment of students with disabilities.[2] After much debate, Congress removed the requirement that students must have a severe discrepancy between ability and achievement in order to be determined to have a learning disability. IDEA replaced the discrepancy provision with permission to states and districts to use data on student responsiveness to intervention in making service eligibility decisions. We provide an extensive discussion of assessing Response to Intervention in Chapter 7, "Assessment in Multi-Tiered Systems of Support." Congress also specified that states must have measurable goals, standards, or objectives for all students with disabilities.

Americans With Disabilities Act of 1990

The **Americans With Disabilities Act (ADA)** is the law that requires public entities, such as local and state government, and public accommodations to provide appropriate access to their activities for individuals with disabilities. It is most often cited in court cases involving either employment of people with disabilities or appropriate education

---

2. The title Individuals With Disabilities Education Improvement Act was used to refer to the amendments, but the statute is still referred to as the Individuals With Disabilities Education Act and the acronym IDEA is still used to refer to the law.

in colleges and universities for students with disabilities. Simply put, most public entities and public accommodations must provide access (e.g., building ramps), transportation (e.g., special buses or wheelchair lifts), or accommodations (e.g., sign language interpreters at plays and musical events) necessary to enable people with disabilities to participate in its services and events.

Americans With Disabilities Act Amendments of 2008

In 2008, Congress reauthorized and revised the Americans With Disabilities Act. The **Americans With Disabilities Act Amendments of 2008 (ADAA)** is the name of the new law, which includes changes primarily for the purpose of clarifying the criteria for making decisions about eligibility for entitlements such as special education services. The term *504/ADAA impairment* is used to refer to those students who qualify as having a disability under Section 504/ADAA, but who are not eligible for special education and related services under IDEA. As long as they also meet the "need" criterion, they are entitled to accommodations and modifications as a protection under Section 504/ADAA.

Family Educational Rights and Privacy Act of 1974

PROGRESS MONITORING CHECK

Through the **Family Educational Rights and Privacy Act of 1974 (FERPA)**, educational agencies that receive federal funds must allow all parents access to and the ability to amend their child's educational records until the child turns 18, at which time the associated rights are conferred to the student. In order to share identifiable information outside of the school setting, consent from a student's parents or guardians is needed. The associated rules are further explained in Chapter 23, "Principles and Practices for Collaborative Teams," and are also incorporated within IDEA.

Ethical Codes

Professionals who assess students have the responsibility to engage in ethical behavior. Most professional associations have put together sets of standards to guide the ethical practices of their members; many of these standards relate directly to assessment practices. Ethical standards relevant to the concerns of education professionals are the ethical principles of the Council for Exceptional Children (CEC, www.cec.sped.org), National Education Association (NEA, www.nea.org), National Association of School Psychologists (NASP, www.nasponline.org), and American Psychological Association (APA, www.apa.org). In our work with teachers and related services personnel, we consistently have found that the most helpful set of ethical principles and guidelines are the *Professional Standards of the National Association of School Psychologists* published in 2020 and available for download on their website.

In publishing ethical and professional standards, the associations express serious commitment to promoting high technical standards for assessment instruments and high ethical standards for the behavior of individuals who work with assessments. Here, we cite a number of important ethical considerations, borrowing heavily from NASP's (2020) *Principles for Professional Ethics*, APA's (2016) *Ethical Principles of Psychologists and Code of Conduct*, NEA's (2020) *Code of Ethics for Educators*, and CEC's (2015) *Ethical Principles and Practice Standards*, which each are the published ethical codes for the respective professional organizations. We have not cited the standards explicitly, but we have distilled from them a number of broad ethical principles that guide assessment practices and behavior.

Four Broad Ethical Principles

The term *ethics* generally refers to a system of principles of conduct that guide the behavior of an individual. Codes of ethics serve to protect the public. However, ethical conduct is not synonymous with simple conformity to a set of rules outlined as principles and professional standards. Instead, it often requires careful thought and use of a decision-making process. Given that every situation is different, it is impossible to provide an ethical approach for each situation one might encounter. A professional must have good knowledge of the given situation to know how best to apply the relevant principles and standards in a given context. NASP's code of ethics (2020) is organized around four broad ethical themes: respecting the dignity and rights of all persons; professional competence and responsibility; honesty and integrity in professional relationships; and responsibility to schools, families, communities, the profession, and society. We briefly explain these four broad ethical themes in the sections that follow, and describe a process to guide ethical decision-making for situations in which you are uncertain of how to proceed.

Respecting the Dignity and Rights of All Persons

This broad principle means that we always recognize that students and their families have the right to participate in decisions that affect student welfare, and that students have the right to decide for themselves whether they want to share their thoughts, feelings, and behaviors.

Those who assess students regularly obtain a considerable amount of very personal information about those students. Such information must be held in strict confidence. A general ethical principle held by most professional organizations is that confidentiality may be broken only when there is clear and imminent danger to an individual or to society. Results of pupil performance on tests must not be discussed informally with school staff members. Formal reports of pupil performance on tests must be released only with the permission of the persons tested or their parents or guardians, and only for professional purposes and only with persons who have a legitimate *need to know*. Professionals are to release confidential information only within the strict boundaries of relevant privacy statutes.

Professional Competence and Responsibility
(Responsible Caring or Beneficence)

The ethical codes of all helping professions share a common theme referred to generally as the beneficence principle. **Beneficence**, or responsible caring, means educational professionals do things that are likely to maximize benefit to students or at least do no harm. This means that educational professionals always act in the best interests of the students they serve. The assessment of students is a social act that has specific social and educational consequences. Those who assess students use assessment data to make decisions about the students, and these decisions can significantly affect an individual's life opportunities. Those who assess students must accept responsibility for the consequences of their work, and they must make every effort to be certain that their services are used appropriately. In short, they are committed to the application of professional expertise to promote improvement in the quality of life available to the student, family, school, and community. For the individual who assesses students, this ethical standard may mean refusing to engage in assessment activities that are desired by a school system but that are inappropriate or have the potential for harm that outweighs benefit.

Specific provisions under this broad ethical principle include engaging only in assessment practices for which one is qualified and competent. We must all recognize the boundaries of our professional competence. Those who are entrusted with the responsibility for assessing and making decisions about students have differing degrees of competence. Not only must professionals regularly engage in self-assessment to be aware of their own limitations, but also they should recognize the limitations of the techniques they use. For individuals, this sometimes means refusing to engage in activities in areas in which they lack competence. It also means using techniques that meet recognized standards and engaging in the continuing education necessary to maintain high standards of competence. As a professional who will assess students, it is imperative that you accept responsibility for the consequences of your work and work to offset any negative consequences of your work.

School psychologists or members of child study teams are expected to ensure that the effects of their recommendations and intervention plans are monitored and modified when necessary. They also are responsible for maintaining the highest standards for professional practices in assessment, including assessments that use technology such as computer assisted and digital formats for assessment and interpretation, virtual reality assessment, distance assessment, and telehealth assessment.

The **competence** principle also requires competence in selection and use of appropriate assessment instruments (those that are technically adequate and appropriate for use with specific students). Competence also includes responsible school-based record keeping, including knowledge of the conditions under which parents may inspect student records and test protocols.

Those who assess students are to make provisions for maintaining confidentiality in the storage and disposal of records. When working with minors or other persons who are unable to give voluntary informed consent, assessors are to take special care to protect these persons' best interests. Those who assess students are expected to maintain test security. It is expected that assessors will not reveal to others the content of specific tests or test items. At the same time, assessors must be willing and able to back up their decisions with test data.

Honesty and Integrity in Professional Relationships

As schools become increasingly diverse, professionals must demonstrate sensitivity in working with people from different cultural and linguistic backgrounds and with children who have different types of disabilities. Assessors should have experience working with students of diverse backgrounds and should demonstrate competence in doing so, or they should refrain from assessing and making decisions about such students.

Responsibility to Schools, Families, Communities, One's Profession, and Society

Those who are entrusted to educate students have responsibilities to the societies and communities in which they work. This means behaving professionally and not doing things that reflect badly on one's employer or profession. As professionals, we are responsible for promoting healthy school, family, and community environments, respecting and obeying laws, contributing to our profession by supervising, mentoring, and educating professional colleagues, and ensuring that *all* students can attend school, learn, and develop their personal identities in environments free from discrimination, harassment, violence, and abuse (Jacob et al., 2022). Children are recognized as being especially vulnerable in our society, and often the students with whom we work (especially students with disabilities) are among the most vulnerable. We have a responsibility to protect their rights.

Those who assess students are responsible for selecting and administering tests in a fair and nonbiased manner. Assessment approaches must be selected that are valid and that provide an accurate representation of students' skills and abilities and avoid being influenced by their disabilities. Tests are to be selected and administered so as to be racially and culturally nondiscriminatory, and students should be assessed in their native language or primary mode of communication (e.g., braille).

How Do You Resolve an Ethical Dilemma?

How do you decide what kinds of actions are ethical? There are two excellent sources in which you can study specific cases and learn how professionals resolve specific kinds of ethical dilemmas. One source is a textbook by Jacob et al. (2022), and the other is a book of ethical cases by Armistead et al. (2011). School personnel often encounter ethical dilemmas within the complex educational settings they work in. Dailor and Jacob (2011) surveyed members of NASP and reported that issues of child abuse (28%), risky child and adolescent behavior (25%), tensions between test security and record sharing (25%), and administrative pressure to engage in unethical actions (17%) were the most common ethical dilemmas they faced. Diamond et al. (2021) provide a model that encourages school personnel to consider how diversity and equity issues are present in their work and how their decisions may reinforce systemic inequities or support socially just practice. The model provides the most up-to-date set of steps practitioners should go through in solving ethical dilemmas. We show the six-step model in Box 3.1. The model encourages school personnel to take into account ecological factors as they resolve dilemmas. It is not intended to serve as a checklist but rather as a resource to assist school personnel in keeping cultural factors at the forefront as they are confronted with ethical dilemmas.

BOX 3.1

DECIDE Ethical Decision-Making Model

Step 1. Define the problem. To systematically solve a problem or respond to a dilemma, it is important to first understand fully what the problem or dilemma entails. In this first step, the objective is to identify key elements of the situation. Questions to consider include: What has happened or is happening? Who is involved? Who has been impacted or may be impacted (both directly and indirectly)?

Step 2. Ecological framework. Once the specifics of the problem or dilemma have been outlined, it is important to look at the situation through an ecological framework and identify any cultural or contextual factors that may have been overlooked in Step 1. What individual characteristics and identities, system level variables, and interactions may be notable? Characteristics can include (but are not limited to) "race, ethnicity, color, religion, ancestry, national origin, immigration status, socioeconomic status, primary language, gender, sexual orientation, gender identity, gender expression, disability, or any other distinguishing characteristics" (NASP, 2020, p. 44). Beyond individual characteristics, it is also critical to identify contextual variables that may be influencing the situation. An ecological framework accounts for influencing factors such as family members and structure, peers, school and work systems, neighborhoods, resources, social conditions, economic systems, and policies. Questions to consider include: What cultural variables are present? What contextual variables are present? What intersectionality is present? What systemic influences are present? How might power, systemic racism, or implicit biases be influencing the situation? Is this situation part of a larger systemic pattern (e.g., within the school, community, neighborhood)? Have any voices or perspectives been left out of the conversation? This step provides space to consider how to engage in socially just practice. To further clarify what is meant by socially just practice, "social justice requires promoting nondiscriminatory practices and the empowerment of families and communities. School psychologists enact social justice through culturally responsive professional practice and advocacy to create schools, communities, and systems that ensure equity and fairness for all children" (NASP, 2021).

Step 3. Consider ethical, legal, and policy guidelines. In this step, identify all ethical, legal, and policy guidelines that are relevant to the problem or dilemma. Consider these guidelines collectively and identify any conflicts. Consider consultation at this step, as applicable, with direct supervisors, special education directors, other school psychologists, and legal counsel for the school district. Questions to guide this step include: What laws are relevant to this situation? What ethical standards are relevant to this situation? What district policies are relevant to this situation? Is there other relevant guidance to consider (e.g., position statements from professional organizations, technical assistance papers)? Is there anyone you should consult with as you move through this step (e.g., district legal counsel, special education director, supervisor, other school personnel)?

Step 4. Identify the rights and responsibilities of all parties. In this step, identify all individuals or groups involved in the situation, both directly and indirectly, and articulate their rights and responsibilities. Keep in mind the cultural and contextual factors from Step 2 and the legal, ethical, and policy guidelines from Step 3. Questions to guide this step include: Who is directly involved in or impacted by this situation? What are their rights? What are their responsibilities?

Step 5. Determine courses of action and consequences. In this step, identify several possible courses of action to respond to the problem or dilemma, and consider the possible outcomes or consequences for each. Keep in mind the cultural and contextual factors identified in Step 2. Consider consultation at this step, as applicable, with supervisors, special education director, district equity and inclusion director, legal counsel, cultural brokers, and other school psychologists. Questions to guide this step include: What are the ethical, legal, and policy ramifications associated with each option? Do the proposed actions and anticipated consequences align with a socially just, antidiscriminatory, and antiracist practice?

Step 6. Establish a plan. In this final step, identify a decision, make a plan to enact the decision, and monitor the outcome. Ensure that the final decision aligns with legal, ethical, and policy guidelines and is consistent with a socially just practice, taking into consideration cultural and contextual factors of those involved and impacted by the situation. Questions to guide this step include: Does the decision align with legal, ethical, and policy guidelines? Does the decision align with a socially just, antidiscriminatory, and antiracist practice? What is the plan to monitor the outcome of the decision? Who will be responsible for following up, and what is the proposed timeline? How will you know when the problem or dilemma has been resolved?

Source: Adapted from Diamond et al. (2021).

Professional Standards on Assessment

Those who assess students adhere to professional standards on assessment. The *Standards for Educational and Psychological Testing* were developed by a joint committee of the American Educational Research Association, the American Psychological Association, and the National Council on Measurement in Education (2014) and specify a set of requirements for test development and use. It is imperative that those who develop tests behave in accordance with the standards, and that those who assess students use instruments and techniques that meet the standards.

In Parts III and IV of this text, we review commonly used tests and discuss the extent to which those tests meet the standards specified in *Standards for Educational and Psychological Testing*. We provide information to help test users make informed judgments about the technical adequacy of specific tests. There is no federal or state agency that acts to limit the publication or use of technically inadequate tests. Only by refusing to use technically inadequate tests will users force developers to improve them. After all, if you were a test developer, would you continue to publish a test that few people purchased and used? Would you invest your company's resources to make changes in a technically inadequate test that yielded a large annual profit to your firm if people continued to buy and use it the way it was?

3.2
PROGRESS MONITORING CHECK

PROGRESS 3.1 MONITORING CHECK

1. Name three major laws that affect assessment
2. How do the major components of IDEA (individualized educational plan, least restrictive environment, protection in evaluation procedures, and due process) affect assessment practices?
3. Special education is, as we promised you, a field of acronyms. SWD are entitled to services under IDEA; others, who are labeled ADHD, are not eligible for services under IDEA but once received services under ADA and are now eligible under ADAA/504. Students with disabilities are put on an IEP, but school personnel do not have to write one for SW/OD. Students with disabilities are entitled to a FAPE, PEP, and education in the LRE. Translate these sentence in a way that your mother or grandmother could understand.

1. Identify the ethical principles that you believe should guide the behavior of individuals in two of the following professions: plumber, stockbroker, grocery store manager, used car salesman, physician, bartender, and professor. Then write a brief paragraph on why you selected the principles and how they differ for different professions. Are there commonalities?

2. How do the broad ethical principles of beneficence, competence boundaries, respect for the dignity of persons, confidentiality, and fairness affect assessment practices?

3. What are two practices in which you can engage to support the development of technically adequate tests?

CHAPTER 4

Test Scores and Norms

LEARNING OBJECTIVES

1. Describe the quantitative concepts that deal with scales of measurement, characteristics of distributions, average scores, measures of dispersion, and correlation.
2. Explain how test performances are made meaningful through criterion-referenced, standards-referenced, and norm-referenced interpretations.
3. Describe how norms are constructed to be proportionally representative of the population in terms of important personal characteristics (e.g., gender and age), to contain a large number of people, to be representative of today's population, and to be relevant for the purposes of assessment.

School personnel are expected to use the results of tests that they receive through-out their professional careers. Correct usage requires educators to understand the meaning of the scores reported for those tests. Suppose you decide to review the school folders of students who will be in your class in the fall. You learn that Willis has an IQ of 87 and scored at the 22nd percentile on a measure of reading vocabulary. Elaine earned a grade equivalent of 4.2 on a math test. Overall, 65% of your students earned scores of "proficient" in reading on the state test last spring; 22% of your students earned scores of "basic." Most of your class also scored at the state median on the measure of writing. Obviously, this information is supposed to mean something to you and could affect how you will teach. What do these scores mean? Should they affect the instructional decisions you will make?

Understanding the meaning of many test scores requires knowledge of basic statistical concepts. The first section of this chapter reviews quantitative concepts that will be needed by those who want to understand assessment and the use of assessment information to make decisions about students in special and inclusive education.

Descriptive Statistics

We use descriptive statistics to describe or summarize data. In testing, the data are scores: several scores on one individual, one score on several individuals, or several scores on several individuals. Descriptive statistics are calculated using the basic mathematical operations of addition, subtraction, multiplication, and division, as well as simple exponential operations (squares and square roots); advanced knowledge of mathematics is not required. Although many calculations are repetitive and tedious, calculators and computers facilitate these calculations, and test authors usually provide tables of all the pertinent descriptive statistics. This chapter deals with the basic concepts needed for an understanding of descriptive statistics: scales of measurement, distributions, measures of central tendency, measures of dispersion, and measures of relationship (correlation).

Basic Statistical Notation

A number of symbols are used in statistics, and different authors use different symbols. Table 4.1 lists the symbols that we use in this book. The summation sign (Σ) means "add the following"; X denotes any score. The number of scores in a distribution is symbolized by N; n denotes the number of scores in a subset of a distribution. The arithmetic average (mean) of a distribution is denoted by $\overline{X}$. The variance of a distribution is symbolized by S^2, and the standard deviation by S.

Scales of Measurement

The ways in which data can be summarized depend on the kind of scale in which the scores are expressed. There are four types of measurement scales: nominal, ordinal, ratio, and equal interval (Stevens, 1951).

The four scales are distinguished on the basis of the relationship between adjacent, or consecutive, values on the measurement scale. An adjacent value in this case means a potential or possible scale value, rather than an obtained or measured value. In Figure 4.1, the possible val-

TABLE 4.1

Commonly Used Statistical Symbols

Symbol	Meaning
Σ	Summation sign
X	Any score
N	Number of cases
n	Number in subset
$\overline{X}$	Mean
S^2	Variance
S	Standard deviation

ues between 2 inches and 6 inches, measured in intervals of eighths of an inch, are depicted. Any two consecutive points on the scale (for instance 3⅛ and 3¼ inches) are adjacent values. Any two points on the scale that have values between them (for instance 3⅛ inches and 4¼ inches) are not adjacent points. Of course, different scales have different adjacent values—adjacent intervals larger or smaller than ⅛ of an inch.

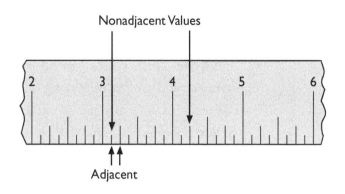

FIGURE 4.1. Adjacent and nonadjacent values.

Nominal Scales

Nominal scales name the values of the scale, but adjacent values have no inherent relationship. These values can describe attributes (e.g., gender, eye color, race), geographic region where a person resides (e.g., the Pacific Northwest), educational classification (e.g., receiving services for learning disability or emotional disability), and so forth.

Because adjacent values on nominal scales have no inherent relationship, the various mathematical operations cannot be performed on them. For example, numbers on athletic shirts have no mathematical relationship to each other. The player who wears number 80 is not necessarily a better or larger or older player than the player who wears number 79 or number 70; they are just different players. There is no implied rank ordering in the numbers worn on the shirts. It would not make any sense to add up shirt numbers to determine which athletic team is the best. Mathematically, all we can do with nominal scales is determine the frequency of each value (e.g., the number of boys and girls).

Ordinal Scales

Ordinal scales order values from worse to better (e.g., pass-fail, or poor-OK-good-better-best), and there is a relationship among adjacent scores. Higher scores are better than lower scores, but the magnitude of the difference between adjacent values is unknown and unlikely to be equal. Thus, we cannot determine how much better a *better* performance is than a *good* performance or if the difference between *good* and *better* is the same as the difference between *better* and *best*. Because the differences between adjacent values are unknown and presumed unequal, ordinal scores cannot be added, multiplied, divided, or averaged.

Ratio Scales

Ratio scales not only order values but also have two very important characteristics: (1) the magnitude of the difference between adjacent values is known and is equal, and (2) each scale has an absolute and logical zero. Equal differences between adjacent values means that the difference between 4 and 5 pounds, for example, is the same as the difference between 40 and 41 pounds and is the same as the difference between 555 and 556 pounds. Because the differences between adjacent values on equal-interval scales are equal, scores can be manipulated mathematically (e.g., added, multiplied, squared, and so forth). Having an absolute and logical difference means that we can create ratios with any two variables. For example, if John weighs 300 pounds and Bob weighs 150 pounds, John weighs twice as much as Bob.

Equal-Interval Scales

Equal-interval scales are ratio scales that do not have an absolute and logical zero. Consider the information in Figure 4.2. The differences among lines A, B, C, and D are readily measured. We can start measuring from any point, such as from the point where Line S intersects Lines A, B, C, and D. The portion of Line A to the right of S is ½ inch long; that of Line B to the right of S is 1 inch long; that of Line C to the right of S is 1¼ inches long; and that of Line D to the right of S is 1¾ inches long. The lines are measured on an equal-interval scale, and the differences among the lines would be the same no matter where the starting point S was located. However, because S is not a logical and absolute zero, we cannot make ratio comparisons among the lines. Although, when we began measuring from S, we found Line A to measure ½ inch from S and Line B to measure 1 inch from S, the whole of Line B is obviously not twice as long as the whole of Line A.

Most tests do not have a logical or absolute zero. Classroom tests, such as Ms. Smith's arithmetic test (Table 4.2), also lack an absolute zero. Because a student gets none of the problems correct does not mean that the student knows absolutely nothing about arithmetic. Because equal-interval scales lack an absolute zero, we cannot construct ratios with data measured on these scales. For example, Sam (whose raw score total is 22) does not know twice as much about arithmetic as Carole (raw score total 11). Later in this chapter you will learn that all standard scores are equal-interval scales. That we

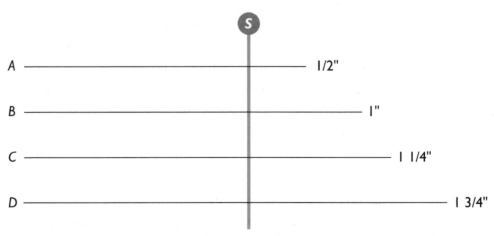

FIGURE 4.2. The measurement of lines as a function of the starting point.

can add, subtract, multiply, and divide data measured on these scales makes them very useful in making complex interpretations of test scores.

Characteristics of Distributions

A **distribution's shape** is a two-dimensional plot of scores by the number of people earning each score. Distributions of equal-interval scores (e.g., student scores on a classroom test) can be described in terms of four characteristics: mean, variance, skew, and kurtosis. The **mean** is the arithmetic average of the scores in the distribution (e.g., the mean height for U.S. women is the average of all U.S. women's heights). The **variance** is an average distance between each score and every other score in the distribution. These characteristics are very important and are discussed repeatedly throughout this book.

Skew refers to the asymmetry of a distribution of scores. In a **symmetrical distribution**, the scores above the mean mirror the scores below the mean. Easy questions are balanced by difficult questions. However, a distribution will be **negatively skewed** when it is easy and many students earn high scores and fewer students earn low scores. That distribution of scores will not be symmetrical. There will be more scores above the mean that are balanced by fewer but more extreme scores below the mean, as shown in Figure 4.3. **Positively skewed distributions** occur when a test is difficult, and many students earn low scores while a few students earn high scores. There are more scores below the mean that are balanced by fewer but more extreme scores above the mean, as shown in Figure 4.3.

Kurtosis describes the peakedness of a curve—that is, the rate at which a curve rises and falls. Relatively flat distributions spread out test takers and are called **platykurtic**.

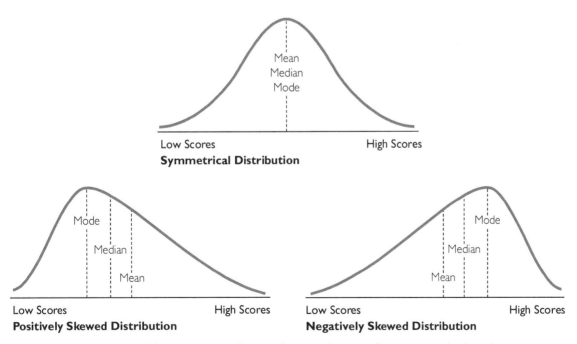

FIGURE 4.3. Relationship among mode, median, and mean for symmetrical and asymmetrical distributions.

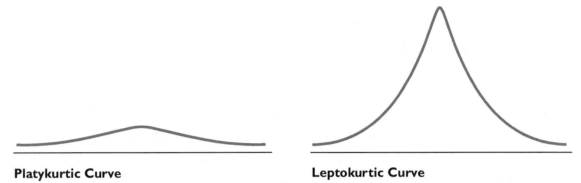

Platykurtic Curve   **Leptokurtic Curve**

FIGURE 4.4. Platykurtic and leptokurtic curves.

(The prefix *plat-* means flat, as in platypus or plateau.) **Leptokurtic** are fast-rising distributions with strong peaks. Figure 4.4 illustrates a platykurtic and a leptokurtic curve.

The normal curve is a particular symmetrical curve. Many variables are distributed normally in nature; many are not. The only value of the normal curve lies in the fact that, for this curve, the proportion of cases that fall between any two points on the horizontal axis of the curve is known exactly.

Average Scores

An **average** gives us a general description of how a group as a whole performed. There are three different averages, sometimes called measures of central tendency: mode, median, and mean. The **mode** is defined as the score most frequently obtained. A mode (if there is one) can be found for data on nominal, ordinal, ratio, or equal-interval scales. Distributions may have two modes (if they do, they are called "bimodal distributions"), or they may have more than two.

The **median** is the point in a distribution above which are 50% of test takers and below which are 50% of test takers. If you rank-order the scores, the median by definition is the middle-occurring score or the average of the two middle-occurring scores given an even number of scores. The median score may or may not actually be earned by a student. For the set of scores 4, 5, 7, and 8, the median is 6, although no one earned a score of 6. For the set of scores 14, 15, 16, 17, and 18, the median is 16, a score that was earned by a student. Medians can be found for data on ordinal, equal-interval, and ratio scales; they must not be used with nominal scales.

The **mean** is the arithmetic average of the scores in a distribution and is the most important average for use in assessment. As shown in Equation 4.1, it is the sum of the scores (ΣX) divided by the number of scores (N); its symbol is $\overline{X}$. The mean, like the median, may or may not be earned by any child in the distribution. Means should be computed only for data on equal-interval and ratio scales.

Eq. 4.1 $$\text{Mean} = \overline{X} = \frac{\Sigma X}{N}$$

Measures of Dispersion

Dispersion tells us how scores are spread out above and below the average score. Three measures of dispersion are range, variance, and standard deviation. The **range** is the distance between the extremes of a distribution; it is usually defined as the highest score less the lowest score. It is a relatively crude measure of dispersion because it is based on only two pieces of information. Range cannot be calculated with nominal data.

The **variance** and the **standard deviation** are the most important indexes of dispersion. The **variance** is a numerical index describing the dispersion of a set of scores around the mean of the distribution. The symbol S^2 is used when describing the variance of a sample; the symbol σ^2 is used when describing the variance of a population. Because the variance is an average, the number of cases in the set or the distribution does not affect it. Large sets of scores may have large or small variances; small sets of scores may have large or small variances. In addition, because the variance is measured in terms of distance from the mean, it is not related to the actual value of the mean. Distributions with large means may have large or small variances; distributions with small means may have large or small variances. The variance of a distribution is computed in Equation 4.2. The variance (S^2) equals the sum (Σ) of the square of each score less the mean $(\overline{X})^2$ divided by the number of scores (N).

$$S^2 = \frac{\Sigma(X - \overline{X})^2}{N}$$ Eq. 4.2

Computational Example—Variance

As an example of computing variance, we use the scores from Ms. Smith's arithmetic test. The first step is to find the mean. Therefore, the scores are added, and the sum (350) is divided by the number of scores (25). The mean in this example is 14. The next step is to subtract the mean from each score; this is done in Table 4.2 in the column labeled $X - \overline{X}$. Note that scores above the mean are positive, scores at the mean are zero, and scores below the mean are negative. These differences $(X - \overline{X})$ are then squared (multiplied by themselves); the squared differences are labeled $(X - \overline{X})^2$. Note that all numbers in this column are positive. The sum of all the squared distances of scores from the mean is 900. The variance equals the sum of all the squared distances of scores from the mean divided by the number of scores; in this case, the variance equals 900/25, or 36.

The variance is important in psychometric theory but has limited application in score interpretation. However, its calculation is necessary to find the standard deviation, which is very important in the interpretation of test scores. The **standard deviation** is a numerical index describing the dispersion of a set of scores around the mean that is calculated as the positive square root of the variance. The symbol S is used when describing the standard deviation of a sample; the symbol s is used when describing the standard deviation of a population.

A standard deviation is frequently used as a unit of measurement in much the same way that an inch or a ton is used. Scores on an equal-interval scale can be transformed into standard deviation units from the mean. The advantage of measuring in standard deviations is that when the distribution is normal, we know exactly what proportion

TABLE 4.2

Computation of the Variance of Ms. Smith's Arithmetic Class

Student	Test Score	X – X̄	(X – X̄)²
Bob	27	13	169
Lucy	26	12	144
Sam	22	8	64
Mary	20	6	36
Luis	18	4	16
Barbara	17	3	9
Carmen	16	2	4
Jane	16	2	4
Charles J.	16	2	4
Hector	14	0	0
Virginia	14	0	0
Frankie	14	0	0
Sean	14	0	0
Joanne	14	0	0
Jim	14	0	0
John	14	0	0
Charles B.	12	–2	4
Jing-Jen	12	–2	4
Ron	12	–2	4
Carole	11	–3	9
Bernice	10	–4	16
Hugh	8	–6	36
Lance	6	–8	64
Ludwig	2	–12	144
Harpo	1	–13	169
SUM	350	000	900

of cases occurs between the mean and the particular standard deviation. As shown in Figure 4.5, approximately 34% of the cases in a normal distribution always occur between the mean and one standard deviation either above or below the mean. Thus, approximately 68% of all cases occur between one standard deviation below and one standard deviation above the mean (34% + 34% = 68%). Approximately 14% of the cases occur between one and two standard deviations below the mean or between one and two standard deviations above the mean. Thus, approximately 48% of all cases occur between the mean and two standard deviations either above or below the mean (34% + 14% = 48%). Thus, approximately 96% of all cases (48% + 48%) occur between two standard deviations above and two standard deviations below the mean.

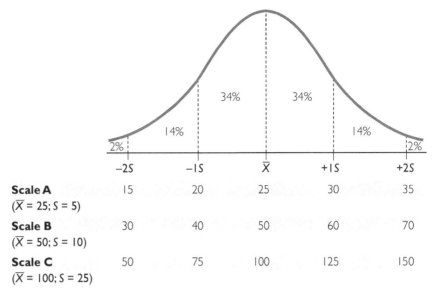

	−2S	−1S	X̄	+1S	+2S
Scale A (X̄ = 25; S = 5)	15	20	25	30	35
Scale B (X̄ = 50; S = 10)	30	40	50	60	70
Scale C (X̄ = 100; S = 25)	50	75	100	125	150

FIGURE 4.5. Scores on three scales, expressed in standard deviation units.

As shown by the positions and values for scales A, B, and C in Figure 4.5, it does not matter what the values of the mean and the standard deviation are. The relationship holds for various obtained values of the mean and the standard deviation. For scale A, where the mean is 25 and the standard deviation is 5, 34% of the scores occur between the mean (25) and one standard deviation below the mean (20) or between the mean and one standard deviation above the mean (30). Similarly, for scale B, where the mean is 50 and the standard deviation is 10, 34% of the cases occur between the mean (50) and one standard deviation below the mean (40) or between the mean and one standard deviation above the mean (60).

4.1
PROGRESS MONITORING CHECK

Correlation

Correlation quantifies relationships between variables. **Correlation coefficients** are numerical indices of the relationship between two variables; they tell us the extent to which any two variables (correlations among three or more variables are called multiple correlations) go together—that is, the extent to which changes in one variable are reflected by changes in the second variable. Correlation coefficients are expressed as a decimal value with a sign (+ or −) that indicates the direction of the relationship. When low values of one variable are associated with low values of a second variable this indicates a positive correlation. When low values of one variable are associated with high values on the second variable, this is a negative correlation. The decimal number can range in value from .00 to either +1.00 or −1.00. and indicates the magnitude of the relationship. A correlation coefficient of either +1.00 or −1.00 indicates a perfect relationship between two variables. Thus, if you know a person's score on one variable, you can predict that person's score on the second variable without error. Correlation coefficients between .00 and 1.00 (or −1.00) allow some prediction, and the more extreme the coefficient, the greater its predictive power. Therefore, a correlation value of "0" tells us that what happens with one variable has nothing to do with what happens with another variable (they are perfectly unrelated). A correlation of .20 (or −.20) tells us that knowledge of performance on test A tells us at least a little bit about performance on test B, while a correlation of .80 (or −.80) tells us that performance on one test tells us a lot about performance on the other test.

Correlation coefficients are very important in assessment. In the next chapter, the section on reliability shows how correlations are used to estimate the amount of error associated with measurement, and the section on validity shows how correlation coefficients are used to provide evidence of validity for a test. Please see the Advanced Information About Correlation online resource.

*ONLINE
RESOURCE*

Scoring Student Performance

Tests and systematic observations occur in structured, standardized situations. Tests require the presentation of standardized materials to an individual in a predetermined manner in order to evaluate that individual's responses, using predetermined criteria. Systematic observations require the use of predetermined definitions of behavior to be observed at predetermined times and settings.

How an individual's responses are quantified depends on the materials used, the intent of the test author, and the diagnostician's intention in choosing the procedure. If we were interested only in determining whether a student had learned a specific fact or concept (e.g., "What is 3 + 5?"), we would make explicit the criteria for what constitutes a correct response and would classify the student's response as right or wrong. If we were interested in determining if a student had learned a finite set of facts (e.g., the sums of all combinations of two single-digit numbers), we could classify the student's response to each fact as right or wrong. Teachers frequently use this approach for the most essential (and frequently the most basic) information that a student must master. More often we would quantify a student's performance as the number or percentage of facts known.

It is usually impractical or impossible to assess all the facts and relationships that might be tested. For example, it seems unlikely that anyone could make up a test to assess a student's knowledge of every aspect of all Shakespeare's plays; however, even if that were possible, administering all the possible questions to a student would be virtually impossible. Even when we cannot test all of the information, we may still want to know how much of the topic students have learned. To do this, testers ask a few questions and estimate students' knowledge based on their responses to those questions. In testing jargon, we use a sample of items (that is, a test) to estimate performance on the domain (all of the possible items). When we estimate a student's performance on an entire domain from the performance on a sample of items, we assume that the sample of items is a fair representation of the domain. In this situation, individual items have little importance beyond estimating performance on the domain.

Subjective Versus Objective Scoring

There are two approaches to scoring a student's response: subjective and objective. **Subjective scoring** relies on private criteria that can and do vary from tester to tester. Subjective scores have been repeatedly shown to be influenced by extraneous and irrelevant variables such as a student's race, gender, appearance, religion, or even given name (Ysseldyke et al., 1981).

Objective scoring is based on observable public criteria. When multiple examiners or observers use objective scoring procedures to evaluate student performance, they obtain the same scores. Because objective scoring leads to systematically better decision making, the Individuals With Disabilities Education Act requires objective measurement (*Federal Register* 71(156), August 14, 2006).

Summarizing Student Performance

When a single behavior or skill is of interest and assessed only once, evaluators usually employ a dichotomous scoring scheme: right or wrong, present or absent, and so forth. Typically, the correct or right option of the dichotomy is defined precisely; the wrong option is defined by default. For example, a correct response to "1 + 2 = ?" might be defined as "3, written intelligibly, written after the ? sign, and written in the correct orientation"; a wrong response would be one that fails to meet one or more of the criteria for a correct response.

A single response can also be awarded partial credit that can range along a continuum from completely correct to completely incorrect. For example, a teacher might objectively score a student response and give partial credit for a response because the student used the correct procedures to solve a mathematics problem even though the student made a computational error. Partial credit can be useful when trying to document slow progress toward a goal. For example, in a life-skills curriculum, a teacher might scale the item "drinking from a cup without assistance," as shown in Table 4.3. Of course, each point on the continuum requires a definition for the partial credit to be awarded.

When an evaluation is concerned with multiple items, a tester may simply report how a student performed on each and every item. More often, however, the tester summarizes

TABLE 4.3

Drinking From a Cup

Level	Definition
Well	Drinks with little spilling or assistance
Acceptable	Dribbles a few drops
Learning	Requires substantial prompting or spills
Beginning	Requires manual guidance

the student's performance over all the test items to provide an index of total performance. The sum of correct responses is usually the first summary index computed.

Although the number correct provides a limited amount of information about student performance, it lacks important information that provides a context for understanding that performance. Four summary scores are commonly used to provide a more meaningful context for the total score: percent correct, accuracy, fluency, and retention.

Percent Correct

Percent correct is widely used in a variety of assessment contexts. The **percent correct** is calculated by dividing the number correct by the number possible and multiplying that quotient by 100. This index is best used with *power tests*—tests for which students have sufficient time to answer all of the questions.[1]

Percentages are given verbal labels that are intended to facilitate instruction. The two most commonly used labels are "mastery" and "instructional level." Mastery divides the percentage continuum in two: Mastery is generally set at 90 or 95% correct, and nonmastery is less than the level of mastery. The criterion for mastery is arbitrary, and in instructional settings we frequently set the level for mastery too low.

Some assessments divide the percentage range into three segments: frustration, instructional, and independent levels. When material is too difficult for a student, it is said to be at the *frustration level*; this level is usually defined as material for which a student knows less than 85% of it. An *instructional level* provides a degree of challenge where a student is likely to be successful, but success is not guaranteed; this level is usually defined by student responses between 85 and 95% correct. The *independent level* is defined as the point where a student can perform without assistance; this level is usually defined as student performance of more than 95% correct. For example, in reading, students who decode more than 95% of the words should be able to read a passage without assistance; students who decode between 85 and 95% of the words in a passage should be able to read and comprehend that passage with assistance; and students who cannot decode 85% of the words in a passage will probably have great difficulty decoding and comprehending the material, even with assistance.

Accuracy

Accuracy is the number of correct responses divided by the number of attempted responses multiplied by 100 (the result is a percentage). Accuracy is appropriately used when an assessment precludes a student from responding to all items. For example, a teacher may ask a student to read orally for 2 minutes, but it should not be possible for that student (or any other student) to read the entire passage in the time allotted.[2] Thus,

---

1. A situation in which there are more opportunities to respond than time to respond is termed a *free operant*.

Benny may attempt 175 words in a 350-word passage in 2 minutes; if he reads 150 words correctly, his accuracy would be approximately 86%—that is, $100 \times (150/175)$.

Fluency

Fluency is the number of correct responses per minute. Teachers often want their students to have a supply of information at their fingertips so that they can respond fluently (or automatically) with cognitive ease. For example, teachers may want their students to recognize sight words without having to sound them out, recall addition facts without having to labor over the solution, or supply Spanish words for their English equivalents. Criterion rates for successful performance are usually determined empirically. For example, readers with satisfactory comprehension usually read connected prose at rates of 100 or more words per minute, depending on their grade level. (See, e.g., Hasbrouck, 2010; Daane et al., 2005).

Retention

Retention refers to the percentage of learned information that is recalled. Retention may also be termed recall, maintenance, or memory of what has been learned. Regardless of the label, it is calculated in the same way: Divide the number recalled by the number originally learned, and multiply that ratio by 100%. For example, if Helen learned 40 sight vocabulary words and recalled 30 of them 2 weeks later, her retention would be 75%—that is, $100\% \times (30/40)$. Because forgetting becomes more likely as the interval between the learning and the retention assessment increases, retention is usually qualified by the period of time between attainment of mastery and assessment of recall. Thus, Helen's retention would be stated as 75% over a 2-week period.

Interpreting Test Performance

There are three common ways to interpret an individual student's performance in special and inclusive education: criterion-referenced, standards-referenced, and norm-referenced.

Criterion-Referenced Interpretation

When we are interested in a student's knowledge about a single fact, we compare a student's performance against an objective and absolute standard (criterion) of performance. Thus, to be considered **criterion-referenced**, there must be a clear, objective criterion for each of the correct responses to each question, or to each portion of the question if partial credit is to be awarded.

---

2. To avoid having students practice making errors while developing basic skills, they should not be given homework (independent practice) until they are at the independent level.

Standards-Referenced Interpretation

In large-scale assessments used for accountability purposes, school districts must ascertain the degree to which they are meeting state and national achievement standards. To do so, states specify the qualities and skills that competent learners need to demonstrate. Interpretation of an individual's performance based on comparison to these state standards is considered a **standards-referenced** interpretation.

Standards-referenced assessments consist of four components:

- *Levels of performance:* The entire range of possible student performances (from very poor to excellent) is divided into a number of bands or ranges. Verbal labels that are attached to each of these ranges indicate increasing levels of accomplishment. For example, a performance might be rated on a four-point scale: *poor, emerging, proficient,* and *advanced* performance.
- *Objective criteria:* Each level of performance is defined by precise, objective descriptions of student accomplishment relative to the task. These descriptions can be quantified.
- *Examples:* Examples of student work at each level are provided. These examples illustrate the range of performance within each level.
- *Cut scores:* These scores provide quantitative criteria that clearly delineate student performance level.

Norm-Referenced Interpretations

Sometimes testers are interested in knowing how a student's performance compares to the performances of other students—usually students of similar demographic characteristics (age, gender, grade in school, and so forth); these are considered **norm-referenced** interpretations. In order to make this type of comparison, a student's score is transformed into a **derived score**. Two types of norm-referenced scores are derived scores: developmental scores and scores of relative standing.

Developmental Scores

There are two types of developmental scores: developmental equivalents and developmental quotients. **Developmental equivalents** may be age equivalents or grade equivalents and are based on the average performance of individuals. Suppose the average performance of 10-year-old children on a test was 27 correct. Furthermore, suppose that Horace answered 27 questions correctly. Horace answered as many questions correctly as the average of 10-year-old children. He would earn an age equivalent of 10 years. An **age equivalent** means that a child's raw score is the average (the median or mean) performance for that age group. Age equivalents are expressed in years and months; a hyphen is used in age scores (e.g., 7-1 for 7 years 1 month old). If the test measured mental ability, Horace's score would be called a mental age; if the test measured language, it would be called a language age. A **grade equivalent** means that a child's raw score is the average (the median or mean) performance for a particular grade. Grade equivalents are expressed in grades and tenths of grades; a decimal point is used in grade scores (e.g., 7.1). Age-equivalent and grade-equivalent scores are interpreted as a performance equal to the average of *X*-year-olds and the average performance of *X*th graders, respectively.

There are major problems with developmental scores. Although teachers often like age- and grade-equivalent scores because on the surface they seem easy to understand, their interpretation requires great care. The following problems occur in the use of developmental scores.

- *Systematic misinterpretation:* Students who earn an age equivalent of 12-0 have merely answered as many questions correctly as the average for children 12 years of age. They have not necessarily performed as a 12-year-old child would; they may well have attacked the problems in a different way or demonstrated a different performance pattern from many 12-year-old students. For example, a second grader and a ninth grader might both earn grade equivalents of 4.0, but they probably have not performed identically. We have known for more than 40 years that younger children perform lower-level work with greater accuracy (for instance, successfully answered 38 of the 45 problems attempted), whereas older children attempt more problems with less accuracy (for instance, successfully answered 38 of the 78 problems attempted) (Thorndike & Hagen, 1978).

- *Need for interpolation and extrapolation:* Average age and grade scores are estimated for groups of children who are never tested. Interpolated scores are estimated for groups of students between groups actually tested. For example, students within 30 days of their eighth birthday may be tested, but age equivalents are estimated for students who are 8-1, 8-2, and so on. Extrapolated scores are estimated for students who are younger and older than the children tested. For example, a student may earn an age equivalent of 5-0 even though no child younger than 6 was tested. Thus, these values are estimated and may not always hold true.

- *Promotion of typological thinking:* An average 12-0 pupil is a statistical abstraction. The average 12-year-old is in a family with 1.2 other children, 0.8 of a dog, and 2.3 automobiles; in other words, the average child does not exist. Average 12-0 children more accurately represent a range of performances, typically the middle 50%.

- *Implication of a false standard of performance:* Educators expect a third grader to perform at a third-grade level and a 9-year-old to perform at a 9-year-old level. However, the way in which equivalent scores are constructed ensures that 50% of any age or grade group will perform below age or grade level, because half of the test takers earn scores below the median.

- *Tendency for scales to be ordinal, not equal interval:* The line relating the number correct to the various ages is typically curved, with a flattening of the curve at higher ages or grades. Figure 4.6 is a typical developmental curve. Thus, the amount of learning required to attain an interval of gain in the final score is not equivalent across all score intervals (e.g., to gain from 9.5 to 9.6 is not the same as 9.1 to 9.2). Because the scales are ordinal and not based on equal interval units, scores on these scales should not be added or multiplied in any computation.

To interpret a developmental score (e.g., a mental age), it is usually helpful to know the age of the person whose score is being interpreted. Knowing developmental age as well as chronological age (CA) allows us to judge an individual's relative performance. Suppose that Ana earns a mental age (MA) of 120 months. If Ana is 8 years (96 months) old, her performance is above average. If she is 35 years old, however, it is below average. The relationship between developmental age and chronological age is often quantified as a developmental quotient. For example, the equation for a *ratio IQ* is shown in Equation 4.3.

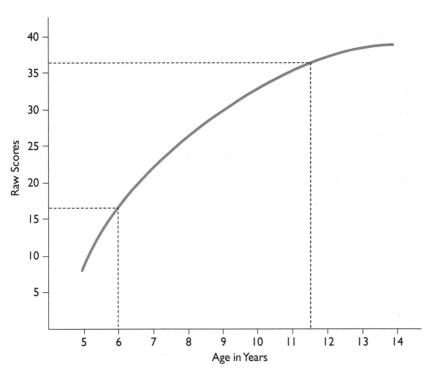

FIGURE 4.6. Mean number correct for 10 age groups: an example of arriving at age-equivalent scores.

All the problems that apply to developmental levels also apply to developmental quotients.

Eq. 4.3
$$IQ = \frac{MA \text{ (in months)}}{CA \text{ (in months)}} \times 100$$

Scores of Relative Standing

Scores of relative standing compare a student's performance to the performances of similar (in age or grade) students. In essence, these scores tell us the percentage or proportion of students who earned better or worse scores. These scores have the following advantages:

- They mean the same thing regardless of a student's age or the content being tested.
- They allow us to compare one person's performance on several tests—for example, Jerry's scores on math, science, and language subtests.
- They also allow us to compare several people on the same test, for example Jerry, Mary, and Tony on a math subtest.

The interpretation of test scores would be far more difficult if the scores had different means and standard deviations. Consider comparing students' heights measured on different scales. Suppose, for example, George is 70 inches tall, Bridget is 6 feet 3 inches tall, Bruce is 1.93 meters tall, and Alexandra is 177.8 centimeters tall. To compare their heights, it is necessary to transform the heights into comparable units. In feet and inches, their heights are as follows: George, 5 feet 10 inches; Bridget, 6 feet 3 inches; Bruce, 6 feet 4 inches; and Alexandra, 5 feet 10 inches. Scores of relative standing put raw scores into comparable units, such as percentiles or standard scores.

Percentile Family. The percentile family includes percentiles, deciles, quartiles, etc. **Percentile ranks (percentiles)** are derived scores that indicate the percentage of people whose scores are at or below a given raw score. Although percentiles are easily calculated, test authors usually provide tables that convert raw scores on a test to percentiles for each age or grade of test takers. Interpretation of percentiles is straightforward. If Bill earns a percentile of 48 on a test, Bill's test score is equal to or better than those of 48% of the test takers to whom he is being compared. (It is also correct to say that 53% of the test takers earned scores equal to or better than that of Bill). Theoretically, percentiles can range from 0.1 to 99.9—that is, a performance that is equal to or better than those of one-tenth of 1% of the test takers to a performance that is equal to or better than those of 99.9% of the test takers. The 50th percentile rank is the median.

Computational Example—Percentile Ranks

Percentile ranks can be used when the scale of measurement is ordinal or equal-interval. They are derived scores indicating the percentage of people whose scores are at or below a given raw score. The percent correct is not the same as the percentage of people scoring at or below a given score. Percentiles corresponding to particular scores can be computed by the following four-step sequence.

1. Arrange the scores that could be earned by the students from the highest to lowest (that is, best to worst).
2. Record the number of students earning each score.
3. Compute the percentage of students earning each score.
4. Compute the percentage of students with scores below each score.
5. Add the percentage of students with scores below the score to one-half the percentage of students with scores at the score to obtain the percentile rank.

Mr. Greenberg gave a test to his developmental reading class, which has an enrollment of 25 children. Table 4.4 shows the scores earned by the students, arranged from highest to lowest. Subsequent columns show the number of students who earned each score, the percentage of all 25 students who earned each score, and the percentage of students who were below each particular score. In the last group of columns, the percentile rank is computed.

TABLE 4.4

Computing Percentile Ranks for a Hypothetical Class of 25

	Percentile Ranks						
Score	Number of Students Earning This Score	Percentage of Students Earning This Score	Percentage of Students Below the Score	+	Half of Percentage of Students at the Score	=	Percentile
50	2	8	92	+	$(\frac{1}{2})(8)$	=	96
49	0						
48	4	16	76	+	$(\frac{1}{2})(16)$	=	84
47	0						
46	5	20	56	+	$(\frac{1}{2})(20)$	=	66
45	5	20	36	+	$(\frac{1}{2})(20)$	=	46
44	3	12	24	+	$(\frac{1}{2})(12)$	=	30
43	2	8	16	+	$(\frac{1}{2})(8)$	=	20
42	0	—					
41	0	—					
40	2	8	8	+	$(\frac{1}{2})(8)$	=	12
39	0	—					
38	1	4	4	+	$(\frac{1}{2})(4)$	=	6
—							
—							
—							
24	1	4	0	+	$(\frac{1}{2})(4)$	=	2

Only one child scored 24; this single score is 1/25 of the class, or 4%. No one scored lower than 24, so 0% (0/25) of the scores are below 24. The child who scored 24 received a percentile rank of 2 because $0 + (\frac{1}{2})(4) = 2$.

Again only one child scored 38. Thus, 4% of the total (1/25) scored at 38, and 4% of the total scored below 38. Therefore the percentile rank corresponding to a score of 38 is as follows: $4 + (\frac{1}{2})(4) = 6$.

Two children earned a score of 40, and two children scored below 40. The percentile rank for a score of 40 is 12. The same procedure is followed for every score obtained. The best score in the class, 50, was obtained by two students. The percentile rank corresponding to the highest score in the class is 96.

The interpretation of percentile ranks is based on the percentage of people. All students who score 48 on the test have a percentile rank of 84. These four students have scored as well as or better than 84% of their classmates on the test. Similarly, an individual who obtains a percentile rank of 21 on an intelligence test has scored as well as or better than 21% of the people in the norm sample. Although percentiles are easy to understand, they are also easy to misunderstand. The primary problem with percentile values is the common misunderstanding that gaining some number of percentile-equivalent points will reflect the same amount of learning gain. Improving from the 50th to the 54th percentile is not the same amount of gain as improving from the 95th to the 99th percentile, for example.

Because the percentile rank is computed using one-half the percentage of those obtaining a particular score, it is not possible to have a percentile rank of either 0 or 100. Generally, percentile ranks contain decimals, so it is possible for a score to receive a percentile rank of 99.9 or 0.1. The 50th percentile rank is the median.

Occasionally, a score is reported as a percentile band. The two most common are deciles and quartiles:

- **Deciles** are bands of percentiles that are 10 percentile ranks in width; each decile contains 10% of the norm group. The first decile ranges from 0.1 to 9.9; the second ranges from 10 to 19.9; the 10th decile goes from 90 to 99.9.
- **Quartiles** are bands of percentiles that are 25 percentiles wide; each quartile contains 25% of the norm group. The first quartile ranges from the 0.1 to 24.9 percentile; the fourth quartile contains percentiles 75 to 99.9.

Standard Score Family. Standard scores are derived scores with a predetermined mean and standard deviation. Although a distribution of scores can be transformed to produce any predetermined mean and standard deviation, there are five commonly used standard-score distributions: z scores, T scores, deviation IQs,[3] normal-curve equivalents, and stanines.

Z scores, the most basic standard score, transform raw scores into a distribution in which the mean is always equal to 0 and the standard deviation is always equal to 1, regardless of the mean and standard deviation of the raw (obtained) scores. Any raw score can be converted to a z score by using Equation 4.4.

$$z = \frac{X - \bar{X}}{S}$$ Eq. 4.4

---

3. When it was first introduced, the IQ was defined as the ratio of mental age to chronological age, multiplied by 100. Because the standard deviation of mental ages varied by age, ratio IQs also had different percentiles at different ages. For this and other reasons, ratio IQs were largely abandoned by the 1960s.

Positive *z* scores are above the mean; negative *z* scores are below the mean. The greater the magnitude of the number, the more above or below the mean is the score. *Z* scores are interpreted as being *X* number of standard deviations above or below the mean. When the distribution of scores is bell-shaped or normal, we know the exact percentile that corresponds to any *z* score.

Because signs and decimals may be awkward in practical situations, *z* scores often are transformed to four other standard scores: *T* scores, IQs, normal curve equivalents, and stanines. The general formula for changing a *z* score into a different standard score is given by Equation 4.5, where S and SS stand for standard score.

Eq. 4.5 $$SS = \bar{X}_{ss} + (S_{ss})(z)$$

- A *T score* is a standard score with a mean of 50 and a standard deviation of 10. A person earning a *T* score of 40 scored one standard deviation below the mean, whereas a person earning a *T* score of 60 scored one standard deviation above the mean.
- *IQs* are standard scores with a mean of 100 and a standard deviation of usually 15. A person earning an IQ of 85 scored one standard deviation below the mean, whereas a person earning an IQ of 115 scored one standard deviation above the mean.
- *Normal curve equivalents* (NCEs) are standard scores with a mean equal to 50 and a standard deviation equal to 21.06. Although the standard deviation may at first appear strange, this scale divides the normal curve into 100 equal intervals.
- *Stanines* (short for standard nines) are standard-score bands that divide a distribution into nine parts. The first stanine includes all scores that are 1.75 standard deviations or more below the mean, and the ninth stanine includes all scores 1.75 or more standard deviations above the mean. The second through eighth stanines are each 0.5 standard deviation in width, with the fifth stanine ranging from 0.25 standard deviations below the mean to 0.25 standard deviations above the mean.

Standard scores are frequently more difficult to interpret than percentile scores because the concepts of means and standard deviations are not widely understood by people without some statistical knowledge. Thus, standard scores may be more difficult for students and their parents to understand. Aside from this disadvantage, standard scores offer all the advantages of percentiles plus an additional advantage: Because standard scores are equal-interval, readers can understand gains between score intervals as equivalent gains and scores can be combined (e.g., added or averaged).[4]

---

4. Standard scores also solve another subtle problem. When scores are combined in a total or composite, the elements of that composite (e.g., 18 scores from weekly spelling tests that are combined to obtain a semester average) do not count the same (that is, they do not carry the same weight) unless they have equal variances. Tests that have larger variances contribute more to the composite than tests with smaller variances. When each of the elements has been standardized into the same standard scores (e.g.,

Cautionary Comments on Interpreting Scores

Test authors include tables in their test manuals to convert raw scores into derived scores. Thus, test users do not have to calculate derived scores. Standard scores can be transformed into other standard scores readily; they can be converted to percentiles without conversion tables only when the distribution of scores is normal. In normal distributions, the relationship between percentiles and standard scores is known. Figure 4.7 compares various standard scores and percentiles for normal distributions. When the distribution of scores is not normal, conversion tables are necessary in order to convert percentiles to standard scores (or vice versa). These conversion tables are test-specific, so only a test author can provide them. Moreover, conversion tables are always required in order to convert developmental scores to scores of relative standing, even when the distribution of test scores is normal. If the only derived score available for a test is an age equivalent, then there is no way for a test user to convert raw scores to percentiles. However, age or grade equivalents can be converted back to raw scores, which can be converted to standard scores if the raw score mean and standard deviation are provided.

The selection of the particular type of score to use and to report depends on the purpose of testing and the sophistication of the consumer. In our opinion, developmental scores should never be used. Both laypeople and professionals readily misinterpret these scores. In order to understand the precise meaning of developmental scores, the

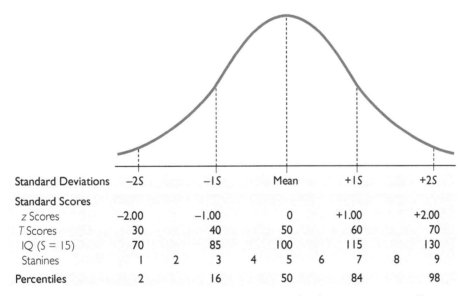

Standard Deviations	−2S		−1S		Mean		+1S		+2S
Standard Scores									
z Scores	−2.00		−1.00		0		+1.00		+2.00
T Scores	30		40		50		60		70
IQ (S = 15)	70		85		100		115		130
Stanines	1	2	3	4	5	6	7	8	9
Percentiles	2		16		50		84		98

FIGURE 4.7. Relationship among selected standard scores, percentiles, and the normal curve.

weekly scores) will carry exactly the same weight when they are combined. Moreover, the only way a teacher can weight tests differentially is to standardize all the tests and then multiply by the weight. For example, if a teacher wished to count the second test as three times the first test, the scores on both tests would have to be standardized, and the scores on the second test would then be multiplied by three before the scores were combined.

interpreter must generally know both the mean and the standard deviation and then convert the developmental score to a more meaningful score, which is a score of relative standing. Various professional organizations (e.g., the International Reading Association, the American Psychological Association, the National Council on Measurement in Education, and the Council for Exceptional Children) also hold very negative official opinions about developmental scores and quotients.

Standard scores are convenient for test authors. Their use allows an author to combine subtests and to give equal weight to various test components or subtests. Their utility for the consumer is twofold. First, if the score distribution is normal, the consumer can readily convert standard scores to percentile ranks. Second, because standard scores are equal-interval scores, they are useful in analyzing strengths and weaknesses of individual students and in research.

We favor the use of percentiles. Percentiles can be a useful way to convey an individual's relative standing in a group. These unpretentious scores require the fewest assumptions for accurate interpretation. The scale of measurement need only be ordinal, although it is very appropriate to compute percentiles on equal-interval or ratio data. The distribution of scores need not be normal; percentiles can be computed for any shape of distribution. Professionals, parents, and students readily understand them. Most important, however, is the fact that percentiles tell us nothing more than what any norm-referenced derived score can tell us—namely, an individual's relative standing in a group. Reporting scores in percentiles may remove some of the aura surrounding test scores, but it permits test results to be presented in terms users can understand. The downside to the use of percentile scores is that they are generally not useful for screening or program evaluation as all systems want to perform better than the 50th percentile. For example, systems may wish to pay their teachers at the 70th percentile equivalent salary for the United States. This does not mean that the new salaries will be 20% more than the old salaries if the old salaries were at the 50th percentile. Also, when attaining a percentile equivalent is the goal, it does not convey a level of performance that is necessarily meaningful or useful to the person or system for which the goal has been set. And theoretically, if all other systems are using the same approach, then the 50th percentile mark will only become an escalating target which might be a good thing for academic achievement, but might not be ideal for something like salary which could outpace system capacity and create system contraction in hiring.

PROGRESS
MONITORING
CHECK

Normative Sample

The most obvious use of normative samples is to provide the derived scores associated with a test taker's raw scores. A **normative sample** (also referred to as a "**standardization sample**" or "**norms**") is the sample of individuals to whom an individual is compared when one obtains a derived score. In practice, testers do not actually calculate percentiles, standard scores, or developmental scores. They use norm tables developed by the test author and based on the standardization sample. Testers merely select the appropriate norm table and find the derived scores (i.e., the percentiles, standard scores, and developmental scores) corresponding to raw scores earned by the test taker.

Because they are used to interpret a test taker's score, norm tables "should refer to clearly described populations. These populations should include individuals or groups with whom test users will ordinarily wish to compare their own examinees" (AERA et al., 2014, p. 104). Not only must they contain individuals with relevant characteristics and experiences, but also those characteristics and experiences must be in the same proportion as the target population to which the test taker will be compared.

Important Characteristics

What makes a characteristic relevant depends on the construct being measured. Some characteristics have a clear, logical, and empirical relationship to a person's development, and several characteristics have an indirect, empirical relationship. Following are brief discussions of the most commonly considered developmental and sociocultural characteristics: sex, age, grade in school, acculturation of parents, race and ethnic identification, geography, and intelligence.

Sex

To date, it is common practice for test publishers to stratify their norm samples on the basis of **sex** or **gender**, including both males and females in the appropriate proportion found in the general U.S. population (approximately 48% male and 52% female). It may no longer be necessary to do so. We can think of only a few instances in which gender is a relevant defining characteristic for conditions requiring differential educational interventions. For example, color blindness is due to a sex-linked recessive gene and the incidence of color blindness globally is one in 12 for males and one in 200 for females. Four times as many males as females evidence the condition of autism. So the developer of a test used to identify color blindness or autism would want to provide separate norms for boys and girls.

In reviewing tests you should examine whether the test authors provide empirical evidence showing that their test is not biased against males or females, that for some reason males or females systematically score higher on the test. If score differences vary by sex, that could be evidence of bias in the assessment.

Age

Chronological age is clearly related to maturation for a number of abilities and skills, and norms frequently use age groups of 1 year. However, we have known for 50 years or more that different psychological abilities develop at different rates.[5] Consequently, tests may use norms with narrower or wider age ranges. When an ability or skill is developing

---

5. Guilford, 1967, pp. 417–426.

rapidly (e.g., locomotion in infants and toddlers), the age range of a norm group may be much narrower than 1 year—e.g., 6-month norms. For mature adults whose skills and abilities have stabilized, the age range may be several years (e.g., norms for persons 59 to 65 years of age, 65 to 70 years of age). The months or years spanned by an age group is an empirical question. Test authors may rely on research with other similar tests or the results with their own test in deciding the range of ages in a norm group.

Grade in School

All achievement tests should measure learned facts and concepts that have been taught in school. The more grades completed by students (that is, the more schooling), the more they should have been taught. Thus, the most useful norm comparisons are usually made to students of the same grade, regardless of their ages.[6] It is also important to note that students of different ages are present in most grades; for example, some 7-year-old children may not be enrolled in school, some may be in kindergarten, some in first grade, some in second grade, and some even in third grade.

Acculturation of Parents

Acculturation is an imprecise concept that refers to an understanding of the language (including conventions and pragmatics), history, values, and social conventions of society at large. Nowhere are the complexities of acculturation more readily illustrated than in the area of language. Acculturation requires people to know more than standard American English; they must also know the appropriate contexts for various words and idioms, appropriate volume and distance between speaker and listener, appropriate posture to indicate respect, and so forth.

Because acculturation is a broad and somewhat diffuse construct, it is difficult to define or measure precisely. Typically, test authors use the socioeconomic status of the parents (usually some combination of education and occupation of the parents) as a very general indication of the level of acculturation of the home. The socioeconomic status of a student's parents is strongly related to scores on all sorts of tests, including intelligence, achievement, adaptive behavior, and social functioning. Historically the children of middle- and upper-class parents have tended to score higher on such tests (see Gottesman, 1968; Herrnstein & Murray, 1994). Whatever the reasons for such differences in child attainment, norm samples certainly must include all segments of society (in the same proportion as in the general population) in order to be representative.

Racial Identity

Race is particularly relevant to our discussion of norms for two reasons. First, the scientific and educational communities have often been insensitive and occasionally blatantly

---

6. In situations where students are not grouped by grade, it may be necessary to use age comparisons.

racist (e.g., Down, 1866/1969). As recently as 1972, the *Stanford-Binet Intelligence Scale* excluded non-White individuals from the standardization sample. Although such overt discrimination is rare today, individuals of color still face subtle forms of discrimination and limited opportunities.

Second, persistent racial differences in *tested* achievement and ability remain, although these differences continue to narrow. Scientists and philosophers have long tried to understand why this might be so, and they have offered a variety of explanations—genetics, environment, interactions between genes and environment, poor test construction, and more recently, structural racism.[7] However, although trying to unravel the interactions among explanations may be interesting scientifically and politically, such an endeavor is far beyond the scope of this text. What is important for our purposes is an understanding that these differences must be considered in developing norm groups, selecting assessments, and interpreting the results.

Geography

There are systematic differences in the attainment of individuals living in different **geographic regions** of the United States, and various psychoeducational tests reflect these regional differences. Most consistently, the average scores of individuals living in the southeastern United States (excluding Florida) are often lower than the average scores of individuals living in other regions of the country. Moreover, community size, population density (that is, urban, suburban, and rural communities), and gains or losses of population have also been related to academic and intellectual development.

There are several seemingly logical explanations for many of these relationships. For example, well-educated young adults tend to move away from communities with limited employment and cultural opportunities. When better-educated individuals leave a community, the average intellectual ability and educational attainment in that community decline, and the average ability and attainment of the communities to which those individuals move increase. Regardless of the reasons for geographical differences, test norms should include individuals from all geographic regions, as well as from urban, suburban, and rural communities.

Intelligence

Intelligence is related to a number of variables that are considered in psychoeducational assessment. Intelligence is certainly related to achievement because most intelligence tests were actually developed to predict school success. Correlations are generally positive but decline as students age. For elementary school students, the correlation may be as high as $r = .7$, but they tend to drop for high school and college students (Atkinson et al., 1993).

---

7. We also note that perhaps as much as 90% of observed racial and cultural differences can be attributed to socioeconomic differences.

Because language development and facility are often considered an indication of intellectual development, intelligence tests are often verbally oriented. Consequently, they tend to correlate with scores on tests of linguistic or psycholinguistic ability. Various perceptual tasks are also used on intelligence tests. Items assessing perceptual abilities appeared on intelligence tests as early as Thurstone's *Primary Mental Abilities* test in 1941.

The full range of intellectual ability must be considered in the development of norms for perceptual and perceptual-motor tests. Historically, norms have been biased by such practices as limiting the sample to students enrolled in and attending school (usually general education classes), excluding individuals with intellectual disability, or selecting only students of *average* intelligence. Such practices inflate test means, restrict the standard deviation, and bias derived scores.

Other Considerations

Norms Are Plural

Most tests have multiple normative samples that are collectively referred to as the **norm sample**. For example, the norm sample of an achievement test may contain 2,600 students from kindergarten through 12th grade. However, that group consists of 200 students in 13 norm groups. If that achievement test also had separate norms for boys and girls at each grade, there would be 26 norm groups of 100 students each. Therefore, when we test a second-grade boy, we do not compare his performance with the performances of 2,600 students in the total norm sample. Rather, we compare the boy's performance to 200 second graders (or to 100 second-grade boys if there are separate norms for boys and girls).

The number of subjects in each norm group should be large enough to guarantee stability. If a sample is very small, another group of participants might have different means and standard deviations. Second, the number of participants should be large enough to represent infrequent characteristics. For example, if about 1% of the population is Native American, a sample of 25 or 50 people will be unlikely to contain even one Native American. Third, there should be enough subjects so that there can be a full range of derived scores. In practice, 100 participants in each normative group are considered the minimum.

It is crucial that various kinds of people in each normative sample be included in the same proportion as occur in the general population. Each norm group must be representative, not just the aggregated or combined sample. Representativeness should be demonstrated for each norm group.

Age of Norms

For a norm sample to be representative, it must represent the current population. Levels of skill and ability change over time. Skilled athletes of today run faster, jump higher, and are stronger than the best athletes of a generation ago. Some of the improvement can be attributed to better training, but some also can be attributed to better nutrition and societal changes. Similarly, intellectual and educational performances have increased from generation to generation, although these increases are neither steady nor linear.

For example, on norm-referenced achievement tests, considerably more than half the students score above the average after the test has been in use for 5 to 7 years. In such cases, the test norms are clearly dated because only half the population can ever be above the median (Linn et al., 1990). While some increase in tested achievement can be attributed to teacher familiarity with test content (Linn et al., 1990), there is little doubt that some of the changes represent real improvement in achievement.

There are probably multiple causes for these increases. Certainly, the computer revolution forever changed the availability of information. Never before has there been so much knowledge accessible to so many people. Students of today know more than did the students in 2000. Students of today also probably know less than will the students in 2025.

The important point is that old norms tend to overestimate a student's relative standing in the population erroneously because the old norms are too easy. The point at which norms become outdated will depend in part on the ability or skill being assessed. With this caution, it seems to us that 15 years is about the maximum useful life for norm samples used in ability testing; 7 years appears to be the maximum for norm life for achievement tests. Although test publishers should assure that up-to-date norms are readily available, test users ultimately are responsible for avoiding the inappropriate use of out-of-date norms (AERA et al., 2014, p. 104).

Specialized Norms

National norms are the most appropriate if we are interested in knowing how a particular student is developing intellectually, perceptually, linguistically, or physically. However, sometimes educators are interested in comparing a test taker to a particular subgroup of the national population. The term **specialized norms** refers to all comparisons that are not national. One type of specialized norm is referred to as local norms. **Local norms** may be based on an entire state, school district, or even a classroom. These norms are useful in ascertaining the degree to which individual students have profited from their schooling and also in retrospective interpretations of a student's performance.

Special population norms are a second type of specialized norm sample. These norms are based on personal characteristics or attainment. For example, the *American Association on Intellectual and Developmental Disabilities' Adaptive Behavior Scale* compares a student's score to those of individuals with intellectual disabilities. Other tests used in career and college guidance are standardized on individuals in specific trades or professions.

4.3

PROGRESS MONITORING CHECK

A third type of norms are called growth norms. **Growth norms** are used to assign percentiles and standard scores to differences in scores from one test to another (e.g., the amount of gain from pretest to posttest) over a specified amount of time. Growth scores have unique issues of score reliability that are discussed in the next chapter. See also the *Advanced Information About Finding a Representative Sample of People* online resource.

4.2
ONLINE
RESOURCE

Ensuring Fairness in Using Test Scores

One fundamental assumption in assessment is that a test is administered, scored, and interpreted by a competent examiner. Test publishers specify in the manuals for most tests the kinds of credentials needed to administer, score, and interpret tests, and these requirements differ for different kinds of tests. For example, individually administered achievement tests can be administered by classroom teachers who have basic training in test administration. Administration of diagnostic reading or math tests takes formal training in diagnostic testing, the kind of training one usually received in a Master's degree program or Certificate of Advanced Graduate Study program in Education. Use of measures of intelligence or socioemotional behavior requires formal training in administration, scoring, and interpretation of such measures. It is imperative that test users stay within their bounds of competence in administering and using tests.

Those who interpret test results must know the meaning of different kinds of scores. Misunderstanding scores can lead to harmful errors in decision making. We can best illustrate this by a personal story. A professional colleague of one of the authors, let's call her Mrs. Hansen, had a daughter, Kate. Kate transferred schools and, because she had been a bit apprehensive about transferring, her mother asked her how her classes were going after the first couple of days in her new school. Kate reported that school seemed fine except for her math class. She indicated that they were doing things that she had done years earlier in her previous school. A week later she reported that this was still the case. Her mother, a special education teacher, contacted the school to ask about Kate's math class. The school counselor, Mr. Norwood, confirmed what Kate had told her mother. "Math is the only class in which we track students, and Kate's IQ on her group intelligence test is in the low 90s. So she is placed in a class with students of similar ability."

Mrs. Hansen was stunned. Kate had been screened for gifted placement in her previous school and had an IQ in the 120s on an individually administered test of intelligence. Mrs. Hansen asked if she could see the test results. She located the score of 92 and recognized that it was a *percentile* score, not an IQ. The counselor said that he would correct the error "next semester." The mother said that the end of the week would be more acceptable.

Imagine if Kate had not had a mother who questioned her about her school work. More importantly, few students have mothers who would understand the distinction between an IQ and a percentile score. The error in test score interpretation would lead to an error in placement and would harm the student.

Similarly, using tests whose norm groups are not representative of the students being tested results in unfair comparisons and potential errors in interpreting test scores. And, importantly, those who assess students should be gathering data for the purpose of making decisions about the students. They should be gathering enough data to make good decisions. Federal law talks about comprehensive decisions. It also talks about multiple measures and multiple methods of assessment for purposes of decision making. At the same time, it is important not to over-test students. Administering far more measures than necessary for purposes of making a decision is just as bad as not gathering enough information. Those who assess students must strive for precision and accuracy in decision making.

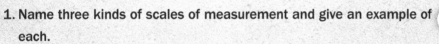

1. Name three kinds of scales of measurement and give an example of each.
2. Why is it important to know about measures of dispersion?
3. Distinguish between mean, median, and mode. In the list of scores below, identify each.

    1, 3, 4, 4, 5, 6, 6, 6,9

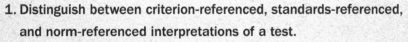
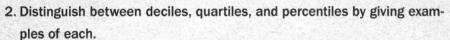

1. Distinguish between criterion-referenced, standards-referenced, and norm-referenced interpretations of a test.
2. Distinguish between deciles, quartiles, and percentiles by giving examples of each.
3. Explain the statistical meaning of the following scores: percentile, *z* score, IQ, NCE, age equivalent, and grade equivalent.

1. Why is acculturation of the parents of students in normative samples important?

2. Identify five important characteristics to take into account when examining the normative population for a test.

3. Age of norms is an important consideration. How old should a test be before you quit using its norms to make normative comparisons?

4. Growth norms are being used increasingly to report on student performance. What are growth norms, what do they tell you about a student's performance, and when should you use them?

CHAPTER 5

Technical Requirements: Reliability and Validity

LEARNING OBJECTIVES

1. Understand the basic concept of reliability, what it is, how it is estimated, and the factors that affect it.
2. Explain the basic information used in test validation.

Reliability

Every day school personnel conduct assessments—mostly they test and they observe—to get information to make educational decisions. For assessments to be useful they must be administered, scored, and interpreted correctly. However, correct administration, scoring, and interpretation is not sufficient to ensure that assessment results will be meaningful. Assessment results must be generalizable. Except for school-specific rules (e.g., no running in the halls), nothing a student learns in school has any value unless it can be generalized to life outside of school. The very nature of schooling presumes students will generalize what they have learned. **Reliability,** in measurement, is the extent to which it is possible to generalize from the items of a test score or observation made at a specific time, by a specific person to a similar performance on the same items at a different time, or by a different person. When assessment results cannot be generalized, they are in error; the results are incorrect. The errors associated with each of the three dimensions—selected items, times, raters—are independent of each other (i.e., uncorrelated) and additive. **Measurement error** is the sum of the three dimensions of error.[1]

Suppose Mr. Jeffreys wanted to know if his students could name the cursive uppercase letters of the alphabet. Because there are only 26 letters, he could test every letter. Students' scores on that test would be their *true scores* on the domain. Suppose Mr. Jeffreys did not want to test every letter, instead preferring to test a smaller sample of letters—for example, five letters. Students' means on all of the possible five-letter tests would be their true scores for five-letter tests. Some of those tests (e.g., *B, C, Q, E, O*) would be much easier than the average of all five-letter tests. Students would earn scores that were higher than their true scores—the average of all five-letter tests. Other tests (e.g., *J, Q, Y, Z, A*) would be much harder than the average of all five-letter tests. Students would earn scores that were lower than their true scores. The differences between students' true scores and their obtained scores are errors. The errors in this example are random and, thus, uncorrelated with true scores. In the long run, the average (mean) of random errors will equal zero. Across a large number of samples, the samples of test items that raise scores are balanced by samples that lower scores.

On achievement tests dealing with beginning material and with certain types of behavioral observations, it is occasionally possible to assess an entire domain (e.g., arithmetic facts). In such cases, the obtained score is a student's true score, and there is no need to estimate the reliability of the test's item sample. However, usually it is not possible or feasible to assess an entire domain, even in the primary grades. In more advanced curricula, it is usually impossible to assess an entire domain—especially when that domain is a hypothetical construct (such as intelligence or visual perception). Therefore, in these cases, the reliability of the item sample should always be estimated.

The same argument can be made for reliability (generalizability) over time. If we are only interested in performance on one occasion, that one occasion makes up the entire domain. The student's performance at that time is the student's true score. Obviously there very few single performances that would comprise an entire domain—felonies, acts of heroism. Thus, performance must generalize over time such that assessing a child on Tuesday does not give a different result than assessing the child on Thursday or in an afternoon versus a morning session.

Similarly, if we are only interested in the evaluations of one person or committee, those evaluations make up the entire domain. The performance as assessed by that one person constitutes the entire domain, and the students' scores are their true scores. Although such a situation is difficult to imagine in schools, personal evaluations are frequently all that matters outside of school. For example, your evaluation of the food at a restaurant is probably the only evaluation that is important to you in determining whether the food was good. The degree to which assessment scores may not general-

---

1. Unlike measurement error that is random, **bias** is measurement error that is systematic and predictable. Bias affects a person's (or group's) score in one direction. Bias inflates people's measured abilities above their true abilities. Bias can also deflate people's measured abilities below their true abilities.

ize across items, time, and assessors is quantified during a test's development and can be summed together to represent the error variance (difference from true score) in the scores.

Although there is always some degree of error, the important question is how much error is attached to a particular score? Unfortunately, a direct answer to this question is usually not directly available. To estimate both the amount of error attached to a score and the amount of error in general, two statistics are needed: a reliability coefficient for the particular generalization and the standard error of measurement.

Reliability Coefficient

The reliability coefficient is a special use of a correlation coefficient. The symbol for a correlation coefficient (r) is used with two identical subscripts (e.g., r_{xx} or r_{aa}) to indicate a reliability coefficient. The **reliability coefficient** indicates the proportion of variability in a set of scores that reflects true differences among individuals. If there is relatively little error, the ratio of true score variance to obtained score variance approaches a reliability index of 1.00 (perfect reliability); if there is a relatively large amount of error, the ratio of true score variance to obtained score variance approaches .00 (total unreliability). Thus, a test with a reliability coefficient of .90 has relatively less error of measurement and is more reliable than a test with a reliability coefficient of .50. Subtracting the proportion of true-score variance from 1 yields the proportion of error variance in the distribution of scores. Thus, if the reliability coefficient is .90, 10% of the variability in the distribution is attributable to error.

All other things being equal, we want to use the most reliable procedures and tests that are available. Since perfectly reliable tests are quite rare, the choice of test becomes a question of minimum reliability for the specific purpose of assessment. We recommend that the minimum standards for reliability presented in Box 5.1 be used in applied settings.

Three Types of Reliability

In educational and psychological assessment, we are concerned with three types of reliability or generalizations: generalization to other similar items, generalization to other times, and generalization to other observers. These three generalizations have different names (that is, item reliability, stability, and interobserver agreement) and are separately estimated by different procedures.

Item Reliability. There are two main approaches to estimating the extent to which we can generalize to different samples of items: alternate-form reliability and internal consistency.

Alternate-form reliability represents the correlation between scores for the same individuals on two different forms of a test. These forms (1) measure the same trait or skill to the same extent, and (2) are standardized on the same population. Alternate forms offer essentially equivalent tests (but not identical items); sometimes, in fact, they are

BOX 5.1

Minimum Standards for Test Reliability According to Test Purpose

- If test scores are to be used for administrative purposes and are reported for groups of individuals, a reliability of .60 should be the minimum standard. This relatively low standard is acceptable because group means are not as affected by a test's lack of reliability as individual scores.

- If weekly (or more frequent) testing is used to monitor pupil progress, a reliability of .70 should be the minimum. This relatively low standard is acceptable because random fluctuations can be taken into account when a behavior or skill is measured often.

- If the decision being made is a screening decision (e.g., a recommendation for further assessment), there is still a need for higher reliability. For screening devices, we recommend a standard of .80.

- If a test score is to be used to make an important decision concerning an individual student (e.g., tracking or special education placement), the minimum standard should be .90.

called equivalent forms. The means and variances for the alternate forms are assumed to be (or should be) the same. In the absence of error of measurement, any subject would be expected to earn the same score on both forms. To estimate the reliability of two alternate forms of a test (e.g., form A and form B), a large sample of students is tested with both forms. Half the subjects receive form A and then form B; the other half receive form B and then form A. Scores from the two forms are correlated. The resulting correlation coefficient is a reliability coefficient.

Internal consistency is the second approach to estimating the extent to which we can generalize to different test items and is a measure of the extent to which items in a test correlate with one another. It does not require two or more test forms. Instead, after a test is given, it is split into two halves that are correlated to produce an estimate of reliability. For example, suppose we wanted to use this method to estimate the reliability of a 10-item test. The results of this hypothetical test are presented in Table 5.1. After administering the test to a group of students, we divide the test into two 5-item tests by summing the even-numbered items and the odd-numbered items for each student. This creates two alternate forms of the test, each containing one half of the total number of test items. We can then correlate the sums of the odd-numbered items with the sums of the even-numbered items to obtain an estimate of the reliability of each of the two halves. This procedure for estimating a test's reliability is called a *split-half reliability estimate*.

It should be apparent that there are many ways to divide a test into two equal-length tests. If the 10 items in our full test are arranged in order of increasing diffi-

TABLE 5.1

Hypothetical Performance of 20 Children on a 10-Item Test

| | Items | | | | | | | | | | Total | | |
Child	1	2	3	4	5	6	7	8	9	10	Total Test	Evens Correct	Odds Correct
1	+	+	+	−	+	−	−	−	+	−	5	1	4
2	+	+	+	+	−	+	+	+	−	+	8	5	3
3	+	+	−	+	+	+	+	−	+	+	8	4	4
4	+	+	+	+	+	+	+	+	−	+	9	5	4
5	+	+	+	+	+	+	+	+	+	−	9	4	5
6	+	+	−	+	−	+	+	+	+	+	8	5	3
7	+	+	+	+	+	−	+	−	+	+	8	3	5
8	+	+	+	−	+	+	+	+	+	+	9	4	5
9	+	+	+	+	+	+	−	+	+	+	9	5	4
10	+	+	+	+	+	−	+	+	+	+	9	4	5
11	+	+	+	+	+	−	+	+	+	+	6	2	4
12	+	+	−	+	+	+	+	+	+	+	9	5	4
13	+	+	+	−	−	+	−	+	−	−	5	3	2
14	+	+	+	+	+	+	+	−	+	+	9	4	5
15	+	+	−	+	+	−	−	−	−	−	4	2	2
16	+	+	+	+	+	+	+	+	+	+	10	5	5
17	+	−	+	−	−	−	−	−	−	−	2	0	2
18	+	−	+	+	+	+	+	+	+	+	9	4	5
19	+	+	+	+	−	+	+	+	+	+	9	5	4
20	+	−	−	−	−	+	−	+	−	−	3	2	1

culty, both halves should contain items from the beginning of the test (that is, easier items) and items from the end of the test (that is, more difficult items). There are many other ways of dividing such a test (e.g., grouping items 1, 4, 5, 8, and 9 and items 2, 3, 6, 7, and 10). The most common way to divide a test is by odd-numbered and even-numbered items (see the columns labeled "Evens Correct" and "Odds Correct" in

Table 5.1). This method of computing internal consistency has fallen out of a favor with some influential groups describing it as "arbitrary and potentially artefactual" (NCII, intensiveintervention.org).

A better method of estimating internal consistency was developed by Cronbach (1951) and is called coefficient alpha. *Coefficient alpha* is the average split-half correlation based on all possible divisions of a test into two parts. In practice, there is no need to compute all possible correlation coefficients; coefficient alpha can be computed from the variances of individual test items and the variance of the total test score and this value is commonly reported by test publishers.

Coefficient alpha can be used when test items are scored pass–fail or when more than 1 point is awarded for a correct response. An earlier, more restricted method of estimating a test's reliability, based on the average correlation between all possible split halves, was developed by Kuder and Richardson. This procedure, called *KR-20*, is coefficient alpha for dichotomously scored test items (that is, items that can only be scored right or wrong).

Stability. **Stability** is the consistency of test scores over time. When students have learned information and behavior, we want to be confident that students can access that information and demonstrate those behaviors at times other than when they are assessed. We would like to be able to generalize today's test results to other times in the future. Educators are interested in many human traits and characteristics that, theoretically, change very little over time. For example, children diagnosed as colorblind at age 5 years are expected to be diagnosed as colorblind at any time in their lives. Color blindness is an inherited trait that cannot be corrected. Consequently, the trait should be perfectly stable. When an assessment identifies a student as colorblind on one occasion and not colorblind on a later occasion, the assessment is unreliable.

Other traits are developmental. For example, people's heights will increase from birth through adulthood. The increases are relatively slow and predictable. Consequently, we would not expect many changes in height over a 2-week period. Radical changes in people's heights (especially decreases) over short periods of time would cause us to question the reliability of the measurement instrument. Most educational and psychological characteristics are conceptualized as being more like height than colorblindness. In other words, we expect reading achievement to increase with length of schooling but to be relatively stable over short periods of time, such as 2 weeks.

Tests used to assess traits and characteristics must produce sufficiently consistent and stable results if those results are to have practical meaning for making educational decisions. When our generalizations about student performance on a domain are correctly generalized from one time to another, the test is said to be stable or to have test–retest reliability. Obviously, the notion of stability excludes changes that occur as the result of systematic interventions to change the behavior. Thus, if a test indicates that a student does not know the long vowel sounds and we teach those sounds to the student, the change in the student's test performance would not be considered a lack of reliability on the part of the measure.

The procedure for obtaining a stability coefficient is straightforward. A large number of students are tested and then retested after a short period of time (preferably 2 weeks later). The students' scores from the two administrations are then correlated, and the obtained correlation coefficient is the stability coefficient.

Interobserver Agreement. Interobserver agreement is the consistency among test scorers. We would like to assume that if any other comparably qualified examiner were to give the test or make the observation, the results would be the same—we would like to be able to generalize to similarly qualified scorers. Suppose Ms. Amig listened to her students say the letters of the alphabet. It would not be very useful if she assigned Barney a score of 70% correct, whereas another teacher (or education professional) who also listened to Barney awarded a score of 50% correct or 90% correct for the same performance. When our scoring or other observations agree with those of comparably trained observers who observe the same behavior at the same time, the observations are said to have interobserver reliability or agreement.[2] Ms. Amig would like to assume that any other education professional would score her students' responses in the same way, otherwise the score will contain error associated with the scorer.

There are two very different approaches to estimating the extent to which we can generalize to different scorers: a correlational approach and a percentage of agreement approach. The *correlational approach* is similar to estimating reliability with alternate forms, which was previously discussed. Two testers score a set of tests independently. Scores obtained by each tester for the set are then correlated. The resulting correlation coefficient is a reliability coefficient for scorers.

Percentage of agreement is more common in classrooms and in applied behavioral analysis. Instead of the correlation between two scorers' ratings, a *percentage of agreement* between raters is computed. Three ways of calculating percent agreement are commonly used: simple agreement, point-to-point agreement, and agreement about occurrences of a behavior.

Simple agreement is calculated by comparing the number of occurrences of a behavior counted by two raters. Divide the smaller number of occurrences by the larger number of occurrences and multiply the quotient by 100. For example, suppose Ms. Amig and her teacher's aide, Ms. Carter, observe Sam on 20 occasions to determine how frequently he is on task during reading instruction. The results of their observations are shown in Table 5.2. Ms. Amig observes 13 occasions when Sam is on task, whereas Ms. Carter observes 11 occasions. Simple agreement is approximately 85%; that is, (11/13) × 100.

---

2. Agreement among observers has several different names. Observers can be referred to as testers, scorers, or raters; it depends on the nature of their actions. Agreement can also be called reliability.

TABLE 5.2

Observations of Sam's On-Task Behavior During Reading, Where "−" Is Off Task and "+" Is On Task

Student	Test Score	X - $\overline{X}$	(X - $\overline{X}$)²
1	+	+	Yes
2	−	−	Yes
3	−	+	No
4	+	+	Yes
5	+	+	Yes
6	+	+	Yes
7	−	−	Yes
8	−	+	No
9	+	+	Yes
10	+	−	No
11	−	+	Yes
12	+	−	Yes
13	+	−	Yes
14	+	−	Yes
15	−	+	Yes
16	+	+	No
17	+	−	Yes
18	−	−	Yes
19	+	−	No
20	+	−	No
Total number of occurrences	13	11	14

The second type of percent agreement, *point-to-point agreement,* is a more precise computation of percent agreement, because each data point is considered. To calculate point-to-point agreement, divide the number of observations for which both observers agree (on both occurrence and nonoccurrence of the behavior observed) by the total number of observations and multiply the quotient by 100. The data from Table 5.2 are summarized in Table 5.3. There are 14 occasions when Ms. Amig's and Ms. Carter's observations agree—nine times that Sam was on task and five times that Sam was off task. Point-to-point agreement is 70%; that is, (14/20) × 100 = 70%.

TABLE 5.3

Summary of Two Observers' Assessments of Sam's On-Task Behavior During Reading

		Ms. Amig		
		–	+	
		2	9	11
Ms. Carter	+	5	4	9
	–	7	13	20

Agreement for occurrence, the third type of interobserver agreement, provides a better measure of agreement than point-to-point agreement when occurrences and nonoccurrences of a behavior differ substantially because point-to-point agreement tends to overestimate the agreement. In other words, if occurrence is very rare, like 5 instances compared to 20 nonoccurrences, but all occurrences were missed by one observer, agreement could still look pretty good at $15/20 \times 100 = 75\%$ but this agreement is inflated by the nonoccurrence agreement of 15. In this case, computing occurrence agreement is a better reflection of the reliability of measurement of occurrence of the behavior of concern. The formula for agreement of occurrence is shown in Equation 5.1, and the data from Table 5.2 is used to calculate agreement of occurrence between the observations of Ms. Amig and Ms. Carter. Of the 14 times that Ms. Amig and Ms. Carter agreed that Sam was on or off task, they agreed nine times that he was on task. The five times they agree that Sam was off task are not of interest and not considered in this calculation. Inserting the numbers into Equation 5.1, the two observers agreed on Sam being on task 60% of the time—$[9 \div (20-5)] \times 100$.

$$\frac{100(N_{agreements\ of\ occurrence})}{N_{observations} - N_{agreements\ of\ occurrence}} = \text{Percentage of Agreement of Occurrence} \qquad \text{Eq. 5.1}$$

Factors Affecting Reliability

Several factors affect a test's reliability and can inflate or deflate reliability estimates: test length, test–retest interval, constriction or extension of range, guessing, and variation within the testing situation.

Test Length. As a general rule, the more items there are in a test, the more reliable the test is; longer tests tend to be more reliable than shorter tests. This fact is especially important when considering internal-consistency estimates of reliability because split-half estimates of reliability actually estimate the reliability of half the test. Therefore, such estimates are appropriately corrected by the formula developed by Spearman and Brown (Spearman, 1910). As shown in Equation 5.2, the reliability of the total test is equal to twice the reliability as estimated by internal consistency divided by the sum of 1 plus the reliability estimate. For example, if a split-half estimate of internal consistency were computed for a test and found to be .80, the corrected estimated reliability would be .89 [i.e., (2)(.8) ÷ (1 + .8). A related issue is the number of effective items for each test taker. Tests are generally more reliable in the middle ranges of scores (e.g., within ±1.5 standard deviation). For a test to be effective at the extremes of a distribution, there must be both enough difficult items for very high-performing pupils and enough easy items for very low-performing pupils. Often, there are not enough very easy and very hard items on a test. Therefore, extremely high or extremely low scores tend to be less reliable than scores in the middle of a distribution.

Eq. 5.2 $\quad r_{xx} = \dfrac{2r_{(\frac{1}{2})(\frac{1}{2})}}{1 + r_{(\frac{1}{2})(\frac{1}{2})}}$

Test–Retest Interval. As previously noted, a person's true abilities can and do change between two administrations of a test. The greater the amount of time between the two administrations, the more likely is the possibility that true scores will change. Thus, when employing stability or alternate-form estimates of reliability, test evaluators must pay close attention to the interval between tests. Generally, the shorter the interval is, the higher the estimated reliability is.

Constriction or Extension of Range. Constriction or extension of range refers to narrowing (constriction) or widening (extension) the range of ability of the people whose performances are used to estimate a test's reliability. When the range of ability of these people is less than the range of ability in the population, a test's reliability will be underestimated. The more constricted the range of ability is, the more biased (underestimated) the reliability coefficient will be. As Figure 5.1 shows, alternative forms of a test produce a strong positive correlation when the entire range of the test is used. However, within any restricted range of the test, as illustrated by the dark rectangular outline, the correlation may be very low. (Although it is possible to correct a correlation coefficient for restriction in range, it is generally unwise to do so.) A related problem is that extension of range overestimates a test's reliability. Figure 5.2 illustrates correlations of scores on alternate-form tests given to students in the first, third, and fifth grades. The scatterplot for each grade, considered separately, indicates poor reliability. However, spelling test scores increase as a function of schooling; students in higher grades earn higher scores. When test authors combine the scores for several grades (or from several ages), poor correlations may be combined to produce a spuriously high correlation. For this reason, tests

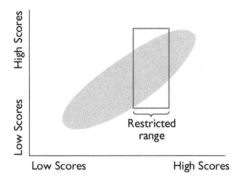

FIGURE 5.1. Constricting the range of test scores and the resulting reduction of the estimate of a test's reliability.

for which scores are expected to improve as individuals age or advance in grade level should provide reliability estimates separately for age/grade groups.

Guessing. Guessing is responding randomly to items. Even if a guess results in a correct response, it introduces error into a test score and into our interpretation of that score. Tests should be constructed to limit the effect of guessing in the final score.

Variation Within the Testing Situation. The amount of error that the testing situation introduces into the results of testing can vary considerably. Children can misread or misunderstand the directions for a test, get a headache halfway through testing, lose their place on the answer sheet, break the point of their pencil, or choose to watch a squirrel eat nuts on the windowsill of the classroom rather than take the test. All such situational variations introduce an indeterminate amount of error in testing and, in doing so, lower reliability. Generally, administration procedures are designed to limit this effect as much as possible (ensuring students understand the directions before beginning, simplifying response formats, conducting assessment in distraction-free environments to the greatest extent possible, knowing when a test administration has been spoiled so the test result can be discarded).

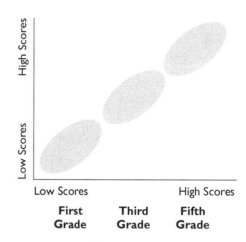

FIGURE 5.2. Extending the range of test scores and the possible spurious increase in the estimate of a test's reliability.

Determining Which Reliability Method to Use

The first consideration in choosing a method of determining a test's reliability is the type of generalization we wish to make. We must select the method that goes with the type of generalization. For example, if we were interested in generalizing about the stability of a score or observation, the appropriate method would be test–retest correlations. It would be inappropriate to use interscorer agreement as an estimate of the extent to which we can generalize to different times. Additional considerations in selecting the reliability method to be used include the following.

- Internal consistency is the most important form of reliability for a test. It sets a limit on other forms of reliability. Conceptually, a test cannot be more reliable over time, for example, than it is within itself. As we review tests in this book, we pay special attention to the internal consistency of each test.

- When one estimates stability, the convention is to retest after 2 weeks. There is nothing special about the 2-week period, but if all test authors used the same interval, it would be easier to compare the relative stability of tests. In examining the test–retest reliability of tests, you should pay special attention to the makeup of the group on whom that reliability was computed. For many tests, test–retest reliability is established on very small groups of a restricted age or grade range in limited geographic areas. For example, information on the test–retest reliability of Test XYZ may be based on the performance of 36 third and fourth graders in Albuquerque, New Mexico. That is a very limited group of students from whom to generalize.

- Many years ago, Nunnally (Nunnally & Bernstein, 1994; Nunnally, 1978) offered a hierarchy for estimating the extent to which we can generalize to similar test items. The first choice is to use alternate-form reliability with a 2-week interval. (Again, there is nothing special about 2 weeks; it is just a convention.) If alternate forms are not available, divide the test into equivalent halves and administer the halves with a 2-week interval, correcting the correlation by the Spearman-Brown formula given above in "Factors Affecting Reliability." When alternate forms are not available and subjects cannot be tested more than once, use coefficient alpha.

- When estimating the extent to which we can generalize among different scorers, we prefer computing correlation coefficients rather than percentages of agreement. Correlation coefficients bear a direct relationship to other indicators of reliability and other uses of reliability coefficients; percentages of agreement do not. We also realize that current practice is to report percentages of agreement and not to bother with the other uses of the reliability coefficient.

Concluding Comments About the Reliability Coefficient

Generalization to other items, times, and observers are independent of each other. Therefore, each index of reliability provides information about only a part of the error associated with measurement. Recently, generalizability theory has emerged as a very promising method to examine types of reliability and interactions between them to estimate overall reliability and to inform use of the test to make reliable decisions (e.g., number of assessment probes needed to make reliable decisions).

In school settings, item reliability is not a problem when we test students on the entire domain (e.g., naming all upper- and lowercase letters of the alphabet). Item reliability should be estimated when we test students on a sample of items from the domain (e.g., a 20-item test on multiplication facts that is used to infer mastery on all facts). Interobserver reliability is usually not a problem when our assessments are objective and our criteria for a correct response clear (e.g., a multiple-choice test). Interobserver reliability should be assessed whenever subjective or qualitative criteria are used to score student responses (e.g., using a scoring rubric to assess the quality of written responses). When students are assessed frequently with interchangeable tests or probes, stability is usually assessed directly prior to intervention by administering tests on 3 or more days until the student's performance has stabilized. If a test is given once, its stability should be estimated, although in practice teachers seldom estimate the stability of their tests.

Standard Error of Measurement

The **standard error of measurement** (*SEM*) is another index of test error and, therefore, reliability. The *SEM* is the average standard deviation of error distributed around people's true scores. Although we can compute standard errors of measurement for scorers, times, and item samples, *SEMs* for item samples are the most frequently calculated.

To illustrate, suppose we wanted to assess students' emerging skill in naming letters of the alphabet and decided to estimate students' knowledge using a 10-letter test. There are many samples of 10-letter tests that could be developed. If we constructed 100 of these tests and tested just one kindergartner, we would probably find a distribution of scores for that kindergartner was approximately normal. The mean of that distribution by definition would be the student's *true score*. The distribution around the true score would be the result of imperfect samples of letters; some letter samples would overestimate the pupil's knowledge, and others would underestimate it. Thus, the variance around the mean would be the result of error. The standard deviation of that distribution is the standard deviation of errors attributable to sampling error and is called the standard error of measurement.

When students are assessed with norm-referenced tests, they are typically tested only once. Therefore, we cannot generate a distribution similar to that shown in Figure 5.3. Consequently, we do not know the test taker's true score or the variance of the measurement error that forms the distribution around that person's true score. By using what we know about the test's standard deviation and its reliability for items, however, we can estimate what that error distribution would be. When estimating the error distribution for one student, test users should understand that the *SEM* is an average; some standard errors will be greater than that average, and some will be less.

The equation for *SEM* equals the standard deviation of the obtained scores (*S*) multiplied by the square root of 1 minus the reliability coefficient, as shown in Equation 5.3. The type of unit (IQ, raw score, and so forth) in which the standard deviation is expressed is the unit in which the *SEM* is expressed. Thus, if the test scores have been

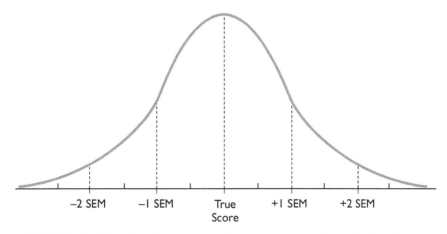

FIGURE 5.3. The standard error of measurement: the standard deviation of the error distribution around a true score for one subject.

converted to *T* scores, the standard deviation is in *T* score units and is 10; the *SEM* is also in *T* score units. From the equation for *SEM*, it is apparent that as the standard deviation increases, the *SEM* increases, and as the reliability coefficient decreases, the *SEM* increases. Similarly, if the reliability coefficient is based on stability, then the *SEM* is for times of testing. If the reliability coefficient is based on different scorers, then the *SEM* is for testers or scorers.

Because measurement error is unavoidable, there is always some uncertainty about an individual's true score. The *SEM* provides information about the certainty or confidence with which a test score can be interpreted. When the *SEM* is relatively large, the uncertainty is large; we cannot be very sure of the individual's score. When the *SEM* is relatively small, the uncertainty is small; we can be more certain of the score.

Eq. 5.3
$$SEM = S\sqrt{1 - r_{xx}}$$

Estimated True Scores

An obtained score on a test is not the best estimate of the true score because obtained scores and errors are correlated. Scores above the test mean have more "lucky" error (error that raises the obtained score above the true score), whereas scores below the mean have more "unlucky" error (error that lowers the obtained score below the true score). An easy way to understand this effect is to think of a test on which Mike guesses on several test items. If all Mike's guesses are correct, he has been very lucky and earns a score that is not representative of what he truly knows. However, if all his guesses are incorrect, Mike has been unlucky and earns a score that is lower than a score that represents what he truly knows.

As it turns out, obtained scores farther above or below the mean tend to be more discrepant from true scores than are obtained scores closer to the mean. Also, as Figure 5.4 illustrates, the less reliable the test is, the greater is the discrepancy between obtained scores and true scores. Nunnally (Nunnally & Bernstein, 1994; Nunnally, 1978) has provided an equation for determining the estimated true score (*X'*), as shown in Equation 5.4. The estimated true score equals the test mean plus the product of the reliability coefficient and the difference between the obtained score and the group mean.[3] Thus, the discrepancy between obtained scores and estimated true scores is a function of both the reliability of the obtained scores and the difference between the obtained score and the mean. It must be remembered that the equation does not give the true score, only the estimated true score.

Eq. 5.4
$$X' = \bar{X} + (r_{xx})(X - \bar{X})$$

---

3. The particular mean that is used has been the subject of some controversy. We believe that the preferred mean is the mean of the demographic group that best represents the particular child. Thus, if the student is Asian and resides in a middle-class urban area, the most appropriate mean would be that of same-age or same-grade Asian students from middle socioeconomic backgrounds who live in urban areas. In the absence of means for particular students of particular backgrounds, we are forced to use the overall mean for the student's age or grade.

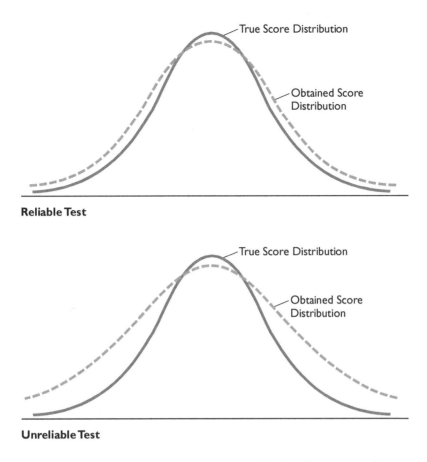

FIGURE 5.4. The discrepancy between obtained scores and true scores for reliable and unreliable tests.

Confidence Intervals

Although we can never know a person's true score, we can estimate the likelihood that a person's true score will be found within a specified range of scores. This range is called a **confidence interval** (c.i.). Confidence intervals have two components. The first component is the score range within which a true score is likely to be found. For example, a range of 80 to 90 indicates that a person's true score is likely to be contained within that range. The second component is the level of confidence, generally between 50% and 95%. The level of confidence tells us how certain we can be that the true score will be contained within the interval. Thus, if a 90% confidence interval for Jo's IQ is 106 to 112, we can be 90% sure that Jo's true IQ is between 106 and 112. It also means that there is a 5% chance her true IQ is higher than 112 and a 5% chance her true IQ is lower than 106. To have greater confidence would require a wider confidence interval. Table 5.4 shows the extreme area for the z scores commonly used to construct confidence intervals. The extreme area is the proportion of cases in the tail of the normal curve—that is, the area from plus or minus X number of standard deviations to the end of the curve. The equations used to calculate a confidence interval are shown in Equations 5.5 and 5.6.

TABLE 5.4

Commonly Used z Scores, Extreme Areas, and Area Included Between Confidence Interval Values

z Score	Extreme Area	Area Between + and −
.67	25.0%	50%
1.00	16%	68%
1.64	5%	90%
1.96	2.5%	5%
2.33	1.0%	98%
2.57	0.5%	99%

Sometimes confidence intervals are implied. A score may be followed by a "±" and a number (e.g., 109 ± 2). Unless otherwise noted, this notation indicates a 68% confidence interval with the number following the ± being the *SEM*. Thus, the lower limit of the confidence interval equals the score less the *SEM* (that is, 109 − 2) and the upper limit equals the score plus the *SEM* (that is, 109 + 2). The interpretation of this confidence interval is that we can be 68% sure that the student's true score is between 107 and 111.

Another confidence interval is implied when a score is given with the probable error (PE) of measurement. For example, a score might be reported as 105 PE ± 1. A PE yields 50% confidence. Thus, 105 PE ± 1 means a 50% confidence interval that ranges from 104 to 106. The interpretation of this confidence interval is that we can be 50% sure that the student's true score is between 104 and 106; 25% of the time the true score will be less than 104, and 25% of the time the true score will be greater than 106.

John Salvia, Professor Emeritus of Special Education at Pennsylvania State University, was co-author of the 13 previous editions of this textbook. John had a strong passion for students learning the importance of the technical adequacy (reliability and validity) of tests. Read his Stakeholder Perspective on the importance of these technical requirements.

Eq. 5.5   Lower limit of c.i. = $X' - (z \text{ score})(SEM)$

Eq. 5.6   Upper limit of c.i. = $X' + (z \text{ score})(SEM)$

Constructing Confidence Intervals

Test manuals frequently table confidence intervals so testers do not have to construct them. However, if a tester needs to construct a confidence interval, the procedures are not difficult although there is some disagreement over which approach is preferred to construct confidence intervals. Nunnally (Nunnally, 1978; Nunnally & Bernstein, 1994) recommend using the *SEM*. Others (e.g., Kubiszyn & Borich, 2003; Sabers et al., 1988) prefer the standard error of estimate (that is, the average standard deviation of true scores around an obtained score.) When test reliability is high, the difference between the two procedures is negligible.

1. Select the degree of confidence—for example, 95%.
2. Find the z score associated with that degree of confidence (e.g., a 95% confidence interval is between z scores of −1.96 and +1.96).

3. Multiply each *z* score associated with the confidence interval (e.g., 1.96 for 95% confidence) by the *SEM*.

4. Find the estimated true score.

5. Add the product of the *z* score and the *SEM* to the estimated true score to obtain the upper limit of the confidence interval; subtract the product of the *z* score and the *SEM* from the estimated true score to obtain the lower limit of the confidence interval.

For example, assume that a person's estimated true score is 75 and the *SEM* is 5. Further assume that you wish to be about 68% sure of constructing an interval that will contain the true score. Table 5.4 shows that a 68% degree of confidence is associated with a *z* score of 1. Thus, about 68% of the time, the true score will be contained in the interval of 70 to 80 [that is, 75 − (1)(5) to 75 + (1)(5)]; there is about a 16% chance that the true score is less than 70 and about a 16% chance that the true score is greater than 80. If you are unwilling to be wrong about 32% of the time, you must increase the width of the confidence interval. Thus, with the same true score (75) and *SEM* (5), if you wish 95% confidence, the size of the interval must be increased; it would have to range from 65 to 85 [that is, 75 − (1.96)(5) to 75 + (1.96)(5)]. About 95% of the time, the true score will be contained within that interval; there is about a 2.5% chance that the true score is less than 65, and there is about a 2.5% chance that it is greater than 85.

Difference Scores

In many applied settings, we are interested in differences between two scores. The differences can take several forms. They can be as simple as the amount of gain from pretest to posttest. *Gap analysis* can be used to compare a student's actual growth to expected growth. Sometimes that growth is expressed in percentiles that compare the amount of growth of similar students (often students with the same pretest score). Differences can be used to compare students' academic achievement with their intellectual abilities. Some educational disorders (e.g., learning disabilities) may require a "significant" discrepancy as a defining characteristic of the disorder; other disorders (e.g., intellectual disability) use the absence of a significant discrepancy to rule out the disorder.

The term *significant discrepancy* can refer to several different kinds of difference (Salvia & Good, 1982): reliable difference, rare difference, and educationally meaningful difference. Here we are concerned with reliable differences, differences that are the result of poor samples of test items, times, or observers/scorers. Two things must be remembered when dealing with difference scores. First, a difference between scores on two different tests (A and B) is a function of four things: the reliability of test A, the reliability of test B, the correlation between tests A and B, and differences in the tests'

**John Salvia, PhD, Professor Emeritus of Special Education,
College of Education, Pennsylvania State University**

As participants on teams making decisions for students with disabilities, teachers, psychologists, supervisors, and providers of related services must base their decisions on assessments that are both reliable and valid. This is a federal and state legal requirement as well as an ethical requirement of several scientific and professional organizations.

Unreliable tests produce results that are inaccurate. We just don't know whose scores are inaccurate and by how much they are off the mark. The good news is that we can calculate a range (i.e., a confidence interval) within which a person's true score falls. Here is an example: If Alice earns the mean score on a test that has .75 reliability, there's about a 25% chance that her true score would be less than the 26th percentile and about a 25% chance that it would be more than the 74th percentile. What is her true percentile rank? We don't know, but we do know that the test is pretty inaccurate. Other types of error are virtually impossible to quantify. For example, if a test's norms are unrepresentative, a score at the 65th percentile means the student performed equal to or better than 65% of whom? We don't know whom because the norms are unrepresentative. Another example, if Alice earns a score at the 40th percentile on a reading test that only requires reading words in isolation, how well does she read text? Again, we don't know, but her score is probably less than the 40th percentile.

Educators make life-altering decisions for some of the neediest students in their charge: eligibility for special education and related services, IEP development, evaluation of student progress, etc. Their decisions also have serious consequences for school districts and taxpayers. Special education decisions are no better than the information on which they are based. The poorer the technical characteristics of an assessment, the less its results can be trusted. The need for technically adequate information applies to commercially developed tests, scales, surveys, questionnaires, etc. It also applies to teacher-made tests and professional impressions. That's why this technical stuff is so important.

norm groups. We can estimate the reliability of difference caused by the first three factors. Second, when the two tests are correlated, the difference between a person's scores on the two tests is almost always less reliable than the scores on which the difference is based. See a summary in Box 5.2. See the online resources for advanced information about difference scores.

ONLINE
RESOURCE

Desirable Standards of Reliability

No test can measure what it purports to measure unless it is reliable. No score is interpretable unless it is reliable. Therefore it is important for test authors to present sufficient information in test manuals for test users to be able to interpret test results

BOX 5.2

Significant Discrepancy

These three can be estimated.

Significant discrepancy can refer to:

- reliable difference
- rare difference
- educationally meaningful difference

A reliable difference between scores on two different tests (A, B) is a function of:

- Reliability of Test A
- Reliability of Test B
- Correlation between Tests A and B*
- Differences in the norm groups of each test

---

*The correlation between Tests A and B is usually less reliable than the scores on which the difference is based.

---

accurately. For a test to be valid (that is, to measure what its authors claim it measures), it must be reliable. Although reliability is not the only condition that must be met, it is a necessary condition for validity.

Test authors and publishers must present sufficient reliability data to allow the user to evaluate the reliability of all test scores that are to be interpreted. Thus, reliability estimates should be presented for any score type (e.g., subtest) when those scores are to be interpreted. Moreover, reliability estimates should be reported for each age and grade. Furthermore, these indices should be presented clearly in tabular form in one place. Test authors should not play hide-and-seek with reliability data. Test authors who recommend computing difference scores should provide, whenever possible, the reliability of the difference (r_{dif}) and the *SEM* of the difference (SEM_{dif}). Once test users have access to reliability data, they can judge the adequacy of the test. Refer to Box 5.1 for our suggested numeric standards for evaluating whether a test has adequate reliability for a given purpose.

5.1
PROGRESS MONITORING CHECK

Validity

"**Validity** refers to the degree to which evidence and theory support the interpretation of test scores for proposed uses of tests." Validity is therefore the most fundamental consideration in developing and evaluating tests. The process of validation involves accumulating relevant evidence to provide a sound scientific basis for the proposed score interpretations. It is the interpretations of test scores for proposed uses that are evaluated, not the test itself. [American Educational Research Association (AERA), American Psychological Association, & National Council on Measurement in Education, 2014, p. 11].

In a real sense, all questions of validity are local, asking whether the testing process leads to correct inferences about a specific person in a specific situation for a specific purpose. A test that leads to valid inferences in general or about most students may not yield valid inferences about a specific student. Two circumstances illustrate this. First, unless a student has been systematically acculturated in the values, behavior, and knowledge found in the public culture of the United States, a test that assumes such acculturation is unlikely to lead to appropriate inferences about that student. Consider, for example, the inappropriateness of administering a verbally loaded intelligence test to a recent U.S. immigrant who does not speak English fluently. Correct inferences about this person's intellectual ability cannot be drawn from the testing because the intelligence test requires not only proficiency in English but also proficiency in U.S. culture and mores.

Second, unless a student has been systematically instructed in the content of an achievement test, a test assuming such academic instruction is unlikely to lead to appropriate inferences about that student's ability to profit from instruction. It would be inappropriate to administer a standardized test of written language (which counts misspelled words as errors) to a student who has been encouraged to use inventive spelling and the use of which has been reinforced. It is unlikely that the test results would lead to correct inferences about that student's ability to profit from systematic instruction in spelling.

Because it is impossible to validate all inferences that might be drawn from a test performance, test authors typically validate just the most common inferences. Thus, test users should expect some information about the degree to which each commonly encouraged inference has (or lacks) validity. Although the validity of each inference is based on all the information that accumulates over time, test authors are expected to provide some evidence of a test's validity for specific inferences at the time the test is offered for use. In addition, test authors should validate the inferences for groups of students with whom the test will typically be used.

Evidence That Test Inferences Are Valid

The process of gathering information about the appropriateness of inferences is called validation. Five general types of evidence are usually considered (AERA et al., 2014, pp. 14–19).

- Evidence based on test content
- Evidence based on internal structure

- Evidence based on relations to other variables
- Evidence based on the consequences of testing
- Evidence based on response processes

These five types of evidence are not discrete. Rather, they are artificial categories that are merely intended to help organize a complex topic. Thus, one could as readily consider evidence based on internal structure to be part of a test's content as easily as a separate type of evidence.

Evidence Based on Test Content

"Test content refers to the themes, wording, and format of the items, tasks, or questions on a test. Administration and scoring may also be relevant to content-based evidence" (AERA et al., 2014, p. 14).

Specifically, we are concerned with the extent to which a test's items actually represent the domain or universe to be measured. It is a major source of evidence for the validation for any achievement test, other education and psychological tests, and observations and ratings. Any analysis of a test's content necessarily begins with a clear definition of the domain or universe that the test's content is intended to represent. Ultimately a test's content validity is determined by the appropriateness of the items included, the importance of items not included, and how the items assess the content.

Appropriateness of Included Items. In examining the appropriateness of the items included in a test, we must ask: Is this an appropriate test question, and does this test item really measure the domain or construct? Consider the four test items from a hypothetical primary (kindergarten through second grade) arithmetic achievement test presented in Figure 5.5. The first item require the student to read and add two single-digit numbers, the sum of which is less than 10. This seems to be a grade-appropriate item for an elementary arithmetic achievement test. The second item requires the student to complete a geometric progression. Although this item is mathematical, the

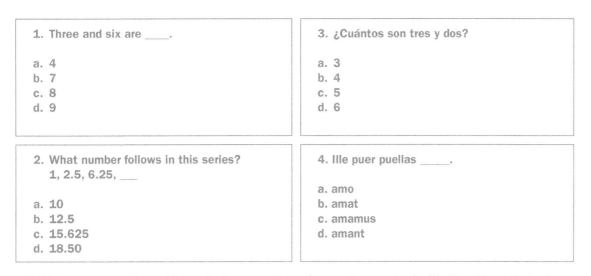

FIGURE 5.5. Sample multiple-choice questions for a primary grade (K–2) arithmetic test.

skills and knowledge required to complete the question correctly are not taught in any elementary school curriculum by the second grade. Therefore, the question should be rejected as an invalid item for an arithmetic achievement test to be used with children from kindergarten through second grade. The third item likewise requires the student to read and add two single-digit numbers, the sum of which is less than 10. However, the question is written in Spanish. Although the content of the question is suitable (this is an elementary addition problem), the method of presentation requires language skills that most U.S. students do not have. Failure to complete the item correctly could be attributed either to the fact that the child does not know Spanish or to the fact that the child does not know that 3 + 2 = 5. Test givers should conclude that the item is not valid for an arithmetic test for children who do not read Spanish. The fourth item requires that the student select the correct form of the Latin verb *amare* ("to love"). Clearly, this is an inappropriate item for an arithmetic test and should be rejected as invalid.

Content Not Included. Test content must also be examined to see if important content is not included. For example, the validity of any elementary arithmetic test would be questioned if it included only problems requiring the addition of single-digit numbers with a sum less than 10. Educators would reasonably expect an arithmetic test to include a far broader sample of tasks (e.g., addition of two- and three-digit numbers, subtraction, understanding of the process of addition, and so forth). Incomplete test content results in an incomplete (and usually invalid) appraisal.

How Content Is Measured. It is clear that how we assess content directly influences the results of assessment. For example, when students are tested to see if they know the sum of two single-digit numbers, their knowledge can be evaluated in a variety of ways. Children might be required to recognize the correct answer in a multiple-choice array, supply the correct answer, demonstrate the addition process with manipulatives, apply the proper addition facts in a word problem, or write an explanation of the process they followed in solving the problem. However, there is an emerging consensus that the methods used to assess student knowledge should closely parallel those used in instruction.[4]

Evidence Based on Internal Structure

Quite similar to evidence for a test's content is a test's internal structure. Internal structure refers to the ways in which test items and subtests represent a test's components and/or total score. Most test domains have more than one dimension or component. For example, reading tests typically assess oral reading and comprehension; math tests typically assess computation and problem solving using whole numbers, fractions, and decimals, and so forth.

---

4. Current theory and research methods as they apply to trait or ability congruence under different methods of measurement are still emerging. Much of the current methodology grew out of Campbell and Fiske's (1959) early work on convergent and discriminant validity and is beyond the scope of this text.

One would rightly expect test authors to present evidence that their tests do have the structure hypothesized. When a test assesses a unidimensional skill or trait, we would expect to see evidence that the test items are homogeneous (e.g., coefficient alpha). When a test is multidimensional, we would expect to find the results of factor analytic studies that demonstrate the congruence between theoretical and obtained factor structure.[5]

When domains are not homogeneous, test authors can jeopardize validity by selecting items on the basis of point-biserial correlations to produce an internally consistent test. Therefore, it is generally a good idea to analyze the structure of a domain, either logically or statistically. When a domain comprises two or more homogeneous classes of test items, homogeneous subtests (representing each factor) can be developed using point-biserial correlations. In this way, the validity of the test can be heightened.

Evidence Based on Relations to Other Variables

The relationship between a new test's results and the results obtained from other tests is of key importance. The evidence falls into two broad categories. First, are the results of the new test consistent (correlated) with the results expected from other measures? The extent to which a person's performance on a criterion measure can be estimated from that person's performance on the assessment procedure being validated is an important indication that a new test is measuring what it is intended to measure. This relationship is usually expressed as a correlation between scores obtained via the new assessment procedure (e.g., a test) and the criterion scores. The correlation coefficient between the new procedure and the criterion is termed a *validity coefficient*. Two types of criterion-related validity are commonly described: concurrent validity and predictive validity. These terms denote the time at which a person's performance on the criterion measure is obtained. *Concurrent criterion-related validity* refers to how accurately a person's current performance (e.g., test score) estimates that person's performance on the criterion measure at the same time. Basically, does a person's performance measured with a new or experimental test allow the accurate estimation of that person's performance on a criterion measure that has been widely accepted as valid? *Predictive criterion-related validity* refers to how accurately a person's current performance (e.g., test score) estimates that person's performance on the criterion measure at a later time. Thus, concurrent and predictive criterion-related validity refer to the temporal sequence by which a person's performance on some criterion measure is estimated on the basis of that person's current assessment; concurrent and predictive validity differ in the time at which scores on

---

5. In addition to making judgments about how appropriately an item fits within a domain, test developers often rely on point-biserial correlations between individual test items and the total score to make decisions about item appropriateness. Items that do not correlate positively and at least moderately (.25 or .30 or more) with the total score are dropped. Retaining only items that have positive correlations with the total score ensures homogeneous test items and internally consistent (reliable) tests. Moreover, when test items are homogeneous, they are likely to be measuring the same skill or trait. Therefore, to obtain reliable tests, test developers are likely to drop items that do not statistically fit the domain.

the criterion measure are obtained. Positive correlations between test scores and other variables can also provide evidence of a test's validity. For example, many skills and abilities are developmental. Thus, we would expect a student's grade level or mental age would correlate positively with chronological age.

The second broad category of evidence demonstrates that the results of the new test are independent (uncorrelated) with other skills or abilities. Sometimes how one measures a skill or ability has more to do with the student's performance than the particular skill or ability being assessed.

Evidence Based on the Consequences of Testing

"Tests are commonly administered in the expectation that some benefit will be realized from the interpretation and use of the scores intended by the test developers. A few of the many possible benefits that might be claimed are selection of efficacious therapies, placement of workers in suitable jobs, prevention of unqualified individuals from entering a profession, or improvement of classroom instructional practices. A fundamental purpose of validation is to indicate whether these specific benefits are likely to be realized. Thus, in the case of a test used in placement decisions, the validation would be informed by evidence that alternate placements, in fact, are differentially beneficial to the persons and the institution." (AERA et al., 2014, p. 19)

Although this type of evidence has been adopted by the joint testing standards committee of the American Educational Research Association, American Psychological Association, and National Council on Measurement in Education, it is important to note that it focuses on how test scores are used, rather than on whether a test provides accurate information. If a test correctly indicates a 10th-grade student cannot read second-grade materials, how a school uses that information has nothing to do with the accuracy of that information. If the school decides nothing is to be done, the test results are accurate; if the school decides to provide the student with ineffective instruction, the test results are still accurate; if the school provides effective remediation, the test results were still correct. However, if tests are indeed used to assign students to ineffective instruction, that particular use of a test could be considered inappropriate and invalid. Therefore, this standard emphasizes the need for test users to use test results in ways that they have good reason to believe will result in positive outcomes and avoid unintended negative outcomes. Because there are so many different factors apart from the accuracy of a test score that influence whether an individual actually derives benefit from its use, we find it impossible to evaluate tests according to this validity standard.

Later in this book we provide reviews of various tests. In those reviews, we focus our analysis of validity on the extent to which there is good reason to believe that for a typical individual, the associated test results can be considered generally accurate. Yet, we encourage readers to think through possible consequences of a test that they choose to use and to consider intended and unintended consequences in their choice to administer and interpret any given test given the purpose of the testing and the needs of the individual student. There is not a handy single metric for this important feature of validity, and yet, thoughtful assessment teams can consider whether the information yielded from any given test is likely to be of use to the student or if instead there is potential for unintended harm and then take steps to maximize benefit and minimize any harm to students. Deciding to use a particular reading test, the results of which will be used by the teacher to sort students into instructional groupings for the year based on their ability, is a practice that might cause some students to receive ineffective instruction and may have little chance of producing benefit to others.

Evidence Based on Response Processes

Response process refers to the way in which students go about answering test questions as well as how examiners go about scoring student responses. In some cases, we want to assess students' skill in using the correct process to solve problems. For example, did they follow the correct mathematical algorithm in solving a long division problem? If a test is intended to measure response processes, we would expect to find evidence that test takers actually are using the desired process. Evidence of this type would include interviews with test takers, having test takers "show their work," having test takers write essays explaining how they arrived at their answers, or having test takers record an audio file explaining how they arrived at their answers.

Factors Affecting Validity

Whenever an assessment procedure fails to measure what it purports to measure, validity is threatened. Consequently, any factor that results in measuring "something else" affects validity. Both unsystematic error (unreliability) and systematic error (bias) threaten validity.

Reliability

Reliability sets the upper limit of a test's validity, so reliability is a necessary but not a sufficient condition for valid measurement. Thus, all valid tests are reliable, unreliable tests cannot be valid, and reliable tests may or may not be valid. The validity of a particular procedure can never exceed the reliability of that procedure because unreliable procedures measure error; valid procedures measure the traits they are designed to measure.

Systematic Bias

Several systematic biases can limit a test's validity. The following are among the most common.

Enabling behaviors and knowledge are skills and facts that a person must rely on to demonstrate a target behavior or knowledge. For example, to demonstrate knowledge of causes of the American Civil War on an essay examination, a student must be able to write. The student cannot produce the targeted behavior (the written answer) without

5.2
PROGRESS MONITORING CHECK

the enabling behavior (writing). Similarly, knowledge of the language of assessment is crucial. Many of the abuses in assessment are directly attributable to examiners' failures in this area. For example, intelligence testing in English of non-English-speaking children at one time was sufficiently commonplace that a group of parents brought suit against a school district (*Diana v. State Board of Education*, 1970). Students who are deaf are routinely given the Performance subtests of the *Wechsler Adult Intelligence Scales* (Baumgardner, 1993) even though they cannot hear the directions. Children with communication disorders are often required to respond orally to test questions. Such obvious limitations in or absences of enabling behaviors are frequently overlooked in testing situations, even though they invalidate the test's inferences for these students.

Test items should demonstrate *differential item effectiveness*, that is they should work the same way for various groups of students. Jensen (1980) discussed several empirical ways to assess item effectiveness for different groups of test takers. First, we should expect that the relative difficulty of items is maintained across different groups. For example, the most difficult item for males should also be the most difficult item for females, the easiest item for White students should be the easiest item for Black students, and so forth. We should also expect that reliabilities and validities will be the same for all groups of test takers.

The most likely explanation for items having differential effectiveness for different groups of people is differential exposure to test content. Test items may not work in the same ways for students who experience different acculturation or different academic instruction. For example, standardized achievement tests presume that the students who are taking the tests have been exposed to similar curricula. If teachers have not taught the content being tested, that content will be more difficult for their students (and inferences about the students' ability to profit from instruction will probably be incorrect).

Unless a test is administered according to the standardized procedures, the inferences based on the test are invalid. As an example of such a *systematic administration error* suppose Ms. Donnelly wishes to demonstrate how effective her teaching is by administering an intelligence test and an achievement test to her class. She allows the students 5 minutes less than the standardized time limits on the intelligence test and 5 minutes more on the standardized achievement test. The result is that the students earn higher achievement test scores (because they had too much time) and lower intelligence test scores (because they did not have enough time). The inference that less intelligent students have learned more than anticipated is not valid; rather, it is an artifact of the testing procedures.

Scores based on the performance of *unrepresentative norms* lead to incorrect estimates of relative standing in the general population. To the extent that the normative sample is systematically unrepresentative of the general population in either central tendency or variability, the differences based on such scores are incorrect and invalid.

Responsibility for Valid Assessment

The valid use of assessment procedures is the responsibility of both the author and the user of the assessment procedure. Test authors are expected to present evidence for the major types of inferences for which the use of a test is recommended, and a rationale should be provided to support the particular mix of evidence presented for the intended uses. Test users are expected to ensure that the test is appropriate for the specific students being assessed (AERA et al., 2014, p. 13).

PROGRESS **5.1**

MONITORING CHECK

1. Explain the concept of measurement error.
2. What does a reliability coefficient of .75 tell you about true-score variability and error variability?
3. Compare and contrast item reliability, stability, and interobserver agreement.
4. What is the difference between simple agreement and point-to-point agreement, and when might you use each appropriately?
5. What is a standard error of measurement?
6. How high should reliability be for purposes of making screening decisions? Instructional decisions? Diagnostic decisions?

PROGRESS **5.2**

MONITORING CHECK

1. Explain evidence of validity based on relations to other measures.
2. Explain evidence of validity based on test content.
3. Explain three factors that can affect a test's validity.

CHAPTER 6

Cultural and Linguistic Considerations in Assessment and Decision Making

To this point in the book you've learned about some of the important foundations of assessment. Now let's imagine working with specific populations of students. Our goal is to ensure that you administer and interpret assessments fully aware that some amount of bias is inherent in all we do and is embedded in the tools we use. Our job is to minimize that known bias in order to maximize the accuracy of the assessment process to support students' lives. Whether you see yourself working in a rural setting, an urban school, a suburban charter school or somewhere else you will have the joy of working with students who have different life experiences than you. Some will have different cultural experiences, different religious beliefs, and some may speak more languages than you or may not yet speak English fluently. The majority of teachers in the United States are White women (77% White women mostly from a middle-class socioeconomic background; Taie & Goldring, 2017) and more than half of the 50 million students in K–12 public schools are from non-White ethnic and racial groups. The National Center for Education Statistics reports that approximately five million students in K–12 schools are classified as limited English proficient (LEP; U.S. Department of Education, National Center for Education Statistics, 2019). **English learners** (ELs, formerly English language learners, ELLs) is the most common term used to broadly categorize students who are and are not designated as LEP who have a first language other than English. When discussing some English learners who have maintained their LEP status for longer periods of time, you may hear the labels "long-term ELs" or "ever ELs." A newer term, but one that is gaining some traction due to the emphasis on asset-based language rather than deficit-based language, is *emerging bilingual* or simply *bilingual* (García & Kleifgen, 2018; Chaparro et al., 2021). Only the LEP label is federally defined. The most inclusive term currently in use is *culturally and linguistically diverse* (CLD). CLD is used to refer to students who may or may not be ELs but who belong to a minoritized cultural or religious group. Students belonging to minoritized groups are those that have been traditionally marginalized or disadvantaged in a range of sectors including but not limited to economics and education. When referring to federal data or laws, we will use the term LEP, but when speaking more generally, we will use ELs and CLD depending on the data and research available.

Let's focus on LEP students for a moment. Five million students out of 50 million means that 10% of students enrolled in public K–12 schools speak at least one language in addition to English. Although we group English learners together under the LEP federal label, this group is extremely diverse. More than 75% of these students speak Spanish as a primary language, but there are more than 400 native languages spoken by this diverse group of students. While nationally, Spanish is the most common first language of students designated as LEP, there are five states where the majority of these students speak another language. For example, in Alaska the Yupik language is the native language of the Native American tribes. This means that the first language of these students, Yupik, was actually the native language of the land long before English speakers arrived. In Vermont, the Nepali language is the most common native language spoken by English learners because of the large Nepalis immigrant community that has settled in the state. It's helpful to consider too that in Vermont only 2% of their student population are designated as LEP (Bialik et al., 2018). You can see through these examples that it will be difficult for any one person to become an expert in the area of assessment for all subgroups of culturally and linguistically diverse students. Similarly, it's impossible for any one test to demonstrate technical adequacy with every subgroup of students.

Disparities in Behavior and Academic Outcomes for CLD Students

It's important not only to understand who the students are that we serve but also the unfortunate disparities that these students face because of systemic issues in our current education system. We have to be aware of the problems so that we can avoid contributing to them and then improve the schools we work with so that the outcomes for CLD students will be better than they have been historically. One disparity faced by students who are Black, American Indian, and Hispanic/Latinx is that they receive more disciplinary actions such as suspensions and expulsions than other students (U.S. Department of Education, 2019; Skiba et al., 2011). Each individual state is different, but there is evidence that some states are worse than others when it comes to disproportionate use of exclusionary discipline practices (i.e., suspension and expulsion) applied to CLD students. Black and Brown students continue to be subjected to suspension (Ksinan et al., 2019) and expulsion (Bal et al., 2019) at higher rates than their White peers. Furthermore, Black and Brown students are also more likely than their White peers to be referred for special education services for behavioral concerns and to be subsequently identified as emotionally disturbed, a special education category defined in part by prolonged patterns of inappropriate behavior (Bal et al., 2019). As a result, Black and Brown children are disproportionately placed in restrictive educational settings (Skiba et al., 2006). Just as Black and Brown children are overrepresented in some areas of special education they are also at-risk for being underrepresented in gifted and talented programs. The following Stakeholder Perspective highlights practices to keep in mind to ensure that African American and Black students in particular are receiving access to gifted and talented programs.

When we look at students who are labeled LEP and those who are labeled as both LEP and as having a disability, both are also at risk for disproportionate receipt of exclusionary discipline practices (Sullivan, 2011). In addition to LEP students specifically, CLD students also fall behind academically. LEP students typically score below their English-only speaking peers on state assessments, even when provided with accommodations. To complicate matters, states have different policies about when you can start assessing an LEP student in the state accountability testing process, so from state to state the policies and the assessments themselves vary, making it difficult to make comparisons on LEP student outcomes.

When it comes to testing CLD students there are potential points of bias that enter into the assessment process, from the behavioral observation, to the reading test, to the teacher report. We must be mindful of these vulnerable points in the decision-making process (Cook et al., 2018). In this chapter we'll share the principles of culturally and linguistically responsive assessment that you can use to decrease bias with the ultimate goal of ensuring positive educational outcomes for students. Next, let's review some of the federal programs in place to protect the rights of English learners and immigrant students.

Stakeholder
PERSPECTIVE

Donna Y. Ford, PhD, Distinguished Professor,
College of Education and Human Ecology, Ohio State University
James L. Moore III, PhD, Vice Provost for
Diversity and Inclusion, Chief Diversity Officer, Ohio State University

We regularly serve as advisors to policy makers, administrators, and coordinators of gifted and talented education (GATE) programs. One of the difficult questions we confront is the extent to which assessments affect access to gifted and talented (GATE) programs and services for culturally different or minoritized students. On a consistent basis, Black and Hispanic students are extensively underrepresented in GATE. For Black students, underrepresentation hovers around 50%. For Hispanic students, it is around 40% (see ocrdata.ed.gov). Eligibility for GATE programs for students in the United States is based on teacher recommendations/referrals, performance on standardized tests of intelligence and achievement, and checklists. Too often, these culturally different students perform lower on all measures compared to White students because the measures have questionable relevance and validity.

When tests and other instruments are invalid, the results do not provide us with accurate information for decision-making purposes; this results in false negatives—gifted and talented students who are not identified but should be. In addition to taking into consideration the standard error of measurement (*SEM*) of each test, decision makers need to adopt a range of proactive equity-minded, culturally responsive practices (Ford et al., 2018, 2020). The notion of *equity* refers to adopting instruments, policies, and procedures that consider the differential needs and experiences of minoritized students compared to White students to support and advocate for them.

At a minimum, equity-minded, culturally responsiveness includes:

- *Linguistic and culturally reduced instruments*, such as nonverbal tests. Culturally different students are less likely to be penalized on such measures because of language

(*continues*)

Legal Considerations

The Every Student Succeeds Act (ESSA; PL 114-95) was reauthorized in 2015 and fully operational in the 2017–2018 school year. A number of the Title Programs are relevant to English learners but one, Title III Language Instruction for English Learners and Immigrant Students, offers the most relevant guidance for this chapter. The goal of Title III is multifaceted and includes supporting educators and school systems to develop and provide effective instructional programs with the goal of English language proficiency and high levels of academic performance for English learners and immigrant students.

differences (e.g., limited English proficient, bilingual, Black English speakers), their lived experiences (e.g., exposure to prejudice and discrimination, lower expectations of them), and social and cultural differences (e.g., higher rates of poverty, and different cultural values, beliefs, norms, behaviors, and styles);

▪ *Universal screening* at multiple grade levels. This practice helps to reduce educator subjectivity, namely negative biases and stereotypes, that contribute to their under-referral of culturally different students for GATE programs and services by providing several different lens on the student's performance. This screening strategy adds objectivity and gives under-referred students greater chances and opportunities to enter the GATE identification and service pool. With universal screening, keep in mind the previous recommendation regarding the instruments adopted.

▪ *Local and building norms.* When local and (preferably) building norms are adopted, culturally different students are compared to students from similar backgrounds and experiences (e.g., culture, language, socioeconomic status, family education, academic performance). As a result, they can be more competitive on intelligence and achievement measures; and

▪ *Equity based numerical goals.* Educators and decision makers must adopt equity in philosophy and actions. To go beyond philosophy by quantifying equity, we recommend a maximum 20% allowance (Ford, 2013). For example, if Black students represent 30% the school district, they should represent a minimum 24% of GATE program enrollment (30% × 80% = 24%). This is not a racial quota.

In order to implement the four practices just shared, educators and decision makers should be trained in both GATE and culturally responsive education. Such preparation helps reduce negative biases and stereotypes, along with discriminatory practices. This training helps educational professionals to be equity-minded and culturally responsive in their thinking and behaviors about GATE students.

Title III also has a goal to support parental and community participation in educational programs.

Title III provides grants and subgrants to states so that they can implement programs that include language testing for students to determine their language proficiency and eligibility for English learner status and programs. There is also an accountability component of Title III. Examples of the metrics included are (a) the number and percentage of students enrolled in English learner programs, (b) the number and percentage who exit the language programs, and (c) the number and percentage of students meeting state academic standards. School district administrators often have the job of collecting this information and reporting it to the state. In your position you may be asked to contribute to the data gathering. At the individual student level, special education teachers, school psychologists, and speech-language specialists are asked to consult with **English language development (ELD)** teachers.

Protections for Students Being Assessed

The principle criteria for protecting EL students during the special education assessment process can be found in the IDEA (PL 108-446). Tests must be selected and administered in such a way that they minimize dependence upon skills that the students lack due to their status as an English learner. If testing is needed for special education eligibility then, to the extent feasible, tests and evaluation materials must be administered in the student's native language or other mode of communication that minimizes the English language load. This principle is echoed in §300.534(b) of the IDEA, which forbids a student to be identified as in need of special education services if the determining factor is limited proficiency in English.

There are many challenges to establishing special education eligibility for students who have already been made eligible for English language development services. The IDEA (§300.304-§300.309) requires that failure to achieve adequately in "oral expression, listening comprehension, written expression, basic reading skills, reading fluency, reading comprehension, math calculation or math problem-solving" be considered indicative of a specific learning disability only if the student has been "provided with learning experiences and instruction appropriate for the child's age or State-approved grade level standards." Students can also qualify by failing to respond to a scientific, research-based intervention. In order to find a student eligible under this category, the associated results cannot be due to limited English proficiency. Furthermore, limited research has been done specifically on interventions to address the needs of ELs, and so it may be difficult to identify and implement an appropriate intervention that both meets the legal requirements and addresses the unique characteristics of students who are ELs.

Limited English proficiency is not to be considered a speech or language impairment. Although it is quite possible for a student with limited English to have a speech or language impairment, that impairment would also be present in the student's native language. Speakers of the student's native language, such as the student's parents, could verify the presence of stuttering, impaired articulation, or voice impairments; the identification of a language disorder would require a fluent speaker of the child's native language. When it is not possible to determine whether a student has a disability, students who are ELs who are experiencing academic or behavioral difficulties still need to have sustained ELD services and other appropriate interventions as long as they are eligible.

Protections for Parents in the Assessment Process

Parents are the principal advocates for their children within the educational system, and the IDEA contains a number of protections for them as well, especially in terms of notice, participation, and consent. For example, §300.503(b) requires that parents receive prior notice if the school intends to initiate or change their child's identification as a student with a disability. That notice must "be provided in the native language of the parent or other mode of communication used by the parent, unless it is clearly not feasible to do so." Although notice is usually in written form, the IDEA also provides that interpreters be used if the native language or mode of communication of the parent is not written language. Parents must be given notice of their procedural safeguards. This notice must be in the parents' native language or other mode of communication if they do not understand English [§300.504(c)]. Schools must take steps to make sure that the parents of a student with a disability have the opportunity to participate in team meetings. To that end, §300.345(e) requires the use of interpreters or other appropriate measures "for parents with deafness or whose native language is other than English." In those instances when parental consent is required (e.g., to conduct an initial assessment of a student to determine special education eligibility), that consent must be given in the parents' native language or mode of communication [§300.500(b)(1)]. With these federal goals and protections in mind, let's discuss how to conduct testing in a culturally and linguistically responsive way.

6.1
PROGRESS MONITORING CHECK

Culturally and Linguistically Responsive Assessment

In response to the disproportionate numbers of students of color enrolled in special education and receiving exclusionary discipline, scholars in the 1990s coined the terms *culturally responsive teaching* (Gay, 1995) and *culturally relevant pedagogy* (Ladson-Billings, 1995). Those terms have evolved to include variations such as *culturally responsive practices* and, more relevant to this chapter, *culturally and linguistically responsive assessment* (NASP, 2015). **Culturally responsive practices (CRP)** is an umbrella term defined as school-based interactions between adults and students that honor students' cultural backgrounds and identities and use this knowledge as an asset from which to build in order to enhance the acquisition of new knowledge and experiences (Gay, 2002). Research-based efforts to integrate CRP into existing school-based practices and interventions have been ongoing, but empirical research on CRP is still emerging (Debnam et al., 2015; Bottiani et al., 2018). Despite these limitations most scholars see the importance of CRP, so much so that professional organizations like the Council on Exceptional Children have held CRP professional development opportunities for their members (e.g., Ford & Gardner, 2016). Professional organizations for school psychologists both at the state level (e.g., Illinois School Psychologists Association, 2017; North Carolina School Psychology Association, 2010) and at the national level (NASP, 2015) have taken the lead on specifically addressing what culturally and linguistically responsive assessment practices look like and we'll draw from those sources in the remainder of this chapter. First, we'll focus on assessing students who are also ELs for special education.

Assessing English Learners for Special Education

When an EL student is referred for intervention, it may be necessary to assess the student to determine if that student is eligible to receive special education services. Recall that about 10% or 5 million of all K–12 students in the United States are designated as LEP. Of those students, about 9% also have been made eligible for special education. Of those 9%, 50% of them have the designation of a specific learning disability (U.S. Department of Education, 2015). However, as you've also learned, there are a limited number of tests that have included ELs in their normative sample and even fewer that have ELs with learning disabilities in their normative samples. As you are called upon to assess EL students in your setting, consider the following culturally and linguistical responsive practices.

Second Language Acquisition Knowledge and Expertise

While it is outside the scope of this book to go into much detail about second language acquisition, ideally assessors have developed their own professional knowledge around how second language acquisition can impact the student's performance in a natural academic setting as well as in formal testing settings. For example, you'll commonly hear English language development teachers talk about basic interpersonal communication skills (BICS). BICS can be thought of as those phrases and functions of language that students learn quickly and become a part of their everyday life in the classroom and with peers. Strong BICS will enable a student to easily speak about what happened at lunch or what they did over the weekend but may not assist them when attempting to understand a science lesson. The student will need strong academic language, sometimes also referred to as cognitive academic language proficiency (CALP), to advance in their content area classes beyond basic skill instruction. In Chapter 15 we discuss phonology, syntax, semantics, and pragmatics, the four major components of language, that have a number of subskills which students will need to develop in English in addition to maturing in their native language use. These elements of language develop at different rates as do a student's ability to demonstrate expressive (articulate thoughts into words) and receptive (comprehend oral and written communication) language. Assessors can begin to guide their own learning through a number of self-study methods including reputable websites such as the Center for Applied Linguistics (cal.org) and colorincolorado.org that offer resources for educators. We've only touched the tip of the iceberg here and there is much more to understand, including calls for educators to reconceptualize how we think about language development and instruction for emerging bilingual students (Flores & Rosa, 2015). With all there is to understand about second language acquisition it's critical that the assessor, a member of the team, the building's ESL teacher, or a consultant provide that expertise and guidance.

Bilingual Consultants

There are more than 400 languages spoken by K–12 students as native languages (U.S. Department of Education, 2015). Some individual schools have a student population that speaks over 100 different languages. Those facts, in combination with the dearth of school psychologists and other specialists with a bilingual certification, make it clear that not all teams or assessors have the expertise needed to assess ELs. In order to address this limitation, recent work has identified a framework for what bilingual consultation for specialists looks like and what formal training an individual might need in order to effectively and appropriately fill this role. In addition to expertise in language acquisition, facility in other core competencies (e.g., acculturation, a/typical development, family engagement, advocacy, use of interpreters, measurement) has been proposed as necessary (Harris & Sullivan, 2017). Within some of these core competencies there are subgroups of knowledge according to tier of support within tiered systems of service delivery (described in Chapter 7). For example, a bilingual consultant might be familiar with the reading screening assessments that are appropriate with ELs as well as typical scores that other EL students have demonstrated. The consultant can then also report the level of scores typically earned by other similar students from the district in the past as a demonstration of a local normative sample for comparison. A consultant can help develop a strength-based plan that includes culturally responsive family engagement practices and, through that process, learn that the family has been experiencing higher than typical levels of acculturative stress that may manifest as mental or physical health challenges and which has likely impacted the student's ability to engage in learning. The primary role of the bilingual consultant would be to assist the team in distinguishing between second language acquisition and language or learning disabilities and help the team develop a culturally and linguistically appropriate education plan (Harris & Sullivan, 2017). Potentially, a bilingual consultant could help a monolingual school psychologist or special education teacher determine the appropriate assessment approach that takes into consideration the student's linguistic skills based on their native language.

Effective Collaboration With Interpreters

While interpreters or bilingual staff can be used to help facilitate instruction or interventions, it is the responsibility of the assessor to be judicious about ways to incorporate an interpreter into the assessment process. There are some cautionary considerations. For example, it is not recommended that an interpreter independently translate a test developed and normed in English because it will invalidate the test. It is not recommended that the tester translate or interpret English-only test directions or content and answer test-related questions in the student's native language unless explicitly stated in the administration guidelines for the test (Council of National Psychological Associations for Advancement of Ethnic Minority Interests, 2016). There are some tests that say a tester can speak to students in their native language before the testing period to build rapport, to make the student feel at ease, and make sure they understand why the testing is taking place, but the tester must clearly state to the student that only English must be spoken when the testing begins if English skills are to be measured.

Norms that are not inclusive of English learners mean that these tests are not useful with this population. Because a monolingual assessor does not know the accuracy of a translator's skills it's imperative that interpreters have the proper training to assist in assessment procedures. In a best-case scenario, districts have set standardized criteria for interpreters and bilingual staff to be used in different school settings (e.g., teacher-parent conferences, IEP meetings, playground monitors). If it is deemed necessary to work with an interpreter during the testing session, then consider the assessment and special education knowledge of the interpreter. They will need to understand the importance of standardization, confidentiality, and have an understanding of the special education process and vocabulary (Rhodes, Ochoa, & Ortiz, 2005). Interpreters are essential members of the student's teams when making linguistically appropriate plans and helping to make parents and guardians feel included and welcomed.

English-Learner Specific Accessibility and Accommodations

Accessibility supports and accommodations are discussed in detail in Chapter 19. Here we'll briefly discuss some designated features and accommodations that are specific to students who have an LEP and a special education designation. One excellent source of information about accessibility and accommodations for ELs is the WIDA Consortium (wida.wisc.edu) based at the Wisconsin Center for Education Research at University of Wisconsin–Madison. The WIDA Consortium has 40 member states, territories, and federal agencies and is committed to the work of providing resources to these partners to advance the academic language and achievement for CLD students. Even if the state you plan to work in is not included in the WIDA consortium you can still download many resources that will guide you in the use of accessibility tools for EL students using different platforms and depending on the skills being tested (i.e., reading, writing, speaking, listening; wida.wisc.edu/assess/accessibility). Another excellent resource is the National Center on Educational Outcomes (NCEO.org) at the University of Minnesota. NCEO researchers compile data on state policies and practices in participation, and practices in accommodations for ELs with and without disabilities. Always review the test administration guidelines, as many manuals will guide you in the types of allowable accommodations to maintain validity. People will commonly think of test modifications such as a side-by-side English/native language version of the test or use of a specialized English dictionary containing the definitions for difficult words, but some accommodations like this are not allowable when trying to assess a student's language proficiency. Other tools that might be allowed are extended time, small group setting, dictating responses to a scribe, and having someone read, explain, or clarify test directions. Many state accommodation policies indicate which accommodations ELs can receive on the statewide test used for accountability purposes. Also consider that if a test allows for any student to ask for the directions to be repeated, then it is not an accommodation specific to EL students, it's just a regular test-administration feature. It's important to keep in mind that many tests have accessibility features like re-reading the directions already built into standardized administration. There remains limited research on the use of accommodations with EL students (Guzman-Orth et al., 2016) so always stick to standardization, use the test's universal design features, and emphasize appropriate test selection criteria to ensure that the tests you are administering to your EL students will help you answer the education questions at hand (WIDA Consortium, 2016). Keep up to date with research on assessment accessibility for ELs with disabilities by regularly reviewing the NCEO website.

Additional Culturally and Linguistically Responsive Practices

Additional practices to aid in understanding the cultural and linguistic background of students in order to improve the assessment process are listed in Box 6.1 and described below.

> **BOX 6.1**
>
> Additional Culturally and Linguistically Responsive Practices
>
> Learn about the communities in which you practice.
> Partner with multicultural consultants and community liaisons.
> Use multimodal assessment practices.
> Evaluate a student's opportunity to learn in their current placement.
> Understand the student's educational and instructional history.

Learn About the Communities in Which You Practice

You don't have to be an expert on every immigrant community your school serves, but with every effort you make to connect and learn about the cultures of your students, you will be better able to serve them and their families. Oversimplifying culture affects how students interact in the learning environment and how teachers interpret student behavior. For example, in some cultures it may be disrespectful for children to make eye contact with adults who are not in their family. This cultural insight will be helpful information if you are asked to assess a student from this culture for autism. To learn more about your students' communities you can attend cultural celebrations, volunteer on community led projects, and encourage your students to talk about their cultures as they feel comfortable and want to share. The simple gesture of listening and asking questions goes a long way to make students and families feel heard and welcomed in the school setting.

In the following Stakeholder Perspective, Mr. Casey Sovo shares some insights about working in Native American communities and with Native American students. Even if your school has only a small percentage of Native American students its critically important to be aware of and sensitive to the many injustices that have occurred to Native American communities so that you can support your students to achieve to their fullest potential.

Partner With Multicultural Consultants and Community Liaisons

It's okay to ask thoughtful questions and to ask for assistance when you're not sure how to proceed. More and more districts are employing multicultural consultants and

**Casey Sovo, MA Arts in Teaching,
Education Program Administrator, Bureau of Indian Education**

As a teacher for 5 years, an education specialist focused on K–3 literacy for 4 years, and now for the last 11 years as an education program administrator for the BIE, I train teachers and principals on how to improve their overall instruction and assessment practices. During these years, I have worked with K–12 schools across the country that serve predominantly Native American students. I'm Comanche and St. Regis Mohawk, and I experienced multiple aspects of the American education system: rural, urban, suburban, public, private, and charter. Here are some of the lessons I've learned and continue to share with colleagues who are new to working with Native American students and their communities.

Assessors of Native American children should always try to understand the context from which the student arrives at the point in time when an assessment is necessary. First, the assessor must believe that the majority of stories and images that we have consumed through mass media are false and derogatory toward Native Americans. Second, the assessor must know that the majority of Native American children, whether rural, urban or suburban, have not had the advantage of Head Start or Pre-K schooling. Therefore, the assessor should understand that in order to confidently assess a Native American child, he or she should approach the situation with the same reverence and humility that one would approach a complete stranger by focusing on first attempting to understand rather than to be understood.

(continues)

community liaisons. These colleagues are hired to improve relations with the community and to better serve students and their families. Invite your district's community liaison to your classroom and they may be able to offer suggestions about how to appropriately interpret student behavior or connect with a struggling student. Get to know your colleagues in these roles so that you have a good working relationship when difficult cases arise.

Use Multimodal Assessment Practices

Over-relying on standardized assessment can be problematic when working with CLD students. Using observations, samples of students' work, surveys, and interviews will ensure that you develop a plan that will truly serve the whole student. Gathering progress monitoring data with measures such as curriculum-based measures (CBM) which have been shown to be valid with English learning samples (Sandberg & Reschly, 2011) will also be essential to determine the extent to which the student is respon-

Native American families and their children have had a difficult, tumultuous, and sometimes deadly relationship with Western education and pedagogy styles since the arrival of the Pilgrims in the 1400s. The U.S. government's policy of Western expansion and support of Christian dogma have run over the long held and prosperous life ways of traditional Native Americans for almost 600 years. It is only logical that Native American families would be suspicious and wary of education officials trying to tell them "what is best" for their student and child when the last 30 years have proven to an overwhelming majority that Native American students who are identified as a student with a disability rarely improve their academic skills well enough to be exited from the special education program within the 13 years of the normal K–12 school routing.

The assessor would do well to remember that all assessments are biased toward one experience or another, favor one perspective over another, or prioritize certain sets of knowledge above others. Therefore, it is important to understand that a Native American child's early life experiences are the best that can be had given the circumstances or family structure, but that does not make one set of experiences better or worse than another.

It is important for assessors to understand that Native American children do not learn differently from other children because they are Native American but that their educational experiences are impacted by geography, rurality, history, access to early learning programs, equity, internet connectivity, electricity, and sometimes even running water. Just the same as other young American children, poverty has no boundaries with regard to color, ethnicity, race, nationality, citizenship, or creed. The purpose of assessment should be to identify the needs of the student and determine the supports that the school can provide to give an equitable opportunity for learning!

sive to previous interventions. Those data can also guide how the team adapts future interventions.

Evaluate a Student's Opportunity to Learn in Their Current Placement

One of the challenges in the special education eligibility process is evaluating the current classroom instruction and the extent to which the student has had sufficient opportunities to learn in that setting. CLD students may experience academic struggles that reflect a dissonance between familiar communication styles and instructional practices leaving them vulnerable to misinterpreting instruction. Many teachers report that they have not had sufficient training to teach EL students. For this reason, it's important that we observe in the classroom to determine if the teacher is using instructional strategies that are effective for CLD students, such as sheltered instruction or explicit instruction (Chaparro et al., 2021). You can also interview classroom teachers to ascertain their training in effective instructional strategies for CLD students and their understanding

BOX 6.2

Sample Questions to Gain an Understanding of Prior Educational Experiences

- How many years of schooling has the student had?

- Were those years of schooling continuous or were there gaps in attendance?

- In any one year in particular were there absences or long gaps in instruction?

- What was the primary language of instruction?

- What subjects were taught to the student?

- Which languages were taught?

- Which languages does the student have literacy skills in?

of their students' linguistic needs or of their students' cultural backgrounds. Classroom teachers can share the types of instructional strategies they use to support CLD students and which of those instructional strategies are engaging for the student. One of the most important pieces in the data collection process is the evaluation not of the student but of the quality of the instruction and the interventions provided to the student.

Understand the Student's Educational and Instructional History

A student's educational history will greatly impact his or her current performance and because most educators are not trained on the education methods of other countries, it's helpful for us to ask important questions about past education experiences (Blatchley & Lau, 2010). For example, in one case a student was thought to be a native Spanish speaker as the father spoke Spanish fluently with school personnel. The student had been enrolled in school consistently in Honduras, but his Spanish was significantly below that of similar students. The student was being tested for Special Education services due to concern over his low Spanish skills and slow English learning. Only after multiple interviews and meetings with the father and the student did it come to light that the student's native language was an indigenous language, Spanish was his second language that he had only recently learned, and English was now his third language. The father was fluent in Spanish and in their native indigenous language and so his language skills did not hint to the school personnel that Spanish might not be their native language. Only through interviews and discussions did this student's full history become known. The student was added to intensive intervention groups, but he was not made eligible for special education. See Box 6.2 for a sample of questions to ask to gain a better understanding of past educational experiences.

What other questions would you add to the list to get to know your student and determine if the learning difficulties were in just one or multiple languages? This section provides an overview of some culturally and linguistically responsive approaches to evaluating CLD students. We've highlighted resources from NASP, CEC, the WIDA Consortium, and two state organizations, Illinois School Psychologists Associate and North Carolina School Psychology Association, but there are other tools out there that can supplement your practice.

6.2

PROGRESS MONITORING CHECK

Alternative Ways to Test Students Who Are ELs

In the following section, we provide information about strategies that are sometimes used when testing students who are ELs. There are four main methods that have been historically implemented: testing in native language, testing in multiple languages, testing with nonverbal tests, and testing in English only. For example, when testing for special education eligibility, it is important to know if the deficit area is present in all of the languages that a student speaks or is limited to only one language. It is necessary to test students in their native language and a second language when enrolled in a dual-language learning program and so some literacy and language tests now offer complimentary forms in both English and Spanish, for example. You may want to test a student in their native language when you're trying to ascertain their education level from previous native language schooling. Because the native language is one that is not common in your area and you do not have a test in that language, you may have to use a nonverbal test to demonstrate a student's ability to learn. These various methods will help you when you are trying to establish an effective instructional plan.

Native Language Testing

In order to have the most accurate information about an EL student's current level of academic and behavioral ability we should first determine a student's language proficiency in English and in their native language. There are several ways to test students using directions and materials in their native language. Multiple tests are currently available in language versions other than English—most frequently, Spanish. These tests run the gamut from tests in English that are translated to those that are re-normed, to those that are specifically developed for another language and culture. The differences among these approaches are significant.

When tests are only translated, the questions may be of different difficulty and readability levels when the same question is asked the same way in two different languages. The difficulty of the vocabulary can vary from language to language. For example, the word *functional* is an English/Spanish cognate—meaning the word is spelled the same and means the same thing in both languages. However, the word is more common in Spanish, so a kindergartener who is a native Spanish speaker may know the word, but the same age native English speaker might not know the word because it isn't introduced into the curriculum until upper elementary and it doesn't come up in everyday conversation. Background knowledge can also impact the results from a test,   which is why it is important to use tests that were developed specifically in a language other than English and have been normed with the target population. Use of tests that are simply translated versions of the English version is discouraged. Instead use tests that were developed for the target population and include that population in the normative sample.

Test in Multiple Languages

With the popularity of dual-language instruction programs and even entire schools dedicated to educating students to fluency in multiple languages we have seen a slight increase in the number of assessments that are being developed with the dual-language learner in mind. For example, *Star Reading* is a diagnostic and screening measure that includes *Star Assessments* in Spanish. Similarly, the *IDEA Language Proficiency Test* (IPT) has reading and language progress monitoring assessments in both English and Spanish for students in kindergarten through high school. Some of the commonly used curriculum-based assessments that are discussed in Chapter 8 also have Spanish companions to measure early literacy skills through reading comprehension. For example, DIBELS 8th Edition has a companion Spanish assessment called IDEL. Despite the increased availability of language and literacy measures with parallel forms, these tests still conceive of each language separately. This limits a student's ability to demonstrate their full range of knowledge. For example, a student being tested in English may answer a question in their native language and they may have the answer correct, but because the test is in English the answer is marked as incorrect. The student successfully demonstrated receptive language but not expressive language. Heteroglossic tests, or ones that allow students to answer and be scored in multiple languages (Flores & Rosa, 2015), are still rare because of the complicated process for developing and scoring a standardized reliable measure. There are, however, a number of other language measures available. The Center on Applied Linguistics has created a free, searchable directory of information called the Foreign Language Assessment Directory (FLAD; cal.org/what-we-do/projects /flad). You can use this directory to look up reliability, validity, and other important information for almost 200 tests in more than 90 languages.

Use Nonverbal Tests

Several nonverbal tests are available for testing when native language assessments are not available and testing in English is inappropriate. Depending on the test, developers suggest that their test can be used as a proxy for intelligence, learning ability, and problem-solving skills. This type of test is believed to reduce the effects of language and culture on the assessment of a range of intellectual abilities. Nonverbal tests do not, however, completely eliminate the effects of language and culture. Some tests (see Chapter 17) do not require a student to speak—for example, the nonverbal index of the *Wechsler Intelligence Scale for Children–Fifth Edition*. However, these tests frequently have directions in English. Some tests, for example, the *Comprehensive Test of Nonverbal Intelligence–Second Edition* allow testers to use either oral or pantomime directions. A few tests are exclusively nonverbal, such as the *Leiter International Performance Scale*, a measure of observation skills and problem-solving skills that has instruction delivered by pantomime only. Some school districts will use a test like this when a new student is enrolled who cannot be tested in their native language or in English. They use the test as an indicator that the student will be able to join English language development classes without special accommodations. Tests that do not rely on oral directions or responses are more useful because they do not make any assumptions about students' language competence. However, other validity issues cloud the use of performance tests in the schools. For example, the nature of the tasks on nonverbal intelligence tests is usually less related to success in school than are the tasks on verbal intelligence tests.

Moreover, some cultural considerations are beyond the scope of directions and responses. For example, the very nature of testing may be more familiar in U.S. culture than in the cultures of other countries. When students are familiar with the testing process, they are likely to perform better. As another example, students from other cultures may respond differently to adults in authority, and these differences may alter estimates of their ability derived from tests. Thus, although performance and nonverbal tests may be a better option than verbal tests administered in English, they are not without problems.

Test in English Only

Testing in English only represents a monolinguistic view in which the other languages that students bring to their learning environment are ignored and undervalued. Whenever possible, educators should convey the principle that knowledge of multiple languages is an added-value to any individual's life. In fact, learning multiple languages boosts intelligence. In an ideal world all citizens would be multilingual to increase the connections across our global community. In a testing scenario, multilingual competence is very easy to overlook when assessing in only English. "Bilingual" implies equal proficiency in two languages. However, children must learn which language to use with specific people in specific settings. For example, they may be able to switch between English and Spanish with their siblings; speak only Spanish with their grandparents; and use only English with their older sister's husband, who still has not learned Spanish.

Although students can switch between languages, sometimes called translanguaging or code switching, they may not be equally proficient in both languages. They may not be equally competent or comfortable in using both languages, regardless of the context or situation. These students tend to prefer one language or the other for specific situations or contexts. For example, Somali may be spoken at home and in the neighborhood, whereas English is spoken at school. Moreover, when two languages are spoken in the home, the family may develop a hybrid language borrowing a little from each. These factors complicate the testing of bilingual students. Some bilingual students may understand academic questions better in English, but the language in which they answer can vary. If the content was learned in English, they may be better able to answer in English. However, if the answer calls for a logical explanation or an integration of information, they may be better able to answer in their native language. Finally, it cannot be emphasized strongly enough that language dominance is not the same as language competence for testing purposes. Because a student appears to know more Spanish than English, it does not mean that the student knows enough Spanish to be tested in that language. Because students' skills in language comprehension usually precede their skills in language production, performance tests with oral directions might be useful with some students. However, the testers should have objective evidence that a student sufficiently comprehends academic language for the test to be valid. If testing in English-only, then it is strongly recommended that a robust method for other sources of data be collected, such as those listed previously in this chapter.

Another Option to Consider

There is another option that we have not yet mentioned. It may sound strange coming from the authors of a book on assessment, but it's worth noting that sometimes the best option may be to not assess at all with any standardized testing tools. In select cases there may be cultural and other experiences which may make assessment scenarios a damaging experience which contributes to harming the child and their education experience. In some cultures, answering questions about yourself may be seen as self-aggrandizing, competitive, and immodest, and parents may not give permission to allow a student to receive one-on-one assessment. In this example, these cultural values work against any rationale we could provide to proceed with standardized testing.

The impact of traumatic experience is very real and should be considered before testing new CLD students who you are just learning about or are new to the school or country. Some children who are refugees may have been traumatized by civil strife in their native countries or by a hazardous journey to the United States. In some cases, just the sight of someone with a clipboard and official-looking clothes can trigger fear or a traumatic memory causing more harm than good. Even when that is not the case, male-female relations may be subject to cultural differences. Female students may be hesitant to speak to male teachers; male students (and their fathers) may not see female teachers as the professionals that they are. Children may be hesitant to speak to adults from other cultures. Some research suggests that it may be easier for children to work with examiners of the same race and cultural background (Goldhaber et al., 2015). Finally, some immigrant students and their families may have little experience with the types of testing done in U.S. schools. Consequently, at the very least, these students may lack test-taking skills, and at worst, students and families may think they are in trouble or that the testing of their student will in some way jeopardize the family's immigration status. All of the example scenarios are reasons for following the culturally and linguistically responsive approaches listed earlier and for considering postponing testing until the student feels safe in the school settings and testing can be constructive rather than harmful.

6.3
PROGRESS
MONITORING
CHECK

1. Describe which legal protections are provided to students with LEP designation in the special education eligibility process.
2. Which protections does IDEA offer parents of students with LEP designation in the special education eligibility process?

1. Define culturally-responsive teaching in your own words.
2. Give three examples of how you can apply culturally-responsive practices to the assessment process?
3. Why is it important to consider culture and language when assessing students for special education services?

1. If you are going to test a CLD student for special education eligibility what are four methods to contemplate?
2. Describe the advantages of a multi-lingual assessment approach.
3. Explore some of the websites and professional associations mentioned in this text.
4. Identify additional professional associations that offer guidance on the assessment of CLD students.

PART II

Providing Support and Monitoring Student Progress

CHAPTER 7

Assessment in Multi-Tiered Systems of Support

LEARNING OBJECTIVES

1. Define and describe Response to Intervention (RTI) and Multi-tiered Systems (MTSS) of support (MTSS) concepts that underlie school assessment practices.
2. List the fundamental assumptions in assessing RTI.
3. Describe dimensions of assessment (specificity and frequency) in MTSS models.
4. Indicate evidence for and against the effectiveness of RTI and MTSS.

When the first editions of this textbook were written shortly after President Gerald Ford signed the Education for All Handicapped Children Act in 1975, assessment practices were pretty robotic and stereotypic. Students with disabilities had just won the right to a free and appropriate public education. At that time, the U.S. Department of Education had specified 10 disability conditions and a set of eligibility criteria for each condition. Students who met those criteria *and* who demonstrated a need for special education could be declared eligible for special education services. Individualized Education Program (IEP) teams were required by law to make eligibility and intervention planning decisions. Students whose scores on intelligence tests were two standard deviations below average and who demonstrated maladaptive behavior in their everyday environment could be labeled "mentally retarded" (the term used at the time) and receive special education services, usually in a separate classroom. Students who demonstrated a significant discrepancy between their performance on an intelligence test and their performance on achievement tests, and who demonstrated a disorder in performance on one or more measures of psychological processes, could be labeled "learning disabled" and receive special education services.

Over time, largely as a function of research findings and the push for data-driven decision-making practices in schools, names for conditions changed, and robotic, stereotypic assessment practices fell out of favor. In the early days of special education, the focus of educational efficacy was defined mostly via process indicators, such as how many children were present and served in particular programs. There was little attention to who was being selected for such programs and how much benefit they derived from being served in the programs. Beginning in about 2001, several policy documents and legislative actions turned the focus of education from process to results, with radical implications for assessment and instructional practices for all students. The No Child Left Behind Act (NCLB) of 2002 established the clear expectation that schools would implement evidence-based instructional practices and engage in data-based assessment of student outcomes, measuring and reporting the success of schools in meeting the proficiency criteria established in each state. (We discuss these events in much greater detail in Chapter 22.) The reauthorization of the Individuals With Disabilities Educational Improvement Act (IDEA) of 2004 and its accompanying regulations in 2006 brought about increased attention to two important concepts: Response to Intervention and the development of multi-tiered systems of supports for matching instruction/intervention to student needs.

RTI and MTSS Defined

Research, policy, and legislation came together to recommend that the most pragmatic way to evaluate whether children could learn, was to teach them using evidence-based practices and measure their response. This process was called **Response to Intervention (RTI)** early on, and later the term **multi-tiered systems of support (MTSS)** was added. RTI now commonly means the primary metric that is used for decision making about intervention success or the need for intensification of intervention, whereas MTSS refers to the larger framework. In this chapter, we will use MTSS to refer to the framework for decision making and RTI as the metric that fuels MTSS decisions (e.g., begin intervention, intensify instruction, refer for an eligibility evaluation).

At the heart of special and remedial education remains matching instructional content, methods, and pace to the needs and skills of students who are not making as much academic progress as expected. Students begin instruction with differing skills and needs. As shown in Figure 7.1, within MTSS all students receive universal supports within general education, this level is considered Tier 1. However, many students will require additional, more targeted supports to help them succeed. Targeted supports are also sometimes referred to as supplemental supports, or Tier 2. For a small percentage of students even these targeted supports are not enough; they require intensive supports to succeed; intensive supports are also referred to as tertiary or Tier 3 supports. Students

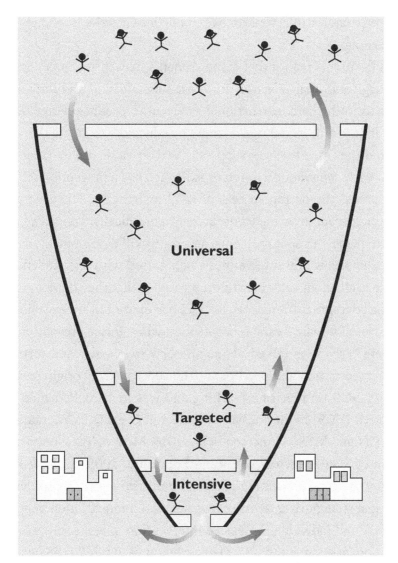

FIGURE 7.1. Students receive multiple tiers of support that increase in intensity if they are not successful in school.

are provided with instruction that can be adjusted flexibly, throughout the school year, depending on their needs for more or less intensive supports. In this chapter we discuss the two important concepts of RTI and MTSS and describe assessment practices within each of those two sets of practices.

Features of RTI and MTSS

Good instruction is effective for most students. However, the extent to which any program or intervention will be effective with an individual student is unknown. Program or intervention effectiveness is affected by the unique characteristics of the students and their teachers. A supplemental program with strong support in the research literature may not necessarily address the skills with which students at a particular school are struggling. Therefore, it is important to monitor student progress over time to know whether a program or intervention, when applied, has the intended positive impact on student learning.

MTSS reflects this reality that some students may thrive in general education while others struggle and that relatively low-cost supplemental and individual interventions can be added to the core instructional program to produce better learning for all students. A public health model was adapted by educators to create the multi-tiered aspect of MTSS and the three levels of supports (Walker et al., 1996). Central to MTSS is the notion that early intervention to repair skill gaps has a prevention effect for most learners and improves the overall success of K–12 instruction. The general notion of MTSS is to monitor student progress (continuously, periodically, annually, or with some other degree of frequency) to spot problems, ascertain skill development, or check the efficacy of academic or behavioral interventions being used with the student. Some would say the practice is all about catching children early so that they do not get left behind.

The basic conceptual framework for RTI has existed in the psychological and educational literature for many years; it has its foundation in the prevention sciences (Caplan, 1964), where physicians talked about primary, secondary, and tertiary prevention or treatment. In education and psychology, the concept likely originated in the early work of Lindsley (1964) on precision teaching and was first implemented as an assessment model by Beck (1979) in the Sacajawea Project in Great Falls, Montana. There are many models of RTI and MTSS (Jimerson et al., 2016; McIntosh & Goodman, 2016; National Association of State Directors of Special Education, 2005; Sugai & Horner, 2009), yet all models share certain defining features: universal screening to determine classwide and individual student risk, layers of instructional intensification beginning with core to supplemental and individual, intensive intervention, ongoing progress monitoring, and data collection/assessment to inform decisions at each tier. MTSS begins in general education and involves all students in screening and progress monitoring of core instruction to make adjustments at the program level. As children are advanced to more intensive instruction, it is essential that RTI is monitored which results in the occurrence of two circumstances: assessment increases in frequency and fewer students are served at each tier. Review the graphic in Figure 7.1 to see the three tiers in the RTI model, and then read the story about "Charles" for an example of how a teacher used one type of RTI approach to address a student's needs.

Charles

Charles, a second grader, is the oldest of three children who moved from the city into the suburban West Morgan School District over the summer. Several requests for Charles's records from the city district were never answered. Following the fall screening in Mrs. Buchanon's class, the teacher's worry that Charles was struggling in reading was validated: Charles scored in the risk range and was the lowest scoring reader in the class. Mrs. Buchanon noted that

Charles made lots of errors when reading. After listening to Charles read aloud twice, she decided to tally the number of correct and incorrect words he read. The next time Charles read aloud, he read 18 words correctly in 1 minute and made nine errors. She then allowed him to finish the brief passage. Not surprisingly, he was unable to answer any of the comprehension questions correctly. Clearly, the beginning second-grade material was too difficult for Charles. Mrs. Buchanon tried material at the mid-first-grade level, but it was also too difficult. In beginning first-grade material, Charles read 28 words correctly and made six errors. He was only able to answer one of three comprehension questions correctly.

Mrs. Buchanon decided to use a generally effective instructional strategy to improve Charles's reading. She paired him with Michelle, one of the better readers in the class. Charles would read beginning first-grade material aloud for 5 minutes, and Michelle would follow along as he read and help him correct his errors. Mrs. Buchanon monitored the intervention twice a week. Although Charles seemed to enjoy working with Michelle, his reading performance remained at about 30 words read correctly per minute with six errors.

Mrs. Buchanon then developed an intensified intervention. She assessed Charles's knowledge of letter names and letter sounds. He could name all of the letters, all of the long vowel sounds, none of the short vowel sounds, and all of the common consonant sounds. She worked with him for 2 minutes daily on short vowel sounds and sent worksheets home for Charles to practice with his mother. Charles continued to read with Michelle for 5 minutes every day. However, instead of supplying a correct word for an incorrect one, Michelle provided the correct initial sound of the word before supplying the correct word. After a month, Charles had learned the short "o" and improved his fluency from 30 correct sounds per minute to 45 correct sounds per minute. However, increased accuracy in letter sounds was not accompanied by increases in oral reading comprehension.

At this point, it was clear that Charles was not making the kind of gains he needed to make; he was falling further behind his classmates. Mrs. Buchanon consulted with the school building's intervention assistance team. The team recommended an intensive intervention of explicit instruction targeting phonemic awareness, letter–sound associations, and reading fluency. The team did not specifically target reading comprehension because of the likelihood that Charles's poor comprehension was the result of his lack of reading fluency. Charles received 12 minutes of individual instruction from the reading specialist each day. Data were collected weekly on Charles's reading accuracy and fluency. The reading specialist worked on phonemic awareness activities using magnetic letters to locate beginning, middle, and ending sounds with one-on-one support from the reading specialist. Then the specialist had him read nonsense words for 1 minute to try to beat his score from the day before. Finally, the specialist modeled the first 60 words of a first-grade reading passage, then assisted Charles to read the first 60 words of the passage, providing prompts to decode words, immediate corrective feedback for errors with a repetition loop (i.e., having him reread missed words), and overcorrection for missed words. She then finished the session by having Charles read for 1 minute aloud to try to beat his score from the day before and to monitor his progress each day. He was allowed to count up his correctly read words and earn a small reward for beating his last best score.

Charles progressed consistently in the intensive program. The number of correct words read per minute increased steadily in progressively more difficult reading materials. By the end of the first semester, Charles was reading beginning second-grade material independently. By the end of the second grade, he had caught up to his peers; he was reading end-of-second-grade material independently. The intervention team ended his intervention; however, progress monitoring for Charles continued in the third grade to make sure he maintained his gains. Charles continued to progress at the rate of his peers.

Importance of Assessment

"MTSS is a proactive and preventative framework that integrates data and instruction to maximize student achievement and support students social, emotional, and behavior needs from a strengths-based perspective. MTSS offers a framework for educators to engage in data-based decision making related to program improvement, high-quality instruction and intervention, social and emotional learning, and positive behavioral supports necessary to ensure positive outcomes for districts, schools, teachers, and students" (retrieved from Center on Multi-tiered System of Supports, mtss4success.org /essential-components).

In Figure 7.1 we depicted MTSS as a funnel, with students filtering through the funnel as they need increasing levels of support. Students receive increasingly intensive levels of service and supports until interventions are identified that result in a positive Response to Intervention. Some educators depict the multi-tiered system of supports as a triangle, as shown in Figure 7.2. However, in the past, educators viewed the triangle as having two sides; one side of the triangle was academics and the other side was behavior. MTSS has been conceptualized as the integration of RTI for academics and behavior (McIntosh & Goodman, 2016) with the goal of increasing the effectiveness of interventions because of a focus on a student's academic *and* behavioral needs. Whether a funnel, triangle, or pyramid is used to illustrate the concept, what is communicated by these drawings is that (1) there are individual differences in the intensity of supports that students need in order to be successful, and (2) the numbers of students served decreases as more intensive supports are needed and provided. Assessment helps you figure out what skills and skill deficits students have, the intensity of supports that students need, whether good instruction is happening with students, the extent to which they are profiting from it, and the extent to which teachers and schools are "effective."

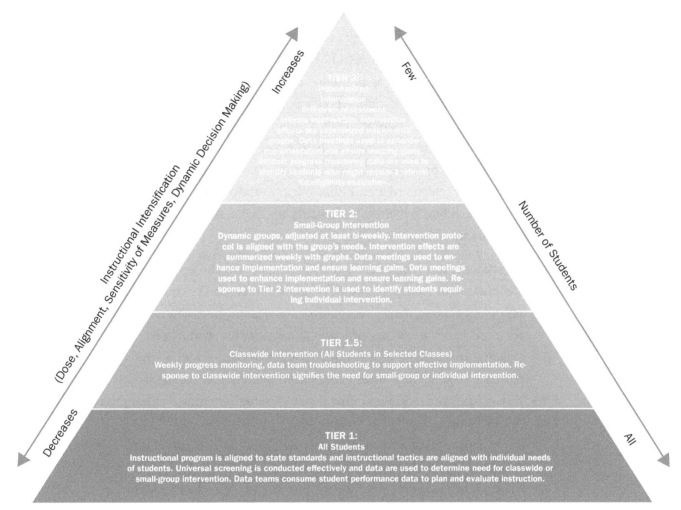

FIGURE 7.2. The multi-tiered system of supports pictured as a triangle. *Note.* Reprinted from Kovaleski et al. (in press) with permission from Guilford Press.

Think of MTSS as a **series of tiers**. Tiers within the funnel or triangle describe the intensity of instruction, not specific places, programs or types of students, or staff. The **first tier** is the core instructional programming made available to all students. Screening tests (e.g., formative assessments) given in the classroom show which students are at risk for reading, math, and other learning difficulties. Brief follow-up tests for those who are at risk may show that a student who has difficulty reading needs additional instruction in word fluency. In the **second tier**, the classroom teacher might provide corrective feedback and extra instruction. In other cases, another educator who has expertise in reading and fluency might teach a small group of students who are having the same difficulty. Students who fail to respond to specific targeted interventions may then be considered for more specialized instruction in the **third tier**, where instruction may occur with increased intensity. Examples of increased intensity include instructional sessions of longer duration, instruction offered daily instead of 3 times a week, or instruction that is more targeted to the student's specific skill gaps. If difficulties persist, a team of educators may complete a comprehensive evaluation to determine eligibility for special education and related services.

Regardless of the intervention within a tier, the goal is to use student performance data to inform ways to provide the type of instruction and educational assistance that the student needs to be successful. Typical assessments in Tier 1 include universal screening and continuous or periodic (e.g., three times per year) progress monitoring to identify students at risk. At Tier 2, typical assessments include diagnostic assessment in academic content areas to inform instruction and intervention as well as progress monitoring designed to help make instructional decisions. At Tier 3, assessment consists primarily of continuous or very frequent collection of information, consideration of referral to a multidisciplinary study team, and assessment designed to determine eligibility for special education services. When correctly implemented, an MTSS results in:

- All students receiving high-quality instruction in the general education setting.
- A reduction of referrals for special education eligibility consideration.
- The use of assessment information by teams of educators to make decisions about all students as they are screened for academic and behavior problems.
- Ongoing monitoring of individual student progress and analysis of the data to pinpoint specific difficulties experienced by individual students.
- At-risk students receiving immediate individual attention without having to wait to be identified as eligible for special education services.
- Consistent, rigorous implementation of progress monitoring and effective interventions.
- All students receiving appropriate instruction prior to consideration for special education placement.

Systems Are Essential for the Implementation of RTI and MTSS

MTSS is all about systems, or the interaction and implementation of systems, through communication protocols and teaming. MTSS involves improvement cycles and communication loops between teams within a school and between teams at the school and at the district level. Improvement cycles involve the notion that we are constantly using data to make improvements, and in this book the improvement cycle is the problem-solving process described in Chapter 20. Figure 7.3 depicts one model of how MTSS is in part defined by teams who use improvement cycles (i.e., problem-solving process) and communication loops (e.g., monthly data shares on Tier 2 outcomes at staff meeting) to support data-based decision making at all levels.

The following is a list of the six essential systems in an MTSS framework:

- *Instruction and Intervention:* There is a continuum of evidence-based and scientifically based curricular materials for all students across tiers that are aligned and complementary in scope.

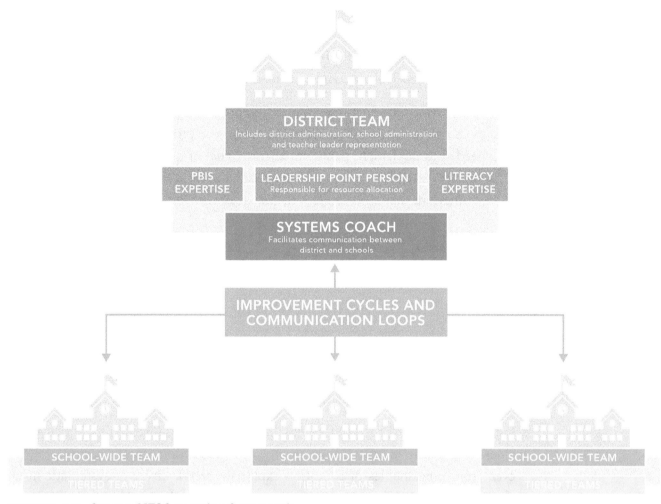

FIGURE 7.3. Oregon MTSS teaming framework.

- *Universal Screening:* All students are given brief, technically adequate, general outcome measures on a regular basis, or other universal data thresholds are used with the purpose of preventatively identifying students at-risk for difficulties.
- *Progress Monitoring:* Students being served by supplemental and intensive intervention are also receiving brief, technically adequate, curriculum-based measures to indicate Response to Intervention. Intervention fidelity is monitored periodically to indicate that the intervention is being delivered as intended.
- *Data-Based Decision Making:* There is a continuum of teams that use data to make decisions about a school's progress toward goals at various levels (e.g., grade, content area, intervention group). Data and rules for using data are shared between teams. Data are also used to monitor how the whole system is working, including quality of classroom and intervention instruction.
- *Professional Development and Coaching:* All school building faculty and staff are offered professional learning opportunities that support the MTSS framework. Coaching is offered and based on data. The impact of these training and coaching opportunities is also monitored for quality.

- *Leadership:* Administrators at the district and school levels have a shared commitment to providing the resources necessary to fully implement and sustain MTSS. Teacher leaders help to build the capacity of all staff so that the commitment to high-quality MTSS is shared and sustained even with staff or principal turnover.

MTSS offers the systems such as communication protocols between teams, the decision rules teams use to make data-based decisions, and the professional development and coaching needed to implement a system with the goal of quantifying a student's RTI. The focus of this book is on assessment in special and inclusive education settings and MTSS is a framework that aims to meet the needs of students in both of these settings.

Fundamental Assumptions in Assessing Response to Intervention

As a metric, RTI is complex because it requires some preconditions that generally most assessments do not require. RTI requires a series of coordinated actions with in-tandem assessment of instruction and child learning and decision making to result in a binary RTI decision (child is responding successfully to intervention or not). There are seven assumptions that underlie the validity of RTI.

- *Instruction occurs* and the student has had access to the instruction. When we assess response to instruction, we assume that instruction actually occurs. However, some philosophies of education explicitly eschew direct or systematic instruction and value a student's discovering content, skills, and behavior.[1] Thus, it is likely that some students could spend their time in instruction-free environments and would stand no chance of being instructed. We also assume, maybe most importantly but rarely measured, that the instruction delivered is generally effective. There needs to be evidence that the instruction that is implemented works for students in general and, more specifically, for students who are the same age and grade as the student being assessed. This means that students are actively engaged in the instruction to learn the content being covered and that instructional strategies and appropriate classroom management works for the majority of the students. This also means that chronic absenteeism is also not an issue. Chronic absenteeism is defined as missing 10% of school days in a school year, which in some districts means that a student misses 2 or 3 days per month. It doesn't seem like much, but the cumulative effect leads to gaps in access to instruction.
- *Instruction occurs as intended.* It is assumed that instruction is implemented in the way in which it is intended to be implemented and that students are actively

---

1. Most parents would prefer that this procedure not be used to teach their children to swim.

engaged in the instruction. Over the past decade, researchers have become increasingly interested in intervention integrity (also sometimes called treatment integrity, implementation integrity, or treatment fidelity). For example, when we assess the extent to which a student responds to phonics instruction, we are assuming that the phonics instruction was implemented as the teacher intended and that the student was actively engaged during instruction.

- *The instruction that is assessed is known to be generally effective.* There needs to be empirical evidence that the instruction that is implemented works for students in general and, more specifically, for students who are the same age and grade as the student being assessed.

- *The measurement system is adequate to detect changes in student learning as a result of instruction.* There are four subcomponents to this assumption.

  - The measurement system reflects the curriculum or assesses the effect of instruction in that curriculum. It is axiomatic that response to instruction must reflect the content being instructed.

  - The measurement system can be used frequently. Frequent measurement is important to avoid wasting a student's and a teacher's time when instruction is not working. It is also important to prevent a student from practicing (and mastering) errors and making them more difficult to correct.

  - The measurement system is sensitive to small changes in student performance. If measurement is conducted frequently, it is unlikely that there will be large changes in student learning. Thus, to be effective, the measurement system must be capable of detecting small, but meaningful, changes in student learning or performance.

  - The measurement system actually assesses student performance, not simply what the teacher does. Clearly, what a teacher does is important because it goes directly to intervention integrity. However, we are primarily interested in whether the student is learning given the correct use of an intervention.

- *There are links between the assessment data and modifications in instruction.* This is the concept of data-driven decision making and reiterates our earlier point that data collected and not used to make decisions are useless. It is assumed that the data are both useful and used for purposes of instructional planning. Student failure to respond to instruction, as determined by the formative measures used, should trigger a change in instruction. Additional data may need to be collected to determine what change has the highest probability of leading to student success; nevertheless, a change would be needed to intensify instruction.

- *There are consequences that sustain improved student outcomes* and *continued implementation of the measurement system.* It is assumed not only that the system is good, but that it is worth keeping in place. In our experience, we have learned that the collection of direct frequent data on student performance is considered both time-consuming and arduous by some teachers. At the same time, teachers tell us that they and their students are "better off" when data are collected. Although many teachers are motivated by their students' progress, it is sometimes necessary to provide rewards to others for data collection if we want them to engage in direct and frequent measurement. These teachers have told us that, if it does not matter to someone that they monitor student progress, they will stop doing so.

- *Assessment of RTI is not setting specific.* It is assumed that RTI are assessed in both general and special education settings.

The RTI decision will not be valid unless the above conditions are met. The RTI decision begins in core instruction and thus, requires certain structures to ensure the ultimate RTI decision is valid. Many of the chapters in this book are relevant to the effective implementation of MTSS and a valid resulting RTI decision (screening, data teams, progress monitoring, using data to make instructional decisions, diagnostic assessment for math and reading, assessment for accountability).

MTSS is no longer a new framework and has been adopted in most states with varying degrees of success. New models are being adopted by state departments of education on a regular basis. For example, over 40 states' departments of education have MTSS or RTI named on their websites (Bailey, 2019). As we prepared this textbook, both the Michigan and Minnesota Departments of Education had just adopted new MTSS Models. Research has persistently demonstrated that the most difficult-to-implement ingredients happen also to be the most important ones if you care about improving system outcomes, making valid RTI decisions, and producing benefit to struggling students. The actions that have always been difficult for schools remain difficult and these include: interpreting the collected data, troubleshooting interventions that are not producing the desired learning gains, collecting adequate integrity data, and responding to low-fidelity data with in-class coaching and support (Silva et al., 2020). Thus, in most systems, even though MTSS has been widely endorsed and adopted, most systems need to continually fine-tune implementation so that MTSS can deliver results for their students.

7.1
*PROGRESS
MONITORING
CHECK*

Another Method for Evaluating RTI—Gap Analysis

Gap analysis involves examining the difference between the actual rate of improvement for a student and the rate of improvement that would be necessary to attain an expected benchmark level by a particular point in time. There are no specific legally defined guidelines or criteria for how small the gap must be to consider the student as demonstrating reasonable progress nor are there specifications about how large the gap must be to consider a student as eligible for special education services. Some states are beginning to specify a magnitude of gap necessary to declare students eligible for special education services under the SLD category. We describe gap analysis further in the chapter on making eligibility decisions.

Blending MTSS and RTI Together

As we have said, MTSS involves a systematic approach to matching student need with instruction and intervention. This process occurs in a series of steps that start with determining risk or need for intervention through universal screening. Next, is selecting the right intervention and effectively deploying and managing that intervention. As needed the next step involves intensifying the intervention systematically and continuing to monitor progress. After pre-specified periods of intervention delivery, teams of educators work on interpreting the data to determine whether the response was sufficient to rule out a possible LD or the response was insufficient which is evidence that the child has an LD and a need for special education. Thus, the validity of the RTI decision requires the correct use of MTSS.

Intervention Features
That Influence Intervention Effect

A valid RTI decision depends upon three intervention features: efficacious intervention, aligned with student needs, and delivered with sufficient integrity.

Intervention Efficacy

If an intervention is to be critical to the validity of the RTI decision, then an intervention that can be expected to work well, when used well, must be selected. This part of the process is like selecting an antibiotic versus essential oils to cure an infection. Research data support that antibiotics, when properly used, cure infection and have minimal or rare side effects that are outweighed by the risk associated with not treating an infection. These data don't exist for essential oils. In academic and behavioral intervention, we should begin with interventions that have good evidence that the treatment itself is generally effective with students who are at the same age and grade as the student being assessed. This is especially true in models that require normative peer comparisons (examinations of student progress relative to that of classmates). Under the requirements of accountability (see Chapter 22), school personnel are expected to use evidence-based interventions. Information about the extent to which interventions are generally effective is found by reviewing the research evidence in support of the treatments.

Fortunately, there are a number of resources that teachers can turn to in order to understand the quality of evidence available for an intervention and what effect sizes have been found in research. The National Center on Intensive Intervention (NCII, intensiveintervention.org) provides Tools Charts for academic (charts.intensiveintervention .org/aintervention) and behavioral (charts.intensiveintervention.org/bintervention) interventions. The tools charts can be filtered by content area (reading, math) and grade level. Readers can view vendor-reported evidence and the NCII expert panel's rating as to the quality of that evidence to select interventions for their setting. Then, the reader can view a listing of consumer report-like ratings of interventions to identify those that have reported strong evidence of their efficacy. One subtlety to understand is that the rating is not an expert rating of the intervention per se, but rather a rating of the research pertaining to the efficacy of interventions. This and other tools can be used to help determine if you're starting with a research-based curriculum or program in the first place.

Correct Alignment of Intervention With Student Need

Let's return to our antibiotic versus essential oil example. Choosing to use an antibiotic was the evidence-based choice, but our work is not done. We now have to select the right antibiotic or the one that will effectively kill the bacteria that is causing the infection, and this step is the second requirement of effective intervention. A generally efficacious intervention must be the right fit for the student's particular learning needs. As an extreme example, selecting a highly effective math intervention (e.g., ROOTS) to address the needs of a reading problem is not good alignment. More subtly, when ROOTS is designed for early numeracy (which it is), it would not be a good fit for a middle schooler struggling with fraction understanding. You must measure student skills to identify skill gaps when selecting an intervention rather than relying solely on what has been shown to be most effective in the research literature.

There is a science to aligning intervention with student need. It is grounded in a framework called the Instructional Hierarchy (Haring et al., 1978) which is enormously useful in designing instruction for core and increasingly intensive intervention. An important element of intensification is the extent to which the intervention is precisely aligned to student needs. More intensive instruction requires more precise assessment to permit more precise alignment. When students are not successful with that type of instruction, more precise information is needed to intensify the instruction. In order to ascertain alignment, you might ask the following questions. Has the student mastered the necessary prerequisite understandings? Does the student need more explicit acquisition support? Does the student require fluency-building intervention? To make these decisions, we assess the student.

We start with the goal understanding, determine whether the student's performance is frustrational (inaccurate and slow), instructional (accurate but slow), or mastery (fluent). When student performance is at mastery, we can move up a skill. When performance is instructional, we can provide fluency-building intervention (high dosage of high-quality practice with delayed corrective feedback, for example). When performance is frustrational, we can provide acquisition instruction (guided practice with modeling and immediate corrective feedback, for example). This alignment is so powerful that when instruction is misaligned (i.e., you give fluency-building instruction when acquisition is needed), you will see learning decelerate. You can use this understanding in core instruction to estimate the type of instruction you should plan. You can also use this understanding to build an intervention for Tiers 2 and 3, specifically selecting which skill to target and what type of intervention to use. As intervention is implemented, progress monitoring data are required to adjust the intervention and maintain its alignment with student need. We'll discuss progress monitoring in more detail in the next chapter. For the time being, it's important to know that assessment can help to determine the correct alignment with the student's need.

Intervention Integrity

As school personnel assess RTI, it is critical to demonstrate that intervention is occurring and that it is occurring in ways that it was intended. Even when we have chosen to use an antibiotic and selected the correct antibiotic for the infection, writing the prescription does not cure the illness. The patient must consistently take the antibiotic as prescribed by the doctor. This challenge is the most pernicious threat to RTI validity. Imagine assessing student RTI, concluding that the student did not respond to the intervention (that the intervention did not work), and then learning later that the intervention either was never put in place or was poorly implemented. Or imagine that a student starts to make substantial progress, but you are not sure what made the difference and thus are not sure what to maintain or change in a student's program.

How can you make sure that interventions are put in place with good integrity? Teachers and interventionists should be trained on the nuances of implementing an intervention. If, for example, teachers are to implement a published program with their classes, it would be important that they know the specifics of that published program. They might attend specific training and work for a time alongside another teacher in a setting where the program is being implemented.

Most interventions fail because they have not been correctly and consistently implemented. Advances in implementation science have taught us that installing interventions without systematically attending to simultaneously supporting their correct adoption and use is futile. The National Implementation Research Network is the hub of current implementation science research and many helpful resources for district and school administrators can be found there. In summary, intervention integrity requires supports (e.g., training and time) to permit the use of the intervention, measurement of integrity, and discussions of how well the intervention was used in tandem with student learning gains or lack thereof.

Intervention Dosage

In the early days of MTSS, intensified instruction was defined on the basis primarily of time. That is, more frequent, longer duration interventions were considered more intensive, as were one-to-one formats and more frequent progress monitoring. What we have learned in the intervening years is that shorter, more frequently occurring interventions produce more robust learning gains. Micro-doses of interventions (e.g., 3-minute interventions delivered multiple times per day) can produce powerful and enduring gains in learning that are superior to more traditionally delivered 20- or 30-minute sessions even when the overall weekly time devoted to intervention is the same. Schools should seek to offer interventions in shorter durations, delivered more frequently, at least daily. Smaller teacher:student ratios during intervention do not produce stronger responses to intervention. In other words, if delivering supplemental intervention in small groups of five students is as intensive as delivering intervention in small groups of two students, then working with five students at one time is more efficient and therefore easier to accomplish each day. Intervention dosage includes the actual delivery of intensified instruction and this is now operationalized by capturing the integrity of the intervention delivered along with an estimate of the precision of measurement and delivery, and the density of the active ingredient in the intervention (e.g., opportunities to respond for a fluency-building intervention). All of these elements are considered superior to time-based estimates of dosage.

Valid RTI decisions require that an efficacious intervention that has been selected based on diagnostic assessment information to be correctly aligned with the student's specific needs. The properly aligned intervention should be implemented at a sufficient dosage for the intervention to work. Assessments are essential for a valid RTI decision as they can either systematically magnify or miss intervention effects based on their design.

In the following Stakeholder Perspective, you will read about MTSS implementation from the vantage point of a district administrator working within a large district. Consider how we've used the phrase, *alignment between assessment and intervention*. Dr. Brahim confirms the importance of alignment between assessment, interventions and professional development.

Stakeholder PERSPECTIVE

Naomi Brahim, EdD, Director of MTSS Behavior, Jefferson County Schools, Louisville, Kentucky

Jefferson County Public Schools (JCPS) is a large urban school district in Louisville, Kentucky, serving approximately 100,000 students at 175 schools. The student population is very diverse, with 60% students of color, 12% receiving ESL services, 65% receiving free or reduced-price lunch, and 7% experiencing homelessness. The district began implementation of a comprehensive systems-focused model in 2016 to explicitly address increasing rates of in-school and out-of-school suspensions as well as ethnic disproportionality in behavior referrals. JCPS relies on the multi-tiered system of supports (MTSS) framework for behavior. We choose to integrate two other aligned practices into our MTSS framework: restorative practices (RP) and positive behavior interventions and supports (PBIS) as vital components to ensure equitable practices are used in schools for all students.

A key element of the MTSS school-based framework is the focus on whole-school training: custodians, clerks, nutrition workers, bus drivers, teachers, and administrators all receive the training. District leadership understands that students interact every day with a myriad of adults, and each interaction is an opportunity to build a positive relationship, teach prosocial skills, and deepen a student's sense of belonging. With that in mind, every district employee who interacts with students has been invited to participate in the training. To incentivize participation, the district has set aside a portion of their yearly budget to pay employees their daily rate for the participation in training. This message made it very clear that the district viewed this training as a priority and valued staff attendance.

PBIS provided the universal multi-tiered system for most of our schools, and then we layered on RP, which we will refer to as the Aligned Cohort. The initial student outcome data showed promising, positive trends of decreasing office referrals for the elementary, middle, and alternative schools participating in the initial pilot of 10 schools that added restorative practices implementation to the MTSS framework in the 2017–2018 school year. The schools that showed a clear, positive impact on a reduction in the number of office discipline referrals had better PBIS fidelity and better RP fidelity. As of May 2021, 29 schools had been trained in how to integrate PBIS and RP into their MTSS framework.

Figure 7.4 shows a decrease in referrals between April 2018 and the same time the previous year for the elementary, high, and alternative schools in the Aligned Cohort compared to the district averages. These early trends showed very positive potential, as this was the first year of implementation for the full model. The impact on suspensions for the high schools was also very promising. Table 7.1 shows the decrease in overall suspension events and repeat suspensions for the high schools in the Aligned Cohort compared to the district averages. Go to our JCPS MTSS website (sites.google.com/jefferson.kyschools.us/jcpsmtss/home) to learn more about our implementation of MTSS for behavior. As a district leader, the rewards to this systematic approach to behavior supports across the tiers has been invaluable in numerous ways that the data only highlights. Our integrated and aligned approach is proof of the power of using data to make decisions combined with training and supporting *all* staff to make a shared commitment to serving *all* students.

What Would MTSS Look Like If It Were Implemented Well?

When MTSS is implemented well you will see the benefit in student outcomes and through measures of implementation fidelity and intervention integrity. The school and district will have the resources necessary which includes evidence-based materials,

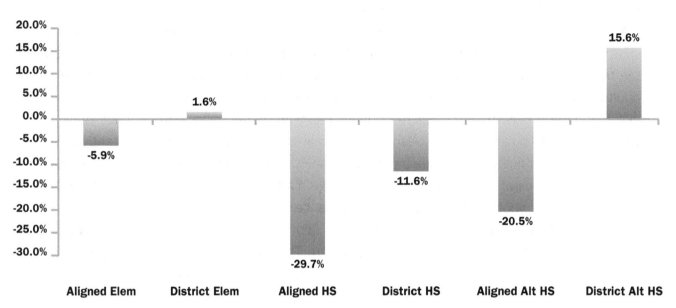

FIGURE 7.4. Percentage average change in referrals for aligned cohort and district averages, 2016–2017 and 2017–2018 school years.

TABLE 7.1

Percentage Change of Suspension Events and Repeat Suspensions for High Schools Only and Aligned Cohorts and District Averages, 2016–2017 and 2017–2018 School Years

High School	Change in Overall Suspensions	Change in Repeat Suspensions
Aligned Cohort Average	−29.0%	−29.9%
District Average	.3%	−5.1%

personnel, and training. If RTI is being implemented well, one would see teachers engaged in evidence-based intervention, monitoring student progress toward intended goals, and adjusting instruction based on student response. Teachers would meet regularly in teams to review and discuss students' progress and there would be clear criteria specified ahead of time indicating desired levels of performance and rates of progress. Frequent communication with parents whose children may be at risk is also encouraged in an MTSS model and the school seeks regular input from all family and community stakeholders. Although MTSS and RTI have been around for decades many schools and districts are currently in the initial phases of implementing MTSS to establish their overall systems for delivery of effective instruction. High-quality implementation of RTI is a challenging process that takes a coordinated effort over a sustained period of time and resources aligned with the practices that we've outlined in this chapter.

MTSS and RTI Resources and Examples

There are many reliable online resources on MTSS and RTI. We'd like to highlight the Center on Multi-Tiered System of Supports (mtss4success.org) at the American Institutes for Research. The website was previously named the National Center on RTI and was funded by the U.S. Department of Education's Office of Special Education Programs from 2011 to 2012. The American Institutes for Research is also home to the National Center on Intensive Intervention, which is referenced later in this book where we discuss data-based individualization (DBI), which takes more specific and focused steps and procedures to serve students with more severe needs. A nonprofit organization called the National Center for Learning Disabilities hosts the RTI Action Network (rtinetwork.org) also with a number of excellent resources. There is also a wonderful series of books which includes titles such as *RTI Applications* (Burns et al., 2012), *RTI Team Building* (Broxterman & Whalen, 2013), *Integrated Multi-Tiered Systems of Support* (McIntosh & Goodman, 2016), *The Data Driven School* (Hyson et al., 2020), *Implementing Response to Intervention in Secondary Schools* (Windram & Bollman, 2016), and *The RTI Approach to Evaluating Learning Disabilities* (Kovaleski et al., in press), that are written for practitioners who are implementing MTSS and RTI. Many of these books offer valuable reproducible handouts that can be used by teachers, teams, and principals. Case studies from Oregon, Florida, and Michigan at the district and state levels are also described in detail (Chaparro et al., 2016; Kincaid & Batsche, 2016; Russell & Harms, 2016). These books offer detailed descriptions of the foundations of problem-solving and RTI strategies, assessment and measurement considerations, evidence-based practices, and lessons learned in implementing MTSS and RTI.

7.2
PROGRESS
MONITORING
CHECK

PROGRESS
7.1

MONITORING CHECK

Write your answers to each of the following questions and then compare your responses to the text.

1. Are MTSS and RTI the same? How are they different?
2. What are the essential elements of MTSS?
3. What are the potential benefits of MTSS implementation?
4. What are the fundamental assumptions in implementing assessment to monitor RTI?

1. What are three essential features or interventions that should be considered when estimating RTI?

2. Why is it important for teachers and assessors to have training not just in assessments but also in the qualities of intervention integrity?

3. Provide a rationale for the importance of alignment between intervention, need, and assessment.

CHAPTER 8

Monitoring Student Progress Toward Instructional Goals

LEARNING OBJECTIVES

1. Describe characteristics of effective progress monitoring tools.
2. Know the defining characteristics of curriculum-based measurement (CBM).
3. Understand different types of CBM and the purposes for which they are used.
4. Explain several approaches to setting instructional goals and deciding when instructional changes are necessary.
5. Identify two diagnostic approaches that can be used with CBM.
6. Identify assessment frameworks that can be used along with progress monitoring to inform instructional changes.

Multi-tiered systems of support (MTSS) and service delivery models include data-based problem-solving of academic and behavior problems as a core component. Progress monitoring is the method by which data are gathered regularly so that timely instructional decisions can be made by the intervention team. Not only is progress monitoring a central element of MTSS, it is also a federally required component in the development of an Individualized Education Program (IEP); progress must be monitored for each goal listed in the IEP. Knowing whether students have mastered a particular skill or have sufficient knowledge about a particular topic is important, but monitoring progress during instruction is the only way for a teacher to make adjustments to instruction to get a better result. To make adjustments to instruction, we need to know whether students are gaining skills and knowledge at a rate that signifies they will experience skill mastery. We need to know when a student's rate of learning is inadequate so that we can make instructional changes in an attempt to improve learning to reach short-term and long-term skill mastery. We also need to know whether students are maintaining, integrating, and generalizing the skills and knowledge they acquire in order to complete more complicated tasks. Systematic methods for monitoring progress toward goals can provide the information needed to make instructional and intervention decisions.

Progress monitoring is the collection of data that are used to determine the effect of instruction and intervention over a certain period of time. Not all progress monitoring is highly systematic and objective. For instance, in a general education setting, teachers often use grades to indicate whether students are making sufficient progress. Grades are a simple way to convey information to parents about general progress at school, but they are highly problematic for progress monitoring in the way we are talking about here. Grades often involve subjective evaluation. They also are problematic for progress monitoring because they may or may not accurately represent a student's actual skills (consider situations in which parents actually do the homework *for* their children!) and they are not incrementally sensitive to changes that a teacher might make to improve instruction. End-of-unit tests may also be used to gauge progress, but this approach does not allow one to know the extent to which a student has maintained or is able to integrate their knowledge across multiple units. More systematic approaches to progress monitoring are necessary to gauge actual progress in skill development toward goals and are the focus of this chapter.

Progress monitoring can be used to measure progress toward grade-level standards and toward individual goals. Furthermore, it can be used to measure progress toward academic, behavioral, and social-emotional goals. There are currently more tools available to monitor progress in the development of basic academic skills such as reading and math that meet basic levels of technical adequacy compared to those available to address behavioral and social-emotional development, and so we focus on measures addressing academic skills in this chapter. Many of these progress monitoring tools are used within MTSS and RTI models to support data-based decision making (Deno et al., 2009); more information about how teams use this process is presented in Chapter 23, "Principles and Practices for Collaborative Teams." Progress monitoring measures can be used to help develop appropriate and specific annual IEP goals for students receiving special education services, such that progress toward these goals can be appropriately monitored throughout the year and instructional changes made when necessary. More information about that process is presented in Chapter 21, "Using Assessment Information to Make Diagnostic/Eligibility Decisions." The current chapter focuses on foundational concepts associated with progress monitoring, provides examples of progress monitoring tools, and provides helpful strategies for setting goals and making decisions about progress.

Research has accumulated on the effects of systematic progress monitoring; this research indicates that systematic progress monitoring has a positive effect on student learning (Bolt et al., 2010; McMaster et al., 2002; Ysseldyke & McLeod, 2007). When effective progress monitoring tools are used, teachers can have greater confidence in their knowledge of whether instruction and interventions are effective. Progress monitoring allows teachers to know if the student is making adequate progress toward the goal. When teachers can observe a student's amount of growth in a set period of time, then the instructional plan can stay the same. If a student's growth drops below the growth needed, then the student is no longer making adequate progress and a change in the instructional plan is warranted. In order to make these decisions throughout the school year, teachers, specialists, and intervention teams need effective tools to monitor progress.

Characteristics of Effective Progress Monitoring Tools

Although most teachers engage in some form of progress monitoring, there are certain qualities that make some approaches better than others for effective learning rate monitoring, problem solving, and goal setting. In general, we consider more systematic approaches to be the most helpful. Next, we highlight several qualities of effective progress monitoring tools.

Direct Measurement of Basic Skills

By direct, we mean that the student is asked to demonstrate the targeted basic skill. Indirect measurement would incorporate perceptions and judgments about the student's skills rather than asking the student to actually demonstrate the given skill. Typically, *probes* or forms are developed and used; these involve a special testing format well-suited to the direct assessment of student skills in a short amount of time to allow for frequent and repeated assessment (a necessary feature for monitoring progress). For example, a student may be asked to read a short passage out loud or may be asked to complete a set of math computation problems during a set time interval.

Representative Sampling of Skills Expected to Be Taught Across the Targeted Time Period

Instead of only measuring what has been taught, progress monitoring usually involves measurement of what has not yet been taught so that we can detect the actual learning gains a student has made that correspond to the instruction provided. When using rate of improvement during instruction, low scores on baseline or initial probes is not problematic. When only end-of-unit tests are used to examine student achievement, it is impossible to know whether a student actually learned anything. A student could earn perfect scores on every end-of-unit test across the course of 1 year and have learned nothing due to already knowing everything prior to receiving instruction. When only end-of-unit tests are used, it is also impossible to know whether a student has maintained knowledge of what was learned because the student may forget what they learned immediately after taking each end-of-unit test. By testing periodically using a representative sampling of what is expected to be learned within a given period of time, it is possible to track the extent to which a student is truly learning and maintaining new knowledge and skills that they are expected to know by the end of the year. For example, many published reading progress monitoring tools do have a representative sampling of end-of-school-year skills.

Efficient and Frequent Administration, Scoring, and Interpretation

Because limited time for progress monitoring administration is a concern for special education teachers, it is important that probes are easy to administer, score, and interpret (Swain & Hagaman, 2020). The more frequently a probe is administered, the quicker one can know when additional intervention is necessary. This can allow for highly responsive instruction and prevent students from practicing errors. In order for the measures to be administered and scored frequently, and not substantially infringe on instructional time, it is important for them to be brief as possible, while still allowing for valid and reliable measurement. Many progress monitoring tools involve time limits to both facilitate measurement of fluency (which is an important dimension of skill mastery) and ensure that the tool can be quickly administered and easily incorporated into busy schedules.

Sensitive to Small Amounts of Change in Skills Over Short Periods of Time

We want to be able to detect whether students are making adequate progress from week to week and month to month. Other tools, such as diagnostic and summative measures, are not designed with frequent administration in mind. For progress monitoring purposes, it is important that the tools provide accurate measurement across a range of skill levels, given that they are often intended to be used across the entire year as students are developing the associated skills. Depending on the skill being measured, probes can be administered as regularly as daily for academic and behavioral skills. Research indicates that, for reading progress monitoring, reliable and useful information can be gathered by intermittent progress monitoring schedules, and weekly progress monitoring is as effective as every 3 weeks (Jenkins & Terjeson, 2011). Varied progress monitoring schedules can obtain similar levels of accuracy thresholds when data are collected for 9 to 12 weeks (Gesel & Lemmons, 2020). In the case of IEP goal monitoring, the data collection will span the entire duration of the school year, increasing the reliability of the observed growth.

Example Progress Monitoring Tools

Currently, there are a growing number of tools available that can be used for the purpose of progress monitoring of academic skills. Evidence for their technical adequacy has been accumulating. The National Center on Intensive Intervention (NCII) is funded by the Office of Special Education programs and operated by the American Institute for Research (AIR). Progress monitoring tool publishers submit their tools and their technical adequacy information rated by national experts. Descriptions of various published progress monitoring packages and information on their associated technical characteristics can be found at intensiveintervention.org/resource/academic-progress-monitoring -tools-chart.

At the website for the Academic Progress Monitoring Tools Chart (enter "NCII Academic Progress Monitoring Tools Chart" into your search engine) you can examine ratings for commonly used academic progress monitoring tools. Ratings change over time as publishers submit new information to the review panels. Tools are rated on three criteria. Tools assessing progress toward performance standards are rated for satisfactory reliability, tools assessing growth over time are rated for their validity, and all tools receive ratings on whether or not they have conducted bias reviews. See Box 8.1 for a list of tools that received satisfactory ratings.

Several of the tools reviewed at the NCII website stem from the development of a set of procedures that are called curriculum-based measurement; others have developed out of computer-based technologies. We describe these two general types in the sections that follow.

Curriculum-Based Measurement Approaches

Developed by Dr. Stan Deno and others at the University of Minnesota Institute for Research on Learning Disabilities in the early 1980s (Deno, 1985; Fuchs et al., 1984), **curriculum-based measurement** (CBM) involves a standardized set of procedures that allow one to directly measure important skills in a relatively short amount of time. CBM procedures have been developed for measur-

---

BOX 8.1

Academic Progress Monitoring Measures Receiving Satisfactory Ratings From the National Center on Intensive Intervention

At the time we prepared this chapter (mid-2021), the following academic progress monitoring measures had received satisfactory ratings for reliability, validity, and bias review:

- *i-Ready Diagnostic and Growth Monitoring in Math* at Grades 4–8
- *i-Ready Diagnostic and Growth Monitoring in Reading/English Language Arts* at Grades K–8.
- *Star Math* at Grades 1–9 and Grade 11
- *Star Reading* at Grades 1–11.

National Center on Intensive Intervention at the American Institutes for Research. (2020, June). *Academic progress monitoring tools chart.* charts .intensiveintervention.org/aprogressmonitoring

BOX 8.2

Characteristics of Traditional CBMs

- Direct measurement of student performance on basic skills.

- Sampling from grade-level instructional materials of things that are intended to be taught for a predetermined period of time (i.e., usually 1 school year).

- Content sampling is typically stratified and purposeful to represent the same types of items and item difficulty across the measures. Similar difficulty across items and measures is important so that changes in performance across time can be attributed to learning (or lack of learning) rather than changes in probe difficulty.

- Common standardized and timed administration procedures.

- Common, preset objective scoring procedures.

ing student progress in reading, math, writing, and vocabulary. See the characteristics of traditional CBMs in Box 8.2.

Fuchs and Deno (1994) distinguished two types of curriculum-based measurement, one they referred to as "general outcome measures" (GOMs) and the other "mastery measurement." In the intervening years, CBM has evolved and improved. There are now essentially two categories of CBM: GOMs and subskill mastery measures (SMMs). The primary difference between these two types of assessment is how general you want the measure to be, as GOMs are more general than SMMs. The more general the measure, the less sensitive it will be for a single point in time assessment in terms of detecting risk. This is because scores are often suppressed due to sampling content that has not yet been taught. GOMs will also be less sensitive to growth that occurs with intervention since they are more general in their content. Stated another way, GOMs will show growth but expected incremental gains will be much smaller since GOMs are designed to detect growth over a longer period of instruction.

General Outcome Measures

These tools measure important outcomes that require maintenance and coordinated use of many skills. The most commonly used **general outcome measure** is oral reading fluency, which requires students to read connected text that is selected to represent end-of-year grade level material. Students are asked to read aloud from a passage for between 1 and 3 minutes and are scored based on the number of words they read correctly per minute. Oral reading requires students to coordinate many different foundational skills (e.g., knowledge of letter sounds, skill and automaticity with blending sounds to produce words, skill in identifying and correctly reading words that don't fit common alphabetic rules) and represents students' ability to read connected text, a skill that is fundamental to academic achievement. Several different but equivalent reading passages (sometimes referred to as "reading probes") are developed to represent the reading level that the student would be expected to attain by the end of the school year, so that the student's performance level can be assessed repeatedly to measure progress. GOMs are typically used to measure progress toward long-term goals, such as a student reading at a certain rate on a grade-level passage by the end of the school year.

Subskill Mastery Measures

Subskill mastery measures typically involve measurement of more narrowly defined skills. They may be prerequisite skills necessary for generalized performance. For example, before children read connected text fluently, they need to master blending consonant-vowel-consonant (CVC) patterns. The teacher may work on CVC patterns using explicit instruction with modeling, guided practice, and timed practice trials. To monitor growth, the teacher will monitor CVCs using unpracticed materials. Once the student is able to perform at mastery on that skill, the teacher may introduce the next skill target in the instructional sequence. If the teacher wanted to monitor generalization gains (sometimes called "transfer"), the teacher might add a measure of words read correctly per minute to see if improving the specific skill problem produces gains on the goal skill.

SMM is especially common in mathematics because mathematics GOMs have been less successful (demonstrated weaker technical adequacy) relative to reading GOMs. This relative weakness of math GOMs has most likely occurred because math involves a greater number of highly related but distinct skills and a GOM can only sample up to approximately four subskills on a given measure. Children typically need to master more than four skills during grade-level math instruction. SMMs are typically used to measure progress toward shorter-term goals that would occur over a quarter or semester during the school year.

Although curriculum-based measurement tools can be used to measure a variety of important basic skills and to predict performance on other higher-level thinking tasks (i.e., reading comprehension, math problem solving), it is important to realize that they are not designed to accurately measure higher-level thinking skills. They can help us identify many students who are likely to struggle in developing these higher-level thinking skills without additional intervention; however, there are some important skills for which there are not currently CBMs available. For example, although CBM methods have been developed to monitor progress in the development of vocabulary terms associated with science, we are not aware of any common CBM methods for measuring student problem solving in science.

When CBM was first developed, educators were encouraged to develop their own equivalent passages or probes based on material that students in a particular grade were expected to cover across the course of the year. Each probe or passage would include randomly selected material that would be covered during the entire year. Years of research have demonstrated that external measures developed and tested to ensure equivalent difficulty, reliability, and validity are superior for conducting CBM. Because time is a major barrier to the use of CBM, we do not recommend creating your own probes. It is a very time-consuming process and more importantly it is difficult to ensure that passages and probes generated in this way are of equivalent difficulty. It's such a difficult task that even probes developed by researchers have been shown to have equivalency concerns across probes (Chaparro et al., 2018). For most teachers and most students using a commercially available CBM assessment suite is advisable.

Many commercial packages of CBM tools have been developed to help schools and teachers use CBM (e.g., Acadience, AIMSweb, DIBELS, easyCBM, Fastbridge Learning, iSTEEP, SpringMath, Star CBM). The technical adequacy of these measures are reviewed and posted on the National Center on Intensive Intervention's Progress Monitoring Tools Chart mentioned earlier in this chapter. In the past decade, the increasing use and application of computer technology in schools has facilitated administration, scoring, management, and interpretation of data used for monitoring student progress. These published CBM tool packages also come with the use of a database that offers online reports and recommendations for student risk level and instructional level. With these online CBM systems, teachers and teams of educators (see Chapter 23, "Principles and Practices for Collaborative Teams") can nimbly gather data, receive guidance in the interpretation of data, and even print reports that are easy to share with various stakeholders including parents and guardians. These CBM tool packages also build on research which recommends that growth be measured and interpreted seasonally, fall to winter and then again for winter to spring (Van Norman & Nelson, 2019a,b). Some tools (e.g., SpringMath) even link assessment directly to specific interventions in a seamless MTSS application. Since its inception in the early 1980s by special education researchers, the science of CBM development and usage has facilitated the scaling-up of MTSS and RTI. Without sound tools it would be difficult to make frequent instructional and placement decisions about students who are struggling with academics and behavior.

Computer-Adaptive Approaches

In addition to approaches that include CBM as their foundation, there are other technology-enhanced assessment systems that are increasingly being used to monitor student progress. Computer-adaptive testing is a common feature of these systems. In computer-adaptive testing, items are selected for administration as the student completes the test. If a student fails to accurately answer an item, an easier item is presented. If a student correctly answers an item, a more difficult item is presented. This process continues until the student's pattern of performance on the test allows for an accurate estimate of his or her current level of skill. When developed to allow for progress monitoring, such tests can be administered repeatedly across the course of a year, and student scores compared to know whether the student is making sufficient progress. Some examples of technology-enhanced progress monitoring tools that involve computer-adaptive testing include Renaissance Learning's *Star Reading* and *Star Math*, Northwest Evaluation Association's *Measures of Academic Progress* (NWEA MAP), Curriculum Associates' i-Ready, and several measures included in FAST. Some of these measures are also reviewed on the NCII Progress Monitoring Tools Chart.

8.1
PROGRESS MONITORING CHECK

Setting Goals

Identifying goals students are to achieve is an essential part of the problem-solving process. A well-defined goal allows a teacher or a data team to have a target to direct their intervention efforts toward. Progress monitoring is the vehicle that allows the team to adjust their efforts when learning is not occurring at the intended rate. In this section, we describe a variety of considerations for setting goals. In some cases, the calculations and approaches are built into the technology that is used for progress monitoring, but we believe that it is necessary for school personnel to have a foundational understanding of various concepts involved in goal setting.

Level Versus Growth

Progress monitoring tools allow school personnel to examine two different dimensions of student achievement: level and growth. In the past, assessment in schools has focused primarily on examining performance levels. The notion here is that those students who meet an expected level of performance are making sufficient progress; those who are not meeting expected levels of performance are not making sufficient progress and may need additional intervention. As more technically adequate tools for progress monitoring have been developed and used, growth in achievement can be determined and used to inform decision making. Monitoring growth during instruction is helpful because it can allow us to know whether a student's rate of learning is higher than before and can ultimately inform decisions about whether certain instructional techniques are more effective than others for selected students. It is the only way to accomplish midway adjustments to instruction as opposed to summative evaluation of post-instruction effects. Thus, progress monitoring is an essential ingredient of prevention. **Rate of improvement (ROI)**, which provides an index of growth, can be calculated. This is also sometimes described as a slope or growth rate. ROI can be thought of as the change in scores divided by the time between the measurements and is typically reported as gains per week in academic interventions. For example, if a student currently reads at 80 words correct per minute, and 4 weeks ago the student read at 70 words correct per minute, the student's ROI would be (80 words correct per minute – 70 words correct per minute) or 10 words gained over 4 weeks or roughly a gain of +2.5 words correct per minute per week.

To calculate the actual ROI, we recommend the use of Ordinary Least Squares regression, which is incorporated within computer-based progress monitoring programs or can be computed using Excel under the function "slope." Ordinary Least Squares regression provides the line of best fit through the available data points and is a more accurate reflection of actual learning gains over time because it accounts better for the variation of the scores. Determining the student's past ROI can help to set the next goal. ROI also allows teams to adjust the intensity of the intervention. If we want the student to learn at a higher ROI then we will need to increase instructional intensity by adding time, opportunities to respond, or other alterable instructional variables.

Comparison Approaches

In progress monitoring, the term *benchmark* is frequently used. Benchmarks can refer to many different things. Sometimes benchmark is used synonymously with *screening*. In a broader application **benchmark** represents a reference standard for a functional criterion that is associated with longer-term success or failure. Students who are described as "meeting benchmark" are often described as making progress toward year-end academic goals. Some existing progress monitoring tools include benchmarks that are connected to state or Common Core standards, such that a student's progress toward these standards can be evaluated (standards-referenced benchmarks). In fact, some year-end accountability assessment systems have been built such that attaining benchmark at one grade forecasts a likelihood of meeting the next year's benchmark all the way up to college admissions testing (e.g., the Aspire assessment system). In this way, systems can examine progress over the course of multiple years of instruction and attempt to move all students toward an aspirational long-term goal. Other existing progress monitoring tools include benchmarks that are connected to information gathered on the performance and typical growth of thousands of same-grade peers from across the nation (norm-referenced benchmarks). Benchmarks can be very helpful in setting appropriate goals for groups of students as well as for individual students.

When specific benchmarks are not available, or if they are considered inappropriate for certain students, there are alternative methods for setting goals. When information on the performance and growth of similar peers is available, this information can be used and is referred to as a local normative sample. For example, one might identify the end-of-year score associated with the 25th percentile for a given student's grade and use that to inform goal setting for a student who is currently scoring at the 10th percentile or below. Or, one might identify the typical growth rate of someone who is scoring at the 10th percentile and set a goal for the student to have a growth rate that is higher than that growth rate. A related term that is increasingly used in discussions of student progress and that some publishers are providing to help with evaluating the progress of individual students is **student growth percentile (SGPs)**. An individual student's growth percentile is determined by comparing the target student's growth to the growth of similar peers who scored at the same initial level as the target student. A growth percentile score greater than 50 indicates above average growth compared to students who scored at the same level during initial testing. Growth percentiles can be helpful given that growth rates may vary substantially depending on the level at which a student is currently performing. There are also drawbacks to using SGPs because they do not account for the notion that growth is impacted by many factors including the time of the school year, the alignment of the instruction and assessment, and instructional conditions to name a few examples. Further, the distributions of growth rates at any given percentile are collected from large samples for which instruction was not controlled (i.e., was highly variable) so that SGPs are likely to be unstable as decision metrics. SGPs alone may be useful to guide individual goal setting in conjunction with other information described in this chapter. SGPs have not yet met the technical adequacy criteria necessary to be used for decision making in the absence of more compelling instructional information (e.g., dosage, integrity, type of intervention) and in the absence of more extensively evaluated SGP development.

If information on peer performance is not available or is considered inappropriate for setting goals for a particular student, it may be appropriate to use the student's existing growth rate or ROI to inform goal setting. For instance, one might set a goal for an individual student's ROI to increase by a certain amount. However, it is important to recognize that in some cases, setting individual goals that are considerably higher than benchmark levels can be problematic. We have heard of situations in which a teacher set a very high oral reading fluency goal for high-achieving students, such that the goal is far beyond the threshold considered necessary or optimal for comprehension. As a result of such a goal, a student might be coached to merely read faster and not necessarily to read effectively. It is therefore important to keep in mind whether the given goal is an appropriate target for instruction or if a different focus is necessary.

Moderate Versus Ambitious Goals

The above-mentioned approaches are intended to offer some guidance for goal setting. Although there have been considerable advances in progress monitoring because of the technical adequacy of widely available measures, there still remains some uncertainty in the goal-setting process. We know that setting goals and monitoring student progress toward those goals is important and helpful, we still are left wondering what levels are most appropriate. If goals are always set at such high levels that they are never met, this can become very frustrating for everyone involved (e.g., teachers, parents, students). However, if goals are set at levels that are not challenging to meet, this may correspond to less effective teaching and learning in the long run. The challenge is to identify goals that are both possible to attain and high enough to stimulate the use of highly effective instruction.

Some technology-enhanced assessment programs offer goal setting tools that allow teachers to select goals that are considered either "moderate" or "ambitious." A recent study involving such a tool showed that although most teachers selected moderate goals, those teachers who selected ambitious goals were notably successful in terms of students meeting those goals (Ysseldyke et al., 2015). Although more research in this area is needed, we think that it is likely in the best interests of students to set ambitious goals.

In the following Stakeholder Perspective, a longtime school psychologist shares her observations on the shifts in assessment and the benefits of CBM in her practice.

Knowing When to Make an Instructional Change

Because progress monitoring tools are brief, they may not have particularly strong levels of reliability. Scores often vary from administration to administration, and that variation may be due to error rather than true differences in student achievement. When graphed over time (see Chapter 9 and Chapter 11 for more information on data displays), the associated student performance data may show up in the form of data points that are

Kim Hosford, PhD, School Psychologist, Southern Oregon Education Service District and Ashland School District

I have been a school psychologist for nearly 30 years and have worked primarily in rural school districts of varying sizes in Oregon. I also worked in Iowa, where I was able to learn to use curriculum-based measures (CBM). When I began my career in the early 1990s, curriculum-based measurement was a fairly new assessment approach. I had no training in CBM in my graduate program and no exposure in my practicum or internship. When I attended my first CBM training offered by Dr. Mark Shinn, one of the prominent researchers behind CBM, my practice completely shifted. To me, use of CBMs made sense. I thought it was a great idea to use tools that allowed us to directly measure students' skills that could be linked directly to develop interventions. Unfortunately, the full potential of CBM didn't get realized until nearly 20 years later. School psychologists were very much entrenched in the notion that standardized tests were necessary to identify learning issues, and the test creators and publishers were happy to allow that practice to be perpetuated. In Oregon, it wasn't until the Department of Education added a Response to Intervention eligibility for Specific Learning Disabilities (SLD) and required a progress monitoring component for SLD eligibility that CBMs took hold. In my opinion, this was great, but CBMs are not about making eligibility decisions. The real value of these tools is their ability to convey a picture of ongoing student performance in real time, which is invaluable for the "who, what, and how much" of intervention decision-making.

Over the course of the past 15 years, I've been able to use a wide variety of these tools as they've become available. Some are completed in quick, one-on-one sessions, while students complete others on the computer. The wide variety of available tools make the selection process difficult for districts. The tools I have personally found most useful to support school teams in identifying which students need intervention support and the type of supports required are those that assess fluency, that we administer one-on-one, and that we can do with relative frequency. These tools are well crafted, and within a matter of weeks we are able to determine if our intervention is having the desired effect based on the pattern the data present. This alone has been a boon, as it has largely removed the biases from the equation and simply allows us to consider student performance over time given the curriculum, instruction, and environment we provide. This is a far more powerful position as it then allows us to adjust the things we can to intensify, if and where needed, to support student growth. In my practice, in the larger scope of continuous improvement, progress monitoring is one of most powerful approaches we can use to move the system forward to benefit all kids.

scattered and it can be difficult to detect a trend. If someone were to make a decision based on only two initial data points that showed a decreasing trend, a corresponding decision to make an instructional change may be informed by estimates that are not accurate. To avoid making such mistakes, it is important to use specific guidelines for decision making that account for the high potential for error.

First, when making decisions about which progress monitoring tools to use, it is important to examine evidence that publishers provide for (a) reliability of the level scores, and (b) reliability of slope/growth or ROI scores. Higher reliability means that one can be more confident that the associated scores represent true achievement or growth differences. In addition, collecting more data can improve the reliability of the information that you have. In other words, it is often best to wait until you have administered the tool several times to make decisions about whether or not the student is making sufficient progress.

Over time, several widely accepted guidelines have emerged for making decisions using CBM data. Similar to the approach noted in Chapter 11 for behavioral data, data from CBM administrations can be graphed over time and aimlines constructed that connect initial or baseline performance to a particular goal for level at a future point in time. When using this approach, a common guideline, called a data-point rule, is that one should wait until a specific number of data points have been collected before examining the data to make a decision. Some research indicates that it is advisable to make a change after four data points fall below the aimline, assuming that the data are being collected weekly (Fuchs et al., 2014) or more often. This criterion will vary depending on the frequency of the progress monitoring schedule. Similarly, there are multiple methods, such as visual analysis and Ordinary Least Squares linear regression, for establishing and evaluating the trendline before making an instructional decision. It can be difficult for novice educators to make instructional decisions using these methods without training (Nelson et al., 2017), which strengthens the rationale for working with a collaborative team or using technology tools that assist with such ongoing data interpretation.

Progress monitoring and instructional decisions must be informed by the tools being used, the intensity of the intervention, fidelity of intervention implementation, plus other factors such as the time of school year. Teams must monitor when recent data points fall consistently below the aimline in order to determine if an instructional change is needed. A slightly more sophisticated approach involves constructing a trendline and examining whether the trendline has a similar or greater slope than that represented by the aimline. An excellent demonstration of this entire process can be found in an article by Lemons et al. (2014) where the authors use a specific case to demonstrate all of the steps in the progress monitoring data use process to make decisions when delivering intensive interventions. If you need to manually create a trendline and do not have specific software or a database to support you, we suggest using Excel. Enter your data into an Excel worksheet and create a scatterplot. Using the chart tools, you can select layout and then linear trendline. When you plot your aimline on the same graph, you can estimate if the student's ROI is above or just at the aimline. Such a slope would suggest that the intervention is currently sufficient for helping the student meet the goal by the appointed time. If the trendline is less steep than the aimline or has a downward slope, this would indicate that an instructional change is needed. With some technology-enhanced assessment tools, the current ROI (also called growth rate or slope) may be calculated automatically within the assessment system, and so the current ROI can be compared to a desired ROI to know if an instructional change is needed. If the current ROI is lower than desired, an instructional change may be necessary. Other technology-enhanced programs may automatically prompt the teacher that an instructional change is necessary based on an internal formula that is applied to the student-performance data that are collected. The best methods for making instructional decisions continue to be a developing area of education research. Current research suggests that, as in other areas of assessment for special and inclusive education, data teams may be best off using multiple methods (e.g., trendline analysis and the 4-data-point rule) together to decide when to make intervention changes (Van Norman & Nelson, 2019a).

Fairness Considerations When Progress Monitoring

In this chapter we have focused on progress monitoring at the individual student level. If you're working in an MTSS model then you will know that progress monitoring can also be used to look at the progress of a small group receiving the same intervention. If the majority of the students in an intervention group are not making adequate progress, then we have a systems-level fidelity issue. Perhaps the students are placed in the wrong group or the teacher has not been trained in effective use of the intervention materials. Remember when evaluating the impact of interventions that sometimes it is necessary to look at a group of students and not just one student at a time. This level of decision making will fall under the purview of collaborative teams for Tiers 2 and 3. When focusing only on one student at a time, it is important to recognize that tools used for progress monitoring can provide information to indicate that an instructional change is needed, but they do not necessarily provide information on which change should be made.

One mistake that we have heard some school professionals make is to focus on using a progress monitoring tool alone to make decisions about how to change instruction. For instance, some teachers who use oral reading fluency to monitor progress begin to focus entirely on interventions to develop reading fluency as opposed to doing a more careful analysis of other skills that the student might need in order to develop reading fluency (e.g., phonemic awareness, phonics). Although in some cases error analysis can be conducted using progress monitoring probes to pinpoint areas in need of additional instruction, additional assessment is usually needed to identify what instructional changes are needed. Additional curriculum-based frameworks for diagnosing student's difficulties in ways that can help in the design of effective interventions are available. Curriculum-based evaluation (Hosp et al., 2014) and curriculum-based assessment (Gickling & Thompson, 1985) are broad assessment approaches that both include progress monitoring as well as additional assessment strategies that can help identify instructional targets. The NCII promotes the use of data-based individualization (DBI), which is also a framework for closely monitoring a student's responsiveness to a validated strategic or supplemental intervention that is offered through what are typically labeled Tier 2 or Tier 3 services in an MTSS model. DBI offers the procedural pathway from delivering an intervention to progress monitoring a student's response. When a student is not making adequate progress, diagnostic data are collected and the intervention is adapted and progress is again monitored. The curriculum-based evaluation, assessment, and DBI frameworks allow one to link assessment information to a potentially highly effective intervention. Using a standardized framework and considering intervention impact on groups of students as well as individuals will increase the fairness of our progress monitoring intervention delivery systems.

8.2
PROGRESS MONITORING CHECK

PROGRESS 8.1

MONITORING CHECK

Write your answers to each of the following questions and then compare your responses to the text.

1. What are the defining characteristics of curriculum-based measurement?
2. Describe three different types of CBM.
3. Describe the purposes for each of the three types of CBM.
4. Go to the NCII Progress Monitoring Tools Chart and read the review of one CBM tool mentioned in this section.

PROGRESS 8.2

MONITORING CHECK

1. Give an example of a reading level goal. Give an example of a reading growth goal
2. How would you describe rate of improvement to a colleague?
3. How would you describe rate of improvement to a parent?
4. What are some potential problems in using only progress monitoring tools to inform the nature of instructional changes?

PART III
Using Formal Measures

CHAPTER 9

How to Evaluate a Test

This chapter has been one of the most popular chapters of the previous 13 editions of this textbook. Students in assessment courses, teachers, school psychologists, counselors, and school administrators repeatedly tell us that they find very useful a step-by-step guide on how to evaluate a test. They regularly use such a guide to evaluate specific tests that have already been used, such as unfamiliar tests reported in a multidisciplinary evaluation. In other instances, they use such a guide when they are looking for a test that can be used to evaluate a specific student or group of students. There are a number of reference books that provide reviews of tests, but most of these fall short of giving school personnel the specific information they need. The Mental Measurements Yearbook series now published by the Buros Center for Testing at the University of Nebraska includes consumer-oriented test reviews that provide information to promote and encourage informed test selection. Typical test review entries include descriptive information, two professional reviews, and reviewer references. The most recent publication is *The Twenty-First Mental Measurements Yearbook* (Carlson et al., 2020). One can go to the website for buros.org to obtain a complete list of tests reviewed in all 21 editions of the Mental Measurements Yearbooks, and one can subscribe to an online service to read test reviews.

Another useful publication is *Tests in Print X* (Anderson et al., 2022). This source provides information about test purposes, intended population, administration times, scores, price, publisher, and test authors. It does not include information about the behaviors sampled by specific tests nor information on the technical adequacy of tests. Though restricted to review of achievement tests, a useful publication is *The Achievement Test Desk Reference* (Flanagan et al., 2006) intended for use primarily in learning disabilities identification. Finally, school personnel can use as a reference the Tools Charts published by the National Center on Intensive Intervention (intensiveintervention.org). The Tools Charts display ratings of research evidence provided by vendors in support of their assessments and interventions. Ratings are provided via a rigorous, anonymous review process by an external technical review committee of experts who review evidence using specific criteria.

Basic Evaluation Questions

It is essential that testers understand that they—not test authors or publishers—are ultimately responsible for accurate and appropriate inferences about the specific students whom they test. Whether evaluating a test that has already been administered or looking for a test to use, educators deal with the same questions.

- Is the test's content appropriate?
- Is the test appropriate for the students to be tested and the decisions to be made?
- Are the testing procedures appropriate?
- Is the test technically adequate?

Is the Test's Content Appropriate?

Making sure that a test's content is relevant involves more than the names of its subtests. Valid testing of student achievement requires that test content match instructional content. Test and instruction match when what is taught is tested in the same way that it is taught. It also requires testing only content that has been taught. The content of ability tests is a somewhat different matter. These tests usually require test takers to perform some sort of mental or physical manipulation of content. On achievement tests if students are not familiar with the content, failure to manipulate the content does not indicate lack of ability. For example, test takers may be asked to identify the similarity among atlas, dictionary, and thesaurus. If they do not know what a thesaurus and atlas are, they cannot identify the common attribute (a reference book).

The age of the test is also important. Generally, tests that were published or most recently updated 15 or more years ago should not be used unless absolutely necessary (e.g., it is the only test available to assess a specific domain or newer tests lack adequate norms, reliability, or validity). When dealing with older tests, it is a good idea to contact the publisher to make sure that you are considering the most recent version of a test. It is a waste of time to evaluate a test that is not the latest edition or one that will be replaced soon by a newer version.

Is the Test Appropriate for the Student?

Content that is generally appropriate may still not be appropriate for all students of the same age or grade. Students with physical and sensory handicaps often require extensive test accommodations. However, students who are not identified with a disability may also need test accommodations. Such students include students from different language and cultural backgrounds, students who are very anxious or distractible, or students who read or process information slowly.

Some tests can be administered to groups whereas others must be administered individually. Group tests can be appropriately administered to an individual student, but the converse is not true. Individual tests cannot be used with groups of students.

Is the Tester Qualified to Administer the Test?

Some tests require special training to administer. Other tests may require a specific license or credential to even inspect or purchase the test. In addition to having the necessary credentials to use a test, testers must also be thoroughly familiar with the test itself. First-time users should practice administering and scoring the test.

Is the Test Technically Appropriate?

SIn chapters 4 and 5, we discussed the major technical considerations in test development and use. When evaluating a specific test it is necessary to understand that each piece of information is probably not of equal importance. For example, while several types of technical features affect an achievement test's validity, content validity is usually the most important. It is also important to understand that some types of information are seldom provided by test authors and publishers. For example, test authors seldom provide information about the curriculum in which the students in the norm group were instructed.

9.1
PROGRESS MONITORING CHECK

An examination of the technical aspects of a test goes beyond checking to determine if specific information relating to important standards is provided; we also consider the quality of the evidence presented. Evaluating the evidence presented in test materials requires a "prove or show me" mindset. One should expect that test authors will tend to make their tests look as good as they can. Test authors must demonstrate to potential users that their tests provide accurate educational and psychological information that can be properly used to draw inferences about students.

The Evaluation Process

1. Acquire All Relevant Materials

Usually, this means purchasing a copy of the manual for the test. Sometimes publishers will give or lend specimen kits; usually now they must be purchased. Tests are not just sold by the company that owns the copyright; the same test kit may be sold by different publishing companies. In our experience, the company that owns a test's copyright is often more willing to provide a specimen kit.

It is also helpful to have a copy of the *Standards for Educational and Psychological Testing* (American Educational Research Association, American Psychological Association, and the National Council on Measurement in Education, 2014). This monograph provides brief explanations of the various criteria and the evidence to demonstrate that the criteria have been met.

2. Specify the Test's Most Important Characteristics

Generally speaking, what makes some types of evidence more important than others is a function of the students being tested, the domain being assessed, and the purpose of testing. For example, evidence of content validity is usually more important for achievement tests than ability tests; evidence of internal consistency is more important than stability (e.g., test–retest reliability) when tests are given frequently. It's a good idea to make a list of the important characteristics and space to indicate your rating of the evidence provided.

3. Review the Test

We begin a test review by locating the evidence presented by the author. Often, we find neatly organized test manuals that have useful chapter titles, subsections, and indexes so that we can readily find the sections we seek (e.g., reliability). Even when a test manual is organized carefully, we often must extract the evidence we are seeking from large tables or appendices.

When test materials are not well organized or use idiosyncratic terminology, locating the evidence is more difficult. In such instances, we need to assemble all materials. (Because we often need to have all of them open at once, we will need a large workspace.) Then, we begin reading and making notes on the important types of evidence for our purpose: content, testing procedures, scores, norms, reliability, and validity. It does not matter where one starts; however, validity and usefulness of inferences based on test scores are better left for last.

Test's Purposes. We generally begin our reviews by finding the uses that the author recommends for a test. For example, the authors of the *Gray Oral Reading Test–Fifth Edition* (Wiederholt & Bryant, 2012, p. 4) state that their test is intended to (1) identify students with reading difficulties, (2) aid in the diagnosis of reading disabilities, (3) aid in determining particular kinds of reading strengths and weaknesses, (4) document students' progress in reading as a consequence of special intervention programs, and (5) be used in research of the abilities of schoolchildren. Thus, if one of the test's intended purposes is the reason we are giving the test, we would look in the test manual for evidence that the test can be used effectively for that purpose. It is the responsibility of the author to provide that evidence.

Test Content and Assessment Procedures. We first look for a definition of the domain being assessed and then examine the test's content to see if it represents that domain. Some test manuals contain extensive descriptions of the domains they assess. Other manuals merely name the domains, and those names can imply a far broader assessment than the test content actually provides. For example, the *Wide Range Achievement Test 4* (Wilkinson & Robertson, 2006) claims to measure reading. However, cursory examination of the test's content reveals that it only assesses letter identification, word recognition, and comprehension of sentences using a modified cloze[1] procedure. Thus, if we are interested in a more comprehensive assessment of reading achievement, we might find this test unsuitable for the type of decision we wish to make.

We also examine testing procedures. Some tests use very well-defined testing procedures; the test specifies exactly how test materials are to be presented, how test questions are to be asked, if and when questions can be restated or rephrased, and how and when students can be asked to explain or elaborate on their answers. Other tests use less well-specified testing procedures—that is, flexible directions and procedures. In either case, the directions and procedures should contain sufficient detail so that test takers can respond to a task in the manner that the author intended. When test authors provide adaptations and accommodations for students who lack the enabling skills to take the test in the usual manner, the author should provide evidence that the adaptations and accommodations produce scores with the same meaning as those produced by non-adapted, non-accommodated procedures. Generally, the more flexible the materials and directions, the more valid the test results will be for students with severe disabilities. For example, the *Scales of Independent Behavior–Revised* (Bruininks et al., 1984) can be administered to any respondent who is thoroughly familiar with the person being assessed. In any case, the procedures followed during our own administration or use of the test must mirror those that were used in the collection of the technical adequacy and norm data for the test.

It is also necessary to examine how test content is tested. Specifically, we look for evidence that the test's content and scoring procedures represent the domain. Evidence may include any of the following, alone or in combination:

- Comparisons of tested content with some external standard. For example, the Common Core State Standards specify standards for specific content and skills to be mastered and describe what mastery looks like specific to those skills.
- Comparisons of tested content with the content tested by other accepted tests.
- Expert opinion.
- Reasoned rationale for the inclusion and exclusion of test content as well as assessment procedures.
- *Scores.* The types of derived scores available on a test should be the most straightforward piece of evidence about a test. Information about the types of scores might be found in several places: in a section on scoring the test, in a section on

---

1. In a cloze procedure, one or more words are removed from a sentence, and the test taker is asked to replace the missing word with a contextually appropriate one.

norms, in a separate section on scores, in a section on interpreting scores, or on a scoring form.

We must consider if the types of scores lead to correct inferences about students. For example, norm-referenced scores lead to inferences about a student's relative standing on the skills or abilities tested. Such scores are appropriate when a student is being compared to other students, for example, when trying to determine if a student is lagging behind peers significantly. Such scores are not appropriate when trying to determine if a student has acquired specific information (e.g., knows the meaning of various traffic signs) or skills (e.g., can read fluently material at grade level). On the other hand, knowing that a student can perform accurately and fluently with grade-level material provides no information about how that performance compares to the performances of other similarly situated students.[2] If test authors use unique kinds of scores (or even scores that they create), it is their responsibility to define the scores. For example, the *Woodcock-Johnson Psychoeducational Battery III Normative Update* (Woodcock et al., 2001) created a "W-Score" as one unit of analysis.

Norms. Whenever a student's score is interpreted by comparing it to scores earned by a reference population (that is, scores earned by other test takers who comprise the normative sample), the reference population must be clearly described (AERA et al., 2014, p. 104). For example, whenever a student's performance is converted to a percentile or some other derived score, it is essential that the normative sample be composed of a sufficient number of test takers to whom we would ordinarily want to compare our student's performance.

A word of caution is warranted. In developing test norms, several thousand students may actually be tested, but not all of those students' scores may be used. Scores might be dropped for any one of several reasons:

- Demographic data are missing (e.g., a student's gender or age might not be noted).
- A student failed to complete the test or an examiner inadvertently failed to administer all items.
- A student failed to conform to criteria for inclusion in the norm group (e.g., he or she may be too old or too young).
- A score may be an outlier (e.g., a fifth grader may correctly answer all of the questions that could be given to an adult).

Thus, the number of students initially tested will not be the same as the number of students in the norm group.[3]

---

2. We repeat the warning that grade equivalents do not indicate the level of materials at which a student is instructional. A grade equivalent of 3.0 does not indicate that a student is accurate or fluent in 3.0 materials. More likely, 3.0 materials are far too difficult for a person with a grade equivalent of 3.0.

3. The difference between the number of students tested and the number of students actually used in the norms is of relevance only when a number of students are dropped and the validity of the norming process is therefore called into question.

Good norms are based on far more than just the age (or grade) and sex of students. Norms must be generally representative of all students of that age or grade. Thus, we would expect students from major racial and ethnic groups (that is, European Americans, African Americans, Asian Americans, and Hispanic Americans) to be included. We would also expect students from throughout the United States as well as students from urban, suburban, and rural communities to be included. Finally, we would expect students from all socioeconomic classes to be included. Moreover, we would expect that the proportions of students from each of these groups would be approximately the same as the proportions found in the general population. Therefore, we look for a systematic comparison of the proportion of students with each characteristic to the general population for each separate norm group. For example, when the score of a 9-year-old girl is compared to those of 9-year-old girls in general, we look for evidence that the norm group of 9-year-old girls (1) consists of the correct proportions of students of various races as designated in the U.S. census (census.gov/topics/population/race/about.htm), (2) contains the correct proportion of Latinx/Hispanic students, (3) contains the correct proportion of students from each region of the country and each type of community, and so forth. Because some authors do not use weighting procedures, we do not expect perfect congruence with the population proportions. However, when the majority group's proportion differs by 5% or more from its proportion in the general population, we believe the norms may be problematic. We recognize that this is an arbitrary criterion; but it seems generally reasonable to us.

Datedness of norms is also an important issue. Publishers are expected to keep norms updated. While there is no hard and fast rule on how often tests should be re-normed, it would seem practical that norms should not be more than 12 to 15 years old. For this reason, it is common practice for some publishers to publish normative updates for tests that have been in publication for more than 10 years or so.

When making a decision about the appropriateness of a test for an individual student you should always ask yourself the question, "To what extent is this student like those on whom the test was standardized?" If the norm group does not include students who are like those with whom you want to use the test, then using the test to provide scores of relative standing is inappropriate.

Reliability. For every score that is recommended for interpretation, a test author must provide evidence of reliability. First, every score includes all domain and norm comparisons scores. Domain scores are scores for each area or subarea that can be interpreted appropriately. For example, an author of an achievement test might recommend interpreting scores for reading, written language, and mathematics; an author might recommend interpreting scores for oral reading and reading comprehension, whereas another author might use oral reading and reading comprehension as intermediate calculations that should not be interpreted. This recommendation means that for every subscore that will be interpreted, that subscore must meet the technical adequacy standards detailed in Chapter 4 for the purpose for which the subscore is being reported. Next, norm comparison means specifying each normative group to which a person's score could be compared (e.g., a reading score for third-grade girls, for second-grade boys, or for fifth graders). Thus, if an author provides whole year norms for students in the first through third grades in reading and mathematics, there should be reliability information for 6 scores—that is, 3 (grades) multiplied by 2 (subject matter areas). If there were whole-year norms for students in the first through the 12th grades in three subject matter areas, there would be 36 recommended scores—that is, 12 grades multiplied by 3 subject matter areas. In practice, it is not unusual to see reliability information for 100 or more domain-by-age (or grade) scores.[4]

As we have already learned, reliability is not a unitary concept. It refers to the consistency with which a test samples items from a domain (that is, item reliability), to the stability of scores over time, and to the consistency with which testers score responses. Information about a test's item reliability as well as its stability estimates must be presented; these indices are necessary for all tests. Information about interscorer reliability is only required when scoring is difficult or not highly objective. Thus, we expect to see estimates of item reliability and stability (and perhaps interscorer agreement) for each domain or subdomain by norm–group combination. If there are normative comparisons for reading and mathematics for students in the first through third grades, and item reliability and stability were estimated, there would be 12 reliability estimates: six estimates of item reliability for reading and mathematics at each grade and six estimates of stability for reading and mathematics at each grade.

Given modern computer technology, there is really no excuse for failing to provide all estimates of internal consistency. Collecting evidence of a test's stability is far more expensive and time-consuming. Thus, we often find incomplete stability data. This can occur in a couple of ways. One way is for authors to report an average stability by using standard scores from a sample that represents the entire age or grade range of the test.[5] Although this procedure gives an idea of the test's stability in general, it provides no information about the stability of scores at a particular age or grade. Another way authors incompletely report stability data is to provide data for selected ages (or age ranges) that span a test's age range. For example, if a test were intended for students in kindergarten through sixth grade, an author might report stability for first, third, and fifth grades.

It is not enough, however, for a test merely to contain the necessary reliability estimates. Every reliability estimate should be sufficient for every purpose for which the test was intended. Thus, tests (or subtests) used in making high-stakes educational decisions (e.g., special education eligibility) for students should have reliability estimates

---

4. Note that information about reliability coefficients applies to any type of score (e.g., standard scores, raw scores, and so forth). Information about standard errors of measurement is specific to each type of score.

5. Note that information about reliability coefficients applies to any type of score (e.g., standard scores, raw scores, and so forth). Information about standard errors of measurement is specific to each type of score.

of .90 or higher. Also, each test (and subtest) must have sufficient reliability for each age or grade at which it is used. For example, if a reading test were highly reliable for all grades except second grade, it would not be suitable for use with second graders.

Finally, when test scoring is subjective, evidence of interscorer agreement must be provided. Failure to report this type of evidence severely limits the utility of a test.

Validity. The evaluation of a test's general validity can be the most complicated aspect of test evaluation. Strictly speaking, a test found lacking in its content, procedures, scores, norms, or reliability cannot yield valid inferences (i.e., cannot be valid). Regardless of the domains they assess, all tests should present convincing evidence of general validity. General validity refers to evidence that a test measures what its authors claim it measures. Thus, we would expect some evidence for content validity, criterion-related validity, and construct validity.

However, we expect more. Test authors should also present evidence that their test leads to valid inferences for each recommended purpose of the test. For example, if test authors claim their test can be used to identify students with learning disabilities, we would expect to see evidence that use of the test leads to correct inferences about the presence of a disability. When these inferences rely on the use of cutoff scores, there should be evidence that a specific cutoff score is valid. For example, there is much discussion among those who screen children for reading or behavior disorders that the screening tests predict later disorders. Evidence of such claims should be provided in test manuals. Similarly, if test authors claim their test is useful in planning instruction, evidence is needed. Evidence for a standardized test's utility in planning instruction would consist of data showing how a test score or profile can be used to find instructional starting points—and the accuracy of those starting points.

Making a Summative Evaluation. In reaching an overall evaluation of a test, it is a good idea to remember that it is the test authors' responsibility to convince potential test users of the usefulness of their test. However, once you, the test administrator and interpreter, use a test, you—not the test author—become responsible for test-based inferences.

Test-based inferences can only be correct when a test is properly normed, yields reliable scores, has evidence for its general validity, and was correctly administered according to standard administration directions. If evidence for any one of these components is lacking or insufficient (e.g., the norms are inadequate or the scores are unreliable), then the inferences cannot be trusted. Having found that a test is generally useful, it is still necessary to determine if it is appropriately used with the specific students you intend to test for the purpose you are testing. Of course, a test that is not generally useful will not be useful with a specific student.

4. Make a Summative Decision

The summative decision answers the questions we asked in Box 5.1. Are the results of this test accurate enough to use in making screening, diagnostic, instructional planning, and outcomes decisions? The criteria for each of these decisions is different because the consequences of each decision are different. Making long-term life-altering decisions about individual students requires the highest quality of evidence. When making decisions about groups of students, individual errors tend to balance out so a somewhat lower quality of evidence can be used. Regardless of the decision, test interpreters must be transparent about the quality of the data they present.

PROGRESS

9.1

MONITORING CHECK

1. Justify a "prove it" approach to evaluating a test.
2. What reliability estimates should be reported in a test manual?
3. Where in a test manual would you look to learn about the kinds of students who participated in the norms sample for a test? What information would you look for?
4. How can an educator learn about a test's technical adequacy?

CHAPTER 10

Screening

Screening is a familiar concept to most of us. We have participated in screening during our lives in a number of ways, with one of the most familiar being vital screenings when we visit our healthcare providers. Routine checking of height, weight, blood pressure, and temperature allows healthcare providers to note when our well-being may be at risk so that further assessment and possibly corrective treatments can be undertaken to prevent negative health outcomes. For example, an elevated temperature could indicate an infection; high blood pressure could indicate a number of heart-related problems that should be investigated further and either ruled out or treated; and being underweight could signify inadequate nutrition. The screening itself is not therapeutic. Rather, the screening detects a condition that we may not know about, and once we know about it, therapeutic actions can be taken to prevent harm. Routine cancer screenings like mammograms can lead to detection of breast cancer before other symptoms are apparent, allowing for more effective early intervention and saving lives.

Academic screening functions in much the same way. Routine screening to ensure children are meeting expected academic milestones or benchmarks for performance allows us to rapidly detect risk and then ideally do something to prevent that risk from becoming a reality for students. In education, academic screenings typically involve short reading, math, and writing assessments that are delivered in the regular classroom by the child's regular classroom teacher. Generally, the teacher administers these assessments in a single session to the entire class at one time. Assessments may be given in a paper-and-pencil format or they may be administered via the computer. Many commercial academic screening tools exist that permit accurate identification of risk in literacy, math, and writing.

Some teachers reading this chapter may think of screening as the type of developmental readiness screenings that used to be prevalent as part of formal entry into kindergarten or first grade. These screenings are not commonly used (or at least not commonly useful) anymore because they have been replaced by more actionable screenings that are yoked to early instruction and emerging skill proficiencies that when weak can signal school teams to arrange early intervention for students. Developmental screenings are still administered as part of pediatric well visits during a child's early years, but these are distinct from the type of academic screenings on which we will focus in this chapter.

One of the most important research findings of the 20th century has been the discovery that academic difficulties could be detected early in a child's learning, and that when detected, corrective interventions could not only remediate but prevent future problems (O'Connell et al., 2009; Torgesen, 1999). In fact, one of the most encouraging research findings of many decades has been that specific learning disability may be a largely preventable condition for the vast majority of susceptible children (Torgesen, 2001). Critically, academic screening is necessary to realize this protective benefit of intervention.

As a result, Reading First, No Child Left Behind and the subsequent Every Student Succeeds Act, subsequent policy guides (*National Reading Panel* report), and state and local regulatory procedures in K–12 schools related to the Individuals With Disabilities Act (IDEA) have emphasized the importance of early and ongoing academic screening to detect risk. Screening is often described as "universal" because it includes all students in a school as opposed to, for example, only a subset of students about whom a teacher may have raised a concern. Universal screening is important because one purpose of screening is to find students who are likely to fail academically without some form of targeted instructional intensification or support.

Unfortunately, however, many systems fail to experience the full potential benefit of screening when they simply collect and report, but do not really interpret and plan corrective actions based on those interpretations. As Shinn has said many times, "Don't screen if you won't intervene" (Shinn & Malecki, in preparation). The purpose of screening, whether it be medical or academic, is to provide the right therapeutic actions to avoid the bad outcome that would certainly happen if effective therapy were not delivered. So to really understand the power of screening, we must take a step backward and think about the first purpose of screening, which is to evaluate program health or the degree to which the school's educational effort is meeting the needs of most students in the school. In schools where large percentages of students are not meeting expected learning outcome standards at expected grade levels, that is a sign that the educational program is not adequate. It is unfair, unjust, and ultimately not valid to identify individual students in such a context. Rather, the program itself must be identified as flawed in some way. Subsequent efforts to meet the needs of individual students in that setting have to account for the flawed programming by including instructional trials in subsequent assessment. If children make learning gains when given high-quality instruction in short trials, that is powerful evidence that the child does not have a disability. Further, such instructional trials (and widespread student learning gains) can be used to drive system-reform efforts, for example, engaging in literacy improvement in the school or district. In Figure 10.1, Class 1, the class on the left, finds that six of 36 students perform below the screening benchmark at screening, but Class 2, the class on the right, finds that 18 of 36 students perform below the expected benchmark. Class 2 has a classwide problem that should cause the teacher and the data teams to troubleshoot and supplement core instruction for all students in the class before attempting to identify individual students for further assessment and intervention.

Academic screening is now commonplace in schools. Virtually all students in the United States are screened in reading at least once per year. Most are screened in other areas (e.g., math, writing, social-emotional development) and often are screened up to

Class 1: 17% of Students
Score Below Screening Benchmark

Class 2: 50% of Students
Score Below Screening Benchmark

This Class Does Not Have
a Classwide Learning Problem

This Class Has a Classwide
Learning Problem

FIGURE 10.1. In this example, two classes are shown. The first class (on the left) has 6 of 36 students scoring below the screening benchmark, whereas the second class (on the right) has 18 of 36 students scoring below the screening benchmark.

three times per year. Schools often coordinate screening through their supplemental intervention or multi-tiered systems of support structures. Once children are referred for evaluation, a great deal of information is available to the assessment team to consider during eligibility determination and subsequent individualized education planning for students who qualify for special education.

Because collection of screening data is now commonplace, many systems are facile in conducting schoolwide screening each year. The challenge for most systems, however, is correct interpretation and action based upon screening data. In other words, most systems over-collect and under-consume their abundant screening data. In 1975, Maynard Reynolds famously said that "in today's context, the measurement technologies ought to become integral parts of instruction designed to make a difference in the lives of children and not just a prediction about their lives" (p. 15).

In the space that follows, we will offer some pragmatic guidelines for collecting, interpreting, and acting upon screening data so that the protective benefits associated with screening can be attained.

10.1
PROGRESS MONITORING CHECK

Screening Measures Should Be Brief

Many screening measures can be administered in only a few minutes to the entire class at one time. Curriculum-based measurement (CBM) directly measures student's skills in reading by having children read aloud for 1 minute and recording the number of words read correctly in a grade-level passage. CBMs in mathematics directly measure math skill by having students complete problems of a given skill type for 2-4 minutes and scoring the answers as answers or digits correct during the timed interval. CBMs in writing provide a story prompt (e.g., "If I had a million dollars, I . . .") and direct the student to write for 3 minutes following a 1-minute thinking period. Writing CBM is scored in a number of ways, but the simplest is the number of words written in 3 minutes. All of these measures have been demonstrated to yield stable or reliable scores that correlate moderately to strongly with scores on more comprehensive measures in each skill area, and can be used to determine whether a student is experiencing risk. Ideally, the teacher administers screening measures following standardized directions, scores the measures, and uses a web-based system to display screening results by class and student in each academic area.

Screening Measures Should Be Aligned With Grade-Level Content

The measure should be well-aligned with grade-level learning expectations (not too hard and not too easy). This alignment is easy to verify by considering the state standards used by your school, your own school's pacing guide, and the actual content used on the screening measure. Some measures generate composite scores and sometimes these can be somewhat opaque to teachers who may not readily see what types of items are being assessed and what subscores are used to generate a composite score. In addition to examining reliability, validity, and accuracy values associated with all reported and interpreted scores, it is important to verify that the content itself reflects grade-level learning expectations. In mathematics, one problem with many screening systems is that the measures emphasize simple computations that reflect below-grade-level learning expectations. This approach can result in a better distribution of scores (i.e., more normal distribution) but it is an approach that will not work well for screening because it will potentially be too easy for students and students who pass the screening may be at risk to fail the year-end test.

Screening Measures Should Yield Technically Adequate Scores

The National Center on Intensive Intervention (NCII) maintains a website (intensiveintervention.org) and a screening "Tools Chart" that summarizes vendor-reported evidence for commonly used screening tools in schools. The chart can be sorted by grade level and content area so that users can readily identify available tools at their grade level in their area of interest (e.g., reading). The chart provides the vendor-supplied evidence in support of reliability, bias, validity, and decision accuracy in a standard format. Additionally, the NCII review process uses a team of experts in screening assessment to evaluate the vendor-supplied data and provides a "consumer-report" type summary of the quality of the research evidence supplied by the vendor. The chart is a handy way for teachers to verify publisher claims and to select tools that have solid evidence that they are technically valid for screening.

In screening, the most important technical feature is called **classification accuracy**. These are the data that represent the overall accuracy of the measure in forecasting the outcome that we are concerned about (e.g., academic proficiency usually defined as passing the year-end test in a content area). Classification accuracy reflects the percent correct decisions that can be made using the screening measure. In the example in Figure 10.2, we compare the accuracy of two screeners. The first screening measure is reading CBM, whereby a teacher reads for 1 minute with each student in the class and assigns a words read correctly per minute score to each student. In this example, we know reading CBM generally identifies 90% of students who are going to fail the year-end test in reading. In the case of the first screening, we can be pretty confident that students who fail the screening need intervention (to avoid likely reading failure) and those who pass the screening, can most likely be ruled out as needing intervention. The second screening is a hypothetical rating scale. In this example, we estimate that the rating scale correctly identifies only 50% of students who are likely to fail the year-end test. On the second screening, it would be foolish to conclude that students who pass the screening do not need intervention (because we would fail to give intervention to half the students

FIGURE 10.2. This figure shows the accuracy of two screeners. The screener on the left correctly detects 5.4 of 6 students who need intervention and 24 of 30 students who do not need intervention for an overall percentage correct identification of 82%. The screener on the right correctly detects 3 of 6 students who need intervention and 18 of 30 students who do not need intervention for an overall percentage correct identification of 58%.

who really needed it). So in comparing these two screenings, we see that reading CBM correctly identifies 5.4 of the 6 children who will fail the year-end test, whereas the rating scale correctly identifies three of the six children who will fail the year-end test. Data teams would be wise to select the first screening for use in their classrooms.

But the overall percentage of correct decisions attained from a given screening does not tell us all we need to know about the accuracy of that screening measure. It is possible for a screening to appear to attain a high level of accuracy (e.g., 90%) when the screening is actually so inaccurate as to be worthless in a given setting. Let's say that a screening indicates that zero of 30 cases score below the threshold for determining risk, but three of those cases truly were at risk. The overall percent accuracy of the screening would be 90%, but for the students for whom the screening was most critical (the three students who truly were at risk), the test was 0% accurate. A more thorough understanding of screening accuracy can be understood with three values: the measure's **sensitivity**, the measure's **specificity**, and the **base rate** of risk in the setting in which the screening is being used. We will define these shortly, but first we must understand how we decide whether a student is at risk in the first place.

Screening scores and criterion scores occur on a continuum as in Figure 10.3. If we obtain scores for CBM words read correctly per minute for all students in fourth grade, we will see a distribution of scores that looks like the one shown in Figure 10.3.

Reading Screening

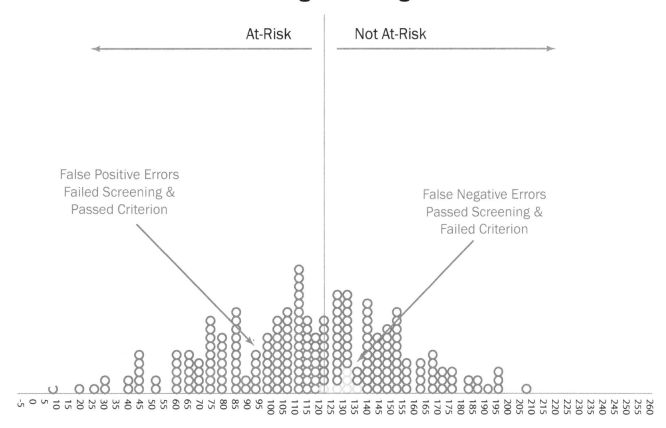

FIGURE 10.3. Reading screening.

We then apply a cut score, which is a threshold of performance above which we say a student truly is not at risk and below which we say a student truly is at risk. In Figure 10.3, 123 words read correct per minute (wc/min) is the cut score that signifies lack of risk in reading. Thus, all students below 123 wc/min will be considered "at risk" in reading, whereas all students at or above 123 wc/min will be considered not at risk.

One of the challenges in the screening literature in education is that the way we separate (or dichotomize) truly-at-risk and truly-not-at-risk groups can be somewhat arbitrary. In medicine, understanding accuracy can be simpler when death is the outcome. That outcome is not continuous; rather, death is binary in nature as one cannot be a "a little bit dead" or, alternatively, "very dead." Therefore, predicting death (and avoiding it, at least for the short-term) is meaningful. In education, "truly not at risk" is often the student who scores at the level of performance that is considered "proficient" on the year-end test. Other **criterion** outcomes are possible in education, too, such as meeting the ACT readiness benchmark in math in Grade 11, graduating from high school, or being admitted to college.

To understand these values, we can think of two groups of students: one group truly is at risk and the other group truly is not at risk according to the outcome criterion of our choice. Each student in these two groups can have two screening results: they can

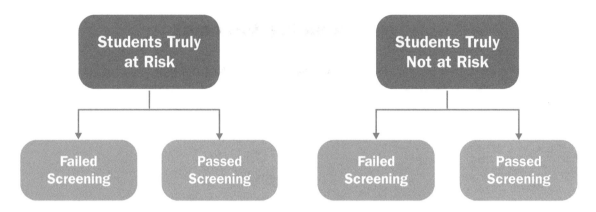

FIGURE 10.4. Screening results of four distinct groups.

pass the screening or they can fail the screening as shown in Figure 10.4. This creates four distinct groups that result when we screen.

In academic screening, just like medical screening, a positive result indicates a problem, so in our case a "positive" case is one that has failed the criterion. This terminology originates from a patient having positive symptoms on a screening, which indicates the underlying condition for which we are screening in the first place. For example, a positive cancer screening is not good news but rather indicates the possibility of a cancer. A "negative" case, on the other hand, is good news in screening. In academic screening, this is a student who has passed the criterion.

Because these are our four possible groups, we can also show them as in Figure 10.5. Now we are ready to understand sensitivity and specificity, which are the most important metrics in screening accuracy. These values are wonderfully practical, useful, and easy to interpret. They go beyond simple correlation to quantify the utility of a screening with a specific cut score used in a specific setting as to the accuracy of the decisions that can be made based upon the scores. So any student will fall into one of the four cells as shown in Figure 10.5, reflecting one of the four possible outcomes of screening. First, all of the students who failed the criterion appear in the left-hand column, whereas all of the students who passed the criterion appear in the right-hand column. Sensitivity reflects the number of truly at-risk students who were correctly detected by the screening (left-hand column), and specificity reflects the number of truly not-at-risk students who were correctly detected by the screening (right-hand column).

There are other classification accuracy metrics that are highly useful in screening, including likelihood ratios and posterior probabilities, and interested readers can read other sources that provide greater detail on those metrics (e.g., Kovaleski et al., in press). However, for all classification accuracy metrics, students are sorted into one of the four cells as shown in Figure 10.5. From these raw or estimated case counts in each cell, all screening accuracy metrics are computed, with sensitivity and specificity being the most basic metrics.

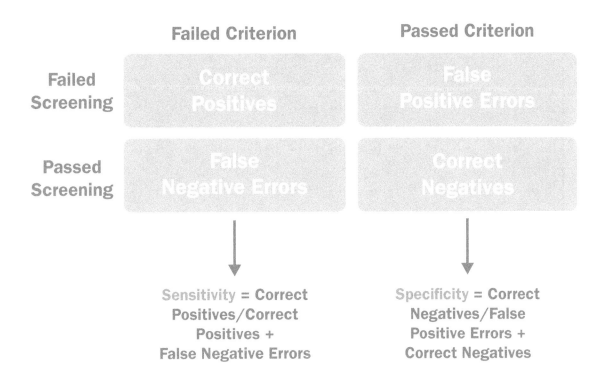

FIGURE 10.5. The calculation of sensitivity and specificity comes directly from the proportions of false-positive and false-negative decision errors.

Let's use an example. In seventh grade, all 207 students participated in winter screening for mathematics. Three CBM screening measures were used and one is shown here in Figure 10.6. In this example, students earned scores of total answers correct in 4 minutes for a screening assessment solving inverse operations using addition and subtraction. These students also received a year-end test score in mathematics later that spring on the state accountability measure.

The proficiency criterion for math is set by the state and on this measure is set at a standard score of 3629 (shown with a vertical line on Figure 10.6). The screening cut score is 6, so students scoring six answers correct per 4 minutes or higher have passed the screening (shown with a horizontal line on Figure 10.6). This allows us to see visually the number of cases that fall into each of the four categories. Looking at the data this way makes it easy to see that the raw number of cases in each category can be transferred to the four-cell contingency table as in Figure 10.7, and from there sensitivity is calculated as 78% and specificity is calculated as 81%.

Looking at the data plotted this way, it is also easy to see that if we move the screening threshold up or make the screening more rigorous and difficult to pass, more students will fail. This will reduce the number of false-negative errors, but it will automatically cause an increase in false-positive errors. The same is true when lowering the screening threshold or making the screening easier to pass (the number of false-positive errors will be reduced, but the number of false-negative errors will go up accordingly). That

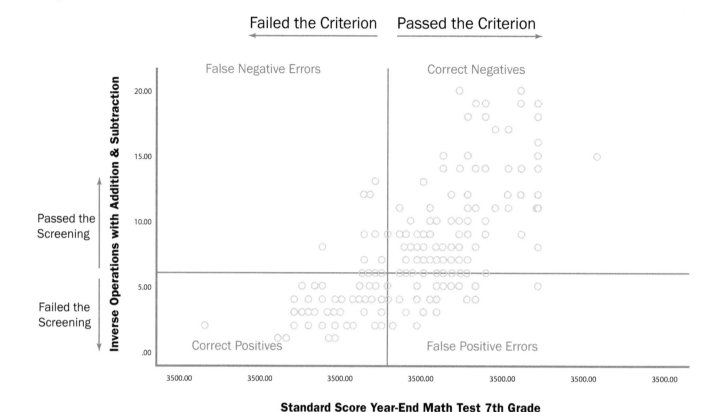

FIGURE 10.6. Screening scores plotted against year-end test scores allow us to see the numbers of correct and incorrect decisions that are used to calculate sensitivity and specificity. (Multiple students can earn the same score, so circles can be superimposed; thus, the number of circles shown in the graph looks fewer than the numbers in the green boxes below.)

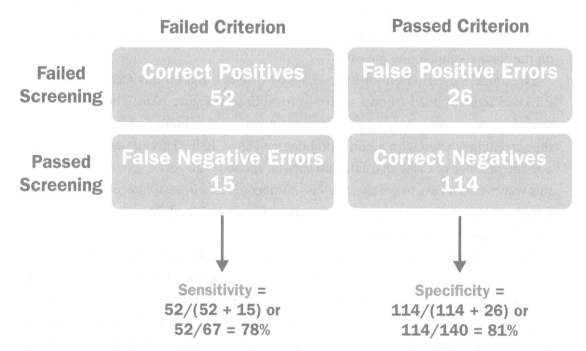

FIGURE 10.7. Using the counts in each cell, we calculate sensitivity and specificity.

trade-off is a reality of screening and is one that vendors must consider when setting their thresholds to be useful.

Thus, readers must understand that sensitivity and specificity must be considered in tandem when selecting and interpreting screening data. Before screening, one cannot know whether a student will be truly at risk or truly not at risk (that is the point of screening) and therefore, neither metric will tell the user the whole story on its own with regard to screening accuracy. Often systems will prioritize sensitivity as the most critical metric at screening, with specificity considered second as an indication of how burdensome the interventions will be. In other words, a screening can be 100% sensitive when it fails every student exposed to it, but this would burden the follow-up systems such as to make the screening useless. The idea is to use the most sensitive measure that comes at the lowest cost to specificity, for example (90% sensitivity/80% specificity is a good balance).

Generally speaking, sensitivity or the capacity to detect (i.e., not miss) truly at-risk students is the most important function of screening. Specificity or the capacity to detect true negatives is the most important feature of diagnostic tests. Sensitive measures are useful for ruling out risk, whereas specific measures are useful for ruling in risk. Another way to think about academic screening is to emphasize sensitive and highly efficient measures at the first stage of screening, which reduces the sample to be screened further and to follow-up with measures that have greater specificity (or will reduce the number of false-positive errors while keeping the true positives in the sample).

Typically, screening tools must meet rigorous accuracy criteria for their data to receive a strong rating on a site like the NCII Tools Chart. On the NCII site, you can select "Tools Charts" and then select "Academic Screening" and the tools chart for academic screening will open up. From there, you can select filters by grade and content area to refine the list. After you have narrowed down your choices, you can even select individual screening tools to display and compare on a single page. The tools chart technical advisory committee includes experts in screening assessment who follow a rigorous rubric to evaluate screening tools on their classification accuracies (e.g., sensitivity and specificity), psychometric data (e.g., reliability and validity), their evidence on lack of bias, and their usability features. The criteria that tools must meet to attain a full bubble (the highest rating), a half-bubble, or an empty bubble are detailed right on the site. You can also click into each tool and read information about the tool including cost and implementation details that are provided by vendors. The tools chart is updated regularly, so we refer readers directly to the site to review academic screenings and select the screening that best meets your needs. Screenings that currently earn high ratings for their technical evidence include Acadience's DIBELS Next, i-Ready, SpringMath, and *Star Reading*. The chart is updated regularly, so we encourage you to look directly at the chart and examine the data that are pertinent to your content area (reading or math) and the specific grade level in which you work.

Screening Systems Must Be Efficient

Most systems can gain efficiency in their screening process. One of the common pitfalls in screening is the belief that giving more screening measures at the same screening occasion will improve accurate decision making. Some school-based personnel will even refer to this process as "triangulating their data." This assumption is problematic in screening because it invites an over-collection of screening data that generally does not result in a more accurate decision, but instead takes instructional time and probably contributes to "paralysis by analysis." In other words, data teams end up with a lot of screening data and then are not sure how to act upon those data, especially if the data disagree. One of the conclusions apparent from screening research is that giving multiple screening measures for the same academic content area at the same time does not improve accuracy. Therefore, teams will be wise to take an inventory of which screening measures are being used in their schools and to pare down the number of screening measures administered. Typically, a single, high-quality screening measure in each key content area is sufficient for decision making. The time spent on unnecessary screening can then be repurposed toward more frequent progress monitoring for children who receive intervention. Similarly, sometimes teams believe that a different measure has to be used to satisfy each requirement that may be set forth by a district. For example, a system may require universal screening in reading for all students as part of their MTSS, and the state may require dyslexia screening. Sometimes, teams believe that separate measures must be administered to satisfy both requirements, which is not true. When a single measure can be administered to satisfy multiple requirements, then we recommend that approach. As a general rule of thumb, the most accurate and most efficient assessment (in time, dollars, and utility) will be the optimal screening measure for your setting.

10.2

PROGRESS
MONITORING
CHECK

Universal Versus Targeted Screening

Teachers might wonder, "Should all students be included in screening? What if the student is being served in special education and I know the student will perform poorly on the screening?" Because the purpose of screening is to identify risk in programs and in individual students, it is important to include all students in the screening process. When all students are included in screening, we can understand the percent of students on track by class grouping and grade level, by demographic subgroup (e.g., girls versus boys), and by other factors that might be important to us in evaluating how well our program of instruction is meeting the needs of the students in our school. For example, we might look at the percent of third-grade students meeting the expected reading benchmark at fall and winter screenings as an indication of how much improvement was attained in the fall semester of instruction. We might further examine the percent of students meeting the reading benchmark who recently moved into the district or who participated in small-group instruction with the reading coach. When we look at the data at the program level, it helps us ask questions about our program effects and make thoughtful adjustments to get better results for our students as a whole. We can only evaluate program effects when all students are included in screening. The other purpose of screening is to find individual students who may be at risk. When a student is excluded from the screening process, they might be overlooked as needing intervention. Schools should take care to include all students in screening and to conduct make-up sessions with students who were absent during the screening especially since children experiencing academic risk are often also children who tend to be absent from school more frequently.

Under What Conditions Might Targeted Screening Be Recommended?

When new students move into the school, the school might want to give students a brief period of acclimation and this can be accomplished by screening when the student first arrives and after a brief period of adjustment to the new school. It could also be the case that when program effects appear weak, subsequent screening might occur more frequently to verify that program effects are improving (or stated another way, risk is declining with program improvements). Finally, when learning is first occurring, for example, with passage reading in first grade, more frequent screening can allow for more rapid detection of risk. To accomplish this, children who have demonstrated success on the terminal skill can be exited from further screening, but children who are not yet at mastery can continue to be exposed to the screening until mastery is expected, at which time children could be recommended for supplemental instruction if they are not at mastery. Schools might also wish to repeat academic screening for students exiting intervention groups to verify success on the original criterion that caused them to be recommended for intervention in the first place.

How Often Should Screening Occur?

Screening should occur at least twice per year, at fall and winter. Ideally, data teams in schools decide how often to screen based upon how they will use the data. That is, screening is conducted to answer specific questions that will lead to specific instructional changes as a result of the screening. Fall screening allows most systems to determine child risk early in the school year and to deliver intervention to children who are experiencing academic risk. Fall screening also provides a useful baseline by which to speculate about program needs and to make subsequent program changes. Winter screening provides a useful follow-up to evaluate whether program changes are having the desired effect and to determine continued or new child risk. Occasionally a spring screening can make sense if the system will use the spring screening data to evaluate improvements made following the winter screening and to plan supplemental instruction that may unfold during the summer months or guide early fall decisions about students for the following year.

Who Should Administer the Screening Measures?

Ideally, the teacher leads the collection of academic screening data in the classroom. When direct skill assessments are used that are brief and meaningful, the teacher is best positioned as the familiar adult to help students perform their best. The teacher also gains valuable first-hand knowledge about student performance. Occasionally, a teacher may be surprised to see a child perform better on a brief timed assessment than he or she might have predicted. The teacher also can observe the types of errors students show and especially error patterns that may be shared by many students, and this information can help the teacher know what misconceptions need to be addressed in subsequent instruction. Conducting screening in the classroom is also highly efficient and allows the teacher to be equipped to contribute to data-team decision making about classroom instruction and individual student risk.

Norm-Referenced Risk Thresholds Can Be Problematic

Because academic screening measures are standardized and norm-reference groups are available for many commercial tools, it is relatively straightforward to identify students as being at risk based on a norm-referenced criterion. In academic screening, however, there are two problems with norm-referenced screening criteria of which teachers and teams should be aware. First, when the base rate of risk is high, the score distribution will be affected and discriminating who is truly at risk in that context becomes mathematically error-prone (VanDerHeyden, 2010, 2011, 2013). Second, knowing that a student has performed below the 20th or 40th percentile on a measure at screening is not the same as knowing that the student has performed at a level of performance for which the student has an 80% or greater probability of failing the year-end test, not retaining the skill in 2 months, or not being able to use the learned skill to solve novel problem presentations. The second type of criterion is often referred to as a benchmark criterion. The key is that it is a level of performance that is associated with some functional criterion that teachers and parents care about (i.e., comprehension, passing a year-end test, retaining the learned skill). Many teachers want to provide intervention to any student who has a high probability of failing the year-end test, not just an arbitrary lowest-performing subset of students. Many vendors use normative criteria to determine risk; others use benchmark criteria. Systems should be aware of which criteria are used by their screening tool so that they can correctly interpret for parents and for follow-up actions. Systems can also evaluate their own datasets over time to verify the accuracy of the screening tools used in their own settings with their own students, asking what percentage of students who failed last year's reading test also failed the winter screening in reading (i.e., sensitivity) (Nelson et al., 2016).

How Should the Screening Results Be Shared?

Screening data should be summarized in graph form with a reference for interpretation right on the graph. Providing a tabular listing of scores does not help teachers interpret the data. Instead, graphing performance and clearly indicating which students are on track and which students are at risk and in need of further assessment and intervention is the key decision of screening, so those data need to be made clear. First, are most students in the class meeting expected benchmarks for performance? If not, what about other classes at the same grade level? Where large percentages of students by class or by grade are not performing as expected, then the first order of business should be enhancing core instruction for all students. Additionally, many systems will consider adding a classwide intervention to bolster academic performance for the class as a whole and provide a dataset from which to more accurately determine which individual students are truly at risk. In classes where many children score below benchmark, screening errors (inaccurate screening decisions) become very likely while at the same time the teacher will feel the impossible burden of having too many children appearing to be in need of intervention. In those cases, classwide intervention within a short number of weeks can greatly reduce the number of students recommended for individual intervention while also making those recommendations more accurate.

In Figure 10.8, we can see the scores of all students in a class relative to the expected level of performance. In this case, most students are scoring in the risk range, indicating a classwide learning problem in mathematics.

In Figure 10.9, on the other hand, most students are performing above the expected level of performance. In this case, only three children score in the risk range. If most students in the class are doing well, then children who score below the expected benchmark can be identified for intervention. Thus, this screening can be used to readily identify the three students for follow-up assessment and potentially intervention.

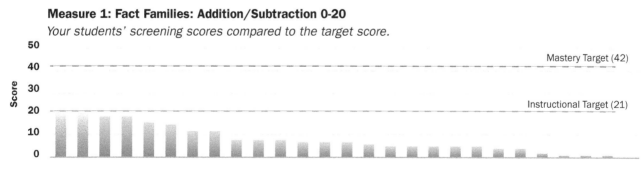

FIGURE 10.8. Classwide screening graph that shows most students in the class are performing in the range considered to be at risk.

Measure 1: Multiply 1 Digit by 2–3 Digit w/ & w/o Regrouping

Your students' screening scores compared to the target score.

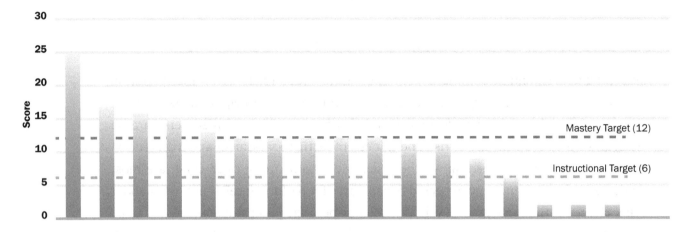

FIGURE 10.9. Classwide screening graph that shows only three children are performing in the range that is considered to be at risk.

What Actions Should the Screening Result In?

Screening itself does not directly produce a benefit to students. Rather, attaining screening benefits requires teachers and data teams to correctly interpret screening data and take action. One of the primary purposes of assessment set forth in this book is to benefit learning for all students, and this intended benefit includes students in special education. The key to effective or even adequate screening is to interpret and take action based on the screening data. The first step is to identify and begin to make a plan to remediate systemic (i.e., classwide) learning problems. These can be addressed by working with school leaders to improve instruction in the classroom. Planned instructional improvements can be implemented, and their effects can be evaluated at the next screening. If the improvements are working, then teams should see greater percentages of students meeting screening benchmarks. The second step is to identify and provide supplemental intervention to students who perform in the risk range at screening when the majority of their classmates are thriving in the same environment. If supplemental and intensive interventions are having the desired effect, then children who receive those supports should move out of the risk range on subsequent screenings.

Enhancing Fairness in Screening

The key to fairness in screening is to understand the reality that screening data without interpretive and therapeutic actions are not useful. When screening does not lead to intervention, the screening data can do more harm than good. Schools may misuse such information to lower their expectations for student learning or to sort students into groupings for which instruction is not really changed or intensified. When this happens, and it is very common, this is a miscarriage of justice. On the other hand, systems and teachers can adopt the following screening practices to ensure that the screening measures produce scores and results that are equitable for all learners.

First, all children should participate in screening, using rigorous grade-aligned content. Second, the results of the screening should first be examined at the program level. When large numbers of children score in the risk range, program-wide improvements should be initiated and subsequent screenings can be used to determine whether such changes are producing risk reduction in the system. Third, data should be disaggregated by race, disability status, and other categorical variables for which students may not experience equity. Disaggregated assessment scores can signify the need for adults to intensify instruction and allocate resources differentially to provide all learners equitable access to the general education core curriculum. Fourth, systems can preserve resources devoted to screening so that they may be spent in instruction by adopting efficient screening practices and using professional time to summarize and act upon the collected screening data.

PROGRESS 10.1
MONITORING CHECK

1. How does screening produce benefits for children?
2. State two purposes for screening.
3. How do you know whether there is a classwide problem or an individual problem?

PROGRESS 10.2
MONITORING CHECK

1. Identify four important considerations in screening
2. Why is it important that screening tests be technically adequate?
3. Differentiate between a false positive and a false negative.
4. Differentiate between sensitivity and specificity.

CHAPTER 11

Assessing Behavior Through Observation

Teachers are constantly monitoring themselves and their students. Sometimes they are just keeping an eye on things to make sure that their classrooms are safe and goal oriented, to anticipate disruptive or dangerous situations, or to keep track of how things are going in a general sense. Often, teachers notice behavior or situations that seem important and require their attention: the fire alarm has sounded, Harvey has a knife, Betty is asleep, Jo is wandering around the classroom. In other situations, often as a result of their general monitoring, teachers look for very specific behaviors to observe: social behaviors that should be reinforced, attention to task, performance of particular skills, and so forth.

When assessment does not rely on permanent products (that is, math assignments and physical creations such as a table in shop or an argumentative essay), observation is usually involved. Clearly, social behavior, learning behavior (e.g., attention to task), and aberrant behavior (e.g., hand flapping) are all suitable targets of observation. Obviously, behavioral observation can be an integral part of assessing physical and mental states, physical characteristics, and educational disabilities as well as monitoring student progress and attainment. Although nonsystematic observational approaches can be helpful for gathering initial information about student behavior, we emphasize the use of systematic observation for making important decisions about whether substantial instructional changes are necessary for individual students due to their behavioral characteristics.

Approaches to Observation

Quantitative or Qualitative

There are two basic approaches to observation: qualitative and quantitative. Through qualitative observation an observer monitors the situation and memorializes the observations in a narrative, the most common form being anecdotal records. **Qualitative observations** can describe behavior as well as its contexts (that is, antecedents and consequences), and usually occur without predetermining the behaviors to be observed or the times and contexts in which to observe. Good anecdotal records contain a complete description of the behavior and the context in which it occurred and can set the stage for more focused and precise quantitative observations. We stress *systematic observation*, a quantitative approach to observation. Although we note in a later section of this chapter some examples of nonsystematic observations that may be useful, we focus most of the chapter on systematic observations. Measuring behavior through **systematic observation** is distinguished by five steps that occur in advance of the actual observations: (1) The behavior is defined precisely and objectively, (2) the characteristics of the behavior (e.g., frequency) are specified, (3) procedures for recording are developed, (4) the times and places for observation are selected and specified, and (5) procedures are developed to assess interobserver agreement. Behavioral observations can also vary on a number of other dimensions, as described below.

Live or Aided

Quantitative analysis of behavior can occur in real time or after the behavior has occurred by means of devices such as video or audio recorders that can replay, slow down, or speed up records of behavior. Observation can be enhanced with technology. For example, tools such as the Swivl™ robot camera sits on a tripod and tracks the teacher as they move around the classroom. After the instructional period, the video gets loaded to a secure cloud storage. However, observation can also occur with only the observer's unaided senses.

Obtrusive Versus Unobtrusive

Observations are called **obtrusive** when it is obvious to the person being observed that he or she is being observed. The presence of an observer makes observation obvious; for example, the presence of a practicum supervisor in the back of the classroom makes it obvious to student teachers that they are being observed. The presence of observation equipment makes it obvious; for example, a video camera with a red light on makes it obvious that observation is occurring. Something added to a situation can signal that someone is observing. For example, a dark, late-model, four-door sedan idling on the side of the road with a radar gun protruding from the driver's window makes it obvious to approaching motorists that they are being observed; a flickering light and noise coming from behind a mirror in a testing room indicates to test takers that there is someone or something watching from behind the mirror.

When observations are **unobtrusive**, the people being observed do not realize they are being watched. Observers may pretend that they are not observing or observe from hidden positions. They may use hidden cameras and microphones.

Unobtrusive observations are preferable for two reasons. First, people are reluctant to engage in certain types of behavior if another person is looking. Thus, when antisocial, offensive, or illegal behaviors are targeted for assessment, observation should be conducted surreptitiously. Behaviors of these types tend not to occur if they are overtly monitored. For example, Billy is unlikely to steal Jayden's lunch money when the teacher is looking; Rosie is unlikely to bully Natalia in front of teachers; and Dillon is unlikely to spray-paint gang graffiti on the front doors of the school when other students are present.

The second reason that unobtrusive observations are preferable is that the presence of an observer alters the observation situation. Observation can change the behavior of those in the observation situation. For example, when a principal sits in the back of a probationary teacher's classroom to conduct an annual evaluation, both the teacher's and the students' behavior may be affected by the principal's presence. Students may be better behaved or respond more enthusiastically in the mistaken belief that the principal is there to watch them. The teacher may write on the chalkboard more frequently or give more positive reinforcement than usual in the belief that the principal values those techniques. Observation can also eliminate other types of behavior. For example, retail stores have long used mounted cameras to discourage shoplifting and now many private homes use digital security cameras to deter package theft from their front doors.

When the target behavior is not antisocial, offensive, highly personal, or undesirable, obtrusive observation may be used provided the persons being observed have been desensitized to the observers and/or equipment. It is fortunate that most people quickly become accustomed to observers in their daily environment—especially if observers make themselves part of the surroundings by avoiding eye contact, not engaging in social interactions, remaining quiet and not moving around, and so on. Observation and recording can become part of the everyday classroom routine. In any event, obtrusive observation should not begin until the persons to be observed are desensitized and are acting in their usual ways.

Contrived Versus Naturalistic

Contrived observations occur when a situation is set up before a student is introduced into it. For example, a playroom may be set up with toys that encourage aggressive play (such as guns or punching-bag dolls) or with items that promote other types of behavior. A child may be given a book and told to go into the room and read or may simply be told to wait in the room. Other adults or children in the situation may be partners of the observer and may be instructed to behave in particular ways. For example, an older child may be told not to share toys with the child who is the target of the observation, or an adult may be told to initiate a conversation on a specific topic with the target child.

In contrast, **naturalistic observations** occur in settings that are not contrived. For example, specific toys are not added to or removed from a playroom; the furniture is arranged as it always is arranged. Increasingly, school personnel gather data in naturally occurring classroom situations.

Two Formats for Nonsystematic Behavioral Observation

Although the focus of this chapter is on conducting systematic observations, we think it is important to highlight two nonsystematic formats for behavioral observation that teachers and school support professionals may find useful: Antecedent Behavior Consequence (ABC) event recording and Direct Behavior Ratings (DBR).

ABC Event Recording

ABC event recording is a qualitative observational method in which the observer records descriptions of the behaviors of interest, along with the antecedents and consequences that correspond to the behaviors of interest. *Antecedents* include what is happening right before the behavior occurs and may include things like what the student has been asked to do or any related teacher or peer communication that occurs right before the behavior of interest. *Consequences* are what happens right after the behavior occurs and may include things like the provision of a time-out, peer laughing/attention, teacher redirection, or teacher praise. To complete an ABC event recording observation, the observer takes notes for a given time interval in a way that allows for categorization of the behaviors observed according to the ABC framework. At times an observer might

TABLE 11.1

Observations of Zack's Behavior

Day:	Monday
Context:	Sustained silent reading: all students in their own seats. Zack was on task for activities other than independent seat work.
Antecedents:	I tell the class to take out their novels and begin reading where they had left off on Friday.
Behavior:	Zack takes out his novel but does not open it. He fidgets a minute or two and then gets out of his seat, wanders around the room, talks to Cindy and Marie.
Consequences:	The girls initially ignore Zack, and then tell him to go away. Zack giggles, and I scold him and tell him to return to his seat. Zack is falling behind in reading.
Day:	**Tuesday**
Context:	Science activity center: students working on time unit.
Antecedents:	I tell the class to write up their observations from their measurement experiments independently.
Behavior:	Zack requires help to find his lab book. After writing a few words, he gets up to sharpen his pencil but ends up strolling around the room. He talks to Cindy and Marie again.
Consequences:	The girls complain that Zack is bothering them again. Zack says he was just asking them about the project. I tell him to get back to work or he will get a time out. Zack is falling behind in science.
Note:	Zack was on task for activities other than independent seat work.
Day:	**Wednesday**
Context:	Sustained silent reading—all students in their own seats.
Antecedents:	I tell the class to take out their novels and begin reading where they had left off on Monday.
Behavior:	Zack puts his head down on the open pages of his novel. After about 5 minutes, he gets up and wanders around again.
Consequences:	Time out. Zack is far behind his peers in completing his novel.
Note:	Zack was again on task for activities other than independent seat work.

also make note of a setting event, or an event that occurs before the antecedent that may influence the student's behavior. For example, if the student didn't eat breakfast or had a disagreement on the morning bus, those situations would be noted as setting events. The academic task can be an important setting event (e.g., math core instruction, small-group instruction, independent seatwork). The ABC information may be used to (a) better define the behavior of interest for more systematic observation in the future, and (b) develop some initial hypotheses about the function of a student's behavior that might later be tested and used to develop a behavioral intervention plan (see Chapter 18 for more information on conducting functional behavioral assessments). In Table 11.1 we illustrate a teacher's narrative recording of a student, Zack. She decided to record Zack's behavior because he was repeatedly getting out of his seat and wandering around the room. She wanted to identify the context, antecedents, consequences, and specific features of Zack's behaviors. The approach is considered nonsystematic.

Direct Behavior Rating

Direct behavior rating is a quantitative observational method that has become more widely recognized and used for both assessment and intervention in the area of behavioral supports. It is also used to facilitate communication about a student's behavioral progress. Although it includes some aspects of systematic observation it does not require precise behavioral definitions, nor does it typically involve specifying the defining characteristic of the behavior or determining inter-observer agreement. For these reasons, we consider it a nonsystematic observation technique. The appeal of DBRs is in their simplicity and in their malleability.

The overall procedure is as follows: a target behavior and observational time period is selected, an individual (typically the teacher) rates the student or groups of students on the target behavior, and the rating is communicated to someone else (typically the targeted students and parents). Target behaviors, numbers of students to be rated, frequency of ratings, communication methods, and any associated reinforcement for behavioral improvements are determined in advance, but can be manipulated to address situational needs. For example, a teacher might decide to target an individual student's performance on following the directions the first time during transitions (e.g., gym class to academic instruction time, academic instruction time to outdoor recess). At each identified transition time, the student would be given a rating on a scale of 0–100% for the estimated percent of time the student followed the directions the first time during the given transition. This information could be communicated to the student as well as sent home to the parents each day. Although quantitative in nature, DBRs do not involve a highly systematic approach to data collection when compared to what is described in later sections of this chapter. Because of this, it may be the case that there is greater error evident in the ratings. However, research is growing on the helpfulness and adequacy of the technical qualities for DBRs (Briesch et al., 2016). Chafouleas et al. (2009) describe their potential for use within a multi-tiered system of support model. You can learn more about this approach and download associated materials at the website for direct behavior ratings (dbr.education.uconn.edu).

11.1
PROGRESS MONITORING CHECK

Defining Behavior for Systematic Observations

Through systematic observations, behavior is usually defined in terms of its topography, its function, and its characteristics. The function that a behavior serves in the environment is not directly observable, whereas the characteristics and topography of behavior can be measured directly.

Topography of Behavior

Behavioral topography refers to the way in which a behavior is performed. For example, suppose the behavior of interest is holding a pencil to write and we are interested in Patty's topography for that behavior. The topography is readily observable: Patty holds the pencil at a 45-degree angle to the paper, grasped between her thumb and index finger; she supports the pencil with her middle finger; and so forth. Paul's topography for holding a pencil is quite different. He holds the pencil with his whole hand making a fist around the pencil and switches back and forth between his left and right hand and so forth.

Function of Behavior

The **function of a behavior** is the reason a person behaves as they do or the purpose the behavior serves. Obviously, the reason for a behavior cannot be observed; it can only be inferred. Sometimes, a person may offer an explanation of a behavior's function—for example, "I was screaming to make him stop." We can accept the explanation of the behavior's function if it is consistent with the circumstances, or we can reject the explanation of the function when it is not consistent with the circumstances or is unreasonable. Other times, we can infer a behavior's function from its consequences. For example, Johnny stands screaming at the rear door of his house until his mother opens the door and then runs into the backyard and stops screaming. We might infer that the function of Johnny's screaming is to have the door opened. Behavior typically serves one or more of five functions: (1) social attention from peers or adults/communication; (2) access to tangibles or preferred activities; (3) escape, delay, reduction, or avoidance of aversive tasks or activities; (4) escape or avoidance of other individuals; and (5) internal stimulation (Alberto & Troutman, 2005).

Measurable Characteristics of Behavior

The measurement of behavior, whether individual behavior or a category of behavior, is based on four characteristics: duration, latency, frequency, and amplitude. These characteristics can be measured directly (Shapiro & Kratochwill, 2000).

Behaviors that have discrete beginnings and endings may be assessed in terms of their **duration**—that is, the length of time a behavior lasts. The duration of a behavior is usually standardized in two ways: average duration and total duration. For example, in computing average duration, suppose that Janice is out of her seat four times during a 30-minute activity, and the durations of the episodes are 1 minute, 3 minutes, 7 minutes, and 5 minutes. In this example, the average duration is 4 minutes—that is, (1 + 3 = 7 + 5)/4. To compute Janice's total duration, we add 1 + 3 + 7 + 5 to conclude that she was out of her seat a total of 16 minutes. Often, total duration is expressed as a rate by dividing the total occurrence by the length of an observation. This proportion of duration is often called the "prevalence of the behavior." In the preceding example, Janice's prevalence is .53 (that is, 16/30).

Latency refers to the length of time between a signal to perform and the beginning of the behavior. For example, a teacher might ask students to take out their books. Sam's latency for that task is the length of time between the teacher's request and Sam's placing his book on his desk. For latency to be assessed, the behavior must have a discrete beginning (like the teacher's instruction to take out their books).

For behaviors with discrete beginnings and endings, we often count **frequency**—that is, the number of times the behaviors occur. When behavior is counted during variable time periods, frequencies are usually converted to rates. Using rate of behavior allows observers to compare the occurrence of behavior across different time periods and settings. For example, three episodes of out-of-seat behavior in 15 minutes may be converted to a rate of 12 per hour.

Alberto and Troutman (2005) suggest that frequency should not be used under two conditions: (1) when the behavior occurs at such a high rate that it cannot be counted accurately (e.g., many stereotypic behaviors, such as foot tapping, can occur almost constantly) and (2) when the behavior occurs over a prolonged period of time (e.g., cooperative play during a game of Monopoly).

Amplitude refers to the intensity of the behavior. In many settings, amplitude can be measured precisely (e.g., with noise meters). However, in the classroom, it is usually estimated with less precision. For example, amplitude can be estimated using a rating scale that calibrates the amplitude of the behavior (e.g., crying might be scaled as "whimpering," "sobbing," "crying," and "screaming"). Amplitude may also be calibrated in terms of its objective or subjective impact on others. For example, the objective impact of hitting might be scaled as "without apparent physical damage," "resulting in bruising," and "causing bleeding." More subjective behavior ratings estimate the internal impact on others; for example, a student's humming could be scaled as "does not disturb others," "disturbs students seated nearby," or "disturbs students in the adjoining classroom."

Selecting the Characteristic to Measure

The behavioral characteristic to be assessed should make sense; we should assess the most relevant aspect of behavior in a particular situation. For example, if Burl is wandering around the classroom during the reading period, observing the duration of that behavior makes more sense than observing the frequency, latency, or amplitude of the behavior. This is because it is the length of time away from his academic work that is the primary problem rather than the number of times he is away from his work. If Camilla's teacher is concerned about her loud utterances, amplitude may be the most salient characteristic to observe. If Molly is always slow to follow directions, observing her latency makes more sense than assessing the frequency or amplitude of her behavior. For most behaviors, however, frequency and duration are the characteristics measured.

Sampling Behavior

As with any assessment procedure, we can assess the entire domain if it is finite and convenient. If it is not, we can sample from the domain. Important dimensions for sampling behavior include the contexts in which the behaviors occur, the times at which the behaviors occur, and the behaviors themselves.

Contexts

When specific behaviors become the targets of intervention, it is useful to measure the behavior in a variety of contexts. Usually, the sampling of contexts is purposeful rather than random. We might want to know, for example, how Jesse's behavior in the resource room differs from his behavior in the general education classroom. Consistent or inconsistent performance across settings and contexts can provide useful information about what events might set the occasion for the behavior. Differences between the settings in which a behavior does and does not occur can provide potentially useful hypotheses about *setting events* (that is, environmental events that set the occasion for the performance of an action) and *discriminative stimuli* (that is, stimuli that are consistently present when a behavior is reinforced and serve to bring out behavior even in the absence of the original reinforcer).[1] For example, one of the authors of this book has a cat that only meows outside a child's door in the morning when the alarm has signaled that food will be forthcoming (because the feeder is now awake). The alarm is the discriminative stimulus that signals food will be available, which occasions the cat to meow and probably the feeder to feed him faster, thereby reinforcing meowing. Bringing behavior under the control of a discriminative stimulus is often an effective way of modifying it. For example, students might be taught to finish their work quickly when the "activity bank for early finishers" is available at school.

Similarly, consistent or inconsistent performance across settings and contexts can provide useful information about how the consequences of a behavior are affecting that behavior. Some consequences of a behavior maintain, increase, or decrease behavior. Thus, manipulating the consequences of a behavior can increase or decrease its occurrence. For example, assume that Joey's friends usually laugh and congratulate him when he makes a sexist remark and that Joey is reinforced by his friends' behavior. If

---

1. Discriminative stimuli are not conditioned stimuli in the Pavlovian sense that they elicit reflexive behavior. Discriminative stimuli provide a signal to the individual to engage in a particular behavior because that behavior has been reinforced in the presence of that signal.

his friends could be made to stop laughing and congratulating him, Joey would probably make fewer sexist remarks.

Times

With the exception of some criminal acts, few behaviors are noteworthy unless they happen more than once. Behavioral recurrence over time is termed **stability** or **maintenance**. In a person's lifetime, there are almost an infinite number of times to exhibit a particular behavior. Moreover, it is probably impossible and certainly unnecessary to observe a person continuously during his or her entire life. Thus, temporal sampling is always performed, and any single observation is merely a sample from the person's behavioral domain.

Time sampling always requires the establishment of blocks of time, termed **observation sessions**, in which observations will be made. A session might consist of a continuous period of time (e.g., 1 school day). More often, sessions are discontinuous blocks of time (e.g., every Monday for a semester or during daily reading time). It is important to remember that any observation is simply a sampling of behavior at a specific time and for a period of time. Thus, we are always making inferences to how a person behaves in a larger timeframe and in any larger sample of behavior.

Continuous Recording

Observers can record behavior continuously within sessions. They count each occurrence of a behavior in the observation session; they can time the duration or latency of each occurrence within the observation session.

When the observation session is long (e.g., when it spans several days), continuous sampling can be very expensive and is often intrusive. Two options are commonly used to estimate behavior in very long observation sessions: the use of rating scales and time sampling. In the first option, rating scales are used to estimate one (or more) of the four characteristics of behavior. Following are some examples of such ratings:

- *Frequency:* A parent might be asked to rate the frequency of a behavior. How often does Paige usually pick up her toys—always, frequently, seldom, never?
- *Duration:* A parent might be asked to rate how long Bernie typically watches TV each night—more than 3 hours, 2 or 3 hours, 1 or 2 hours, or less than 1 hour?
- *Latency:* A parent might be asked to rate how quickly Marisa usually responds to requests—immediately, quickly, slowly, or not at all (ignores requests)?
- *Amplitude:* A parent might be asked to rate how much of a fuss Jessica usually makes at bedtime—screams, cries, begs to stay up, or goes to bed without fuss?

In the second observation option, duration and frequency are sampled systematically during observation intervals. Three different sampling plans have been advocated: whole-interval recording, partial-interval recording, and momentary time sampling.

Time Sampling

Continuous observation requires the expenditure of more resources than does discontinuous observation. Therefore, it is common to observe for a sample of times within an observation session.

In **interval sampling**, an observation session is subdivided into intervals during which behavior is observed. Usually, observation intervals of equal length are spaced throughout the session, although the recording and observation intervals need not be the same length. Three types of interval sampling and scoring are common.

In **whole-interval sampling**, a behavior is scored as having occurred only when it occurs throughout the entire interval. Thus, it is scored only if it is occurring when the interval begins and continues through the end of the interval.

Partial-interval sampling is quite similar to whole-interval recording. The difference between the two procedures is that in partial-interval recording, an occurrence is scored if it occurs during any part of the interval. Thus, if a behavior begins before the interval begins and ends within the interval, an occurrence is scored; if a behavior starts after the beginning of the interval, an occurrence is scored; if two or more episodes of behavior begin and end within the interval, one occurrence is scored.

Momentary time sampling is the most efficient sampling procedure. An observation session is subdivided into intervals. If a behavior is occurring at the last moment of the interval, an occurrence is recorded; if the behavior is not occurring at the last moment of the interval, a nonoccurrence is recorded. For example, suppose we observe Robin during her 20-minute reading period. We first select the interval length (e.g., 10 seconds). At the end of the first 10-second interval, we observe if the behavior is occurring; at the end of the second 10-second interval, we again observe. We continue observing until we have observed Robin at the end of the 60th 10-second interval.

Salvia and Hughes (1990) summarized a number of studies investigating the accuracy of these time-sampling procedures. Both whole-interval and partial-interval sampling procedures provide inaccurate estimates of duration and frequency.[2] Momentary time sampling provides an unbiased estimate of the proportion of time that is very accurate when small intervals are used (that is, 10- to 15-second intervals). Continuous recording with shorter observation sessions is the better method of estimating the frequency of a behavior.

Behaviors

Teachers and psychologists may be interested in measurement of a particular behavior or a constellation of behaviors thought to represent a trait (e.g., cooperation). When an observer views a target behavior as important in and of itself, only that specific behavior is observed. However, when a specific behavior is thought to be one element in a

---

2. Suen and Ary (1989) have provided procedures whereby the sampled frequencies can be adjusted to provide accurate frequency estimates, and the error associated with estimates of prevalence can be readily determined for each sampling plan.

constellation of behaviors, other important behaviors within the constellation must also be observed in order to establish the content validity of the behavioral constellation. For example, if taking turns on a slide were viewed as one element of cooperation, we should also observe other behaviors indicative of cooperation (such as taking turns on other equipment, following the rules of games, and working with others to attain a common goal). Each of the behaviors in a behavioral constellation can be treated separately or aggregated for the purposes of observation and reporting.

Observations are usually conducted on two types of behavior. First, we regularly observe behavior that is desirable and that we are trying to increase. Behavior of this type includes all academic performances (e.g., oral reading or science knowledge) and prosocial behavior (e.g., cooperative behavior or polite language). Second, we regularly observe behavior that is undesirable or may indicate a disabling condition. These behaviors are harmful, stereotypic, inappropriately infrequent, or inappropriate at the times exhibited.

- *Harmful behavior:* Behavior that is self-injurious or physically dangerous to others is almost always targeted for intervention. Self-injurious behavior includes such actions as head banging, eye gouging, self-biting or self-hitting, smoking, and drug abuse. Potentially harmful behavior can include leaning back in a desk or being careless with reagents in a chemistry experiment. Behaviors harmful to others are those that directly inflict injury (e.g., hitting or stabbing) or are likely to injure others (e.g., pushing other students on stairs or subway platforms, bullying, or verbally instigating physical altercations). Unusually aggressive behavior may also be targeted for intervention. Although most students will display aggressive behavior, some children go far beyond what can be considered typical or acceptable. These students may be described as hot-tempered, quick-tempered, or volatile. Overly aggressive behavior may be physical or verbal. In addition to the possibility of causing physical harm, high rates of aggressive behavior may isolate the aggressor socially.
- *Stereotypic behavior:* Stereotypic behaviors, or stereotypies (e.g., hand flapping, rocking, and certain verbalizations such as inappropriate shrieks), are outside the realm of culturally normative behavior. Such behavior calls attention to students and marks them as behaving in ways that are developmentally atypical or unusual to untrained observers. These behaviors are often physically and emotionally exhausting for the student exhibiting the behavior and have been demonstrated to interfere with skill acquisition. Stereotypic behaviors are often targeted for intervention.
- *Infrequent or absent desirable behavior:* Incompletely developed behavior, especially behavior related to physiological development (e.g., walking), is often targeted for intervention. Intervention usually occurs when development of these behaviors will enable desirable functional skills or social acceptance. Shaping is usually

used to develop absent behavior, whereas reinforcement is used to increase the frequency of behavior that is within a student's repertoire but exhibited at rates that are too low.

- *Normal behavior exhibited in inappropriate contexts:* Many behaviors are appropriate in very specific contexts but are considered inappropriate or even abnormal when exhibited in other contexts. Usually, the problems caused by behavior in inappropriate contexts are attributed to lack of stimulus control. Behavior that is commonly called "private" falls into this category; elimination and sexual activity are two examples. The goal of intervention should be not to get rid of these behaviors but to confine them to socially appropriate conditions. Behavior that is often called "disruptive" also falls into this category. For example, running and yelling are very acceptable and normal when exhibited on the playground; they are disruptive in a classroom.

A teacher may decide on the basis of logic and experience that a particular behavior should be modified. For example, harmful behavior should not be tolerated in a classroom or school, and behavior that is a prerequisite for learning academic material must be developed. In other cases, a teacher may seek the advice of a colleague, supervisor, or parent about the desirability of intervention. For example, a teacher might not know whether certain behavior is typical of a student's culture. In yet other cases, a teacher might rely on the judgments of students or adults as to whether a particular behavior is troublesome or distracting for them. For example, are others bothered when Bob reads problems aloud during arithmetic tests? To ascertain whether a particular behavior bothers others, teachers can ask students directly, have them rate disturbing or distracting behavior, or perhaps use sociometric techniques to learn whether a student is being rejected or isolated because of his or her behavior. The sociometric technique is a method for evaluating the social acceptance of individual pupils and the social structure of a group: Students complete a form indicating their choice of companions for seating, work, or play. Teachers look at the number of times an individual student is chosen by others. They also look at who chooses whom. Because children learn best in environments where the opportunity to earn reinforcement is high, the likelihood of punishment is low, and the child feels a sense of acceptance and belonging. The teacher can be a key actor in helping adjust the environment to better support the behavior of all students and to create an effective learning space for children. The teacher can also be a key actor in helping children develop skills to improve the alignment between behavior and classroom norms and student behavioral and social skill.

For infrequent prosocial behavior or frequent disturbing behavior, a teacher may wish to get a better idea of the magnitude and pervasiveness of the problem before initiating a comprehensive observational analysis. Casual observation can provide information about the frequency and amplitude of the behavior; carefully noting the antecedents, consequences, and contexts may provide useful information about possible interventions if an intervention is warranted. If casual observations are made, anecdotal records of these casual observations should be maintained.

Conducting Systematic Observations

Preparation

Careful preparation is essential to obtaining accurate and valid observational data that are useful in decision making. Five steps should guide the preparation for systematic observation:

1. *Define target behaviors.*
    *   Use definitions that describe behavior in observable terms.
    *   Avoid references to unobservable, internal processes (e.g., understanding or appreciating).
    *   Anticipate potentially difficult discriminations and provide examples of instances and noninstances of the behavior. Include subtle instances of the target behavior, and use related behaviors and behavior with similar topographies as noninstances.
    *   State the characteristic of the behavior that will be measured (e.g., frequency or latency).

2. *Select contexts.* Observe the target behavior systematically in at least three contexts: the context in which the behavior was noted as troublesome (e.g., in reading instruction), a similar context (e.g., in math instruction), and a dissimilar context (e.g., in physical education or recess).

3. *Select an observation schedule.*
    *   Choose the session length. In schools, session length is usually related to instructional periods or blocks of time within an instructional period (e.g., 15 minutes in the middle of small-group reading instruction).
    *   Decide between continuous and discontinuous observation. The choice of continuous or discontinuous observation will depend on the resources available and the specific behaviors that are to be observed. When very low-frequency behavior or behavior that must be stopped (e.g., physical assaults) is observed, continuous recording is convenient and efficient. For other behavior, discontinuous observation is usually preferred, and momentary time sampling is usually the easiest and most accurate for teachers and psychologists to use. When a discontinuous observation schedule is used, the observer requires some equipment to signal exactly when observation is to occur. This can be facilitated through use of computer programs or audio recording devices. One student or several students in sequence may be ob-

served. For example, three students can be observed in a series of 5-second intervals. A computer tablet or other audio device would signal a need to record every 5 seconds. On the first signal, Jim would be observed; on the second signal, Erin would be observed; on the third signal, Amanda would be observed; on the fourth signal, Jim would be observed again; and so forth.

4. *Develop recording procedures.* The recording of observations must also be planned. When a few students are observed for the occurrence of relatively infrequent behaviors, simple procedures can be used. The behaviors can be observed continuously and counted using a tally sheet or a wrist counter. When time sampling is used, observations must be recorded for each time interval; thus, some type of recording form is required. In the simplest form, the recording sheet contains identifying information (e.g., name of target student, name of observer, date and time of observation session, and observation-interval length) and two columns. The first column shows the time interval, and the second column contains space for the observer to indicate whether the behavior occurred during each interval. More complicated recording forms may be used for multiple behaviors and/or multiple students. When multiple behaviors are observed, they are often given code numbers. For example, "out of seat" might be coded as 1, "in seat but off task" might be coded as 2, "in seat and on task" might be coded as 3, and "no opportunity to observe" might be coded as 4. Such codes should be included on the observation record form. Figure 11.1 shows a simple form on which to record multiple behaviors of students. The observer writes the code numbers in the box corresponding to the interval. Complex observational systems tend to be less accurate than simple ones. Complexity increases as a function of the number of different behaviors that are assessed and the number of individuals who are observed. Moreover, both the proportion of target individuals to total individuals and the proportion of

Observer: *Mr. Kowalski*

Date: *2/15/21*

Times of observation: *10:15 to 11:00*

Observation interval: *10 sec*

Instructional activity: *Oral reading*

Students observed:

S1 = *Henry J.*
S2 = *Bruce H.*
S3 = *Joyce W.*

Codes:

1 = out of seat
2 = in seat but off task
3 = in seat, on task
4 = no opportunity to observe

	S1	S2	S3
1	___	___	___
2	___	___	___
3	___	___	___
4	___	___	___
5	___	___	___
.			
.			
.			
179	___	___	___
180	___	___	___

FIGURE 11.1. A simple recording form for three students and two behaviors.

target behaviors observed to the number of target behaviors to be recorded also have an impact on accuracy. The surest way to reduce inaccuracies is to keep things relatively simple.

5. *Select the means of observation.* The choice of human observers or technology tools will depend on the availability of resources. If electronic recorders are available and can be used in the desired environments and contexts, they may be appropriate when continuous observation is warranted. If other personnel are available, they can be trained to observe and record the target behaviors accurately. Training should include didactic instruction in defining the target behavior, the use of time sampling (if it is to be used), and the way in which to record behavior, as well as practice in using the observation system. Training is always continued until the desired level of accuracy is reached. Observers' accuracy is evaluated by comparing each observer's responses with those of the others or with a criterion rating (usually a previously scored videotape). Generally, very high agreement is required before anyone can assume that observers are ready to conduct observations independently. Ultimately, the decision of how to collect the data should also be based on efficiency. For example, if it takes longer to desensitize students to an obtrusive video recorder than it takes to train observers, then human observers are preferred.

Data Gathering and Types of Error

Observers should prepare a checklist of equipment and materials that will be used during the observation and assemble everything that is needed, including an extra supply of recording forms, spare pens or pencils, and something to write on (e.g., a clipboard or tabletop). When technology recording tools (e.g., an online app, digital camera, or a computer tablet) are used, equipment should be checked before every observation session to make sure it is in good working condition and fully charged. Also, before the observation session, the observer should check the setting to locate appropriate vantage points for equipment or furniture. During observation, care should be taken to conduct the observations as planned. Thus, the observer should make sure that he or she adheres to the definitions of behavior, the observation schedules, and recording protocols. Careful preparation can head off trouble.

As with any type of assessment information, two general sources of error can reduce the accuracy of observation. **Random error** in observational processes can result in over or underestimates of behavior. **Systematic error** in observational processes reflects consistent errors that (once identified) can be predicted; they bias the data in a consistent direction—for example, behavior may be systematically overcounted or undercounted.

Random Error

Random errors in observation and recording usually affect observer agreement. Observers may forget behavior codes, or they may use the recording forms incorrectly. Because changes in agreement can signal that something is wrong, the accuracy of observational data should be checked periodically. The usual procedure is to have two people observe and record on the same schedule in the same session. The two records are then compared, and an index of agreement (e.g., point-to-point agreement) is computed. Poor agreement suggests the need for retraining or for revision of the observation procedures. To alleviate some of these problems, we can provide periodic retraining and allow observers to keep the definitions and codes for target behaviors with them. Finally, when observers know that their accuracy is being systematically checked, they are usually more accurate. Thus, observers should not be told when they are being observed but to expect their observations to be checked.

One of the most vexing factors affecting the accuracy of observations is the incorrect recording of correctly observed behavior. Even when observers have applied the criterion for the occurrence of a behavior correctly, they may record their decision incorrectly. For example, if 1 is used to indicate occurrence and 0 is used to indicate nonoccurrence, the observer might accidentally record 0 for a behavior that has occurred. Inaccuracy can be attributed to three related factors.

Lack of familiarity with the recording system: Observers definitely need practice in using a recording system when several behaviors or several students are to be observed. They also need practice when the target behaviors are difficult to define or when they are difficult to observe.

Insufficient time to record: Sufficient time must be allowed to record the occurrence of behavior. Problems can arise when using momentary time sampling if the observation intervals are spaced too closely (e.g., 1- or 5-second intervals). Observers who are counting several different high-frequency behaviors may record inaccurately. Generally, inadequate opportunities for observers to record can be circumvented by electronic recording of the observation session; when observers can stop and replay segments of interest, they essentially have unlimited time to observe and record.

Lack of concentration: It may be difficult for observers to remain alert for long periods of time (e.g., 1 hour), especially if the target behavior occurs infrequently and is difficult to detect. Observers can reduce the time that they must maintain vigilance by taking turns with several observers or recording observation sessions for later evaluation. Similarly, when it is difficult to maintain vigilance because the observational context is noisy, busy, or otherwise distracting, electronic recording may be useful in focusing on target subjects and eliminating ambient noise. Inaccurate observation is sometimes attributed to lack of motivation on the part of an observer. Motivation can be increased by providing rewards and feedback, stressing the importance of the observations, reducing the length of observation sessions, and not allowing observation sessions to become routine.

Systematic Error

Systematic errors are difficult to detect through inter-observer agreement procedures because they may likely influence all observers' ratings in the same direction at the same time. To minimize such error, three steps can be taken.

1. *Guard against unintended changes in the observation process.*[3] When assessment is carried out over extended periods of time, observers may talk to each other about the definitions that they are using or about how they cope with difficult discriminations. Consequently, one observer's departure from standardized procedures may spread to other observers. When the observers change together, modifications of the standard procedures and definitions will not be detected by examining interobserver agreement. Techniques for reducing changes in observers over time include keeping the scoring criteria available to observers, meeting with the observers on a regular basis to discuss difficulties encountered during observation, and providing periodic retraining.

2. *Desensitize students.* The introduction of equipment or new adults into a classroom, as well as changes in teacher routines, can signal to students that observations are going on. Overt measurement can alter the target behavior or the topography of the behavior. Usually, the pupil change is temporary. For example, when Janey knows that she is being observed, she may be more accurate, deliberate, or compliant. However, as observation becomes a part of the daily routine, students' behavior usually returns to what is typical for them. This return to typical patterns of behavior functionally defines desensitization. The data generated from systematic observation should not be used until the students who are observed are no longer affected by the observation procedures and equipment or personnel. However, sometimes the change in behavior is permanent. For example, if a teacher was watching for the extortion of lunch money, Robbie might wait until no observers were present or might demand the money in more subtle ways. In such cases, valid data would not be obtained through overt observation, and either different procedures would have to be developed or the observation would have to be abandoned.

3. *Minimize observer expectancies.* Sometimes, what an observer believes will happen affects what is seen and recorded. For example, if an observer expects an intervention to increase a behavior, that observer might unconsciously alter the criteria for evaluating that behavior or might evaluate approximations of the target behavior as having occurred. The more subtle or complex the target behavior, the more susceptible it may be to expectation effects. The easiest way to avoid expectations during observations is for the observer to be blind to the purpose of the assessment. When video or audio tools are used to record behavior, the

---

3. Technically, general changes in the observation process over time are called instrumentation problems.

order in which they are evaluated can be randomized so that observers do not know what portion of an observation is being scored. When it is impossible or impractical to keep the purpose unknown to observers, the importance of accurate observation should be stressed and such observation rewarded.

Data Summarization and Criteria for Evaluation

Depending on the particular characteristic of behavior being measured, observational data may be summarized in different ways. When duration or frequency is the characteristic of interest, observations are usually summarized as rates (that is, the prevalence or the number of occurrences per minute or other time interval). Latency and amplitude should be summarized statistically by the mean and the standard deviation or by the median and the range. All counts and calculations should be checked for accuracy.

Once accurate observational data have been collected and summarized, they must be interpreted. Behavior is interpreted in one of four ways:

- *A behavior's presence is an absolute criterion.* Behaviors evaluated in this way include those that are unsafe, harmful, and/or illegal.
- *A behavior can be compared to the behavior of others.* This comparison is generally called a normative comparison. Normative data may be available for some behaviors or, in some cases, data from behavior rating scales and tests. Social comparisons can be made using a peer whose behavior is considered appropriate. The peer's rate of behavior is then used as the standard against which to evaluate the target student's rate of behavior.
- *The social tolerance for a behavior can also be used as a criterion.* For example, the degree to which different rates of out-of-seat behavior disturb a teacher or peers can be assessed. Teachers and peers could be asked to rate how disturbing the out-of-seat behavior of students who exhibit different rates of behavior is. In a somewhat different vein, the contagion of the behavior to others can be a crucial consideration in teacher judgments of unacceptable behavior. Thus, the effects of different rates of behavior can be assessed to determine whether there is a threshold above which other students initiate undesirable behavior.
- *Progress toward objectives or goals is frequently used as a standard against which to evaluate behavior.* A common and useful procedure is graphing data against an aimline. As shown in Figure 11.2, an

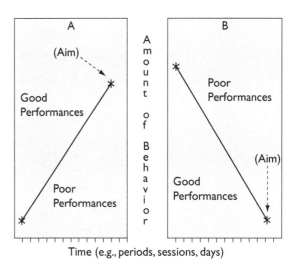

FIGURE 11.2. Aimlines for accelerating and decelerating behavior.

aimline connects a student's measured behavior at the start of an intervention with the point (called an aim) representing the terminal behavior and the date by which that behavior should be attained. When the goal is to accelerate a desirable behavior (Figure 11.2A), student performances above the aimline are evaluated as good progress. When the goal is to decelerate an undesirable behavior (Figure 11.2B), student performances below the aimline are evaluated as good progress. Adequate progress is progress that meets or exceeds the desired rate of behavior change.

Technology and Observation

Over the past decade, new technologies have been developed that can assist with systematic observations. Traditionally, systematic observations have required observers to pay close attention to both a stopwatch and the child they are observing, while at the same time recording their observations using paper and pencil. After collecting the data, the observer needed to develop a way to organize, analyze, summarize, and display the results. Today software programs are available for use on handheld mobile devices (tablets and smart phones) and these can be used to record and analyze pupil behavior. One example of these is the *Direct Behavior Rating-Single Item Scale* (DBR-SIS; charts.intensiveintervention.org/progressmonitoring/tool/?id=f79232cf4c4bbd63), which reflects a teacher's rating of the proportion of time a student was observed to engage in a specific behavior using a scale from 0 (never) to 10 (always) during a specified observation time. DBR-SIS is used in classrooms to observe both academic and social behaviors using tablets. A new experimental technology-based observational system is being increasingly used to conduct student observations at Tiers 2 and 3. Called the Multi-Option Observation System for Experimental Studies (MOOSES) (Tapp, 2021), it is used to record and analyze individual student behavior. Mobile devices, tablets, and associated applications help reduce several associated burdens on observers by automatically prompting observers at set time intervals to provide information and allowing for automatic summarization and display of the information collected.

Although these programs can facilitate more accurate, efficient, and less obtrusive collection and use of observational data, it remains important for users to critically examine programs they are considering for use to determine if the programs will allow for appropriate data collection, analysis, and use. More specifically, it is important to ensure that a particular program will allow coding and analysis approaches that fit the nature of the behaviors intended to be observed. We unfortunately have encountered observational programs that involve coding of behaviors using methods that are not in alignment with the nature of the behavior to be observed. For example, they may be programmed to measure "off-task" behavior using a frequency count during an observational session rather than through use of a momentary time-sampling approach when the latter would be more appropriate for the given behavior. It therefore remains essential for users to have solid foundational knowledge and skills associated with defining, measuring, summarizing, and evaluating behavior to make appropriate use of the associated technologies.

Fairness in Observing Students

Bias can and does occur in the process of gathering observational data. When observers go into classrooms for the purpose of gathering data on student behavior it typically is in response to a concern raised by a teacher, parent, administrator or someone else about that student's behavior. It is typical for an observer to expect to see the behaviors of concern evidenced by the student. Observers must be careful that they observe what actually goes on in classrooms rather than what they expect to see or want to see.

It is likely for an observer to hold prior knowledge or subjective feelings about individual students. Observers need to be careful that they do not hold inappropriate stereotypes and that they do not let such stereotypes interfere with objective observations of students and objective analyses of observational data.

1. What is the distinction between a qualitative and a quantitative observation? Give an example of each.
2. What is an unobtrusive observation. Give an example of one.
3. Differentiate between a contrived and a naturalistic observation and give an example of each.
4. What do the A, B, and C stand for in an ABC event recording?
5. What are the advantages of a DBR?

1. How does the topography of a behavior differ from the function of a behavior?
2. Give examples of behaviors for which you would want to observe and record duration, latency, frequency, and amplitude.
3. Give examples of instances in which you would want to do whole-interval recording rather than partial-interval recording.

PROGRESS 11.3

MONITORING CHECK

1. What four steps should you go through in preparing to sample behaviors in a classroom?

2. Differentiate between random and systematic error.

3. Describe two observation systems that can be used on iPads, tablets, or smart phones.

CHAPTER 12

Assessment of Academic Achievement With Multiple-Skills Measures

LEARNING OBJECTIVES

1. Describe factors to consider in selecting an achievement test.
2. Explain the reasons why we assess academic achievement.
3. Describe and compare representative individually administered achievement tests.
4. Explain how to get the most out of an achievement test.

Many different kinds of achievement tests are administered to the students who attend today's schools. It is important that you know why the tests are administered and that you understand the specific kinds of tests that will be described in this chapter.

Purposes of Achievement Testing

Teacher-Made Tests

Teachers design tests to ascertain the extent to which their students have learned or are learning what has been taught or assigned. Student achievement is the basis on which teachers make decisions about student skill development, student progress and instructional problems, and grades. Teachers also use the information they receive from teacher-made tests to make judgments about the extent to which they should modify their instruction ("Are students mastering what I teach?") and about their own effectiveness as teachers.

Screening

We described the use of achievement tests for the purpose of making screening decisions in Chapter 10. These tests are administered to identify students with skill deficits, to distinguish individual deficits from entire classroom deficits, and to identify students who may need further diagnostic evaluations.

Outcomes / Accountability

Since the early 1990s, schools have been required to assess students in order to provide information to states. In turn, states have been required to provide information to the federal government on the extent to which all students are making progress toward specific educational standards. Over time, the standards have changed, as well as the requirements for participation, especially for students with disabilities. In Chapter 20, we describe the history of changes in accountability requirements and in the achievement testing programs that have accompanied those requirements.

Diagnosis / Eligibility and Intervention Planning

Many of the achievement tests that are administered in schools are given for the purpose of making diagnostic or eligibility decisions. They are given by school psychologists or special education teachers for the purpose of deciding whether students demonstrate significant enough skill deficits to be eligible for special education services. The tests are given for the purpose of planning instructional interventions, especially at Tiers 2 and 3 of multi-tier systems of support models. Specially trained school personnel administer the tests for the purpose of instructional planning or as part of IEP teams developing specific intervention plans.

   In this chapter we describe and discuss achievement tests that assess skills in multiple domains (reading, mathematics, writing, science, spelling, etc.). In subsequent chapters we will discuss diagnostic achievement tests that assess skills in single domains.

Individual Versus Group-Administered Achievement Tests

If you talk to your parents or grandparents, you will learn that they spent many hours each year during their schooling taking group-administered achievement tests. These tests served the multiple purpose of screening and outcomes evaluation. The results of student performance on these tests were used to identify students who were behind their peers and were in need of remedial or compensatory instruction, students who were in need of enrichment, or students who might need special educational assistance (remember that there was no "special education" or services for "handicapped students" until after 1975). Performance on group tests was also used to make comparisons among classrooms within schools, schools within districts or states, and even among states. The group tests included measures like the *Iowa Tests of Basic Skills, Stanford Achievement Tests, California Achievement Tests, Terra Nova,* and *Metropolitan Achievement Tests.* The first few editions of this textbook included extensive reviews of those tests. Students spent five to eight hours scattered over multiple days each spring taking these very long achievement tests. It usually took many weeks to score the tests and results often were not available until the fall of the next school year when they were of limited use in making screening and instructional-planning decisions. Over time, the use of these tests declined so that today you will seldom see them used in schools.

The multiple skills achievement tests we describe in this chapter are all individually administered.

To Whom or What Are the Test Scores Compared?

Achievement tests may be referenced differently. It is important that you know whether the tests you use or the tests you receive results on are norm-referenced, standards-referenced, curriculum-based, or computer-adaptive.

Norm-Referenced Tests

Norm-referenced tests are standardized on groups of students who should be representative of the U.S. school-age population. They tell you how an individual student performed relative to others at their age or grade level. Further, it is useful to consider the student to whom you might give the test and the context within which you will interpret their results to identify if the norm-reference group is a logical fit (i.e., represents the student who will be tested and the way in which you will interpret the results). For example, if private parochial or charter schools wished to use an achievement test for their own program evaluation and to determine how an individual student is achieving grade-level understandings, it might be more meaningful to compare the student to a norm sample specifically collected from private parochial or charter schools. These schools differ from public schools in key ways, including their admission and dismissal policies.

Standards-Referenced Tests

Standards-referenced tests are achievement tests in which student performance is compared to specific standards, usually state performance standards. For example, the *Florida State Assessment* is a standards-referenced test in which student performance is compared to the Florida state education standards.

Criterion-Referenced Tests

Criterion-referenced tests are another name for standards-referenced tests. These tests are used to compare a person's knowledge or skills against a predetermined standard, learning goal, performance level, or other criterion. With criterion-referenced tests, each person's performance is compared directly to the standard, without considering how other students perform on the test. Standards- and criterion-referenced tests yield functional information about skill mastery in how likely the child is to attain forthcoming academic benchmarks over time. Use of these standards is common in accountability testing and schools often set goals for improvement that involve moving more students into higher proficiency categories over time. Publishers provide information about how their criterion is set for each category of performance, and readers of this book may be surprised to know that this generally involves a team of school professionals working with the publisher during the test-development phase to determine what each level of performance should be in terms of sample test items.

Curriculum-Based Measures

Curriculum-based measures (CBM) are designed to assess progress toward general outcomes. CBMs involve a standardized set of measures of important skills that can be administered in a relatively short amount of time. CBM measures have been developed in reading, math, writing, spelling, and vocabulary. They provide direct measurement of student performance on basic skills using common standardized, timed administration procedures, and preset objective scoring procedures. Depending on the content area, probes may be selected randomly from grade-level instructional materials of things that are intended to be taught for a predetermined period of time (e.g., 1 school year or seasonally from fall to winter). Recently, off-the-shelf packages of CBM tools have been developed to help schools and teachers use CBM (e.g., AIMSweb, DIBELS Next, Easy CBM, SpringMath, Star CBM).

Curriculum-Based Assessments

Curriculum-based assessment (CBA) is an evaluation process that makes use of academic content selected directly from material taught. A key characteristic of CBA is that teachers are assessing precisely what they teach, which is not always the case with indirect or norm-referenced assessments that do not necessarily reflect the specific material covered in particular classrooms.

Computer-Adaptive Tests

In computer-adaptive testing, items selected for administration are based on the student's performance on earlier items. The tests allow teachers to pinpoint the student's precise level of skill development.

Computer-Administered Tests

Increasingly achievement tests are being administered by computer rather than using paper and pencil. The tests can be norm-referenced, standards-referenced, or curriculum-based. As with all tests, test publishers should provide data to indicate that computer-based assessment is both reliable and valid for the purposes it will be used.

In this chapter we concentrate on describing and discussing the individually administered tests of multiple skills that are used in making diagnostic/eligibility and instructional planning decisions. They are among the measures most frequently used by IEP teams in making such decisions. Multiple-skill achievement tests evaluate knowledge and understanding in several curricular areas, such as reading, spelling, math, and/or language. These tests are intended to assess the extent to which students have profited from schooling and other life experiences, compared with other students of the same age or grade.

Considerations for Selecting an Achievement Test

In selecting an individually administered multiple skill achievement test, teachers must consider six factors: content validity, opportunity to learn, response mode, state standards, relevance of norms, and technical adequacy.

Content Validity

Teachers must first evaluate evidence for content validity, the most important kind of validity for achievement tests. Many multiple-skill tests have general content validity—the tests measure important concepts and skills that are generally part of most curricula. This validity makes their content suitable for assessing general attainment.[1] However, if a test is to be used to assess the extent to which students have profited from school instruction—that is, to measure student achievement—more than general content validity is required: the test must match the instruction provided. This tenet of assessment can be confusing to new assessors who might have heard critiques about school systems "teaching to the test," implying that when there is a strong alignment between instructional content and test content that somehow the assessment scores are compromised, less reliable, or inflated. In fact, an achievement test is designed to test how well students have acquired academic skills that they are expected to have been taught at their grade level. *Tests that do not match instruction lack content validity, and decisions based on such tests should be restricted.*

Opportunity to Learn

Second, when making decisions about content validity for students with disabilities, educators must consider the extent to which the student has had an opportunity to learn

---

1. "Achievement" generally refers to content that has been learned as a product of schooling. "Attainment" is a broader term referring to what individuals have learned as a result of both schooling and other life experiences.

the content of the test. In some situations, students with disabilities have not had adequate access to instruction in the skills measured on multiple-skill achievement tests. In these cases, a low score on such a test may reflect lack of instruction rather than the influence the school has had on the student's development of academic skills.

Response Mode of the Subtests

Third, educators who use achievement tests for students with disabilities need to consider whether the stimulus–response modes of subtests may be exceptionally difficult for students with physical or motor problems. Tests that are timed may be inappropriately difficult for students whose reading or motor difficulties cause them to take more time on specific tasks. (Many of these issues are described in greater detail in Chapter 19, "Accessibility Supports and Accommodations").

State Standards

Fourth, educators must consider the state education standards for the state in which they work. In doing so, they should examine the extent to which the achievement test they select measures the content of their state standards. One consideration, of course, is to use data from the state test rather than administering yet an additional achievement test.

Relevance and Appropriateness of Norms

Fifth, educational professionals must evaluate the adequacy of each test's norms by asking whether the normative group is composed of the kinds of individuals to whom they wish to compare their students. If a test is used to estimate general attainment, a representative sample of students from throughout the nation is preferred. However, if a test is used to estimate achievement compared to other students within a school system, local norms are better. In addition to asking questions about relevance, test users need to be concerned about the datedness of norms. For example, what if you find that an achievement test was last normed 20 years ago? Times have changed significantly over 20 years and it would be unethical and inappropriate to use tests that old to make normative comparisons.

Technical Adequacy

Finally, teachers should examine the extent to which a total test and its components have the reliability necessary for making decisions about what students have learned. Recall that when used for purposed of making screening decisions, tests or subtests should have reliabilities that exceed .80. You will note in this chapter that the subtests of most of the most commonly used achievement tests have reliabilities that exceed .80, though not always. Individually administered achievement tests are often used in making special education eligibility decisions, for which recommended reliability of all subtests is .90. Only some of the achievement measures reviewed have subtests whose reliabilities exceed the commonly recommended standard of .90.

Specific Individually Administered Tests of Academic Achievement

In Table 12.1 we provide information on commonly used multiple-skill measures of academic skills. Of the tests we review, the most commonly used are the *Woodcock-Johnson Tests of Achievement–Fourth Edition* and the *Wechsler Individual Achievement Test–Fourth Edition* (WIAT 4).

12.1
PROGRESS
MONITORING
CHECK

Getting the Most Out of an Achievement Test

The achievement tests described in this chapter provide the teacher with overall scores in areas such as word meaning and math computation skills. Although overall scores can help in screening children, they generally lack the specificity to help in planning individualized instructional programs. The fact that Francis earned a standard score of 85 on the Mathematics Problem Solving subtest of the WIAT 4 does not tell us what math skills Francis has and has not mastered. In addition, a teacher cannot rely on test names as an indication of what is measured by a specific test. For example, a reading standard score of 115 on the *Wide Range Achievement Test 5* (WRAT 5; Wilkinson & Robertson, 2017) tells a teacher nothing about reading comprehension or rate of oral reading. Teachers typically have other information, such as scores from cumulative records or their own observations of student performance that they can use along with test scores to make judgments about the reasonable level at which to instruct students and the specific skills that need to be taught.

A teacher must look at any test in terms of the behaviors sampled by that test. Here is a case in point. Suppose Richard earned a standard score of 70 on a spelling subtest. What do we know about Richard? We know that Richard earned enough raw score points to place him two standard deviations below the mean of students in the norm sample who are enrolled in the same grade as he is. That is all we know without going beyond the score and examining the kinds of behaviors sampled by the test. The test title tells us only that the test measures skill development in spelling. However, we still do not know what Richard did to earn a score of 70.

First, we need to ask, "What is the nature of the behaviors sampled by the test?" Spelling tests can be of several kinds. Richard may have been asked to write a word read by his teacher, as is the case in the Spelling subtest of the WRAT 5. Such a behavior sampling demands that he recall the correct spelling of a word and actually produce that correct spelling in writing. On the other hand, Richard's score of 70 may have been earned on a spelling test that asked him just to recognize the correct spelling of a word. For example, the Spelling subtest of the *Peabody Individual Achievement Test–Revised/Normative Update* (PIAT-R/NU) presents the student with four alternative spellings of a word (e.g., "empti," "empty," "impty," and "emity"), and the teacher asks a child to point to the word *empty*. Such an item demands recognition and pointing, rather than recall and production. Thus, we need to look first at the nature of the behaviors sampled by the test.

TABLE 12.1

Commonly Used Comprehensive Tests of Academic Achievement

Title, Author(s), and Publisher	Skills Assessed	Norms	Reliability Evidence	Validity Evidence
Diagnostic Achievement Battery–Fourth Edition (DAB-4) Newcomer, 2014, PRO-ED	Listening comprehension, phonics and word identification, reading comprehension, punctuation/capitalization, spelling, mathematics reasoning, and mathematics calculation	Standardized on a sample of 1,310 students from 25 states stratified on the basis of geographic region, race, gender, Hispanic status, exceptionality status, parental education, and household income. Ages 6 to 14.	Internal consistency reliabilities for subtests range from .73 to .90, with only the listening comp subtest having reliabilities below .80. Reliabilities for composites range from .89 to .97. Test–retest reliabilities for subtests exceed .80, and for composites they exceed .90.	Arguments for content validity based on test selection procedures and item analysis. Evidence of criterion/predictive validity based on moderate to high correlations with other achievement tests.
Kaufman Test of Educational Achievement–Third Edition Kaufman, A. & Kaufman, N., 2014, Pearson	Assesses achievement in the areas of reading (letter and word recognition, nonsense word recognition, reading comprehension, reading vocabulary, word recognition fluency, decoding fluency, silent reading fluency), mathematics (math concepts and applications, math computation, math fluency), writing (written expression, spelling, writing fluency), oral language (listening comprehension, oral expression, associational fluency), and language processing (phonological processing, object naming facility, letter naming facility).	Age norms on 2,050 students and grade norms on 2,600 students stratified on basis of gender, ethnicity, parental education, and geographic region. Based on 2012 U.S. Census. Ages 4 to 24.	Internal consistency reliability for composites range from .54 to .99. Test–retest reliabilities for composites range from .72 to .91.	Limited evidence for content validity. Evidence for concurrent/predictive validity based on moderate to high correlation with other achievement measures, primarily the WIAT-III and the *WJ III Tests of Achievement*.

Title, Author(s), and Publisher	Skills Assessed	Norms	Reliability Evidence	Validity Evidence
Wechsler Individual Achievement Test–Fourth Edition Breaux, K. C., 2020, Pearson	Four core composite scores (reading, written expression, math, total achievement) and 20 subtests (phonemic proficiency, word reading, listening comprehension, alphabetic writing fluency, reading comprehension fluency, math problem solving, orthographic fluency, sentence composition, oral expression, oral reading fluency, essay composition, pseudoword decoding, sentence writing fluency, numerical operations, decoding fluency, spelling, math fluency addition, math fluency subtraction, math fluency multiplication, and orthographic closure). Some tests are administered only at specific grades and one should consult the test manual.	Ages 4 to 50; Grades PK to 12. Grade norms are based on 2,100 examinees in PK–12, with both fall and spring norms developed. Age norms are based on 1,832 individuals, most of whom were included in the grade norms. Standardization sample was stratified on basis of grade, age, sex, race/ethnicity, parent or self education level, and geographic region matched to the 2018 census.	Internal consistency reliabilities range from .74 to .97, with the exception of alphabetic fluency where the internal consistency coefficient is .64. Only 15 of 27 subtests have reliabilities that exceed .80.	Arguments for content validity and response processes validity are based on how the test was developed. The author presents good evidence for convergent and discriminant validity in support of construct validity. Moderate correlations with other achievement measures like the KTEA-3 support concurrent and predictive validity.
Wide Range Achievement Test–Fifth Edition Wilkinson & Robertson, 2017, Pearson	Four subtests (word reading, spelling, math computation, and sentence comprehension); reading composite (word reading + sentence comprehension)	Ages 5 to 85+; Grades K to 12. Two parallel forms. Norms stratified on basis of parent educational level, race/ethnicity, region, and gender matched to 2015 census. Grade norm sample: 2,150 examinees split into fall and winter sample. Age norms sample 5 to 85+: 2,355 examinees, most from age norms sample.	Internal consistency for age norms from .85 to .96 for subtests and >.95 for reading composite; internal consistency for grade norms. 82 to .97 for subtests and >.94 for reading composite. No test–retest reliability reported in WRAT 5 manual.	Arguments for content validity and response processes are based on content development. Evidence for construct validity is based on the results of a number of studies showing good convergent and discriminant validity. Correlations with other achievement measures are moderate, though students in general earn slightly higher scores on the other measures' validity.

(continues)

TABLE 12.1 (*continued*)

Title, Author(s), and Publisher	Skills Assessed	Norms	Reliability Evidence	Validity Evidence
Woodcock-Johnson IV Tests of Achievement Shrank, McGrew, & Mather, 2014, Riverside	Broad reading, basic reading skills, reading comprehension, reading comprehension-extended, reading fluency, mathematics, broad mathematics, math calculation sills, math problem solving, written language, broad written language, basic writing skills, written expression	7,416 individuals, ages 2 to 90 in more than 46 states, selected using a stratified sampling plan that controlled for 12 variables.	Median reliabilities for achievement clusters are all above .90.	Good evidence for both content and predictive validity.

Second, we must look at the specific items a student passes or fails. This requires going back to the original test protocol to analyze the specific nature of skill development in a given area. We need to ask, "What kinds of items did the child fail?" and then look for consistent patterns among the failures. In trying to identify the nature of spelling errors, we need to know, "Does the student consistently demonstrate errors in spelling words with long vowels? With silent *e*'s? With specific consonant blends?" and so on. The search is for specific patterns of errors, and we try to ascertain the student's relative degree of consistency in making certain errors. Of course, finding error patterns requires that the test content be sufficiently dense to allow a student to make the same error at least twice.

Let's return to Richard again and his score of 70. We also have no idea how the rest of Richard's grade mates or classmates in his actual school would have performed on the same test (unless we administered the test to the whole grade or class). It is theoretically possible for a child to appear to have a very low score relative to a national sample, and yet, perform above the average in his or her actual class or grade. This scenario commonly occurs in cases where the grade as a whole is low-performing and could be an indication that instruction has not adequately covered the expected grade-level content as prescribed by state and local standards.

Individually administered multiple skills achievement tests are also useful in IEP planning. Read the Stakeholder Perspective by Lisa Persinger to see how she has used to *Woodcock-Johnson IV Achievement Battery* in IEP planning.

Ensuring Fairness in Assessment of Academic Achievement

In making sure an achievement test is fair to students, it is critical to be certain they have had an opportunity to learn the material assessed by the test at the grade level in which they are placed. Unless the content assessed by an achievement test reflects the content of the curriculum to which they have been exposed, the results are meaningless. Students will not have had a formal opportunity to learn the material tested. When students are tested on material they have not been taught, or tested in ways other than those by which they are taught, the test results will not measure what they may have learned. Jenkins and Pany (1978) compared the contents of four reading achievement tests with the contents of five commercial reading series at Grades 1 and 2. Their major concern was the extent to which students might earn different scores on different tests of reading achievement simply as a function of the degree of overlap in content between tests and curricula. Jenkins and Pany calculated the grade scores that would be earned by students who had mastered the words taught in the respective curricula and who had correctly read those words on the four tests. Grade scores are shown in Table 12.2. It is clear that different curricula result in different performances on different tests.

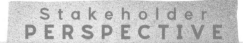

Lisa L. Persinger, PhD, Faculty, Northern Arizona University

Before I began teaching future school psychologists, I was a full-time school psychologist for 7 years in Arizona and Colorado. On my team, we found the *Woodcock-Johnson Tests of Achievement* (WJ) to be a valuable source of information for writing an IEP. My team has worked to develop a deeper understanding of student reading and writing problems, so we started giving all the standard and extended subtests in these areas. As a result, we have increased our confidence in skill targets on the IEP.

For example, we used error analysis of the student's performance on the subtests to develop goals as well as justify the accommodations. We found that the error analysis on real and nonsense word reading was well aligned with a standard phonics screener, saving time for the teacher on specifying the baseline in the phonics goals. For older students with dyslexia, we found that giving the standard administration of the writing samples and then testing the limits about a week later by having the student dictate their sentences allowed us to get a much stronger sense of the student's ability to compose using their natural vocabulary and language skills. The difference between the handwritten responses and the dictated responses allowed us to create more individualized goals as well as justify when speech-to-text was going to provide a powerful difference for the student. Subsequently, we asked the students to edit their dictated responses so that we could identify how their editing skills stack up in their own text versus that on the editing subtest. These translated into specific target skills and baselines for the IEP, such as identifying and/or correcting errors in medial punctuation, capitalization, spelling, or word choice.

When we use the *Woodcock-Johnson Tests of Achievement*, we've also easily created baselines that can be converted to percentages or ratios for our IEP goals. For example, "Johnny identified 1 of 5 punctuation errors (incorrect or omitted punctuation) in 3 sentences" can be reflected as the baseline for his editing goal in writing. In some cases we've used the raw score from the math fluency subtest (number of math facts answered correctly in the timed period) as a baseline and then used curriculum-based measures with similar math facts for progress monitoring the students with math fact fluency goals on their IEPs. Using a combination of tools like curriculum-based measures with the WJ has strengthened our IEP development and the implementation of the students' plans. In short, we've been able to quantify student performance on WJ discrete tasks to create accurate baselines that correspond well to classroom performance.

The data produced by Jenkins and Pany are now more than 40 years old. Yet the table is still the best visual illustration of issues with limited test-curriculum overlap. Shapiro and Derr (1987) showed that the degree of overlap between what is taught and what is tested varied considerably across tests and curricula. Also, Good and Salvia (1988) dem-

TABLE 12.2

Grade-Equivalent Scores Obtained by Matching Specific Reading Test Words to Standardized Reading Test Words

		MAT			
Curriculum	PIAT	Word Knowledge	Word Analysis	SDRT	WRAT
Bank Street Reading Series					
Grade 1	1.5	1.0	1.1	1.8	2.0
Grade 2	2.8	2.5	1.2	2.9	2.7
Keys to Reading					
Grade 1	2.0	1.4	1.2	2.2	2.2
Grade 2	3.3	1.9	1.0	3.0	3.0
Reading 360					
Grade 1	1.5	1.0	1.0	1.4	1.7
Grade 2	2.2	2.1	1.0	2.7	2.3
SRA Reading Program					
Grade 1	1.5	1.2	1.3	1.0	2.1
Grade 2	3.1	2.5	1.4	2.9	3.5
Sullivan Associates Programmed Reading					
Grade 1	1.8	1.4	1.2	1.1	2.0
Grade 2	2.2	2.4	1.1	2.5	2.5

Note. From "Standardized Achievement Tests: How Useful for Special Education?" by J. Jenkins and D. Pany, *Exceptional Children*, 44 (1978), 450. Copyright 1978 by The Council for Exceptional Children. Reprinted with permission.

onstrated significant differences in test performance for the same students on different reading tests. They indicate the significance of the test curriculum overlap issue, stating:

> Curriculum bias is undesirable because it severely limits the interpretation of a student's test score. For example, it is unclear whether a student's reading score of 78 reflects deficient reading skills or the selection of a test with poor content validity for the pupil's curriculum. (p. 56)

1. Identify at least four important considerations in selecting a specific achievement test for use with the fifth graders in your local school system.

2. Describe the major advantages and disadvantages of using individually administered, multiple-skill achievement tests.

3. A new student is assessed in September using the WRAT 5. Her achievement test scores (using the *Woodcock-Johnson Achievement Tests IV*) are forwarded from her previous school and place her in the 90th percentile overall. However, the latest assessment places her only in the 77th percentile. Give three possible explanations for this discrepancy.

CHAPTER 13

Using Diagnostic Reading Measures

LEARNING OBJECTIVES

1. Understand why we assess reading.
2. Understand the foundations of scientifically based reading research, including the importance of connecting assessment to instruction and intervention.
3. Identify the areas assessed by diagnostic reading tests, including oral reading, comprehension, word-attack, reading recognition, and reading-related behaviors.
4. State some of the critical considerations of appropriate use of diagnostic reading measures.

Why Do We Assess Reading?

Think back to when you were a child learning to read. Who was your reading teacher? Was it a teacher or a parent? Perhaps you are someone who figured out the reading code seemingly on your own. Now think of someone who struggled with learning to read. How might poor reading skills impact someone's life? Reading is one of the most fundamental skills that teachers teach and that students learn. For non-fluent readers, life in school is likely to be difficult even with appropriate curricular and testing accommodations and adaptations. Life after school with poor reading skills can lead to constrained opportunities and less options for employment. Reading is arguably the most critical skill that teachers teach in early elementary school. Students who have not learned to read fluently by the end of third grade are unlikely ever to read fluently (Adams, 1990). Research is clear that explicit and evidence-based instruction closely tied to formative assessment is the practice that assists struggling readers to attain literacy (Torgesen et al., 1999; Vaughn & Fletcher, 2020). Explicit evidence-based reading intervention is necessary to prevent reading failure for some children but is still beneficial for other students. In other words, evidence-based reading intervention benefits most students in a classroom and harms none, even those who were not really at risk for reading failure.

Early universal screening is essential to prevent reading failure. The goal for early and ongoing screening of reading skills is to identify struggling students early enough to prevent long-term reading failure. Screening is also recommended for middle school students. At the elementary and middle school levels it is recommended that universal screening occur three times per year. At the secondary level it is not common practice, nor recommended, to screen all ninth-grade students in reading, but in fact some high school students do need support in reading. High school students with poor reading skills can be identified by first examining year-end state tests results for the student for the most recent years of schooling. Screening data and reading intervention data, if any, that may have been collected during middle school should be available in the student's permanent file. Universal screening at the high school level is different from other levels in that formative assessment are not administered multiple times per year for all students. Instead, year-end state test scores are used. Sometimes this happens in 10th grade only, while in other states testing might occur in ninth grade and 11th grade. If the student's year-end English language arts test scores are in the nonproficient range and the student is exhibiting poor academic performance in high school, then reading screening should be conducted to verify basic reading skills or alternatively to plan for reading intervention if reading skills are interfering with grade-level success (Shinn et al., 2016). Formative assessment systems, such as screening, partnered with evidence-based instruction can prevent or ameliorate reading challenges that will eventually impact other content areas. The canon of reading research demonstrates that teachers can successfully provide intensive systematic intervention in foundational reading skills to improve long-term reading outcomes for elementary school students (Gersten et al., 2008). There is also evidence that older students can benefit from intensive interventions in reading comprehension and in content areas like social studies, including students with identified reading disabilities (Vaughn & Fletcher, 2020).

In elementary schools screening tests are universal, meaning they are administered to all students to evaluate core instruction and to identify students in need of intervention. Progress monitoring is used to assess students receiving Tier 2 and Tier 3 supports. In this chapter, we'll discuss diagnostic tests which are most often used at Tiers 2 and 3 (supplemental and intensive) in the multi-tiered system of supports (MTSS) model for both elementary and secondary students. There are two primary purposes for using diagnostic reading tests. First, diagnostic tests are administered to students who are experiencing difficulty learning to read. In this case, tests identify a student's skills and lack of skills so that educators can plan appropriate interventions. Second, they are administered to ascertain a student's initial or continuing eligibility for special services. Tests given for this purpose are used to compare a student's skill level to the skills of other students at the same grade level.

In the past, diagnostic reading tests have been administered to evaluate the effects of instruction across a school but it has been determined that screening assessments better serve this purpose. Diagnostic tests are not useful for program evaluation because lengthy individually administered tests tend to be an inefficient way to evaluate instruction for large groups of students. Additionally, diagnostic tests are less capable of detecting small but important gains in learning by individual students. Thus, teachers should use curriculum-based assessments to monitor students' daily or weekly progress during instruction. This was also discussed in Chapter 8, "Monitoring Student Progress Toward Instructional Goals."

Because reading skills are fundamental to success in our society, they should be closely monitored. When screening indicates a need for intervention, diagnostic tests should be administered to inform instructional adjustments that can be made to address specific needs or skill gaps of the student. When used appropriately, diagnostic reading tests can help us to precisely identify skill gaps and tailor instruction to those needs so that students can learn to read.

Note that there are a small percentage of students, some with low-incidence disabilities, who can learn basic reading skills when given highly effective instruction, but may need additional supports to advance beyond basic reading skills. Fortunately, technologies such as text-to-speech converters and computer screen-readers are making it increasingly possible for such students to access printed information without the prerequisite reading skills. At the same time, technology supports brings up a new dilemma: Under what conditions should we reduce reading intervention efforts in order to focus more on teaching a student to use technology-based accessibility methods (e.g., computer screen-readers, text-to-speech (TTS) software)? It's critical that answers to difficult questions such as this one, are made by teams of educators with family stakeholders using the best data available. Some of these accommodations may actually facilitate reading development, and so we believe that their use should be considered on a case-by-case basis, particularly for those students with the most severe reading difficulties. Overall, it is essential that we operate under the assumption that each student will learn to read when we assess, instruct, and intervene appropriately and with prevention in mind.

Scientifically Based Reading Research Foundations

For 150 years, educators have at times been acrimoniously divided over how to teach reading. In the early days of public education, observations of reading were too crude to indicate more than that the reader looked at print and said the printed words or answered questions about the content conveyed by those printed words. Consequently, theorists speculated about the processes occurring inside the brain of the reader. One theory that emerged based on these speculations was that students learn how to read by sight and should be taught to recognize whole words and the shapes of words, not how to decode individual sounds within words. This theory was referred to as whole language and dominated curricula, teacher training, and reading instructional models in the 1980s and 1990s. Experimental data did not and still does not support the whole language theory. Examples of charismatic features of the whole language theory are to provide rich and interesting books for young readers and encourage students to use pictures and context clues to guess at a word. In actuality, providing students with interesting and rich literature is a commonly held value not specific to whole language theory. But research has demonstrated that relying on context clues often results in unskilled readers misunderstanding the text. Specifically, whole language discouraged strategies like mapping letter–sound relationships (phonological skill) to decode or sound out words and promoting fluency in reading. Beginning in the 1980s researchers in psychology and education began to study and demonstrate that learning to read is an unnatural process for which explicit teaching in decoding is necessary for most children to successfully learn to read. This body of work is called Scientifically Based Reading Research (SBRR), the Science of Reading, or simply Reading Science.

Reading, unlike other areas of instruction, benefits from research across multiple disciplines. Of course, educational psychology and special education researchers have significantly contributed to Reading Science, but we have also learned from scholars in the fields of cognitive psychology, neuroscience, and linguistics. Across these fields there is a commonly agreed-upon model of reading that is called the simple view of reading (Gough, 1990). The formula of the simple view of reading is that decoding times language comprehension amounts to reading comprehension. Embedded within decoding and language comprehension are a number of subskills which when combined create fluent decoding and comprehension. Through the Science of Reading we know about the critical subskills of decoding including phonemic awareness, alphabetic knowledge, and phonological awareness. **Phonemic awareness** is the knowledge that there are individual sounds that make up words. **Alphabetic knowledge** is the idea that there are graphemes or symbols that are letters that have a meaning. **Phonological awareness** begins to blend the two previous concepts—that there are graphemes that represent phonemes. Beginning readers must understand how words are made up of sounds before they need to read, or in other words they require, *phonemic awareness*, the ability to recognize and manipulate **phonemes** (i.e., individual sounds). Beginning readers must initially associate **graphemes** (alphabet letters) with phonemes. Beginning readers learn these associations, known as **decoding**, best through explicit phonics instruction. Next, beginning readers must decode fluently in order to comprehend what they are reading. After students become fluent decoders, they can read increasingly challenging material. This material often contains advanced vocabulary that students must be taught. It contains more complex sentence structure, more condensed and abstract ideas, and perhaps less literal and more inferential meaning. This process describes the transition of "learning to read" to "reading to learn" that begins in the early elementary and continues in middle, high school and beyond.

By 1967 there was substantial evidence that systematic instruction in phonics produced more successful readers (Bond & Dykstra, 1967; Chall, 1967), which resulted in a confluence of policy and legislative events in education including the formation of the National Reading Panel, the initial passage of the No Child Left Behind Act, and the emergence of data-based decision-making models like MTSS to promote literacy for all students. Explicit and systematic phonics instruction is the most effective and efficient method for teaching beginning reading and for ameliorating reading problems for older students. Empirical evidence repeatedly demonstrates that instruction and intensive intervention anchored to Reading Science leads to more fluent readers with good comprehension and is effective for a range of learners including English learners, students with disabilities, and students from marginalized communities (Foorman et al., 1998; Gunn et al., 2000; National Institute of Child Health and Human Development, 2000; Rayner et al., 2001; Wanzek et al., 2016). Because the data are so clear about the benefits of reading instruction based on the Science of Reading, teachers might presume that they will teach in a school where effective practices are commonly accepted and effectively deployed. Yet, research continues to report that most student teachers are ill-equipped in how to teach reading based on the Science of Reading. This makes teachers susceptible to published curricula and, unfortunately, many curricula still persist either fully grounded in whole language philosophies or maintaining remnants of whole language tactics within an otherwise mediocre reading curriculum. Thus, some teachers must find their own pathways to understand the Science of Reading and seek to align teaching practices with whatever curriculum is used at their school. Teachers can also be important advocates for the adoption of curricula that genuinely embed the Reading Science into their materials and methodologies.

Misconceptions About Reading Development

While learning more about how students begin to read, scholars also learned that some long-held beliefs were not valid. For example, it is incorrect to say that unskilled readers read letter by letter, but skilled readers read entire words and phrases as a unit. Actually, skilled readers read letter by letter and word by word, but they do it so quickly that they appear to be reading words and phrases (see, for example, Snow et al., 1998). It is also incorrect to say that fluent readers rely heavily on context cues to identify words (Share & Stanovich, 1995). Fluent readers do use context cues to verify their decoding accuracy. Non-fluent readers also rely on context clues because they lack skill in more appropriate word-attack skills and unfortunately, they make erroneous conclusions from context clues without correct decoding skills to guide them. Such errors can be subtle and yet change the meaning altogether of what the student is reading. For example, substituting "a" for "the" can change the meaning of a passage altogether because "the" implies exclusivity whereas "a" implies there are many options. Similarly, substituting "are" for "were" changes the tense or timing context of the passage. These may seem like subtle errors, but they are detrimental to comprehension and are best avoided by teaching children to correctly read the words.

Another misconception about learning to read is that reading skills develop innately within children, like maturity, and some students will not fully develop until third grade whereas other students develop their reading skills in kindergarten. The truth is that there is a range of learners and some students will learn how to read with fewer instructional opportunities to learn than other students. But the idea that if we just wait the student will eventually "get it" is completely wrong. Reading is not like maturity; it will not develop with age. In order to learn, students must be taught. With effective instruction, the anatomy of the brain is changed as a complex neural connection is made between the brain regions responsible for object recognition and language (Dehaene, 2009). In fact, Reading Science demonstrates that students who initially struggle with learning to read can ultimately reach grade-level reading performance with intensive intervention that targets specific skills. The instruction should be offered daily and in small groups. Reading assessments can help educators determine when it is time to intervene and generally can offer a data-based approach to reading instruction.

Today, despite clear evidence indicating the essential role of phonics in reading and strong indications of the superiority of comprehensive reading programs with direct and explicit instruction in phonics (Stuebing et al., 2008), some widely used curricula continue to use ineffective practices or minimize phonics instruction (Student Achievement Partners, 2020). This may explain why most students who are referred for psychological assessment are referred because of reading problems, and why most of these students have problems in phonological awareness and fluent decoding or word-level reading.

The Science of Reading also informs the assessment of reading. Educators' views of how students learn to read and how students should be taught influences their beliefs about reading assessment. Thus, diagnostic testing in reading can be caught in the middle of the debate. While this is becoming less problematic as more teachers are trained in the Science of Reading and more publishers incorporate SBRR into their curricula, there are still a multitude of students who are not receiving or benefitting from scientifically based reading instruction. As with all assessments it is important to make the connection between the skills that you are testing, the tests that you use to measure those skills, and the recommendations made to guide instruction.

PROGRESS
MONITORING
CHECK

Skills Assessed by Diagnostic Reading Tests

Reading is a complex skill. The ultimate goal of reading is to comprehend written material with efficiency, but students need opportunities to learn to integrate many subskills to reach that end. Beginning readers rely heavily on a complex set of decoding skills that can be assessed holistically by having a student read orally to assess decoding accuracy and fluency. Decoding skills may also be measured analytically by having students apply these skills in isolation (e.g., using their phonological awareness skills to read nonsense words). Once fluency in decoding has been attained, readers are expected to go beyond the comprehension of simple language and ideas to the process of understanding and evaluating what is written. In upper elementary grade levels, teachers transition to teaching students to read in order to learn a wide range of content. Advanced readers rely on different skills (e.g., linguistic competence and abstract reasoning) and different facts (e.g., vocabulary and prior knowledge). Comprehension may be assessed by having a student read a passage that deals with an esoteric topic and is filled with abstract concepts and content-specific vocabulary. Sentences in that passage may have complicated grammar with minimal redundancy and no context clues. At the secondary level, if a student has been identified by poor performance on state language arts test and other measures of reading comprehension, it may be necessary to drill down to test for basic reading skills. Because of the link between behavior and academics you may find a high school student acting out to avoid a class, may actually have a hidden reading deficit. Diagnostic reading assessments can assist educators at both the elementary and secondary levels. Now let's discuss some of the common types of skills and tasks measured in diagnostic reading tests.

Word-Attack Skills

Morphological word knowledge helps students to decode and comprehend unfamiliar vocabulary words. Words contain free morphemes (such as *farm*, *book*, and *land*) and bound morphemes (such as *-ed*, *-s*, and *-er*). **Word-attack**, or word analysis, skills are the demonstration of morphological knowledge and are used to derive the pronunciation or meaning of a word through a morphological approach including phonics and structural analysis. **Phonic analysis** is the use of letter–sound correspondences and sound blending to identify words. **Structural analysis** is a process of breaking words into morphemes, or meaningful units.

Because lack of word-attack skills can contribute to reading difficulties, a variety of subtests of commonly used diagnostic reading tests specifically assess morphological skills. Subtests that assess word-attack skills range from such basic assessments as analysis of skill in associating letters with sounds to tests of syllabication and blending. Generally, for subtests that assess skill in associating letters with sounds, the examiner reads a word aloud and the student must identify the consonant–vowel–consonant cluster or digraph that has the same sound as the beginning, middle, or ending letters of the word. Syllabication subtests present polysyllabic words, and the student must either divide the word orally into syllables or circle specific syllables.

Blending subtests, on the other hand, are of three types. In the first method, the examiner may read syllables out loud (e.g., "wa-ter-mel-on") and ask the student to pronounce the word. In the second type of subtest, the student may be asked to read word parts and to pronounce whole words. In the third method, the student may be presented with alternative beginning, middle, and ending sounds and asked to produce a word.

Word Recognition Skills

Subtests of diagnostic reading tests that assess a pupil's word recognition skills are designed to ascertain what some educators call "sight vocabulary." In the past, sight words were thought to just be words that a student memorized and while there is some truth to that notion, sight words are much more reliant on decoding than many realized. As you're reading this sentence you do not need to sound out any of the words because you are a fluent reader, so essentially all of these words have become sight words for you. A student learns the correct pronunciation of letters and words through effective instructional experiences. The more a student is exposed to specific words and the more familiar those words become to the student, the more readily they recognize those words and are able to decode them fluently. Most readers of this book immediately recognize the word *hemorrhage* and do not have to employ phonetic skills to pronounce it. On the other hand, a word such as *sphenopalatine* is not a part of the sight vocabulary for most of us. Such words slow us down; we must use phonetics to analyze and read them.

Word recognition subtests form a major part of most diagnostic reading tests. Some tests expose words for brief periods of time (usually one-half second) to determine whether students can process words quickly. Students who recognize many words are said to have good word recognition skills. Other subtests assess letter recognition, recognition of words in isolation, and recognition of words in context.

Oral Reading

A number of tests and subtests are designed to assess the accuracy and/or fluency of a student's oral reading. Oral reading tests consist of a reading passage that varies in length depending on grade level. The examiner notes reading errors and behaviors that characterize the student's oral reading.

Rate of Reading

Fluency is a seemingly easy to understand term in the context of reading, but it is actually more complex than you might think (Cummings & Petscher, 2016). You know when you hear a student read out loud whether you would call them a fluent reader or not. But in this context, a good reader might also be called fluent if they recognize words quickly (without having to rely on phonetic analysis) and are in a good position to construct meaning of sentences and paragraphs. That good reader would also have to be accurate. Accuracy, correctly decoding a word, plus decoding at a rate that comprehension is facilitated, combine to create the construct of fluency (rate + accuracy = fluency).

First, let us consider rate. Readers who decode words at a slow rate have problems comprehending what they read, and the problems become more severe as the complexity of the reading material increases. Indeed, reading rate partnered with accuracy is an excellent general indicator of reading achievement. As a consequence, increasingly more states are including reading fluency as part of their comprehensive reading assessment systems. To obtain the rate of reading either silently or orally the test must be timed so that a rate per minute can be estimated.

Nonetheless, many commercially available diagnostic reading tests do not assess reading fluency and the timing of reading tests is more common when using formative assessments such as curriculum-based measurement. However, there are some exceptions. For example, the *Gray Oral Reading Test–Fifth Edition* (GORT-5) is timed. A pupil who reads a passage on the GORT-5 slowly but makes no errors in reading may earn a lower score than a rapid reader who makes one or two errors in reading.

Oral Reading Errors

Oral reading requires that students decode the word that is printed on the page correctly, which represents the accuracy portion of our fluent reader formula. However, all errors made by a student are not equal. It is important to carefully read the scoring directions for a test to know how specific errors are handled; each test handles these a bit differently. Some errors are relatively unimportant to the extent that they do not affect the student's comprehension of the material. Other errors are ignored. Examiners may note characteristics of a student's oral reading that are not counted as errors. Self-corrections are not counted as errors. Disregarded punctuation marks (e.g., failing to pause for a comma or to inflect vocally to indicate a question mark) are not counted as errors. Repetitions and hesitations due to speech handicaps (e.g., stuttering or stammering) are not counted as errors. Dialectic accents are not counted as mispronunciations. Other characteristics of a student's oral reading that may be of concern but may not count as errors include inappropriate head movement, finger pointing, loss of place, and lack of prosody (e.g., lack of expression or reading in a monotone voice).

Here are some examples of ways that oral reading may be scored on a test that you administer:

Gross Mispronunciation of a Word: A gross mispronunciation is recorded as an error when the pupil's pronunciation of a word bears so little resemblance to the proper pronunciation that the examiner must be looking at the word to recognize it. An example of gross mispronunciation is reading "encounter" as "actors."

Partial Mispronunciation of a Word: A partial mispronunciation can be one of several different kinds of errors. The examiner may have to pronounce part of a word for the student (an aid); the student may phonetically mispronounce specific letters (e.g., by reading "red" as "reed"); or the student may omit part of a word, insert elements of words, or make errors in syllabication, accent, or inversion.

Omission of a Word or Group of Words: Omissions consist of skipping individual words or groups of words.

Substitution of One Meaningful Word for Another: Substitutions consist of the replacement of one or more words in the passage by one or more different meaningful words. The student might read "dense" as "depress." Some oral reading tests require that examiners record the specific kind of substitution error. Substitutions are classified as meaning similarity (the words have similar meanings), function similarity (the two words have syntactically similar functions), graphic/phoneme similarity (the words look or sound alike), or a combination of the preceding.

Repetition: Repetition occurs when students repeat words or groups of words while attempting to read. In some cases, if a student repeats a group of words to correct an error, the original error is not recorded, but a repetition error is. In other cases, such behaviors are recorded simply as spontaneous self-corrections.

Inversion, or Changing of Word Order: Errors of inversion are recorded when the child changes the order of words appearing in a sentence. For example, the student reads "it was a pretty day" as "was it a pretty day." They have decoded the words accurately, but the inversion changes the meaning of the sentence.

Reading Comprehension

Diagnostic tests assess five different types of reading comprehension:

Literal comprehension entails understanding the information that is explicit in the reading material.

Inferential comprehension means interpreting, synthesizing, or extending the information that is explicit in the reading material.

Critical comprehension requires analyzing, evaluating, and making judgments about the material read.

Affective comprehension involves a reader's personal and emotional responses to the reading material.

Lexical comprehension means knowing the meaning of key vocabulary words.

In our opinion, the best way to assess reading comprehension is to give readers access to the material and have them restate or paraphrase what they have read.

Poor comprehension has many causes. The most common is poor decoding, which affects comprehension in two ways. First, if students cannot convert the graphemes (i.e., letters that represent sounds) to words, they cannot comprehend the message conveyed by those words. The second issue is more subtle. When students expend all of their mental resources on sounding out the words, they will not have the cognitive resources left to process the word meaning. For that reason, increasing reading fluency frequently diminishes problems in comprehension.

Another cause for poor reading comprehension is that students may not have received effective instruction on how to read for comprehension. Metacognition skills such as self-monitoring comprehension and rereading a sentence that was difficult to understand are skills that are helpful for students to be taught. Students can be taught to enhance their comprehension by using strategies such as summarizing the main idea, and integrating material with previous knowledge. Finally, individual characteristics can interact with the assessment of reading comprehension. For example, in an assessment of literal comprehension, a reader's memory capacity can affect comprehension scores unless the reader has access to the passage while answering questions about it or re-telling its gist. In addition, the extent to which a student has background information and interest in the topic area may affect the student's score. For instance, if a student has substantial prior knowledge about basketball and a passage on which the student is tested is about basketball, the student's score may reflect existing knowledge rather than current reading comprehension skills.

Although many of the same processes are involved in comprehending different types of texts, it is important to recognize that the skills necessary can vary slightly depending on genre or *type* of reading material. For instance, effective comprehension of narrative text may require one to read from beginning to end, and understand concepts such as characters, plot, and setting whereas effective comprehension of informational text may involve use of navigational tools such as the table of contents and index and understanding of how to comprehend information presented in diagrams. It is possible for a student to have strong comprehension skills for one type of genre and not for another. For this reason, it may be necessary to assess student comprehension skills across a wide variety of genres.

Other Reading and Reading-Related Behaviors

A variety of subtests that fit none of the aforementioned categories are included in diagnostic reading tests as either major or supplementary subtests. Examples of such tests include oral vocabulary, spelling, handwriting, and auditory discrimination. In most cases, such subtests are included simply to provide the examiner with additional diagnostic information.

Critical Considerations When Using Diagnostic Reading Measures

There are three major problems in the diagnostic assessment of reading strengths and weaknesses. The first is the problem of *curriculum match*. Students enrolled in different reading curricula or whose teachers use different instructional programs have different opportunities to learn specific skills. Reading instruction programs differ in the skills that are taught, in the emphasis placed on different skills, in the sequence in which skills are taught, and in the time at which skills are taught. Tests differ in the skills they assess. Thus, it can be expected that pupils studying different curricula and experiencing different instructional programs will perform differently on the same reading test. It can also be expected that pupils studying the same curriculum and experiencing the same instructional programs will perform differently on different reading tests. Assessors must be very careful to examine the match between skills taught in the students' curriculum and instructional program and skills tested. Most teachers' manuals for reading instructional programs include a listing of the skills taught at each level in the

13.2
PROGRESS MONITORING CHECK

series. Many authors of diagnostic reading tests now include in test manuals a list of the objectives measured by the test. Assessors should carefully examine the extent to which the test measures skills that have been covered during classroom instruction. Ideally, assessors would select specific parts of tests to measure exactly taught content. To the extent that there is a difference between what has been taught and what is tested, the test is not a valid measure.

A second problem is the *selection of tests that are appropriate for making different kinds of educational decisions*. We noted that there are different types of diagnostic reading tests. In making classification decisions, educators must administer tests individually. They may either use an individually administered test or give a group test to one individual. For making instructional planning decisions, the most precise and helpful information will be obtained by giving individually administered criterion-referenced measures. Educators can, of course, systematically analyze pupil performance on a norm-referenced test, but the approach is difficult and time-consuming. It may also be futile because norm-referenced tests usually do not contain enough items on which to base a diagnosis. When evaluating individual pupil progress, assessors must consider carefully the kinds of comparisons they want to make. If they want to compare pupils with same-grade peers, norm-referenced measures are useful. If, on the other hand, they want to know the extent to which individual pupils are mastering curriculum objectives, criterion-referenced measures are the diagnostic tests of choice.

The third problem is one of *generalization*. Assessors are faced with the difficult task of describing or predicting student performance in reading. Yet reading itself is difficult to describe, being a complex behavior composed of numerous subskills. Those who engage in reading diagnosis will do well to describe student performance in terms of specific skills or subskills measured (such as recognition of words in isolation, listening comprehension, and oral reading fluency), being careful to avoid over parsing subtest scores. Test interpreters should limit their predictions to making statements about probable performance of specific reading skills, not probable performance in reading in general. Using the reading diagnostic measures are just one part of making important education decisions for students. Diagnostic reading assessments serve their intended purpose when connected in a comprehensive assessment system to screening and progress monitoring (covered in Chapter 8, "Monitoring Student Progress Toward Instructional Goals," and Chapter 10, "Screening").

Commonly Used Diagnostic Reading Assessments

There are many diagnostic reading tests on the market. Schools and districts have a test library for testing professionals to use in specific cases. Information about some of the commonly used and easy-to-obtain measures is summarized in Table 13.1. In the case of a few of the tests, you'll notice that the test has not been normed within the last 10 years. Despite this limitation we have chosen to include some of these tests because we know from our experience and colleagues that these tests remain popular in school, clinical, and in education research settings. As with all of the assessments listed in this book, you'll want to choose an assessment that will help you answer your case-specific questions in order to develop an effective educational plan for the student.

Ensuring Fairness in Assessment of Reading Skills

It's important to remember that in order for assessment or instruction to be fair it does not need to be identical for all students. There is no one simple flow chart that will apply to all students. However, your decision to use a specific test must be defensible and reasoned. As test administrators and educators, it is our responsibility to determine the equitable and fair use and interpretation of diagnostic reading assessments that does not lead to over- or under-representation of students from minoritized populations. If you use the guiding principle that the primary reason for assessing reading skills is to plan appropriate reading instruction for individual students, then you will have a compass pointing you in the direction of fairness at all times. This approach entails aligning instruction to a student's level of skill development; thus, pinpointing the student's level of skill development in various areas. This alignment is essential to give teachers the knowledge to make those matches both with the curriculum and with the quality and intensity of the instructional delivery. Our role is to select tests that sample relevant skills, as quickly as possible, in nonbiased ways, and that link to the curriculum as directly as possible. A strength of reading skill measures in general, as opposed to measures of cognitive processes, is this direct link to specific reading skills. Reading skill measures are thus, low-inference measures that lead directly to recommended intervention actions.

Diagnostic reading assessments serve the purpose of identifying skill deficits. In this chapter we have identified formal and standardized diagnostic measures. This type of measure generally requires that the person administering the measure is trained and will administer and interpret the assessment for the intended purpose. Sometimes it can delay testing if a specialist is needed to administer the measure. Because timeliness of assessment is also an important consideration when applying fairness as a principle it should be noted that there are also informal, quick to administer reading diagnostic tests that a classroom teacher can use to get students access to intervention sooner. Examples of these measures include a phonics inventory, a word reading list, or an error analysis of a reading screening or progress monitoring measure already collected. A free training module on the use of informal diagnostic assessments, Informal Academic Diagnostic Assessment: Using Data to Guide Intensive Instruction, can be found at the National Center on Intensive Intervention website (intensiveintervention.org). Timeliness in testing and treatment, partnered with appropriate selection of assessments that closely align with instruction, can ensure the fairness principle is followed.

TABLE 13.1

Commonly Used Diagnostic Reading Measures

TITLE, AUTHOR(S), AND PUBLISHER	SKILLS ASSESSED	NORM GROUP	RELIABILITY EVIDENCE	VALIDITY EVIDENCE
Comprehensive Test of Phonological Processing–Second Edition (CTOPP-2) Wagner, Torgesen, & Rashotte (2013) PRO-ED	Phonological awareness, phonological memory, and rapid naming are three kinds of phonological processing abilities measured. Subtests include elision, blending words, sound matching, phoneme isolation, memory for digits, nonword repetition, rapid digit naming, rapid letter naming, rapid color naming, rapid object naming, blending nonwords, and segmenting nonwords.	Normed on 1,900 individuals in six states. Ethnically and racially nationally representative samples and stratified by ages 4 to 24.	Composite scores have a coefficient alpha of .85 or higher. Overall alternate-form reliability is .85 or higher for all composite scores. Internal consistency and alternate-form reliability is also demonstrated for subgroups of students based on race, learning disabled, and sex.	The authors report on three types of validity: content-description, criterion-prediction, and construct-identification. Item bias was examined using differential item functioning (DIF) and demonstrated no racial, gender, and ethnicity bias. Criterion-prediction validity Correlations between the CTOPP-2 and other tests of phonological awareness and other early literacy skills range from .66 to .82. Confirmatory factor analysis displayed strong model fit.
Gray Oral Reading Tests–Fifth Edition (GORT-5) Wiederholt & Bryant (2012) PRO-ED	Oral Reading and Reading Comprehension are the skills measured for ages 6 to 23. Subskills measured are rate, accuracy, passage comprehension, and oral reading.	Normed from 2009 through 2010 on 2,556 Individuals ages 6 to 23 from 33 states. Nationally representative in geographic region, race, gender, Hispanic status, parental educational attainment, income, and exceptionality status.	Alternate-form coefficient alpha of .91 or higher for all age intervals. Alternate-form test–retest immediate reliability ranges from .82 to .90. Alternate-form test–retest delayed reliability ranges from .77 to .88. Overall, the oral reading quotient is sufficiently reliable for making important decisions for individual students.	Item bias was examined using differential item functioning (DIF) and demonstrated little to no racial, gender, and ethnicity bias. Correlations with other reading tests varied from large to very large magnitudes, .54 to .85, with average correlations from .68 on the Accuracy subtest to .77 on the Oral Reading Index subtest. Criterion-prediction validity was strengthened by the sensitivity and specificity metrics including low numbers of false positives.

TITLE, AUTHOR(S), AND PUBLISHER	SKILLS ASSESSED	NORM GROUP	RELIABILITY EVIDENCE	VALIDITY EVIDENCE
Group Reading Assessment and Diagnostic Evaluation (GRADE) Williams (2001) Pearson	Five areas of reading are assessed for PK–12: Prereading includes picture matching, picture differences, verbal concepts, and picture categories. Reading readiness includes sound matching, rhyming, letter recognition, same and different words, phoneme-grapheme correspondence. Vocabulary includes of word reading, word meaning, and vocabulary. Comprehension includes Sentence and Passage comprehension. Oral language is measured by listening comprehension.	16,408 students were included in the spring and 17,024 were included in the fall sample in the late 1990s. Numbers of students tested in each grade ranged from 808 (seventh grade, spring) to 2,995 (kindergarten, spring). Geographic region characteristics were presented without disaggregating results by grade and were compared to the population data as reported by the U.S. Census Bureau (1998).	Total test coefficient alphas were calculated as measures of internal consistency for each form of the test, for each season of administration (fall and spring). These ranged from .89 to .98. Subtest–subtest combination coefficients ranged from .45 (Listening Comprehension, Form B, 11th grade, spring administration) to .97 (Listening Comprehension, Form A, preschool, fall administration). Of the 350 coefficients calculated, 99 out of 350 met or exceeded .90. Test–retest correlation coefficients ranged from .77 (fifth-grade students taking Form A of Level 5) to .98 (fourth-grade students taking Form A of Level 4). Alternate-form reliability ranged from .81 to .94.	The author presents three types of validity: content, criterion-related, and construct validity. Criterion-related coefficients ranged from .61 to .90 and was performed with a limited sample of elementary and middle school students. An attempt to demonstrate construct validity used correlations between scores, ages, and special education eligibility status with a small group of students.
i-Ready Curriculum Associates, (2018) Curriculum Associates	Three versions span Grades K–12 (Diagnostic, Growth, and Standards Mastery). Six Strands are measured (High Frequency Words, Phonics, Phonological Awareness, Reading Comprehension Literature, Reading Comprehension Informational Text, Vocabulary).	2016 norms included 3.9 million assessments taken by over 1 million students from over 4,000 schools. Stratified on sex, ethnicity, urbanicity, region, and free and reduced lunch level.	Internal consistency coefficients range from .70 to .95 for domain scores and .91 to .97 overall. Test–retest reliability of .70 to .88 is reported.	Content validity based on content development and review. Criterion/predictive validity based on Lexile linking and Quantile linking studies showing moderate to high relationship to performance on PARCC, SBAC, and several state assessments. Studies showing validity of setting growth targets.

(continues)

TABLE 13.1 (*continued*)

TITLE, AUTHOR(S), AND PUBLISHER	SKILLS ASSESSED	NORM GROUP	RELIABILITY EVIDENCE	VALIDITY EVIDENCE
MAP® Growth NWEA, 2019, NWEA	Assesses Reading Comprehension, Understanding of Genre and Text, and Vocabulary. The *Technical Manual* includes an extensive list of specific skills assessed matched to instructional areas and sub-areas	This is a standards-referenced test matched to the Common Core State Standards. The test includes an item bank of more than 42,000 items aligned to CCSS. A separate document entitled *MAP Growth Norms* (Thum & Hansen, 2015) is used to obtain norm-referenced scores like percentiles.	Internal consistency coefficients range from .86 to .91. Test–retest reliability coefficients range from .77 to .82.	Extensive evidence for content validity, based primarily on item development, is provided in the technical manual. Evidence for predictive/criterion validity is based on high correlations with performance on end of year state tests.
Star Reading Renaissance Learning, Inc. (2017)	A K–12 standards-based adaptive test aligned to the Common Core State Standards as well as other state and national reading and language arts standards. The five broad skills measured are: word knowledge and skills, comprehension strategies and constructing meaning, analyzing literary text, understanding author's craft, and analyzing argument and evaluating text. Those broad skills represent 46 skills.	Samples of 100,000 students in each grade level from first through 11th were included in the reliability analyses. Data were collected from 2013 through 2016 from a national representative sample stratified on geographic region, district socio-economic status, and district/school size.	Internal consistency coefficients range from .91 to .98. Alternate-form reliability ranges from .81 to .87.	Evidence for content validity, based primarily on item development, is provided in the technical manual. Evidence for concurrent and predictive validity is based on correlations with performance on end of year state tests. Concurrent validity for Grades 1 to 6 were on average .71 and predictive validity was on average .74 and predictive validity was on average .71. For Grades 7 to 12 the average concurrent validity was .72 and the average predictive validity was .80.

TITLE, AUTHOR(S), AND PUBLISHER	SKILLS ASSESSED	NORM GROUP	RELIABILITY EVIDENCE	VALIDITY EVIDENCE
Test of Reading Comprehension–Fourth Edition (TORC-4) Brown, Wiederholt, & Hammill, PRO-ED (2008)	First published in 1978 it has evolved to currently include five subtests in this fourth edition: relational vocabulary, sentence completion, paragraph construction, text comprehension, contextual fluency. The scaled scores from the five subtests are combined to create the Reading Comprehension index, an overall composite score. The test is normed on students from 7 to 17 years of age.	The normative sample of 1,942 students from 14 states is nationally representative of 2005 U.S. census data.	Reliability has been established for subgroups within the normative sample including by gender, race, ethnicity, and identified learning disability, gifted and talented, and ADHD. Internal consistency coefficients range from .90 to .99 on all subtests and each age range and .97 to .98 on the overall composite reading comprehension score.	Item bias was examined using differential item functioning (DIF) and demonstrated negligible racial, gender, and ethnicity bias for the majority of items with less than 4% of items or 5 or fewer items out of 124 having a potential bias. Criterion-prediction validity was demonstrated by measured by demonstrating correlations with four measures of literacy ranging from .51 to .78 with the reading comprehension composite score. Criterion test validity was demonstrated with a range of literacy tests including the WJ-III Broad Reading cluster and found that students scored similarly on the TORC-4 and the criterion tests.
Test of Silent Contextual Reading Fluency–Second Edition (TOSCRF-2) Hammill, Wiederholt, & Allen (2014), PRO-ED	Efficiently assesses the silent reading ability of students ages 7 through to 24 years by adapting reading passages used in the Gray Oral Reading (Wiederholt & Bryant, 2012) and Silent Reading (Wiederholt & Blalock, 2000) Tests.	2,375 students from 29 states were included in the nationally representative sample from 2009 to 2012. Geographic region, gender, race, ethnicity, household income, and parents' education were all included as stratified variables.	Alternate-form reliability across the four forms ranges from .97-.90. Average test–retest reliability ranges from .84 to .94 depending on the sample subgroup.	Criterion-prediction validity is demonstrated by reporting the correlations between the TOSCRF and nine other literacy assessments across 11 studies. The average correlation between the TOSCRF first and second edition with the other measures was .73 with a range of .41 to .89 depending on the measure and type of sample. Sensitivity median is reported at .74 and the specificity index is .90 which suggests an adequate diagnostic accuracy for the intended purposes.

(continues)

TABLE 13.1 (*continued*)

TITLE, AUTHOR(S), AND PUBLISHER	SKILLS ASSESSED	NORM GROUP	RELIABILITY EVIDENCE	VALIDITY EVIDENCE
Test of Silent Word Reading Fluency–Second Edition (TOSWRF-2) Mather, Hammill, Allen, & Roberts (2014); PRO-ED	Silent reading ability is composed of subskills of word identification, word comprehension, and silent word reading fluency.	2,429 students from 35 states were assessed from 2009 to 2012. Individuals ages 6 to 24 were a part of the normative sample. Less than 1% of the sample identified as having a traumatic brain injury, visual impairment, or physical/health impairment. Geographic region, gender, race, parental education, household income, and Hispanic status were used as stratification variables.	Internal consistency reliability coefficients ranged from .83 or above for all stratification subgroups including people with learning disabilities (.93), language impairments (.91). Test–retest reliability was .90 on average and ranged from .84 to .93 depending on grade level.	Correlations with 39 reading measures, 7 spelling measures, and 2 orthographic measures are reported that range from .51 (WJ-R Passage Comprehension) to .92 (*Test of Orthographic Competence*).

Several tests have normative samples that were collected more than 15 years ago. According to APA, achievement tests standardized more than 15 years ago are not be used to make normative comparisons.

1. Why is it important to assess students' reading skills?
2. Describe the foundational reading skills as identified by Reading Science.

MONITORING CHECK

1. What is assessed in word attack, oral reading and reading comprehension?
2. Why is curriculum match an important consideration in choosing a diagnostic reading test?

MONITORING CHECK

CHAPTER 14

Using Diagnostic Mathematics Measures

LEARNING OBJECTIVES

1. Understand why we administer and use diagnostic math tests.
2. Explain the ways in which mathematics is taught.
3. Identify the skills sampled by diagnostic mathematics tests.
4. Understand how to use diagnostic math assessment for intervention planning.

Diagnostic assessment in mathematics is designed to identify specific strengths and weaknesses in skill development most commonly for the purpose of planning intervention. We have learned that assessment in schools occurs on a continuum: screening to determine risk at the class and student level, progress monitoring to generate data for instructional decision making, summative evaluation or performance at key intervals, and diagnostic assessment to develop interventions for struggling students. In multitiered systems of support (MTSS), math interventions can be delivered at the whole-class level, in small groups, and individually. Diagnostic assessment helps teachers know which skills to target at each tier.

Because mathematics proficiency is logically hierarchical with new understandings building on earlier understandings, diagnostic math assessment is also logical. Because the successful performance of all mathematical operations depends on the successful performance of other operations (e.g., multiplication depends on addition), it is easier to specify sequences of skill development which become the basis for assessment targets when screening, monitoring progress, developing interventions, and making decisions about intervention response.

Why Do We Assess Mathematics?

There are several reasons to assess students' mathematics knowledge and skills. First, diagnostic math tests are intended to provide sufficiently detailed information so that teachers and intervention teams can ascertain a student's mastery of specific math skills and plan individualized and supplemental math instruction. Second, some diagnostic math tests provide teachers with specific information on the kinds of items students in their classes pass and fail. This gives teachers information about the extent to which the curriculum and instruction in their classes are working, and it provides opportunities to identify common skill gaps for reteaching to better promote mastery of important math skills. Finally, diagnostic math tests are occasionally used to make eligibility decisions. Therefore, diagnostic math tests are often used to establish special learning needs and eligibility for programs for children with learning disabilities in mathematics.

Diagnostic math assessment has evolved over the years. Now that year-end tests are available that evaluate math performance relative to state standards, summative evaluation of student progress at the program level relies on year-end accountability tests. Year-end accountability assessments can also be useful at the student level to signify a need for intervention in subsequent grades, alert teachers to gaps in skill proficiencies that might be addressed via intervention to improve performance on subsequent tests, and document below age- or grade-level standards toward meeting the eligibility criteria for a learning disability in math. Thus, broad diagnostic math measures that are not aligned with state standards, such as the *Test of Mathematics Ability* (TOMA), *Comprehensive Mathematical Abilities Test* (CMAT), *KeyMath*, and others, have declined in use in most systems. Simultaneously, advances in direct skill measures, such as those used to accomplish screening and progress monitoring, have proliferated. Direct skill measures allow greater specificity in identifying whole class and individual student needs for supplemental and individual intervention. Wherever possible, a recursive process of teaching and direct skill assessment has become the basis for planning, adjusting, and even evaluating instruction using measures and tool packages such as *Star Math* (renaissance.com), *MAP Growth* (nwea.com), FASTT Math (scholastic.com), easyCBM (easyCBM.com), and more traditional paper-and-pencil-based CBM measures like those used by SpringMath (sourcewelltech.org) and Acadience Math K–6 (acadiencelearning .org). These measures are more efficient than earlier, more traditional diagnostic math tests and offer greater specificity and economy in selecting skill targets for intervention, greater sensitivity for evaluating gains in Response to Intervention (RTI), and the flexibility needed to align the measures with core instruction and grade-level expectations.

Tests like the TOMA-3, *Test of Mathematical Abilities–Third Edition* (proedinc.com), which have excellent psychometric properties, remain useful primarily during evaluation procedures to determine eligibility for those students who do not have existing test scores from year-end testing. However, such measures are rarely used to develop interventions, to inform instruction, or to evaluate intervention effects.

In this chapter, we begin with an explanation of the evidence pertaining to effective core math instruction. The primary determinant of who will be identified as needing intervention (and therefore needing diagnostic math assessment to build intervention) is the core instructional program. Unfortunately, the quality of core instruction is highly variable across schools and therefore, teachers must be equipped with some background to know how to ensure students are provided with adequate core instruction prior to identifying them as needing supplemental intervention.

Instructional Debates in Math

Since 2005, proficiency scores in math have gotten worse and gaps for minoritized students have widened (nationsreportcard.gov/mathematics). Only about one in four 12th-grade students is considered to be proficient in mathematics, and this value has remained unchanged since 2005. Math achievement is a major concern serving as an economic barrier for three out of four children in preventing successful enrollment and completion of post-secondary education. Poor math proficiency is thus associated with worse economic trajectories for the vast majority of U.S. schoolchildren.

There have been decades of debate about how best to teach math. In the 1950s, mathematics emphasized the mastery of basic facts and algorithms, deductive reasoning, and proofs; teachers explained, modeled, and gave corrective feedback. With the launch of Sputnik in 1957 and the Soviet lead in space exploration, some reacted by blaming the way in which science and mathematics were taught in U.S. schools. The old way was thought to stifle creativity and understanding.

In the 1960s, *new math* became popular in teacher-education programs in colleges and universities. Set theory, number bases, and the commutative, associative, and distributive properties became part of the curriculum. However, it soon became clear that the new math curricula were not improving student performances. In the mid-1970s, *Why Johnny Can't Add* convincingly criticized the many shortcomings of new math and advocated a return to more traditional mathematics curricula.

In the 1980s, new math was replaced by a constructivist approach to math instruction, which remains popular today, and which we will refer to as "minimally guided instruction" (Kirschner et al., 2006). This approach provided students with the freedom to select activities that fit their interests and prior experiences. Using concrete materials (like objects for counting), students created their own subjective mathematical understandings using their own curiosity, thoughts, and conclusions. Teachers were expected to orchestrate situations in which their students constructed knowledge with little or no help from the teacher and these methods have been given many names including "discovery learning" and "inquiry-based instruction." Tactics like allowing students to wrestle with challenging math content as a mechanism to attain "deeper understanding" when they finally made the correct independent discovery (a process called "productive struggle") and having students learn new understandings outside of class and then teach the teacher the new understanding (a process called "flipped classrooms") are just two examples of popular tactics that have been promoted as superior ways to teach math using minimally guided instructional principles.

Minimally guided instruction emerged out of a desire to promote more than rote understanding or memorization of algorithms and to instead help students understand the coherent nature of numbers, operations, and problem solving. Advocates of minimally guided instruction argued that teaching the procedures necessary in the algorithm to solve the problem produced shallow understanding and did not result in students understanding the algorithm. Advocates alleged that procedural instruction resulted in students understanding the algorithm like a memorized trick that would be easily forgotten, an allegation that was probably true. In effect, minimally guided instruction largely turns the responsibility for learning over to the student. It is a powerful example of how well-intended ideas and desires (i.e., to promote deeper understanding) can lead to inadvisable tactics occurring in practice. When practices are implemented in classrooms without experimental evaluation, children are subjected to unconsented experimentation and important instructional opportunities are lost. Minimally guided math instruction has led to block schedules (treating longer-duration class intervals as a mechanism for improving learning), prolonged use of manipulatives or counters or counting tactics in lieu of teaching algorithms, cooperative learning arrangements where students are intended to wrestle with challenging math content and discover the correct solutions without adult guidance. All of these tactics have been shown to be inferior in research and to cause worsened, rather than better, learning.

By 2001, it was clear that advice for how to teach math might be causing more harm than benefit to math achievement in the United States. Jon Star (2005) wrote an important article detailing how the concepts of procedural skill and conceptual understanding had really been falsely pitted against each other, and the point of this article was to make plain the abysmal failings of minimally guided instruction as a mechanism to establish this poorly defined construct of "deeper conceptual understanding." Star explained that procedural knowledge is not necessarily rote knowledge and that as students work with procedures, their conceptual understanding is improved and vice versa. A series of experiments by independent research teams published in prestigious academic journals over the next 15 years demonstrated this reality: Excellent math instruction works in concert to teach procedural skill and conceptual knowledge daily.

Decades of research in several fields including cognitive science, school psychology, and special education have demonstrated that minimally guided instruction is not only not helpful for students, but actually produces measurable harm to students who require effective instruction to attain minimal math proficiencies. Despite early acknowledgment of these scientific findings in policy advice including the *Adding It Up* report in 2001 and all subsequent policy documents (e.g., *National Mathematics Advisory Panel Report*, 2008), minimally guided instruction continues to take instructional space in school, much to the misfortune of students.

Evidence-Based Math Instruction

The Institute for Education Sciences (IES) from the U.S. Department of Education has published two practice guides in the last two decades summarizing experimental data and making targeted recommendations for evidence-based instruction in mathematics (Fuchs et al., 2021). Based on the evidence, these recommendations are as follows:

- provide systematic instruction
- actively teach mathematical language
- use concrete-representational-abstract sequencing in math instruction
- use number lines when teaching to help students understand quantity and operational effects on quantity
- provide deliberate instruction in solving word problems
- use timed activities to build fluency

The body of math instruction research published in cognitive science, school psychology, and special education is an overwhelming indictment of minimally guided instruction as a primary means of teaching new math understandings.

But like many ideas in education, even when the evidence shows that certain tactics do not work and may even cause harm, it can take decades for them to fade away from daily use in schools. VanDerHeyden and Codding (2020) summarized a number of prevalent and popular myths in math instruction that are often conveyed to teachers in their training programs and professional-development experiences. These myths include that conceptual understanding must be established before procedural skill can be developed, that directly teaching an algorithm is harmful, that discovered solutions produce deeper understanding than solutions that are taught using explicit instruction, that timed assessment and instruction causes student anxiety, and that targeting student's executive function skills will promote stronger math achievement. These beliefs are problematic because they often interfere with teacher use of effective practices during core instruction. Effective instruction, by definition, is instruction that produces learning when it is used. See the Stakeholder Perspective by Jared Campbell, Statewide Lead Consultant for Mathematics Initiative at Pennsylvania Training and Technical Assistance Network (PaTTAN).

In summary, new teachers should not be surprised to encounter strong feelings about math instruction. When there is debate, returning to the science of effective instruction

Jared Campbell, MEd, Statewide Lead for Mathematics Initiative, Pennsylvania Training and Technical Assistance Network (PaTTAN)

Mathematics teachers need to begin their educational careers understanding that the reality of teaching is much broader than the courses they received in their teacher preparation program. There is a limited amount of time to prepare teachers to enter the classroom; programs must be selective with course content. The goal of a teacher program is to prepare teachers for entry into the profession, not mastery. Becoming a master teacher is a lifelong endeavor. Being a teacher involves a lifetime of learning that changes as research evolves, as school systems adjust, as educational priorities shift, and as your students change.

The reality is that your general-education teacher-training program likely prioritized research in general education. There are research efforts in the fields of behavior, special education, and school psychology that will come to play a major role in improving your craft. You must study educational research from multiple perspectives.

Professional development in the general-education arena is often strategy heavy. As a teacher, I have experienced trainings that showed us a bunch of instructional strategies with the hopes that we might try just one. Often, there was no guidance about when to utilize any particular strategy. I would go back to my room, do my best, and hope for the best. If it went well I would consider it a good strategy, and I would continue using it. If it did not go well, I would simply move on. I never considered the fact that I may not have done the strategy correctly or that it may not have been what my students needed at that time. At that time, I was naive to the research of other disciplines such as school psychology.

Had I known about the Instructional Hierarchy, I would have considered how my students' performance indicated the types of evidence-based practices that would have been helpful. Then I could have made a better instructional match. Had I known about implementation science, I would have solicited coaching supports to ensure successful usage of those practices. I would offer these points for consideration for young math teachers as they strive to enhance their professional learning:

- Do not rely on general-education–focused teacher organizations alone. Instead, validate and integrate these ideas with other fields of education research.
- Knowledge of instructional strategies will not be enough. You must be sure quality research supports their use and be able to match them to students' needs through the Instructional Hierarchy.
- Data are necessary to make an instructional match and to determine its effect on student performance.
- Fluency has its place in mathematics learning. In fact, building fluency is what ensures students can do something easily enough so that they can flexibly apply it to and integrate it with other mathematical ideas later.

can help to ensure all children are provided access to effective instruction. After all, there is no such thing as one-size-fits-all instructional tactics, but rather tactics that can work for the right problem when properly used at a given moment in time, which is the purpose of diagnostic math assessment. We recommend that you follow the IES practice guide recommendations to deliver instruction in your classroom. We also recommend that you use a strong system of progress monitoring to evaluate instructional tactics to make sure that they work for your students. We will detail what to assess and how to assess it for intervention planning in the remaining sections of this chapter.

Skills and Understandings That Should Be Assessed in Math

Fortunately, knowing what skills children should master in what order during K–12 instruction has become much easier since 2000. First, the National Council for Teachers of Mathematics (NCTM) took a step forward when they published *Principles and Standards for School Mathematics*. This publication recognized that certain learning standards were important for students to master during K–12 math instruction and arrived in concert with the requirement for states to articulate standards and measure progress toward standards as part of educational accountability. In 2006, NCTM published *Curriculum Focal Points for Prekindergarten Through Grade 8 Mathematics*, and this was a bigger step forward because it brought both recognition that some standards "mattered" more than others and installed a prioritization scheme, which was enormously helpful at the time. In 2009, the Common Core State Standards (CCSS) were published, which improved upon the Focal Points because they offered greater specificity of skills. Now, most state math standards are very similar to the CCSS even when they do not officially use CCSS. Thus, the CCSS standards are an excellent starting place to understand which skills to assess to determine whether students are on track in their math instruction and to develop effective interventions when they are not.

Diagnostic Assessment of Math in MTSS

Math assessment begins with screening. As detailed in Chapter 10, screening can be used to evaluate programs of instruction and to identify individual students who are in need of supplemental intervention in MTSS. Screening in mathematics typically involves direct assessment of specific computational skills that are aligned with grade-level content. Generally, these assessments are timed and follow the basic standard procedures of curriculum-based measurement.

When a student is identified as needing intervention, the intervention team has to collect additional data to build an effective intervention, which is where diagnostic assessment becomes the next step in the process. The first goal of the assessment is to identify the skill or skills that should be targeted during intervention. Beginning with grade-level expectations (starting with the state standards or the Common Core), the teacher can examine an instructional calendar if one is provided by the district. An instructional calendar specifies which skills are to be mastered on a timeline for the school year. Thus, the teacher has an organizing scheme to sequence and pace instruction during math, using the textbook and other tools to support instruction. The teacher can also assess student proficiency directly to understand whether students have mastered the taught understanding or whether more instruction and practice is needed to reach mastery.

Starting with the expected skill, the teacher can then map out logical prerequisite skills that enable success on the problem skill. Let's work through an example in Figure 14.1.

Let's say that a second-grade student is struggling with adding two-digit numbers with and without regrouping. The teacher can directly assess that skill. If the student's performance is in the at-risk range, the teacher can then assess addition of two-digit numbers without regrouping to determine if the trouble is specific to the regrouping skill. If the student's performance is still in the risk range, the teacher can then assess sums to 20 to determine if addition of basic facts is causing the student's trouble. If performance is still in the risk range, the teacher can assess still simpler facts, sums to 9. Assessment can continue in finer slices until the teacher identifies the specific skill that is causing the student to have trouble with the goal skill. Identifying a logical sequence of skills is sometimes referred to as building a task or skill hierarchy.

Once the teacher identifies the starting intervention skill, the teacher can then select an intervention tactic that is useful for establishing accurate performance and understanding (e.g., an acquisition intervention) or an intervention that is useful for building fluency. For example, if the student scores in the risk range on addition with regrouping, but scores in the mastery range for addition without regrouping, then the teacher

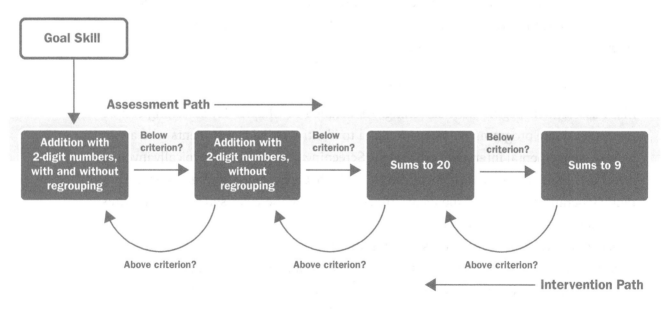

FIGURE 14.1. Possible sequence of assessment to determine intervention target for a second-grade student.

will use an intervention that targets conceptual understanding of place value properties. Most likely the teacher will work with expanded notation and mapping quantities on a number line along with explicit procedural instruction to establish understanding of how to regroup accurately within an addition algorithm. Once the child becomes accurate, then the teacher would change the intervention to provide intervals of practice and goals for improvement.

Progress Monitoring Assessment Following Diagnostic Assessment

Once the teacher has selected the right intervention and begun working with the student, progress must be monitored. Weekly assessment of the skill being targeted via intervention is important to permit adjustment of the intervention (e.g., increasing task difficulty in increments until the goal skill is mastered). If, for example, the student's intervention began with sums to 20, then once the weekly score for sums to 20 reached the mastery range, the teacher would change the skill to addition of two-digit number without regrouping and continue with intervention. Weekly monitoring of the goal skill is important to verify generalization or transfer (i.e., the skill being targeted in intervention is producing the desired return in improving the skill that the child needs to be on grade level). In this example, that means assessing addition of two-digit numbers with regrouping each week.

Specific Diagnostic Mathematics Tests

In Table 14.1, we provide specific information on commonly used diagnostic mathematics tests. We show the authors of each test, the age or grade range for which the test is intended to be used, specific skills assessed by each test, the nature of the norm group, and information on the reliability and validity of each measure. Note that several of the diagnostic mathematics tests have not been updated for nearly 20 years and users should use the norms for those tests with utmost caution.

Ensuring Fairness in Mathematics Testing

Diagnostic math measures were prevalent before year-end accountability assessments were developed but have declined in their practical use in classrooms today because they are not very useful for developing interventions. Because diagnostic assessment is mostly needed to build interventions and research has demonstrated that brief assessments of direct skills connected to grade-level learning expectations are superior in efficiency and specificity to pinpoint math skill gaps and intervention needs, external/broader math measures are rarely used. Instead, direct skill measures are more commonly used for intervention planning. When a child is being evaluated for a possible

TABLE 14.1

Commonly Used Diagnostic Mathematics Tests

Test, Author(s), & Publisher	Skills Assessed	Norms	Reliability Evidence	Validity Evidence
Group Math Assessment Diagnostic Evaluation (G*MADE) Williams, 2004, Pearson	Math Concepts and Communication, Operations and Computation, Process and Applications	First, a bias study was conducted on 10,000 students to see if the test was biased on the basis of gender, race/ethnicity, or geographic region. Then, the test was normed on >28,000 students in K–12 stratified on the basis of geographic region, community type, and socioeconomic status. The norm sample is outdated.	Internal consistency reliabilities exceed .74 and 90% exceed .80. Test–retest reliabilities exceed .80 with the exception of .78 for level 4, form A.	Content validity based on mapping to NCTM Math Standards. Several studies support adequate criterion predictive validity based on correlations with other math achievement measures.
KeyMath-3 Diagnostic Assessment Connolly, 2007, Pearson	Numeration, Algebra, Geometry, Measurement, Data Analysis and Probability, Mental Computation and Estimation, Addition and Subtraction, Multiplication and Division, Foundations of Problem Solving, Applied Problem Solving	Standardized on 3,630 individuals ages 4-6 to 21 years of age using demographic characteristics from the 2004 census. Crosstabs are reported. In addition, representative samples of students with emotional disturbance, learning disabilities, speech/language disturbance, intellectual disability, and developmental delay were included in the norms.	Internal consistency coefficients for students in K and first grade are low. At other grades, reliability coefficients generally exceed .80. Test–retest reliabilities exceed .80 with the exception of the Foundations of Problem Solving subtest (.70) and the Geometry subtest (.78).	Evidence for content validity is good based on correlation with NCTM standards. Evidence for criterion/predictive validity is moderate based on correlations with KeyMath-3 normative update and G*MADE.
Test of Mathematical Abilities–Third Edition (TOMA-3) Brown, Cronin, & Bryant, 2013, PRO-ED	Four core subtests (Mathematical Symbols and Concepts, Computation, Mathematics in Everyday Life, Word Problems); one supplemental subtest (Attitude Toward Math)	Normed on 1,456 students in 21 states stratified on the basis of gender, region, ethnicity, Hispanic status, exceptionality status, household income, and parental education based on the 2011 census.	Internal consistency reliabilities for subtests range from .86 to .93 and for composite from .96 to .97. Test–retest reliabilities exceed .8 with one exception.	Content validity based on item selection and differential item function analysis; criterion/predictive validity based on moderate to high correlations with CMAY and on confirmatory factor analysis.

Test, Author(s), & Publisher	Skills Assessed	Norms	Reliability Evidence	Validity Evidence
Test of Early Mathematics Ability–Third Edition (TEMA-3) Ginsburg & Baroody, 2003, PRO-ED	Informal math (Numbering Skills, Number Comparisons, Calculations, Concepts); formal Math (Numeral Literacy, Mastery of Number Facts, Calculation Skills, Understanding of Concepts)	Standardized on 1,228 children (637 took form A and 591 took form B) in 15 states. Stratified on the basis of geographic region, gender, race, ethnicity, family income, educational level of parents, and disabling condition. The size of the norm group was very limited and the norms are now outdated.	Internal consistency reliability for form A range from .92 to .95 and for form B from .95 to .95. Test–retest reliabilities range from .82 to .93.	Content validity based on item selection and criterion/predictive validity established by moderate to high correlations with relevant subtests of KeyMath R/NU, WJIV Achievement, DAB3, and YCAT.
Comprehensive Mathematical Abilities Test–Second Edition (CMAT-2) Hresko, Herron, & Sherbenou, 2022, PRO-ED	Core composites (General Mathematics, Basic Calculations, Mathematical Reasoning); supplemental composites (Advanced Calculations, Practical Applications); global composite (Global Mathematics Ability); six core subtests (Addition; Subtraction; Multiplication; Division; Problem Solving; Charts, Tables, and Graphs); six supplemental subtests (Algebra, Geometry, Rational Numbers, Time, Money, Measurement)	Standardized on 1,173 students in 32 states stratified on the basis of gender, geographic area, race, educational attainment of parents, residence, ethnicity, and family income based on the 2019 census.	Coefficient alpha reliabilities range from .83 to .92 for subtests and from .93 to .99 for composites.	Content validity is based on item development and systematic match of items to curricula and to NCTM Math Standards. Criterion related validity was established by showing moderate to nearly perfect correlations with performance on KeyMath-3 DA, SAGES-3, TOMA-3, and WJIV ACH.
MAP Growth Assessment NWEA, 2019	Mathematics K–12 assesses skills ranging from counting and cardinality to advanced calculation skills, while Specific High School Mathematics assesses skills in Algebra I, II, Geometry and Integrated Mathematics I, II, and III. Extensive lists of specific skills assessed matched to instructional areas are included in the technical manual NWEA, 2019),	This is a standards-referenced test comprised of an item bank containing more than 42,000 items aligned to Common Core State Standards and CTM standards. A separate publication entitled *MAP Growth Norms* (Thum & Hansen, 2015) is used to obtain standard scores such as percentiles.	Internal consistency coefficients range from .86 to .98, while test–retest reliability coefficients range from .83 to .92.	Content validity is based on extensive item development and studies of item match and DIF. Content/predictive validity was established by showing moderate to high prediction of scores on end-of-year state mathematics tests.

(continues)

TABLE 14.1 *(continued)*

Test, Author(s), & Publisher	Skills Assessed	Norms	Reliability Evidence	Validity Evidence
Star Math Renaissance Learning, 2021	Computer-adaptive test that assesses skills in four domains (Numbers and Operations; Algebra; Geometry and Measurement; Data Analysis, Statistics, and Probability). Fifty-four skill sets and over 790 core skills contained in an item bank of over 6,000 items.	Standardized in 2017 on 1,917,271 students with separate norms in fall (1,347,950 students) and spring (976,130 students). Students drawn from all 50 states and D.C. and stratified on the basis of gender, geographic region, school size, and district socioeconomic status. A unified set of norms was produced so that scores on *Star Reading* and *Star Math* could be compared.	Internal consistency reliabilities range from .85 to .94. Test–retest reliabilities are best represented by alternate forms reliabilities because in computer-adaptive testing each administration is a new form. Alternate-form reliabilities range from .67 to .84.	Content validity evidence is based on item selection and development and match to state and national standards. Factor analysis studies were conducted to show the unidimensionality of *Star Math*. Criterion/predictive validity was established by showing high predictions of scores on end-of-year state tests and by showing moderate to high correlations with other measures like NWEA MAP and *Terra Nova*.
i-Ready Diagnostic and Growth Curriculum Associates, 2018	Four strands (Algebra, Geometry, Measurement, Numbers and Operations)	2016 norms included 3.9 million assessments taken by over 1,000,000 students from over 4,000 schools. Norms were stratified on the basis of sex, ethnicity, urbanicity, region, and free/reduced-price lunch level. Separate norms are available for fall, winter, and spring.	Internal consistencies for domain scores range from .74 to .96 and from .92 to .96 for overall math score. Test–retest reliabilities range from .71 to .89.	Content validity is based on item selection and development matched to content of mathematics curricula. Quantile linkage studies were conducted demonstrating moderate to high relationship to performance on PARCC, SBAC, and several state assessments.
SpringMath Education Research and Consulting, 2013, Sourcewell Technology	Measures 145 skills in seven areas (Combining Whole Numbers and Variables; Taking Whole Numbers and Variables; Factors, Products, Exponents, with Whole Numbers; Quantity Discrimination, Ordinal Position and Place Value; Solve for Unknowns; Create Equivalent Quantities)	No norms per se. Decision rules are mastery measurement, trials to criterion, or rate of improvement (ROI) compared to same-class peers' median rate of improvement given the same intervention.	Alternate-form reliabilities range from .77 to .88. Model-based reliability findings found that variance across generate alternate forms attributable to the probe were trivial (less than 5%). Most variance was explained at the student level. Reliability coefficients were greater than .7 on the first trial (ranged from .74 to .92) and .8 (range from .83 to .95) at all grade levels.	Specificity, sensitivity, and the lower bound of the confidence interval around the area under the curve (indicating discriminant validity) all met or exceeded .80 for measures at all grades except kindergarten, for which sensitivity was .79. Additional evidence for convergent and discriminant validity based on moderate correlations ($r = .4$ to $r = .6$) with end-of-year tests in math and low correlations with end-of-year tests in reading.

LD in math and does not have available year-end accountability data to determine below age- or grade-level achievement in math, an external/broad diagnostic math measure could be useful. Assessment teams must exercise caution in using an external diagnostic math assessment during eligibility evaluation because the math assessment may not be well aligned with the program of instruction that the student has received. Thus, math intervention data are enormously protective where global measures might be disconnected from the child's instructional experience. If the student has a low achievement score but also has data to indicate that the student is mastering the content introduced during core instruction or has had a strong response to supplemental small-group or individual intervention, then the team must consider that the diagnostic math test was not reflective of the child's true capacity for achievement because the poor achievement might be due to lack of instruction in the skills assessed.

The history of ineffective mathematics instruction and assessment, similar to that of reading in the previous chapter, still lingers in today's classrooms and unfortunately students pay the price with poor outcomes and sometimes stress and anxiety as well. Teachers also pay a price because they've invested precious time on ineffective practices that don't lead to the outcomes that they desire for their students. Using mathematics assessment across the tiers from universal screening to diagnostic and progress monitoring will ensure that teachers have the information they need to make instructional decisions.

*14.1
PROGRESS
MONITORING
CHECK*

Write your answers to each of the following questions and then compare your responses to the text.

1. Describe the trends in student math performance over the past 40 years.
2. Why is minimally-guided instruction an ineffective method for teaching mathematics?
3. Describe one effective mathematics instructional tactic.
4. How does effective progress monitoring support intervention implementation?

CHAPTER 15

Using Oral and Written Language Measures and Measures of Receptive Vocabulary

LEARNING OBJECTIVES

1. Know why we assess oral and written language.
2. Understand how cultural and language background may influence performance on language tests.
3. Be familiar with commonly used measures or oral language, written language, and picture–vocabulary tests.
4. Describe ways to make language assessment fair.

Jill's fifth-grade teacher and her parent expressed concerns to the problem-solving team at Brownville Elementary School. The teacher had read about students with what was called central auditory processing disorders (CAPD) and thought Jill demonstrated all the characteristics of that disorder. Her behavior in the classroom was characterized as often off task, and she had difficulty attending to tasks and following oral directions, was easily distracted by noise, made frequent requests for repetition of information, confused similar letter sounds, often appeared not to be listening, and had poor memory skills. The teacher and parent completed checklists indicating concerns with central auditory processing. At the recommendation of the Teacher Assistance Team, Jill was taken to her family doctor to address concerns about attention challenges and to rule these out as a possible reason for classroom-performance issues. A trial of medication for attention-deficit disorder was completed and Jill showed remarkable improvements in attention and focus but continued to struggle with what appeared to be listening and comprehension components of classroom activities. The speech-language pathologist was brought in to assess Jill's language skills as well as make recommendations about audiological assessment for CAPD.

Jill was administered the *Clinical Evaluation of Language Fundamentals* test. The results were surprising: Her receptive language standard score was 91 and expressive language standard score was 76. This child did not have a CAPD but, rather, expressive language impairment. She could understand and process what was taking place and being asked of her, but she could not organize or formulate her responses well. The speech-language pathologist recommended extensive language therapy to address expressive language. As a result, Jill was able to demonstrate appropriate expressive language skills. Language testing is a vital component of assessing which language disabilities are and are not present and help specialists to avoid making inappropriate intervention recommendations and eligibility decisions.

In this chapter, we discuss three kinds of measures: tests of oral language, tests of written language, and measures of receptive and expressive vocabulary. Until the mid-1980s, measures of receptive vocabulary were used by school personnel as indices of intellectual functioning. They were criticized because they were, in fact, measures only of receptive vocabulary. We'll review several of those measures in this chapter—the *Peabody Picture Vocabulary Test–Fifth Edition* (Dunn, 2019), the *Receptive One-Word Picture Vocabulary Test–Fourth Edition* (Martin & Brownell, 2011), and the *Ortiz Picture Vocabulary Acquisition Test* (Ortiz, 2018)—to highlight some of the limitations and strengths of language and vocabulary tests.

The assessment of language competence should include evaluation of a student's skill in both comprehension and expression of language in a spoken and/or written format. There are four major communication processes: oral comprehension (listening and comprehending speech), written comprehension (reading), oral expression (speaking), and written expression (writing). In assessing language skills, it is important to break language down into processes and measure each one. Each language process makes different demands on a person's ability to communicate and a student's ability to participate in the learning environment. Performance in one area does not always predict performance in the others. For example, a child who has typical comprehension does not necessarily have typical production skills. Also, a child with average expressive skills may have problems with receptive language. Therefore, a complete language assessment will include examination of both oral and written reception (comprehension) and expression (production).

Educators, psychologists, linguists, and speech-language pathologists often have different perspectives on which skills make up language. These different views have resulted in the development of a plethora of tests designed to assess language skills or abilities, each with an apparently unique method of assessing language. The terminology used to describe the behaviors and skills assessed can be confusing as well. Terms such as morphology, semantics, syntax, and supralinguistic functioning are used, and sometimes different test authors use different terms to mean the same thing. One author's vocabulary subtest is another's measure of "lexical semantics." We define language as a code for conveying ideas—a code that includes phonology, semantics, morphology, syntax, and pragmatics. These terms are defined as follows:

Phonology: The hearing and production of speech sounds. The term *articulation* is considered a synonym for phonology.

Semantics: The study of word meanings. In assessment, this term is generally used to refer to the derivation of meaning from single words. The term *vocabulary* is often used interchangeably with semantics.

Morphology: The use of affixes (prefixes and suffixes) to change the meaning of words used in sentences. Morphology also includes verb tense ("John is going" versus "John was going").

Syntax: The use of word order to convey meaning. Typically, there are rules for arranging words into sentences. In language assessment, the word *grammar* is often used to refer to a combination of morphology and syntax.

Pragmatics: The social context in which a sentence occurs. Context influences both the way a message is expressed and the way it is interpreted. For example, the sentence, "Can you close the door?" can have different meanings to a student sitting closest to an open door in a classroom and a student undergoing physical therapy to rehabilitate motor skills. According to Carrow-Woolfolk (1995), contexts that influence language comprehension and production include:

- Social variables, such as the setting and the age, roles, relationships, cultural background, and number of participants in a discourse.
- Linguistic variables produced by the type of discourse (which might be a conversation, narrative, lecture, or text).
- The intention, motivation, knowledge, and style of the sender.

Supralinguistics: A second order of analysis required to understand the meaning of words or sentences. For example, much language must be interpreted in a non-literal way (sarcasm, indirect requests, and figurative language). Dad may say that the lawn looks like a hay field, when he is actually implying that he wants his child to cut the grass. Mom may say that the weather is "great," when she really means that she is tired of all the cloudy and rainy weather.

Throughout this chapter we use "**comprehension**" as a synonym for receptive language and "**production**" as a synonym for expressive language. Table 15.1 defines each of the basic language components for receptive and expressive modalities.

TABLE 15.1

Language Subskills for Each Channel of Communication

	Channel of Communication	
Language Component	**Reception (Comprehension)**	**Expression (Production)**
Phonology	Hearing and discriminating speech sounds	Articulating speech sounds
Morphology and syntax	Understanding the grammatical structure of language	Using the grammatical structure of language
Semantics	Understanding vocabulary, meaning, and concepts	Using vocabulary, meaning, and concepts
Pragmatics	Understanding a speaker's or writer's intentions	Using awareness of social aspects of language
Ultimate language skill	Understanding spoken or written language	Speaking or writing

Why Assess Oral and Written Language?

There are two primary reasons for assessing language abilities. First, well-developed language abilities are desirable in and of themselves. The ability to converse and to express thoughts and feelings is a goal of most individuals. Those who have difficulties with various aspects of language are often eligible for special services from speech-language therapists or from special educators. Second, various language processes and skills are believed to underlie subsequent development. Students who experience language difficulties have also been shown to experience behavior disorders (Chow & Wehby, 2018), learning disabilities, and reading disorders (Adlof et al., 2010).

Written language and spelling are regularly taught in school, and these areas are singled out for assessment in the Individuals With Disabilities Education Act. Written and oral language tests are administered for the purposes of screening, instructional planning and modification, special education eligibility, and progress monitoring. Read the Stakeholder Perspective by Amy VanOrman, an experienced speech-language pathologist in a rural community in central Michigan, as she describes the kinds of language difficulties she sees in the students she works with.

Considerations in Assessing Oral Language

Those who assess oral language must give consideration to cultural and linguistic background and the developmental status of those they assess.

Stakeholder PERSPECTIVE

Amy VanOrman, Speech-Language Pathologist, Greenville Public Schools, Greenville, Michigan

I have held the position of speech-language pathologist in one school district for the past 22 years. Our district, located in Western Michigan, is semirural. Our students are predominantly white, and 50% are eligible for the federal free and reduced-lunch program. I have many stories about trends I've observed over time, but across all those years I have consistently seen vocabulary as a major factor impacting language development. In graduate school I learned that research has long demonstrated a significant vocabulary gap between students from high and low socioeconomic households. Every day as I work with my students, I witness these gaps firsthand. The majority of my students lack background knowledge that can come from reading books or having books read to them. They have not had real-life experiences that promote vocabulary and development. The vocabulary gaps I see go beyond just not being exposed to words or not understanding words. My students struggle to make connections with the words they do know. Often, understanding the context of when and where to use a word is also a challenge because they lack comprehension of the words they are being exposed to in school. I observe how their lagging skills in the areas of vocabulary comprehension and use impacts them across all academic content areas. We are constantly fighting the battle to prevent students from falling further behind because they lack the vocabulary skills to support their continued learning in the curriculum. My job as a speech-language pathologist often focuses on vocabulary exposure, vocabulary growth, and developing strategies for my students to use in the classroom. Instructionally I focus on increasing their ability to understand, talk, and write about the words they encounter in their school journey.

Assessment is a critical part of my job. But without instruction, there's no point to identifying these vocabulary gaps. I've seen the impact of using vocabulary assessment to identify significant gaps so that we can offer effective vocabulary intervention and how it helps students overcome their initial vocabulary gaps.

Cultural and Language Diversity

Cultural and linguistic background must be considered in assessing oral language competence. Although most children in the United States learn English as their first language, the form of English they learn depends on where they were born, who their parents are, and so on. There are many dialects that have been recognized from across the country that differ from Standard English, which is typically used in schools and on language assessments. For example, in central Pennsylvania, a child might say, "My hands need washed," instead of the standard "My hands need to be washed." In New York City, a child learning African American Vernacular English or Black English might say, "He be running," instead of "He is running." These and other culturally determined alternative constructions and pronunciations are not incorrect, nor are they inferior; they are specific to a region or a community, and they are appropriate and serve a critical function within the child's surrounding community. Use of specific dialects does not indicate intelligence or education level and instead might indicate strength-based characteristics such as adaptability and community engagement (American Psychological Association, Task Force on Resilience and Strength in Black Children and Adolescents, 2008). Children should be viewed as having a language disorder only if they exhibit disordered production of their own primary language or dialect.

Cultural background is particularly important when the language-assessment devices that are currently available are considered. Ideally, a child should be compared with others in the same language community. There should be separate norms for each language community, including Standard American English. There are calls for tests to be culturally responsive and in the case of language tests especially to have items as unbiased as possible. Unfortunately, the norm samples of most language tests are heterogeneous, and scores on these tests may not be valid indicators of a child's language ability. Without explicit instruction, differences in how a student pronounces a word—for example, "birfday" for "birthday"—may complicate learning to decode (Gatlin & Wanzek, 2015). These differences should be identified as an instructional target and not an indicator of disability. If there is a mismatch between the English dialect that students are fluent with and the Mainstream American English that the test employs, the child's score cannot be considered a valid indicator of language ability.

15.1
PROGRESS MONITORING CHECK

Developmental Considerations

Age is a major consideration in assessment of the child's language. Language acquisition is developmental. Some sounds, linguistic structures, and even semantic elements are correctly produced at an earlier age than others. Thus, it is not unusual or indicative of a language disorder for a 2-year-old child to say "kitty house" for "the cat is in the house," although the same phrase would be an indication of delay or disorder in a 4-year-old. It is important to be aware of developmental norms for language acquisition and to use those norms when making judgments about a child's language competence.

Considerations in Assessing Written Language

There are two major components of written language: content and form. The **content** of written expression is the product of considerable intellectual and linguistic activity: formulating, elaborating, sequencing, and then clarifying and even revising ideas; choosing the precise word to convey meaning, and so forth. Moreover, much of what we consider to be content is the result of creative endeavor. Our ability to use words to excite, to depict vividly, to imply, and to describe complex ideas is far more involved than simply putting symbols on paper. The **form** of written language is far more mechanistic than its content. For writer and reader to communicate, three sets of conventions or rules are used: penmanship, spelling, and style rules.

The most fundamental rules deal with **penmanship**, the formation of individual letters and letter sequences that make up words. Although letter formation tends to become more individualistic with age, there are a limited number of ways, for example, that the letter A can be written and still be recognized as an A. Moreover, there are conventions about the relative spacing of letters between and within words. **Spelling** is also rule governed. Although American English is more irregular phonetically than other languages, it remains largely regular, and students should be able to spell most words by applying a few phonetic rules. For example, we have known since the mid-1960s that approximately 80% of all consonants have a single spelling (Hanna et al., 1966). Short vowels are the major source of difficulty for most writers. The third set of conventions involves style. **Style** is a catchall term for rule-governed writing, which includes grammar (such as parts of speech, pronoun use, subject-verb agreement, verb voice, and mood) and mechanics (such as punctuation, capitalization, abbreviations, and referencing).

The conventions of written language are tested on many standardized achievement tests. However, the spelling words that students are to learn vary considerably from curriculum to curriculum and from teacher to teacher. For example, Ames (1965) examined seven spelling series and found that they introduced an average of 3,200 words between the second and eighth grades. However, only approximately 1,300 words were common to all the series; approximately 1,700 words were taught in only one series. Moreover, those words that were taught in several series varied considerably in their grade placement, sometimes by as many as five grades. Spelling is closely related to reading and being able to assess whether a student is able to spell as a result of instruction can provide teachers with valuable instructional guidance (Al Otaiba & Hosp, 2010).

Capitalization and punctuation are also assessed on the current forms of several achievement batteries. Again, standardized tests are not well suited to measuring achievement in these areas because the grade level at which these skills are taught varies so much from one curriculum to another. To be valid, the measurement of achievement in these areas must be closely tied to the curriculum being taught. For example, pupils may learn in kindergarten, first grade, second grade, or later that a sentence always begins with a capital letter. They may learn in the sixth grade or several grades earlier that commercial brand names are capitalized. Students may be taught in the second or third grade that the apostrophe in "it's" makes the word a contraction of "it is" or may still be studying "it's" in high school. Finally, in assessing word usage, organization, and penmanship, we must take into account the emphasis that individual teachers place on these components of written language and when and how students are taught.

The more usual way to evaluate a student's written work is to use a written expression rubric that parallels the curriculum. In this way, teachers can be sure that they are measuring precisely vocabulary, spelling, and styles that have been taught. Most teacher's editions of language arts textbook series contain scope-and-sequence charts

15.2
PROGRESS
MONITORING
CHECK

that specify the objectives that are taught in each unit. From these charts, appropriate criterion-referenced and curriculum-connected assessments can be developed. There are also some rubrics available in the research literature and advances are being made in the validation of standardized curriculum-based written-expression measures for use as progress monitoring tools in upper elementary through middle school (e.g., Truckenmiller et al., 2020).

Specific Oral and Written Language Tests

In Table 15.2 we list commonly used measures of oral and written language. We show the test names, authors, and publishers as well as most recent date of publication. We provide a list of subtests and composites measured by the tests, indicate the nature of the group on whom the tests are standardized, and report indices of reliability and validity. Choice of measures to be used will depend largely on the extent to which the behaviors sampled by the tests are those that one wants to sample. It should be noted that few of the tests are standardized on specific cultural or language norm groups. Users may want to pay attention to this feature. None of the language tests provide crosstabs for norms. That is, they do not indicate, for example, the numbers of specific racial groups that were from the Northwest, Southeast, etc. Failure to provide this information does not let the user know if 80% of the African American persons in the norm groups were from the Northeast, for example. Developers of language measures, as well as all tests, could do a better job of providing descriptions of normative samples and efforts taken to develop an unbiased or culturally responsive test.

Use Caution When Evaluating Validity

We caution users of language measures to use a "buyer beware" approach when evaluating the validity of language measures. First, the content validity of all of the language measures is established by the test authors arguing that they believe their measure assesses what they think comprises the aspects of language they set out to assess. They say they reviewed the literature or relied on expert opinion to establish that fact. Most posit some theory of language and then put forth arguments to show that their test assesses components of the theory they put forth. In establishing criterion/predictive validity, authors of language tests nearly always correlate their measures or subtests of their measures with other measures or subtests similarly named. Findings of moderate to high correlations with similarly named subtests, along with findings of low correlations with differently named subtests, are cited as evidence of criterion validity. So we get the same kind of validity argument as is made for measures of cognitive processes, perceptual processes, or perceptual-motor processes. The processes said to be assessed are test-identified and test-named and then validated by tests. This validity argument is a bit circular and does not verify existence of deficits, disorders, or dysfunctions in the test- named and test-identified processes.

TABLE 15.2

Commonly Used Oral and Written Language Tests

Test, Author(s), & Publisher	Skills Assessed	Norms	Reliability Evidence	Validity Evidence
Clinical Evaluation of Language Fundamentals–Fifth Edition (CELF-5) Semel, Wiig, & Secord, 2019	Observational Rating Scale, Sentence Comprehension, Linguistic Concepts, Word Structure, Word Classes, Following Directions, Formulated Sentences, Recalling Sentences, Understanding Spoken Paragraphs, Word Definitions, Sentence Assembly, Semantic Relationships, Reading Comprehension, Structured Writing, Pragmatics Profile, Pragmatics Activities Checklist	>3,000 children, adolescents, and young adults ages 5-0 to 22-11 stratified by age, sex, race/ethnicity, geographic region, and parent/caregiver education level and matched to 2020 census.	Internal consistency reliabilities range from .70 to .95. Test–retest reliabilities ranging from .64 to .90.	Content validity based on arguments that content assessed is appropriate to intended language constructs. Response processes based on evidence that examinees use the processes when responding to test items. Evidence for construct validity based on internal correlation and factor structure.
Comprehensive Receptive and Expressive Vocabulary Test–Third Edition (CREVT-3) Wallace & Hammill, 2013, PRO-ED	Two subtests (Receptive and Expressive Vocabulary); one composite (General Vocabulary)	Standardized on 1,535 persons in 29 states ages 5-0 to 89-11. Stratified on basis of gender, geographic region, race, Hispanic status, exceptionality status, and educational attainment of parents. Matched to 2011 U.S. census.	Internal consistency reliabilities range from .85 to .95 for subtests and .91 to .96 for composite. Internal consistency reliabilities also provided for specific subgroups. Test–retest reliabilities range from .85 to .99 for subtests and composite.	Arguments for content validity are based on selection of subtests and items. Criterion/predictive validity based on demonstration of moderate correlations with other picture vocabulary (EOWPVT, PPVT-2) and other vocabulary tests (WISC III vocabulary).
Expressive One-Word Picture Vocabulary Test–Fourth Edition Martin & Brownell, 2011, Academic Therapy Publications	Expressive Vocabulary	Co-normed with ROWPVT-4 on 2,400 persons ages 2-0 to 103 in 26 states. Examiners picked people randomly and then publisher stratified sample on basis of age, gender, race/ethnicity, and parent/self-educational level	Internal consistency coefficients range from .93 to .97. Test–retest reliability is .98 on an unspecified number of students.	Low to moderate correlations with scores on the ROWPVT-4 and with WISC-4 VCI (.43). Neither of the criterion measures seems to be an assessment of expressive vocabulary. Thus, a weak index of validity.

TABLE 15.2 (*continued*)

Test, Author(s), & Publisher	Skills Assessed	Norms	Reliability Evidence	Validity Evidence
Expressive Vocabulary Test 5 Williams, 2019, NCS Pearson	Expressive Vocabulary	See PPVT 5 above	Internal consistency reliabilities range from .94 to .98. Test–retest reliabilities range from .86 to .92.	Content validity based on literature review and expert opinion, concurrent validity based on correlation with EVT 2, PPVT 5, CELF 5, and KTEA 3 brief. All correlations in moderate range.
Illinois Test of Psycholinguistic Abilities–Third Edition (ITPA-3) Hammill, Mather & Roberts, (2001), PRO-ED	Twelve subtests (Spoken Analogies, Spoken Vocabulary, Morphological Closure, Syntactic Sentences, Sound Deletion, Rhyming Sequences, Sentence Sequencing, Written Vocabulary, Sight Decoding, Sound Decoding, Sight Spelling, Sound Spelling; three composites (General Language Composite, Spoken Language Composite, Written Language Composite)	Standardized on 1,522 people in 27 states stratified on the basis of geographic region, gender, race, residence, ethnicity, family income, and educational level of parents.	Internal consistency coefficients for subtests and composites range from .75 to .97. Test–retest reliabilities range from .86 to .97.	Content validity based on the argument that subtests and items are anchored to psycholinguistic theory. Argument for criterion-related validity based on demonstration of moderate correlations of subtests with measures of same or similar constructs.
Oral and Written Language Scales–Second Edition (OWLS-2) Carrow- Woolfolk, 2011, Pearson	Four subtests (Listening Comprehension, Oral Expression, Reading Comprehension, Written Expression); two composites (Written Language Composite, Oral Language Composite)	Normed on 2,123 students stratified on basis of gender, race/ethnicity, parents' education level, and geographic region matched to 2009 census.	Internal consistency reliabilities range from .93 to .99 for subtests and from .96 to .99 for composites. Test–retest reliabilities for subtests range from .73 to .94.	Evidence for validity is based on arguments that the test aligns with the theory on which it is based while there is not necessarily evidence for the theory. Correlations with comparable subtests on the CELF-4 are relatively low.
Ortiz Picture Vocabulary Acquisition Test Digital Format Ortiz, 2018, Multi Health Systems Inc.	Receptive Vocabulary	Two norm samples (English and English Learners).	Internal consistency reliability .98 for Forms A and B. Test–retest reliabilities range from .72 to .81 .	Evidence for content validity based on expert opinion. Evidence for construct validity based on convergent and discriminant validity and moderate correlations with performance on other measures of receptive vocabulary.

Test, Author(s), & Publisher	Skills Assessed	Norms	Reliability Evidence	Validity Evidence
Peabody Picture Vocabulary Test–Fifth Edition Dunn, 2019, NCS Pearson	Receptive Vocabulary	Normed along with EVT 3 on 2,720 individuals between ages 2-6 to 90 years stratified on the basis of age, sex, race/ethnicity, geographic region, and parent/caregiver education matched to 2017 census.	Internal consistency reliabilities range from .97 to .98. Test-retest reliabilities range from .75 to .84.	Content validity based on literature review and expert opinion, concurrent validity based on correlation with PPVT 4, CELF 5, KTEA 3, and EVT 3. All correlations in moderate range.
Receptive One-Word Picture Vocabulary Test–Fourth Edition Martin & Brownell, 2011, Academic Therapy Publications	Receptive Vocabulary	Co-normed with EOWPVT-4 on 2,400 persons ages 2-0 to 103 in 26 states. Examiners picked people randomly and then publisher stratified sample on basis of age, gender, race/ethnicity, and parent/self-educational level.	Internal consistency coefficients range from .94 to .98. Test-retest coefficient .97 on an unspecified number of students.	Low to moderate correlations with scores on the WISC-4 VCI (.39) and the EOWPVT (.69). Neither of these tests seem to be measures of receptive vocabulary. Thus, a weak index of validity.
Test of Auditory Comprehension of Language–Fourth Edition Carrow-Woolfolk (2014)	Three subtests (Vocabulary, Grammatical Morphemes, Elaborated Phrases and Sentences); one composite (Receptive Language Composite)	Normed along with TEWL on 1,205 children ages 3-0 to 12-11 in 26 states stratified on the basis of geographic region, gender, race, Hispanic status, exceptionality type, household income, and educational attainment of parents.	Internal consistency reliabilities across ages range from .91 to .99; internal consistency for the composite ranges from .97 to .98. Test-retest reliabilities across ages range from .66 to .90.	The author makes a case for the content validity of the test by specifying and defending a model of language development, then showing how items were selected and the test format designed to meet the language model. Criterion-predictive validity evidence is based on evidence of moderate relationship to performance on the CELF-4, DAB-4, TEXL, and OWLS-2.
Test of Auditory Perception–Fourth Edition Martin & Brownell, 2018, Academic Therapy Publications	11 subtests (Processing Oral Directions, Word Discrimination, Phonological Deletion, Phonological Blending, Syllabic Blending [supplemental]; Number Memory Forward, Word Memory, Sentence Memory, Number Memory Reversed [supplemental], Auditory Comprehension, Auditory Figure Ground [supplemental])	Normed on 2,023 children, adolescents and adults ages 5-0 to 23-11 in 40 states standardized using the 2010 census on the basis of gender, ethnicity, Hispanic origin, educational level of parents, region, metro location, and disability status.	Internal consistency coefficients relatively low for subtests, ranging from .64 to .89. Test-retest reliabilities .63 to .92 on a limited sample of students.	Based on relationship to CELF-5 receptive language index. Very limited.

(continues)

TABLE 15.2 (continued)

Test, Author(s), & Publisher	Skills Assessed	Norms	Reliability Evidence	Validity Evidence
Test of Expressive Language Carrow-Woolfolk & Allen	Three subtests (Vocabulary, Grammatical Morphemes, Embedded Phrases and Sentences); one composite (Expressive Language Index)	Normed along with TACL-4 on 1,205 children ages 3-0 to 12-11 in 26 states stratified on the basis of geographic region, gender, race, Hispanic status, exceptionality type, household income, and educational attainment of parents	Internal consistency reliability coefficients across age groups range from .91 to .98. Test–retest reliability coefficients range from .85 to .96.	The authors establish content validity by describing their language model, arguing that the test meets the requirements of the model, and describing their rationale for selection of items and format. Criterion-predictive validity is established by showing moderate correlations with other measures: CELF-4, DAB-4, TACL-4, and OWLS-2.
Test of Language Development–Intermediate–Fifth Edition (TOLD-I:5) Hammill & Newcomer, 2020, PRO-ED	Six subtests (Sentence Combining, Picture Vocabulary, Word Ordering, Relational Vocabulary, Morphological Comprehension, Multiple Meanings); six composites (Listening, Organizing, Speaking, Grammar, Semantics, Spoken Language)	Standardized on 1,012 children 8-0 to 17-11 in 29 states with approximately 100 at each age level stratified on basis of gender, geographic region, race, Hispanic status, parent educational level, and household income.	Internal consistency reliabilities for subtests range from .86 to .98 while composites all exceed .94. Test–retest reliabilities for composites all exceed .87.	The authors provide a rationale for selecting subtests as the basis for content validity. Criterion-predictive validity evidence is based on correlations with TACL, DTLA-5, and TOLD-P:4. Examination of sensibility of performance by specific disability subgroups and differentiation of disability groups.
Test of Language Development–Primary–Fifth Edition (TOLD-P:5) Newcomer & Hammill, 2019, PRO-ED	Nine subtests (Picture Vocabulary, Relational Vocabulary, Oral Vocabulary, Syntactic Understanding, Sentence Imitation, Morphological Completion, Word Discrimination, Phonemic Awareness, Word Articulation); six composites (Listening, Organizing, Speaking, Grammar, Semantics, Spoken Language)	1,007 children ages 4 to 8 in 31 states stratified on basis of geographic region, race, Hispanic status, gender, parent education, and household income.	Internal consistency for subtests ranges from .81 to .93 while it ranges from .87 to .97 for adolescents and adults. Test–retest reliabilities range from .81 to .92 for adolescents and .83 to .95 for adults. Evidence for content validity.	Content validity justified based on subtest selection and test format. Criterion/prediction validity based on correlations with TOLD-P:4, TACL-4, CELF-5, and *Young Children's Achievement Test-2*.

Test, Author(s), & Publisher	Skills Assessed	Norms	Reliability Evidence	Validity Evidence
Test of Orthographic Competence Mather, Roberts, Hammill, & Allen, PRO-ED	Nine subtests (Signs and Symbols, Grapheme Matching, Homophone Choice, Punctuation, Abbreviations, Letter Choice, Word Scramble, Sight Spelling, Word Choice); four composites (Conventions, Spelling Accuracy, Spelling Speed, Orthographic Ability)	Normed on 1,512 individuals stratified on the basis of race, Hispanic status, parent education level, household income, exceptionality status, and gender.	Coefficient alpha reliabilities for subtests range from .81 to .98. Test–retest reliability coefficients range from .75 to .96.	The authors develop a description of what they believe orthographic competence is and represents, and they state a rationale for subtest and item selection. They provide correlations of performance on the TOC-2 with performance on other measures that they argue support their concept of orthographic competence. The other measures are not necessarily measures of something called orthographic competence.
Test of Written Language–Fourth Edition (TOWL-4) Hammill & Larsen, 2008, PRO-ED	Vocabulary, Spelling, Punctuation, Logical Sentences, Sentence Combining	Normed on 2,206 students (200 at each age range) stratified on basis of geographic region, gender, ethnicity, family income, educational level of parents, and disability status.	Internal consistency reliabilities for subtests range from below .60 to above .90 and are limited other than for screening purposes. Test–retest reliabilities also range from <.60 to >.90.	Content validity is based on the way the test was developed and arguments that it assesses appropriate content. Construct validity is based on correlation with measures of similar constructs, with such correlation being in the moderate range.
Woodcock-Johnson IV Tests of Oral Language Shrank, McGrew & Mather, 2014, Riverside	Eight oral language clusters (Oralion, Abbreviation, Letter Choice Language, Broad Oral Language, Oral Expression, Listening Comprehension, Phonetic Coding, Speed of Lexical Access); nine subtests (Picture Vocabulary, Oral Comprehension, Segmentation, Rapid Picture Naming, Sentence Repetition, Understanding Directions, Sound Blending, Retrieval Fluency, Sound Awareness)	Standardized on 7,416 individuals stratified on twelve individual and community variables.	Internal consistency reliabilities for subtests range from .77 to .96. No data on test–retest reliabilities.	Evidence for content validity based on item selection. Evidence for criterion/predictive validity based on moderate to high correlations with CELF-4, PPVT-4, CASL, and OWLS.

(continues)

How Do We Ensure Fairness in Language Assessments?

We wish there were an easy answer to this question. According to the National Center for Education Statistics, in 2018–2019, 19% of K–12 students had a speech or language impairment (U.S. Department of Education, 2020). One of the authors of this book has a daughter who is a speech-language therapist in a predominantly White, rural, economically impoverished community in northern Michigan. Students in that community demonstrate a large number of speech and language problems. Another author of this book has worked in suburban schools with large percentages of students who spoke multiple languages. Questions at the intersection of dual-language development and language disability regularly occurred. Specialists in both dual-language development and disability will need to fully understand their local context and community in order to properly select the best methods of assessment toward the ultimate objective of identifying useful instructional information. It may be that the same assessments can be used in both settings, but most likely that will not be the case. Instead, a multimodal approach will serve specialists the best.

From a practical standpoint, it is difficult to find language tests whose norms include students like those one is assessing. For this reason, it is a good idea to conduct non-standard spontaneous language samples in addition to samples of behavior using formal measures. Second, many standardized tests that are useful in identifying language disorders in children are not very useful in planning treatments that will lead to improved language competence in homes and classrooms. The treatments may lead to raising scores on subtests of measures, but not in daily functioning.

In today's language assessment environment, with a plethora of multicultural and socioeconomic variation within caseloads, a clinician is bound to encounter many children who differ in one or more respects from the normative sample of a particular test. Indeed, the teacher or clinician is likely to see children who do not match the normative sample of a standardized test. When this occurs, the clinician must interpret the scores derived from these tests conservatively or decide an informal curriculum-based measure might be more appropriate. Information from nonstandard assessment becomes even more important, and the clinician should obtain reports from parents, teachers, and peers regarding their impressions of the child's language competence. As previously noted, it is inappropriate to treat multicultural language differences as if they were language disorders. However, the clinician performing an assessment must judge whether the child's language is disordered within their native language community and what impact such disorders may have on classroom performance and communication skills generally.

Written language assessments usually are scored holistically and subjectively. Holistic evaluations tend to be unreliable. Subjective scoring and decision making are susceptible to the biasing effects associated with racial, ethnic, social class, gender, and disability stereotypes. We believe the best alternative to holistic and subjective scoring schemes is to use a measure of writing fluency as an indicator of content generation. Two options have received some support in the research literature: (1) the number of words written (Shinn et al., 1988) and (2) the percentage of correctly written words (Isaacson, 1988).

The second problem in choosing good measures of written expression is in identifying a match between what is taught in the school curriculum and what is tested. The great variation in the time at which various writing skills and conventions are taught renders a general test of achievement inappropriate. Commercially available written language measures have doubtful validity for planning individual programs and evaluating the progress of individual students.

We recommend that teachers and related services personnel construct curriculum-based or criterion-referenced tests that closely parallel the curricula followed by the students being tested. In cases in which normative data are required there are three choices: (1) select measures that most closely parallel the curriculum, (2) develop local norms, or (3) select individual students for comparison purposes. Care should be exercised in selecting methods of assessing language tests. For example, it is probably better to test students in ways that are familiar to them. Thus, if the teacher's weekly spelling test is from dictation, then spelling tests using dictation are probably preferable to tests requiring the students to identify incorrectly spelled words. Language assessments can cover a range of skills from spelling, to writing, to oral comprehension. By carefully considering student characteristics, opportunities to learn, curriculum, and information needed to improve instructional outcomes, a fair and useful interpretation will be more likely.

1. Describe five processes associated with communication.
2. Explain how cultural and/or language background may play a role in determining appropriate language expectations.

1. What are the two major components of written language?
2. Why are two commonly found assessments of language in the classroom?

CHAPTER 16

Using Measures of Perception and Perceptual-Motor Skills

LEARNING OBJECTIVES

1. Understand why perceptual-motor tests are used in schools.
2. Know that there is now empirical evidence for the validity of most perceptual and perceptual-motor measures.
3. Know that perceptual and perceptual-motor tests have very limited use in planning academic interventions but may be useful in planning treatments for weaknesses in motor skills.

Clint is an 8-year-old second grader with noticeable motor difficulties and considerable difficulty learning basic reading skills. When he was 6 years old, his teacher referred him for a psychoeducational evaluation and the Individualized Education Program (IEP) team identified him as a student with developmental disabilities in visual–motor development and early reading skills. The IEP team recommended work on development of skills thought to underlie reading difficulties before engaging in intensive reading instruction. The team recommended an adaptive physical education program along with visual motor services in a special education resource room. The special education resource teacher worked with Clint on tracing patterns, reproduction of geometric designs, rhythm tapping, tracing paths through mazes, and figural discrimination and generalization skills (finding shapes that differed from one another or that were alike). In adaptive physical education, the focus was on balance (balancing on one leg, balancing on his toes, and walking on a balance beam) and locomotor skills such as jumping in place with both feet together, hopping, skipping, marching in place, and swinging his arms when walking.

For all of first grade, Clint participated in the perceptual and motor training. The IEP team met to draft an IEP for second grade. The team noted that Clint was better in directionality, rhythm, and throwing, and his printing and fine motor skills showed good improvement. He still had difficulty in balance and tasks requiring left-to-right movements. He had made little progress in reading. Clint's special education teacher wondered if time spent focusing on development of visual and motor skills might better have been spent teaching him to read.

We include the story of Clint to illustrate the dilemma faced by teachers and other school personnel today. In U.S. schools, there are two "camps" of professionals who hold fundamentally different views about the importance of assessment and treatment of perceptual-motor processes or abilities thought to underlie the development of academic skills. One "camp," with its origins in the work of psychologists and educators in the 1960s to 1980s, holds the view that when young learners experience reading (and sometimes math, writing, or other academic) difficulties, intensive academic instruction should be delayed until underlying deficits thought to cause those difficulties are alleviated or remediated. The other "camp" believes that learning problems should be addressed head-on with direct instruction in the skill development deficit area (e.g., by teaching the child to read). Those who believed strongly in remediation of underlying deficits designed assessments and treatment programs to remediate perceptual-motor problems (Barsch, 1966; Doman et al., 1960; Kephart, 1971), visual perceptual problems (Frostig, 1968), auditory perceptual problems (Reynolds & Wepman, 1987), psycholinguistic problems (Kirk & Kirk, 1971), or problems in sensory integration (Ayers, 1981; Johnson & Mykelbust, 1967). Although many of these approaches were recognized as lacking merit (see, for example, Arter & Jenkins, 1979; Mann, 1979; Ysseldyke & Salvia, 1974) and have subsequently been abandoned because of lack of evidence of their efficacy, some (such as sensory integration) persist today. Recently, professional interest in process deficits as a possible cause of learning disabilities has increased and the option of identifying process disorders continues as one option in the identification alternatives in the federal guidelines that accompany the requirements for identifying students with a learning disability. Ongoing professional interest is also evidenced by front-page articles in major professional association publications that highlight assessment of central information processing disorders (Fairchild & Gadke, 2018).

Why Are Perceptual-Motor Tests Used in Schools?

Note that the heading of this section is "Why *are* perceptual-motor tests used?" not "Why *should* perceptual-motor tests *be* used?" While subtle, the distinction is important. We are not advocating for the use of these tests, rather reporting on the ways in which school personnel use them. There are six ways in which they are used. Sometimes the tests are used as screening measures under the belief that early detection of perceptual-motor problems will enable school personnel to treat them before they can interfere with school learning. Second, perceptual-motor tests are administered to students experiencing school learning problems to see if they also have perceptual-motor problems. If the students score low on both academic measures and perceptual-motor measures, then it is thought that perceptual-motor problems may be causing academic problems and remedial programs are instituted to treat the perceptual-motor deficits and dysfunctions, although research does not support this causal connection.

Third, perceptual-motor measures have been used in assessments to determine if a student meets the eligibility criteria for special education services under the label "learning disabled." One option permitted by federal guidelines for declaring students learning disabled is to demonstrate that they have failed to respond to multiple evidence-based interventions applied with good integrity over a sufficient period of time. The other, as would be the case here, is to demonstrate that they have a disorder in one or more psychological processes as evidenced by low-level performance on one or more technically adequate measure of perceptual-motor processes.

Fourth, some states still have a category of disabilities called "perceptually handicapped" or "perceptually disabled" and require students to receive low scores on perceptual-motor tests to receive services under this label.

Fifth, perceptual-motor tests may be administered to identify deficiencies in motor skills with the intent of providing remedial instruction designed to remediate those motor deficiencies. This seems to us the one legitimate use of perceptual-motor tests. Finally, although an important use and one that is outside the scope of context of this book, perceptual-motor tests are used by clinical psychologists as adjunct measures in the diagnosis of traumatic brain injury or emotional disturbance in school-age children.

Specific Perceptual-Motor Measures

In Table 16.1 we list representative perceptual or perceptual-motor tests used in today's schools. We list authors of the tests, ages the test is designed to be used with, describe the kinds of perceptual or perceptual-motor skills assessed by each test, describe the normative samples for each test, and provide information on test reliability.

Technical Adequacy of Perceptual-Motor Measures

The technical adequacy of perceptual-motor measures, as for all measures, is a function of three factors: the extent to which the students on whom the tests are used are like those on whom the tests were normed, the reliability of the tests, and the validity of the tests. We briefly examine these factors as they relate to perceptual-motor measures in general.

TABLE 16.1

Representative Tests of Perceptual and Perceptual-Motor Skills

Test	Authors & Publisher	Skills Assessed	Norms	Reliability Evidence
Beery-Buktenica Developmental Test of Visual-Motor Integration	Beery, Buktenica, & Beery, 2010, Pearson	One core task (Visual Perception) and two supplemental tasks (Visual Perception, Motor Coordination)	Standardized on 1,737 individuals ages 1–18. Current adult norms are unchanged from fifth edition and are based on 1,021 adults ages 19–100. Stratified on the basis of age, gender, residence (rural, urban), ethnicity, and parental education.	Internal consistency of childhood measure .78 to .95 and of adult measure .71 to .90. Test–retest reliability .88.
Bender Visual-Motor Gestalt Test	Brannigan, Decker, & Bender, 2003, Pearson	Copying Geometric Designs	4,000 individuals ages 4–85 stratified on the basis of race/ethnicity, education level of parents, and geographic region, but excluding students with exceptionalities and students in special education. The norms are too dated to be used in important decision making.	All but four internal consistency reliability coefficients >.90 and these exceed .80. Test–retest reliability is lower.
Developmental Test of Auditory Perception (DTAP)	Reynolds, Voress, & Pearson, 2008, PRO-ED	Language Auditory Perception Index, Non-Language Auditory Perception Index, Background Noise Index, No Background Noise Index, Composite Index	Normed on 1,920 students from only 13 states stratified on the basis of geographic area, race, Hispanic status, gender, parent education, and exceptionality status.	Internal consistency reliability coefficients range from .67 to .96 with 70% exceeding .80. Test–retest reliabilities range from .65 to .91.
Developmental Test of Visual Perception–Third Edition (DTVP-3)	Hammill, Pearson, & Voress, 2014, PRO-ED	Five subtests (Eye-hand Coordination, Copying, Figure-Ground, Visual Closure, Form Constancy) and three composites (Visual-Motor Integration, Motor-Reduced Visual Perception, General Visual Perception)	Normed on 1,035 students from 27 states stratified on the basis of geographic region, gender, race/ethnicity, Hispanic status, parent education, household income, and exceptionality status	Internal consistency reliabilities range from .74 to .95 for subtests with many <.90. Internal consistency for composites exceeds .90. Test–retest reliabilities for subtests are in .60s and for composites in .70s.

Test	Authors & Publisher	Skills Assessed	Norms	Reliability Evidence
Full Range Test of Visual-Motor Integration (FMTVMI)	Hammill, Pearson, Voress, & Reynolds, 2006, PRO-ED	Visual-Motor Integration	Three different norm samples totaling 3,153 individuals. Original *Test of Visual-Motor Integration* normed in 1992 on children ages 5–10, second unspecified number of children and adolescents tested in 1995, and third sample tested in 2000. Added together to form norms, a precarious practice.	Internal consistency for two of the age groups (5- to 10-year-olds and 11- to 74-year-olds) with 100% of coefficients >.80 and 42% greater than .90. Test–retest >.85 for both age ranges on very limited samples.
Koppitz Developmental Scoring System for the Bender Visual-Motor Gestalt Test–Second Edition (Koppitz-2)	Reynolds, 2007, PRO-ED	Copying Geometric Designs	Standardized on 4,000 individuals ages 4–85 stratified on the basis of race/ethnicity, education level of parents, and geographic region but excluding students with exceptionalities and students in special education.	Internal consistency reliabilities >.80 and test–retest reliabilities are lower.
Motor-Free Visual Perception Test–Fourth Edition (MVPT-4)	Calaruso & Hammill, 2015, Academic Therapy Publications	Skill categories (Spatial Relationships, Visual Discrimination, Figure-Ground, Visual Closure, Visual Memory)	Standardized on >2,700 individuals from 25 states stratified on the basis of gender, ethnicity, Hispanic status, geographic location, and education level.	Internal consistency reliabilities .70 to .87 with reliabilities below .80 for weight age groups. Test–retest reliability .76.
Test of Visual-Perceptual Skills–Fourth Edition	ATP Assessments, 2017, Academic Therapy Publications	Six subtests (Visual Discrimination, Spatial Relationships, Form Constancy, Sequential Memory, Visual Figure-Ground, Visual Closure)	Standardized on 1,790 individuals in 28 states stratified on the basis of gender, ethnicity, Hispanic status, parent education, geographic region, urban/suburban v. rural, and disability status.	Internal consistency reliabilities from .48 to .90 for individual subtests, with 18 coefficients below .70. Test–retest reliabilities .46 to .81.

First, as we examine the measures reviewed in Table 16.1 note that most are standardized on limited samples. If you examine the technical manuals for most of the tests you will observe that the method used for gathering normative data was to contact customers of test publishers and ask them to participate in the norming of new measures. Then those customers were asked to select individual students in their area who met specific demographic characteristics (e.g., two White girls whose parents had college degrees). They administered the new measures and submitted the results to the publisher who constructed the norms to match census characteristics based on factors like gender, race/ethnicity, geographic region, and parental income. Note that all of the perceptual-motor measures were standardized in a limited number of states. And none of the test manuals include data on crosstabs as we discussed in the chapter on norms. That is, we are not provided with information on how many of the Black boys came from the Northeast, or how many of the White students whose parents had college educations were girls, etc.

Second, note that reliability of most of the perceptual-motor measures is only high enough that the measures could only be used for screening purposes, presuming subsequent diagnostic assessments would use measures with stronger reliability coefficients. As we noted in the chapter on reliability, internal consistency reliabilities must exceed .90 for those measures to be used to make important diagnostic decisions about students. Few of the composites for perceptual-motor measures have reliabilities that exceed .90 and almost none of the subtest measures exceed .90. Perceptual-motor measures should not be used in making important decisions (such as diagnostic/eligibility decisions) that would have a significant effect on students life opportunities.

Third, establishing evidence for the validity of perceptual-motor measures is problematic. Notice that there is no "validity column" in Table 16.1. Authors of measures of perceptual-motor skills struggle to demonstrate the validity of their tests. To establish validity, of course, the authors need to show that the tests are valid for the purposes for which they are designed. Authors of perceptual-motor tests indicate the purpose of their measures in various ways, but typically indicate that their measures are designed to measure aspects of some underlying theory of perceptual or perceptual-motor development. Further, validity coefficients are a function of reliability such that measures with weak reliability coefficients would not be able to attain strong validity coefficients.

When you read the technical manuals for perceptual-motor measures you will see claims for validity like, "The XYZ Test is standardized on a large sample of students, simple to administer, provides easy to follow and comprehensive scoring directions, is widely used in clinical practice, and is widely used in research." None of these claims has anything to do with the primary requirement of demonstrating that the test measures what its author claims it measures. Most authors base validity claims on theory-based or logic-based arguments. They state theories of perceptual development and then try to show how their measure meets the requirements of their theory without empirical evidence for the validity of the theory itself. Or, they put forward extensive logic-based arguments regarding perceptual or motor development and contend that their measure assesses that development. And, most often they contend that their measure of perceptual-motor development assesses perceptual-motor development because student performance on the measure correlates moderately with student performance on other measures that allegedly assess perceptual-motor development. Missing is evidence that student performance on perceptual-motor measures provides school personnel with useful and necessary information for diagnostic or instructional planning purposes. Or, that there are aptitude-by-treatment interactions: that students who earn low scores on the tests profit from one particular method of instruction while those who earn high scores profit from a competing method of instruction or no instruction.

16.1
PROGRESS
MONITORING
CHECK

In the Interest of Fairness to Students

School personnel administer perceptual-motor tests for two primary reasons: to identify deficits in motor development that need to be remediated in order to further a child's motor development, or to identify perceptual or perceptual-motor disorders that presumably underlie and/or cause reading or other academic problems and that allegedly must be remedied before the student can proceed to learn. Much of the theoretical importance of perceptual-motor assessment is not well-grounded. The mechanisms by which perceptual-motor development affects reading are seldom specified and have not been validated. Thus, theorists may opine that perceptual-motor skills are necessary for reading, but they do not specify what those skills are and how they affect reading. Further, substantial evidence debunks the notion of selecting interventions to correct for measured sensory process preferences or strengths (commonly called "learning styles") as a way to improve learning. Widely used vision treatments as a means to improve reading performance have similarly been thoroughly disproven and policy groups recommend against these practices.

The practice of perceptual-motor assessment is linked directly to perceptual-motor training or remediation. There is an appalling lack of empirical evidence to support the claim that specific perceptual-motor training facilitates the acquisition of academic skills or improves the likelihood of academic success. Kavale and Mattson (1983) conducted a meta-analysis of 180 studies of the effectiveness of perceptual-motor training. They concluded that perceptual-motor training is not an effective intervention technique for improving academic, cognitive, or perceptual-motor variables, and that perceptual-motor assessment and training should be questioned as an effective intervention for children in special education. More importantly, major professional associations and insurance companies have taken strong stands against the practice of perceptual-motor assessment and training. For example, Cigna Insurance Company specifically denies coverage for visual-perceptual training of any kind, citing position statements of the American Academy of Pediatrics, the American Academy of Ophthalmology, and the American

Academy of Ophthalmology and Strabismus. They conclude their position statement on coverage of visual-perceptual training with the following statement:

> Visual perceptual training has been proposed as a treatment for learning disabilities or disorders; however, it is considered behavioral training and educational/training in nature. Evidence in the published, peer-reviewed scientific literature does not indicate that visual perceptual therapy is a treatment for any type of learning disability or disorder. The available evidence does not support the conclusion that visual perceptual training will improve learning skills or treat the underlying cause of the learning disability. (aapc.com/codes/webroot /upload/general_pages_docs/document/mm_0410_coveragepositioncriteria _visual_perceptual_training.pdf)

Douglas Fuchs, Research Professor at Vanderbilt University and Institute Fellow at the American Institutes for Research, is an expert on assessment in special and inclusive education. Read his Stakeholder Perspective on the current role of perceptual-motor assessment and training.

When the purpose of perceptual-motor assessment is to identify specific important perceptual and motor behaviors that children have not yet mastered, some of the tests reviewed in this chapter may provide useful information; performance on specific items will indicate the extent to which specific skills (e.g., tracing a circle) have been mastered. Yet there is no support for the use of perceptual-motor tests in planning instruction designed to facilitate academic learning or to remediate academic difficulties. Using such measures for such purposes is unfair to children and youth. It is also unfair to lead teachers to think that if they spend valuable instructional time teaching a student perceptual and/or perceptual-motor skills then the student's reading skills will improve.

Stakeholder
PERSPECTIVE

Douglas Fuchs, PhD, Research Professor at Vanderbilt University and Institute Fellow at the American Institutes for Research

Before addressing perceptual-motor training, I will start with a brief history of the learning disabilities (LD) construct to provide context. In the 1950s and 1960s, before LD gained currency, children's academic difficulties were often attributed to presumed brain injury, sustained pre- or postnatally. Research by Werner and Strauss suggested that those with and without putative brain injury could be distinguished from one another by subtle behaviors like inattention. These behaviors became codified as "minimal brain dysfunction" (MBD) syndrome. Schools were established for MBD children like the Cove School in Racine, Wisconsin. By the mid-1960s, however, Samuel Kirk and other academics had rejected the MBD perspective, partly because of persuasive critiques by Herbert Birch and others that described MBD as a diagnosis usually made in the absence of credible evidence of brain injury. Kirk and colleagues such as Barbara Bateman, Newell Kephart, and Marianne Frostig promoted diagnostic prescriptive instruction (DPI) as a more defensible explanation of the LD construct.

DPI was favored because it was based on well-known information-processing models—comprising components like the decoding of visual, auditory, and haptic stimuli—and it was operationalized by measures considered by Kirk and others as "behavioral," meaning observable, verifiable, and valid, not as inferential. Because model components like visual and auditory decoding were seen as necessary prerequisites for skill acquisition, the teaching of academic skills like recognizing words in print was put on hold as the students' processing "abilities" were exercised and presumably strengthened. Perceptual-motor functioning, or the coordination of visual perception with fine motor or gross motor performance, was considered an important "ability." For many students with disabilities, perceptual-motor training (e.g., walking balance beams), supplanted academic instruction at one or more grade levels.

By the time I arrived at the University of Minnesota in the mid-1970s to begin my doctoral work, DPI had been dismissed as an explanation of the LD construct and as an evidence-based approach to help students with LD. As expressed in a 1979 review by Judith Arter and Joseph Jenkins, this was mostly because researchers failed to find that abilities training, including perceptual-motor training, improved students with disabilities' school performance, a basic assumption held by DPI advocates like Kirk. By the mid-1980s, special educators in universities and in the schools reoriented their efforts away from abilities training and towards the direct, explicit teaching of academic skills. For the most part, this remains the case today.

1. Identify five ways in which school personnel use measures of perception and perceptual-motor skills.
2. Identify one way in which it might be legitimate to use measures of perception or perceptual-motor skills to plan interventions for students.
3. List two problems in the evidence for the validity of measures of perception and perceptual-motor skills.
4. What issues are present in using the norms for perceptual-motor tests?

CHAPTER 17

Using Measures of Intelligence and Cognitive Processes

LEARNING OBJECTIVES

1. Explain how student characteristics, particularly opportunity to learn, can affect student performance on intelligence tests.
2. Identify behaviors commonly sampled on intelligence tests.
3. Understand and discuss theories that form the foundation of many intelligence tests used today.
4. Identify factors that are commonly interpreted using intelligence tests.
5. Identify the various types of intelligence tests and their relative merits and limitations.
6. Name three commonly used verbal measures of intelligence and three commonly used nonverbal measures of intelligence.
7. Understand several dilemmas in using intelligence tests in schools.

No other area of assessment has generated as much attention, controversy, and debate as the testing of what we call "intelligence." For centuries, philosophers, psychologists, educators, and laypeople have debated the meaning of intelligence. Numerous definitions of the term intelligence have been proposed, with each definition serving as a stimulus for counterdefinitions and counterproposals. Several theories have been advanced to describe and explain intelligence and its development. Some theorists argue that **intelligence** is a general ability that enables people to do many different things, whereas other theorists contend that there are multiple intelligences and that people are better at some things than others. Some argue that, for the most part, intelligence is genetically determined (hereditary), inborn, or something you get from your parents. Others contend that intelligence is, for the most part, learned—that it is acquired through experience. Most theorists today recognize the importance of both heredity and experience, including the impact of parental education, parental experience, maternal nutrition, maternal substance abuse, and many other factors. However, most theorists take positions on the relative importance of these factors.

Both the interpretation of group differences in performance on intelligence tests and the practice of testing the intelligence of schoolchildren have been topics of recurrent controversy and debate. In some instances, the courts have acted to curtail or halt intelligence testing in the public schools; in other cases, the courts have defined what constitutes intelligence testing. Debate and controversy have flourished about whether intelligence tests should be given, what they measure, and how different levels of performance attained by different populations are to be explained.

During the past 30 years, there has been a significant decline in the use of intelligence tests in schools as a result of several factors. Teachers and related services personnel have found that knowing the score (IQ or mental age) a student earns on an intelligence test has not been especially helpful in making decisions about specific instructional interventions or teaching approaches to use. It has at best provided them with general information about how rapidly to pace instruction. Also, it is argued that scores on intelligence tests too often are used to set low expectations for students, resulting in diminished effort to teach students who earn low scores. This has been the case especially with students who were labeled as having an intellectual disability on the basis of low scores on intelligence tests. In cases in which specific groups of students (such as African American or Latinx students) have earned lower scores on tests and this has resulted in disproportionate placement of these groups of students in special education or in diminished expectations for performance, the courts have found intelligence tests discriminatory and mandated an end to their use.

Most importantly, researchers over the past 20 years or so have repeatedly and conclusively shown the significant limitations of efforts to use scores on intelligence tests, and especially profiles of student strengths and weaknesses, on measures of cognitive processes for instructional planning purposes. Burns (2016) summarized the results of more than 200 studies synthesized in seven meta-analyses and reported that a small to negligible effect was found for cognitive assessment and intervention on math and reading improvements. He concluded, "IQ tells us very little about how well a student will respond to interventions" (p. 27).

McGill et al. (2018) reviewed evidence for the use of profile analyses and examinations of cognitive strengths and weaknesses on cognitive measures in planning instruction. They concluded that there is a lack of empirical support for such practices. Based on an extensive review of the research, Fletcher and Miciak (2017) concluded that the bulk of empirical evidence continues to support *not* using cognitive profile analyses for diagnostic and intervention planning decisions.

As we have noted repeatedly, the primary purpose of assessment is to plan interventions that will lead to improved instruction that will enhance students' academic and/or behavioral competence. In the absence of sound evidence that the use of intelligence tests or measures of cognitive processes does so, we advise they not be used. In the interest of informing readers, we devote a chapter to information on measures of intelligence or cognitive processes and their use. Read the Stakeholder Perspective by Dr. Dan Reschly, Professor Emeritus at Vanderbilt University and an authority on the interpretation of student performance on intelligence tests, as he describes the merits and limitations of using cognitive measures and intelligence tests in schools today.

No one has seen a specific thing called "intelligence." Rather, we observe differences in the ways people behave—either differences in everyday behavior in a variety of situations or differences in responses to standard stimuli or sets of stimuli; then we attribute those differences to something we call intelligence. In this sense, intelligence is an inferred entity—a term or construct we use to explain differences in present behavior and to predict differences in future behavior.

We have repeatedly stressed the fact that all tests, including intelligence tests, assess samples of behavior. Regardless of how an individual's performance on any given test is viewed and interpreted, intelligence tests—and the items on those tests—simply sample behaviors. A variety of different kinds of behavior samplings

Stakeholder PERSPECTIVE

Dan Reschly, Professor Emeritus, Vanderbilt University

Intellectual assessment (IQ) dominated determination of eligibility in special education and inclusive education during the 20th century. Although with some changes in eligibility determination over the last 15 years and accompanying revisions in assessment practices, evidence exists of some decline in IQ testing. Despite the prominence of IQ testing for over a century, special and remedial education do not require IQ testing.

The first special education programs in large U.S. cities were established in the late 19th century *before* the development of the tests that were the forerunners to current IQ tests (Hendrick & MacMillan, 1989; Kode, 2002). Descriptions of the children in those classes and their struggles with achievement in the standard curriculum would be familiar to modern general and special educators. Most would be classified today as children with mild intellectual disability (MID) or specific learning disability (SLD). Moreover, concerns about and diagnoses of severe reading problems and the use of the term *dyslexia*, often classified as SLD today, also predate the development of IQ tests. IQ testing was not essential to the roots of special education and is less essential today.

(continues)

"Very likely the importance of IQ at any age level has been overrated. After school entrance it is clear that mental testing adds little to that knowledge of child ability that could be secured by an analysis of academic records based on reliable and cumulative measurements in standard school subject matter," (Stoddard, 1940, p. 6; emphasis added).

As a practitioner, over the years I realized that IQ tests were interpreted too often as saying too much and saying too little about the children and youth experiencing learning and behavioral problems. *Saying too much* through many professionals and non-professionals thinking that the IQ score indicated who could and could not learn, and *saying too little* because the IQ score had little relevance to planning academic and behavioral interventions and even less about how to evaluate and revise interventions that were not effective.

Modern procedures using direct assessment methods (curriculum-based measurement and behavior assessment) allow us to realize Stoddard's assertion that continuously monitoring academic and behavior performance against goals and revising interventions when not sufficiently effective is far more beneficial to students than determining a static IQ score.

IQ testing is still essential in some areas such as classification of students with MID but becomes largely irrelevant even in this area when alternative disability identification criteria are used and the focus is squarely on identification and treatment of behavior and achievement problems. IQ testing is an old technology that has declined in recent years and is likely to further decline in the future.

are used to assess intelligence; in most cases the kinds of behaviors sampled reflect a test author's conception of intelligence. The behavior samples are combined in different ways by different authors based on how they conceive of intelligence. In this chapter, we review the kinds of behaviors sampled by intelligence tests, with emphasis on the psychological demands of different item types, as a function of pupil characteristics. We also describe several ways in which intelligence theorists and test authors have conceptualized the structure of intelligence.

In evaluating the performance of individuals on intelligence tests, teachers, administrators, counselors, and diagnostic specialists must go beyond the names of the tests and the scores they produce to examine the kinds of behaviors sampled on the test. They must be willing to question the ways in which test stimuli are presented, to question the response requirements, and to evaluate the psychological demands placed on the individual.

Why Do We Assess Intelligence?

Given the controversy surrounding the measurement of intelligence, and the many important questions that remain about whether scores on intelligence tests can meaningfully inform instructional decisions, you might wonder why they are used in schools today. We do know that in some U.S. school districts they are not ever administered. However, in the majority of school districts across the United States, they are used to inform special education eligibility decisions, particularly decisions about whether a student qualifies for special education services as either a student with an intellectual disability or a student with a learning disability. In many districts, students with particularly low scores on intelligence tests for which there is additional corroborating information suggesting both limited intelligence, and limited adaptive behavior, can qualify for special education services as a student with an intellectual disability. Using intelligence test scores to inform decisions about whether students have learning disabilities, however, is much more risky; but, it is still a common practice in schools today.

The Effect of Opportunity to Learn, Cultural-Linguistic Background, and Age on Student Performance on Intelligence Tests

Acculturation is the most important characteristic to consider in evaluating performance on intelligence tests. **Acculturation** refers to a process an individual goes through in adapting to a new culture, and often depends on an individual's particular set of background experiences and opportunities to learn in both formal and informal educational settings. These experiences and opportunities to learn, in turn, depend on the person's initial culture and the culture to which the person is now exposed, the experiences available in the person's environment, and the length of time the person has had to assimilate those experiences. The culture in which an individual lives and the length of time the person has lived in that culture may influence the psychological demands presented by a test item. Simply knowing the kind of behavior sampled by a test is not enough because the same test item may create different psychological demands for people undergoing different experiences and acculturation.

Suppose, for example, that we assess intelligence by asking children to tell how hail and sleet are alike. Children may fail the item for very different reasons. Consider Juan (a student who recently moved to the United States from Honduras) and Marcie (a student born and raised in Michigan). Juan has no experience with hail and sleet, so he stands little chance of telling how hail and sleet are alike; he will fail the item simply because he does not know the meanings of the words and has no relevant background experience having lived most of his life in the tropics of Honduras and is new to Texas. Marcie may know what hail is and what sleet is, but she fails the item because she is unable to integrate these two words into a conceptual category (precipitation). The psychological demand of the item changes as a function of the children's knowledge. For the child who has not learned the meanings of the words, the item assesses vocabulary. For the child who knows the meanings of the words, the item is a generalization task.

In considering how individuals perform on intelligence tests, we need to know how opportunity to learn and cultural-linguistic background affect test performance. Items on intelligence tests range along a continuum from items that sample fundamental psychological behaviors that are relatively unaffected by the test taker's learning history to items that sample primarily learned behavior. To determine exactly what is being assessed, we need to know the background of the student. Consider the following item:

> Jeff went walking in the forest. He saw a porcupine that he tried to take home for a pet. It got away from him, but when he got home, his father took him to the doctor. Why?

For a student who knows what a porcupine is, that a porcupine has quills, and that quills are sharp, the item can assess comprehension, abstract reasoning, and problem-solving skill. The student who does not know any of this information may very well fail the item. In this case, failure is due not to an inability to comprehend or solve the problem but to a deficiency in background experience.

Similarly, we could ask a child to identify the seasons of the year. The experiences available in children's environments are reflected in the way they respond to this item. Children from central Illinois, who experience four discernibly different climatic conditions, may well respond "summer, fall, winter, and spring." Children from central Pennsylvania, who also experience four discernibly different climatic conditions but who live in an environment in which hunting is prevalent, might respond "buck season, doe season, small game, and fishing." Within specific cultures, both responses are logical and appropriate; only one is scored as correct.

Items on intelligence tests also sample different behaviors as a function of the age of the child assessed. Age and acculturation are positively related: Older children in general have had more opportunities to acquire the skills and cultural knowledge assessed by intelligence tests. The performances of 5-year-old children on an item requiring them to tell how a cardinal, a blue jay, and a swallow are alike are almost entirely a function of their knowledge of the word meanings. Most college students know the meanings of the three words; for them, the item assesses primarily their ability to identify similarities and to integrate words or objects into a conceptual category. As children get older, they have increasing opportunities to acquire the elements of the collective intelligence of a culture.

The interaction between acculturation and the behavior sampled determines the psychological demands of an intelligence test item. For this reason, it is impossible to define exactly what any one intelligence test would assess for any one student. Identical test items place different psychological demands on different children. Thirteen kinds of behaviors sampled by intelligence tests are described later in this chapter. These types of behavior will vary in their psychological demands based on the test taker's experience and acculturation. Given the great number of potential questions that could be asked for each type of question as well as the number of combinations of question types, the number of questions is practically infinite.

In order to limit the effect of linguistic differences on students' scores on intelligence tests, nonverbal tests of intelligence are frequently administered. However, nonverbal tests only reduce concerns about linguistic differences; the influence of cultural differences or opportunity to learn remain.

Behaviors Sampled by Intelligence Tests

Regardless of the interpretation of measured intelligence, it is a fact that intelligence tests simply sample behaviors. This section describes the kinds of behaviors sampled, including discrimination, generalization, motor behavior, general knowledge, vocabulary, induction, comprehension, sequencing, detail recognition, analogical reasoning, pattern completion, abstract reasoning, and memory.

PROGRESS MONITORING CHECK

Discrimination

Intelligence test items that sample skill in discrimination usually present a variety of stimuli and ask the student to find the one that differs from all the others. Figure 17.1 illustrates items assessing discrimination. Items a and b assess discrimination of figures, items c and d assess symbolic discrimination, and items e and f assess semantic discrimination. In each case, the student must identify the item that differs from the others.

Generalization

Items assessing generalization present a stimulus and ask the student to identify which of several response possibilities goes with the stimulus. Figure 17.2 illustrates several items assessing generalization. In each case, the student is given a stimulus element and is required to identify the one that is like it or that goes with it.

Motor Behavior

Many items on intelligence tests require a motor response. The intellectual level of very young children, for example, is often assessed by items requiring them to throw objects, walk, follow moving

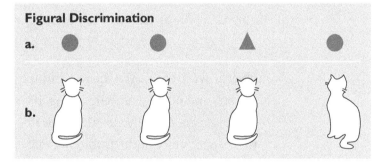

FIGURE 17.1. Items that assess figural, symbolic, and semantic discrimination.

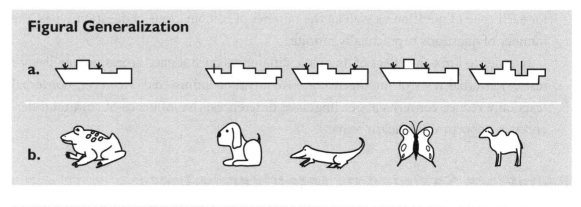

FIGURE 17.2. Items that assess figural, symbolic, and semantic generalization.

objects with their eyes, demonstrate a pincer grasp in picking up objects, build block towers, and place geometric forms in a recessed form board. Most motor items at higher age levels are actually visual–motor items. The student may be required to copy geometric designs, trace paths through a maze, or reconstruct designs from memory.

General Knowledge

Items on intelligence tests sometimes require a student to answer specific factual questions, such as "In what direction would you travel if you were to go from Poland to Argentina?" and "What is the cube root of 8?" Essentially, such items are like the kinds of items in achievement tests; they assess primarily what has been learned.

Vocabulary

Many different kinds of test items are used to assess vocabulary. In some cases, the student must name pictures, and in others, he or she must point to objects in response to words read by the examiner. Some vocabulary items require the student to produce oral definitions of words, whereas others call for reading a definition and selecting one of several words to match the definition.

Induction

Induction items present a series of examples and require the student to induce a governing principle. For example, the student is given a magnet and several different cloth, wooden, and metal objects and is asked to try to pick up the objects with the magnet. After several trials, the student is asked to state a rule or principle about the kinds of objects that magnets can pick up.

Comprehension

There are three kinds of items used to assess comprehension: items related to directions, to printed material, and to societal customs and mores. In some instances, the examiner presents a specific situation and asks what actions the student would take (e.g., "What would you do if you saw a train approaching a washed-out bridge?"). In other cases, the examiner reads paragraphs to a student and then asks specific questions about the content of the paragraphs. In still other instances, the student is asked questions about social mores, such as, "Why should we keep promises?"

Sequencing

Items assessing sequencing consist of a series of stimuli that have a progressive relationship among them. The student must identify a response that continues the relationship. Four sequencing items are illustrated in Figure 17.3.

Detail Recognition

Tests or test items that assess detail recognition evaluate the completeness and detail with which a student solves problems. For instance, items may require a student to count the blocks in pictured piles of blocks in which some of the blocks are not directly visible, to copy geometric designs, or to identify missing parts in pictures. To do so correctly, the

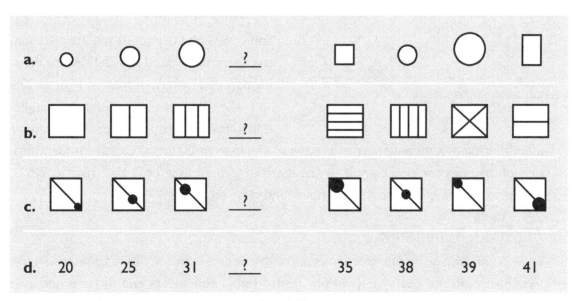

FIGURE 17.3. Items that assess sequencing skill.

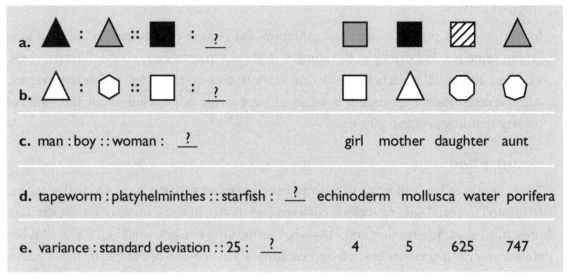

FIGURE 17.4. Analogy items.

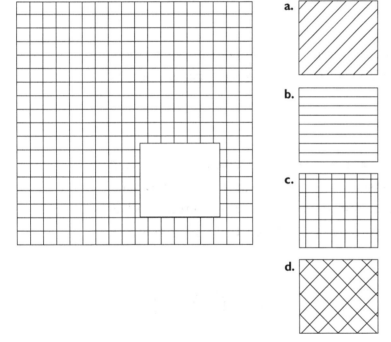

FIGURE 17.5. A pattern completion item.

student must attend to detail in the stimulus drawings and must reflect this attention to detail in making responses.

Analogical Reasoning

"A is to B as C is to ___ " is the usual form for analogies. Element A is related to element B. The student must identify the response having the same relationship to element C as B has to A. Figure 17.4 illustrates several different analogy items.

Pattern Completion

Some tests and test items require a student to select from several possibilities the missing part of a pattern or matrix. Figures 17.5 and 17.6 illustrate two different completion items. The item in Figure 17.5 requires identification of a missing part in a pattern. The item in Figure 17.6 calls for identification of the response that completes the matrix by continuing both the triangle, circle, rectangle sequence and the solid, striped, and clear sequence.

Abstract Reasoning

A variety of items on intelligence tests sample abstract reasoning ability. The *Stanford–Binet Intelligence Scale,* for example, presents absurd verbal statements and pictures and asks the student to identify the absurdity. In the *Stanford–Binet* and other scales, arithmetic reasoning problems are often thought to assess abstract reasoning.

Memory

Several different kinds of tasks assess memory: repetition of sequences of digits presented orally, reproduction of geometric designs from memory, verbatim repetition of sentences, and reconstruction of the essential meaning of paragraphs or stories. Simply saying that an item assesses memory is too simplistic. We need to ask: Memory for what? The psychological demand of a memory task changes in relation to both the method of assessment and the meaningfulness of the material to be recalled.

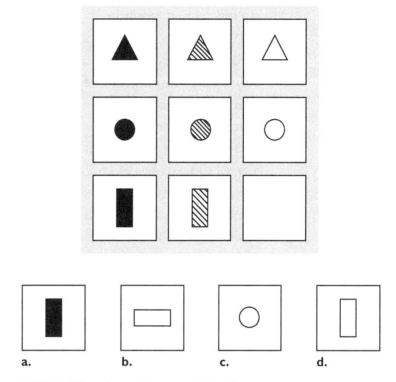

FIGURE 17.6. A matrix completion item.

Theories That Have Informed Intelligence Testing

Early in the study of intelligence, it became apparent that the behaviors used to assess intelligence were highly related to one another. Charles Spearman, an early 20th-century psychologist, demonstrated that a single statistical factor could explain the high degree of intercorrelation among the behaviors. He named this single factor **general intelligence** (g). Although he noted that performance on different tasks was influenced by other specific intelligence factors, he argued that knowing a person's level of g could greatly improve predictions of performance on a variety of tasks. Today, nearly every intelligence test allows for the calculation of an overall test score that is frequently considered indicative of an individual's level of g in comparison to same-age peers.

Later, it became clear that different factor structures would emerge depending on the variables analyzed and the statistical procedures used. Thurstone (1941) proposed an alternative interpretation of the correlations among intelligence test behaviors. He conducted factor analyses of several tests of intelligence and perception, and he concluded that there exist seven different intelligences that he called "primary mental abilities": verbal comprehension, word fluency, number, space, associative memory, perceptual speed, and reasoning. Although Thurstone recognized that these different abilities were often positively correlated, he emphasized multiplicity rather than unity within the construct of intelligence. This approach to interpreting intellectual performance was further expanded by Raymond Cattell and his student John Horn. Cattell suggested the existence of two primary intelligence factors: fluid intelligence and crystallized intelligence. **Fluid intelligence** refers to basic processes of reasoning and other mental abilities that depend minimally on prior learning and acculturation. Fluid intelligence is considered independent of learning, experience and education. **Crystallized intelligence** represents the knowledge and skill one acquires over time from learning and experience. Some tests of intelligence provide separate composite scores for behaviors that are representative of fluid and crystallized intelligence. The fluid intelligence score might represent performance on tasks such as memorizing and later recalling names of symbols or recalling unrelated words presented in a particular sequence. A crystallized intelligence score might represent performance on items that measure vocabulary or general knowledge. John Horn and John Carroll expanded on this theory to include additional intelligence factors, now called the **Cattell–Horn–Carroll (CHC) Theory**. These factors include general memory and learning, broad visual perception, broad auditory perception, broad retrieval ability, broad cognitive speediness, and decision/reaction time/speed. CHC Theory is the theory on which one of the most commonly used tests, the *Woodcock-Johnson IV Tests of Cognitive Abilities*, is based.

Commonly Interpreted Factors and Cognitive Processes on Intelligence Tests

17.2
PROGRESS
MONITORING
CHECK

As you encounter the use of measures of intelligence or cognitive processes in schools, you will encounter the names of various test factors, clusters, indexes, and processes. We describe several common (and overlapping) terms in Table 17.1.

Types of Intelligence Tests

Depending on what types of decisions are being made, as well as the specific characteristics of the student, different types of intelligence tests might be selected for administration. We describe three different types in the following sections.

Individual Tests

Individually administered intelligence tests are most frequently used for making diagnostic (including exceptionality, eligibility, and educational placement) decisions. Federal special education guidelines specify the use of intelligence tests in declaring students eligible for services under the label "intellectual disability." State special education eligibility guidelines and criteria typically specify that the collection of data about intellectual functioning must be included in the decision-making process for eligibility and placement decisions for the condition of "intellectual disability and may also do so for other disability conditions. Guidelines further specify that these data must come from individual intellectual evaluation by a certified school psychologist. Districts may have more specific guidelines than those provided by the state.

TABLE 17.1

Common Intelligence Test Terms, Associated Theorists and Tests, and Examples of Associated Behaviors Sampled

Term	Definition	Theorists	Tests	Example of a Behavior Sampled
Attention	Alertness	Das, Naglieri	CAS-2	When given a target figure and many distracting stimuli, the individual must quickly select those that are identical to the target figure.
Auditory perception/ processing	Ability to analyze, manipulate, and discriminate sounds	Cattell, Horn, Carroll	WJ-IV	When given a sound, the examinee must name words that begin with that sound.
Cognitive efficiency/ speediness	Ability to process information quickly and automatically	Cattell, Horn, Carroll	WJ-IV	When given a worksheet with rows of letter patterns, the examinee must circle the two sets of letter patterns that match in each row.
Comprehension knowledge	Communication and use of acquired knowledge	Cattell, Horn, Carroll	WJ-IV	When provided a word, the examinee must provide a word that has the same meaning.
Fluid reasoning/ intelligence	Efficiency with which an individual learns and completes various tasks	Cattell, Horn, Carroll	WJ-IV	When given a set of information, examinee must determine and apply a rule for the information.
Long-term retrieval/ delayed recall	Ability to store and easily recall information at a much later point in time	Cattell, Horn, Carroll	WJ-IV	After listening to a story, examinee must recall details from the story.
Perceptual speed	Ability to identify patterns		WJ-IV	When given a worksheet with rows of number patterns, examinee must circle the two sets of numbers that match in each row.
Planning	Ability to identify effective strategies to reach a particular goal	Das, Naglieri	CAS-2	When given a legend that pairs numbers with a set of symbols, and a series of numbered boxes, the examinee must write the corresponding symbols in the appropriate boxes.

(continues)

TABLE 17.1 (*continued*)

Term	Definition	Theorists	Tests	Example of a Behavior Sampled
Processing speed	Ability to quickly complete tasks that require limited complex thought	Cattell, Horn, Carroll	WJ-IV, WISC-V	When presented with a key for converting numbers to symbols, the individual must quickly write down the associated symbols for the numbers that are presented.
Quantitative reasoning	Ability to reason with numbers	Cattell, Horn, Carroll	WJ-IV	When given a series of numbers that fit a pattern but one number is missing, the examinee must provide the missing number.
Short-term memory or working memory	Ability to quickly store and then immediately retrieve information within a short period of time	Cattell, Horn, Carroll	WISC-V, WJ-IV	The examiner says several numbers, and the individual must repeat them accurately in backward order.
Simultaneous processing	Extent to which one can integrate pieces of information into a complete pattern	Das, Naglieri	CAS-2	When asked a question verbally and presented with figures, the individual must pick the figure that answers the question.
Successive processing	Extent to which one can recall things presented in a particular order	Das, Naglieri	CAS-2	When given a set of words, the individual must repeat them back in the same order.
Verbal comprehension	"Verbal abilities utilizing reasoning, comprehension, and conceptualization" (WISC-V Examiner's Manual p. 6,)		WISC-V	The individual must verbally express how two things are similar.
Visual perception/ processing	Integrating and interpreting visual information	Cattell, Horn, Carroll	WJ-IV	When given various shapes and a corresponding set of pieces, the examinee must identify which pieces make up the shape.

Group Tests

Group-administered intelligence tests are seldom used these days in schools. When they are used, they are administered as screening devices to identify those students who differ enough from average intelligence to warrant further assessment. In these cases, the tests' merit is that teachers can administer them relatively quickly to large numbers of students. The tests suffer from the same limitations as any group test: They can be made to yield qualitative information only with difficulty, and they require students to sit still for approximately 20 minutes, to mark with a pencil, and, often, to read. During the past 30 years, it has become increasingly common for school districts to eliminate the practice of group intelligence testing. When administrators are asked why they are doing so, they cite the limited relevance of knowing about students' capabilities and the importance of knowing about the subject matter skills (such as for reading and math) that students do and do not have. They also indicate that teachers find it very difficult to use the results of student performance on intelligence tests for instructional purposes and that schoolwide intellectual screening programs are not cost effective. We do not recommend their use due to cost, error, and lack of benefit and utility.

Nonverbal Intelligence Tests

A number of nonverbal tests are among the most widely used tests for assessment of intelligence, particularly when there are questions about the intelligence of a child who is not proficient in English or who is deaf or hard of hearing. Some nonverbal tests are designed to measure intelligence broadly; others are called "picture–vocabulary tests." The latter are not measures of intelligence; rather, they measure receptive vocabulary. In picture–vocabulary tests, pictures are presented to the test taker, who is asked to identify those pictures that correspond to words read by the examiner. Some authors of picture–vocabulary measures state that the tests measure receptive vocabulary; others equate receptive vocabulary with intelligence and claim that their tests assess intelligence. Because the tests measure only receptive vocabulary, they should not be used to make eligibility decisions. Measures of receptive vocabulary are reviewed in Chapter 15, "Using Oral and Written Language Measures and Measures of Receptive Vocabulary."

In the remainder of this chapter, we provide information on the most commonly used verbal and nonverbal measures of intelligence. Detailed information about specific behaviors sampled by subtests of each measure can be obtained by going to the websites for the publishers of each test. In Table 17.2, we list commonly used verbal measures of intelligence, and in Table 17.3 we list commonly used nonverbal measures of intelligence. The most commonly used verbal measures are the *Wechsler Intelligence Scale for Children–Fourth Edition* and *Woodcock-Johnson Cognitive Battery–Fourth Edition*. The other verbal tests are used much less frequently. The nonverbal measures we list are used about equally.

For each measure we list the authors and publisher and then show the subtests and/or composite scores that are provided for the test. We also indicate the nature of the normative groups, as these provide the comparison groups for the students for whom tests are used. We summarize data on reliability for subtests and composites. Recall that the most critical kind of reliability is internal consistency reliability as calculated most often by coefficient alpha. Internal consistency sets an upper limit on other kinds of reliability and the validity of a measure. When available we provide information on test–retest reliability for each of the measures. Recall that for tests to be used to make important decisions about students the tests should have reliabilities that exceed .90. The measures

TABLE 17.2

Commonly Used Verbal Measures of Intelligence

Test	Authors and Publisher	Abilities Measured	Norms	Reliability Evidence
Cognitive Assessment System–Second Edition (CAS-2)	Naglieri, Das, & Goldstein, 2014, PRO-ED	Planning, Attention, Simultaneous Processing, Successive Processing; six supplemental scores	1,342 children and adolescents stratified on the basis of age, gender, race, Hispanic status, geographic region, ethnicity, parental education, and household income.	Full-Scale IQ reliability is .95, while reliabilities of individual subtests range from .86 to .93.
Detroit Tests of Learning Ability–Fifth Edition	Hammill, McGhee & Ehrler, 2019, PRO-ED	General Cognitive Ability; two domain composites (Reasoning Ability, Processing Ability); six subdomain composites (Acquired Knowledge, Verbal Comprehension, Nonverbal Problem Solving, Verbal Memory, Nonverbal Memory, Processing Speed)	Normed on 1,383 individuals ages 6-0 to 17-11 stratified by age to conform to the characteristic of the 2015 census.	Internal consistency reliability coefficients range from .79 to .90 for subtests, .87 to .95 for subdomain composites, and .95 to .98 for domain composites.
Kaufman Assessment Battery for Children–Second Edition	Kaufman, A. & Kaufman, N., 2004, Pearson	Three global scales (Fluid and Crystalized Index, Mental Processing Index, Nonverbal Index); four scales (Sequential, Simultaneous, Learning, Planning)	Normative update in 2018 on 700 individuals.	Reliability of global scales is .94 to .97.
Wechsler Intelligence Scale for Children–Fifth Edition	Wechsler, 2014, Pearson	Verbal Comprehension, Visual Spatial Reasoning, Fluid Reasoning, Working Memory, Processing Speed, Full-Scale IQ	2,200 children ages 6-0 to 16-11 stratified on the basis of age, sex, race/ethnicity, parent education level, and geographic region according to the 2012 census. A sample of children from special groups were included at each age group to accurately represent the population of children enrolled in school.	Because the Coding, Symbol Search, Naming Speed, Symbol Translation, and Cancellation subtests are timed, reliability estimates for those subtests are based on test–retest coefficients. Internal consistency coefficients are reported for all other subtests. Reliabilities for subtests range from .81 to .94 and for Full-Scale IQ from .96 to .97.
Woodcock-Johnson Cognitive–Fourth Edition	Shrank, Mather & McGrew, 2014, Riverside	Comprehension-Knowledge, Fluid Reasoning, Long-Term Retrieval, Visual Processing, Auditory Processing, Cognitive Processing Speed, Short-Term Working Memory	Normed on 7,416 individuals stratified on 12 individual and community variables.	There are 18 cognitive tests, and scores are provided for clusters of tests. Reliabilities for clusters are for the most part .90 and above.

we review all have internal consistency reliabilities for full-scale IQs and for composite scores that exceed .90. Few have high enough reliabilities for subtests; subtest scores should not be used to make important decisions, although you will see this invalid use of subtest score interpretation occur in practice. We have not included a column on validity in our tables, as the validity of measures of intelligence and cognitive abilities is suspect. This is discussed in the next section.

TABLE 17.3

Commonly Used Nonverbal Measures of Intelligence

Test	Authors and Publisher	Abilities Measured	Norms	Reliability Evidence
Comprehensive Test of Nonverbal Intelligence– Second Edition (CTONI-2)	Hammill, Pearson, & Wiederholt, 2009, PRO-ED	Subtests (Picture Analogies, Geometric Analogies, Picture Categories, Geometric Categories, Pictorial Sequences, Geometric Sequences); composites (Pictorial Scales, Geometric Scales, Full Scale)	2,827 individuals in 10 states stratified on the basis of geographic region, gender, race, Hispanic status, education attainment of parents, and family income matched to the 2007 census.	Internal consistency for subtests .80s to .90s and internal consistency for composites all exceed .90. Test–retest reliabilities are lower.
Leiter International Performance Scale–Third Edition	Roid, Miller, Pomplun, & Koch, 2013, Stoelting	Subtests (Figure Ground, Form Completion, Classification/Analogies, Sequential Order, Visual Patters, Attention Sustained, Forward Memory, Reverse Memory, Nonverbal Stroop Incongruent Incorrect, Nonverbal Stroop Congruent Correct, Nonverbal Stroop Effect); 3 composite scores (Nonverbal IQ, Nonverbal Memory, Processing Speed)	Normed on 1,603 individuals ages 3 to 75 stratified on the basis of gender, age, race/ethnicity, educational level of parent/adult, and geographic region matched to the 2008 census.	Internal consistency for nonverbal IQ from .94 to .98, for composite scores from .82 to .92, and for subtest scores from .78 to .95. Test–retest reliabilities are low (below .80).
Test of Nonverbal Intelligence– Fourth Edition (TONI-4)	Brown, Sherbenou, & Johnson, 2010, PRO-ED	Full-Scale IQ	1,272 individuals stratified on the basis of geographic region, gender, race, Hispanic status, education attainment of parents, and family income based on the 2005 census.	Internal consistency reliabilities exceed .90 at all age levels. Test–retest reliabilities range from .84 to .88.

(continues)

TABLE 17.3 (*continued*)

Test	Authors and Publisher	Abilities Measured	Norms	Reliability Evidence
Universal Nonverbal Intelligence Test–Second Edition (UNIT-2)	Bracken & McCallum, 2016, PRO-ED	Subtests (Symbolic Memory, Nonsymbolic Quantity, Analogic Reasoning, Spatial Memory, Numerical Series, Cube Design) composites (Memory, Reasoning, Symbolic, Nonsymbolic, Abbreviated Battery, Standard Battery)	1,603 individuals representative of the 2014 census. Stratified on the basis of geographic region, gender, race, Hispanic status, exceptionality status, household income, and educational attainment of parents.	Test–retest reliabilities are lower for subtests (.62 to .94) and for composite scores (.75 to .93).
Wechsler Nonverbal Intelligence Scale	Naglieri & Wechsler, 2006	6 subtests (Matrices, Coding, Object Assembly, Recognition, Spatial Span, Picture Arrangement)	Normed on 1,323 individuals stratified on the basis of age, gender, race/ethnicity, educational level, and geographic region.	Internal consistency reliability for full-scale IQ is .91; internal consistency reliability for subtests ranges from .74 to .91.

Validity of Measures of Intelligence and Other Cognitive Processes

When you open the manual to an intelligence test, you will find that the authors nearly always include in the very beginning of the manual a definition of "intelligence," and they always define it as a unitary or multiple factor and use a theory (sometimes their own) of intelligence like the CHC Theory, Spearman's *g*, or PASS theory (Planning, Attention-Arousal, Simultaneous, and Successive) to describe the components of intelligence. For example, the *Woodcock-Johnson IV Cognitive Tests* are built on the CHC Theory of intelligence, and the subtests and components assessed are designed to measure aspects of intelligence as posited in that theory. The *Cognitive Assessment System–Second Edition* is built on the PASS theory of intelligence.

In making a case for the validity of their tests, authors of intelligence tests argue that their tests measure what they are designed to measure by making a case that the subtests of their tests measure components of intelligence as posited in the theories on which the tests are built. Yet, at the same time, there is little evidence for the validity of the theories. The validity sections of test manuals for intelligence tests, then, are composed nearly exclusively with evidence that the factors assessed by the test align with factors in the theory on which the test was built. Further, it is typically shown that student performance on the measures of intelligence or cognitive processes correlate highly with their performance on other measures of cognitive processes or intelligence. Almost never do we find evidence about relevance to instruction—that is, information showing that performance on the measures informs educators how to instruct students.

The primary use of individually administered intelligence tests is for diagnostic purposes. They are used in making eligibility decisions, primarily in deciding whether students have an intellectually disability. The federal definition of the disability condition "intellectually disabled" includes specification of four levels of intellectual disability and assigns an IQ range to each level as follows: mild (IQ 52–69), moderate (IQ 36–51), severe (IQ 20–35), and profound (IQ 19 or below). So, Individualized Education Program (IEP) teams must administer an individual intelligence test as part of the process of deciding whether students are eligible for special education services under the intellectual disability label.

Within federal guidelines, students may be classified as having a learning disability by two alternative methods, one of which involves demonstration that the student fails to respond to evidence-based instruction. Federal guidelines specifically prohibit classifying a student as having a learning disability based on a significant discrepancy between performance on an intelligence test and a measure of achievement. Again, however, you will see that this incorrect test use occurs in practice. Federal guidelines permit the use of cognitive assessment of strengths and weaknesses to satisfy one criterion necessary for determining a student has a learning disability; however, the student must still demonstrate inadequate academic achievement (typically operationalized by performing below the 10th percentile on a norm-referenced valid achievement test). Lack of instruction as the cause of low achievement must be systematically ruled out as a separate criterion in addition to other rule-outs (e.g., sensory deficits). Thus, even when a team chooses to use cognitive assessment as the basis for satisfying part of the eligibility criteria to determine learning disability, assessment teams must conduct instructional trials to rule out lack of instruction as causing poor performance (Kovaleski et al., in press).

Because learning disabilities are the most prevalent disability and the use of cognitive tests to determine learning disability has been a significant source of scholarly debate, teachers will be wise to understand exactly how cognitive tests may be properly used in the eligibility process and what their specific limitations are. For example, cognitive tests cannot be used to demonstrate low achievement, nor can they be used to rule out lack of instruction, two additional criteria that are necessary to determine learning disability. Unfortunately, there is a track record in the United States of students being made eligible for special education for learning disabilities without meeting state or local criteria (Shepard & Smith, 1983; Sheppard et al., 1983). Even today, intelligence-achievement discrepancy may be used in schools where it is specifically prohibited because of its demonstrated lack of validity.

Fairness in Assessment of Intelligence and Cognitive Processes

How do we ensure that measures of intelligence and other cognitive processes are used fairly and in the best interest of children and youth? In short, it is difficult to do so.

First, it is important to remember that in educational settings, assessment is a process of collecting information (data) for the purpose of making decisions for or about students. In Chapter 1, we reviewed the kinds of decisions made and pointed out that the end goal is enhancement of student academic and behavioral competence. Tests are administered for the purpose of helping us plan interventions that will lead to improved competence. When tests do not help plan instructional interventions that will lead to improved outcomes, then the use of those tests is a waste of time and potentially harmful to students.

We have noted in this chapter that intelligence tests and measures of other cognitive processes assess hypothetical constructs that are of limited use in planning instructional interventions that lead to improved educational outcomes. Hence, knowing the results of student performance on these tests is of limited use in helping students. As with any other tests, measures of intelligence and cognitive processes sample behaviors, and performance on any one test must be interpreted in light of the behaviors sampled by the test. Performance must also be understood in light of the student's opportunity to learn, cultural background, and age. If these factors are taken into account, then performance on an intelligence test may be helpful to IEP teams in the process of making decisions about eligibility for special education services under the label "intellectual disability." Otherwise, school personnel are advised to stick to measures of skill development in academic and behavioral content areas as they plan instructional interventions for students.

PROGRESS 17.1
MONITORING CHECK

1. Identify two alternative reasons why there has been a decline in the use of intelligence tests in schools over the past 20 years.
2. How does opportunity to learn affect a student's performance on an intelligence test?
3. How does a student's background experiences affect their performance on an intelligence test?
4. Obtain a copy of an intelligence test and examine five items. What behaviors are sampled by each of the items?

PROGRESS 17.2
MONITORING CHECK

1. Describe four commonly interpreted intelligence factors.
2. Identify one commonly interpreted intelligence factor and indicate how the information obtained using that factor might be used to plan an instructional program for a fourth-grade student.
3. When might you decide to use the *Woodcock -Johnson III Cognitive Test* rather than the WISC IV?

CHAPTER 18

Using Measures of Social and Emotional Behavior

LEARNING OBJECTIVES

1. Understand why we assess social-emotional functioning and adaptive behavior.
2. Identify key considerations in the assessment of social-emotional and adaptive behavior.
3. Identify several methods for assessing social-emotional functioning and one common method for assessing adaptive behavior.
4. Understand the components of a functional behavioral assessment.

Mental health and social-emotional competency has been found to be positively related to many important educational outcomes, including academic performance, pro-social behavior, and perceptions of school climate. There are no shortage of modern-day life challenges that can present barriers to the mental health and well-being of children and teens alike. Whether it be within the context of social media or in-person interactions, research has shown that young people are lonelier than people older than 72 (Grant & Sweet Grant, 2019) and are experiencing anxiety and depression at rates higher than previous generations (Bitsko et al., 2018; U.S. Department of Health and Human Services, Center for Disease Control and Prevention, 2019). In one national survey, 74% of teens and young adults said they experienced anxiety about their everyday life, 70% wished they had more friends, and 62% experienced other people putting them down (Pew Research Center, 2019). The term *social-emotional learning* was only officially coined in 1994, but even before then teachers long valued the mental health and social and emotional functioning of their students. We now have decades of research to demonstrate that social-emotional functioning and mental health affect and, in turn, are affected by the development of student academic skills.

Since 1994 there has been an explosion in the availability of social-emotional learning programs, curricula, and assessments in schools. The Collaborative for Academic, Social, and Emotional Learning (CASEL) has taken a multidisciplinary approach to define five broad areas of competency: self-awareness, self-management, social awareness, relationship skills, and responsible decision making. These five competencies have been used to develop social and emotional learning curricula (e.g., Carrizales-Engelmann et al., 2016) because of the direct connection to students' well-being and academic achievement (Durlak et al., 2011). When students either lack or fail to demonstrate a certain repertoire of expected behavioral, coping, and social skills, their academic learning can be hindered. The reverse is also true: School experiences can impact student social-emotional well-being and related behaviors. To be successful in school, students frequently need to engage in certain prosocial behaviors, such as taking turns and responding appropriately to criticism. Other behaviors, such as name calling and uttering self-deprecating remarks, may cause concern and can denote underlying social and emotional problems. In Chapter 11, "Assessing Behavior Through Observation," we noted that teachers, psychologists, social workers, and other diagnosticians systematically observe a variety of student behaviors. In this chapter, we discuss additional methods and considerations for the assessment of behaviors variously called social, emotional, and problem behaviors.

In addition, it is important for students to adapt to their physical and social environments, to stay safe, and avoid danger. This is often referred to as adaptive behavior. For instance, looking both ways before crossing a road, selecting appropriate attire for a cold day, and being able to navigate your way home from a reasonable distance away are all examples of **adaptive behaviors**. In addition to appropriate responses to the demands of the immediate environment, adaptive behavior requires preparation for responses to probable future environments. Certain behaviors (e.g., smoking or drug use) can have life-threatening future consequences. Similarly, acquiring more education or job training and saving money increase the likelihood of thriving in later years. Adaptive behavior varies by age; adults are typically expected to take reasonable care of themselves (by managing their own health, dressing, eating, and so on), to work, and to engage in socially acceptable recreational or leisure activities. In children and adolescents, the behaviors of interest are of two kinds. We assess behaviors that demonstrate age-appropriate independence and responsibility. We also assess those behaviors that are believed to enable the development or acquisition of desired adult behaviors.

In the past it was primarily the responsibility of the classroom teacher to identify students with externalizing and internalizing problem behaviors. Identifying troubling externalizing behaviors was easier than identifying students with internalizing behavior concerns, which lead to missed opportunities for intervention and outreach. With the increased attention on reducing bullying behaviors and improving overall school climate, it is more common to find schools implementing schoolwide social and emotional well-being programs. In this chapter, we take a closer look at some of the assessment practices for students who have already been identified through universal screening or teacher nomination to intervention planning teams or multidisciplinary teams.

Why Do We Assess Social-Emotional and Adaptive Behavior?

There are two major reasons for assessing social-emotional and adaptive behaviors: (1) identification and classification and (2) intervention planning. First, some disabilities are defined, in part, by inappropriate behavior. For example, the regulations for implementing the Individuals With Disabilities Education Act (IDEA) describe in general terms the types of inappropriate behaviors that are indicative of emotional disturbance. Thus, to classify a pupil as having this disability and in need of special education, educators need to assess social and emotional behaviors. IDEA also requires that in order to be eligible for special education services under the category of intellectual disability, there must be evidence of both low intelligence and limited adaptive behavior, and so adaptive behavior must be assessed as part of the assessment of students suspected of having an intellectual disability.

Second, assessment of social-emotional and adaptive behavior will hopefully lead to appropriate intervention. For students whose disabilities are defined by inappropriate behaviors, the need for intervention is obvious. However, the development and demonstration of social and coping skills, and the reduction of problem behavior, are worthwhile goals for all students. Many students will benefit from social-emotional or behavioral interventions even if they are not eligible for special education services. In order to make decisions about student placement and progress, behaviors are monitored and assessed to learn whether the treatment has been successful, and the desired behavior has produced more general improvements in the child's life. Schools are often the first mental health provider for students in need and therefore educators need to be prepared with a range of assessment techniques in order to develop effective services.

Important Considerations in the Assessment of Social-Emotional Functioning and Adaptive Behavior

The appropriateness of social and emotional behavior, as well as adaptive behavior, may vary according to the age of a student, the setting in which the behavior occurs, the frequency or duration of the behavior, and the intensity of the behavior. For example, it is not uncommon for preschool students to cry in front of other children when their parents send them off on the first day of school. However, the same behavior would be considered atypical if exhibited by an 11th grader. It would be even more problematic if the 11th grader cried every day in front of her peers at school. Some behaviors are of concern even when they occur infrequently, if they are very intense, for example, a tantrum, striking a peer, or running away from the classroom. The appropriateness of social-emotional behavior is also shaped by societal and cultural expectations. Consider how we respond to two students getting in a fight. Some cultures may talk to the students about why this behavior is inappropriate and harmful. In other cultural environments, it may be acceptable and even encouraged for students to find resolution to their own disagreement even if it involves violence.

Although some social and emotional problems that students experience are clearly apparent, others may be much less easily observed, even though they have a similar negative effect on overall student functioning. Externalizing problems, particularly those that contribute to disruption in classroom routines, are easily detected. Excessive shouting, hitting or pushing of classmates, and talking back to the teacher are behaviors that are not easily overlooked. Internalizing problems, such as anxiety and depression, are often less readily identified. These problems might be expressed in the form of social isolation, excessive fatigue, or self-destructive behavior. In assessing both externalizing and internalizing problems, it can be helpful to identify both behavioral excesses (for instance, out-of-seat behavior or interrupting) and deficits (such as social isolation or low rate of initiations to peers) that can then become targets for intervention.

Sometimes students fail to behave in expected ways because they do not have the requisite coping or social skills; in other cases, students may actually have the necessary skills but fail to demonstrate them under certain conditions. This dichotomy highlights the importance of distinguishing between skill deficits and performance deficits in the assessment of social behavior. If students never demonstrate certain expected social behaviors, they may need to be instructed explicitly in that grouping of social skills. An interventionist might model the expected behavior for the student or small group of students. If the behavior is expected to be demonstrated across all contexts, an intervention may need to take place in the various settings in order for the student to master the appropriate behavior across settings. Through assessment and observation, it may be possible to detect specific contingencies in specific environments that increase or at least maintain the behavior. An analysis of associated environmental variables can help determine how best to intervene.

Assessing Social-Emotional and Adaptive Behavior

Four methods are commonly used to gather information about social and emotional functioning: observation, interviews, rating scales, and functional behavioral assessment. **Direct observation** of social and emotional behavior is often preferred, given that the results using this method are generally accurate. However, obtaining useful observational data across multiple settings can be time-consuming and expensive, particularly when the behavior is very limited in frequency or duration. Internalizing problems can go undetected unless specific questions are asked, or specific external behaviors are exhibited. Sometime these indicators of internalizing problems are subtle and are therefore less readily detected. The use of rating scales and interviews can often allow for more efficient collection of data across multiple settings and informants, which is particularly important in the assessment of social-emotional behavior. The use of rating scales with adult respondents is the most common way adaptive behavior is measured. Observational procedures were discussed in Chapter 11, "Assessing Behavior Through Observation"; the remaining methods are described in the following sections.

Interviews

Interviews are most often used by experienced professionals to gain information about the perspectives of various knowledgeable individuals, as well as to gain further insight into a student's overall patterns of thinking and behaving. Interviews can be conducted with parents and caregivers, with other educators in the building and with community members such as coaches or religious leaders as long as they have knowledge of the student behavior in various settings. Descriptions of a range of interview techniques are outside the scope of this book. However, in our experience, school psychologists, special educators, school social workers, counselors, and even administrators or community liaisons are called on to conduct interviews with parents, caregivers, and the student themselves to try to understand the source of the behavioral and emotional issues and devise possible solutions. Some school districts have set interview questions that must be asked of parents and caregivers to document medical history. There are many variations on the interview method—most distinctions are made along a continuum from structured to semi-structured. *Behavioral interviews* are an important part of the process to gather information in one or more of the following areas of functioning and development: medical/developmental history, social-emotional functioning, educational progress, and community involvement. Behavioral interviews will be helpful in the problem identification and data collection phases of the problem solving process (Whitcomb, 2018). *Motivational interviewing* (Miller & Rollnick, 2013) is a specific interviewing process that provides a scientifically based procedure to foster a collaborative relationship between the clinician and the client—in our case, usually students and families. The focus is on good listening and giving good advice by asking questions and offering information that help the client discover their own motivation for changing their behavior. Interviewing in this way becomes a method of communication that can be used in the initial assessment process and also in the intervention development phase to find an intervention that will be suitable for the student, teachers, and the parents or caregivers.

Rating Scales

Generally, a parent, teacher, peer, or "significant other" in a student's environment is asked to rate the extent to which that student demonstrates certain desirable or undesirable behaviors. Raters are often asked to determine the presence or absence of a particular behavior and may be asked to quantify the amount, intensity, or frequency of the behavior. Rating scales are popular because they are easy to administer and can be considered a low-cost assessment tool in comparison to observations and interviews. They can also provide useful information about a student's level of functioning over time. They bring structure to an assessment or evaluation and can be used in almost any environment to gather data from almost any source. The important concept to remember is that **rating scales** provide an index of someone's perception of a student's behavior. Different raters will probably have different perceptions of the same student's behavior and are likely to provide different ratings of the student; each is likely to have different views of acceptable and unacceptable expectations or standards. Students may also be asked to complete a rating scale or a self-report of the behaviors and emotions they experience in different settings. In general, surveys and self-reports should be supplemented by the other assessment methods mentioned because bias will always influence how raters score a student.

Just as is the case for academic skills, assessment of social-emotional behavior and mental health occurs at each tier within an educational system, with increasing comprehensiveness and frequency of assessment occurring at higher tiers. One procedure that has been developed to incorporate multiple methods in the assessment of social and emotional behavior, and that resembles a multi-tiered approach to assessment, is *multiple gating* (Walker & Severson, 1992). This procedure is used in the *Systematic Screening for Behavior Disorders* (Walker et al., 2014), which involves the systematic screening of all students using brief rating scales. The screening is followed by the use of more extensive rating scales, interviews, and observations for those students who are identified as likely to have social-emotional problems. Multiple gating may help limit the number of undetected problems, as well as target time-consuming assessment methods toward the most severe problems.

Functional Behavioral Assessment and Analysis

An assessment strategy that has become more commonly used to address problem behavior is **functional behavioral assessment (FBA)**. FBA defines the problem behavior, the environmental conditions under which it occurs, and the consequences that predictably follow the behavior in order to identify the purpose or "function" the behavior serves for the student (Crone et al., 2015). It involves the integration of data from a variety of sources to meaningfully inform intervention efforts. Those who conduct FBAs may use a variety of different assessment methods and tools (e.g., interviews, observations, and rating scales), depending on the nature of the student's behavioral difficulties. Once an FBA has been conducted, a function-based behavior intervention plan (sometimes called a behavior support plan) can be developed that has a high likelihood of reducing the problem behavior. According to IDEA 2004, an FBA must be conducted for any student undergoing special education eligibility evaluation in which problem behavior is of concern. An FBA must also be conducted (or reviewed) following a manifestation determination review[1] in which the associated suspensions from school are determined to be due to the child's disability. FBAs are to be conducted by those who have been appropriately trained.

18.1
PROGRESS
MONITORING
CHECK

Steps for Completing a Functional Behavior Assessment

Although a variety of different tools and measures might be used to conduct an FBA, certain steps are essential to the process. The purpose of conducting an initial FBA is to design an individualized behavior intervention plan to prevent challenging behavior and teach and reinforce replacement skills (Strickland-Cohen & Horner, 2015). The steps are as follows:

1. Define the Behavior

Behavior is complicated. The goal of the FBA process will include interviews and observations that will be used to define the behavior or behaviors so that a thorough and effective behavior plan can be developed and implemented. Students may display a variety of problematic behaviors and in some cases a behavior support plan will need to address multiple behaviors (O'Neill et al., 2014). For example, Annie may exhibit a variety of problematic behaviors, including excessive crying, repeatedly banging her head against her desk until she develops bruises, and noncompliance with teacher directions; a support team will need to address all of these behaviors. It may be that a dangerous behavior receives more intervention resources, but having a clear picture of all of the behaviors is important. Behavior should be defined such that it is observable, measurable, and specific (see Chapter 8, "Monitoring Student Progress Toward Instructional Goals," for ways in which behaviors can be measured). A review of records, interviews with teachers and caregivers, and direct observations are typically necessary when defining problematic behaviors.

2. Identify Potential Setting Events and Antecedents

Once the behavior has been carefully defined, it is necessary to identify any patterns associated with occurrences of the behavior. In doing so, it is important to identify setting events and antecedents.

---

1. A manifestation determination review must be conducted when a student receiving special education services has been the recipient of disciplinary action that constitutes a change of placement for more than 10 days within a school year.

Setting events represent events that make the student particularly sensitive to the antecedents and consequences associated with the problem behavior. For example, a setting event might include being sleep deprived the night before school. This setting event might make a student more likely to be sensitive to a teacher's request for her to finish work quickly. This, in turn, could lead the student to refuse to do her work in response to the teacher's request. Setting events occur before an instance of the problem behavior but are not restricted by time. A setting event could be that the student is staying with one parent when the student prefers to stay with the other parent, a change in home that occurs every 2 weeks. Variables such as medication, physical or medical problems (e.g., pain), number of people in a space, and daily routines like diet and sleep can be areas to investigate for setting event information.

Antecedents are events that occur immediately before the problem behavior. Examples of antecedents include being asked to complete a particular task or having a particularly disliked person enter the room. The person conducting the FBA will gather information, observations, and interviews about the time of day and the location (the when and where) the behavior occurs most often. The antecedents may also be a specific person or group of people. Sometimes an antecedent is a specific activity such as doing homework or attending a certain class. An important step in the process of developing a behavior intervention plan is identifying non-examples of antecedents. For instance, if a student refuses to do a math worksheet when requested by one teacher but not by another teacher, the team can gather more information to learn if the specific staff member is the antecedent rather than the presentation of a math worksheet. This example is a good reminder that whenever an FBA is conducted, the assessor should also include identifying any academic deficits that may be contributing to challenging behavior. Examining academic screening and progress monitoring data will provide useful information as antecedents are being identified.

3. Identify the Consequences

Consequences are events that occur after the behavior and are hypothesized to impact the likelihood that the behavior will occur or not occur in the future. For example, the consequence for a student tearing up a paper that he or she does not want to work on may be that the student does not have to complete the difficult task presented on the paper. If a student hits another student in the arm, the consequence may be that he is sent to the office and the student misses the remainder of class. The question is then: Did the student punch the other student to gain peer and adult attention, was the subject matter difficult and the student wanted to escape the lesson, or perhaps both? This question of why the student engages in the behavior leads to our next step.

4. Develop a Hypothesis About the Function of the Behavior

Using information that is collected about setting events, antecedents, and consequent events through record review, interview, and observation, one can begin to develop hypotheses about the function of the behavior. In Chapter 11, "Assessing Behavior Through Observation," we described several different functions of behavior, including social attention/communication; access to tangibles or preferred activities; escape, delay, reduction, or avoidance of aversive tasks or activities; escape or avoidance of other individuals; and internal stimulation (Carr, 1994).

5. Test the Hypothesized Function of the Behavior

Although this step is typically considered part of a functional behavioral analysis (as opposed to a functional behavioral assessment), it is important to verify that your hypothesis about the function of the behavior is correct. Otherwise, the associated intervention plan may not work. By manipulating the antecedents and consequences, one can determine whether the function is correct. For example, if it is assumed that escape from difficult tasks is a function of the student's problematic behavior of tearing up assignments, one could provide tasks that the student finds easy and enjoys and examine whether he or she tears up the paper. The teacher could instead give brief breaks from the task based on the student's completion of portions of the task. If the student completes more of the task and stops tearing up assignments, this would provide evidence that the function of the behavior is to escape from a difficult task. If the behavior continues at the same rate, even when task difficulty is reduced and breaks from the task are provided for problem completion, one might test out a different hypothesis. For example, if the student commonly is reprimanded and put on a time-out with an instructional aide present for tearing up the paper, another hypothesis might be that receiving attention from the teacher or instructional aide is a function of the student's problematic behavior. To test this, the teacher and instructional aide could provide special attention to the student more frequently when the student is engaged with the task, while also ignoring mild disruptions and having the student complete time-outs without the teacher assistant present. If this corresponds to better work completion and less tearing up of assignments, then attention is likely the function of the behavior.

6. Develop a Behavior Intervention Plan

Although this step is carried out after the actual FBA, it is important to know how to use the assessment data that are collected to inform the development of an intervention plan. A behavior intervention plan should include the following:

Identifying, Teaching, and Reinforcing a Replacement Behavior

As part of the behavior intervention plan, the support team needs to identify a behavior that the student can use to address the identified function in an appropriate manner. For example, if the function of a problematic behavior (such as tearing up work) is escape from a difficult task, the student might be taught how to request a break from the difficult task, such that the same function (escape) would be met when the student engages in a more appropriate behavior (such as work completion). In tandem, additional instruction might be provided to ensure that the student has the academic skills needed to complete the difficult task. Although some might initially think that teaching replacement behaviors (such as to ask for a break and have it granted) results in a lowering of standards, it is important to highlight that having the student ask for a break is more socially appropriate than tearing up an assignment, and it is a step in the right direction. Until the students' academic skills improve, the strategy of asking for a break is a good intermediary. In order to ensure that the student makes use of newly taught replacement behaviors, the intervention plan might include an incentive for when the student initially makes appropriate use of the replacement behavior. Strategies to make the task easier or less aversive to the student are numerous and could include providing adult assistance via explicit instruction, interspersing or alternating difficult problems with easier problems, and using easy problems and very gradually increasing problem difficulty as student proficiency improves.

Effectively Addressing Setting Events and Antecedents

Behavior intervention plans may include an alteration of the conditions surrounding setting events and antecedents in an effort to prevent or decrease the likelihood that the problematic behavior will occur. For example, if escape from difficult items presented on a worksheet is the function of a behavior, and the antecedent is the presentation of those difficult items, the teacher might set up an activity to begin with a few very easy tasks, followed by a medium task, more easy tasks, and perhaps one difficult task toward the end. If peer attention is the function of a behavior, the teacher might choose to introduce challenging tasks in small-group instruction, with one-on-one adult instruction, or when other students are not present so that peer attention is reduced or not available.

Effectively Establish Consequences to Reinforce Alternative Appropriate Behaviors

Behavior intervention plans will include the identification of strategies that can provide similar and equally efficient reinforcers. Consider an example where Kai's problem behavior is getting out of his seat repeatedly during a lesson to talk to the teacher and obtain her attention. The behavior-plan alteration to the reinforcing consequence could be for Kai to access her attention by raising his hand and having the teacher call on him within 3 seconds. In addition to calling on Kai, the teacher would deliver behavior-specific praise, saying, "Kai, thank you for raising your hand." Similarly, if Kai were to engage in the undesired behavior, the teacher would plan to minimize her attention to allow the desirable behaviors to become more efficient at serving the function of the behavior than the problem behavior.

Actively Supporting the Use of the Behavior Intervention

Once a behavior intervention plan is developed, it is important to also create a method for measuring implementation integrity as well as a monitoring strategy to determine whether the behavioral intervention plan is effectively reducing the student's problem behavior and increasing the alternative behaviors. Monitoring the integrity and fidelity of the plan can be monitored by a simple checklist, observations, or other sources of teacher and student reports.

Models of who will conduct an FBA and how the FBA will be conducted vary according to district. Some school districts provide their school psychologists, special education teachers, and other behavior specialists with training on how to conduct a complex FBA with integrity and consistency. Some districts specify that behavior specialists or school psychologists conduct complex FBAs but ask special education teachers to conduct basic FBAs within their classrooms. Basic FBAs are not as thorough as complex FBAs but can quickly generate data to develop a classroom specific behavior plan. Of the four assessment methods for social-emotional and behavioral problems, the FBA requires the most specialized knowledge. Comprehensive training to conduct FBAs is useful to increase the capacity of the school to deliver function-based interventions (Strickland-Cohen et al., 2016). Although it is not common, a proactive approach to addressing the social, emotional, and behavioral needs of students by conducting universal screening for mental health and social-emotional problems is recommended (Dineen et al., 2021). It is important for educators using these universal screening systems to understand that ethical and high-fidelity implementation requires teams to be responsive to the data to detect the need for interventions to improve student mental health and behavior (Reinke et al., 2020). Schools today are one of the largest mental health providers, With the increasing focus on school climate and social-emotional well-being, assessment methods such as FBAs are an invaluable part of your toolbox.

Stakeholder PERSPECTIVE

Ileana Umaña, MA, NCSP, BCBA, School Psychology Doctoral Candidate, Texas A&M University

I have been fortunate to work in highly diverse school districts as a teacher, school psychologist, and board-certified behavior analyst. I am also a bilingual clinician, and most of the students I work with are culturally and linguistically diverse (CLD). I've learned that all data, including test data and any data used in intervention planning, should be interpreted with a CLD lens. If the behavior is determined to be expected in the student's culture, it will lead to different approaches than if atypical. Given that schools and communities are a melting pot of different cultures and cultural norms, it is important to attend to these factors when interpreting data.

When assessing CLD students, it is important to pay particular attention to differences in behavior reports at home and at school. These can often be indicators of differing expectations or cultural norms. For example, I was assigned to assess a student who did not talk during her school day and was thought to have selective mutism. The parent interview revealed that they expect children to respond to conversations with adults rather than start them. Further, due to religious beliefs, the student was expected not to mingle with the opposite sex. Understanding these cultural and religious norms provided great insight into both the student's behavior and how to assess the student and address teacher concerns.

More recently, I worked with a child exhibiting anxiety and frequent tantrums. The parent interview did not match the information they shared on rating scales. The parents spoke candidly and shared their many concerns, but when presented with clinical verbiage in the rating scale to describe the same behavior, they did not indicate their concerns. When asked, the parents shared that culturally, they thought many of the words felt inappropriate and would only be used for extreme circumstances. They did not feel right in applying them to their child. Through this discussion, we were able to identify that indeed some of the behavior was more extreme even if the parents didn't feel comfortable labeling it as such on a rating scale. Using both the rating scale and the interviews allowed us to confirm behaviors of concern and an appropriate intervention plan.

In all of the roles I've held in schools, I have found it extremely important to expand my knowledge of cultural groups so that I can enhance my assessment practices with students from a variety of backgrounds. Through constantly learning about our students' backgrounds and communities, we can understand the dangers of having umbrella assumptions about cultural groups. We can also grow more comfortable with conversations around how culture, language, and religion impact student lives and therefore our assessment practices.

Commonly Used Measures of Social and Emotional Behavior

PROGRESS
MONITORING
CHECK

In this chapter we've discussed the systems, procedures, and foundations for the measurement of social and emotional behavior. There are also a number of published measures that are standardized and have demonstrated sufficient technical adequacy with a variety of target populations. Table 18.1 lists some commonly used measures that you'll encounter both in the school system and in clinical settings. Remember that the standardization procedures for each measure should always be followed and that more than just one measure and one method of data collection often will be needed to develop a comprehensive support plan for students.

TABLE 18.1

Commonly Used Measures of Social and Emotional Behavior

Test, Author(s), & Publisher	Ages	Skills	Norms	Reliability Evidence	Validity Evidence
Behavioral and Emotional Rating Scale–Third Edition Epstein, Pierce, & Lambert, 2002, PRO-ED	Teacher Rating Scale ages 5-0 to 18-11; Parent Rating Scale ages 5-0 to 18-11; Youth Rating Scale ages 11-0 to 18-11	TRS, PRS, and YRS each consist of a battery of scales that measure five dimensions: interpersonal strengths, family involvement, intrapersonal strengths, school functioning, and affective strength. A composite score is provided for each of the three rating scales.	Teacher Rating Scale norms are based on a sample of 1,435 children between 5-0 and 18-11 in 38 states. Parent Rating Scale was normed on 1,032 children between ages 5-0 and 18-11 in 28 states. Youth Rating Scale was normed on 600 children between 11-0 and 18-0 in 27 states. Samples were stratified by age to conform to projected U.S. school-age characteristics for 2019.	Internal consistency coefficients range from .89 to .96 for TRS, .97 for PRS, and range from .80 to .88 for YRS. Internal consistency for composite scale is .94. Test–retest reliabilities for subscales range from .66 to .80.	Evidence for content validity is based on the authors' strong development of their rationale for selecting a strength-based approach and selection of specific subscale content and format. Extensive bias studies revealed little or no bias with regard to gender, race, or Hispanic status. Evidence for criterion-related validity is all based on validity studies with the BERS-2 and the argument that this is appropriate because none of the items changed for BERS-2 and BERS-3. Moderate-to-high correlations are reported in studies comparing the BERS-2 to the *Child Behavior Checklist, Social Skills Rating Scale, SSRS, and Scale for Assessing Emotional Disturbance.*

(continues)

TABLE 18.1 (*continued*)

Test, Author(s), & Publisher	Ages	Skills	Norms	Reliability Evidence	Validity Evidence
Behavior Assessment System for Children–Third Edition, Behavioral and Emotional Screening Systems (BASC-3 BESS) Reynolds & Kamphaus, 2015, Pearson	Ages 2 to 25 years	Composed of five forms: Teacher Preschool, Teacher Child/Adolescent, Parent Preschool, Parent Child/Adolescent, Student Child/Adolescent. Four risk indices are indicated by the teacher and parent forms: behavioral and emotional risk, externalizing risk, internalizing risk, adaptive skills risk. The Student form can be used to generate scores on the internalizing, self-regulation, and personal adjustment indices. Spanish language forms are also available.	Data was collected from a representative sample of the U.S. in regard to gender, race/ethnicity, geographic region, and special education eligibility. More than 9,000 forms were collected from 2013–2014.	Median internal consistency reliabilities for all Teacher and Parent forms range from .81 to .96. Student forms range from .77 to .94. Test–retest reliabilities for the Behavioral and Emotional Risk Index (BERI) range from .86 (Teacher Child/Adolescent form) to .91 (Teacher Preschool and Parent Child/Adolescent forms). Interrater reliabilities of the BERI across all forms range from .65 to .74.	The Conners 3 Teacher form and the BASC-3 BESS Teacher form BERI correlated at .66. The Parent form of the Conners 3 and the BASC-3 BESS correlated at .65. Correlations between the BASC-3 BESS Child/Adolescent form and the Children's Depression Inventory 2 (CDI 2) are reported at .64 (BERI), .51 for the internalizing risk index, and .58 for the self-regulation index. Appropriately, the personal adjustment risk index on the Student form and the CDI 2 had a negative correlation of -.61.
FAST™ Social, Academic, & Emotional Behavior Risk Screener (SAEBRS) Kilgus, & von der Emse, 2015, Illuminate Education	Ages 5 to 18 years	Teachers rate each student in their classroom on 19 items that measure three subdomains: Social Behavior, Academic Behavior, and Emotional Behavior and one broad domain of Total Behavior.	The SAEBRS was normed on 7,808 students in 687 schools in 265 districts in 29 states stratified on race, gender, Hispanic status, free/reduced-lunch status, and geographic region roughly approximating nationwide demographics.	Internal consistency is reported to be .98 Omega coefficient. Test–retest reliability was established for fall to winter (.78), winter to spring (.82), and fall to spring (.73).	Concurrent validity was reported for teachers of students in Grades K-5 with the SSIS-Social Skills (.88), SSIS-Problem Behaviors, (-.89), SSIS-Academic Competence (.61); BASC-3 BESS (-.93); SRSS (-.84); SIBS (-.67). Although the measures are reported to be used with students in Grades 6–12, it is unclear if validity studies have been conducted for the older grades.

Test, Author(s), & Publisher	Ages	Skills	Norms	Reliability Evidence	Validity Evidence
Systematic Screening for Behavior Disorders–Second Edition Walker, Severson, & Feil, 2014, Ancora Publishing	Grades K–12	There are three stages involved in the SSBD system. Stage 2 includes the use of the Teacher Rating Scale to calculate a score on the Critical Event Index, the Adaptive Behavior Index, and the Maladaptive Behavior Index. In this way, the SSBD captures risk for both internalizing and externalizing behaviors.	The normative sample included data on over 6,743 students from 10 different sites across the U.S.	Interrater reliabilities between teachers and assistant teachers of the same children were reported as ranging from .48 to .79, with a median coefficient of .71. Test–retest reliabilities after 6 months had a median correlation of .77.	Concurrent validity was established with the *Behar Scale* and had a median correlation of .69. The SSBD and the *Connors Scale* have a median correlation of .80.
Vineland Adaptive Behavior Scales–Third Edition (Vineland-3) Sparrow, Cicchetti, & Saulnier, 2016, Pearson	Ages birth to 90	There is an Interview form, a Parent/Caregiver form, and a Teacher form that measure three broad domains of adaptive skills: communication, daily living skills, and socialization, resulting in the Adaptive Behavior Composite (ABC) score. A Spanish translated Parent/Caregiver form is available.	Norms were collected in 2014–2015 from a sample of 2,560 people each for the Parent form and the interview and from 1,415 teachers. The sample aimed to be nationally representative on gender, race/ethnicity, and region. They also stratified on highest level of education. The sample included participants with IDEA eligibility for a disability.	Internal consistency range from .86 to .99. Test–retest reliability mean for domains range from .64 to .92.	Correlations between *Vineland–Third Edition* Parent/Caregiver Rating Form and the *Bayley Scales of Infant and Toddler Development–Third Edition*, range from .67 to .81. The *Vineland–Third Edition* Teacher Rating Form and *Adaptive Behavior Assessment System–Third Edition*, range from .75 to .91.

Note. FAST™ Social, Academic, & Emotional Behavior Risk Screener (SAEBRS) is the only behavior screening tool to be reviewed on the National Center on Intensive Intervention website (https://charts.intensiveintervention.org/bscreening). Readers are encouraged to read the detailed review.

Write your answers to each of the following questions and then compare your responses to the text.

1. Why do we assess social-emotional functioning?
2. What are two important considerations in the assessment of social-emotional functioning?
3. What are four methods for assessing social-emotional functioning?
4. Name a limitation to using just one assessment method.

1. Describe the steps that you would follow in conducting a functional behavioral assessment.
2. If a student has a stomachache and asks to go home sick before each test what might be the function of the behavior? What assessment method would you use to verify the hypothesized function?
3. Describe how the results from a functional behavioral assessment can be used to develop an intervention.

CHAPTER 19

Accessibility Supports and Accommodations

Although the use of well-designed tests with strong evidence of reliability and validity can enhance assessment decision making, it does not result in optimal measurement for every student. For some students, the way in which a test is administered under standard conditions may actually prohibit their demonstration of the knowledge and skills being measured. Some tests require that a student have specific skills and knowledge in order to demonstrate what is being measured. For example, tests that require students to print their answers in a test booklet can make it difficult for students with motor impairments to demonstrate their knowledge. Some tests require that students remain focused for long periods of time at a desk; this can make it difficult for students with hyperactivity problems to demonstrate their knowledge. Other tests require that students listen to directions that are read to them by a test administrator. This clearly is difficult for students who are deaf or hard of hearing. Changes in the ways in which tests are administered or in the way in which the student responds may be needed for the student to demonstrate their true knowledge or skill. In the previous editions of this book we talked about changes made in the presentation, setting, response, or timing/scheduling of a test that may or may not influence the construct that is measured. We distinguished between testing adaptations, accommodations, and modifications. Thinking about accommodations has changed significantly over the past 30 years or so, especially with advances in assessment technology, so that it is best now to think about accommodations within the broader context of standards-based instruction and accessibility supports in instruction and assessment.

Recall that we assess students for the purpose of making four primary kinds of decisions: screening decisions, diagnostic (including eligibility) decisions, instructional/intervention decisions, and outcomes decisions. Students take individual tests as part of making the first three kinds of decisions, and they take large-scale, group-administered state tests as part of making outcomes/accountability decisions. In this chapter we will be discussing the use of accessibility supports and accommodations for making individual decisions as well as for making large-scale accountability decisions. Keep these distinctions in mind as you read.

Why Care About Accessibility Supports and Testing Accommodations?

There are many reasons why it is important to understand appropriate ways in which to provide accessibility supports and test accommodations. The reasons we discuss in this chapter include the increased diversity in today's schools and legal requirements for all students to be appropriately measured toward the same standards.

Increased Diversity

Student diversity has increased substantially in the past decade. As we discuss in chapters 1 and 6, schools are more diverse, both in terms of the numbers of students from different socio-cultural and language backgrounds and in terms of the cultures they represent. However, in addition to racial, ethnic, and cultural differences, students enter school with a diverse set of academic background experiences and opportunities. Within the same classroom, students often vary considerably in their academic skill development. Educators face two clear challenges: (1) designing instruction that will be effective for the range in skills and abilities that likely exist among students in the same class, and (2) using assessments that will evaluate validly the large range in student skills.

Since the mid-1970s, considerable attention has been focused on including all students in neighborhood schools and general education settings. Much attention has been focused on including students who are considered to have developmental, physical, or emotional disabilities. As federal and state officials create educational policies, they are now compelled to make them for all children and youth, including those with severe disabilities. Also, as policymakers attempt to develop practices that will result in improved educational results, they rely on data from district- and state-administered tests. However, relying on assessment data presents challenges associated with deciding who to include in the multiple kinds of assessments and the kinds of changes that can be made to include them.

Although meaningful assessment of the skills of such a diverse student population is challenging, it is clear that all students need to be included in large-scale assessment programs. If students are excluded from large-scale assessments, then the data on which policy decisions are made represent only part of the school population. If students are excluded from accountability systems, they may also be denied access to the general education curriculum. If data are going to be gathered on all students, then major decisions must be made regarding the kinds of data to be collected and how tests are to be adapted to include students with special needs. Historically, there has been widespread exclusion of students with disabilities from state and national testing (McGrew et al., 1995; Thompson & Thurlow, 2001; Thurlow, 2014). Participation in large-scale assessments is now recognized by many educators and parents as a critical element of equal opportunity and access to education. Thurlow and Thompson (2004) report that all states now require participation of all students. Furthermore, all states now have accommodation policies that indicate how students can participate in large-scale assessment programs with accommodations. However, many questions remain about which participation and accommodation strategies are the best for particular students. It is up to school teams to determine which accommodations are appropriate for individual students.

Changes in Educational Standards

Part of major efforts to reform or restructure schools has been a push to specify high standards for student achievement and an accompanying push to measure the extent to which schools meet those high standards. It is expected that schools will include students with disabilities and English learners in assessments, especially those completed for accountability purposes.

As we have noted earlier, instruction in U.S. schools is designed so as to enable students to meet sets of state standards in academic content areas. Standards-based instruction originated in the 1990s when President Bill Clinton signed Goals 2000 (PL 103-227) in 1994. Task forces and committees of U.S. educators attempted to specify a set of goals. In a set of concentrated activities under the general heading "Goals 2000," students with disabilities were held to the same standards on state assessments as their peers without disabilities. Educators discussed accommodations and modifications that would be necessary to enable students with disabilities to participate in state assessments, and debates occurred about the extent to which various assessment accommodations affected the validity of test results. Researchers have studied the extent to which various accommodations affected the validity of tests (e.g., Bolt & Ysseldyke, 2006; Helwig & Tindal, 2003), and test companies published lists of accommodations along with ratings of the extent to which those accommodations affected the validity of tests (e.g., Sheinker et al., 2004).

A second paradigm shift took place in the early 2000s (Larson et al., 2020). This shift grew out of the work on **universal design**[1] in assessment and was embodied in President George W. Bush's signing of the No Child Left Behind Act portion of the Elementary and Secondary Education Act of 2001, including the requirement that measurable gains in achievement in math, English language arts, and writing needed to be shown by all students each year. Accessibility supports began being offered to all students, including those who did not have designated disabilities but still had challenges that those supports could address. With advances in technology and developments in technology enhanced assessments, the Race to the Top Initiative of 2009 funded consortia of states to develop technology-based assessments of English language arts and mathematics. States began using a three-tiered assessment framework comprised of universal features, designated features, and accommodations. **Universal features** were defined as accessibility supports that are available to all students as they access instructional or assessment content. **Designated features** were defined as accessibility supports that are available for use by any student for whom the need has been indicated by an educator (or team of educators including the parents or guardians and the student when appropriate) who is familiar with the characteristics and needs of the student. **Accommodations** were defined as changes in procedures or materials that ensure equitable access to instructional or assessment content and generate valid assessment results for students with disabilities and English learners who need them. They do not reduce expectations for learning. See the Stakeholder Perspective from Sheryl Lazarus, who describes how provision of accessibility supports and accommodations have changed over the past 15 to 20 years.

19.1
PROGRESS
MONITORING
CHECK

The Need for Accurate Measurement

It is critical that the assessment practices used for gathering information on individual students provide accurate information. Without accommodations, testing runs the risk of being unfair and inaccurate for certain students. Some test formats make it more difficult for students with disabilities to understand what they are supposed to do or what the response requirements are. Students with specific kinds of disabilities sometimes find it impossible to respond in a way that can be evaluated accurately unless changes are made. However, changing aspects of test presentation, setting, response, and timing/scheduling without carefully considering what the test is designed to measure can

---

1. "Universal design started in architecture before expanding to other fields, and entails designing and developing products or processes for the greatest range of human characteristics possible (Bergstahler, 2012). For educational assessments, universal design might take the form of including diverse students in field tests, using plain language, or designing a simple test interface." (Larson et al., 2020, p. 246)

Sheryl Lazarus, Director, National Center on Educational Outcomes, University of Minnesota

Historically, many students, including many students with disabilities (as well as many English language learners), were excluded from tests because they were unable to access them. Assessments were often designed with little thought of the accessibility needs of many students. In the early 1990s, only a handful of states had policies to indicate which accommodations were allowed for students with disabilities on state summative assessments (and there was no consideration that students other than students with disabilities might need accommodations).

The reauthorization of the Individuals With Disabilities Education Act (IDEA) in 1997 required that students with disabilities participate in assessments and be provided with accommodations. This was further reinforced for summative tests used for accountability by the 2001 reauthorization of the Elementary and Secondary Education Act (ESEA) known as No Child Left Behind (NCLB).

By 2001, all states had accommodations policies that indicated which accommodations could be used by students with disabilities. As accommodations became more widely available, many more students were able to participate in assessments. At that time there was limited research on the effects of accommodations, and often the studies were not designed in ways that provided clear findings about the effects of specific accommodations. The provision of accommodations was often controversial; there was limited agreement on when it was appropriate to use accommodations, and there were concerns that students who used accommodations were getting an "unfair advantage." There was more general acceptance of accommodations commonly used by students with physical disabilities (e.g., braille, magnification) than of accommodations needed by students with less visible disabilities (e.g., extended time, calculator, read aloud). Some states also began to develop accommodations policies for English language learners.

In the early 2010s, states and consortia began to develop technology-based assessments, and many states implemented them by 2015. Many accommodations were now embedded within the test platform (e.g., text to speech, magnification). As the shift to technology-based assessment occurred, there was a concurrent paradigm shift in the thinking about accessibility that focused on accessibility for all. New frameworks were developed that shifted the focus from making decisions about accommodations for students with disabilities and English language learners to new approaches that were inclusive of students without an identified disability or English language learner status. In these frameworks, there typically were universal features, such as embedded highlighters, which any student could use, and designated features which must be designated in advance but which are available for any student who needed them, as well as accommodations for students with disabilities, English language learners, and English language learners with disabilities.

The transformation of accommodations designed for a few to accessibility designed for all means that although accessibility challenges continue to exist, assessments today are more accessible than ever.

also result in poor measurement. Decisions about which changes facilitate more accurate measurement for a particular test, and about which students should receive the associated changes, can be very difficult and ultimately involve subjective decision making about the capacity to measure what the test is intended to measure with and without accommodations. For example, if a child has a learning disability in reading and the child needs to take a math exam that requires lots of reading, a logical accommodation for that child might be to have the test read aloud to the student so that the reading difficulty does not interfere with the assessment of the child's math skill.

It Is Required by Law

By law, students with disabilities have a right to be included in assessments used for accountability purposes, and accommodations in testing should be made to enable them to participate. This legal argument is derived largely from the 14th Amendment to the U.S. Constitution (which guarantees the right to equal protection and due process of law). The Individuals With Disabilities Education Act guarantees the right to education and due process. Also, Section 504 of the Rehabilitation Act of 1973 indicates that it is illegal to exclude people from participation solely because of a disability. If a student is receiving special education services due to an educational disability, that student's instructional and testing accommodations should be documented on an Individualized Education Program (IEP). If a student with a disability does not necessarily need special education services but instead simply needs accommodations to allow appropriate participation in the general curriculum, then the student's accommodation needs are documented on what is commonly referred to as a 504 Plan.

The Americans With Disabilities Act of 1992 mandates that all individuals must have access to exams used to provide credentials or licenses. Agencies administering tests must provide either auxiliary aids or modifications[2] to enable individuals with disabilities to participate in assessment, and these agencies may not charge the individual for costs incurred in making special provisions. Changes that may be provided include an architecturally accessible testing site, a distraction-free space, or an alternative location; a test schedule variation or extended time; the use of a scribe, sign language interpreter, reader, or adaptive equipment; and modifications of the test presentation or response format.

Considerations for Promoting Test Accessibility

The extent to which accessibility supports and accommodations are needed depends in part on the way in which an assessment program is designed. When test development involves careful consideration of the unique needs of all students who may eventually participate, less "after-the-fact" changes in test conditions will be needed. Application of

---

2. The ADA's use of the term *modification* is different than the definition we provide. In this case, the ADA's use of *modification* can be likened to our use of the term *accommodation*.

the principles of universal design to assessment can improve accessibility, such that appropriate testing for all students is promoted. Universal design for assessment involves careful consideration of the needs of all individuals who might need to participate in the test when the test is first developed. For more information on universal design for assessment, you can go to the Universal Design of Assessments section of the website of the National Center on Educational Outcomes (nceo.info).

Fortunately, new technologies are making it increasingly possible for students to access material in ways that best address their needs. The increasing use of computers and electronic tablets during instruction and testing makes it possible for students to customize the font size, brightness, and even language in which materials are presented to meet their individual needs. Screen-reading and speech recognition programs make it possible for students who have difficulty reading and writing to access and respond to written material. However, it is still up to test developers and users to determine which basic skills are important to teach and test, and to correspondingly monitor which changes are appropriate under various conditions. Furthermore, students may need considerable training and experience manipulating and using these features to make the most out of them during instruction and testing. Six factors can impede getting an accurate picture of students' abilities and skills during assessment: (1) the students' ability to understand assessment stimuli, (2) the students' ability to respond to assessment stimuli, (3) the nature of the comparison [norm group or performance description], (4) the appropriateness of the spread of items across difficulty levels, including easy (or basal) or difficult (or ceiling), (5) the students' exposure to the curriculum being tested (opportunity to learn), and (6) the nature of the testing environment.

Ability to Understand Assessment Stimuli

Assessments are considered unfair if the test stimuli are in a format that, because of a disability, the student does not understand or cannot access. For example, tests only available in print are considered unfair for students with severe visual impairments. Tests with oral directions are considered unfair for students with certain hearing impairments. In fact, because the law requires that students be assessed in their primary language and because the primary language of many deaf students is not English, written assessments in English are considered unfair and invalid for many deaf students. When students cannot understand test stimuli because of a sensory or intellectual disability that is unrelated to what the test is targeted to measure, accurate measurement of the targeted skills is hindered by the sensory or intellectual disability. Results or interpretations from such a test are invalid, and failure to provide an accommodation is illegal.

Ability to Respond to Assessment Stimuli

Tests typically require students to produce a response. For example, intelligence tests require verbal, motor (pointing or arranging), or written (including multiple-choice) responses. To the extent that physical or sensory limitations inhibit accurate responding, these test results are invalid. For example, some students with cerebral palsy may lack sufficient motor ability to arrange blocks. Others may have sufficient motor ability but have such slowed responses that timed tests are inappropriate estimates of their abilities. Yet others may be able to respond quickly but expend so much energy that they cannot sustain their efforts throughout the test. Not only are test results invalid in such instances, but also the use of such test results is prohibited in such cases by federal law.[3]

Normative Comparisons

Norm-referenced tests are standardized on groups of individuals, and the performance of the person assessed is compared with the performance of the norm group. To the extent that the test was administered to the student differently than the way it was administered to the norm group, you must be very careful in interpreting the results. To allow for appropriate comparisons, these tests typically have very specific rules for how they are to be administered. Adaptations of measures requires changing either stimulus presentation or response requirements. The adaptation may make the test items easier or more difficult, and it may change the construct being measured. Although qualitative or criterion-referenced interpretations of such test performances are often acceptable, norm-referenced comparisons can be flawed. The *Standards for Educational and Psychological Testing* (American Educational Research Association et al., 2014) specify that when tests are adapted, it is important that there is validity evidence for the change that is made. Otherwise, it is important to describe the change when reporting the score and to use caution in score interpretation.

Appropriateness of the Level of the Items

Tests are often developed for students who are in specific age ranges or who have a particular range of skills. They can sometimes seem inappropriate for students who are either very high or very low functioning compared to same-grade peers. Assessors are tempted to give out-of-level tests when a grade-appropriate test contains either an insufficient number of easy items in general or not enough easy items for the specific student being assessed. Of course, when out-of-level tests are given and norm-referenced interpretations are made, the students are compared with a group of students who differ

---

3. Those who assess students must always be aware of the consequences of their decisions to provide accommodations. We see in practice very liberal decisions to allow students with learning disabilities to take timed tests with no time limits. Practitioners assume that children with learning disabilities have processing deficits, processing deficits mean that timed testing is unfair, and that children with learning disabilities should not be timed during assessment. The problem, of course, is that such a rule causes harm because it deprives students of more valid and accurate formative assessment to drive instruction in the classroom when they can never be timed. If they cannot be timed, we simply cannot reliably ascertain skill mastery. Those who assess must think about how the assessment will be used and conditions under which timing might be avoided versus conditions under which brief timed assessments could be useful unless a student has specific motor limitations and there is no norm sample or benchmark criterion that is representative/meaningful for that particular student.

from them. We have no idea how same-age or same-grade students would perform on the given test. Out-of-level testing occasionally may be appropriate to identify a student's current level of educational performance or to evaluate the effectiveness of instruction. It is inappropriate for accountability purposes.

Exposure to the Curriculum Being Tested (Opportunity to Learn)

One of the issues of fairness raised by the general public is the administration of tests that contain material that students have not had an opportunity to learn. This same issue applies to the making of decisions about accessibility supports and accommodations. Students with sensory impairments may not have had an opportunity to learn the content of test items that use verbal or auditory stimuli. Students receiving special education services who have not had adequate access to the general education curriculum have not had the same opportunity to master the general education curriculum.

To the extent that students have not had an opportunity to learn the content of the test (that is, they were absent when the content was taught, the content is not taught in the schools in which they were present, or the content was taught in ways that were not effective for the students), they probably will not perform well on the test. Their performance will reflect more a lack of opportunity to learn than limited ability.

Environmental Considerations

Students should be tested in settings in which they can demonstrate maximal performance. If students cannot easily gain access to a testing setting, this may diminish their performance. Tests should always be given in settings that students with disabilities can access with ease. The settings should also be quiet enough to minimize distractibility. Also, because fatigue is an issue, tests may need to be given in multiple short sessions (broken up with breaks) so fatigue does not interfere with the valid assessment of the student's skills.

Types of Accessibility Supports and Test Accommodations

It is always difficult to identify the extent to which specific accessibility supports or accommodations are considered to invalidate a student's performance on a test. Assessment specialists have struggled with validity issues since accommodations began being used, and the body of research on validity has grown exponentially. The Council of Chief State School Officers worked with groups of researchers who study validity issues for students with disabilities, and they recently published a very helpful manual on accessibility supports (Lazarus et al., 2021). You should read through that manual to identify the kinds of accessibility supports that are considered to have little to significant effect on the validity of test scores.

19.1
PROGRESS
MONITORING
CHECK

ONLINE
RESOURCE

As you read about accountability, accessibility, and accommodations the terminology sometimes gets confusing. You may want to consult a very helpful online glossary of measurement terms published by the National Council on Measurement in Education and available on their website at ncme.org/resources/glossary.

Recommendations for Making Accommodation Decisions for Individual Students

There are major debates about the kinds of changes that should be permitted during testing for accountability purposes. There are also major arguments about the extent to which adaptations in testing destroy the technical adequacy of tests used for determining instructional needs and eligibility for special education. We think there are some reasonable guidelines for best practice in making decisions about individuals, and we offer some guidelines here. We first provide recommendations for making accommodation decisions on tests that are commonly used to make decisions about individuals (e.g., diagnostic and instructional planning for exceptional children). Then, we provide recommendations for making accommodation decisions on tests that are typically administered at the group level and used for accountability purposes.

When Planning Instruction and Making Instructional Decisions

When making decisions about what to teach, it is important to collect information about the student's current skills in a way that the student can adequately demonstrate his or her knowledge. For example, if you want to know whether students have specific math problem-solving skills, it may be necessary to present the questions in an oral format rather than a written format to students who cannot yet accurately read. Otherwise, students may fail to answer correctly because they cannot read the item, even though they have mastered the math problem-solving skills and you would continue to plan your instruction around the given math problem-solving skill even when the student already has mastered that skill.

However, if you are using data from tests with specific standardized administration procedures and intending to compare to a normative sample, it is important to follow the rules set forth in the administration manual. Published tests are increasingly providing specific rules for testing with accommodations in administration manuals. Such rules should be carefully consulted when using these tests for determining students' instructional needs and making diagnostic/eligibility decisions.

Some related recommendations follow:

- Conduct all assessments in the student's primary language or mode of communication. The mode of communication is that normally used by the person during instruction (such as sign language, braille, or oral communication); however, note that there are additional considerations that should be made in assessing students who are English language learners (see Chapter 6, "Cultural and Linguistic Considerations in Assessment and Decision Making"). Loeding and Crittenden (1993, p. 19) note that for students who are deaf, the primary communication mode is either a visual–spatial, natural sign language used by members of the American Deaf Community called American Sign Language (ASL), or a manually coded form of English, such as Signed English, Pidgin Sign English, Seeing Essential English, Signing Exact English, or Sign-Supported Speech/English. Therefore, they argue, "traditional paper-and-pencil tests are inaccessible, invalid, and inappropriate to the deaf student because the tests are written in English only."

- Make accommodations in format when the purpose of testing is not substantially impaired. For example, a student might be allowed to provide an oral response instead of a written response if the purpose is not to measure writing skills. Or a student might be given more frequent breaks when completing a task if the purpose is not to measure his or her ability to attend for long periods of time. It should be demonstrated that the accommodations assist the individual in responding but do not provide content assistance (e.g., a scribe should record the response of the person being tested—not interpret what the person says, include his or her additional knowledge, and then record a response). Personal assistants who are provided during testing, such as readers, scribes, and interpreters, should be trained in how to provide associated accommodations to ensure proper administration.

- Make normative comparisons only with groups whose membership includes students with background sets of experiences and opportunities like those of the students being tested. For example, if you provide a signed interpretation of a norm-referenced test, you should only compare the student's results with those of a group of students who also had the test signed using the same language.

During Accountability Testing

Many other accommodation recommendations can be implemented when collecting assessment data to make decisions about groups of students, specifically for the purpose of making accountability decisions. Decisions about which accommodations to provide should be made separately for each individual student determined to need them; however, decisions are often guided by state accommodation policies. Thurlow et al. (2003) suggest the following about accommodation decision making for the purpose of accountability:

- States and districts should have written guidelines for the use of accommodations in large-scale assessments used for accountability purposes.

- Decisions about accommodations should be made by one or more persons who know the student, including the student's strengths and weaknesses.
- Decision makers should consider the student's learning characteristics and the accommodations currently used during classroom instruction and classroom testing.
- The student's category of disability or program setting should not influence the decision.
- The goal is to ensure that accommodations have been used by the student prior to their use in an assessment—generally, in the classroom during instruction and in classroom testing situations. New accommodations should not be introduced for the district or statewide assessment.
- The decision is made systematically, using a form that lists questions to answer or variables to consider in making the accommodation decision. Ideally, classroom data on the effects of accommodations are part of the information entered into decisions. Decisions and the reasons for them should be noted on the form.
- Decisions about accommodations should be documented on the student's IEP.
- Parents and older students should be involved in the decision by either participating in the decision-making process or being given the analysis of the need for accommodations and by signing the form that indicates accommodations that are to be used.

PROGRESS MONITORING CHECK

Accommodation decisions made to address individual student needs should be reconsidered at least once a year, given that student needs are likely to change over time. See the Stakeholder Perspective by Savannah Treviño-Casias, who describes her experience of receiving proper test accommodations.

Ensuring Fairness in Making Accessibility and Accommodations Decisions

The content of the sections of this chapter was written with the concept of fairness always in mind. Accessibility supports and accommodations are made with one purpose in mind: to level the playing field for all students. We provide accessibility supports so that all students are able to demonstrate their true knowledge and skills. In the recommendations section of this chapter we provided suggestions about how best to enhance fairness. As we indicated, the list of accessibility supports and accommodations changes often as technology advances enable new kinds of accommodations to be made and as researchers demonstrate the extent to which specific accommodations are valid with specific kinds of learners. The focus must always be on equal access to instruction and assessment for all learners.

Savannah Treviño-Casias, Graduate Student

I remember sitting in a math class: I was frozen and all I could focus on was being surrounded by the sound of pencils moving on paper. My fellow classmates were way ahead of me on that month's math exam. I looked down at my exam and I was lost. I knew I had practiced for weeks leading up to this point, and I had spent hours working on homework and almost every evening after school working with a tutor to understand the material that I was going to be tested on. My mind was clouded with fear, anxiety, and all the math facts I had spent so much time learning. By the time I attempted a few of the questions, I was overwhelmed and kept mixing up my math facts. Before I knew it, class was over and I had barely finished half of the exam.

This was how all of my exams went for years. Eventually, I was evaluated for special education services in the sixth grade. I was finally diagnosed with a learning disability and I was granted accommodations for my in-class learning and on my exams.

What a difference it made when I took my first exam with testing accommodations! I remember it clearly: I sat down alone in a small testing room, just me and my exam. I had a memory aid on hand if needed, double the testing time, and I could take frequent breaks to refocus and process what was on the exam. I felt free, I felt confident, and I felt like I could actually do well on the exam. I had done my part to learn the material, and I had spent hours outside of class working with my tutors, my mom, and my special education teacher to learn and understand what I was going to be tested on. With my testing accommodations, I was able to show my teachers that I was capable, I was smart, and I wanted to learn.

My testing accommodations followed me throughout high school, into college, and now in graduate school. I am a strong advocate for students with disabilities receiving testing accommodations because we deserve to have an equal opportunity to show our capabilities and our strengths. Ever since I first took an exam with testing accommodations, I have never been the same. I know that I am talented and capable, but my testing accommodations gave me confidence in all areas of my academic life. They boosted my self-esteem and improved my capacity to become the successful and competent graduate student that I am today. I have been able to tackle every exam I have taken, including the SAT, GRE, and graduate-level examinations. Testing accommodations have contributed so much to my life, and I am eternally grateful for them.

1. School personnel used to talk about testing accommodations and now they talk about accommodations as one part of accessibility supports. Describe the distinction between these terms.
2. Identify three reasons why school personnel should care about accessibility supports and accommodations in assessment.
3. How have changes in thinking about educational standards affected thinking about accessibility supports over the past 20 or 30 years?

1. Define and give two examples of universal features.
2. Define and give two examples of designated features.
3. Define and give two examples of accommodations.
4. What are two ways in which you might improve the process of deciding the kinds of accommodations to make for third graders in Buffalo Elementary School?
5. What are some ways in which you might improve the process of making large-scale accountability decisions in your state?

PART IV

Using Assessment Information to Make Educational Decisions

CHAPTER 20

Using Assessment Information to Make Intervention Decisions

LEARNING OBJECTIVES

1. Identify several common reasons why individual students struggle in school.
2. Define various sources of information that can inform targeted instructional changes.
3. Identify the steps in a problem-solving process to make intervention decisions.
4. Describe how an Individualized Education Program is designed to provide the necessary instruction and services.

In the earlier chapters we discussed many of the nuts and bolts of assessments. We defined important concepts like reliability and validity and looked at different assessments for different purposes. Now let's take a closer look at how we use these assessments to make critical instructional decisions. As a teacher in general, special, and inclusive settings you're going to use your own observation skills partnered with the various sources of data you and your colleagues collect to make important decisions about the impact of an intervention plan or the proper instructional program for a student. The assessment tools and strategies discussed in earlier chapters can be used to assist in making many of these decisions. In this chapter, we are primarily concerned with the decisions that teachers make about the effectiveness of instruction for students who are at risk and for students who have disabilities, and the procedures that can be used in making these decisions.

Both general and special educators share responsibility for students with disabilities. General educators are largely responsible for identifying general education students who are experiencing sensory, learning, behavior or social-emotional problems. They are also responsible for addressing those problems with or without the assistance of other educators. Both general and special educators share responsibility for the education of students with disabilities who are instructed in general education classrooms. Special educators are additionally responsible for students whose disabilities are so severe that they cannot be educated in general education settings even with a full complement of related services and classroom accessibility supports and accommodations.

It is important to realize that in many cases, it is nearly impossible to know ahead of time who will require special education services. Interventions must be implemented with integrity, and data collected to understand the needs of each student who is struggling.

Children with moderate or severe disabilities usually are identified before the age of 3 or 4 years and enroll in school as students with disabilities. Approximately 40% of all students will experience difficulty during their school career. Most of these problems will be successfully addressed in general education by regular educators. When students' challenges are not addressed successfully and in a timely fashion by general educators, those students are often referred to multidisciplinary teams to ascertain if they have a disability and are in need of or eligible for special education. In the first section of this chapter "Early Identification of Disabilities," we deal with those decisions that precede entitlement to special education. With a strong Response to Intervention (RTI) or multi-tiered system of supports (MTSS) model in place, many of the instructional decision-making processes and procedures described may be highly systematized. In the second half of this chapter "Decisions Made in Special Education," we discuss the different types of data used in the process to determine instructional placement of eligible students.

Early Identification of Disabilities

The overwhelming majority of children enter school under the presumption that they do not have disabilities. However, educators know that some of these students have disabilities that may not be apparent to parents. Because disabilities are likely to be less severe if special services are provided early, federal regulations (§300.111 Child Find) require states to have policies and procedures to ensure all children with disabilities who need special education and related services are located, evaluated, and identified. This requirement, generally referred to as **child find**, means that local school districts and other agencies must inform parents of available services through strategically placed flyers, notices in local newspapers, and so forth.

The purpose of universal screening by school districts is to identify students who are at-risk early for learning difficulties and in that process, they will also identify students who have disabilities. Some children may have undiagnosed sensory difficulties (i.e., vision or hearing difficulties) that are not apparent to parents, physicians, or teachers. Therefore, schools routinely screen all children to identify undetected hearing and vision problems and to provide services for those who need them. Sensory screening is sometimes conducted by a school nurse with the intention of finding children who require diagnosis by a healthcare professional—a hearing specialist such as an audiologist or a vision specialist such as an optometrist or ophthalmologist. With cutbacks in school budgets schools in most states no longer have a school nurse, and if learning concerns arise parents and guardians are encouraged to take their child to the local clinic or pediatrician for vision and hearing testing. A vision or hearing deficit may be identified, but then a decision must be made about how to improve the deficit. The critical point is that screening, by itself, cannot be used to identify a student with a disability. Screening, whether for glasses or for reading difficulties, is just the first step toward identifying struggling students as soon as possible in their schooling so we can avoid recreating old "wait to fail" models that considered just giving a child more time to learn as the intervention instead of developing a preventive, data-based, action-oriented plan. The sooner we screen and identify risk, the sooner we can develop and implement interventions, and the sooner the student will be successful.

Early Identification of Academic Difficulties

Once students are in elementary school it is more common for universal screening to be conducted in reading, math, and behavior. Some of the students in general education will not make adequate progress toward individual, classroom, or state goals. In academic areas for which universal screening is conducted, these students can be identified early for further assessment to determine the extent to which additional academic supports are needed. In areas in which such screening is not conducted at a particular school, teachers must recognize when a student is struggling and not making adequate progress. The threshold of recognition varies from teacher to teacher and may be a function of several factors: teacher skill and experience, class size, availability of alternative materials and curriculum, ability and behavior of other students in the class, and the teacher's tolerance for atypical progress or behavior. Generally, when a student is performing academically at a rate that is between 20 and 50% of the rate of other students, a teacher has reason to be concerned. Teachers will likely be concerned when a student

- repeatedly asks questions that indicate that he or she does not understand new material.
- does not know material that was previously taught and thought to be mastered.
- makes numerous errors and few correct responses.
- does not keep up with peers, in general, or in their instructional groups.
- is so far behind peers that the student cannot be maintained in the lowest instructional group in a class—that is, the student becomes instructionally isolated.
- changes from doing good or acceptable work to doing poor or unacceptable work.

Why a student is having academic difficulty is seldom clear at this point in the decision-making process. There are multiple reasons for school failure, and these reasons may often interact with one another. The reasons for these differences generally fall into two broad categories: ineffective instruction or individual differences. It can be particularly helpful to focus on identifying reasons for a student's academic difficulties that can be addressed through intervention rather than reasons that are out of the confines of the school day. Focusing on what can be influenced by teachers during the school day is best and allows for intervention by school personnel.

Ineffective Instruction

Some students make progress under almost any instructional conditions. When students with emerging skills and a wealth of background knowledge enter a learning situation, such students merely need the opportunity to continue learning and developing skills. These students often learn despite ineffective instructional methodology. However, some students enter a learning situation with underdeveloped skills and require much more precision in the delivery of effective instruction. Without good instruction, these students are in danger of becoming casualties of the educational system. This situation can occur in at least five ways.

Students' lack of prerequisite knowledge or skill. Some students may lack the prerequisites for learning specific content. In such cases, the content to be learned may be too difficult because the student must learn the prerequisites and the new content simultaneously. For example, Mr. Santos may give Alex a reader in which he knows only 70% of the words. Alex will be forced to decode vocabulary that he's unfamiliar with while trying to comprehend what he is reading. Chances are that he will not comprehend the material because he must read too many unknown words.

Insufficient instructional time. The school curriculum may be so cluttered with special events and extras that sufficient time cannot be devoted to core content areas. Students who need more extensive and intensive instruction in order to learn may suffer from the discrepancy between the amounts of instruction (or time) they need and the time allocated to teaching them.

Teachers' lack of subject matter knowledge. The teacher may lack the skills to teach specific subject matter. For example, in some rural areas, it may not be possible to attract physics teachers, so the biology teacher may have to teach the physics course and try to stay one or two lectures ahead of the students.

Teachers' lack of pedagogical knowledge. A teacher may lack sufficient pedagogical knowledge to teach students who are not independent learners. Although educators have known for a very long time about teaching methods that promote student learning (see Stevens & Rosenshine, 1981), this information is not as widely known to teachers and supervisors as one would hope. Thus, some educators may not know how to present new material, structure learning opportunities, provide opportunities for guided and independent practice, or give effective feedback.

Teachers' commitment to ineffective methods. A teacher may be committed to ineffective instructional methods. A considerable amount of effort has gone into the empirical evaluation of various instructional approaches. Yet much of this research fails to find its way into teacher preparation programs and therefore doesn't make it into classrooms. For example, a number of school districts have purchased curricula that are not based on the Science of Reading and do not include phonics instruction. However, the empirical research has been clear for a long time that early and systematic phonics instruction leads to better reading outcomes (Adams, 1990; Foorman et al., 1998; Pflaum et al., 1980). Previous chapters have recommended resources that you can access to identify evidence-based instructional tactics (e.g., the NCII tools charts at intensiveintervention .org). In the online resources we provide a list of websites to discover scientific- and evidence-based curricula and interventions. Through these websites, you can identify evidence-based instructional tactics.

ONLINE
RESOURCE

Individual Differences

A few students make little progress despite systematic application of sound instructional practices that have been shown to be generally effective. There are at least three reasons for this.

> *Student abilities affect learning.* Struggling learners often require more practice or a much higher dosage of opportunities to respond along with more precise use of explicit instruction to acquire various skills and knowledge.
>
> *Students differ in level of engagement.* While some students may find a particular subject inherently interesting and be motivated to learn, others may find the content to be boring and require additional incentives to engage in the instruction being offered. We've heard wonderful stories of struggling students who make great academic or behavioral gains when instruction includes favorite topics and hobbies. Efforts to make the practice part of instruction more game-like with opportunities to earn rewards and praise can increase engagement.
>
> *Cultural differences can affect academic learning and behavior.* For example, teachers are sometimes ill-equipped to teach students from different cultures, thus increasing the importance for all teachers to learn about culturally responsive pedagogy. Teachers should prepare themselves by learning about the cultures of the students in their classrooms in order to provide culturally relevant examples to illustrate concepts and ideas. For example, a teacher might re-examine lessons about national holidays such as Thanksgiving and Martin Luther King Jr. Day to incorporate student perspectives on how these days may be painful reminders of the systemic oppression of their communities. We have much to learn about how to teach and assess with culturally responsive practices; therefore, it is always relevant to consider potential cultural impacts. It is still too common for activities in classrooms to be developed in accordance with the "mainstream" culture which might be less engaging for students who celebrate different traditions in their homes. Thoughtful

teachers can conduct such activities to ensure inclusivity of all students which creates a more engaging learning opportunity for all students.

Early Identification of Behavioral Difficulties

Some students may fail to meet behavioral expectations. As discussed in Chapter 7, "Assessment in Multi-Tiered Systems of Support," any behavior that falls outside the range typically expected—for example, too much or too little expectation, too much or too little assertiveness—can be problematic in and of itself. In other cases, a behavior may be problematic because it interferes with learning. Finally, behavior that is dangerous to the student or the student's classmates cannot be ignored.

As is true with academic learning problems, the reason a student is having behavioral difficulty may be unclear. Among other possibilities, the problem may lie in the teacher's lack of classroom behavior-management skills, a lack of behavioral skill on the part of the student, or a combination of both. Providing task materials that are aligned with students' academic skills (or providing support when the work is highly challenging) is an effective method to prevent disruptive behaviors during instruction (Witt et al., 2004).

A teacher may lack sufficient knowledge, skill, or willingness to structure and manage a classroom effectively. Many students come to school with well-developed interpersonal and intrapersonal skills, and such students easily adjust to classroom behavioral expectations and can be coached in almost any setting. Other students enter the classroom with less-developed skills. For these students, a teacher needs much more explicit classroom management skills. In a classroom in which the teacher lacks these skills, the behavior of such students may interfere with their own learning and the learning of their peers. Thus, a teacher must know how to manage classroom behavior and be willing to do so. Classroom management is one of the more challenging topics in education, and often teachers' personal values and beliefs affect their willingness to create a positive and safe learning space in their classrooms. Fortunately, for some time there has been extensive empirical research supporting the effectiveness of various management techniques (see Alberto & Troutman, 2005; Simonson, 2008; Sulzer-Azaroff & Mayer, 1986).

Even when teachers use generally effective management strategies, they may be unable to manage some student's behaviors effectively. For example, some students may seek any kind of attention—positive or negative. Other students may not get enough sleep or nutritious food to be alert and ready to participate and learn in school. Thus, generally effective management strategies may be ill-suited to a particular student. Because there is seldom a perfect relationship between undesirable behavior and its cause, it is impossible to know *a priori* whether a student's difficulties are the result of different life experiences, lack of structured learning, or flawed management techniques without modifying some of the management strategies and observing the effect of the modifications. See Chapter 18, "Using Measures of Social and Emotional Behavior," for more information about how to determine the function of a behavior in order to increase the alignment between the presumed function of the student's undesirable behavior and an intervention that meets the function in a more appropriate way.

Increasing Teacher Competence and School Capacity

Many academic and behavioral problems can be remediated or eliminated when teachers intervene quickly and effectively. When teachers recognize that students are experiencing difficulties, they do act quickly and can usually provide those students with a little extra help. But with so many students in a general education classroom, interventions that require a lot of teacher time and expertise may not be feasible.

When teachers are unable to remediate or eliminate the problem, they need help. Help can come in two basic forms: increasing teachers' competence through coaching and professional development so that they can handle the problem themselves, and/or bringing additional resources to bear on the problem. The former may consist of informal consultation with other teachers, an instructional coach, or building specialists. The latter may consist of Title I services or discussing the concerns with the intervention assistance team to develop and install a behavior intervention plan.

20.1
PROGRESS MONITORING CHECK

The Intervention Assistance Team

An intervention assistance team can provide more intensive interventions for students, short-term consultation, continuous support, or information, resources, or training for teachers who request help. By providing problem-specific support and assistance to teachers, those teachers become more skillful in their work with students. Although the team's makeup and job titles vary by state, team members should be skilled in areas of learning, assessment, behavior management, curriculum modification, and interpersonal communication.

Intervention assistance teams (see Chapter 23, "Principles and Practices for Collaborative Teams") provide a range of interventions in the general education classroom, as supplemental support, or pull-out interventions prior to services being offered in special education settings. Obviously, students do not need, and should not receive, special education when better teaching or behavioral management would allow them to make satisfactory progress in general education settings. Children have a right to receive support needed for their education to occur in a least restrictive setting (i.e., general education classrooms wherever possible). Thus, when a teacher seeks more intensive help for students, the first form of help offered should be providing more precise explicit instruction, strategies, and evidence-based curricular materials.

The goals of intervention assistance are to remediate student difficulties before they become disabling; to provide remediation in the least restrictive environment; and to verify that if the problems cannot be resolved effectively, they are not caused by the school (that is, to establish that the problems are unique to the individual student).

Traditionally, four (Bergen & Kratchowill, 1990) or five (Graden et al., 1983) stages of intervention activities have been identified, depending how making a formal request for service is counted: (1) making a formal request for services, (2) clarifying the problem, (3) designing the interventions, (4) implementing the interventions, and (5) evaluating the interventions' effects. Early on, special educators adopted the term *referral* to designate a request that a student be evaluated for special education eligibility and entitlement. In many schools the intervention assistance team provides support for Tier 2 interventions but does not handle requests for special education evaluations. When Tier 2 interventions are unsuccessful then classroom teachers will often work with a multidisciplinary team which includes specialists, like school psychologists, social workers, and special education teachers. We consider the work of the multidisciplinary team to be the start of the referral process for special education which we'll discuss later in this chapter. First, we'll discuss how teams can use standardized procedures to make decisions.

Intervention Assistance Team Process

Within an MTSS model it is critical that the team follow prescribed decision guidelines to determine the interventions with which to match students. Sometimes and especially when the teacher is bringing a student to a team discussion, schools will have the teacher fill out a form to provide the team with information about the challenges that the student has been facing as well as some of the low-cost strategies that the teacher has used in the classroom (e.g., changing a student's seat location). More often, teams identify students directly during collaborative meetings following universal screening in the school. When the teacher brings the concern to the intervention assistance team or the multidisciplinary team they should feel confident that all students will receive the best supports available in a standardized method. Defining and following decision guidelines are an essential component to establishing this trust and in the equitable distribution of limited resources. Decision guidelines should be multifaceted and require a variety of data and information. For example, in a school working on high rates of absenteeism, any student with a specific number of absences (e.g., 5 days or more in 1 month) in a specific period of time may be eligible for an intervention even if their grades and behavior are currently not suffering. For behavior, a student with two or more office discipline referrals may be nominated for team attention to identify the student's source of difficulty and to develop a plan to prevent further issues and support future success. Each school year building leadership should define the decision guidelines and make sure all building staff are aware of the guidelines.

Once the decision guidelines are established, teams, both intervention assistance and multidisciplinary, can use a problem-solving approach for each student concern brought to the team for discussion. In the field of special education the problem-solving process was first introduced in the 1980s (Bransford & Stein, 1984; Deno, 1989; Shinn, 1989) and have evolved to include problem identification, problem definition, exploration of solutions, implementation of solutions, and problem solution/program termination. More recently one model has emerged as multiple studies have demonstrated that teams trained and implementing the model with fidelity have been able to positively impact student outcomes. The Team-Initiated Problem Solving (TIPS; Newton et al., 2012) framework advances the Data-Based Problem-Solving Model (Deno, 1989) especially for schoolwide leadership teams and intervention assistance teams. The data-based individualization process (DBI; Stecker et al., 2005) identified in Chapter 8 and described on the National Center on Intensive Intervention website (intensiveintervention .org/implementation-support/dbi-training-series) is a more direct descendant of Deno's model as it aims to more directly transition a student from the intervention assistance team to the multidisciplinary team and the referral and special education implementation process. Here we'll briefly describe the scientifically based TIPS framework (Horner et al., 2018) as seen in Figure 20.1 which is applicable to any team; whether it be the grade-level team teachers meeting monthly to discuss universal screening data or the intervention assistance team looking at small group intervention data. The six steps in the TIPS framework are:

1. Identify the problem with precision.
2. Identify the goal for change.
3. Identify the solution and implementation plan.
4. Implement the solution with fidelity.
5. Monitor and evaluate the implementation fidelity and impact.
6. Make a decision to maintain, modify, or terminate the plan.

1. Identify the Problem With Precision

In the initial consultation, the intervention assistance team works with the classroom teacher to specify the nature of a problem or the specific areas of difficulty. These difficulties should be stated in terms of observable behaviors, not hypothesized causes of the problem. For example, the teacher may specify a problem by saying that "Jenna does not write legibly" or that "Nick does not complete homework assignments as regularly as other students in his class." The focus is on the discrepancy between actual and desired performance. When the discrepancy can be quantified, this can help establish a baseline performance level to allow for monitoring whether an intervention that is designed and implemented is associated with improvement. When the behavior of concern is an academic behavior, then direct assessment of student's skills referenced against other students' skills in the same instructional setting and against meaningful benchmark criteria that forecast successful learning is necessary to define the problem.

The intervention assistance team may seek additional information. For example, the classroom teacher may be asked to describe in detail the contexts in which problems occur, the student's curriculum, the way in which the teacher interacts with or responds to the student, the student's interactions with the teacher and with classmates, the student's instructional groupings and seating arrangements, and antecedents and consequences of the student's behaviors. When multiple problems are identified, they may be ranked in order of importance for action.

An important characteristic of this step is to define the problem as specifically as possible so a clear goal and plan can be developed. Define the problem with precision by identifying the who, what, when, where, why, and frequency of the problem. Consider these two problem statements. The first is considered precise, the second is not precise. Which statement do you think will be easier to develop a plan?

- Imprecise: Mrs. Rollins is concerned because Lily (who) has started refusing to do her math work (what) and instead puts her head down on her desk and doesn't respond to Mrs. Rollins. This problem is happening a couple times a week (how often) in the classroom (where).

- Precise: Mrs. Rollins is concerned because for the past month (how often) Lily (who) has refused to do math work (what) on Tuesdays and Thursdays (when) only when the students work with their partners in the classroom (where). Mrs. Rollins isn't sure, but she thinks Lily is refusing to do the work because she is a shy student and was not matched with her friend for partner work (why). She successfully completes the work when she doesn't have to work with a partner so we can assume academic skills are not a concern. If we were looking at an academic deficit for the work refusal we would also examine Lily's scores on the last universal screening to define the what in our precision problem statement.

This level of precision is necessary to be able to identify the goals and plans with the greatest chance of success.

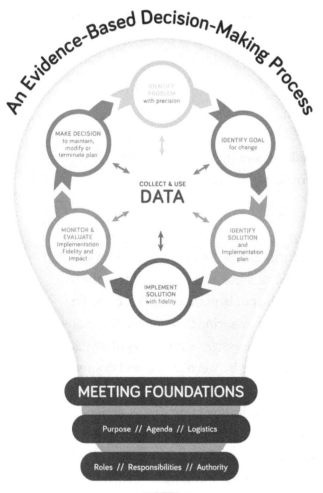

TIPS
Team-Initiated Problem Solving

An Evidence-Based Decision-Making Process

FIGURE 20.1. TIPS framework.

2. Identify the Goal for Change

The step of identifying a goal often goes overlooked in the action planning process. In order to develop a plan, it's important for that plan to be goal oriented. Setting up an intervention plan without having a clear goal in mind is like going on a road trip without knowing where your end destination is located. In the above example, the end goal will be to have Lily participate in the partner work at the first opportunity given. Because she is missing out on important practice opportunities by refusing to participate in group work, the teacher will need to undertake efforts to improve her participation. If Lily has the prerequisite skills to participate, then the teacher may ask an aide to provide assistance to Lily during partner work at the start of intervention with the ultimate goal being Lily participating in partner work without aide assistance when asked to do so in class.

As noted in Chapter 8 ("Monitoring Student Progress Toward Instructional Goals"), the use of systematic progress monitoring tools can help with setting goals. In Lily's case, tracking work completion during partner time will be the data the team must attend to in order to know if the intervention is working. At a minimum, the intervention should bring a student's performance to an acceptable or tolerable level. For academic difficulties, this usually means accelerating the rate of acquisition to close the gap between current performance and the performance desired in the classroom. For students with more variable patterns of achievement, intervention is directed at creating a more stable pattern of performance (unstable academic performance often requires the management of behavioral contingencies to support consistent academic effort).

Setting the criterion for a behavioral intervention involves much the same process as setting targets for academic problems. When the goal is to change behavior, the teacher should select two or three students who are behaving appropriately. These students should not be the best-behaved students but, rather, those in the middle of the range of acceptable behavior. The frequency, duration, latency, or amplitude of their

Intervention Plan

Complete one form for each targeted problem.

Student _____ Gender _____ Date of Birth _____

Referring Teacher _____ Grade _____ School _____

Intervention Objectives

Behavior to be changed:

Criterion for success/termination of intervention:

Duration of intervention:

Location of intervention:

Person responsible for implementing the intervention:

Strategies

Instructional methods:

Instructional materials:

Special equipment:

Signatures

_____   _____
(Referring Teacher)   (Date)

_____   _____
(Member, Teacher Assistance Team)   (Date)

FIGURE 20.2. Intervention plan.

behavior can be used as the criterion. Usually, the behavior of the appropriate students is stable, so the team does not have to predict where they will be at the end of the intervention.

Implicit in this discussion is the idea that the interventions will reach the criterion for success within the allotted time. Thus, the team not only desires progress toward the criterion but also wants that progress to occur at a specific rate or faster. Finally, it is generally a good idea to maintain a written record of the details of the goal for change. This record might be as informal as a set of notes from the team meeting, or it might be a formal document such as the Intervention Plan shown in Figure 20.2. The goal identification step will also become relevant when the team arrives at the final step of the TIPS framework when the status of the problem is evaluated.

3. Identify the Solution and Implementation Plan

Next, the intervention assistance team and the teacher design interventions to remediate the most pressing problems. Initially, the interventions should be based on empirically validated procedures that are known to be generally effective. In addition, parents, other school personnel, and the student may be involved in the intervention. There is a wide selection of published intervention materials and programs that are also based on research. One characteristic of the MTSS framework is that each school has a defined menu of interventions that address some of the more common challenges students face. For example, with behavioral concerns students who are in need of learning self-management skills and receiving positive attention from adults may be assigned to an intervention like Check-In, Check-Out (Hawken et al., 2021) where students check-in at an assigned location with a specific staff member at the start and end of the school day. Throughout the school day, the student might also check in with their classroom teacher to conference and the teacher can give the student behavior-specific praise and the student is reminded and reinforced for appropriate classroom behavior. This is an example of a medium-cost Tier 2 intervention that once in place can serve multiple students who are in need of this boost in positive adult attention and self-management skills.

A major factor determining whether an intervention will be tried or implemented by teachers is feasibility; you can also think about this as contextual fit. Those who conduct assessments and make recommendations about teaching must consider the extent to which the interventions they recommend are doable. Phillips (1990) identified eight major considerations in making decisions about feasibility, which remain relevant today. These considerations are listed and defined in Box 20.1.

The intervention plan should include the following:

- Clear delineation of the skills to be developed or the behavior to be changed
- Methods to be used to effect the change
- Duration of the intervention
- Location of the intervention

BOX 20.1

Considerations in Making Decisions About Feasibility

- *Degree of disruption.* How much will the intervention the teacher recommends disrupt school procedures or teacher routines?

- *Side effects.* To what extent are there undesirable side effects for the student (e.g., social ostracism, loss of instruction), peers, home and family, and faculty?

- *Support services required.* How readily available are the support services required, and are the costs reasonable?

- *Prerequisite competencies.* Does the teacher have the necessary knowledge, motivation, and experience to be able to implement the intervention? Does the teacher have a philosophical bias against the recommended intervention?

- *Control.* Does the teacher have control of the necessary variables to ensure the success of the intervention?

- *Immediacy of results.* Will the student's behavioral change be quick enough for the teacher to be reinforced for implementing the intervention?

- *Consequences of nonintervention.* What are the short- and long-term prognoses for the student if the behaviors are left uncorrected?

- *Potential for transition.* Is it reasonable to expect that the intervention will lead to student self-regulation and generalize to other settings, curriculum areas, or even to other students who are experiencing similar difficulties?

- Names of the individuals responsible for each aspect of the intervention.
- Clear criteria for a successful intervention

4. Implement the Solution With Fidelity

The interventions should then be conducted as planned. To ensure that the intervention is being carried out correctly, a member of the team may observe the teacher using the planned strategy or special materials. Even better, the intervention can be designed to leave "footprints" when it is used. These footprints are called permanent products and include things like completed worksheets or scores. With digital innovations, documenting (and supporting) integrity can include teachers digitally recording sessions and sharing with coaches and teams over the internet. Such direct information about use of the intervention allows for more effective and efficient problem solving at the team level and makes the progress monitoring data more interpretable (i.e., the team can easily see when the intervention was used well and when poor progress was associated with incorrect intervention use). Planning the intervention to leave permanent products of its use also helps the teacher to be aware of and attend to conducting the intervention each day among the multitude of tasks on the teacher's plate.

Data entry can also be an important indicator of intervention treatment integrity. In the Check-In, Check-Out intervention mentioned earlier, the student is given a point card for the day. The student rates themselves and the teacher rates the student on the agreed-upon behavioral expectation (e.g., prepared for class with a pencil and notebook). At the end of the day the point card is turned in and the data are entered. If no data are entered, then the team will be unable to make a decision about the student's progress. If the data are entered but several days or classes are missing because the student or the teacher neglected to rate the student, then the team learns that the student is not receiving the intended daily dosage of the intervention. Another term used for fidelity is treatment integrity. If the desired outcomes are not being observed, then it's important for the team to ask if the intervention is being delivered as it was intended to be delivered. Fidelity or integrity checks can involve having another team member observe intervention delivery to troubleshoot and optimize intervention use. Generally, self-ratings about how well an intervention was used or whether an intervention was used are not an accurate basis for estimating actual intervention use. A student's number of absences may also impact the treatment integrity. Before the team arrives at the next step to evaluate the progress made there must be some assurance or documentation of the quality of the intervention implementation.

5. Monitor and Evaluate the Implementation Fidelity and Impact

The effects of the interventions should be evaluated frequently enough to allow fine-tuning of the teaching methods and materials (see Chapter 8). The frequency of progress monitoring will depend upon on the targeted skills. Generally speaking, we suggest that progress monitoring data be collected and recorded weekly. In the case of behavior monitoring and an intervention like Check-In, Check-Out, progress is monitored multiple times per day. Frequently, student performance is graphed to make pictures of progress. Effective programs designed to increase desired behavior produce results like those shown in Figure 20.3. The student usually shows an increase in the desired behavior (correct responses) and a decrease in the number of errors (incorrect responses). It is also possible for successful programs to produce only increasingly correct responses or only a decrease in errors. Ineffective programs

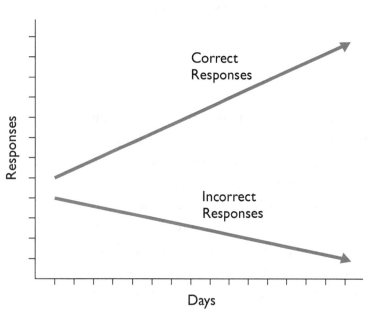

FIGURE 20.3. A successful learning intervention.

show no increase in the desired correct responses, no decrease in the unwanted errors, or both.

Although frequent data collection is important, it is also important to realize that in some cases, substantial intervention time may be needed before intervention effects will be detected. It is therefore important to balance the desire for immediate effects with an understanding that it may take time for a student to respond to an intervention. The team should determine ahead of time how much intervention time should elapse and how much data should be collected before they evaluate the effectiveness of the intervention. This decision is mostly dictated by the sensitivity of measures used for progress monitoring. In most cases, weekly progress monitoring is necessary as the first sign that intervention integrity may require some support. Interventions that are deployed but then unexamined for many weeks are unlikely to be correctly and consistently used. It is a common error in MTSS to fail to actively manage intervention and this is the primary driver of unsuccessful interventions in schools. A high rate of unsuccessful interventions (greater than 10%) should signify the need to fine-tune the team's procedures for deploying and sustaining effective implementation of interventions in classrooms. These criteria are in part what make up the decision guidelines that determine the thresholds of when students will be nominated and served by certain levels of interventions. At this stage in the TIPS process, which is generally between 6 to 10 weeks after an intervention has begun, the team must decide if the plan should be maintained, modified, or terminated.

6. Make a Decision to Maintain, Modify, or Terminate the Plan

To assess a student's rate of behavior change, we graph the acceleration of a desired behavior (or the deceleration of an undesired behavior) with an aimline (see Chapter 8), as shown in Figure 20.4. The aimline connects the student's current level of performance with the point that represents both the desired level of behavior and the time at which the behavior is to be attained. When behavior is targeted for increase, we expect the student's progress to be at or above the aimline (as shown in Figure 20.4); when behavior is targeted for decrease, we expect the student's progress to be at or below the aimline (not shown). Thus, a teacher, the intervention assistance team, and the student can look at the graph and make a decision about the adequacy of progress.

When better than anticipated progress is being made, the teacher or team can decide to set a more ambitious goal (that is, raise the level of desired performance) without changing the goal

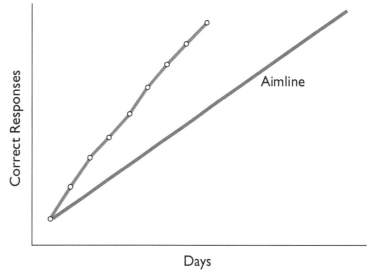

FIGURE 20.4. Student progress with an aimline.

achievement date, or they can set an earlier target for achieving the criterion without changing the level of performance. When inadequate progress is being made, teachers can take several steps to fine-tune the student's program. When adequate progress is being made, the intervention should be continued until the criterion is reached. The intervention assistance team should continue to follow these six steps, using their established decision guidelines to determine when a student should be removed from an intervention.

When to Refer the Student for Multidisciplinary Evaluation

20.2
PROGRESS MONITORING CHECK

When several interventions have been implemented with a high-level of fidelity at each level of MTSS and have not led to sufficient success, the student is likely to be referred for psychoeducational evaluation to ascertain eligibility for special education. Similarly, if the team has repeatedly made adaptations to the intervention and the student continues to need more intensive and individualized instruction in order to reach a desirable rate of improvement, then it may be an indicator that the case should be brought to the multidisciplinary team.

Because RTI is a formalized process that may be used to determine eligibility for Specific Learning Disability (SLD), a formal request for services may be required and might be made on a form similar to that shown in Figure 20.5. When such a form is used, it should contain identifying information (such as teacher and student names), the specific problems for which the teacher is seeking consultation, the interventions that have already been attempted in the classroom, the effectiveness of those interventions, and current academic instructional levels. This information allows those responsible for providing consultation to decide whether the problem warrants their further attention.

Request for Consultation

Student _____ Gender _____ Date of Birth _____

Referring Teacher _____ Grade _____ School _____

Specific Educational/Behavioral Problems:

_____

_____

_____

_____

Current Level or Materials in Deficit Areas:

_____

_____

_____

Specific Interventions to Improve Performance in Deficit Areas and Their Effectiveness:

_____

_____

_____

_____

What Special Services Does the Student Receive (e.g., Title I Reading, Speech Therapy)?

_____

_____

Most Convenient Days and Times for Consultation:

_____

_____

FIGURE 20.5. Request for consultation

Decisions Made in Special Education and Included in an IEP

Approximately 14% of all students who enter school will experience sufficient difficulty to be identified as having a disability at some time during their school career. Most of these students will receive special education services because they need special instruction. Some students with disabilities (such as students with certain chronic health impairments) will not need special education but will require special related services that must be provided under Section 504 of the Rehabilitation Act of 1973.

After students have been determined to be eligible for special education, special education decisions revolve around design and implementation of their Individualized Education Programs (IEPs). An IEP is a blueprint for instruction and specifies the goals, procedures, and related services for an individual eligible student. Assessment data are important for such planning. Numerous books and hundreds of articles in professional and scientific journals discuss the importance of using assessment data to plan instructional programs for students. The Individuals With Disabilities Education Act (IDEA) requires a thorough assessment that results in an IEP. Pupils are treated differentially on the basis of their IEPs. Moreover, most educators would agree that it is desirable to individualize instruction for students in special and inclusive education because the general education programs have not proved beneficial to them. IEPs vary considerably from one school district to another, although they have the same basic structure and are designed to meet the same Federal guidelines. An informative source for understanding what must be included in IEPs is a document entitled "A Guide to the Individualized Education Program." It is available at this website: www2.ed.gov/parents/needs/speced /iepguide/index.html. The guide is interactive and you can search each section for specific information.

The Individuals With Disabilities Education Act of 1997 and subsequent revisions to the Act and its regulations set forth the requirements for IEPs. Instructionally, an IEP is a road map of a student's 1-year trip from point A to point B. This road map is prepared collaboratively by an IEP team that includes the parents and, when appropriate, the student, at least one general education teacher, at least one of the student's special education teachers, a representative of the school administration, an individual who can interpret the instructional implications of evaluation results, and other individuals who have knowledge or special expertise relevant to the student's needs.

Development and implementation of an IEP involves all of the processes involved in program planning more generally, which includes defining a problem, goal-setting, development and implementation of intervention strategies, and evaluation, but in this case they are targeted to address the needs of an individual child. The IEP begins with a description of the student's current educational levels—the starting point of the metaphoric trip. Next, the IEP specifies measurable, annual, academic, and functional goals (the student's destination). The IEP must include a description of how progress toward meeting annual goals will be measured and when progress reports will be provided to parents. The IEP must identify the special education and related services that are based on peer-reviewed research (to the extent practicable) needed by the student in order to reach the goals (the method of transportation and provisions that make the trip possible). Finally, the IEP requires measurement, evaluation, and reporting of the student's progress toward the annual goals (periodic checks to make sure the student is on the correct road and traveling fast enough). Hopefully, these requirements make apparent to you the significant benefit of using MTSS and RTI as part of eligibility determination as the screening, progress monitoring, diagnostic assessment, and subsequent response to intensive individualized intervention is the best basis for knowing what can work to address the student's needs (and what is likely to not work).

Current Levels of Performance

A student's current level of performance is not specifically defined in the regulations for IDEA. However, because current levels of performance are the starting points for instruction, a current level must be instructionally relevant and expressed quantitatively. Although legally permissible, scores from standardized achievement tests are not particularly useful. Even if there is adequate correspondence between test and curricular content, the fact that a student is reading less well than 90% of students in the grade is not useful information about where the teacher should begin instruction. If a student is physically aggressive in the third-grade classroom, that alone is too vague to allow a teacher, parents, and the student to tell whether progress toward acceptable behavior is being made. Although not defined in the IDEA, we think a current educational level in an academic area should be the level at which a student is appropriately instructed. For example, knowing that Sam is at an *instructional* reading level in third-grade materials (i.e., reads that material with between 90% and 95% accuracy) is directly related to where his instruction should begin and suggests where more intensive support should be provided when content area instruction requires comprehension of more challenging text.

Current educational level in behavioral areas should also be quantified. Frequency, duration, latency, and amplitude can be quantified, and the results can be compared to those of a peer who is performing satisfactorily on the target skill or behavior.

Annual Goals

IEPs must contain a statement of measurable annual goals, which meet each educational need arising from the student's disability and ensure the student's access to the general education curriculum (or appropriate activities, if a preschooler). Thus, for each area of need, parents and schools must agree on what should be a student's level of achievement after 1 year of instruction.

In part, the selection of long-term goals is based on the aspirations and prognosis for a student's post-school outcomes. Although these are not formally required by federal law until a special education student reaches 16 years of age, the expected or desired post-school outcomes shape the special education a student receives. For students with pervasive and severe cognitive disabilities, the prognosis may be assisted living with supported employment. With this prognosis, educational goals are likely to center on daily living, social skills, and leisure rather than academic areas. For students with moderate disabilities, the prognosis may be independent living and unskilled or semiskilled employment. With this prognosis, educational goals are likely to be basic academics and vocational skills. For students with mild disabilities, which represents the greatest number of students served in special education in the United States, the prognosis may be professional or skilled employment. For these students, educational goals should prepare students for college or technical schools.

Annual goals are derived directly from a student's curriculum and a student's current instructional levels. When continued academic integration is the desired educational outcome, a student's goals are mastery of the same content at the same rate as peers without disabilities in their same setting. Thus, after 1 year, the student would be expected to be instructional in the same materials as his or her peers. When reintegration is the desired educational outcome, a student's goal depends on where the regular class peers will be in 1 year. For students pursuing alternative programming, the IEP team makes an educated guess about where the student should be after one year of instruction. Increasingly goal setting can be meaningfully informed by information supplied by publishers of progress monitoring instruments. And, as assessments now involves monitoring progress toward instructional goals, goal setting is a far more important activity and a skill that all teachers should have.

Specially Designed Instruction

IDEA defines special education, in part, as specially designed instruction that is provided in classrooms, the home, or other settings (see 34 CFR §300.26). It includes the adaptation of instructional content, methods, or delivery to meet the needs of a student with disabilities.

Currently, the best way to design instruction for students with disabilities is to rely on evidence-based practices (Burns et al., 2017; Sprick et al., 2021; ies.ed.gov/ncee/wwc). Teachers can do several things to make it easier for their students to learn facts and concepts, skills, or behavior. They can model the desired behavior. They can break down the terminal goal into its component parts and teach each of the steps and their integration. They can teach objectives in a variety of contexts with a variety of materials to facilitate generalization. They can provide time for practice, and they can choose the schedule on which practice is done (in other words, they can offer distributed or massed practice). Several techniques that are under the direct control of the teacher can be employed to instruct any learner effectively.

It is important to understand that one of the most profound scientific discoveries of the past century is that effective instruction can be operationalized and benefits all learners. Children identified with learning disabilities do not respond differently to highly effective instruction than children who are not identified with learning disabilities. We now understand that learning disabilities are largely preventable given highly effective early reading instruction (Lyon et al., 2001). Thus, understanding how to deliver highly effective instruction in the classroom is the most important priority of any teacher in general or special education.

Fortunately, delivering highly effective instruction is a well-defined process for which we can make some targeted "how to" suggestions here. When the desired outcomes of learning have been specified and mapped onto a calendar for students in general education, these are the assessment targets by which to assess performance discrepancies and then to drill-down to find useful instructional targets to close those gaps. Assessing expected grade-level skills and understandings allows the teacher to identify where skill deficits exist and then to "sample back" through incrementally easier prerequisite skills to find the student's instructional level, which will be the entry point for intervention. The Instructional Hierarchy (Haring et al., 1978) is the scientific framework for connecting instructional strategies to student proficiency. The learning stages acquisition, fluency, generalization, and adaptation are mapped onto effective teacher behaviors to support students at each phase until they reach mastery of the skills. See The Instructional Hierarchy: SA Scientific Framework for Connecting Instructional Tactics to Student Proficiency (located in the online resources) for a more in-depth description of the instructional hierarchy.

ONLINE
RESOURCE

Research in MTSS and RTI has developed the concept of intensification. Pragmatically, special education should represent the most intensive instruction that can be offered in a school. We can think of special education instruction as the ICU-level instruction in a school, whereas general education may be thought of as urgent care-type instruction. In the early days of RTI, systems attempted to define intervention intensification as more sessions of longer duration with more frequent progress monitoring. The intervening years of research taught us that these dimensions of interventions were not strongly related to intensification. Instead, more intensive interventions are those that are (a) more precisely aligned with student's needs according to the Instructional Hierarchy, and (b) deliver active ingredients of the intervention at a higher dosage. Frequent progress monitoring (weekly) is necessary to enable and sustain correctly aligned intervention tactic and skill/content. Sensitive measures are also necessary to enable and sustain dynamic adjustment of the intervention. Goals are also related to intensification, as more narrowly defined skill targets will produce more rapid improvements than will more general targets.

However, always remember that efficacy is local. We recommend that teachers first rely on general principles that are known and demonstrated to be effective in facilitating learning. Consequently, we must treat our translation of these principles, known to be effective, as tentative. In a real sense, we hypothesize that our treatment will work, but we need to verify that it has worked. The point was made years ago by Deno and Mirkin (1977) and remains true today:

> At the present time we are unable to prescribe specific and effective changes in instruction for individual pupils with certainty. Therefore, changes in instructional programs that are arranged for an individual child can be treated only as hypotheses that must be empirically tested before a decision can be made about whether they are effective for that child. (p. 11)

Teaching is often experimental in nature. When there is no database to guide our selection of specific tasks or materials, decisions must be tentative. The decision maker makes some good guesses about what will work and then implements an instructional program. We do not know whether a decision is correct until we gather data on the extent to which the instructional program actually works. We never know if the program will work until we have tried it and monitored whether a student makes subsequent gains in performance. When instruction fails, asking what is wrong with the learner is the wrong question. Because learning is the most predictable outcome of highly effective instruction, when instruction does not produce the desired return in student learning, we must ask what is wrong with the instruction and make adjustments accordingly. Read the Stakeholder Perspective by Reina Chehayeb, a former classroom teacher and current school psychology doctoral student at Northeastern University, as she describes how she used technology to help her assess and design math instruction.

Related Services

In addition to special instruction, eligible students are entitled to developmental, corrective, and other supportive services if such services are needed in order for the students to benefit from special education; federal legislation uses the term *related services*, which has been widely adopted by states and school districts. Related services include both those not typically provided by schools and those typically provided (34 CFR §300.24).

Schools must provide to students with disabilities a variety of services to which nondisabled students are seldom entitled. Services described in 34 CFR §300.24 include, but are not limited to, the following types:

Audiology. Allowable services include evaluation of hearing, habilitation (e.g., programs in auditory training, speech reading, and speech conservation), amplification (including the fitting of hearing aids), and hearing conservation programs.

Psychological services. Psychological services allowed include testing, observation, and consultation.

Physical and occupational therapy. These therapies can be used to (a) improve, develop, or restore functional impairments caused by illness, injury, or deprivation; and

(b) improve independent functioning. These therapies may also be used with pre-school populations to prevent impairment or further loss of function.

Recreation. Allowable programs include those located in the schools and community agencies that provide general recreation programs, therapeutic recreation, and assessment of leisure functioning.

Counseling services. Either group or individual counseling may be provided for students and their parents. Student counseling includes rehabilitation counseling that focuses on career development, employment preparation, achievement of independence, and integration in the workplace and community; it also includes psychological counseling. Parental counseling includes therapies addressing problems in the student's living situation (that is, home, school, and community) that affect the student's schooling. Parental counseling also includes assistance to help parents understand their child's special needs, as well as information about child development.

Medical services. Diagnostic and evaluative services required to determine medically related disabilities are allowed.

Stakeholder PERSPECTIVE

Reina Chehayeb, MA Education, Doctoral Candidate, Northeastern University, Boston, Massachusetts

I was a second- and third-grade math teacher for 3 years in New York City and recently taught math as part of a research study in Boston. Teachers, including myself, have often used assessment data to guide our instruction in the classroom. Unfortunately, there are two major problems with this: the accuracy of this process as well as its timing. Often, we use assessment data from each math test to group students into different "buckets." In my experience, one of those was almost always an "intervention" bucket, where students were in need of individual or small-group intervention. The tests that fell into this bucket would be analyzed to determine which specific skills each student struggled with. Teachers would provide individualized instruction for these students, who would also have access to manipulatives and other resources such as counting cubes, base-ten blocks, or a number line.

In theory, this works well. Logistically, however, there are issues around the accuracy and timing of this approach. First, most teachers simply do not have the time to parse through students' assessments to find patterns, which can lead to rushed, inaccurate conclusions. Second, there is a major issue with

(continues)

Schools must also provide to students with disabilities the services they typically provide to all children. Thus, schools must provide to students with disabilities, as needed, speech and language services, school health and school social work services, and transportation. School-provided transportation includes whatever is needed to get students to and from school, as well as between schools or among school buildings, including any required special equipment such as ramps. Although these related services are mandatory for students who need them to profit from their special education, there is nothing

waiting until an assessment is over to take action. There is a disservice being done to students when teachers wait and react to test scores rather than deliver interventions proactively throughout the year, especially since most schools still rely on assessments to determine student growth.

Computer programs can help mitigate both of these problems. Using general, classwide assessments, algorithms can analyze student scores to determine not only which students could benefit from an intervention, but what type of intervention is ideal. SpringMath is one example that I've used that helps me to connect assessment to instruction quickly, thus eliminating any concerns about timing. The algorithm used by SpringMath analyzes a whole-class baseline assessment and instantaneously determines whether individual, small-group, or whole-class intervention would be beneficial. The program then generates a neat intervention packet targeting the appropriate skills with a checklist of activities, explicit instructions, and all the worksheets and assessments required to carry out the intervention, as well as a follow-up assessment. After teachers input the data from the follow-up assessment into the program, the process repeats, generating new interventions as appropriate based on who mastered the previous skills, and who may need to revisit them further. If this were to be done by hand, teachers would need additional time allocated throughout the day to analyzing test items, determining patterns, creating and scheduling intervention protocols, and planning for another assessment—all of which SpringMath can do in a matter of seconds.

Using SpringMath, I was better able to monitor student growth than I could in outdated grade books and saw students master skills faster and with a much deeper understanding than I had before. When I didn't see adequate progress, I knew I had an excellent source of information to work with my colleagues in the special education department to determine if any additional testing and intervention was needed. Programs like these also help teachers use their instruction proactively and with consistency throughout the year. With innovative solutions that embrace technology, utilizing the accuracy and timing of interventions to teachers' and students' advantages becomes much more feasible.

to prohibit a school from offering other services. Thus, schools may offer additional services free of charge to eligible students.

Although federal law is very clear about the need to provide related services to students with disabilities, how that need should be established remains unclear. In practice, most schools or parents seek an evaluation by a specialist. The specialist notes a problem and expresses a belief that a specific therapy could be successful and benefit the student. Thus, need is frequently based on professional opinion. We must also note that related services can be very costly, and some school districts try to avoid providing them. We have heard of districts maintaining that they do not offer a particular service even though federal law mandates that service should be provided to students who need it.

Least Restrictive Environment

Federal law expresses a clear preference for educating students with disabilities as close as possible to their home and with their nondisabled peers to the maximum extent appropriate. Education in "special classes, separate schooling or other removal of children with disabilities from the regular educational environment occurs only if the nature or severity of the disability is such that education in regular classes with the use of supplementary aids and services cannot be achieved satisfactorily" (34 CFR §300.550).

Placement Options

A hierarchy of placements ranges from the least restrictive (educating students with disabilities in a general education classroom with a general education teacher who receives consultative services from a special education teacher) to the most restrictive (educating students with disabilities in segregated residential facilities that provide services only to students with disabilities). Between these two extremes are at least five other options:

Instructional support from a special education teacher in the general education classroom. In this arrangement, eligible students remain in the general education classroom in their neighborhood schools, and the special education teacher comes to the student to provide whatever specialized instruction is necessary.

Instructional support from a special education teacher in a resource room. In this arrangement, eligible students remain in a general education classroom for most of the day. When they need specialized instruction, they go to a special education resource room to receive services from a special education teacher. Because districts may not have enough students with disabilities in each school to warrant establishing a resource room program at each school, a student may be assigned to a general education classroom that is not in the student's neighborhood school.

Part-time instruction in a special education classroom. In this arrangement, eligible students have some classes or subject matter taught by the special education teacher and the rest taught in the general education classroom. As is the case with resource rooms, the general education classroom may not be in the student's neighborhood school.

Full-time instruction in a special education classroom, with limited integration. In this arrangement, eligible students receive all academic instruction from a special education teacher in a special classroom. Eligible students may be integrated with nondisabled peers for special events or activities (such as lunch, recess, and assemblies) and nonacademic classes (such as art and music).

Full-time instruction in a special education classroom, without integration. In this arrangement, eligible students have no interaction with their nondisabled peers, and their classrooms may be in a special day school that serves only students with disabilities.

Factors Affecting Placement Choice

The selection of a particular option should be based on the intensity of education needed by the eligible student. The less intensive the intervention needed by the student, the less restrictive the environment; the more intensive the intervention needed by the student, the more restrictive the environment. The procedure for determining the intensity of an intervention is less than scientific. Frequently, there is some correspondence between the severity of disability and the intensity of service needed, but that correspondence is not perfect. Therefore, special education teachers and parents should consider the level of control and precision needed to deliver the needed interventions. The more intensive an intervention is (for instance, requiring highly scripted instructional sequences with a high density of practice opportunities), the more likely it is that the intervention will be provided in more, rather than less, restrictive settings. When more intensive interventions are needed, the student will have less opportunity to participate with peers without disabilities, no matter what the student's placement. Obviously, if students require round-the-clock intervention, they cannot get what they need from a resource room program.

In addition to the nature of needed interventions, parents and teachers may also reasonably consider the following factors when deciding on the type of placement:

Disruption. Bringing a special education teacher into or pulling a student out of a general education classroom may be disruptive. For example, some students with disabilities cannot handle transitions: They get lost between classrooms, or they forget to go to their resource rooms. When eligible students have a lot of difficulty changing schedules or making transitions between events, less restrictive options may not be appropriate.

Well-being of individuals without disabilities. Eligible students will seldom be integrated when they present a clear danger to the welfare of peers without disabilities or teachers. For example, assaultive and disruptive students are likely to be placed in more restrictive environments.

Well-being of the student who has a disability. Many students with disabilities require some degree of protection—in some cases, from nondisabled peers who may tease or physically abuse a student who is different; in other cases, from other students with disabilities. For example, the parents of a seriously withdrawn student may decide not to place their child in a classroom for students with emotional disabilities when those students are assaultive.

Labeling. Many parents, especially those of students with milder handicaps, reject disability labels. They desire special education services, but they want these services without having their child labeled. These parents may prefer consultative or itinerant services for their children.

Inclusion. Some parents are willing to forgo the instructional benefits of special education for the potential social benefits of having their children educated exclusively with peers without disabilities. For these parents, full inclusion is the preferred option.

There are also pragmatic considerations in selecting the educational setting. One very real consideration is that a school district may, for economic reasons, not be able to provide a full range of options. In such districts, parents are offered a choice among existing options unless they are willing to go through a due process hearing or a court trial. A second consideration is instructional efficiency. When several students require the same intervention, the special education teacher can often form an instructional group. Thus, it will probably cost less to provide the special education services. A third consideration is the specific teachers. Some teachers have skill sets particularly matched to some disability types, and parents may well opt for a more restrictive setting because the teacher there is highly regarded. Parents and special education teachers must realize that selecting a placement option can be an imprecise endeavor. Thus, although federal regulations are clear in their preference for less restrictive placements, the criteria that guide the selection of one option over another are variable and influenced by many factors.

Effectiveness of the Instructional Program

IEPs are supposed to result in effective instruction for students with disabilities. IDEA requires that each student's IEP contain a statement detailing the way in which progress toward annual goals will be measured and how parents will be informed of their child's progress (34 CFR §300.347). In addition, IDEA requires IEP teams to review each student's IEP "periodically, but not less than annually, to determine whether the annual goals for the child are being achieved" (34 CFR §300.343). If adequate progress is not being made, IEP teams are required to revise the IEPs of students who are not making expected progress toward their annual goals. An exception to this rule is that according to IDEA 2004, some states may put in place comprehensive multiyear IEPs for those students who have milder disabilities and for whom parents agree a multiyear IEP is sufficient.

PROGRESS
MONITORING
CHECK

Fairness and Using Data to Make Instructional and Placement Decisions

Throughout this book, we have discussed procedures that are useful in collecting information about students' achievement and behavior. We have also discussed how that information can be systematized using graphs and charts. We have offered guidelines about how to reach decisions about a student's progress. All of these discussions are relevant to the decision about the effectiveness of each component of a student's instructional program. Judgments about the simultaneous effectiveness of all of the components of an instructional program are geometrically more complicated. What makes a goal important varies by student. For an aggressive, acting-out student, self-control may be more important than quadratic equations. For a student with a learning disability, learning to read may be more important than improvement in spelling. The key to making these critical decisions both about intervention delivery and instructional placement is that there is a standardized process that guides data-use and decision making. When teams use thresholds, such as five or more absences in a month, the team ensures that students will not get overlooked or slip through the cracks. These decision guidelines are to hold ourselves as educators accountable so that we minimize the influence of our own biases (e.g., we "know" the family, so we won't ask about the increased student absences). When decision guidelines include set timepoints for all intervention plans to be reviewed (e.g., all interventions are reviewed 6 weeks after starting if not earlier) you and your team can be confident that services are being delivered to students in a timely fashion and students are not falling behind because the team is not reviewing their case often enough. As uncomfortable as it is to self-evaluate, the true impact of interventions is often unrealized because the intervention is delivered not according to plan which indicates that maybe the intervention selected didn't have good contextual fit or it wasn't feasible. Collecting fidelity data will boost confidence and transparency in the instructional decision-making process. Just the fact that as a field we agree to work collaboratively in teams demonstrates our willingness to provide supports for any student who needs them. As you have learned, instructional decision making is no easy task. It is best made with colleagues who are also willing to commit to the process to minimize bias and inequities in service delivery and to maximize the positive impact of interventions for students in need.

PROGRESS 20.1 MONITORING CHECK

1. Describe five main reasons how ineffective instruction may contribute to students' academic struggles.
2. Describe how individual differences may contribute to students' behavioral challenges.

PROGRESS 20.2 MONITORING CHECK

1. What are the advantages of an intervention assistance team using a problem-solving model?
2. What are the six steps in the TIPS framework's problem-solving process?
3. Write examples of a precise and imprecise problem statement based on a situation you have observed.

PROGRESS 20.3 MONITORING CHECK

1. What components should be included in an IEP?
2. List three characteristics of specially designed instruction?
3. What are some of the factors that may influence parents' preference for their student's placement?

CHAPTER 21

Using Assessment Information to Make Diagnostic/ Eligibility Decisions

LEARNING OBJECTIVES

1. Identify and define the disabilities recognized by the Individuals With Disabilities Education Improvement Act.
2. Articulate the difference between an RTI approach and a discrepancy approach to identifying students as learning disabled.
3. Explain how the need for special education is established.
4. Describe the composition and responsibilities of multidisciplinary teams.
5. Describe the process for determining eligibility (including procedural safeguards, the requirements for valid assessment, and the team process).
6. Discuss common problems in determining eligibility.

The issue of eligibility for special education hinges on two questions: Does the student have a disability? And if so, does the student need special education? Both questions must be answered in the affirmative to be eligible for special education and related services. Students who have disabilities but do not need special education are not eligible, although they may well be eligible for services under Section 504 of the Rehabilitation Act of 1973. Students who do not have disabilities but need (or would benefit from) special education services are not eligible. Once students have been determined to be eligible for special education, they are automatically entitled to procedural safeguards, special services, altered outcome expectations, and special fiscal arrangements, as discussed in Chapter 3, "Laws, Ethical Codes, and Professional Standards That Impact Assessment."

Official Student Disabilities

Students are classified as having a disability under several laws; three are particularly important: The Americans With Disabilities Act (Public Law 101-336), Section 504 of the Rehabilitation Act of 1973, and the Individuals With Disabilities Education Improvement Act (IDEA; 34 CFR §300.7). In the schools and other educational settings, the following disabilities, enumerated in regulations of the IDEA (34 CFR §300.7), are commonly used: autism, intellectual disability, specific learning disability, emotional disturbance, traumatic brain injury, speech or language impairment, visual impairment, deafness and hearing impairment, orthopedic impairments, other health impairments, deaf–blindness, multiple disabilities, and developmental delay.[1] Identification under §300.306 of the IDEA requires that

- a team (i.e., group of qualified professionals and the parent(s) of the student) determine whether the student has a disability and the student's educational needs.
- a student cannot be determined to have a disability if conditions are caused by (1) a lack of appropriate instruction in reading or math, (2) limited English proficiency, or (3) if the child does not otherwise meet the eligibility criteria.
- the team draws upon information from a variety of sources, including aptitude and achievement tests, input from parents, and teachers, as well as information about the child's physical condition, social or cultural background, and adaptive behavior; and
- the team ensures that information obtained from all of these sources is documented and carefully considered.

§300.8 of the IDEA regulations define the specific disabilities. These definitions are provided below.

Autism

Students with **autism** are those who demonstrate "developmental disability significantly affecting verbal and nonverbal communication and social interaction, generally evident before age 3 that adversely affects a child's educational performance. Other characteristics often associated with autism are engagement in repetitive activities and stereotyped movements, resistance to environmental change or change in daily routines, and unusual responses to sensory experiences. Autism does not apply if a child's

---

1. The definitions in IDEA (excluding the need for special education) are generally used for entitlements under Section 504.

educational performance is adversely affected primarily because the child has an emotional disturbance."

Students with suspected autism are usually evaluated by speech and language specialists and psychologists after it has been determined that some aspects of their educational performance fall outside the normal range and various attempts to remedy the educational problems have failed. Frequently, a speech and language specialist would look for impaired verbal and nonverbal communication. A large proportion of autistic children are mute, an impairment that is readily apparent. Autism in students with speech and language might manifest itself as overly concrete thinking. For example, a student with autism might react to a statement such as "don't cry over spilled milk" quite literally ("I didn't spill any milk"). Another manifestation would be a lack of conversational reciprocity (usually long, often tedious, orations about a favorite subject) and failure to recognize a listener's waning interest. Moreover, this impaired social communication would be a consistent feature of the student's behavior rather than an occasional overexuberance. A psychologist looks for behavior that defines the condition: repetitive activities (e.g., self-stimulating behavior, spinning objects, aligning objects, and smelling objects), stereotyped movements (e.g., hand flapping, rocking, and head banging), resistance to change (e.g., eating only certain foods or having a tantrum when activities are ended). A psychologist may also administer a behavior rating scale (e.g., the *Gilliam Autism Rating Scale*) as an aid to diagnosis. Finally, a psychologist rules out emotional disturbance as a cause of the student's behavior and impairments.

Intellectual Disability

Students with **intellectual disabilities** are those who demonstrate "significantly subaverage general intellectual functioning, existing concurrently with deficits in adaptive behavior and manifested during the developmental period that adversely affects a child's educational performance." Students who are eventually labeled "intellectually disabled" are often referred because of generalized delays: They lag behind their age mates in most areas of academic achievement, social and emotional development, language ability, and, perhaps, physical development.

Usually, a psychologist will administer a test of intelligence that is appropriate in terms of the student's age, acculturation, and physical and sensory capabilities. In most states, students must have an IQ that is two standard deviations or more below the mean (usually 70 or less) on a valid and correctly administered test. However, a test of intelligence is not enough. The pupil must also demonstrate impairments in adaptive behavior. There is no federal requirement that a test or rating scale be used to assess adaptive behavior psychometrically. In practice, most school psychologists will administer an adaptive behavior scale (e.g., the *Vineland Adaptive Behavior Scales–Second Edition*). However, when it is not possible to do so, a psychologist will interview parents or guardians and make a clinical judgment about a student's adaptive behavior.

Specific Learning Disability

A student with a **learning disability** is one who "does not achieve adequately for the child's age or . . . meet state-approved grade-level standards in one or more of the following areas, when provided with learning experiences and instruction appropriate for the child's age or state-approved grade-level standards: oral expression, listening comprehension, written expression, basic reading skills, reading fluency skills, reading comprehension, mathematics calculation, [or] mathematics problem solving" (34 CFR §300.306). In addition, the student's failure to meet age or state standards cannot be due to: a visual, hearing, or motor disability; intellectual disability; emotional disturbance; cultural factors; environmental or economic disadvantage; or limited English proficiency.

To ensure that the lack of progress is not due to lack of appropriate instruction in reading or math, there must be data to demonstrate that the student received appropriate instruction in regular education settings from qualified personnel, that there were repeated assessments of student progress at reasonable intervals, and that assessments of progress were provided to the child's parents (Office of Special Education, n.d.).

Therefore, initial evaluations to ascertain if a student has a learning disability have four components: ruling out other causes of poor achievement, verification of achievement difficulties, documentation of unsuccessful attempts to remediate the achievement difficulties, and evidence of a disorder in a basic psychological process.

Emotional Disturbance

Emotional disturbance means "a condition exhibiting one or more of the following characteristics over a long period of time and to a marked degree that adversely affects a child's educational performance: (1) an inability to learn that cannot be explained by intellectual, sensory, or health factors; (2) an inability to build or maintain satisfactory interpersonal relationships with peers and teachers; (3) inappropriate types of behavior or feelings under normal circumstances; (4) a general pervasive mood of unhappiness or depression; (5) a tendency to develop physical symptoms or fears associated with personal or school problems" [§300.8(c)(4)]. This disability includes schizophrenia but excludes "children who are socially maladjusted, unless it is determined that they have an emotional disturbance." Students who are eventually labeled as having an emotional disorder are often referred for problems in interpersonal relations (e.g., fighting or extreme noncompliance) or unusual behavior (e.g., unexplained episodes of crying or extreme mood swings).

Students suspected of being emotionally disturbed are evaluated by a psychologist after it has been determined that some of their school performance falls outside the normal range and various attempts to remedy the school problems have failed. Requirements for establishing a student's eligibility for emotional disturbance vary among the states. However, multidisciplinary teams usually obtain a developmental and health history from a student's parent or guardian to rule out sensory and health factors as causes of a student's inability to learn. A parent or guardian is usually interviewed about the student's relationships with peers, feelings (e.g., anger, alienation, depression, and fears), and physical symptoms (e.g., headaches or nausea). Parents or guardians may also be asked to complete a behavior rating scale such as the *Behavior Evaluation Rating Scale* to obtain normative data on the student's behavior. Teachers will likely be interviewed about their relationships with the student and the student's relationships with peers at school. They may also be asked to complete a rating scale (e.g., the *Walker–McConnell Scale of Social Competence and School Adjustment*) to obtain normative data for in-school behavior. In addition, a psychologist might be asked to administer a norm-referenced achievement battery to verify that the student's educational performance has been negatively affected by the student's emotional problems.

Traumatic Brain Injury

Students with **traumatic brain injury** have "an acquired injury to the brain caused by an external physical force, resulting in total or partial functional disability or psychosocial impairment, or both, that adversely affects a child's educational performance. Traumatic brain injury applies to open or closed head injuries resulting in impairments in one or more areas, such as cognition; language; memory; attention; reasoning; abstract thinking; judgment; problem solving; sensory, perceptual, and motor abilities; psychosocial behavior; physical functions; information processing; and speech. Traumatic brain injury does not apply to brain injuries that are congenital or degenerative, or to brain injuries induced by birth trauma" [§300.8(c)(12)]. Students with traumatic brain injury have normal development until they sustain a severe head injury. As a result of this injury, they have a disability. Most head injuries are the result of an accident (frequently an automobile accident), but they may also occur as a result of physical abuse or intentional harm (e.g., being shot).

Traumatic brain injury will be diagnosed by a physician, who is usually a specialist such as a neurologist. The need of a student with brain injury for special education will be based first on a determination that the student's school performance falls outside the normal range and various attempts to remedy the educational problems have failed. Next, a school psychologist will likely administer a standardized achievement battery to verify that the student's achievement has been adversely affected and that the child needs specialized supports and interventions.

Speech or Language Impairment

A student with a **speech or language impairment** has "a communication disorder, such as stuttering, impaired articulation, a language impairment, or a voice impairment, that adversely affects a child's educational performance" [§300.8(c)(11)]. Many children will experience some developmental problems in their speech and language. For example, children frequently have difficulty with the *r* sound and say "wabbit" instead of "rabbit." Similarly, many children will use incorrect grammar, especially with internal plurals; for example, children may say, "My dog has four foots." Such difficulties are so common as to be considered a part of normal speech development. However, when such speech and language errors continue to occur beyond the age when most children have developed correct speech or language, there is cause for concern. Not all students who require intervention for speech or language problems are eligible for special education. A student may be eligible for speech or language services but not have a problem that adversely affects his or her school performance. Thus, for a student to be eligible for special education as a person with a speech or language impairment, that student must not only have a speech/language impairment but also need special education.

The identification of students with speech and language impairments proceeds along two separate paths. School personnel identify the educational disability in the same way that other educational disabilities are identified. When extra help from a teacher does not solve the problem, the student is referred to a child study team for intervention. If those interventions fail to remedy the achievement problem, the student is referred for multidisciplinary evaluation. A psychologist or educational diagnostician will likely administer a norm-referenced achievement test to verify the achievement problem. At the same time, speech and language specialists will use a variety of assessment procedures (norm-referenced tests, systematic observation, and criterion-referenced tests) to identify the speech and language disability. If the student has both need and disability, the student will be eligible for special education and related services.

Visual Impairment

A student with a **visual impairment** has "an impairment in vision that, even with correction, adversely affects a child's educational performance. The term includes both partial sight and blindness" [§300.8(c)(13)]. Students with severe visual impairments are usually identified by an ophthalmologist before they enter school. Many students who are partially sighted will be identified by routine vision screening that usually takes place in the primary grades; others will be identified when visual demands increase (e.g., when font size is reduced from the larger print used in beginning reading materials). Severe visual impairment is always presumed to adversely affect educational development, and students with this disability are presumed to need special education services and curricular adaptations (e.g., mobility training, instruction in braille, and talking books). A vision specialist usually assesses functional vision through systematic observation of a student's responses to various types of paper, print sizes, lighting conditions, and so forth.

Deafness and Hearing Impairment

Deafness is an impairment in hearing "that is so severe that the child is impaired in processing linguistic information through hearing, with or without amplification, and that adversely affects a child's educational performance" [§300.8(c)(3)]. A student with a **hearing impairment** has a permanent or fluctuating impairment "that adversely affects educational performance but that is not included under the definition of deafness."

Most students classified as deaf will be identified as such before they enter school. Deafness will be presumed to adversely affect a student's educational development, and students with this disability are presumed to require special education services and curricular adaptations. However, even severe hearing impairments may be difficult to identify in the first years of life, and students with milder hearing impairments may not be identified until school age. Referrals for undiagnosed hearing-impaired students may indicate expressive and receptive language problems, variable hearing performance, problems, and perhaps problems in peer relationships. Diagnosis of hearing impairment is usually made by audiologists, who identify the auditory disability, in conjunction with school personnel, who identify the educational disability.

Orthopedic Impairments

An **orthopedic impairment** is "a severe impairment that adversely affects a child's educational performance. The term includes impairments caused by a congenital anomaly, impairments caused by disease (such as poliomyelitis and bone tuberculosis), and impairments from other causes (such as cerebral palsy, amputations, and fractures or burns that cause contractures)" [§300.8(c)(8)].

Physical disabilities are generally identified prior to entering school. However, accidents and disease may impair a student who previously did not have a disability. Medical diagnosis establishes the presence of the condition. The severity of the condition may be established in part by medical opinion and in part by systematic observation of the particular student. For many students with physical disabilities, the ability to learn is not affected. These students may not require special education classes, but they will need accommodations and modifications to the curriculum—and perhaps the school building—that can be managed through a 504 Plan. For example, a student may require a personal care aide to help with positioning, braces, and catheterization; educational technology (e.g., a voice-activated computer); and transportation to and from school that can accommodate a wheelchair. When such adaptations and accommodations are insufficient to allow adequate school progress, special education is indicated. The specially designed instruction can include alternate assignments, alternative curricula, alternative testing procedures, and special instruction.

Other Health Impairments

Other health impairment "means having limited strength, vitality, or alertness, including a heightened alertness to environmental stimuli, that results in limited alertness with respect to the educational environment that (i) is due to chronic or acute health problems such as asthma, attention deficit disorder or attention deficit hyperactivity disorder, diabetes, epilepsy, a heart condition, hemophilia, lead poisoning, leukemia, nephritis, rheumatic fever, sickle cell anemia, and Tourette syndrome; and (ii) adversely affects a child's educational performance" [§300.8(c)(9)]. Diagnosis of health impairments is usually made by physicians, who identify the health problems, and school personnel, who identify the educational disability. For some students with other health impairments, the ability to learn is not affected. These students may not require special education classes, but they will need accommodations and modifications to the curriculum that can be managed through a 504 Plan. For example, a student may require nursing services to administer medication, times and places to rest during the day, and provisions for instruction in the home. When health impairments adversely affect educational progress even with the curricular adaptations and modifications, special education is indicated.

Deaf–Blindness

Deaf–blindness means "concomitant hearing and visual impairments, the combination of which causes such severe communication and other developmental and educational needs that they cannot be accommodated in special education programs solely for children with deafness or children with blindness" [§300.8(c)(2)].

Only a small number of students are deaf–blind, and their assessment is typically complex. Tests that compensate for loss of vision usually rely on auditory processes; tests that compensate for loss of hearing usually rely on visual processes. Psychological and educational evaluations of students who are both deaf and blind rely on observations as well as interviews of and ratings by individuals sufficiently familiar with the student to provide useful information.

Multiple Disabilities

Multiple disabilities "means concomitant impairments (such as intellectual disability–blindness or intellectual disability–orthopedic impairment), the combination of which causes such severe educational needs that they cannot be accommodated in special education programs solely for one of the impairments. The term does not include deaf–blindness" [§300.8(c)(7)].

Developmental Delay

Although not mandated by IDEA, states may use the category of **developmental delay** for children between the ages of 3 and 9 years who are "(1) experiencing developmental delays, as defined by the state and as measured by appropriate diagnostic instruments and procedures, in one or more of the following areas: physical development, cognitive development, communication development, social or emotional development, or adaptive development; and (2) … need special education and related services" [§300.8(b)]. Diagnosis of developmental delay is usually made by school personnel, who identify the educational disability, and other professionals (such as speech and language specialists, physicians, and psychologists), who identify the delays in the developmental domains.

Ruling Out Other Causes of Poor Achievement

The first sign that a student may have a learning disability is poor academic achievement. Yet, poor academic achievement is not specific to LD. Stated another way, students may demonstrate poor academic achievement for a variety of reasons. In fact, the most likely causes of poor academic achievement are not LD. Thus, those responsible for making the actual determination that a student has a learning disability must rule out these other potential causes for poor achievement. IDEA specifically forbids that the student's achievement problem be the result of a visual, hearing, or motor impairment; intellectual disability; emotional disturbance; or environmental, cultural, or economic disadvantage. The presence of various medical conditions may also be used to rule out a diagnosis of learning disability.

Verification of Achievement Difficulties

It is expected that all students will meet age or grade and local and state achievement standards; however, students with high IQs may fail to meet expectations when their performance is only average. Only students who fail to meet expected age- or grade-level academic standards can be considered for a diagnosis of learning disability. Meeting the criterion of below age- or grade-level academic achievement is a necessary criterion for learning disability. You may encounter systems that have used ability-achievement discrepancy to attempt to meet the eligibility criterion for LD and concluded that a child's advanced capability relative to only average achievement is a discrepancy indicating the child meets eligibility criteria for LD, but this is not a correct interpretation of IDEA criteria. In this case, the child has not met the criterion of below age- or grade-level academic performance, nor has the student demonstrated a need for special education to permit grade-level achievement. Academic difficulties must be verified by direct observation during classroom instruction. In addition, school personnel will likely perform a records review to ascertain the intensity and duration of the problems. Previous grades, teacher comments, and the results of standardized achievement tests (e.g., from Tier 1 screening and year-end accountability assessments) are useful. Finally, individual achievement tests may be administered by a school psychologist or learning specialist. The student may also be evaluated by a speech and language specialist who would look for manifestations of a disorder in producing or understanding language. This specialist may conduct an assessment of a student's spontaneous or elicited language during an interview or play situation; the specialist may administer a formal test.[2] There are no quantitative guidelines in the regulations to indicate a language disorder, but a child with a disability in language would be expected to earn scores that are substantially below average.

---

2. For example, the *Test of Written Language–Fourth Edition* or the *Test of Language Development–Primary, Fourth Edition*.

Documentation of Unsuccessful Attempts to Remediate

Before it can be assumed that a student has a learning disability, educators must demonstrate that the student has had the opportunity to learn—that the teacher has used effective and appropriate teaching methods and curricula. Normally, this means that there have been numerous, documented attempts to remediate the educational problems using at least Tier 2 (targeted) interventions and that these attempts have failed. Meeting this criterion requires repeated assessments in the face of known instructional intensifications that were conducted with strong integrity for a sufficient period of time to detect growth. The assessments should be sensitive to expected learning gains and administered weekly to permit an understanding of Response to Intervention (RTI).

Evidence of a Learning Disability

Either of two approaches can be used to infer that a student has a disorder in a basic psychological process—Response to Intervention or severe discrepancy. Either approach can be used singly or in combination with the other approach. Importantly, if a team elects to use a severe discrepancy approach to determine LD eligibility, they still must take the actions needed to rule out lack of adequate instruction as causing the poor performance. Thus, using Response to Intervention to determine LD eligibility can be more efficient.

Response to Intervention.[3] In this approach, students receive targeted (i.e., Tier 2) interventions. The academic problem is verified, alternative hypotheses about how to remediate the problem are generated, interventions are developed and applied, and assessment data are collected and interpreted. If a student fails to progress or if a student makes insufficient progress after several interventions, there is *prima facie* evidence of a learning disability. However, the rule-outs still apply. The student cannot have an intellectual disability, and so forth. Thus, in this approach, students are thought to have a learning disability when they fail to progress sufficiently after receiving intensive instruction using methods of proven effectiveness (that is, validated by objective, empirical research). We describe more about this approach later in this chapter.

Severe discrepancy. In this approach, students must exhibit a pattern of strengths and weaknesses in performance, achievement, or both, relative to age, state-approved grade-level standards or intellectual development [34 CFR §300.309(a)(2)]. In this approach, a psychologist typically looks for large differences between a student's measured intelligence (i.e., scores on a test of intelligence)[4] and measured achievement (i.e., scores on a standardized test of achievement). A significant difference between ability and achievement is taken as a demonstration of a learning disability when the previously

---

3. Chapter 7 ("Assessment in Multi-Tiered Systems of Support") deals extensively with Response to Intervention.

4. Scores from an intelligence test can also be used to rule out an intellectual disability.

enumerated criteria are present. Schools may also consider a pattern of strengths and weaknesses within a student's achievement (e.g., large differences between reading and mathematics scores on a standardized achievement test). An analysis of strengths and weaknesses is based on differences between scores. Such differences are almost always less reliable than the individual scores on which the differences are based. For example, the difference between reading and math achievement will almost always be less reliable than either the reading or the math achievement score. Difference scores are discussed in more detail in the reliability chapter.

Finally, psychologists may also administer tests to assess specific psychological processes such as visual perception (e.g., the *Developmental Test of Visual Perception*). Low scores may also be used to support a diagnosis of a learning disability.

21.1

PROGRESS MONITORING CHECK

The RTI Approach to Identifying Students With Learning Disabilities

When Congress passed the IDEA in 2004 and the U.S. Department of Education published regulations that accompany that law in 2006, school personnel were given permission to use Response to Intervention as an alternative approach to the identification of students with learning disabilities. Within RTI models, evidence-based instructional interventions are implemented over relatively long periods of time (usually for more than 8 to 12 weeks) and decisions are made about whether or not a student's rate of progress is indicative of responding or not responding to the intervention. Students are considered eligible for special education services if, after experiencing well-implemented evidence-based interventions that were selected based on their measured learning needs they continue to show inadequate progress. In addition to showing slow growth it must be demonstrated that the student is performing at a low level relative to their age-level or grade-level peers and that they do not show evidence of another disability condition (e.g., intellectual disability, emotional disturbance, or visual impairment). There is no federal guidance on how low is low and how slow is slow (Kovaleski et al., 2013).

Within RTI models there may be reliance on norm-referenced tests, though this typically is not the case. Rather, the assessment procedures used are those more closely aligned with the process of teaching and learning: curriculum-based measurement and computer-adaptive measures linked closely to classroom instruction and intervention.

The use of the RTI approach requires systematic monitoring of student progress over time, careful analysis of Rate of Improvement (ROI), and analysis of the gap between observed and expected performance over time. We discuss procedures for calculating ROI and for conducting a gap analysis in Chapter 7. Kovaleski et al. (2013) also provide a very nice description of the steps involved in calculating ROI and in conducting a gap analysis (pp. 61–77 of their book *The RTI Approach to Evaluating Learning Disabilities*). They identify the following steps involved in using an RTI approach to making decisions about eligibility for special education under the label learning disabled.

Step 1. Determine Present Level of Performance (PLOP). Universal screening measures typically are used to determine the student's current level of academic performance in specific content areas. Scores are expressed as standard scores for computer-adaptive tests or in units like words correct per minute for curriculum-based measures. The evaluation team must demonstrate that the student "does not achieve adequately for the child's age or to meet State-approved grade-level standards" across a variety of sources of data.

Step 2. Document Deficiency in the Student's Rate of Improvement (ROI). To accomplish this the team must do the following:

2.1 Calculate the Typical Rate of Improvement for students at that level. Publishers of some curriculum-based packages (like DIBELS Next or Easy CBM) and some computer-adaptive measures (like *Star Reading* and *Star Math*) maintain large databases of student performance that are used to develop norms on typical rates of growth for students at specific age and grade levels. These norms can be used to identify typical ROIs for students who are at the level of performance for the student assessed.

2.2 Set the Instructional Goal or Target. School personnel must decide what outcomes they want students to achieve. If they want students to maintain performance as is, then they set moderate goals. If they want to close the gap between low performance and average (age-level or grade-level) performance, they may set ambitious goals. Some publishers provide tools for goal setting. For example, Renaissance Learning, publisher of the Star Enterprise measures (*Star Reading*, *Star Math*, and *Star Early Literacy*) provides users with a Goal Setting Tool that can be used to set moderate, ambitious, or custom goals for student improvement.

2.3 Monitor Student Progress. Computer-adaptive tests or curriculum-based measures are administered periodically to ascertain the student's rate of improvement.

2.4 Conduct a Progress Monitoring ROI and Benchmark ROI Gap Analysis. In Chapter 7 (MTSS and RTI chapter) we described the procedures one uses to calculate ROI. One can also look up the relationship between the student's actual ROI and the expected ROI on publishers' websites (e.g., the websites for DIBELS Next and Renaissance Learning, publisher of the Star Enterprise measures).

The team can use this information to compute the magnitude of the gap between actual and expected performance, as well as an indication of the number of weeks it would take the student to reach his/her goal. Armed with this information the team can make a decision about whether there is a reasonable gap or significant gap between the student's ROI and the ROI for typical students. If the gap is considered significant or unreasonable, then the student may be declared eligible for special education services. The difficulty here is that there are no rules, guidelines, or published empirical criteria on how large the gap must be to consider the student eligible for special education services. As a "rule of thumb," educators operate under the general consideration that "a student would be sufficiently deficient in level of performance and sufficiently deficient in ROI such that the student would not attain acceptable performance in a reasonable amount of time" (Kovaleski et al., 2013, p. 150). And, of course, the two terms debated are "acceptable performance" and "reasonable amount of time." Generally speaking, educators do not expect students with SLD to catch up to grade level within a period of one year. Rather, they show that given the student's rate of improvement the student will not catch up to the target that is set for him or her in a selected period of time (e.g., 1 year, 2 years).

Hauerwas et al. (2013) conducted an analysis of state-level special education regulations, SLD criteria and guidance documents used to define responsiveness to intervention. They found that some states (Colorado, Connecticut, Pennsylvania, and Oregon as of 2013) provide best practice descriptions about RTI data collection and processes for determining LD eligibility. However, they report that there is no national consensus on how to use RTI data as part of SLD identification.

Step 3. Rule Out Other Disability Conditions. The evaluation team always must rule out other disability conditions like visual, hearing, or physical disability; emotional disturbance; intellectual disability; or autism. The team must also rule out that the student's poor academic performance and growth is due to cultural factors or environmental disadvantage or to limited English proficiency.

Step 4. Document that Low-Level Performance Is Not the Result of Lack of Instruction. The evaluation team must rule out the possibility that lack of instruction is the cause of the student's academic problems. In so doing, the team must demonstrate that the student has been receiving evidence-based core instruction in the general education curriculum and that the instruction has been delivered by a qualified teacher. In addition to this, the team should document the interventions that were implemented at Tiers 2 and 3 and the extent to which the student responded to those interventions.

Step 5. Determine that the Student Needs Special Education. Recall that we have pointed out on several occasions in this textbook that eligibility for special education requires that students meet the criteria for a federally identified disability condition, and need special education services to be successful in school. The previous steps above were focused on demonstrating that the student meets the criteria for learning disability. Determining the "need" for special education services is difficult. Typically such decisions are made based on the intensity of interventions the student needs. Kovaleski et al. (2013) cite Barnett et al. (2004) as providing the best definition of intervention intensity as "qualities of time, effort, or resources that make intervention support in typical environments difficult as intensity increases, establishing a clear role for specialized services" (p. 68). Special education services are those that require enhancements to management and planning, modifications to typical classroom routines, and types of intervention episodes, materials, and change agents not available in the general education classroom. Kovaleski et al. (2013) further describe distinctions of special education when they state that:

"Enhancements to management and planning in special education would include more frequent monitoring of student responding, more frequent progress monitoring, more explicit teacher prompting, and more frequent and detailed communication with parents and professionals. Modifications to typical classroom routines would involve different instructional tasks and assessments, increased assistance to students during instruction, additional practice opportunities, enhanced feedback to students about performance, and unique contingencies for meeting expectations. . . . providing special education presupposes that teaching staff are specially trained to deliver highly explicit instruction and make instructional adjustments based on students' responding" (p. 159)

Establishing Educational Need for Special Education

In addition to having one (or more) of the disabilities specified in IDEA, a student must experience a lack of academic success. This criterion is either implicit or explicit in the IDEA definitions of disabilities. Autism, hearing impairment, intellectual disability, and six other disabling conditions are defined as "adversely affecting a child's educational performance." Multiple disabilities (such as deaf–blindness) cause "severe educational needs." Learning disability results in an "imperfect ability" to learn basic academic skills.

Most students without obvious sensory or motor disabilities are presumed to not have disabilities when they enter school. However, during their education, it becomes clear to school personnel that these students have significant problems. They fail to behave appropriately or to meet state-approved grade-level standards in one or more core achievement areas when provided with appropriate instruction. In short, they demonstrate marked discrepancies from mainstream expectations or from the achievement and behavior of typical peers. The magnitude of the discrepancy necessary to consider a student for special education is not codified, and there are many opinions on this issue.

The presence of a discrepancy alone does not establish need, because there are many causes for a discrepancy. Thus, school personnel usually should engage in a number of remedial and compensatory activities designed to reduce or eliminate the discrepancy. Engaging in remedial efforts not only affords the student protection against misidentification (being falsely identified as having a disability), it is also a legal requirement and provides fruitful information for instructional planning and programming for the student whether that student is served in general or special education. As discussed in Chapter 20, "Using Assessment Information to Make Instructional Decisions," interventions initially may be designed and implemented by the classroom teacher. When the teacher's interventions are unsuccessful, the student is referred to the multi-tiered system of supports (MTSS) team that designs and may help implement further interventions. Need for special educational services for students is established when one of two conditions is met. As we noted in the discussion of RTI approaches in section 2, if a student fails to respond to validated and carefully implemented interventions, need for special education is indicated. Second, as we also noted, successful interventions may be too intensive or extensive for use in regular education. That is, the interventions needed to remediate the student's academic or behavioral deficits are so intrusive, labor-intensive, or specialized that a general education classroom teacher cannot implement them without the assistance of a special education teacher or without seriously detracting from the education of other students in the classroom.

Some students have such obvious sensory or motor problems that they are identified as having a disability before they enter school. From accumulated research and professional experience, educators know that students with certain disabilities (e.g., blindness, deafness, and severe intellectual disabilities) will not succeed in school without special education. Thus, educators (and relevant regulations) assume that the presence of a severe disability is sufficient to demonstrate the need for special educational services.

The Multidisciplinary Team

The determination that a student has a disability is made by a team of professionals called a multidisciplinary team (MDT). The team conducts a multidisciplinary evaluation (MDE) by collecting, assembling, and evaluating information to determine whether a student meets the conditions that define a disability as set forth in IDEA and state law.[5]

Composition of the MDT

IDEA requires that the team have members with the same qualifications as those who must serve on IEP teams and "other qualified professionals, as appropriate" (34 CFR §300.533). Thus, the team must include the student's parents (and the student, if appropriate), a general education teacher, a special education teacher, a representative

---

5. Note that there are two types of teams required under special education law, and the same people may or may not serve on the two types of teams: evaluation teams (usually called MDTs) and Individualized Education Program (IEP) teams (always called IEP teams). In addition, many schools have teacher teams (often called child study teams) that deal with student difficulties before a student is referred for evaluation.

of the school administration, and an individual who can interpret the instructional implications of evaluation results. If the student is suspected of having a learning disability, the team must also include "at least one person qualified to conduct individual diagnostic examinations of children, such as a school psychologist, speech-language pathologist, or remedial reading teacher" (34 CFR §300.540). In practice, school psychologists are usually members of most MDTs.

Responsibilities of the MDT

The team is responsible for gathering information and determining if a student has a disability. In theory, the decision-making process is straightforward. Members of the MDT organize existing student assessment data, determine what additional data are needed to determine eligibility, conduct additional needed assessments (e.g., sensory screenings), and organize and interpret data to determine whether he or she meets the criteria for a specific disability. Thus, the MDT must collect, at a minimum, information required by the definition of the disability being considered. Moreover, federal regulations (34 CFR §300.532) require that a student be "assessed in all areas related to the suspected disability, including, if appropriate, health, vision, hearing, social and emotional status, general intelligence, academic performance, communicative status, and motor abilities."

In reaching its decision about eligibility, the team must do two things. First, it must draw upon information from a variety of sources, including aptitude and achievement tests, parent input, information about response to evidence-based interventions, and teacher recommendations, as well as information about the child's physical condition, social or cultural background, and adaptive behavior. Second, it must ensure that information obtained from all of these sources is documented and considered [§300.306(c)].

The Process of Determining Eligibility

IDEA has established rules that MDTs must follow in determining whether a student is eligible for special education and related services. The first set of rules provides a variety of procedural safeguards intended to provide students and their parents the right to full and meaningful participation in the evaluation process.

Procedural Safeguards

The right to procedural safeguards have emerged over time in response to now almost unimaginable decisions made to certify children as having disabilities and provide them with special education without parent awareness or involvement. As a result, iterations of IDEA have evolved to provide important protections to children. Rather than hoops to jump through, these protections are designed to ensure that parents are aware of and involved in such important life decisions as where and how their children will be educated. As specified in §300.504, school districts and other public agencies must give parents a copy of the procedural safeguards relating to

- independent educational evaluation;
- prior written notice in the native language of the parent or other mode of communication used by the parent;
- parental consent;
- access to educational records;
- opportunity to present complaints to initiate due process hearings;
- the child's placement during pendency of due process proceedings;
- procedures for students who are subject to placement in an interim alternative educational setting;
- requirements for unilateral placement by parents of children in private schools at public expense;
- mediation;
- due process hearings, including requirements for disclosure of evaluation results and recommendations;
- state-level appeals (if applicable in that state);
- civil actions;
- attorneys' fees; and
- the state complaint procedures.

Valid Assessments

Rules established under IDEA require valid and meaningful assessments. School districts and other public agencies must ensure that students are assessed in all areas related to their suspected disabilities, including, if appropriate, health, vision, hearing, social and emotional status, general intelligence, academic performance, communicative status, and motor abilities. The evaluations must be sufficiently comprehensive to identify all of the child's special education and related services needs, whether or not they are commonly linked to the disability category in which the child has been classified.

School districts and other public agencies must ensure that the assessment includes a variety of techniques, including information provided by the parent, that provide relevant information about

- whether the student is a student with a disability; and
- the student's involvement and progress in the general curriculum.

The assessments must be conducted by trained and knowledgeable personnel in accordance with any instructions provided by the producer of the tests. If an assessment is not conducted under standard conditions, a description of the extent to which it varied from standard conditions must be provided in the evaluation report. As specified in §300.304(c), only tests or other evaluation materials may be used that are

- "not racially or culturally discriminatory";
- "administered in the child's native language or other mode of communication" (in addition, for students with limited English proficiency, districts and other public agencies must select and use materials and procedures that measure the extent to which the child has a disability and needs special education, rather than measuring the child's English language skills);
- "selected and administered so as best to ensure that if a test is administered to a child with impaired sensory, manual, or speaking skills, the test results accurately reflect the child's aptitude or achievement level or whatever other factors the test purports to measure, rather than reflecting the child's impaired sensory, manual, or speaking skills (unless those skills are the factors that the test purports to measure)";
- technically sound instruments that may assess the relative contribution of cognitive and behavioral factors, in addition to physical or developmental factors;
- "tailored to assess specific areas of educational need and not merely designed to provide a single general intelligence quotient"; and
- relevant in assisting persons determining the educational needs of the student.

Team Process

The final set of requirements set forth by IDEA concerns the process for determining a student's eligibility for special education and related services. The MDT team follows four steps as specified in §§300.305/306:

1. The team reviews existing evaluation data to determine if additional data are needed.
2. The team gathers any additional data that are needed, ensuring that information obtained from all sources is documented.
3. The team determines if the student is a child with a disability by considering information from a variety of sources (that is, academic screening, year-end accountability tests, if needed, additional achievement or aptitude tests, parent input, teacher recommendations, detailed information about interventions selection, implementation, and progress monitoring data showing the child's response to the intervention, physical condition, social or cultural background, and adaptive behavior) and comparing this information to the state and federal standards for the suspected disability.
4. The team prepares an evaluation report.

In practice, deciding whether a student is entitled to special education can be complex. Sometimes, the problems a student is experiencing can suggest a specific disability to team members. For example, having problems maintaining attention, being fidgety, and being disorganized may suggest the possibility of attention deficit disorder; persistent and major difficulties learning letter–sound correspondences despite many interventions may suggest a learning disability. MDTs should do more than simply confirm a disability. MDTs should adopt a point of view that is, in part, disconfirmatory—a point of view that seeks to disprove the working hypothesis.

Many behaviors are indicative of specific disabilities. For example, stereotypic hand flapping is associated with autism, intellectual disabilities, and some emotional disturbances. Assessors must be open to alternative explanations for the behavior and, when appropriate, collect information that will allow them to reject a working hypothesis of a particular disability. For example, if Tom was referred for inconsistent performance in expressive language, even though his other skills—especially math and science—were average, an MDT might suspect that he could have a learning disability. What would it take to reject the hypothesis that he has such a disability? He would not be considered to have a learning disability if it could be shown that his problem was caused by a sensorineural hearing loss, if his problem arose because his primary language is a dialect of English, if he suffered from recurrent bouts of otitis media (middle-ear infections), and so forth. Therefore, the MDT would have to consider other possible causes of his behavior. Moreover, when there is evidence that something other than the hypothesized disability is the cause of the educational problems, the MDT would need to collect additional data that would allow it to evaluate these other explanations. Thus, MDT evaluations frequently (and correctly) go beyond the information required by the entitlement criteria to rule out other possible disabling conditions or to arrive at a different diagnosis.

Finally, in attempting to establish that a student should be classified with a disability, we often must choose among competing procedures and tests. However, as indicated in Chapter 15, individual tests of intelligence are not interchangeable. They differ significantly in the behaviors they sample and in the adequacy of their norms and reliability and slightly in their standard deviations. A person with a low IQ, but one that is barely withing the normal range may earn an IQ of less than 70 on one or two tests of intelligence but earn scores greater than 70 on two others. Thus, if we had to assess such a student, we could be caught in a dilemma of conflicting information.

The routes around and through the eligibility process are easier to state than to accomplish. First, we should choose (and accord priority to) objective, technically adequate (reliable and well normed) procedures that have demonstrated validity for the particular purpose of classification. Second, we must consider the specific validity. For example, we must consider the culture in which the student grew up and how that culture interacts with the content of the test. A test's technical manuals may contain information about the wisdom of using the test with individuals of various cultures, or the research literature may have information for the particular cultural group to which a student belongs. Often, theory can guide us in the absence of research. Sometimes it is just not possible to test validly, and we must also recognize that fact.

Problems in Determining Special Education Eligibility

Four problems with the criteria used to determine eligibility for special services are especially noteworthy. First, we find the prevalent (but mistaken) belief that special educational services are for students who could benefit from them. Thus, in many circles, educational need is believed to be sufficient for entitlement. Clearly, this belief is contradicted by pertinent law, regulations, and litigation. Students must need the services *and* meet the criteria for a specific disability. Nonetheless, some educators have such strong humanitarian beliefs that when they see students with problems, they want to get those students the services that they believe are needed. Too often, the regulations may be bent so that students fit entitlement criteria.

Second, the definitions that appear in state and federal regulations are frequently very imprecise. The imprecision of federal regulations creates variability in definitional criteria and regulations among states, and the imprecision of state regulations creates variability in application of definitional criteria and regulations among districts within states. Thus, students who are eligible in one state or district may not be eligible in other states or districts. For example, some states and school districts may define a learning disability as a severe discrepancy between measured intellectual ability and actual school achievement. However, there is no consensus about the meaning of "severe discrepancy"; certainly, there is no widely accepted mathematical formula to ascertain severe discrepancy. To some extent, discrepancies between achievement and intelligence are determined by the specific tests used. Thus, one test battery might produce a significant discrepancy, whereas another battery would not produce such a discrepancy for the same student. Other states and school districts may define a learning disability by an inadequate Response to Intervention. Yet, what constitutes an inadequate response can be ambiguous and the validity of the decision depends upon a series of coordinated and correct actions (screening, identification, intervention intensification, progress monitoring, and decision making).

Third, the definitions treat disabilities as though they were discrete categories. However, most diagnosticians are hard-pressed to distinguish between primary and secondary intellectual disability or between primary and secondary emotional disturbance. Also, for example, distinctions between individuals with autism and individuals with severe intellectual disabilities and autistic-like behaviors are practically impossible to make with any certainty.

Fourth, parents may often prefer the label associated with one disability (e.g., autism or learning disability) over the label associated with another (e.g., intellectual disability). Because of the procedural safeguards afforded to students with special needs and their parents, school districts may become embroiled in lengthy and unnecessarily adversarial hearings in which each side has an expert testifying that a particular label is correct even though those labels are contradictory and sometimes mutually exclusive. School personnel find themselves in a no-win situation because the definitions and their operationalizations are so imprecise. As a result, school districts sometimes give parents the label they want rather than what educators, in their best professional judgments, believe to be correct. Districts may be reluctant to risk litigation because parents can frequently find an expert to contradict the district staff members. In some states, special educational services are non-categorical. In these states, a label qualifies a student for special education but does not determine the nature of the special education; that is determined by the individual student's needs, not label, and students with different labels are grouped together for instructional purposes.

21.2
PROGRESS
MONITORING
CHECK

Ensuring Fairness in Making Eligibility Decisions

Schools offer special education services in the belief that students who receive the services are those with disability conditions who need the services in order to benefit from their education. To the extent that students are erroneously identified as having disabilities then the process of declaring them eligible for services harms them. It runs the risk of assigning them to a setting in which they do not belong and to inferior educational services, depriving them of services in general educational settings. Similarly, some students with disabilities do not need special education services in order to profit from education. They are most fairly served in general education settings. All of this is to say that we want to reserve special education services for students who indeed have disabilities and who need them.

Accuracy in assessment, test administration and interpretation, and decision making are critical in making eligibility decisions. All of the requirements of law come together in affecting such decisions: requirements like assessing students in their native language or mode of communication, making certain tests are technically adequate, that norms groups are appropriate, and so forth. And, remember that we are also talking about making sure that students who are eligible for special education services actually are able to receive those services. That they are not overlooked and missed through the same inaccurate and invalid procedures that might overidentify other students for services. It is all about identifying the right students for the right kinds of services with as much accuracy as possible so that all students can receive their legal right to free and appropriate public education.

Write your answers to each of the following questions and then compare your responses to the text.

1. List and define each disability recognized by IDEA.
2. How is the need for special education established?
3. What are the responsibilities of the MDT?
4. What procedural safeguards are guaranteed by IDEA?

1. State three important issues encountered in making eligibility decisions.
2. Distinguish between RTI and discrepancy-based approaches to identification of learning disabilities.
3. What needs to be ruled out in identifying a student as learning disabled?

CHAPTER 22

Using Assessment Information to Make Accountability Decisions

LEARNING OBJECTIVES

1. Know the legal requirements for state and school district assessment and accountability systems specified in federal laws.
2. Understand the two different types of accountability.
3. Define the important terms associated with assessment for the purpose of making accountability decisions.
4. Understand the role that standards play in accountability systems.
5. Understand the purpose of the alternate assessment.
6. Know the important considerations for making decisions about how students participate in accountability systems.
7. Understand important considerations for interpreting assessment information from accountability testing.

Educators who teach students with disabilities or related services personnel who are responsible for the educational programs of students with disabilities need to think about how they will account for the results of the education those students receive. They also need to think broadly about the extent to which schools are producing the results we want them to produce. A special education teacher is not only responsible for teaching children in special education. A special education teacher is a valuable member of the school's instructional team and can help guide the general program of instruction to produce better growth for all learners, if the special education teacher understands how to use assessment data to drive instruction. We need to always be thinking about the extent to which individual students are meeting the goals, standards or outcomes that their schools have set for them, as well as thinking about how we should assess progress toward those goals or standards. Most importantly, we need to think about how individual students with disabilities will participate in state and district assessment and accountability systems. Consider the case of Rocky.

Rocky is a third-grade student diagnosed with autism. He receives instruction in the general education setting for most of his day, although he needs a teacher assistant to assist with implementation of his comprehensive behavior plan. This plan involves providing him with a variety of cues and reminders about the daily classroom schedule and how he is expected to behave during various activities. He has a very difficult time behaving appropriately when there are changes in the classroom schedule; in such cases, he often becomes very anxious, sometimes throws tantrums, and rarely completes his work.

This is the first year that Rocky is expected to complete the statewide assessment used for accountability purposes, and his Individualized Education Program (IEP) team must determine how he can best participate. At first, Rocky's parents are very concerned that he will have an anxious reaction to testing, and they do not want him to participate. His general education teacher is also fearful that he will not be able to focus and complete the test.

Rocky's school district has been warned by the state that it needs to increase its rates of participation of students with disabilities in the statewide assessment; in the past, many students with disabilities were excluded from statewide testing. Rocky's school is under considerable pressure to show that it is including all students, particularly those with disabilities, in the accountability program. At the meeting, the administrator, special educator, and school psychologist explain how important it is for Rocky to participate so the education that he, and students like him, receive can be evaluated to help determine how resources will be allocated throughout the district. They also point out how he is working toward all the same grade-level achievement standards as other students, and that his participation may help them determine what he can and cannot do. They explain the variety of ways in which Rocky can be accommodated during testing. For instance, they can continue to have the teacher assistant implement his behavior management plan. They can role-play in the days prior to the test what the test will be like. Also, they can develop a picture schedule that is similar to the one he uses in the classroom to go along with the testing schedule.

After presenting the underlying rationale for having Rocky participate, as well as the ways in which he could be accommodated during testing, the team agrees that it is appropriate to have Rocky attempt the statewide assessment toward grade-level achievement standards. His teacher assistant is provided specific training on how she can and cannot assist Rocky during testing to ensure that his results are as accurate as possible.

The day of the test is considerably draining for Rocky and his teacher assistant, but Rocky manages to complete the test. Although his total score ends up falling below the proficiency standard, and his teachers question whether it is an optimal measure of his skills and knowledge, his teachers and parents are impressed with the fact that he did not score in the lowest proficiency category. In fact, Rocky was able to correctly answer many of the items on the test; he was able to demonstrate some of what he knew when provided appropriate accommodations during testing.

In this chapter, we examine the collection and use of assessment information for the purpose of making decisions about how students should participate in school, district, and state accountability systems.

A powerful idea dominates policy discussions about schools: the notion that "students should be held to high, common standards for academic performance and that schools and the people who work in them should be held accountable for ensuring that students—all students—are able to meet those standards" (Elmore, 2002, p. 3). It has not always been that way. Until the early to mid-1990s, school personnel focused on the *process* of providing services to students. They provided evidence that they were teaching students, and often evidence that they were teaching specific types of students (e.g., Title I, intellectually disabled, deaf, or disadvantaged students). When administrators were asked about special education students or services, typically they described the numbers and kinds of students who were tested or taught, the settings in which they were taught, or the numbers of special education teachers who tested and taught them (e.g., "We have 2,321 students with disabilities in our district; 1,620 are educated in general education classes with special education supports, and the remainder are in resource rooms, self-contained classes and out-of-school settings; the students are served by 118 special education teachers and 19 related services personnel"). Few administrators could provide evidence for the results or outcomes of the services being provided, in fact, such data really were not available. Since the early 1990s, there has been a dramatic shift in focus from serving students with disabilities to measuring the results of the services provided.

Much of the impetus for this shift to a focus on results was the publication of *A Nation at Risk: The Imperative for Educational Reform* (National Commission on Excellence in Education, 1983). In this document, the then secretary of education revealed the low status of U.S. schoolchildren relative to their counterparts in other nations and reported that "the educational foundations of our society are presently being eroded by a rising tide of mediocrity that threatens our very future as a nation and a people" (p. 5). In this report, the secretary argued that the nation was at risk because mediocrity, not excellence, was the norm in education. Recommendations included more time for learning; better textbooks and other materials; more homework; higher expectations; stricter attendance policies; and improved standards, salaries, rewards, and incentives for teachers. The entire nation began to focus on raising educational standards, measuring performance, and achieving results. Policymakers and bureaucrats, who had been spending a great deal of money to fund special education, began demanding evidence of its effectiveness. In essence, they employed the old saying, "The proof of the pudding is in the eating," arguing that it matters little what you do if it does not produce what you want.

In 1994, the Clinton administration specified a set of national education goals. Called "Goals 2000," these were a list of goals that students should achieve by the year 2000. Additional requirements for large-scale assessment and accountability systems designed to measure the performance and progress of all students toward high standards were included in the general and special education legislation that followed (i.e., No Child Left Behind [NCLB] Act of 2001 and the 1997 and 2004 reauthorizations of the Individuals With Disabilities Education Act) and represented a continued emphasis on promoting high achievement for all students. The tenor of the legislation was that instruction should produce learning and learning could be measured in incremental gains annually. Further, the commitment that all children could grow and attain basic proficiencies was a fundamental shift in U.S. education and therefore educational investments could be examined in light of the cost to produce benefit was exciting new territory. The status of related legislation as we write this chapter is provided in the following section; however, you are encouraged to consult the web for more recent updates.

Legal Requirements

During the 1990s, state educational agencies put forth great efforts in the development of educational standards and large-scale assessment programs to measure student progress toward those standards. However, the extent to which students with disabilities were included in those efforts was minimal. The 1997 reauthorization of the Individuals With Disabilities Education Act (IDEA) included provisions specifying that students with disabilities should participate in states' assessment systems, and that statewide assessment program reports would include information on the extent to which *all* students, including students with disabilities, met state-specified standards. Recognizing that some students with disabilities had unique assessment needs, and that the regular assessment programs might not allow for appropriate measurement of their achievement toward state standards, IDEA 1997 introduced the requirement for IEP teams to determine which accommodations (if any) were needed for individual students to effectively participate in the statewide assessment program. It also required the development of alternate assessments for those students who could not effectively participate in the regular assessment even with accommodations. The 2004 reauthorization of IDEA contains those same requirements.

NCLB included the requirement that states have assessment and accountability systems, and report annually on the performance and progress of all students in reading, math, and science. In 2003, the U.S. Department of Education issued a set of guidelines for alternate assessments that included the concept of alternate achievement standards. The law requires that school systems consider not only how their students are doing as a whole, but also how particular groups of students are doing, with a focus on the following groups: economically disadvantaged, students with limited English proficiency, students receiving special education services, students from major racial/ethnic groups. To be considered successful, schools must succeed with all students. States, school districts, and individual schools are required by law to measure the performance and progress of all students. Schools that don't make adequate yearly progress are subjected to certain sanctions (see the Types of Accountability sections in this chapter for more information on accountability requirements). School personnel need to know how assessment information is used by state education agency personnel to make accountability decisions.

Given the impact of federal legislation on statewide assessment and accountability systems, we anticipate that many things that we write about in this chapter will change by the time it goes to print. Accountability became a cornerstone of education between 1997 and 2004. In the intervening decades, we have seen a softening of some of the requirements initially set forth with great aspiration by NCLB. Years of national data have not produced the results that early accountability advocates hoped for; however, the underlying philosophy that educational investments should produce discernible improvements and basic proficiencies for all students have endured and have led to newer initiatives like the Science of Reading. Thus, we certainly do not expect accountability to go away; in fact, most believe that legislative changes will have an even greater emphasis on holding schools accountable for the achievement of all students and we believe that this expectation creates a healthy tension in systems to always seek to bring benefit to the children we serve. You can find more information about recent legislative changes related to accountability systems and related assessment information by tracking information at the websites for the National Center on Educational Outcomes and the National Center for Research on Evaluation, Standards and Student Testing. Information on the progress of the major assessment consortia can be found at websites for Smarter Balanced Assessment Consortium (SBAC; smarterbalanced.org), Partnership for Assessment of Readiness for College and Careers (PARCC: osse.dc.gov/parcc), Dynamic Learning Maps (DLM; dynamiclearningmaps.org), and National Center and State Collaborative (NCSC; www.ncscpartners.org). The website for the Council of Chief State School Officers (CCSSO; ccsso.org) also regularly contains information on state assessment updates.

Types of Accountability

Accountability systems hold schools responsible for helping all students reach challenging standards, and they provide rewards to schools that reach those standards and sanctions to schools that do not. Today, the consequences of accountability systems are becoming more significant and are often referred to as "high stakes." As we write this chapter, Every Student Succeeds Act (ESSA; a subsequent iteration of NCLB) accountability requirements are in effect, which require state educational agencies to have an accountability system that includes certain key components. However, states may choose to add additional features to their accountability system. Although all states include system accountability, some additionally include accountability for students.

System accountability is accountability designed to improve educational programs and is the focus of federal education reform efforts. ESSA requires that states develop adequate yearly progress (AYP) targets for schools that are based primarily on student progress as measured by statewide assessment programs, assessment participation rates, and student attendance/graduation rates. Schools that do not make AYP in consecutive years experience the following:

- After 2 years of not making AYP, the school must allow students to attend a higher performing school in the district.
- After 3 years of not making AYP, the school must provide supplemental supports to low-achieving disadvantaged students.
- After 4 years of not making AYP, the school must take corrective action that may include replacing school staff or restructuring the organizational structure of the school.
- After 6 years of not making AYP, the school must develop and implement an alternative governance plan.

All states are expected to publicly report on the performance of their students and school systems. States may additionally decide to incorporate additional school rewards and sanctions for schools based on student performance. Among the sanctions that states commonly use are assigning negative labels to schools, removing staff, and firing principals. Rewards include assigning positive labels to schools and giving extra funding to schools or cash awards to staff.

Student accountability is accountability designed to motivate students to do their best. Nothing in NCLB requires that states attach rewards or sanctions to individual student performance; however, some states have chosen to do so. The most common high-stakes use of assessment evidence for individual students is to determine whether a student receives a standard high school diploma or some other type of document. Another type of student accountability, that has appeared is the use of test scores to determine whether a student will move from one grade to another.

The standards-based assessment and accountability movements and the federal laws that accompany them have brought a new assessment vocabulary that includes terms such as *alternate achievement standards, adequate yearly progress,* and *schools in need of improvement.* Some of these terms are used in many different ways in the professional and popular literature. In fact, the multiple uses of the terms cause confusion. The National Council on Measurement in Education publishes a comprehensive Glossary of Measurement Terms that can be accessed at ncme.org/resource/glossary. We think readers will find that resource helpful in identifying the definitions of measurement terms with which they are unfamiliar.

Measuring Whether Students Meet Standards

Assessments completed for outcomes and accountability purposes involve measuring the extent to which students are learning what we want them to learn, or the extent to which school systems are accomplishing what we want them to accomplish. To do this, state education agency personnel must specify the standards that schools and students will work toward. They typically do so by specifying a set of **content standards**, which are statements of the subject-specific knowledge and skills that schools are expected to teach students, indicating what students should know and be able to do. States are required by law to specify academic content standards in reading, math, and science. For quite some time, each state educational agency was expected to develop its own academic content and achievement standards. As a result, standards, and the focus of grade-level instruction, varied across states. Alicia might be taught multiplication in third grade in Michigan, while her cousin Dennis, who lives in Missouri, might not be taught multiplication until fourth grade. This could cause substantial problems for students who move from state to state and consequently miss out on important instruction. Furthermore, statewide assessments designed to hold schools and students accountable for achieving state standards also varied, making comparisons across states inappropriate. Arizona might report having 76% of students proficient on the statewide assessment, and Alaska might report 90% of students proficient. Does this mean Alaskans have higher achievement? Not necessarily—the differences in content and achievement standards (and consequent difference in statewide assessments) might be such that one test is much more difficult than another. Given these and related concerns, the Council of Chief State School Officers (CCSSO) and the National Governors Association Center for Best Practices (NGA Center) led efforts in the development and implementation of Common Core standards through the Common Core State Standards Initiative. Forty-eight states were involved in the development of these standards in math and English/language arts, and 40 states adopted the final standards that were released in June of 2010. In addition, two consortia were formed and were involved in developing assessments to measure progress toward the Common Core standards: the PARCC Race to the Top Assessment Consortium and the Smarter Balanced Assessment Consortium.

The Common Core State Standards (CCSS) included quantifiable benchmarks in English language arts and math at each grade level from kindergarten through high school. The language arts standards mandated the teaching of reading, writing, speaking and listening, language and media and technology, and keyboarding. States could also choose cursive writing as a sixth standard. Math standards mandated the teaching of eight specific principles and specific skill competencies by each grade level. Common Core standards were widely misunderstood in popular media and denigrated by some on the basis that they prescribed particular methods of teaching, which they patently did not and still do not. Rather, they specify skill-based outcomes by certain grade levels as prioritized instructional content targets. For example, Common Core specifies that by third grade, children will multiply fluently with factors to 10. Over time states began rejecting Common Core in political discussions, debates, and decisions so that by the year 2000 we were back to a situation in which states had their own standards with some consortia of states having common standards and common assessments. Fortunately, many states had already updated their standards to create a de facto alignment with Common Core standards and so the result today is more uniformity in learning expectations than existed before Common Core. We recommend teachers make themselves familiar with Common Core standards at your grade level along with the standards published by your state. Common Core standards for math can be located here: corestandards.org/Math/. Common Core standards for English language arts can be located here: corestandards.org/ELA-Literacy/.

For students with disabilities to meet high academic standards and to fully demonstrate their conceptual and procedural knowledge and skills in mathematics, reading, writing, speaking and listening (English language arts), their instruction must incorporate supports and accommodations, including:

- Supports and related services designed to meet the unique needs of these students and to enable their access to the general education curriculum (IDEA 34 CFR §300.34, 2004).
- An IEP that includes annual goals aligned with and chosen to facilitate their attainment of grade-level academic standards.
- Teachers and specialized instructional support personnel who are prepared and qualified to deliver high-quality, evidence-based, individualized instruction and support services.

To participate with success in the general curriculum, students with disabilities, as appropriate, may be provided additional supports and services, such as instructional supports for learning—based on the principles of Universal Design for Learning (UDL)—which foster student engagement by presenting information in multiple ways and allowing for diverse avenues of action and expression.

Many states specify academic content standards in other areas. States must also specify **achievement standards** (sometimes called **performance standards**), which are statements of the levels at which or the proficiency with which students will show that they have mastered the academic content standards. Academic achievement standards use language drawn directly from law, and they have the force of law. States are required to define at least three levels of proficiency (usually called basic, proficient, and advanced). Some states specify more than three levels of proficiency (e.g., they may choose to indicate that a student's level of performance is below basic). The law requires that all students be assessed related to the state content and achievement standards. The state must provide for students with disabilities the reasonable accommodations necessary to measure their academic achievement relative to state academic content and state student academic achievement standards. It is important to know that all students, including students with disabilities, must have access to the same content standards.

The other kind of standards that apply specifically to students with disabilities are alternate achievement standards. Although most students with disabilities are expected to be instructed and assessed according to the grade-level achievement standards, it can be determined that some will work toward alternate achievement standards. **Alternate achievement standards** are expectations for performance that differ in complexity from grade-level achievement standards, but they are linked to those general education standards. States are permitted to define alternate achievement standards to evaluate the achievement of students with the most significant cognitive disabilities.

Standards-based assessment is characterized by specifying what all students can be expected to learn and then expecting that time will vary but that all will achieve the standards. States are required to use assessments of student proficiency relative to academic content standards. The following are reasons why school personnel would want to assess student performance and progress relative to standards:

- To ascertain the extent to which individual students are meeting state standards— that is, accomplishing what it is that society wants them to accomplish
- To identify student strengths and weaknesses for instructional planning
- To allocate supports and resources
- To ascertain the extent to which specific schools within states are providing the kinds of educational opportunities and experiences that enable their students to achieve state-specified standards
- To provide data on student or school performance that can be helpful in making instructional policy decisions (curricula or instructional methodologies to use)
- To decide who should receive a diploma as indicated by performance on tests that measure whether standards are met
- To inform the public on the performance of schools or school districts
- To know the extent to which specific subgroups of students are meeting specified standards

22.1
PROGRESS
MONITORING
CHECK

Alternate Assessment

Regardless of where students receive instruction, all students with disabilities should have access to, participate in, and make progress in the general curriculum. Thus, all students with disabilities must be included in state assessment systems and in state reporting of AYP toward meeting the state's standards. We have noted that states must specify academic content standards and academic achievement standards, and they must have assessments aligned to those standards. To address the needs of students with significant disabilities, states may choose to develop alternate achievement standards that are based on the expectations for all students.

States must include all students in their assessment and accountability systems. However, not all students can participate in the general state assessments, even with assessment accommodations designed to compensate for their specific needs. IDEA 1997 included a provision that by the year 2000 states would have in place alternate assessments intended for use with those students who evidenced severe cognitive impairments. In August 2002, the U.S. secretary of education proposed a regulation to allow states to develop and use alternate achievement standards for students with the most significant cognitive disabilities for the purpose of determining the AYP of states, local education agencies, and schools. In August 2003, the secretary specified that the number of students considered proficient using alternate assessments toward alternate achievement standards could not exceed 1% of all students.

An **alternate assessment** is defined in the NCLB federal regulations (NCLB Regulations, 2003) as "an assessment designed for the small number of students with disabilities who are unable to participate in the regular state assessment, even with appropriate accommodations." It is further indicated that "an alternate assessment may include materials collected under several circumstances, including (1) teacher observation of the student, (2) samples of student work produced during regular classroom instruction that demonstrate mastery of specific instructional strategies . . . or (3) standardized performance tasks produced in an 'on demand' setting, such as completion of an assigned task on test day" (p. 68699). The assessments must yield results separately in both reading/language arts and mathematics, and they must be designed and implemented in a manner that supports use of the results as an indicator of AYP.

Alternate assessments are not simply compilations of student work, sometimes referred to as box or folder stuffing. Rather, they must have a clearly defined structure, specific participation guidelines, and clearly defined scoring criteria and procedures; must meet requirements for technical adequacy; and must have a reporting format that clearly communicates student performance in terms of the academic achievement standards specified by the state. They must meet the same standards for technical adequacy as does the general assessment. It has been a struggle for some states to satisfy this requirement. Alternate assessments may be needed for students with a broad array of disabling conditions, so a state may use more than one alternate assessment.

Alternate assessments can be designed to measure student performance toward grade-level standards or alternate achievement standards. Recall that an alternate achievement standard is an expectation of performance that differs in complexity from a grade-level standard. For example, the Massachusetts Curriculum Frameworks include the following content standard: "Students will identify, analyze, and apply knowledge of the purpose, structure, and elements of nonfiction or informational materials and provide evidence from the text to support their understanding." A less complex demonstration of this standard is "to gain information from signs, symbols, and pictures in the environment"; a more complex demonstration is to "gain information from captions, titles, and table of contents in an informational text" (Massachusetts Department of Education, 2001).

Alternate Assessments Based on Alternate Achievement Standards

The alternate assessment based on alternate achievement standards (AA-AAS) is intended to be used with students with significant cognitive disabilities as determined by each state's eligibility criteria.

National data on who participates in AA-AAS show that most participating students are those with the most significant cognitive disabilities, primarily those with intellectual disabilities, autism, and multiple disabilities. This group includes students who are also English learners (ELs). ELs with disabilities who participate in an AA-AAS, may also take an English language proficiency (ELP) alternate assessment.

Sometimes referred to as the 1% assessment, the 1% now refers to a state-level cap of 1% of all tested students who may participate in this assessment. This cap is meant to avoid inappropriate inclusion of students with disabilities in an alternate assessment. Previously (under No Child Left Behind) the 1% meant that no more than 1% of the total population of tested students could count as proficient for accountability using an AA-AAS.

The achievement of grade-level content by students with significant cognitive disabilities is very different from their general education classroom peers, but the evidence of their work is compelling. Given the right kinds of supports, these students, including ELs with significant cognitive disabilities, are able to learn academic content with reduced complexity, breadth, and depth clearly linked to the same grade-level content as their peers. Researchers and practitioners are working side-by-side to capture the nature of the linkages to the grade-level content in both instruction and in assessment.

Making Participation Decisions for Individual Students

All students, including all students with disabilities, need to be included in accountability systems. Federal law requires that states and districts report annually on the performance and progress of *all* students, including students with disabilities. Teachers, related services personnel, and IEP teams need to make decisions about how individual students will participate. Students with disabilities can participate either by regular assessment, regular assessment with accommodations, or alternate assessment. It is up to the IEP team to decide how to include each student. In making these decisions, the team should answer each of the following questions:

> *What standards is the student working toward?* If the student is working toward the regular content and achievement standards, then he or she should participate in the regular assessment. If the student is working toward alternate achievement standards, then he or she should participate in the alternate assessment.
>
> *Are there specific characteristics of the individual student and/or of the test that may represent barriers to optimal measurement of the targeted skills/knowledge?* The student may have

a specific disability that is such that low test performance would be a result of the disability rather than the student's actual achievement on the skills targeted for measurement. For example, if the student is visually impaired and the reading comprehension test requires reading of printed material, a low score on the printed test may indeed be due to a visual impairment rather than low reading comprehension skills. If such characteristics are present, an accommodation should be considered. For example, if the student is instructed in braille, a braille version of the test may be necessary and appropriate. States typically provide lists of accommodations that may be provided and considered standard for the accountability test, as well as guidelines for making accommodation decisions. In some cases, the list the state provides is not all inclusive, and it is possible to request permission to use other unique accommodations that are deemed necessary for individual students.

Does the student receive accommodations during instruction? Assessment accommodations should be provided only if and when students have had exposure to and experience with those accommodations prior to testing. The accommodation should not be a new experience used for the first time during assessment.

School personnel should always monitor the effects of provision of an accommodation to ensure that it does not adversely affect student performance. And parents (and to the extent possible, students themselves) should be involved in making decisions about the kind of assessment in which the student participates and the accommodations provided.

Understanding Assessment Information Used to Make Accountability Decisions

As a result of accountability system implementation, student assessment data have become much more readily available to the public. Although this public reporting is intended to promote better student instruction and learning, it is important that those who have access to the data know how to appropriately interpret the information. Without these skills, poor judgments and decisions may be made that are harmful to students. For instance, it is important for consumers of accountability information to understand that most tests used for accountability purposes are intended to measure performance of an entire group of students, and that the tests do not necessarily provide reliable data on the skills of individual students. Without this knowledge, consumers may make unwarranted judgments and decisions about individual students based on their test scores.

In addition, it is important for people to recognize that not all students need to be tested in the same way; it is often important for students to be tested using different formats. Some students have special characteristics that make it difficult for them to demonstrate their knowledge on content standards in a traditional paper-and-pencil format. These students may need accommodations to demonstrate their true knowledge. What is most important is that students' knowledge and skill toward the identified achievement standards are measured. Those with assessment expertise can help determine

PROGRESS
MONITORING
CHECK

what accommodations or alternate assessments might be necessary for students to best demonstrate their skills and knowledge.

Write your answers to each of the following questions and then compare your responses to the text.

1. What legal requirements for state and school district assessment and accountability systems are specified in IDEA 2004 and ESSA?
2. What is the difference between system and student accountability?
3. Name and define five important terms used to describe accountability systems.
4. What is the difference between content and achievement standards? Why was there a movement toward the development of Common Core state standards? Why then was the movement rejected?

1. What is an alternate assessment, who is it intended for, and why is it important?
2. What are some important considerations in making participation decisions for students with disabilities?
3. State two important considerations in understanding assessment information that is used for making accountability decisions.

CHAPTER 23

Principles and Practices for Collaborative Teams

LEARNING OBJECTIVES

1. Understand the characteristics and foundations of effective teams.
2. Understand the importance of objectivity, confidentiality, and self-evaluation for effective teaming.
3. Know the types of collaborative teams that are commonly formed in special education and inclusive school settings.
4. Know strategies for effectively including parents, guardians, and students into the collaborative teaming process.

Every school has its own policies and practices that are contextually unique, but there are many facets of the modern education workplace that are common. One of the defining features of working within a multi-tiered systems of support (MTSS) school is that there are collaborative teams that keep the system running smoothly. There are groups of educators that meet regularly to make decisions about everything from the bell schedule to the schoolwide behavioral expectations to aligning available interventions to student needs. Some of these teams are made up of all general education teachers from one grade level, other teams include administrators and a mix of teachers and specialists, while other teams include important stakeholders such as parents and community leaders. Special education teachers, school psychologists, and other specialists are most commonly found on teams that are using data to plan and design instructional interventions and identify appropriate educational placement.

In this chapter, we provide an overview of the many different teams that may be formed to examine assessment data and suggestions for making appropriate team decisions and we'll focus specifically on teams charged with supporting students and teachers in special education and inclusive settings. We offer guidelines for communicating assessment information in both oral and written formats, as well as regulations governing record keeping and the dissemination of information collected in school settings.

Characteristics of Effective School Teams

Many individuals play important roles in promoting student learning; each brings unique expertise that can be useful in the process of decision making. In using assessment data to make decisions, you will work with a range of colleagues who hold a variety of positions and have varying levels of experience and knowledge that may or may not overlap with your own areas of expertise. When working with teams who are making Individualized Education Programs (IEPs), you might work with other special and general educators, administrators, speech–language pathologists, and school psychologists. Depending on your setting, your team might also include social workers, nurses, physicians, physical therapists, occupational therapists, audiologists, counselors, curriculum directors, attorneys, child advocates, and probably many others. IEP teams will always also include parents and guardians reflecting the importance of effective communication and collaboration to effectively promote positive outcomes for students across settings.

Although the expertise offered by each individual on the team can be an asset to decision making, it is important to recognize that group decision making does not necessarily result in better decisions than individual decision making. Some pitfalls of group decision making can be the tendency for groups to concede to the majority opinion regardless of its accuracy, and situations where groups tend to become more extreme in their decision making than what any individual originally intended (Gutkin & Nemeth, 1997). To avoid these pitfalls, it is important to adhere to principles of effective teaming. Fortunately, there is a scientifically based example of effective teaming called the Team-Initiated Problem-Solving framework (Newton et al., 2012). We introduced the TIPS framework in Chapter 20, "Using Assessment Information to Make Intervention Decisions." There are two major components to the TIPS framework shown in Figure 20.1. Previously we described the problem-solving process of the TIPS framework which delineates how a team uses data to make decisions. The other TIPS framework component is called the Meeting Foundation and describes how a team meets efficiently so that they can do the important work of the problem-solving process. In this chapter we'll highlight the Meeting Foundations component of the TIPS framework as one evidence-based method for collaborative teaming.

Meeting Foundations

There are six components of the TIPS Meeting Foundations. These foundations may seem simple at first glance, but by planning and implementing each of these features, the collaborative team can focus on the critical mission at hand: using data to improve outcomes for students. The six components are shared purpose, goals, and function; defined roles; defined responsibilities; established logistics and norms; prepared agenda; and established administrative authority. In the TIPS graphic in Figure 20.1, note that the Meeting Foundations, at the base of the light bulb, make the connection between the lightbulb and electricity; without the Meeting Foundations, the job of problem solving will be more difficult to manage and the team will be left in the dark.

Shared Purpose, Goals, and Function

Unnecessary conflict and inefficiencies in decision making occur when team members do not understand the team's purpose and when their activities do not reflect that purpose. For example, some members of prereferral intervention teams may view the team's purpose as "just one more hoop to jump through" before a referral for evaluation to determine special education eligibility is made, whereas others may view it as an opportunity to identify the conditions under which a student learns best. Those holding the former perspective may be less inclined to put forth substantial effort in associated team activities, which may reduce team effectiveness. The team's purpose, goals, and functions should also include the decision guidelines—or those criteria used to decide how intervention and instructional decisions are made. It is important for the team's purpose and function to be clearly articulated when the team is formed and for all team members to be committed to working toward that goal.

Defined Roles

Team composition needs to be determined carefully, balancing the need for unique expertise and the need for a team to efficiently complete commissioned tasks. Participating team members should be fully aware of the unique expertise that they bring as well as their knowledge limitations. More team members is not always better; managing large teams can be overwhelming and may intimidate important members of the team (e.g., some parents may be intimidated when they walk into a team meeting that includes many school professionals). In addition, large teams may lead to decisions that are informed by just one or two particularly dominant team members. The TIPS Meeting Foundations call for distinctive assigned roles that are specific to the teaming process. Building from research on barriers to effective teaming, it was determined that teams are set up for success when they have members assigned to the roles of meeting facilitator, data analyst, and minute taker. Ideally, there are enough staff so that each role can also be assigned a back-up person that can serve in the role if the primary person is absent. The appointment of these distinctive roles can be helpful in assisting the team in following appropriate organizational procedures and ensure that all team members are fully able to share their expertise and knowledge in ways that facilitate progress toward the team's goal.

Defined Responsibilities

Not only is it helpful to have specific team members identified as the facilitator, data analyst, and minute taker, but the entire team needs to be familiar with the responsibilities of each role. There are responsibilities that should take place before, during, and after the meeting. For example, before the meeting, a general team member should communicate if they will be absent. They should also make sure they complete any assigned tasks from the previous meeting. A facilitator's job is to call the meeting to order at the scheduled time and to ensure that the team sticks to the agenda and has the time needed to address all items. During the meeting, a minute taker's job will include asking follow-up questions if the team moves onto a new topic without completing the action plan for the initial discussion topic. The data analyst will need to review the meeting minutes from the last meeting to determine what data will be needed for the next meeting. They will also need to check in with the facilitator and administrators to see if there are new students and new sources of data that should be gathered to prepare for the next meeting. Although this list isn't exhaustive you can get an idea that collaborative teaming is a complicated process and having defined roles and responsibilities can make the team more efficient and effective.

Established Logistics and Norms

It can often be helpful for teams to develop and implement systematic procedures for operation. How many times have you searched your email to remind yourself of the details of an important meeting? There are meetings in schools every day, and sometimes the meeting is in the library, except on every Tuesday when a parent group is using the library, so the meeting shifts to the third-grade classroom. Logistical details such as the location of the meeting, the duration of the meeting, and team norms set the communication and behavioral expectations. Having these details in place provides a strong foundation so that the meeting can start and end on time, and valuable time is not spent wandering the halls trying to find an available meeting room. Together, team members can establish their agreed-upon meeting norms which can include principles such as "respect each team member's contributions" and "come prepared." Meetings norms should be accessible during the meeting. Some teams post norms on their meeting minutes form or a poster can be displayed in the conference room if the norms hold true across multiple teams. Meetings norms can contribute to a team's sense of self-efficacy when participating members feel that their voice and their time is being respected. It is important for those with minority opinions to be given the opportunity to express their positions and for their ideas to be respected and considered within the group's functioning. Effective problem solving can occur when all individuals are encouraged to contribute.

Prepared Agenda

In many cases, teams may have forms that facilitators use to guide team meetings (see Figure 23.1 for an example of such a form). The facilitator might create a written agenda for team meetings, in which there is time for those who have collected information to present their findings, time for additional input from team members, and time for group decision making. Because such procedures and structures can help teams maintain attention to task and promote efficiency toward addressing the team's goals, the TIPS Meeting Foundation recommends that an agenda be determined before each meeting and the agenda should be emailed to all team members in advance to allow everyone to adequately prepare. When the agenda is set in advance the data analyst can bring the necessary data and the facilitator can budget the time allowed to be able to attend to each item on the agenda. When team members want to discuss important issues that are not associated with the specific decisions to be made, it is important to tactfully address those concerns. Some decisions that school teams make are associated with a substantial amount of conflicting opinion and emotionality. It is important that team meeting facilitators anticipate those discussions that will take more time because of the sensitive nature and prescribe the time needed. When last-minute items get added to an agenda the team may feel rushed, members may feel unheard, and the team will not be able to effectively accomplish their goals. Agendas help the team to set the purpose for the meeting, allocate sufficient time, prepare the necessary data, and address tasks and action plans on the timelines required to meet goals.

Established Administrative Authority

The building principal cannot sit on each and every collaborative team, but it is important that each team have one member that does have administrative authority. Teams are sometimes in the position of needing to establish action plans or intervention plans that call for changing personnel and schedules. For example, a special education teacher alone cannot decide to move an instructional aide from playground supervision to working one-on-one with a student because there is a ripple effect to moving personnel of which the teacher may not be aware. Most school buildings have assistant principals, teachers on special administrative assignment, or mentor teachers that work collaboratively with the building principal and can act as an administrative proxy. These leaders can work with the team to efficiently make the necessary changes to meet the needs of the students and not wait to make a decision until the next meeting in 1 or 2 weeks.

Additional Considerations for Effective Teams
Use Objective Data to Guide Decision Making

Often, educational decisions are made without appropriate attention to relevant student data (Ysseldyke, 1983; Ysseldyke, 1987). Without the appropriate collection of and adherence to using data to guide team decision making, the subjective preferences of team members may take precedence over what is truly in the best interest of the student

Date of meeting: 01/31/2022

Student name: Jesse Johansen

Student's grade: 3

Teacher's name: Darcy Dunlap

School: Eastern Elementary

Name and title of those attending the meeting (note facilitator and recorder): Carrie Court (3rd grade lead teacher), Darcy Dunlap (recorder), Greg Gorter (guidance counselor), Jackie Johansen (mother), Eric Enright (principal, facilitator)

A. Student Strengths (provide brief summary of student strengths; 2–3 minutes)

Jesse has many friends and gets along really well with all the other students. He likes to play soccer and is very good at math.

B. Nature of Difficulties (in 2 minutes, circle all that apply)

Academic

(Reading)   Writing   Spelling   Math   Social Studies   History   Other: _____

Behavioral

Aggression   Attention   Task Completion   Homework   Attendance   Tardiness   Other: _____

Social/Emotional

Depression   (Anxiety)   Peer Relationships   Social Skills   Other: _____

Physical

Body Odor   Headaches   Nausea   Fatigue/Sleeping in Class   Other: _____

C. Summary of Data Collected to Support Difficulties Circled Above (2–3 minutes per area)

Jesse performed in the at-risk range on the Fall and Winter DIBELS benchmarking tasks during third grade. When asked to read in class, his voice becomes shaky, he shuts down, and he refuses to read. His mother reports that he is beginning to not like going to school and doesn't eat his breakfast (most likely due to his nervousness about having to go to school).

D. Prioritization of Difficulties (2–3 minutes)

#1 Most Problematic of the Above Listed Difficulties: Reading (the team believes that his poor skills in reading are what are contributing to his anxiety).

#2 Most Problematic of the Above Listed Difficulties: Anxiety

#3 Most Problematic of the Above Listed Difficulties:

E. Problem Definition in Observable and Measurable Terms (2 minutes)

Currently when presented with a third grade DIBELS benchmark passage, Jesse reads a median of 60 words correctly in one minute.

F. Goal (2 minutes)

Eight weeks from now when presented with a third grade DIBELS benchmark passage, Jesse will read a median of 75 words correctly in one minute.

G. Suggested Intervention Ideas for Addressing #1 of Prioritized Difficulties (15 minutes)

Intervention Idea #1: After school tutoring with an eighth-grade student.

Intervention Idea #2: Flashcards of phonics patterns that Jesse's teacher would administer after school two days per week, and Jesse's mom would administer at home the other three days each week.

Intervention Idea #3: Read Naturally® program that would be administered after school.

FIGURE 23.1. Completed example form to guide initial problem-solving team meeting.

H. Description of Final Intervention Selected (10 minutes)

i. What will the student do? Jesse will be taught how to use the Read Naturally® program, and will practice listening to and reading aloud with the tapes.

ii. How often and when will this occur? Two times a week for 45 minutes after school (Tues./Thurs.).

iii. Who is responsible for implementing the intervention? Jesse's mom and teacher

iv. How will progress be measured? DIBELS progress monitoring probes will be administered once a week.

v. Who is responsible for measuring progress? Jesse's teacher

vi. How, when, and to whom will progress be reported? Progress will be reported at the follow-up meeting, unless four consecutive data points fall below the aim line, in which case an earlier meeting will be convened.

I. Date and Time of Follow-Up Meeting (2 minutes): 02/28/2022

FIGURE 23.1. Completed example form to guide initial problem-solving team meeting.

being served. To obtain and interpret data in an objective manner requires you and your collaborative team to be on the lookout for both data that confirm and disconfirm a hypothesis. Confirmation bias describes the tendency to primarily pay attention to data that confirm one's original hypothesis while disregarding or underemphasizing data that conflict with the original hypothesis (see Nickerson, 1998, for a review). It is therefore important for teams to carefully attend to all collected data and be sure to carefully consider information that is collected which is not aligned with the original hypothesis.

The appropriate use of data to inform decision making can ensure that appropriate practices are put into place and help eliminate conflicting viewpoints on how to proceed. Not all data points will be equally valuable to the decision at hand and it is important to afford priority to the more valuable data. A single data point that goes against the body of evidence should not be the basis for ruling in or ruling out the need for intervention, for example. On the other hand, when there is no disagreement about the need for intervention, it is inefficient and unhelpful to collect multiple data points to support that decision. Teams often believe that over-collecting data will produce a more accurate decision. Sometimes this is called "triangulating data," which implies that one needs three data points that are in agreement to reach a single conclusion. This process is costly and does not make the decision more accurate. Often when data are over-collected, teams can experience "paralysis by analysis," which involves extending or delaying the decision. When decision making is more efficient, teams can collect new information that can be of better use in future decisions concerning the student. For example, when the team uses available adult time to initiate intervention for a student, then the team can use intervention response data as the basis for determining whether additional support or intervention is required.

Ensure Confidentiality—It's the Law!

Confidentiality is of critical importance when a team is responsible for making decisions about special education eligibility. Ultimately, it is against the law to break confidentiality rules, and such breaches can be grounds for termination of employment. Team efficacy decreases and students and families are not served with integrity when a participating member betrays or neglects confidentiality. Beyond confidentiality being a legal right, it is a fundamental element of trust that is necessary for all team members to engage in decision making. A well-functioning team is a team that attends specifically to trust-building actions which requires confidentiality. Team members must feel comfortable to share information, even sensitive information, and to believe that such information will not be used against them but instead will be used to benefit the process, the decision, and ultimately the student.

Regular reminders of confidentiality guidelines can be provided by an administrator, school psychologist, or other team leader, and guidelines can be included in the team norms or meeting minutes. Team facilitators should tell members at the very first meeting that confidentiality is critical and that reminders will be provided regularly. As new people join the team, it's always helpful to restate the importance of confidentiality along with review of the team's purpose and procedures.

Include Regular Evaluations of Team Functioning

Team processes and procedures can always be improved. Just as we evaluate the fidelity of intervention implementation, we can also monitor the fidelity of our teaming procedures. For example, the TIPS framework includes a TIPS Fidelity Checklist for Tier 2 Teams (Todd et al., 2020) that can be used by a team member during the meeting or by a colleague observing the collaborative team. It is important for the team to engage in periodic self-evaluation in order to ensure that it is meeting identified goals and objectives and that it is respectful of all team members' contributions. This can help to ensure that all team members are able to contribute their skills and knowledge in a way that is most beneficial to students.

How well a team functions is directly impacted by the overall context. In MTSS, it is especially important to engage in the hard work outside of the meetings, which means implementing instructional changes, verifying their effective implementation, and monitoring progress to report back to the team. The outside-the-meeting efforts are the most difficult for teams to get done. Teams successfully schedule and attend meetings and collect sufficient screening information. However, the magic of effective teaming comes to fruition when interventions are selected that are in alignment with the students' needs and the contextual variables, and when implementation and progress monitoring is conducted with integrity. Implementing intervention and actively managing that intervention with troubleshooting and sensitive progress monitoring continues to be an area of weakness for most MTSS teams (Burns et al., 2008; Silva et al., 2020). Further, MTSS cannot be used as a valid decision process in the absence of effective intervention management and monitoring. Refer back to chapters 7, 8, and 21 to be reminded of the various ways in which effective teams will use data to make decisions within an MTSS model. As you and the teams that you participate on look for tools to support your procedures, you'll find the following resources helpful. The National Center on Positive Behavioral Interventions and Supports (pbis.org/tools/all-tools#tips) also hosts a number of tools to support the TIPS process including fidelity checklists that support Tiers 1 and 2 teams meeting. The National Center on Intensive Intervention (NCII) has an excellent set of rubrics that teams can use to both evaluate the efficacy of data teams supporting students with Tier 3 interventions and serve as a target to improve your data team process. The NCII tools can be accessed here: intensiveintervention.org/resource/dbi-implementation-rubric-and-interview.

Types of Collaborative Teams

Although all the teams described in this chapter are typically involved in making decisions based on data to support student learning, the teams vary considerably in the types and levels of decisions made and, therefore, the nature of data collected, analyzed, and interpreted. We use broad labels to define the teams discussed here but there are a variety of different terms used to describe similarly functioning teams in the schools and districts you encounter.

Teams That Coordinate Tier 1 Supports
Schoolwide Leadership Teams

With the development of technology for managing large amounts of student data, as well as increased attention to accountability for student outcomes, teams of educational professionals are formed to collect, analyze, and interpret data on students across the entire school or district. The ultimate purpose of these teams is to inform instructional planning and resource allocation at school and district levels such that student achievement is optimized. They can be thought of as teams intended to ensure that the universal level of support within MTSS (core instruction) is effective. Sometimes these teams are referred to as the "universal team" or the "building implementation team." Team members may include those with special expertise in data analysis, curriculum, and instruction. These individuals come together to examine statewide assessment data, results from schoolwide screening efforts, and information on existing educational

Chanda Telleen and Dr. Tina Lawson, Educational Consultants, Pennsylvania Training and Technical Assistance Network (PaTTAN)

The state coordination team of the Pennsylvania Positive Behavior Support Network (PaPBS Network) learned of and recognized the power of the Team Initiated Problem Solving (TIPS) process to increase the fidelity of implementation statewide of a multi-tiered framework of behavior support. Our local team of facilitators struggled when engaging in site-based analysis of the massive amount of data at hand. The need was clear: How can we as a state support productive, efficient, and effective dialogue around the use of school-level data to sustain the implementation of various evidence-based practices? Those of us on the state coordination team looked for a process to efficiently and effectively support the data analysis needed while delivering a comprehensive replicative process to impact over 2,000 schools in our network. With so many teams and so much data, it was clear that TIPS provided a problem-solving and data-based decision-making process that we needed. As a result, TIPS training was provided throughout the commonwealth and continues to be supported through our network of professional development. Below is an example of one facilitator's experience with the TIPS introduction to the training protocol of the PaPBS Network.

I have worked as an educational consultant for the past many years, providing training and technical assistance to building level teams implementing the Positive Behavior Interventions and Supports (PBIS) framework. These teams include an administrator, general education teachers, and an individual with behavioral expertise. Working with teams, I frequently noticed that meetings were often inefficient. Problems were introduced without the use of supporting data, solutions were not well documented, and the overall meeting structure was informal. I introduced the TIPS process to teams and began to observe a shift in the functionality of meetings and an improvement in student outcomes. The teams attended a one-day training and received follow-up coaching. I worked directly with them to strengthen their meeting foundations by ensuring that all members understood meeting roles; a timed agenda was present, meeting attendance was documented, minutes were reflective of the discussion, and to-do items decided upon during the meeting. Meetings began to shift from complaining about problems to using data to identify problems with precision, identify goals for change, identify specific solutions with an articulated action plan, and create strategies for monitoring both fidelity and progress. Teams have shown growth through both the improvement of student outcomes and more satisfaction with the time spent in the meeting.

programming, with the purpose of identifying strategies for improving student achievement at a schoolwide level. Participants on these teams who have specialized expertise in assessment can contribute to the team by (1) helping the school identify methods for collecting relevant data on all students effectively and efficiently, (2) creating and interpreting visual displays of assessment data for the purpose of decision making, (3) recognizing areas in which additional assessment is needed prior to making substantial changes in school programming, and (4) identifying methods for monitoring the effectiveness of any associated changes in school programming.

Grade-Level Teams

These are teams that include all teachers from a particular grade level to meet on a regular basis to discuss curricular planning. These teams can meet as often as needed with all grade-level teachers present. Some schools have scheduled time for a weekly late start school schedule to allow time for teachers to plan and meet in grade-level teams. An administrator or an instructional or behavioral coach may join the meeting monthly or quarterly to support the grade team to identify areas for instructional improvement using available screening and progress monitoring data. Teachers will communicate about instructional targets and dates by which important learning outcomes should be mastered using their instructional calendars. For example, teachers might choose a set vocabulary list for the month and aim to teach approximately the same lessons so that all teachers can help each other reinforce these teaching goals when they encounter students from other classrooms but in the same grade level. These grade-level teams also provide an infrastructure for mentorship. Based on a systematic review of their grade-level data, the team may make recommendations for professional development and changes in school programming. It is helpful to combine concurrent grade levels for a meeting once or twice per year to coordinate instructional sequences and targets across grades (i.e., vertical teaming). *Vertical teaming* allows teachers to talk to each other about skill gaps that they observe at the beginning of their grade-level instruction so that below-grade-level teachers might troubleshoot and adjust their instruction to avoid such gaps in the future.

Informal Parent–Teacher Team

Many teachers work collaboratively with parents and guardians to provide low-cost supports to students in the general education classroom. There are many online applications that teachers use to communicate frequently with parents. If a concern about a student does arise, it will be easier to work with the parent to provide these low-cost supports to students if regular home-school communications are already the norm. Sometimes teachers and parents will exhaust their options or the concerns may be too large for this informal parent–teacher team to meet the needs of the student. In this case the classroom teacher then can work with the parent to bring the concerns to the intervention assistance team in order to conduct a more in-depth problem analysis and brainstorm additional ideas for intervention. Although not legally required to include parents in all intervention planning meetings, it is important to keep open lines of communication and to align school efforts with home-based efforts to support a student as much is possible. A helpful guideline is that for any child who is receiving supplemental intervention with progress monitoring, the teacher should send home the progress monitoring graph with a brief note weekly or as often as progress monitoring is occurring.

Teams That Coordinate Tiers 2 and 3 Supports
Intervention Assistance Teams

Traditionally intervention assistance teams include a couple of grade-level teachers, a special education teacher, a building administrator, and perhaps other specialists. The core function of this team is to provide support to general education classroom teachers or parents who have concerns about an individual student or small groups of students. The team collaboratively defines the specific problem, analyzes the problem in order to develop a targeted intervention plan, implements the intervention plan, monitors the plan implementation and student progress, and evaluates the effectiveness of the plan. This team can coordinate observations, additional academic testing (not intended for special education eligibility purposes), and monitor fidelity of implementation of interventions. If that plan does not lead to the desired progress, then the student's case will be moved to the team that focuses on Tier 3 or individualized instruction and interventions. In other words, as a student is determined to need a higher level of support through the MTSS framework, additional expertise is sought to assist with development of a more intensive intervention. Intervention assistance teams have many names. You might hear them called Tier 2 teams, student study teams, teacher assistance teams, or problem-solving teams. In some models the intervention assistance team is the team that coordinates both Tier 2 and Tier 3 supports so the team might be referred to as the Tiers 2/3 coordination team. Those with expertise in assessment can assist these teams by helping to select and administer assessment tools to define and analyze the problem, as well as to monitor intervention integrity and student progress.

Multidisciplinary Teams

These teams are convened when a student has not made adequate progress following support provided through multiple levels of interventions and is being considered for special education evaluation; the function and activities of these teams are more fully discussed in Chapter 21, "Using Assessment Information to Make Diagnostic/Eligibility Decisions." They are charged with the responsibility of determining whether a student has a disability and is in need of special education services according to the Individuals With Disabilities Education Act (IDEA). Within an MTSS model, this team might also be referred to as a Tier 3 team or a Tier 3 coordination team. A multidisciplinary team is often made up of the general education teacher, special education teacher, a school psychologist, a school counselor, school social worker, an administrator, and other specialists depending on the student case. Parents and guardians are also essential members of the team and will be critical to complete surveys and answers questions about the student's behaviors in different settings with family members and out in the community.

Individualized Education Program Teams

After a student is found eligible for special education services under IDEA, the IEP is developed by a team of individuals who have specialized knowledge in the specific areas of the child's disability, as well as those who will be responsible for carrying out the plan, including the parents or guardians. These teams typically meet on at least an annual basis to review the progress and programming for each student receiving special education services individually. Special education teachers and school psychologists often serve as assessment specialists, and when serving on the IEP team, are often responsible for collecting data through observations, permanent products of student performance, and diagnostic testing. After those data are collected, then each specialist must write up a summary interpreting the data so that the team can build an effective plan that is aligned to the student's needs.

With all of these various data-based collaborative teams in mind you can understand why it's important to employ the characteristics of effective teaming no matter your team's charge. As someone who is called on as an assessment specialist, you will sometimes need to remind your team of the importance of staying focused on the goals at hand by collecting and interpreting the data needed to answer the questions at hand. Through your understanding of assessments, you will ensure that all team members, including parents and guardians, are able to fully contribute to learning plans and effective instruction and intervention can reach the relevant students. In the next section we'll discuss how you can ensure that parents, guardians, and the students themselves can understand the data being presented in order to contribute effectively to the planning process.

23.1
PROGRESS MONITORING CHECK

Communicating Assessment Information to Parents and Students

Parents and guardians usually have more information about certain aspects of their child's life than any other person involved in the assessment process. However, many parents have limited knowledge and skill in understanding assessment and can find it challenging to take in all of the information presented by different individuals and understand what it means in terms of what is best for their child. Given the influential role that they play in the lives of their children, it is crucial that they understand the assessment results; this will allow them to participate fully in the decision-making process. Many parents (as well as other team members) may lack the knowledge to understand assessment results without substantial explanation. Some parents may themselves have disabilities. However, not all parents will lack knowledge or technical expertise; some parents are themselves professionals—psychologists, special educators, attorneys, therapists, and so forth. Other parents will have educated themselves about their child's needs. Regardless of their backgrounds, all parents may need to be empowered to be active and helpful members of school decision-making teams.

A variety of things can limit parent understanding of assessment information and participation in team decision making. Language barriers can clearly hinder effective communication. Many parents may not have a schedule that permits participation in meetings as scheduled by school professionals. They may feel intimidated by various school professionals. They may not recognize the important knowledge that they can bring to the team or not understand how to effectively communicate that knowledge to the team. Parents may have strong emotional reactions to data that are presented about their child's academic successes and failures, which may hinder rational decision making. They may have strong feelings and opinions about the quality of educational services provided to their child and about how their child's needs might best be met by educational professionals. Unfortunately, parents' unique knowledge about their child is often disregarded or ignored by school professionals, who often make decisions prior to team meetings.

Students can also be important contributors to team decision-making, and assessment information needs to be communicated to them in developmentally appropriate ways. Older students are required by law to be included in aspects of IEP decision making; participation in associated meetings can help to ensure that their perspectives and desires are appropriately considered. With advanced information about meeting purposes and procedures, students from a variety of ages can participate in important and meaningful ways (Martin et al., 2006).

Schools can take several steps to make communication with parents and students more effective. Better communication should result in more effective parental and student participation in associated team decision making. Read the Stakeholder Perspective of Kirsten Hood, a school social worker in Michigan, as she describes the importance of relationships between team members, parents, and students.

Communicate With Parents Frequently

In the past, it was often the case that parents were not made aware of difficulties that their child was having until the child was being considered for special education evaluation. When this happens, it can lead to strong emotional reactions and frustration among parents. It can also lead to unnecessary conflict if parents do not think that special education services would be in the best interest of their child. It is important that parents are provided frequent and accurate information on the progress of their child from the very beginning of their child's enrollment in school. By providing this information, parents of those students who are consistently low performing may become more involved in helping to develop intervention plans that may reduce their child's difficulties. Furthermore, when parents receive frequent communication about their child's progress (or lack thereof), they may more readily understand why a referral for special education eligibility evaluation is made. In schools where MTSS is used, communication with parents often occurs more frequently, given that student instruction may shift as students begin receiving different levels of support.

Kristen Hood, School Social Worker, Waverly Community Schools, Lansing, Michigan

As a school social worker in Michigan, I bring specialized knowledge of behavioral interventions to Intervention Assistance Teams. In Michigan, school social workers are required members of Multidisciplinary Teams when the suspected disability is emotional impairment or autism spectrum disorder, and I am a member of an IEP team that provides ongoing direct services to a student when there is need for further social-emotional skill development. Additionally, according to the social work code of ethics, I am obligated to practice cultural competence, which means I help my teams continually assess whether decisions are appropriate and inclusive and evaluate our process and practice to ensure that we are not inadvertently replicating oppression or exclusion of marginalized communities.

Beyond these roles, I also aim to cultivate two critical components for a team's success: rapport and buy-in. No matter how well-organized or well-planned a team system, no matter how well-intentioned or well-reasoned a selected intervention, team experiences are doomed to failure (or at least ongoing struggle) if they are missing rapport and buy-in. Every team member is holding various perceptions and emotions, which are often heightened when student behavior is involved. For instance, a teacher may be feeling overwhelmed, angry, or even frightened of a student's behavior and may be taking the student's behavior personally. They may need support and validation to understand the student's behavior differently. Parents may be feeling sadness and may even have adversarial feelings toward the school or team members based on their past interactions with staff around the problematic behavior. The team must communicate genuine, authentic care and concern for the child's well-being, as well as a sense of optimism, to build rapport with the parent.

Ultimately, nothing is more important than the relationship that team members have with the student. If a student likes you, and feels liked by you, students (and their parents) are more willing to engage with you. If a student doesn't like you, or thinks that you don't like them, students and parents will be much more dismissive and disengaged. It is also essential to directly involve the student whenever possible to allow them input into the team decisions, which makes them more willing to engage in the team's plan.

Mediating all of these competing emotions occurs in daily interactions outside of formal team meetings and ultimately develops trust and respect (rapport). Team members must then authentically demonstrate a willingness to engage in the agreed-upon plan with a shared vision of success (buy-in). In these ways, I apply principles of human behavior across the entire team experience in an ongoing navigation of human emotions and relationships. When the relationships are strong, the team will find success.

Communicate Both the Child's Strengths and Weaknesses

Many parents of students with special needs are often reminded of their child's weaknesses and difficulties in school and may rarely be alerted to their child's successes and strengths. Alternatively, some parents may overvalue their child's relative strengths and ignore or minimize their child's weaknesses. In order to work effectively with parents, and to facilitate creative problem solving as a part of a team, it is important to recognize and communicate about a child's specific strengths and weaknesses.

Translate Assessment Information and Team Communications

Assessment data that are reported to all parents (e.g., statewide assessment results and screening results) should be made available in the parent's primary language or mode of communication. To facilitate participation in team meetings, interpreters should be provided. In order to interpret well, they may need special training in how to communicate the pertinent information to parents, as well as how to ensure that parents' questions, concerns, and contributions have a voice within team meanings. For all parents, even those who have English as their primary language, it is important to avoid jargon and acronyms. The use of figures and graphs to show assessment results can facilitate parent understanding. When students are present, it is important to promote their understanding of assessment information and results, as well. It is a good practice to start with the figure and explain it fully as you would to a friend who may or may not have expertise interpreting such information. You can project the graph onto a screen and walk through the data points—how they were collected, what they mean, and how they logically contribute to the decision at hand. If you do not project the graphs, then attendees should have a printed copy of them. Also, all attendees should have an opportunity to ask questions about the information that you present briefly before the discussion continues.

Understand the Impact of Cultural Differences on the Interpretation of Assessments

As discussed in the chapter on working with students and families from culturally and linguistically minoritized groups it is suggested that a person who understands both the student's culture and educational matters be present (Chaparro et al., 2021). Of course, all teachers should do their best to learn about their students' home cultures but in addition, a district-provided cultural liaison may be available to assist with helping parents to understand the assessment process. This may be necessary even when language differences are not a barrier (e.g., the student is Amish and the culture of the school is not Amish). This culturally responsive approach can help a team prevent misunderstandings. For any family it could be that communication modes that are a normal part of school functioning (e.g., email) are not part of the home environment, and it is important to be aware of these differences.

Schedule Meetings to Facilitate Parent Attendance

Efforts should be made to schedule meetings at a time when parents can be present. Challenges associated with transportation should be addressed. In certain circumstances, it may be necessary for school professionals to meet at a location that is more convenient for parents than the school setting. It may also be necessary for school personnel to communicate directly with an employer, encouraging the employer to allow the parent to be excused from work. This is especially true in communities in which one company (e.g., a paper mill, an automobile factory, or a meat packing plant) is the employer of many parents. In this case, a blanket arrangement could be made in which the company agrees to release the parent for school meetings if a request is made by the school.

Explain the Purpose of Assessment Activities and Potential Outcomes

Whereas school professionals may be very familiar with assessment-related processes and procedures, and associated decisions that are made, parents often are new to the process. It is important to prepare them for what to expect as it relates to administration of assessment instruments and using the results of assessment data that are collected. It is important to let the parents know up front what will be involved in assessing the child (e.g., when it will occur, what assessment materials are used), and how the assessment process will be explained to the child. It can be helpful for school professionals to contact parents before a meeting to explain the purpose of the meeting and what they can expect to happen at the meeting. Parents should be informed of all potential outcomes of a particular meeting (e.g., development of an intervention plan, decision to collect more data, and decision that the student is eligible to receive special education services) so that they have appropriate expectations of decisions that can and cannot be made at the meeting. These norms may seem like simple good manners, but they are often overlooked in busy schools. A helpful exercise is to ask yourself how you would feel if you were going through a visit with a physician specialist for a medical illness and had the experience of the special education team meeting. How would you feel about the medical meeting in terms of introduction, expectations, ability to contribute and be heard, the amount of jargon and accessibility of highly technical information, and the general tone of the interaction? Check in with parents and guardians frequently during the meeting to ensure they understand the purpose of assessments and associated meetings.

Communicate Using Nontechnical Language

By now, you have most certainly recognized that language used in educational circles is full of acronyms. It is important to use nontechnical language whenever possible, and to fully explain other technical terms that may be used so that parents can understand

and contribute to the team discussion. Whereas some parents may understand technical terms associated with assessment data, others may not. It is more appropriate to err on the side of using language that is easier to understand than to assume that parents understand terminology that is used by school professionals. Figures and graphs can help to convey student progress in an understandable way when you carefully describe how to read the graph or table.

Focus on Solutions and Avoid Blame

Just about every school team meeting is intended to promote student achievement, whether directly or indirectly. Accomplishing this goal requires that individual team members focus on alterable rather than unalterable variables. In other words, the team and the student are best served when the focus is on what can be changed in the future to promote student learning rather than dwelling on what has happened in the past. Unfortunately, there can be a tendency to focus on what people may have done or failed to do in the past rather than making plans for the future. Although it is important to learn from past mistakes, team members should focus on solutions to improve student learning. Focusing on past failure can decrease morale and contribute to unnecessary conflict and blame among team members.

Prepare Students for Active Participation in Meetings

Although in some cases it may make sense to hold a meeting without the student present, in many cases, it can be helpful to have the student present in order for the student's interests and desires to be considered. If a student will attend, it is important to prepare them for what the meeting will entail, and when possible, provide training to facilitate active participation of the student in team decision making.

Manage Electronic Communication

The increasing use of technology in schools has strong potential to promote student learning, as noted in several chapters throughout this book. Large files containing student performance data are maintained on computers which allow for more efficient analysis of student data. The use of email and text messages between teachers and parents can also greatly enhance the speed with which information is communicated and to enhance collaboration between parents, guardians, and educators. However, with these advances also comes a need for guidelines to prevent misuse and mishandling of this information, given that such information can be more easily transmitted to those who do not have a right or a need to have the given information. Password protection systems should be used to ensure that only those who have a legitimate need can access specific student information electronically (this includes password-protecting flash drives and electronic files such as test result reports). The use of portable document format (PDF) and basic computer programs like Excel and Word allow the user to easily add passwords to view and edit specific files and offer the added layer of security encryption.

Separate identification codes should be developed and used rather than actual student names and identification numbers within large datasets that include sensitive information. Also, email messages when possible should be encrypted or at least worded in a way that avoids use of actual student names in order to prevent accidental transmission or forwarding to those who do not need the given information. Email communications about students, just as students' records, should be carefully guarded. You can accomplish the goal to maintain privacy and security by using difficult-to-guess passwords and by using only initials to identify students in emails. These security precautions can prevent unintended sharing of private information. Always consult your district technology policies and solicit advice from your district's information technology staff when in doubt or when considering the adoption of new applications and interventions that are based online. In addition to these considerations please see the online resources section on managing records according to federal guidelines. Taken altogether these characteristics of effective teams, the purpose of these various teams, and the inclusion of parents, guardians, and students in the teaming process will help you and your school use assessment to its fullest potential to serve the needs of the students and the supporting educators and families.

23.2
PROGRESS
MONITORING
CHECK

PROGRESS 23.1 MONITORING CHECK

1. Describe the importance of having assigned roles and responsibilities on a team.
2. Describe your potential tasks on the team if you are the data analyst.
3. Name and describe the functions of six types of teams commonly formed in school settings.
4. Why is it important for a collaborative team to self-evaluate team functioning?

PROGRESS 23.2 MONITORING CHECK

1. What are some potential barriers to communicating effectively about assessment with parents?
2. What are some ways to overcome communication barriers with parents?
3. How can you ensure that parents and guardians feel welcome in the school collaborative meeting context?
4. What are some ways to be sure to protect data and your communications with parents?

How to Read and Understand Psychoeducational Reports and State Assessment Reports

Reading and Understanding Psychoeducational Reports

You may have to write psychoeducational reports summarizing the findings of assessments you conduct on students. At the very least, you will be expected to be an informed consumer of the information included in psychoeducational reports. That is no easy task. Why? Because you may have to sort through a lot of information to find what is relevant to the decisions you are trying to make. While there are not as many report writing styles and types as there are report writers, it sometimes seems like that is the case. Reports range from very brief reports that do not include enough information to those in which it is clear that report writers not only collect far too much information but like to hear themselves talk. Many psychological reports contain a lot of information that is not relevant to the primary purpose of schooling: improving the academic and behavioral competence of students. As Lichtenstein (2013a) concluded on the basis of extensive reviews of studies conducted on the intelligibility and usefulness of psychoeducational reports, reports are not written in a way that communicates useful information easily to intended consumers. It is our contention in this chapter, and throughout this book, that the primary purpose of assessing students is to plan and modify interventions that will lead to enhanced academic and behavioral competence. Much of the information included in many reports is extraneous to that need. How do we get the most meaning out of psychoeducational reports? Let's consider first the purposes of those reports.

The Purposes of Psychoeducational Reports

Why are psychoeducational reports written? To whom are those who write them trying to communicate, what information are they trying to communicate, and for what purposes? And, why should you as an educator or related services person want to read the report? More importantly, how can you best understand and use the information contained therein.

First, understand that reports are written for many purposes, only some of which are relevant to what school personnel need. In this chapter we concentrate our discussion on the information that is necessary for purposes of making diagnostic and instructional planning decisions. Children come to the attention of psychologists through a process of referral, usually in response to concerns expressed by parents and/or teachers. So a good psychoeducational report will address those expressed concerns. The report should document, integrate, and synthesize data from a comprehensive evaluation of the student. The report should provide information that can be used by an Individualized Education Program (IEP) team in the process of making decisions about special education eligibility and about instructional needs, goals, intervention alternatives, and services (Carrierre & Hass, 2019).

What Are the Components of Psychoeducational Reports?

While there is no standard set of information that is included in psychoeducational reports, you can expect to find some specific information that you need. You can also expect to find much information that you do not need. This is where we advise you to be very selective in just what information you attend to. It is common for psychologists to include far too much information in their reports, just as it is common for them to gather far too much information. Our bias is that the assessment process, and thus the reporting out of that process, be focused on what matters. That is, we expect that the focus will be on things that the school can actually do something about. Many psychological reports go into extensive information about matters that schools can do little about, for example, the history of the mother's pregnancy when the child is presenting with a problem learning to read. Lichtenstein and Ecker (2019) reviewed many of the textbooks recommending organization of psychoeducational reports and concluded that there was considerable consistency across reports and training courses in their recommendations. Lichtenstein (2013a) and Lichtenstein and Ecker (2019) recommend a consumer-responsive report writing process and list the following as components of the report:

- Identifying/demographic information (includes the student's name, date of birth, age, parent's names, address, date of exam, school and grade, name of examiner, etc.).
- Reasons for referral.
- Background information (includes physical, developmental, social, academic, history of interventions that have been tried and their success, previous evaluations).
- Assessment procedures (a listing of the academic and behavioral measures used).
- Behavioral observations (during assessment and elsewhere, in a variety of settings, formal and informal).
- Intervention history (a review of interventions tried and their success).
- Interviews (including caregivers and teachers).
- Assessment results (test results reported should include scores as well as tables of scores and ranges of scores including where possible confidence intervals. Look for descriptions of behaviors sampled rather than only test names.).
- Clinical impressions.
- Summary and recommendations.

Some break the reporting of test results into sections (e.g., cognitive and memory, academic skills, executive functioning, adaptive functioning, personality, processing abilities). This may or may not be useful, and of course, the number of sections is limited only by the number of domains of tests that are possible to give. As a general rule of thumb, we advise the use of focused reporting which includes information pertinent to the decisions that need to be made. Some systems use standard reports for which a lot of the content can be copied and pasted when building reports for students. While this practice habit may be tempting in its seeming efficiency, it results in reports that are less targeted, less useful, and more difficult to interpret. When the key information is embedded in a sea of information that is not important to the decision at hand, it is easy to overlook or misinterpret the key information that is there.

24.1
PROGRESS
MONITORING
CHECK

Making Sense of It All

As you read a psychoeducational report, you should do so with a pen and paper in hand. You want to come away from the experience with notes on important background considerations for instructional planning, the student's strengths and weaknesses, a clear notion about instructional level in core content areas like reading, math, and written language, and good ideas about instructional strategies that might be effective in educating the student. You should have questions prepared for the person who wrote the report if you do not understand something. Remember that you need to obtain the information you need for intervention planning, but you may also be in the position of conveying report information to caregivers or instructional aides who do not have a background in assessment. We will talk about that later in this chapter. In any event, you want to have ideas about where to start in the intervention process and thoughts about what might work.

As you examine the various sections of a report ask yourself these questions:

Background Information

1. Is there any indication of sensory deficits (visual or auditory difficulties) that will require instructional or assessment accommodations?
2. Are there any specific physical or medical conditions that will limit the student's participation in class or in specific kinds of interventions?
3. Is the child's primary language one other than English, and how will language influence the way in which instruction is delivered?
4. How does the child's cultural background inform specific instructional considerations?
5. To what extent is the information on the success of previous interventions consistent with what I know about the success of interventions I have tried with this student?
6. Is there anything else in the child's background and education history I need to consider in planning instruction?

Behavioral Observations

1. Did the examiner or others observe the child often enough and in enough different settings to get a good picture of how the child behaves and interacts with others?
2. To what extent are the behaviors the child is said to have exhibited consistent with the behaviors I have observed him/her exhibiting?
3. Are the behaviors that were observed relevant to planning and delivering instruction to this student?

List of Assessment Devices Used

1. To what extent am I familiar with the tests that were used?
2. Are the tests that were used relevant to the referral concern and to the goal of enhancing the student's academic and behavioral competence?
3. Is there evidence that the tests used were normed on students like the student who was tested (the criterion of representativeness)?
4. To what extent are the tests that were used technically adequate?
5. To what extent was it necessary to gather information using each of the tests (the criterion of relevance)?

Assessment Results

1. To what extent do I understand the results as they are presented?

2. Are graphs and/or tables presented in a clear and easy to understand manner?
3. When presenting assessment findings does the psychologist describe the behaviors that were sampled by each of the measures, or merely state test names? In either event, do I know the behaviors that were sampled by the tests or subtests?
4. Do I understand the scores and ranges of scores that are reported?
5. Given the information reported (scores and ranges) is it clear to me where the student stands relative to others their age (interindividual comparisons)?
6. Does the information reported give me a good understanding of the child's intraindividual strengths and weaknesses?
7. Do I know the child's instructional level and where to start instruction in the curriculum?
8. Am I given feasible suggestions on intervention strategies that might work with the child?
9. Are the recommendations provided relevant to improving instructional and behavioral outcomes for the student?
10. Are there sufficient resources (e.g., materials, time, instructional aids, administrator support, training) available to support me in my efforts to implement the suggested interventions?

Helping Parents Understand Reports

When parents refer (or agree to the referral) their child for psychoeducational evaluation they typically are worried that something doesn't seem "quite right" about the academic performance or behavior of their child. Without assistance from a professional, most parents do not understand what psychoeducational reports communicate about their child. So, just as we have been talking about the things you need to understand, it is important that professionals help parents understand the content of reports. They need assistance especially in understanding the behaviors sampled by tests, scores and ranges of scores, and the implications of student performance for intervention planning. Lichtenstein and Ecker (2019) conducted an extensive review of research on the extent to which intended consumers of assessment information (parents, teachers, related services personnel, and administrators) understand the content of reports) and indicated that researchers consistently conclude that consumers do not comprehend the content of reports. Lichtenstein and Ecker (2019) and Lichtenstein (2013b,c) recommend a shift in the kinds of reports that school psychologists write to what they call "consumer responsive reports."

Questionable Information in Psychological Reports

There are no limitations on the information that can be included in the reports that school psychologists, clinical psychologists, or school diagnosticians write on the students with whom they work. These professionals practice from their own theoretical frameworks and typically are informed by the training they have received. Each has differing professional beliefs and values, and, of course, the beliefs and values typically are very strongly held. Practitioners engage in differing assessment practices and write different kinds of psychological or psychoeducational reports. Sometimes the reports include questionable information based on questionable practices. The reports may even include information based on assessments that have been shown clearly to be unreliable and invalid. You, the reader, need to be the one to sort this out.

In this text there are several kinds of assessment practices we have not covered. For example, we have not reported on the topic of projective testing because there is very limited empirical support for the validity of projective testing. Projective tests are designed to let a person respond to ambiguous stimuli, presumably revealing hidden emotions and internal conflicts projected by the person into the test. For example, psychologists present sets of ambiguous stimuli such as inkblots, pictures, or incomplete sentences, and the individual responds with the first thought or series of thoughts that come to mind or tells a story about each picture.

We also have not reported in this text on the assessment of executive functioning skills, as there is limited information supporting the validity of assessment of these skills. Some reports include information on proficiency in these skills, including proficiency in adaptable thinking, planning, self-monitoring, self-control, working memory, time management or organization, inhibitory control, attention, set-shifting, and cognitive flexibility.

A third example is the reporting of information on performance of measures of neuropsychological assessment, sensory integration, or perceptual-motor functioning. Again, these are areas in which there is not good evidence for validity, especially predictive validity for the planning of evidence-based interventions; that is, interventions that lead to enhanced academic and behavioral competence for students.

Two Examples of Psychoeducational Reports

Now that you understand the qualities of consumer responsive psychoeducational reports we've provided two very different consumer responsive reports in the online resources for you to review. One is the "Specific Learning Disabilities, Assessment Documentation Form" on a student named Max who is diagnosed with an attention-deficit/hyperactivity disorder. The report is representative of a traditional psychoeducational report from a Midwestern school district. The second, an "Educational Evaluation Report" on Maxine, is from the Heartland Education Agency in Iowa, an agency that long has been a national model for using an multi-tiered system of supports (MTSS) methodology in its assessment and decision-making process. We think you'll find advantages to both types of reports. After reviewing these reports, discuss with your classmates or colleagues how the reports used in your setting could be improved in their consumer responsiveness.

Even when all the assessments conducted meet basic conventions for reliability and validity, you must still review the information in the report with a sense of which assessment results might be prioritized over others given the specific type of decision you are

ONLINE
RESOURCE

ONLINE
RESOURCE

trying to make. Teams can be tempted to over-parse data, selecting a single data point or single data points to make a series of disconnected recommendations. It is important to evaluate the bulk of the evidence and to understand which assessments are useful for ruling in and ruling out specific conclusions and which assessments will be given more weight when the assessment scores "disagree." It is helpful again to remain focused on interpreting the data that are germane to the decision being made.

Understanding State Assessment Reports

Each year, school districts administer to all students a standards-based test designed to assess their performance and progress relative to state grade-level educational standards. Each year, state education agencies (SEAs) issue reports designed to provide parents, teachers, and the general public with information on the performance and progress of individual students, classrooms, schools, districts, and their entire state based on the performance of students on those state assessments. Reports are always issued in aggregate, that is, on groups of students. Assessment results for individual students are confidential and may be released only in accordance with the Family Educational Rights and Privacy Act (FERPA). This act was discussed in Chapter 3.

School personnel need to be able to understand the information included in state assessment reports. In this section of this chapter we provide you with some general guidelines on what to look for and how to interpret information typically included in state assessment reports. Understand, though, that reports differ significantly from state to state. States have different standards, different expectations for performance levels, different terminology, different assessment systems, use different kinds of tests and test content, and report test results in a variety of ways. In the following pages, we list the questions you should ask and let you know what you should look for. As you begin reading this section, go to the website for the state test report for the state in which you live (or the state in which your college or university is located). Conversely, if you are taking a class, your instructor may want to assign different students to review the state test websites for different states so that comparisons can be made. In preparing this section, we relied extensively on the websites for the state tests in Florida, Texas, Colorado, Minnesota, California, and New York.

Questions You Should Ask
What Content Is Assessed and at What Grade Levels?

All states assess students in reading, mathematics, and science. All also provide assessments of English language proficiency. Some call the reading tests "measures of English language arts" because they include a measure of writing. It is critical, though, that you look beyond test names to look at the content assessed by the tests. Do not be satisfied with knowing the domains assessed (math calculation, algebra). Look more specifically at the kinds of behaviors sampled by the domains. Most states assess students in Grades

3 through 8 and again in Grade 10 or Grade 11. Look at the specific grade levels at which students are assessed and look at the types of questions that are used to assess student performance in each content area.

What Kinds of Reports Are Issued?

State education agency assessment personnel issue many different kinds of reports, and those differing reports often are intended for different audiences. All SEAs issue student reports, reporting data on the performance (and sometimes growth) of individual students, which are intended for parent and student use. Other kinds of reports issued include reports at the classroom, school, district, and state level, which are intended for educators mostly for the purpose of program evaluation and accountability. You would consult these differing kinds of reports depending on the information you needed. For example, if you wanted to compare assessment results across school districts in Pennsylvania, you would look at the state report to see if data are disaggregated by school district. If they are not, you would look to see if there is a separate report by district. At the time we prepared this book, we checked the websites for representative SEAs and examined the kinds of reports they issue. While there are similarities in reports issued, there are also interesting differences. For example, Florida issues annual reports showing student performance in English language arts, mathematics, social studies, and science at each of five achievement levels. They do so separately for districts and schools within districts. New York issues reports showing proficiency rates in math and ELA by grade, race, for New York City multilingual learners, and for New York City students with disabilities. The neighboring state of New Jersey does not go into quite as much detail, showing proficiency levels for all students and then separately broken down by race, gender, English learners, students with disabilities, and students who are economically disadvantaged.

The state of California is part of the Smarter Balanced Assessment Consortium (SBAC), and each year they issue a report showing the percentage of students in each school who exceed standards, meet standards, nearly meet standards, and have not met standards. They do so in ELA and mathematics and have results broken out by grade level, race, and gender. The report also indicates the percentage of change in students meeting the standards between the current school year and the previous school year. In Texas, data are reported broken down by five proficiency levels (e.g., approaches grade level), and separately for race/ethnicity, special education status (enrolled in special education or not) and English learner status (yes/no). Data are reported for student, district, and state performance in reading, mathematics, science, social studies, English, and biology at select grade levels.

What Performance Indicators Are Used?

Different states use different performance indicators. All report performance levels regarding mastery of standards, but a wide variety of labels is used to describe those levels. For example, the Minnesota Department of Education uses four achievement level descriptors (does not meet, partially meets, meets, and exceeds). These descriptors are used to describe performance relative to grade-level standards, and the first two are considered "not proficient" while the latter two are considered "proficient" for accountability purposes. Florida uses five descriptors (inadequate, below satisfactory, satisfactory, proficient, and mastery). Colorado also uses five descriptors, but different terminology (did not yet meet expectations, partially met expectations, approached expectations, met expectations, and exceeded expectations). Critically, the level of performance that signifies proficiency in one state may differ from another state.

In addition to level of performance, states increasingly are reporting on growth from year to year. Some include student growth percentiles. You may see trend analyses or growth analyses in the reports you examine. Some states also report scaled scores or percentile ranks (though scores like student growth percentiles, scaled scores, and percentiles may be included in separate technical reports that are hard to find). Occasionally state reports will include Lexiles (a numeric representation of a student's reading ability based on a text's readability level).

How Are Assessment Data Reported?

State education agency personnel use a variety of ways to report information to stakeholders. The most common approaches are by means of tables or graphs. To understand the information in these reports or to help others understand the information contained therein, you will need to know how to read those tables and graphs. Review the state reports at the website you chose earlier and examine the ways in which student, classroom, district, or state performance are depicted. Are bar graphs or line graphs used? If so, look at the key to understand what data are being displayed. Consider the y-axis to understand magnitude of change and especially consider any reference points that reflect proficiency or other key outcomes that are important in interpreting the data. Practice explaining the data to a colleague or classmate to increase your comfort level reading graphs and reports. Parents are generally more comfortable understanding norm-referenced data (how my child compares to other children in his or her performance) and may need some explanation to interpret the results in different ways (e.g., which intervention provided the most benefit to my student; what level of performance is powerful evidence of ongoing and future success in mastering associated skills versus what level of performance signifies risk).

You can expect to be able to answer the following questions from information displayed on state accountability reports.

Who Participated in the Assessments?

State education agencies are required to include all students in their state assessments. Students must participate in the regular assessment with or without accommodations; those with significant cognitive disabilities may participate in an alternate state assessment. SEA personnel are required to report annually the numbers of students who participated in the state assessment, and they must do so by specific subgroups, including students with disabilities, English learners, gender, specific racial groups, and economically disadvantaged students. You should examine the state assessment reports to see if they do indeed report on the numbers of students in each of the subgroups who participated and on the performance of students in those subgroups. Note that states are exempted from reporting on the performance of students in any group (e.g., English learners) if the number of students in the subgroup is so small that reporting of scores might disclose the scores of individual students.

Even though states are required to have all students participate in their assessments, some states change the criteria for participation in the general assessment versus the alternate assessment, or they change their criteria for receiving assessment accommodations from year to year. If this is the case, this should be indicated in footnotes to graphs or tables or in specific notes in the reports.

Are Data Reported Separately for Various Required Subgroups?

The Every Student Succeeds Act (ESSA) requires that SEAs publish annual reports on the performance of all students including all students with disabilities. Further, it is required that states report on the performance of specific racial subgroups of students, students who are English learners, students receiving free and reduced-price lunch, and students in each of the federally defined disability categories. They must do so by grade level.

Does the Report Include Information on Content Standards Mastery?

State reports provide school personnel with information on the performance and growth of the students in their districts and classrooms. The information is useful to the extent that it is helpful in planning interventions for individual students or helps school personnel make changes in their curricula or instructional approaches to help all of their students correct skill weaknesses or gaps. All states are required to have lists of content standards that students must master by the end of specific grade levels. They must also specify criteria to indicate when those content standards have been mastered. You should examine the extent to which the state reports provide district personnel with specific information on the extent to which individual students in their classrooms have mastered specific content. Failing to interpret state testing data in this way is a missed opportunity to use the results to improve programs of instruction. Teachers need to know what skills students are expected to master, the types of assessment questions that will be asked to determine skill mastery, and then what the results of those assessments are to determine whether instruction was successful or whether improvements can be made in the next year.

Some teachers may find it confusing that a cohort of students in fourth grade is compared to a different cohort of students who are in fourth grade the following year, but that is the correct way to examine the data for the question at hand. When evaluating a program of instruction, the goal is to evaluate learning changes that are linked to the program of instruction. If you were to compare a cohort of specific students in fourth grade and then fifth grade, you would be evaluating that unique group of students who received two programs of instruction (Grades 4 and 5). Because generally you cannot change which students attend your school, the appropriate level of analysis is the program of instruction, which can be changed. The presumption here is that cohorts of students are similar enough in performance across grades that changes in performance can mostly be attributed to the program of instruction (not the unique grouping of students). Incidentally, historical events that occur in a given year can impact program evaluation. For example, at the time this book was written, schools were documenting learning losses that resulted from widespread shutdowns of schools and altered schedules and instructional formats that affected learning. Such events must be considered when interpreting assessment results at the program level.

Does the Report Indicate the Extent to Which Students With Disabilities Were Provided Accessibility Supports and Accommodations?

As we indicated in Chapter 17, students who are entitled to instructional accommodations are also entitled to accommodations in assessment. States must provide students with disabilities accommodations when they take state assessments. So, for example, students who have visual impairments and who use large print during instruction are entitled to use large print during assessments. SEA personnel must indicate in the state report the numbers of students who took the state test with accommodations.

Does the Report Indicate the Numbers of Students With Disabilities Who Took an Alternate Assessment?

According to the provisions of ESSA, up to 1% of students (those with significant cognitive disabilities) may take an alternate assessment. SEA personnel must report the numbers of students at each grade level who took an alternate assessment.

24.2
*PROGRESS
MONITORING
CHECK*

How Did Students in Your State Compare to Students in the Nation?

You cannot compare the state test performance of students in one state with the state test performance of students in another state. State tests differ significantly from state to state, as does the assignment of proficiency levels. Comparisons should be limited to within-state comparisons. Any effort to compare students across states would require looking at scores on the National Assessment of Educational Progress (NAEP), a test administered periodically by the U.S. Department of Education's National Center for Education Statistics.

MONITORING CHECK

1. What are the primary purposes of psychoeducational reports?
2. What steps can be taken to improve communication between report writers and the consumers of psychoeducational reports?
3. How can you help parents understand psychoeducational reports?
4. What are the typical components of a psychoeducational report?

MONITORING CHECK

1. What are the most important kinds of information to look for when you read a state assessment report?
2. Why does the federal government require that state departments of education report performance data separately by subgroups?

REFERENCES

Adams, M. (1990). *Beginning to read: Thinking and learning about print*. MIT Press.

Adlof, S. M., Catts, H. W., & Lee, J. (2010). Kindergarten predictors of second versus eighth grade reading comprehension impairments. *Journal of Learning Disabilities, 43*(4), 332–345. https://doi.org/10.1177/0022219410369067

Alberto, P. A., & Troutman, A. C. (2005). *Applied behavior analysis for teachers* (7th ed.). Prentice-Hall.

Al Otaiba, S., & Hosp, J. (2010). Spell it out: The need for detailed spelling assessment to inform instruction. *Assessment for Effective Intervention, 36*(1), 3–6. https://doi.org/10.1177/1534508410384478

American Educational Research Association (AERA), American Psychological Association, & National Council on Measurement in Education. (2014). *Standards for educational and psychological testing*. American Educational Research Association.

American Psychological Association. (2016). *Ethical principles of psychologists and code of conduct*.

American Psychological Association, Task Force on Resilience and Strength in Black Children and Adolescents (2008). *Resilience in African American children and adolescents: A vision for optimal development*. https://www.apa.org/pi/families/resources/resiliencerpt.pdf

Americans With Disabilities Act Amendments of 2008, PL 110-295. 42 USCA § 12101. (2008).

Americans With Disabilities Act of 1990, 42 U.S.C. § 12101 *et seq.* (1990).

Ames, W. (1965). A comparison of spelling textbooks. *Elementary English, 42*(2), 146–150, 214.

Anderson, N. A., Schlueter, J. E., Carlson, J. F., & Geisinger, K. F. (Eds.). (2022). *Tests in print X*. Buros Center for Testing.

Armistead, L. D., Williams, B. D., & Jacob, S. (2011). *Professional ethics for school psychologists: A problem-solving model casebook* (2nd ed.). Wiley.

Arter, J. A., & Jenkins, J. R. (1979). Differential diagnosis–prescriptive teaching: A critical appraisal. *Review of Educational Research, 49*(4), 519–555. https://doi.org/10.3102/00346543049004517

Atkinson, R. L., Atkinson, R. E., Smith, E. E., & Bem, D. J. (1993). *Introduction to psychology* (11th ed.). Harcourt Brace.

ATP Assessments. (2017). *Test of Visual Perceptual Skills–Fourth Edition*. Academic Therapy Publications.

Bailey, T. R. (2019, September 20). *Is MTSS the new RTI? Depends on where you live*. Center on Multi-Tiered System of Supports at the American Institutes for Research. https://mtss4success.org/blog/mtss-new-rti-depends-where-you-live

Bal, A., Betters-Bubon, J., & Fish, R. E. (2019). A multi-level analysis of statewide disproportionality in exclusionary discipline and the identification of emotional disturbance. *Education and Urban Society, 51*(2), 247–268. https://doi.org/10.1177/0013124517716260

Barnett, D. W., Daly, E. J., Jones, K. M., & Lentz, F. E. (2004). Response to intervention: Empirically based special service decisions from single-case designs of increasing and decreasing intensity. *The Journal of Special Education, 38*, 66–79. https://doi.org/10.1177/00224669040380020101

Barsch, R. (1966). Teacher needs–motor training. In W. Cruickshank (Ed.), *The teacher of brain-injured children* (pp. 183–195). Syracuse University Press.

Baumgardner, J. C. (1993). *An empirical analysis of school psychological assessments: Practice with students who are deaf and bilingual* [Unpublished doctoral dissertation]. University of Minnesota, Minneapolis.

Beck. R. (1979). *Great Falls precision teaching project: Report for joint dissemination and review panel*. Great Falls Public Schools.

Beery, K., Buktenica, N. & Beery, N. (2010). *Developmental Test of Visual-Motor Integration–Sixth Edition.* Pearson. https://doi.org/10.1037/t48947-000

Bergen, J. R., & Kratochwill, T. R. (1990). *Behavioral consultation and therapy.* Plenum Press.

Bergstahler, S. (2012). *Universal design in education: Principles and applications.* University of Washington. http://www.washington.edu/doit/sites/default/files/atoms/files/Universal-Design-Education-Principles-Applications.pdf

Bialik, K., Scheller, A., & Walker, K. (2018, October 25). *6 facts about English language learners in U.S. public schools.* Pew Research Center. https://www.pewresearch.org/fact-tank/2018/10/25/6-facts-about-english-language-learners-in-u-s-public-schools

Bitsko, R. H., Holbrook. J. R., Ghandour, R. M., Blumberg, S. J., Visser, S. N., Perou, R., & Walkup, J. (2018). Epidemiology and impact of health care–provider diagnosed anxiety and depression among US children. *Journal of Developmental & Behavioral Pediatrics, 39*(5), 395–403. https://doi.org/10.1097/DBP.0000000000000571

Blatchley, L. A., & Lau, M. Y. (2010). Culturally competent assessment of English language learners for special education services. *Communiqué, 38*(7), 25.

Bolt, D. M., Ysseldyke, J. E., & Patterson, M. J. (2010). Students, teachers, and schools as sources of variability, integrity, and sustainability in implementing progress monitoring. *School Psychology Review, 39*(4), 612–631. https://doi.org/10.1080/02796015.2010.12087746

Bolt, S. E., & Ysseldyke, J. E. (2006). Comparing DIF across math and reading/language arts tests for students receiving a read-aloud accommodation. *Applied Measurement in Education, 19,* 329–355. https://doi.org/10.1207/s15324818ame1904_6

Bond, G., & Dykstra, R. (1967). The cooperative research program in first-grade reading instruction. *Reading Research Quarterly, 2,* 5–142.

Bottiani, J. H., Larson, K. E., Debnam, K. J., Bischoff, C. M., & Bradshaw, C. P. (2018). Promoting educators' use of culturally responsive practices: A systematic review of inservice interventions. *Journal of Teacher Education, 69*(4), 367–385. https://doi.org/10.1177/0022487117722553

Bracken, B., & McCallum, R. S. (2016). *Universal Nonverbal Intelligence Test–Second Edition.* Multi-Health System Inc.

Bransford, J., & Stein, B. S. (1984). *The ideal problem solver: A guide for improving thinking, learning, and creativity.* W. H. Freeman.

Breaux, K. C. (2020). *Wechsler Individual Achievement Test–Fourth Edition: Technical and interpretive manual.* NCS Pearson.

Briesch, A., Chafouleas, S., & Riley-Tillman, C. (2016). *Direct behavior rating: Linking assessment, communication, and intervention.* Guilford Press.

Brown, V., Sherbenou, R., & Johnson, D. (2010). *Test of Nonverbal Intelligence–Fourth Edition.* PRO-ED.

Brown, V. L., Cronin, M. E., & Bryant, D. R. (2013). *Test of Mathematical Abilities–Third Edition.* PRO-ED.

Broxterman, K., & Whalen, A. J. (2013). *RTI team building: Effective collaboration and data-based decision making.* Guilford Press.

Bruininks, R., Woodcock, R., Weatherman, R., & Hill, B. (1996). *Scales of Independent Behavior–Revised: Comprehensive manual.* Riverside Publishing Company.

Burns, M. K. (2016). Effect of cognitive processing assessments and interventions on academic outcomes: Can 200 studies be wrong? *Communiqué, 44*(5), 26–29.

Burns, M. K., Peters, R., & Noell, G. H. (2008). Using performance feedback to enhance the implementation integrity of the problem-solving team process. *Journal of School Psychology, 46*(5), 537–550. https://doi.org/10.1016/j.jsp.2008.04.001

Burns, M. K., Riley-Tillman, T. C., & Rathvon, N. (2017). *Effective school interventions: Evidence-based strategies for improving student outcomes* (3rd ed.). Guilford Press.

Burns, M. K., Riley-Tillman, T. C., & VanDerHeyden, A. M. (2012). *RTI applications.* Guilford Press.

Calaruso, R., & Hammill, D. (2015). *Motor-Free Visual Perception Test–Fourth Edition.* Academic Therapy Publications.

Campbell. D., & Fiske, D. (1959). Convergent and discriminate validation by the multitrait-multimethod matrix. *Psychological Bulletin, 56*(2), 81–105.

Caplan, G. (1964). *The principles of preventive psychiatry.* Basic Books.

Carlson, J. F., Geisinger, K. F., & Johnson, J. L. (2020). *The twenty-first mental measurements yearbook.* Buros Center for Testing.

Carr, E. G. (1994). Emerging themes in the functional analysis of problem behavior. *Journal of Applied Behavior Analysis, 27*(2), 393–399. https://doi.org/10.1901/jaba.1994.27-393

Carrierre, J. A., & Hass, M. (2019, October 23). *Writing useful and understandable psychoeducational reports.* Presentation at the meeting of the California Association of School Psychologists, Long Beach, CA.

Carrizales-Engelmann, D., Feuerborn, L. L., Gueldner, B. A., & Tran, O. K. (2016). *Merrell's strong kids: A social & emotional learning curriculum—Grades 3–5* (2nd ed.). Brooke's Publishing.

Carrow-Woolfolk, E. (1995). *Manual for the listening comprehension and oral language subtests of the Oral and Written Language Scales.* American Guidance Service.

Carrow-Woolfolk, E. (2011). *Oral and Written Language Scales–Second Edition (OWLS-2).* Western Psychological Services.

Carrow-Woolfolk, E. (2014). *Test of Auditory Comprehension of Language–Fourth Edition.* PRO-ED.

Carrow-Woolfolk, E., & Allen, E. (2022). *Test of Expressive Language.* PRO-ED.

Center on Multi-Tiered System of Supports at the American Institutes for Research. (2021, May 1). *Essential components of MTSS.* https://mtss4success.org/essential-components

Chafouleas, S. M., Riley-Tillman, T. C., & Christ, T. J. (2009). Direct behavior rating (DBR): An emerging method for assessing social behavior within a tiered intervention system. *Assessment for Effective Intervention, 34*, 195–200. https://doi.org/10.1177/1534508409340391

Chall, J. (1967). *Learning to read: The great debate.* McGraw-Hill.

Chaparro, E. A., Green, A., Linan-Thompson, S., & Batz, R. (2021). Classroom to casa: Implementing multi-tiered systems of support for emerging bilinguals. *Preventing School Failure, 65*(4), 1–9. https://doi.org/10.1080/1045988X.2021.1937022

Chaparro, E. A., Helton, S., & Saddler, C. (2016). Oregon's effective behavioral and instructional support systems initiative: Implementation from district and state-level perspectives. In K. McIntosh & S. Goodman (Eds.), *Multi-tiered systems of support: Integrating academic RTI and school-wide PBIS* (pp. 267–286). Guilford Press.

Chaparro, E. A., Stoolmiller, M., Park, Y., Baker, S. K., Basaraba, D., Fien, H., & Mercier Smith, J. (2018). Evaluating passage and order effects of oral reading fluency passages in second grade: A partial replication. *Assessment for Effective Intervention, 44*(1), 3–16. https://doi.org/10.1177/1534508417741128

Chow, J. C., & Wehby, J. H. (2018). Associations between language and problem behavior: A systematic review and correlational meta-analysis. *Educational Psychology Review, 30*, 61–82. https://doi.org/10.1007/s10648-016-9385-z

Collaborative for Academic, Social, and Emotional Learning. (2014). *What is SEL? Skills and competencies.* https://casel.org/what-is-sel/

Cook, C. R., Duong, M. T., McIntosh, K., Fiat, A. E., Larson, M., Pullmann, M. D., & McGinnis, J. (2018). Addressing discipline disparities for black male students: Linking malleable root causes to feasible and effective practices. *School Psychology Review, 47*(2), 135–152. https://doi.org/10.17105/SPR-2017-0026.V47-2

Council for Exceptional Children. (2015). *Ethical principles and practice standards.*

Council of National Psychological Associations for the Advancement of Ethnic Minority Interests. (2016). *Testing and assessment with persons & communities of color.* American Psychological Association. https://www.apa.org/pi/oema

Cronbach, L. (1951). Coefficient alpha and the internal structure of tests. *Psychometrika, 16*, 297–334. https://doi.org/10.1007/BF02310555

Crone, D. A., Hawken, L. S., & Horner, R. H. (2015). *Building positive behavior support systems in schools: Functional behavioral assessment* (2nd ed.). Guilford Press.

Cummings, K. D., & Petscher, Y. (Eds.). (2016). *The fluency construct: Curriculum-based measurement concepts and applications.* Springer.

Curriculum Associates. (2012). *i-Ready assessments technical manual.*

Daane, M. C., Campbell, J. R., Grigg, W. S., Goodman, M. J., & Oranje, A. (2005). *Fourth-grade students reading aloud: NAEP 2002 special study of oral reading* (NCES 2006-469). U.S. Department of Education, Institute of Education Sciences, National Center for Education Statistics, U.S. Government Printing Office.

Dailor, A. N., & Jacob, S. (2011). Ethically challenging situations reported by school psychologists: Implications for training. *Psychology in the Schools, 48*(6), 619–632.

Debnam, K. J., Pas, E. T., Bottiani, J., Cash, A. H., & Bradshaw, C. P. (2015). An examination of the association between observed and self-reported culturally proficient teaching practices. *Psychology in the Schools, 52*(6), 533–548. https://doi.org/10.1002/pits.21845

Dehaene, S. (2009). *Reading in the brain: The science and evolution of a human invention.* Viking Penguin Group.

Deno, S. L. (1985). Curriculum-based assessment: The emerging alternative. *Exceptional Children, 52,* 219–232. https://doi.org/10.1177/001440298505200303

Deno, S. L. (1989). Curriculum-based measurement and special education services: A fundamental and direct relationship. In M. R. Shinn (Ed.), *Curriculum-based measurement: Assessing special children* (pp. 1–17). Guilford Press.

Deno, S. L., & Mirkin, P. (1977). *Data-based program modification: A manual.* Council for Exceptional Children.

Deno, S. L, Reschly, A. L., Lembke, E. S., Magnusson, D., Callender, S. A, Windram, H., & Stachel, N. (2009). Developing a school-wide progress-monitoring system. *Psychology in the Schools, 46*(1), 44–55. https://doi.org/10.1002/pits.20353

Diamond, E., Whalen, A., Kelley, K. K., & Davis, S. (2021). DECIDE. An ethical decision-making model supporting a socially just practice. *Communiqué, 49*(8), 4, 6–7.

Diana v. State Board of Education, C-70: 37RFT (N. D. Cal. 1970).

Dineen, J. N., Chafouleas, S. M., Briesch, A. M., McCoach, D. B., Newton, S. D., & Cintron, D. W. (2021). Exploring social, emotional, and behavioral screening approaches in U.S. public school districts. *American Educational Research Journal, 59*(1), 146–179. https://doi.org/10.3102/00028312211000043

Doman, R., Spitz, E., Suckerman, E., Delacato, C., & Doman, G. (1967). Children with severe brain injuries: Neurological organization in terms of mobility. In E. C. Frierson & W. B. Barbe (Eds.), *Educating children with learning disabilities.* Appleton-Century-Crofts.

Doman R. J., Spitz E. B., Zucman E., Delacato C. H., & Doman G. (1960). Children with severe brain injuries: Neurological organization in terms of mobility. *Journal of the American Medical Association. 174*(3), 257–262. doi:10.1001/jama.1960.03030030037007

Dunn, D. M. (2019). *Peabody Picture Vocabulary Test–Fifth Edition.* NCS Pearson.

Durlak, J. A., Weissberg, R. P., Dymnicki, A. B., Taylor, R. D., & Schellinger, K. B. (2011). The impact of enhancing students' social and emotional learning: A meta-analysis of school-based universal interventions. *Child Development, 82*(1), 405–432. https://doi.org/10.1111/j.1467-8624.2010.01564.x

Education for All Handicapped Children Act of 1975, 20 U.S.C. § 1400 *et seq.* (1975).

Education for All Handicapped Children Act of 1975, 20 U.S.C. § 1400 *et seq.* (1975 & amend. 1986).

Education for All Handicapped Children Act of 1975, Pub. L. No. 94-142, 89 Stat. 773 (1975). https://www.govinfo.gov/content/pkg/STATUTE-89/pdf/STATUTE-89-Pg773.pdf

Education Research and Consulting Service, Inc. (2013). SpringMath (Version 2.2.1). Sourcewell Technology. https://www.springmath.org

Elmore, R. (2002). *Bridging the gap between standards and achievement.* The Albert Shanker Institute.

Eunice Kennedy Shriver National Institute of Child Health and Human Development, National Institutes of Health, Department of Health and Human Services. (2000). *Report of the National Reading Panel. Teaching children to read: Reports of the subgroups* (00-4754). U.S. Government Printing Office.

Every Student Succeeds Act (2015), Pub. L. No. 114-95 § 114 Stat. 1177 (2015–2016).

Every Student Succeeds Act, 20 U.S.C. § 6301 (2015). https://www.congress.gov/bill/114th-congress/senate-bill/1177

Every Student Succeeds Act, Pub. L. No. 114-95, Stat. 1177 (2015). https://www.govinfo.gov/content/pkg/BILLS-114s1177enr/pdf/BILLS-114s1177enr.pdf

Fairchild, L., & Gadke, D. (2018). Central auditory processing disorder: Considerations and cautions for school psychologists. *Communiqué, 47*(1), 1, 27–31.

Family Educational Rights and Privacy Act (FERPA), 20 U.S.C. § 1232g (1974).

Flanagan, D., Ortiz, S., Alfonso, V. C., & Mascolo, J. T. (2006). *The achievement test desk reference: A guide to learning disability identification.* Wiley.

Fletcher, J. M., & Miciak, J. (2017). Comprehensive cognitive assessments are not necessary for the identification and treatment of learning disabilities. *Archives of Clinical Neuropsychology, 32*, 2–7. https://doi.org/10.1093/arclin/acw103

Flores, N., & Rosa, J. (2015). Undoing appropriateness: Raciolinguistic ideologies and language diversity in education. *Harvard Educational Review, 85*(2), 149–171. https://doi.org/10.17763/0017-8055.85.2.149

Foorman, B., Francis, D., Fletcher, J., Schatschneider, C., & Mehta, P. (1998). The role of instruction in learning to read: Preventing reading failure in at-risk children. *Journal of Educational Psychology, 90*(1), 37–55. https://doi.org/10.1037/0022-0663.90.1.37

Ford, D. Y., & Gardner, R. (2016, October). *Culturally relevant instruction: Teaching for everyone's success!* Presentation for CEC Learning Library. https://exceptionalchildren.org/webinar/culturally-relevant-instruction-teaching-everyones-success

Frostig, M. (1968). Education for children with learning disabilities. In H. Myklebust (Ed.), *Progress in learning disabilities* (pp. 234–266). Grune & Stratton.

Fuchs, D., Fuchs, L. S., & Vaughn S. (2014). What is intensive instruction and why is it important? *TEACHING Exceptional Children, 46*(4), 13–18. https://doi.org/10.1177/0040059914522966

Fuchs, L. S., & Deno, S. L. (1994). Must instructionally useful performance assessment be based in the curriculum? *Exceptional Children, 61*(1), 15–24. https://doi.org/10.1177/001440299406100103

Fuchs, L. S, Deno, S. L., & Mirkin, P. K. (1984). The effects of frequent curriculum-based measurement and evaluation on pedagogy, student achievement, and student awareness of learning. *American Educational Research Journal, 21*(2), 449–460. https://doi.org/10.3102/00028312021002449

Fuchs, L. S., Newman-Gonchar, R., Schumacher, R., Dougherty, B., Bucka, N., Karp, K. S., Woodward, J., Clarke, B., Jordan, N. C., Gersten, R., Jayanthi, M., Keating, B., & Morgan, S. (2021). *Assisting students struggling with mathematics: Intervention in the elementary grades* (WWC 2021006). National Center for Education Evaluation and Regional Assistance, Institute of Education Sciences, U.S. Department of Education. http://whatworks.ed.gov

García, O., & Kleifgen, J. (2018). *Educating emergent bilinguals: Policies, programs and practices for English learners* (2nd ed.). Teachers College Press.

Gay, G. (1995). Building cultural bridges: A bold proposal for teacher education. *Multicultural education: Strategies for implementation in colleges and universities, 4*, 95–106.

Gay, G. (2002). Culturally responsive teaching in special education for ethnically diverse students: Setting the stage. *International Journal of Qualitative Studies in Education, 15*(6), 613–629. https://doi.org/10.1080/0951839022000014349

Gersten, R., Compton, D., Connor, C. M., Dimino, J., Santoro, L., Linan-Thompson, S., & Tilly, W. D. (2008). *Assisting students struggling with reading: Response to intervention and multi-tier intervention for reading in the primary grades. A practice guide* (NCEE 2009-4045). National Center for Education Evaluation and Regional Assistance, Institute of Education Sciences, U.S. Department of Education. http://ies.ed.gov/ncee/wwc/publications/practiceguides

Gesel, S. A., & Lemons, C. J. (2020). Comparing schedules of progress monitoring using curriculum-based measurement in reading: A replication study. *Exceptional Children, 87*(1), 92–112. https://doi.org/10.1177/0014402920924845

Gickling, E. E., & Thompson, V. P. (1985). A personal view of curriculum-based assessment. *Exceptional Children, 52*(3), 205–218. https://doi.org/10.1177/001440298505200302

Gilliam, J. (2014). *Gilliam Autism Rating Scale–Third Edition*. PRO-ED.

Ginsburg, H. P., & Baroody, A. J. (2003). *Test of Early Mathematics Abilities–Third Edition*. PRO-ED.

Goldhaber, D., Theobald, R., & Tien, C. (2015). *The theoretical and empirical arguments for diversifying the teacher workforce: A review of the evidence* (CEDR Working Paper No. 2015-9). University of Washington Bothell, Center for Education Data & Research. http://eric.ed.gov/?id=ED574302

Good, R. H., & Salvia, J. A. (1988). Curriculum bias in published norm-referenced reading tests: Demonstrable effects. *School Psychology Review, 17*(1), 51–60.

Gottesman, I. (1968). Biogenetics of race and class. In M. Deutsch, I. Katz, & A. Jensen (Eds.), *Social Class, Race, and Psychological Development* (pp. 11–51). Holt, Rinehart, and Winston.

Gough, P. (1990). The simple view of reading. *Reading and Writing, 2*(2), 127–160.

Graden, J., Casey, A., & Bonstrom, O. (1983). *Prereferral interventions: Effects on referral rates and teacher attitudes* (Research Report No. 140). University of Minnesota, Institute for Research on Learning Disabilities.

Grant, A., & Sweet Grant, A. (2019, December). Stop trying to raise successful kids. The Atlantic. https://www.theatlantic.com/magazine/archive/2019/12/stop-trying-to-raise-successful-kids/600751

Gunn, B., Biglan, A., Smolkowski, K., & Ary, D. (2000). The efficacy of supplemental instruction in decoding skills for Hispanic and Non-Hispanic students in early elementary school. *The Journal of Special Education, 34*(2), 90–103. https://doi.org/10.1177/002246690003400204

Gutkin, T. B., & Nemeth, C. (1997). Selected factors impacting decision making in prereferral intervention and other school-based teams: Exploring the intersection between school and social psychology. *Journal of School Psychology, 35*(2), 195–216. https://doi.org/10.1016/S0022-4405(97)00005-8

Guzman-Orth, D., Laitusis, C., Thurlow, M., & Christensen, L. (2016). Conceptualizing accessibility for English language proficiency assessments. *ETS Research Report Series, 2016*, 1–12. https://doi.org/10.1002/ets2.12093

Hammill, D. D., Pearson, N. A., & Voress, J. K. (2014). *Examiner's manual: Developmental Test of Visual Perception–Third Edition*. PRO-ED.

Hammill, D. D., & Larsen, S. (2008). *Test of Written Language–Fourth Edition*. PRO-ED.

Hammill, D. D., Mather, N., & Roberts, R. (2017). *Illinois Test of Psycholinguistic Abilities–Third Edition*. PRO-ED.

Hammill, D. D., McGhee, J., & Ehrler, W. (2019). *Detroit Tests of Learning Aptitude–Fifth Edition*. PRO-ED.

Hammill, D. D., Pearson, N., & Wiederholt, L. (2009). *Comprehensive Test of Nonverbal Intelligence–Second Edition*. PRO-ED.

Hammill, D. D., & Newcomer, P. (2020). *Test of Language Development–Intermediate–Fifth Edition*. PRO-ED.

Hanna, P., Hanna, J., Hodges, R., & Rudoff, E. (1966). *Phoneme-grapheme correspondence as cues to spelling improvement*. U.S. Department of Health, Education, and Welfare.

Haring, N. G., Lovitt, T. C., Eaton, M. D., & Hansen, C. L. (1978). *The fourth R: Research in the classroom*. Charles E. Merrill Publishing Co.

Harris, B., & Sullivan, A. L. (2017). A framework for bilingual school consultation to facilitate multitier systems of support for English language learners. *Journal of Educational and Psychological Consultation, 27*(3), 367–392. https://doi.org/10.1080/10474412.2017.1307758

Hasbrouck, J. (2010). *Developing fluent readers*. Read Naturally, Inc.

Hauerwas, L. B., Brown, R., & Scott, A. N. (2013). Specific learning disability and response to intervention: State level guidance. *Exceptional Children, 80*(1), 101–120. https://doi.org/10.1177/001440291308000105

Hawken, L. S., Crone, D. A., Bundock, K., & Horner, R. H. (2021). *Responding to problem behavior in schools: The check-in, check-out intervention* (3rd ed.). Guilford Press.

Helwig, R., & Tindal, G. (2003). An experimental analysis of accommodation decisions on large-scale mathematics tests. *Exceptional Children, 69*(2), 211–225. https://doi.org/10.1177/001440290306900206

Herrnstein, R., & Murray, C. (1994). *Intelligence and class structure in American life*. The Free Press.

Horner, R., Newton, J. S., Todd, A., Algozzine, B., Algozzine, K., Cusumano, D., & Preston, A. I. (2018). A randomized wait-list controlled analysis of team-initiated problem solving professional development and use. *Behavioral Disorders, 43*(4), 444–456. https://doi.org/10.1177/0198742917745638

Hosp, J. L., Hosp, M. K., Howell, K. W., & Allison, R. (2014). *The ABCs of curriculum-based evaluation: A practical guide to effective decision making*. Guilford Press.

Howell, K. W., & Morehead, M. K. (1987). *Curriculum-based evaluation for special and remedial education: A handbook for deciding what to teach*. Merrill.

Hresko, W. P., Schlieve, P. L., Herron, S. R., Swain, C., & Sherbenou, R. J. (2003). *Comprehensive Mathematical Abilities Test (CMAT)*. PRO-ED.

Hyson, D. M., Kovaleski, J. F., Silberglit, B., & Pedersen, J. A. (2020). *The data-driven school: Collaborating to improve student outcomes*. Guilford Press.

Illinois School Psychologist Association. (n.d.). *ISPA professional practice guidance: English learner assessment*. https://www.ilispa.org/assets/docs/ResourceLibrary/ellprofessionalpractices.pdf

Individuals With Disabilities Education Act of 1990, 20 U.S.C. § 1400 *et seq.* (1990 & amend. 1997).

Individuals With Disabilities Education Improvement Act of 2004, 20 U.S.C. § 1400 *et seq.* (2004).

Isaacson, S. (1988). Assessing the writing product: Qualitative and quantitative measures. *Exceptional Children, 54*(6), 528–534. https://doi.org/10.1177/001440298805400606

Jacob, S., Decker, D., Lugg, E., & Diamond, E. (2022). *Ethics and law for school psychologists*. Wiley.

Jenkins, J., & Pany, D. (1978). Standardized achievement tests: How useful for special education? *Exceptional Children, 44*(6), 448–453. https://doi.org/10.1177/001440297804400606

Jenkins, J., & Terjeson, K. J. (2011). Monitoring reading growth: Goal setting, measurement frequency, and methods of evaluation. *Learning Disabilities Research and Practice, 26*(1), 28–35. https://doi.org/10.1111/j.1540-5826.2010.00322.x

Jensen, A. R. (1980). *Bias in mental testing.* The Free Press. https://doi.org/10.1017/S0140525X00005161

Jimerson, S. R., Burns, M. K., & VanDerHeyden, A. M. (Eds.). (2016). *Handbook of response to intervention: The science and practice of multi-tiered systems of support* (2nd ed.). Springer. https://doi.org/10.1007/978-1-4899-7568-3

Johnson, D., & Myklebust, H. (1967). *Learning disabilities: Educational principles and practices.* Grune & Stratton.

Kaufman, A., & Kaufman, N. (2018). *Kaufman Assessment Battery for Children.* Pearson.

Kavale, K., & Mattson, M. D. (1983). "One jumped off the balance beam": Meta-analysis of perceptual-motor training. *Journal of Learning Disabilities, 16*(3), 165–173. https://doi.org/10.1177/002221948301600307

Kephart, N. (1971). *The slow learner in the classroom.* Merrill.

Kincaid, D., & Batsche, G. (2016). Florida's multi-tiered support systems for academics and behavior. In K. McIntosh & S. Goodman (Eds.), *Multi-tiered systems of support: Integrating academic RTI and school-wide PBIS* (pp. 287–304). Guilford Press.

Kirk, S., & Kirk, W. (1971). *Psycholinguistic disabilities.* University of Illinois Press.

Kirschner, P. A., Sweller, J., & Clark, R. E. (2006). Why minimal guidance during instruction does not work: An analysis of the failure of constructivist, discovery, problem-based, experiential, and inquiry-based teaching. *Educational Psychologist, 41*(2), 75–86. https://doi.org/10.1207/s15326985ep4102_1

Kovaleski, J. F., VanDerHeyden, A. M., & Shapiro, E. S. (2013). *The RTI approach to identifying learning disabilities.* Guilford Press.

Kovaleski, J. F., VanDerHeyden, A. M., & Shapiro, E. S. (in press). *The RTI approach to evaluating learning disabilities* (2nd ed.). Guilford Press.

Ksinan, A. J., Vazsonyi, A. T., & Jiskrova, G. K. (2019). National ethnic and racial disparities in disciplinary practices: A contextual analysis in American secondary schools. *Journal of School Psychology, 74,* 106–125. https://doi.org/10.1016/j.jsp.2019.05.003

Kubiszyn, T., & Borich, G. (2003). *Educational testing and measurement: Classroom application and practice* (7th ed.). Wiley.

Ladson-Billings, G. (1995). Toward a theory of culturally relevant pedagogy. *American Journal of Educational Research, 32*(3), 465–491. https://doi.org/10.3102/00028312032003465

Langdon, J., Down, H. Observations on an ethnic classification of idiots. *Heredity* 21, 695–697 (1966). https://doi.org/10.1038/hdy.1966.69

Larson, E. D., Thurlow, M. L., Lazarus, S. L., & Liu, K. K. (2020). Paradigm shifts in states' assessment accessibility policies: Addressing challenges in implementation. *Journal of Disability Policy Studies, 30*(4), 244–252. https://doi.org/10.1177/1044207319848071

Lazarus, S. S., Goldstone, L., Wheeler, T., Paul, J., Prestridge, S., Sharp, T., Hochstetter, A., & Warren, S. (2021). *CCSSO accessibility manual: How to select, administer, and evaluate use of accessibility supports for assessment and instruction for all students.* Council of Chief State School Officers.

Lemons, C. J., Kearns, D. M., & Davidson, K. A. (2014). Data-based individualization in reading. *TEACHING Exceptional Children, 46*(4), 20–29. https://doi.org/10.1177/0040059914522978

Lichtenstein, R. (2013a). Writing psychoeducational reports that matter: A consumer-responsive approach. *Communiqué, 42*(3), 1, 28–30.

Lichtenstein, R. (2013b). Writing psychoeducational reports that matter: A consumer-responsive approach. Part 2. *Communiqué, 42*(4), 1, 10–13.

Lichtenstein, R. (2013c). Writing psychoeducational reports that matter: A consumer-responsive approach. Part 3. *Communiqué, 42*(4), 1, 9–12.

Lichtenstein, R., & Ecker, B. (2019). *High impact assessment reports for children and adolescents: A consumer-responsive approach.* Guilford Press.

Lindsley, O. R. (1964). Direct measurement and prosthesis of retarded behavior. *Journal of Education, 147,* 68–81.

Linn, R., Graue, R., & Sanders, N. (1990). Comparing state and district test results to national norms: The validity of claims that "Everyone is above average." *Educational Measurement: Issues and Practice, 9*(3), 5–14.

Loeding, B. L., & Crittenden, J. B. (1993). Inclusion of children and youth who are hearing impaired and deaf in outcomes assessment. In J. E. Ysseldyke & M. L. Thurlow (Eds.), *Views on inclusion and testing accommodations for students with disabilities.* University of Minnesota, National Center on Educational Outcomes.

Lyon, G. R., Fletcher, J. M., Shaywitz, S. E., Shaywitz, B. A., Torgesen, J. K., Wood, F. B., Schulte, A., & Olson, R. (2001). Rethinking learning disabilities. In C. E. Finn Jr., A. J. Rotherham, & C. R. Hokanson Jr. (Eds.), *Rethinking special education for a new century* (pp. 259–287). Thomas B. Fordham Foundation.

Mann, L. (1979). *On the trail of process: A historical perspective on cognitive processes and their training.* Grune & Stratton.

Markwuardt, F. (1998). *Peabody Individual Achievement Test–Revised: Normative Update.* American Guidance Service.

Martin, J. E., VanDycke, J. L., Christensen, W. R., Greene, B. A., Gardner, J. E., & Lovett, D. L. (2006). Increasing student participation in their transition IEP meetings: Establishing the self-directed IEP as an evidence-based practice. *Exceptional Children, 72*(3), 299–316. https://doi.org/10.1177/001440290607200303

Martin, N. A., & Brownell, R. (2011). *Receptive One-Word Picture Vocabulary Test–Fourth Edition.* Academic Therapy Publications.

Martin, N. A., & Brownell, R. (2018). *Test of Auditory Perception–Fourth Edition.* Academic Therapy Publications.

Massachusetts Department of Education. (2001). *Resource guide to the Massachusetts curriculum frameworks for students with significant disabilities—English language arts section.* www.doe.mass.edu/mcas/alt/rg/ela.pdf

Mather, N., Roberts, R., Hammill, D. D., & Allen, E. (2022). *Test of Orthographic Competence.* PRO-ED.

McGill, R. J., Dombrowski, S. C., & Canivez, G. L. (2018). Cognitive profile analysis in school psychology: History, issues, and continued concerns. *Journal of School Psychology, 71,* 108–121. https://doi.org/10.1016/j.jsp.2018.10.007

McGrew, K. S., Algozzine, B., Ysseldyke, J. E., Thurlow, M. L., & Spiegel, A. N. (1995). The identification of individuals with disabilities in national databases: Creating a failure to communicate. *The Journal of Special Education, 28*(4), 472–487. https://doi.org/10.1177/002246699502800406

McIntosh, K., & Goodman, S. (2016). *Integrated multi-tiered systems of support: Blending RTI and PBIS.* Guilford Press.

McMaster, K., Fuchs, D., Fuchs, L. S, & Compton, D. L. (2002). Monitoring the academic progress of children who are unresponsive to generally effective early reading intervention. *Assessment for Effective Intervention, 27*(4), 23–33. https://doi.org/10.1177/073724770202700404

Miller, W. R., & Rollnick, R. (2013). *Motivational interviewing: Helping people change* (3rd ed.). Guilford Press.

Naglieri, J., Das, J., & Goldstein, A. (2014). *Cognitive Assessment System–Second Edition.* PRO-ED.

National Association of School Psychologists. (2015). *The provision of school psychological services to bilingual students* [Position statement].

National Association of School Psychologists. (2020). Principles for professional ethics. In *NASP professional standards.* https://www.nasponline.org/standards-and-certification/professional-ethics

National Association of State Directors of Special Education. (2005). *Response to intervention: Policy considerations and implementation.*

National Center for Education Statistics. (2019). *Digest of education statistics.* U.S. Department of Education.

National Center on Intensive Intervention. (n.d.). *Informal academic diagnostic assessment using data as a guide for intensive intervention.* https://intensiveintervention.org/resource/informal-academic-diagnostic-assessment-using-data-guide-intensive-instruction-dbi

National Center on Intensive Intervention at the American Institutes for Research. (2020, June). *Academic progress monitoring tools chart.* https://charts.intensiveintervention.org/aprogressmonitoring

National Commission on Excellence in Education. (1983). *A nation at risk: The imperative for educational reform.* U.S. Government Printing Office.

National Council of Teachers of Mathematics. (2000). *Principles and standards for school mathematics: Standards 2000.*

National Council of Teachers of Mathematics. (2006). *Curriculum focal points for prekindergarten through grade 8 mathematics.*

National Education Association. (2020). *Code of ethics for educators.*

National Governors Association Center for Best Practices & Council of Chief State School Officers. (2010). *Common Core State Standards.*

National Institute of Child Health and Human Development. (2000). *Report of the National Reading Panel. Teaching children to read: An evidence-based assessment of the scientific research literature on reading and its implication for reading instruction* (NIH Publication 00-4). U.S. Government Printing Office.

National Mathematics Advisory Panel. (2008). *Foundations for success: The final report of the national mathematics advisory panel.* U.S. Department of Education. https://files.eric.ed.gov/fulltext/ED500486.pdf

NCLB Regulations. (2003, December 9). New regulation about assessment of children who have significant cognitive impairments. *Federal Register, 68*(236), 68697–68708.

Nelson, P. M., Van Norman, E. R., & Christ, T. J. (2017). Visual analysis among novices: Training and trend lines as graphic aids. *Contemporary School Psychology, 21*(2), 93–102. https://doi.org/10.1007/s40688-016-0107-9

Nelson, P. M., Van Norman, E. R., & VanDerHeyden, A. M. (2017). Reduce, reuse, recycle: The longitudinal value of local cut scores using state test data. *Journal of Psychoeducational Assessment, 35*(7), 683–694. https://doi.org/10.1177/0734282916658567

Newcomer, P. (2014). *Diagnostic Achievement Battery–Fourth Edition.* PRO-ED.

Newcomer, P., & Hammill, D. (2019). *Test of Language Development–Primary–Fifth Edition.* PRO-ED.

Newton, S. J., Horner, R., Algozzine, B., Todd, A. W., & Algozzine, K. (2012). A randomized wait-list controlled analysis of the implementation integrity of team-initiated problem solving process. *Journal of School Psychology, 50*(4), 421–441. https://doi.org/10.1016/j.jsp.2012.04.002

Nickerson, R. S. (1998). Confirmation bias: A ubiquitous phenomenon in many guises. *Review of General Psychology, 2*(2), 175–220. https://doi.org/10.1037%2F1089-2680.2.2.175

No Child Left Behind Act of 2001, 20 U.S.C . 70 § 6301 *et seq.* (2002).

North Carolina School Psychology Association. (2010). *Referring and evaluating English language learners for programs and services for children with special needs: Professional practices.*

Northwest Education Agency. (2019). *MAP growth technical manual report.*

Nunnally, J. (1978). *Psychometric theory* (2nd ed.). McGraw-Hill.

Nunnally, J., & Bernstein, I. (1994). *Psychometric theory* (3rd ed.). McGraw-Hill.

O'Connell, M. L., Bolt, T., & Warner, K. E. (Eds.). (2009). *Preventing mental, emotional, and behavioral disorders among young people: Progress and possibilities.* National Research Council on the Prevention of Mental Disorders and Substance Abuse Among Children, Youth and Young Adults, National Academies Press.

O'Neill, R. E., Albin, R. W., Storey, K., Horner, R. H., & Sprague, J. R. (2015). *Functional assessment and program development for problem behavior: A practical handbook* (3rd ed.). Cengage Learning.

Ortiz, S. (2018). *Ortiz Picture Vocabulary Acquisition Test.* Multi Health Systems.

Pew Research Center. (2019, February 20). *Most U.S. teens see anxiety and depression as a major problem among their peers.* https://www.pewresearch.org/social-trends/2019/02/20/most-u-s-teens-see-anxiety-and-depression-as-a-major-problem-among-their-peers

Pflaum, S., Walberg, H., Karegianes, M., & Rasher, S. (1980). Reading instruction: A quantitative analysis. *Educational Researcher, 9*(7), 12–18. https://doi.org/10.3102/0013189X009007012

Phillips, K. (1990). *Factors that affect the feasibility of interventions.* Workshop presented at Mounds View Schools, unpublished.

Rayner, K., Foorman, B., Perfetti, C., Pesetsky, D., & Seidenberg, M. (2001). How psychological science informs the teacher of reading. *Psychological Science in the Public Interest, 2*(2), 31–73. https://doi.org/10.1111/1529-1006.00004

Rehabilitation Act of 1973, 29 U.S.C. § 701 *et seq.* (1973).

Rehabilitation Act of 1973, Section 504, 29 U.S.C. § 794(a). (1973).

Reinke, W. M., Herman, K. C., Thompson, A., Copeland, C., McCall, C. S., Holmes, S., & Owens, S. A. (2020). Investigating the longitudinal association between fidelity to a large-scale comprehensive school mental health prevention and intervention model and student outcomes. *School Psychology Review, 50*(1), 17–29. https://doi.org/10.1080/2372966X.2020.1870869

Renaissance Learning (2021). *Star Math technical manual.*

Reynolds, C. R. (2007). *Koppitz Developmental Scoring System for the Bender Gestalt Test–Second Edition.* PRO-ED.

Reynolds, C. R., & Kamphaus, R. W. (2015). *Behavior Assessment System for Children–Third Edition: Manual.* Pearson.

Reynolds, C. R., Voress, J., & Pearson, N. S. (2014). *Developmental Test of Auditory Perception.* PRO-ED.

Reynolds, M. C. (1975). Trends in special education: Implications for measurement. In W. Hively & M. C. Reynolds (Eds.), *Domain-referenced testing in special education.* University of Minnesota Leadership Training Institute/Special Education.

Reynolds, W., & Wepman, J. (1987). *Wepman's Auditory Discrimination Test.* Western Psychological Services.

Rhodes, R. L., Ochoa, S. H., & Ortiz, S. O. (2005). *Assessing culturally and linguistically diverse students: A practical guide.* Guilford Press.

Russell, C., & Harms, A. (2016). Michigan's integrated behavior and learning support initiative: A statewide system of support for MTSS. In K. McIntosh & S. Goodman (Eds.), *Multi-tiered systems of support: Integrating academic RTI and school-wide PBIS.* Guilford Press.

Sabers, D., Feldt, L., & Reschly, D. (1988). Appropriate and inappropriate use of estimated true scores for normative comparisons. *The Journal of Special Education, 22*(3), 355–358.

Salvia, J., & Good, R. H. (1982). Significant discrepancies in the classification of pupils: Differentiating the concept. In J.T. Neisworth (Ed.), *Assessment in special education* (pp. 77–82). Aspen Systems.

Salvia, J., & Hughes, C. (1990). *Curriculum-based assessment: Testing what is taught.* Macmillan.

Sandberg, K. L., & Reschly, A. L. (2011). English learners: challenges in assessment and the promise of curriculum-based measurement. *Remedial and Special Education, 32*(2), 144–154. https://doi.org/10.1177/0741932510361260

Semel, E., Wiig, E., & Secord, W. (2013). *Clinical Evaluation of Language Fundamentals–Fifth Edition.* Pearson.

Shapiro, E. S., & Derr, T. (1987). An examination of overlap between reading curricula and standardized reading tests. *The Journal of Special Education, 21*(2), 59–67.

Shapiro, E. S., & Kratochwill, T. (Eds.). (2000). *Behavioral assessment in schools: Theory, research, and clinical foundations* (2nd ed.). Guilford Press.

Share, D., & Stanovich, K. (1995). Cognitive processes in early reading development: A model of acquisition and individual differences. *Issues in Education: Contributions from Educational Psychology, 1,* 1–57.

Sheinker, A., Barton, K. E., & Lewis, D. M. (2004). *Guidelines for inclusive test administration 2005.* Monterey, CA: CTB/McGraw-Hill. http://www.ctb.com/media/articles/pdfs/general/guidelines_inclusive.pdf

Shepard, L. A., & Smith, M. L. (1983). An evaluation of the identification of learning disabled students in Colorado. *Learning Disability Quarterly, 6,* 115–127.

Shepard, L. A., Smith, M. L., & Vojir, C. P. (1983). Characteristics of pupils identified as learning disabled. *American Educational Research Journal, 20,* 309–331.

Shinn, M., Tindal, G., & Stein, S. (1988). Curriculum-based measurement and the identification of mildly handicapped students: A review of the literature. *Professional School Psychology, 3*(1), 69–85. https://doi.org/10.1037/h0090531

Shinn, M. R. (Ed.). (1989). *Curriculum-based measurement: Assessing special children.* Guilford Press.

Shinn, M. R., & Malecki, C. (in preparation). *Curriculum-based measurement (CBM) use in screening students for basic skills performance discrepancies.* Curriculum-Based Measurement.

Shinn, M. R., Windram, H. S., & Bollman, K. A. (2016). Implementing response to intervention in secondary schools. In S. Jimerson, M. Burns, & A. VanDerHeyden (Eds.), *Handbook of response to intervention: The science and practice of multi-tiered systems of support* (2nd ed.) (pp. 563–586). Springer.

Shrank, F., Mather, N., & McGrew, K. (2014a). *Woodcock-Johnson IV Cognitive Battery.* Riverside Publishing.

Shrank, F., Mather, N., & McGrew, K. (2014b). *Woodcock-Johnson IV Tests of Achievement.* Riverside Publishing.

Shrank, F., McGrew, K., & Mather, N. (2014). *Woodcock-Johnson IV Tests of Oral Language.* Riverside Publishing.

Silva, M. R., Collier-Meek, M. A., Codding, R. S., Kleinert, W. L., & Feinberg, A. (2020). Data collection and analysis in response-to-intervention: A survey of school psychologists. *Contemporary School Psychology, 25,* 554–571. https://doi.org/10.1007/s40688-020-00280-2

Simonson, B. (2008). Evidence-based practices in classroom management: Considerations for research to practice. *Education and Treatment of Children, 31*(3), 351–380. https://doi.org/10.1353/etc.0.0007

Skiba, R. J., Horner, R. H., Chung, C. G., Rausch, M. K., May, S. L., & Tobin, T. (2011). Race is not neutral: A national investigation of African American and Latino disproportionality in school discipline. *School Psychology Review, 40*(1), 85–107. https://doi.org/10.1080/02796015.2011.12087730

Skiba, R. J., Poloni-Staudinger, L., Gallini, S., Simmons, A. B., & Feggins-Azziz, L. R. (2006). Disparate access: The disproportionality of African American students with disabilities across educational environments. *Exceptional Children, 72*(4), 411–424. https://doi.org/10.1177/001440290607200402

Snow, C., Burns, M., & Griffin, P. (1998). *Preventing reading difficulties in young children*. National Academy Press.

Spearman, C. (1910). Correlation calculated from faulty data. *British Journal of Psychology, 3*(3), 271–295. https://doi.org/10.1111/j.2044-8295.1910.tb00206.x

Sprick, R., Coughlin, C., Garrison, M., & Sprick, J. (2021). *Interventions* (3rd ed.). Ancora Publishers.

Star, J. (2005). Reconceptualizing procedural knowledge. *Journal for Research in Mathematics Education, 36*(5), 404–411.

Stecker, P. M., Fuchs, L. S., & Fuchs, D. (2005). Using curriculum-based measurement to improve student achievement: Review of research. *Psychology in the Schools, 42*(8), 795–820. http://dx.doi.org/10.1002/ pits.20113

Stevens, R., & Rosenshine, B. (1981). Advances in research on teaching. *Exceptional Education Quarterly, 2*(1), 1–9. https://doi.org/10.1177/074193258100200106

Stevens, S. S. (1951). Mathematics, measurement, and psychophysics. In S. S. Stevens (Ed.), *Handbook of Experimental Psychology* (pp. 1–49). Wiley.

Strickland-Cohen, M. K., & Horner, R. H. (2015). Typical school personnel developing and implementing basic behavior support plans. *Journal of Positive Behavior Interventions, 17*(2), 83–94. https://doi.org/10.1177/1098300714554714

Strickland-Cohen, M. K., Kennedy, P. C., Berg, T. A., Bateman, L. J., & Horner, R. H. (2016). Building school district capacity to conduct functional behavioral assessment. *Journal of Emotional and Behavioral Disorders, 24*(4), 235–246. https://doi.org/10.1177/1063426615623769

Student Achievement Partners. (2020). *Comparing reading research to program design: An examination of teachers college units of study*. https://achievethecore.org/page/3240/comparing-reading-research-to-program -design-an-examination-of-teachers-college-units-of-study

Stuebing, K. K., Barth, A. E., Cirino, P. T., Francis, D. J., & Fletcher, J. M. (2008). A response to recent reanalyses of the National Reading Panel Report: Effects of systematic phonics instruction are practically significant. *Journal of Educational Psychology, 100*(1), 123–143. https://doi.org/10.1037/0022-0663.100.1.123

Suen, H., & Ary, D. (1989). *Analyzing quantitative behavioral observation data*. Lawrence Erlbaum Associates.

Sugai, G., & Horner, R. H. (2009). Responsiveness-to-intervention and school-wide positive behavior supports: Integration of multi-tiered system approaches. *Exceptionality, 17*(4), 223–237. https://doi.org/10.1080/09362830903235375

Sullivan, A. L. (2011). Disproportionality in special education identification and placement of English language learners. *Exceptional Children, 77*(3), 317–334. https://doi.org/10.1177/001440291107700304

Sulzer-Azaroff, B., & Mayer, G. R. (1986). *Achieving educational excellence: Using behavior strategies*. Holt, Rinehart, and Winston.

Swain, K. D., & Hagaman, J. L. (2020). Elementary special education teachers' use of CBM data: A 20-year follow-up. *Preventing School Failure: Alternative Education for Children and Youth, 64*(1), 48–54. https://doi .org/10.1080/1045988X.2019.1678009

Taie, S., & Goldring, R. (2017). *Characteristics of public elementary and secondary school teachers in the United States: Results from the 2015–16 National Teacher and Principal Survey, First Look* (NCES 2017-072). U.S. Department of Education. National Center for Education Statistics.

Tapp, J. (2021). *Multi-option observation system for experimental studies (MOOSES)*. Kennedy Center, Vanderbilt University.

Thompson, S. L., & Thurlow, M. L. (2001). *State special education outcomes: A report on state assessment activities at the beginning of the new decade*. University of Minnesota, National Center on Educational Outcomes.

Thorndike, R. L., & Hagen, R. (1978). *Measurement and evaluation in psychology and education*. Wiley.

Thurlow, M. L. (2014). Accommodations for challenge, diversity, and variance in human characteristics. *Journal of Negro Education, 83*(4), 442–464. https://doi.org/10.7709/jnegroeducation.83.4.0442

Thurlow, M. L., Elliott, J. L., & Ysseldyke, J. E. (2003). *Testing students with disabilities: Practical strategies for complying with district and state requirements* (2nd ed.). Corwin Press.

Thurlow, M. L., & Thompson, S. (2004). *2003 state special education outcomes*. University of Minnesota, National Center on Educational Outcomes.

Thurstone, T. G. (1941). Primary mental abilities in children. *Educational and Psychological Measurement, 1,* 105–116.

Todd, A. W., Horner, R. H, Algozzine, B., Chaparro, E. A., & Nese, R. N. T. (2020). *Team initiated problem solving fidelity checklist for tier 2 (TIPS-FC-T2).* University of Oregon, Educational and Community Supports. https://www.pbis.org/resource/tips-fidelity-checklist-tier-2-brief

Torgesen, J. K., Alexander, A. W., Wagner, R. K., Rashotte, C. A., Voeller, K. K., Conway, T. (2001). Intensive remedial instruction for children with severe reading disabilities: Immediate and long-term outcomes from two instructional approaches. *Journal of Learning Disabilities, 34*(1), 33–58. https://doi.org/10.1177/002221940103400104

Torgesen, J. K., Wagner, R. K., Rashotte, C. A., Rose, E., Lindamood, P., Conway, T., & Garvan, C. (1999). Preventing reading failure in young children with phonological processing disabilities: Group and individual responses to instruction. *Journal of Educational Psychology, 91*(4), 579–593. https://doi.org/10.1037/0022-0663.91.4.579

Truckenmiller, A. J., McKindles, J. V., Petscher, Y., Eckert, T. L, & Tock, J. (2020). Expanding curriculum-based measurement in written expression for middle school. *The Journal of Special Education, 54*(3), 133–145. https://doi.org/10.1177/0022466919887150

U.S. Department of Education. (2015). *Number and percent of children ages 3 through 5 and students ages 6 through 21 served under IDEA, Part B, by LEP status and state, 2014–15.* https://www2.ed.gov/programs/osepidea/618-data/static-tables/2014-2015/part-b/child-count-and-educational-environment/1415-bchildcountandedenvironment-4.xlsx.

U.S. Department of Education, EDFacts Data Warehouse (EDW). (2014–15). SEA File C141, LEP Enrolled. Extracted April 3, 2017.

U.S. Department of Education, National Center for Education Statistics, Common Core of Data (CCD). (2019). *Local education agency universe survey, 2017–18.* See *Digest of Education Statistics* 2019, table 204.20. https://nces.ed.gov/programs/coe/indicator_cgf.asp#info

U.S. Department of Education, Office of Special Education Programs, Individuals With Disabilities Education Act (IDEA) database, https://www2.ed.gov/programs/osepidea/618-data/state-level-data-files/index.html#bcc;and National Center for Education Statistics, National Elementary and Secondary Enrollment Projection Model, 1972 through 2029.

U.S. Department of Health and Human Services, Centers for Disease Control and Prevention. (2019). *Data and statistics on children's mental health.* https://www.cdc.gov/childrensmentalhealth/data.html

Van Norman, E. R., & Nelson, P. M. (2019a). Assessing the consequential validity of early literacy progress monitoring data: An investigation of the accuracy of decision rules to evaluate response to instruction. *School Psychology, 34*(5), 512–520. http://dx.doi.org/10.1037/spq0000321

Van Norman, E. R., & Nelson, P. M. (2019b). An evaluation of the use of seasonal goal lines to improve the accuracy of curriculum-based measurement of reading decision rule recommendations. *Assessment for Effective Intervention, 46*(3), 167–177. https://doi.org/10.1177/153450841987224

VanDerHeyden, A. M. (2010). Determining early mathematical risk: Ideas for extending the research. *School Psychology Review, 39*(2), 196–202. https://doi.org/10.1080/02796015.2010.12087773

VanDerHeyden, A. M. (2011). Technical adequacy of response to intervention decisions. *Exceptional Children, 77*(3), 335–350. https://doi.org/10.1177/001440291107700305

VanDerHeyden, A. M. (2013). Universal screening may not be for everyone: Using a threshold model as a smarter way to determine risk. *School Psychology Review, 42*(4), 402–414. https://doi.org/10.1080/02796015.2013.12087462

VanDerHeyden, A. M., & Codding, R. S. (2020). Belief-based versus evidence-based math assessment and instruction: What school psychologists need to know to improve student outcomes. *Communiqué, 48*(5), 1, 20–25.

Vaughn, S., & Fletcher, J. M. (2020). Identifying and teaching students with significant reading problems. *American Educator, 44*(4), 4–11, 40. https://www.aft.org/ae/winter2020-2021/vaughn_fletcher

Walker, H., Severson, H., & Feil, E. (2014). *Systematic screening for behavior disorders* (2nd ed.). Ancora Press.

Walker, H. M., Horner, R. H., Sugai, G., Bullis, M., Sprague, J. R., Bricker, D., & Kaufman, M. J. (1996). Integrated approaches to preventing antisocial behavior patterns among school-age children and youth. *Journal of Emotional and Behavioral Disorders, 4*(4), 194–209. https://doi.org/10.1177/106342669600400401

Walker, H. M., & Severson, H. H. (1992). *Systematic screening for behavior disorders* (2nd ed.). Sopris West.

Wallace, G., & Hammill, D. (2013). *Comprehensive Receptive and Expressive Vocabulary Test–Third Edition*. PRO-ED.

Wanzek, J., Vaughn, S., Scammacca, N., Gatlin, B., Walker, M. A., & Cpain, P. (2016). Meta-Analyses of the effects of tier 2 type reading interventions in grades K–3. *Educational Psychology Review, 28*, 551–576. https://doi.org/10.1007/s10648-015-9321-7

Wechsler, D. (2014). *WISC-V technical and interpretive manual*. NCS Pearson.

Whitcomb, S. A. (2018). *Behavioral, social, and emotional assessment of children and adolescents*. Routledge.

WIDA Consortium. (2016). *The WIDA accessibility and accommodations framework: Considerations influencing the framework's development*. https://wida.wisc.edu/sites/default/files/resource/WIDA-Accessibility-Accommodations-Framework.pdf

Wiederholt, L., & Bryant, B. (2001). *Examiner's manual: Gray Oral Reading Tests–Third Edition*. PRO-ED.

Wilkinson, G. S., & Robertson, G. S. (2017). *Wide Range Achievement Test–Fifth Edition*. Pearson.

Williams, C. (2019). *Expressive Vocabulary Test–Fifth Edition*. Pearson.

Windram, H., & Bollman, K. (2016). *Implementing response to intervention at the secondary level*. Solution Tree.

Witt, J. C., VanDerHeyden, A. M., & Gilbertson, D. (2004). Troubleshooting behavioral interventions: A systematic process for finding and eliminating problems. *School Psychology Review, 33*(3), 363–383. https://doi.org/10.1080/02796015.2004.12086254

Woodcock, R. W., McGrew, K. S., & Mather, N. (2001). *WJ-III Tests of Cognitive Abilities and Tests of Aachievement*. Riverside Publishing.

Ysseldyke, J. E. (1987). Classification of handicapped students. In M. C. Wang, M. C. Reynolds, & H. J. Walberg (Eds.), *Handbook of special education: Research and practice* (Vol. 1, pp. 253–271). Pergamon.

Ysseldyke, J. E., & McLeod, S. (2007). Using technology tools to monitor response to intervention. In S. R. Jimerson, M. K. Burns, & A. M. VanDerHeyden (Eds.), *Handbook of response to intervention* (pp. 396–407). Springer.

Ysseldyke, J. E., & Salvia, J. A. (1974). Diagnostic-prescriptive teaching: Two models. *Exceptional Children, 41*(3), 181–186. https://doi.org/10.1177/001440297404100305

Ysseldyke, J. E., Stickney, E., & Has, A. (2015, February). *Using growth norms to set instructional goals for struggling students* [Paper]. Annual meeting of the National Association of School Psychologists, Orlando, FL.

INDEX

Page numbers in bold and italics refer to tables and figures, respectively. Page numbers followed by *n* indicate notes.